COLOR
ENCYCLOPEDIA OF
GEMSTONES

COLOR ENCYCLOPEDIA OF GEMSTONES

Second Edition

Joel E. Arem, Ph.D., F.G.A.

VAN NOSTRAND REINHOLD COMPANY
—— New York ——

This book is dedicated to Abraham "Edge" Goldstein of Brooklyn, New York. His love of minerals and gems and his generosity and willingness to share his knowledge with others have been an inspiration to three generations of hobbyists. I consider myself fortunate to be numbered among those whom Edge considers his close friends.

Copyright © 1977, 1987 by **Van Nostrand Reinhold Company Inc.**
All photographs copyright © 1977, 1987 by Joel E. Arem
Library of Congress Catalog Card Number: 86-26759
ISBN: 0-442-20833-2

Printed in the United States of America

Van Nostrand Reinhold Company Inc.
115 Fifth Avenue
New York, New York 10003

Van Nostrand Reinhold Company Limited
Molly Millars Lane
Wokingham, Berkshire RG11 2PY, England

Van Nostrand Reinhold
480 La Trobe Street
Melbourne, Victoria 3000, Australia

Macmillan of Canada
Division of Canada Publishing Corporation
164 Commander Boulevard
Agincourt, Ontario M1S 3C7, Canada

16 15 14 13 12 11 10 9 8 7 6 5 4 3 2

Library of Congress Cataloging-in-Publication Data
Arem, Joel E., 1943-
    Color encyclopedia of gemstones.
    Bibliography: p.
    Includes index.
    1. Precious stones. I. Title.
QE392.A69 1987   553.8′03′21   86-26759
ISBN 0-442-20833-2

Contents

Preface

The first edition of this encyclopedia was published a decade ago, and some remarkable changes have occurred in the gemstone marketplace during this interval. Although diamond still retains its place as the most popular and esteemed of all gemstones, the extremely wide gap in this leadership position versus colored stones has narrowed. There is a large and growing demand for all kinds of gemstones, especially brightly colored stones that can be worn as fashion accessories. Beaded jewelry has become an item of immense popularity; pearls have seen a huge revival. Rare gemstones such as tanzanite and tsavorite have made the transition from collector items to market staples. Even such barely commercial stones as andalusite, iolite, sphene, chrysoberyl, and some of the feldspars are becoming more widely known and distributed. The long-speculated and long-awaited birth of a large and active collector market for gemstones cannot be far off.

About thirty new species may now be added to the list of cut gems, along with some new varieties, such as malaya garnet. Previously unknown localities have yielded large and spectacular crystals of rare species, such as anglesite, which in turn have yielded record-size faceted gemstones. More and more dealers are aware of the growing value of exotic gem species; the list of known taaffeites has thus grown from a handful of gems to perhaps more than fifty known cut stones, and more will surely be identified.

On the commercial side, the Argyle deposits of Australia have become the most important diamond discoveries of the century, adding as much as 50 percent to the proven world reserve of diamond. Unfortunately, most of the Australian diamonds are not suitable for cutting as gems, so while the amount of diamond in these deposits is immense, the total value is not as large as might be guessed. However, there seems to be an unusually high percentage of brightly colored diamond in the Australian deposits, including some extraordinary pink material. So-called fancy colored diamonds (in truth, *colored gemstones*) may well become the most eagerly sought and highly prized of all gems before the next edition of this book is published.

The growing popularity of colored gemstones has made it crucial that a sensible, scientific, precise, consistent, and universally accepted method of color grading be developed. The immense pool of capital in pension plans and trust accounts will never touch gems as wealth-preservation vehicles until such grading is an established fact. Many grading systems have been proposed. All of them, without exception, have the same basic failing, that is, despite the pseudo-scientific appearance of "number systems" for estimating color, clarity, cut, and so forth, they are all based on *visual estimation.* This is also true of diamond, an amazing fact considering that a multimillion dollar investment market rose and fell based on "certification" with a built-in variability as high as 20–30 percent. Large money pools will never be invested in any product that must be defined in such loose terms, with the consequent potential for immediate loss on liquidation as large as the upper end of the range of grading error.

Only objective, scientific, machine-based grading will solve this problem. This implies the acceptance by the gemstone field of terminology that is universally applied in other industries where color is equally important (paints, textiles, plastics), such as Munsell color designations. Also, the variability of color grading by such machines must be reduced to less than 5 percent, a formidable challenge indeed considering the complexity of measuring color in materials where pleochroism, cutting proportions, and inclusion-scattering are all potential sources of error.

The gemstone field is also continually searching for

new, useful, simple, and nondestructive methods of testing. It is likely that considerable development will occur during the next decade in perfecting both luster-measurement systems (which obviate the problem of measuring high refractive indices) and thermal measurement devices, which blazed to prominence as a means of rapidly distinguishing between diamond and cubic zirconia.

Synthetic gems have become a fact of life in the gemstone trade. In fact, most people associate the name *spinel* with birthstone simulants made of synthetic spinel and do not even realize that natural spinels are rare, durable, and beautiful gems. Synthetic ruby, emerald, and sapphire have become important marketplace commodities in their own right and have a bright future. For as gemstones become increasingly rare and demand for them grows, gemstone prices will rise to a point where very fine stones are out of reach of all but a tiny percentage of potential buyers. Synthetic gems provide the look and durability of these fine, rare gems at a fraction of their cost. Unfortunately, the crystal growers are enticed by a far greater monetary reward than are the gem scientists who build detection equipment. Inevitably, a small percentage of artificial gemstones will foil even the best laboratories. The markets will not be disrupted as long as this percentage remains small. Also, the physical properties of most synthetic gems are within (or overlap) the range of properties of their natural counterparts; detection is therefore based primarily on characteristic inclusions, some of which are definitive proof of origin. Thus, although a high degree of internal perfection adds measurably to the value of a gemstone, total perfection can be a real liability in the case of emerald and corundum gems. That is, small, hard-to-see inclusions allow the origin of a gemstone to be proven; a truly flawless gemstone may be extremely rare and potentially valuable, but may also be impossible to prove as natural!

Laboratory products such as cubic zirconia have established markets of their own, apart from and not competitive with those for natural stones. Such products are popular because we live in an age of aspiration, where television dramas about wealth and power have the highest ratings, an age where the trappings of wealth have mass appeal. Gemstones have long been used as a means of displaying affluence, and it is therefore not surprising that the demand for gems continues to rise while the supply continues to fall.

The new section on synthetic gem materials is especially timely. Synthetic gems have been in the marketplace for some time (in the case of ruby more than a century) and have caused much confusion and concern. A number of excellent books have been published on synthetic gemstones, but they all seem to focus on the technology and history of these materials. The chapter on synthetics in this second edition is designed primarily to be useful to gemologists. The information is presented in the same format as for natural gemstones and summarizes the essential literature on the subject. The reader is referred to the books listed in the bibliography for details of manufacturing methods, history, and so forth. Also, the entire subject of gemstone treatment (color alteration and enhancement) is left for other texts.

There is little doubt that many superb, large, and unique gemstones exist that have not been mentioned in the current work, despite a major effort to keep abreast of the appearance of such gems. Many of the cutters who produce these rare objects do not keep detailed notes, and once they have been spirited away into private or museum collections, it becomes enormously difficult to track them all down. A plea is once again extended to readers of this book to supply me with any information that will make future editions more comprehensive, accurate, and useful; thanks are gratefully extended to those individuals who took the time to comment on the first edition with the aim of helping to make future editions better. Some of the comments received as long ago as 1977 have finally been incorporated into this current work.

It is my hope that the *Color Encyclopedia of Gemstones* will increasingly become the most-used handbook for quickly needed information about gemstones, as well as the text most used by an increasingly large and active group of gemstone collectors who are fascinated by the range of color and beauty displayed by many rare gemstone species and varieties. If these collectors play an active role in providing a continuing stream of information and comments about the book, it will then be ever more useful to those who need it most and who will shape the gemstone market of the future.

JOEL E. AREM
P.O. Box 5056
Laytonsville, MD
20879

Acknowledgment

Many people assisted in the production of the first edition of the *Color Encyclopedia of Gemstones*. Many of these people also assisted in the preparation of this revision, as did a number of other friends and colleagues.

Those involved in the first edition include Floyd Beattie, Casper Beesley, Karen Breau, Bernard Cirlin, Carlton Davis, Denver Museum of Natural History, William Dippel, Pete J. Dunn, Mike Evick, Gemological Institute of America, A. Edge Goldstein, Alberta Gordon, Elvis Gray, Mike Gray, A. V. Gumuchian, George Harlow, John Holcombe, William T. Huff, Kuhn's Baltic Amber Specialties, William Larson, Jim Leone, Richard T. Liddicoat, Betty Llewellyn, Joseph Longstreth, Barry Nathan, C. D. ("Dee") Parsons, William Pinch, John Saul, Sonja Schwartzman, John Sinkankas, Kenneth Sumner, Lillian Turner, Martin Zinn.

Thanks to those who assisted in some way with the second edition: Cos Altobelli, Jean DeMouthe, Ernest Fairbanks, Gordon V. Axon, Myrtle Granger, George Bruce, Bart Cannon, Charles Leavitt, Jr., W. W. Hanneman, Don Hoover, Arthur T. Grant, Grant Waite, Michael O'Donoghue, Peter Keller, Victor Yount, Eugene S. Love, Sean Sweeney, David Brackna, Richard E. McCarty, John T. McCasland, Thomas Chatham, and Sarabeth Koethe.

Very special thanks are extended to C. D. ("Dee") Parsons, master cutter and collector extraordinaire, who assembled a unique collection of rare species and catseye gems for shipment to the author to be photographed for the second edition. This irreplaceable package was lost in the U.S. mail. Dee's invaluable assistance in the preparation of the first edition of the encyclopedia made it possible for many gem species to be photographed in color for the first time.

I am grateful to the Minolta Camera Corp. for providing the superb diagrams reproduced in the section on color measurement technology.

I welcome comments, criticisms, additions, and corrections in the hope of making future editions of this book more accurate, comprehensive, and useful. Please address all correspondence to Dr. Joel E. Arem, P.O. Box 5056, Laytonsville, MD 20879.

Introduction

Gemstones are among humans' most treasured objects. They have been held in high esteem throughout history by all societies in all parts of the world. The histories of certain individual gemstones can be traced over a span of centuries, and gems have the same associations of wealth, prestige, status, and power as gold and silver.

In the earliest periods of civilization, people became curious about natural objects, including minerals. Minerals are naturally occurring inorganic chemical elements and compounds. Scientists today have amended this definition in light of discoveries about the arrangements of atoms in crystals. A mineral species is therefore also defined in terms of a definite crystalline structure. The chemical composition of a mineral may vary but only within defined limits. If the composition varies outside these defined limits, the mineral may be given a new name and considered a distinct species.

Early humans discovered pebbles and fragments of various brightly colored minerals in fields and stream beds, on mountain slopes, and in barren deserts. Some of these were made into ornaments. Others were ascribed mystical powers or symbolic religious significance. For centuries gem materials held a position of tremendous influence in human affairs. However, there was no science of gemology. The primary attribute of any gemstone was color, yet no reliable ways existed for differentiating minerals of the same or similar colors. It is not surprising that confusion reigned in both the literature and the marketplace. There are literally hundreds of references to gemstones in the Bible. Yet in many cases it is not known today exactly what stones were being described. Some incorrect names that were in use nearly two thousand years ago are still employed today!

The modern science of gemology is a relatively recent development. Fairly accurate methods of chemical analysis existed more than one hundred years ago. Yet even as recently as 1910 the nature of the internal structure of crystals was not firmly established. When X-rays first revealed the magnificent atomic geometry of crystals in the years following 1914, mineralogy, chemistry, and gemology all entered a new age of sophistication.

Progress, however, often adds complications and problems. At the same time that some scientists worked to improve identification methods, others developed ways of duplicating nature's gem masterpieces in the laboratory. Accurate detection technology was, in a sense, developed just in time to prevent collapse of the market for various gemstones.

A large part of the value of a fine gem lies in its scarcity as a rare natural object. People are therefore less likely to spend a large sum of money for a stone that might turn out to be a laboratory product. The overall question of the reasons for the value of gems is complex and will be discussed in following pages.

Gemology, in the last decades of the twentieth century, is at a major turning point in its growth. Worldwide affluence has created an unprecedented demand for gems of fine quality, vastly raising their cost. Political problems in gem-producing areas have created restrictions in the supply of gem materials, further raising gem prices. Synthesis technology is developing new materials with very desirable properties that are never found in nature, as well as laboratory equivalents of the more valuable natural gemstones. It has become essential to devise ways to distinguish natural and synthetic materials as well to as reveal simulations and methods of color enhancement by chemical and physical treatment.

This book is an encyclopedia of gemstones. It is an attempt to provide basic information about all the mineral species that have been cut as gems, including their color varieties. This introduction must first, however, speak to the most basic question at hand: What is a gem?

WHAT IS A GEM?

World literature abounds with references to *precious* and *semiprecious* gems. These terms are used even today, without rigor, by the public and jewelry trade alike. Just what do these terms mean?

In antiquity, the so-called precious stones were diamond, ruby, emerald, sapphire, pearl, and occasionally opal. The dictionary *(Webster's New Collegiate Dictionary,* 7th ed., 1967) defines *precious* as "of great value or high price"; *semiprecious* is defined as meaning "of less commercial value than precious".

This indicates clearly that *precious* is a marketing term, applying to any expensive item. It is worth noting that a diamond can be purchased for as little as $200 per carat, yet certain colors of garnet are currently selling at prices over $1,000 per carat. Garnet has always been regarded as semiprecious, so it is obvious that these terms, as applied to gems, have little relevance or meaning. Therefore, aside from considerations of historical usage, the terms *precious* and *semiprecious* should be completely abandoned.

We are still left with the fundamental issue: What is a gem?

Nobody will argue with the statement that diamond, ruby, sapphire, and emerald are gems. Opal is a gem, as are jade, lapis, garnets, and turquoise. However, what do we do with andalusite, diopside, and sphene?

A material, to be considered a gem, must have beauty, durability, and scarcity, according to most accepted authorities, but all of these terms are subjective and open to wide interpretation. Opal, a gem, has hardness of only 5.5 on Mohs' scale (see page 15), which is really too soft to wear in a ring. Opal is also quite fragile and brittle and may crack spontaneously because of internal dehydration. If durability is a major criterion, opal is not a very good gem. Yet it *is* a gem and has always been considered as such because of its other properties and beauty.

Proustite, a silver arsenic sulfide, is a rare mineral that is seldom faceted, and then only for collectors. Its red color is one of the richest in the mineral kingdom, far surpassing in intensity the hue of most rubies. Anyone who sees a cut proustite is likely to comment on its great beauty. There may be fewer than fifty cut proustites in the entire world, so the scarcity factor is indisputable. Is a cut proustite a gem or not?

Zoisite has been known as a mineral for decades. It is usually gray or pinkish and opaque and seldom cut, even by collectors of the unusual. Then in the late 1960s fine, blue-violet, transparent zoisite crystals were discovered in Tanzania, and a few stones were cut from them. The cut stones were sold to a few collectors and connoisseurs of unusual faceted minerals. Eventually one of the world's major jewelry establishments, Tiffany & Co., noted that cut blue zoisite resembles fine sapphire, dubbed the new material *tanzanite* and launched a major promotion of the "new gemstone." Today, tanzanite is accepted as a gem and large stones bring rather high prices. Here is an example of a mineral that was not a gem by accepted criteria before 1967 but *became* a gem by promotion. This is a double standard that leads one to ask for an objective criterion in the definition of a gem.

The dictionary is again consulted, and we find that a gem is "a precious or sometimes semiprecious stone cut and polished for ornament." If we omit the terms relating to price, as discussed earlier, we have the basis of a simple and unambiguous definition.

A gem is any mineral cut and polished for ornamental purposes.

There are more than three thousand known minerals. Any of them could be used as a gem if it were found in a form solid, massive, or attractive enough to warrant the effort of cutting. The definition of a mineral is unambiguous. The definition allows for all the rare and unusual materials that have been cut and that heretofore have been difficult to classify or discuss. My definition of a gem is thus very tight, but we must allow for several exceptions, which are considered gems through the necessity of thousands of years of acceptance as such. These exceptions are pearl, coral, and amber. Pearl and coral actually are made up of mineral material (calcite and aragonite) but created through the agency of organic processes. Amber is the petrified, hardened sap of ancient pine trees and is an organic material.

The term *ornamental material* could be more aptly applied to amber and coral, as well as ivory, jet, shell, and wood. All of these are natural materials of organic origin that are polished and used in jewelry, but they would not be called *gems* under the proposed terminology.

A problem in nomenclature now arises regarding manufactured compounds and crystals that are sometimes cut for jewelry purposes. The term *synthetic* is derived from words that mean, literally, put together (from components), which, by itself, is noncommittal as to origin. The terms *created* and *cultured* have also been used in regard to laboratory products. The public has come to accept the term *synthetic* in connection with jewelry stones created in the laboratory. It should always be remembered, however, that a synthetic gemstone is a contradiction in terms, since a gem is by definition a mineral, which is a *naturally* occurring material.

The following classification avoids the confusions of current usage: a *gem* is a mineral cut and polished for ornamental use; a *gemstone* is a crystal, fragment, or pebble of gem material (this term is also used to describe the cut stone); a *jewel* is a combination of gemstone and metal setting allowing the gem to be worn easily; a *synthetic* is a manufactured material that may either be physically and chemically equivalent to a mineral, or a compound unknown in nature but that can be grown in transparent crystals suitable for cutting; a *simulant* is a material that resembles another (usually more costly) material (for example, glass used as a substitute for ruby or emerald). A *homocreate* is a manufactured substance with properties in the range of those displayed by the natural substance it is intended to duplicate; that is, a homocreate is a synthetic that specifically *is* physically and chemically equivalent to a mineral.

SCOPE OF THIS BOOK

Unlike other books about gems, this work does not provide history and lore of stones, descriptions of occurrences, mining and cutting techniques, or market and price data that are rapidly outdated. It is, rather, a comprehensive compendium of data organized in a format that provides rapid access to the basic properties of gemstones, especially those data that would be useful in identification.

The book's major asset is the large array of color plates. The photographs are a result of nearly fifteen years of concentrated effort to develop specific techniques for gem photography. The ultimate goal is to capture on film the exact color of a faceted gemstone, while displaying to best advantage the cut and brilliance derived from the cutting. At the same time, hot spots or specular reflections from individual facets must be avoided, and the gem as pictured should have solidity and dimension, rather than appear flat or look like a painting. It is a major photographic challenge to achieve all these features simultaneously. The color plates in this book represent my current stage of technical competence, as modified by the limitations of converting color transparencies to images on paper, and there is considerable room for improvement. In many cases, however, the photos clearly show the degree of birefringence in a gem and also inclusions that are present, making the photos especially useful to the gemologist concerned with such matters.

There are nearly 250 species included in this volume. It must be remembered, of course, that any mineral species can be considered a gemstone if suitable cutting material can be found. Some minerals have been known for decades or centuries but have not been considered gem materials because pieces of sufficient size, cohesion, or transparency have never been available. This situation may change at any time with respect to a given mineral, so the list of gem species will undoubtedly increase with time.

The data presented herein were compiled from many sources. The primary sources are standard reference works in the mineralogical and gemological literature. These provided a framework of basic information about all the species covered. Gaps were then filled by research into the periodical literature of mineralogy and gemology. This yielded current information about localities, new gemstones, additional basic data, and some information on gemstone sizes. In some cases, as in the case of dispersion, mineralogical data were reworked into a form more familiar to the gemologist. Specifically, a Hartman dispersion net was used to plot refractive index vs. wavelength information, and the interval B–G was extracted and reported as the dispersion of the material in question.

Spectral data are provided only where a spectrum is distinctive enough to be useful in identification. Some spectra are complex and variable for a given mineral species, and in such cases the text lists only the pervasive or especially diagnostic lines.

Information on stone sizes comes from diverse sources. These sources include the standard literature, specialized books on specific gems (such as amber, pearl, opal, and diamond) and personal communications from cutters, dealers, collectors, and museum curators. There are sure to be omissions in noting the existence of large and important gems, for which I assume full responsibility. Such omissions can be eliminated in future editions through the assistance of readers of this book in sending me relevant information (see page vii).

Information on wearing characteristics of gems is inferred from analysis of mineral properties, comparison with other gems typically worn in jewelry, or from direct observation. No attempt has been made to disparage any particular gemstone, but rather an effort has been made to offer realistic advice on the liabilities and care of gems. The aim is the prevention of loss due to mishandling of more fragile or softer gems. Some gemstones are poor choices for ringstones, but make lovely earring or pendant stones.

The information presented in the text portion of this book is highly condensed. A basic familiarity with the principles and terminology is assumed, although a brief summary of important concepts is presented in the following pages. Further information is easily obtained from the many excellent specialized books available to interested readers, as listed in the Bibliography (see page 236).

In this edition I have used the new names for Ceylon, Rhodesia, and S.W. Africa: Sri Lanka, Zimbabwe, and Namibia, respectively. However, although Madagascar is now officially the Malagasy Republic, I have retained the older name for simplicity and familiarity.

Sins of omission, in preparing a book of this type, are invariably made and easily criticized. It is likely that many of the finest stones in existence are not on display but rather are held in private collections. There are probably a number of mineral species that have been faceted by hobbyists and either never reported in the literature or inadequately referenced. In all such cases, a plea is again made for assistance from readers in making future editions of this work more complete, comprehensive and accurate.

THE NATURE OF GEMS

As we have seen, gems are, with few exceptions, minerals. Minerals are naturally occurring chemical elements and compounds. Every mineral is characterized by a definite crystalline structure and a chemical composition that varies within defined limits.

The universe is made of atoms, which are the basic chemical units of matter. Every chemical element consists of atoms of a type characteristic of that element. Within the atom are yet smaller particles, some of which have electrical (+ or −) charges. The positively charged particles are called *protons* and are concentrated in the center or *nucleus* of the atom. Negatively charged particles, called *electrons,* surround the nucleus.

An isolated atom is electrically neutral because the number of positive charges within it is balanced by an equal number of negative charges. However, atoms may borrow electrons from each other, some atoms thus acquiring a net + charge and some a net − charge. Charged atoms are called *ions*. Positive ions are known as *cations*, and negative ions are called *anions*.

An atom that loses an electron seldom gives it up entirely. Usually the loan is half-hearted, and the donor atom shares the electron(s) with the recipient atom. Neither atom will give up the electron(s) completely, and the result is an endless tug-of-war that keeps the atoms involved joined together.

In some cases, however, atoms do gain or lose electrons entirely and become ions. But the atom losing an electron thus acquires a positive charge, and a neutral atom gaining an electron becomes negatively charged. Since it is a basic law of nature that unlike charges attract each other, the ions are held close to each other in a way similar to the atoms merely sharing electrons.

The forces holding atoms together are called *bonds*. Electron sharing produces *covalent* bonds, which are usually very strong. The second example mentioned above, involving the attraction of ions, is called an *ionic* bond. Other types of bonds are generally weaker than these bond types.

A group of atoms held together by bonds in such a way as to form a cohesive unit is called a *molecule*. The molecule is the smallest amount of a chemical compound that displays all the characteristics of the compound.

At a temperature of absolute zero (−273°C), atoms are completely at rest and do not vibrate. At all temperatures above this, however, atoms are in motion. At high temperatures, atomic vibration is so violent that bonds may form but are immediately broken. This is the situation in a gas or vapor, where atoms and molecules fly about at random and occupy all the space available to them.

At lower temperatures atoms stay in contact for a longer period of time, and may become bonded together but still retain a large degree of freedom of motion. This is the characteristic of liquids, in which atoms slide over each other but remain essentially in contact. Lowered temperatures further slow down atomic vibrations and prevent the atoms from breaking the bonds that form as a result of electrical attraction.

If the vibration is slowed down enough, the atoms become locked in fixed positions relative to one another. Every atom in a given mixture of atom types tries to surround itself with specific kinds of other atoms, all at fixed distances and relative positions. This becomes a kind of unit of pattern in three dimensions. The pattern is analogous to wallpaper, in which a (perhaps geometric) unit of pattern is repeated at regular intervals. The repetition of molecular pattern units in three dimensions results in a *crystal structure*.

Crystal structures are both repetitive and symmetrical. One can discern, within a structure, planes of atoms of a specific type. These may be bonded to adjacent planes of atoms of a different type. If these bonds happen to be weak, the plane of bonds may be a zone of structural weakness in the material. On a macroscopic scale, the crystal might tend to split along such planes.

Furthermore, light traveling through the material interacts with the atoms in the crystal structure. The interaction involves the light energy itself and the electrons surrounding the atoms in the structure. Bonds between atoms are, in a sense, regions in which electrons are more highly concentrated, and therefore bond energies in a structure are localized in regions between specific sets of atoms. Bond strengths within a crystal vary greatly in direction. Consequently, light is affected in different ways, depending on the path it takes through the crystal.

Crystal properties are directional, because the bonding within a crystal structure varies with direction, as well as the types of atoms involved. This concept is critical in understanding the properties of gems and minerals.

CRYSTAL STRUCTURES AND PROPERTIES

All solids are crystals, and every mineral is characterized by a crystal structure. Different minerals may have structures that are built of similar or even identical pattern units. However, no two minerals have exactly the same structural pattern *and* chemical composition.

A glass is rigid but is not considered a true solid because the atoms within it are not organized in a long-range periodic array. A glass may form when, upon cooling from a molten state, a material solidifies before the atoms can arrange themselves into a pattern. The strong bonds linking the atoms together overcome random motion of the atoms, and the material may become both rigid and hard. There is no single temperature at which all the bonds loosen and allow the atoms to move again. Consequently, glasses have no specific melting point but rather soften gradually and eventually begin to flow. Obsidian and tektites are examples of naturally occurring glasses.

Chemical composition and structure both play a role in determining the properties of a mineral or gemstone. For example, consider the minerals halite (NaCl) and cerargyrite (AgCl). Both substances crystallize in the isometric system, form cube-shaped crystals, and are colorless and transparent. The crystal structures are identical: each chlorine atom is surrounded by six metal atoms at equal distances. A plane of atoms in the structure parallel to a cube face would contain rows of alternating chlorine and metal atoms in both minerals.

The properties of these minerals, however, are very different. The specific gravity of halite is 2.17, that of cerargyrite is 5.55! The refractive index of halite is 1.54, whereas that of cerargyrite is 2.07. These large differences may be attributed to the presence of silver in cerargyrite as opposed to sodium in halite.

In the above instance, the structures and compositions of the minerals discussed are very simple, and the metal atoms are major essential components of the formulas. A study of mineral properties reveals, however, that even small variations in chemistry can have a major effect on physical properties. This applies both to different minerals with slightly different formulas and to variations in chemistry within a single mineral species.

A good example of this is the mineral beryl, which is beryllium aluminum silicate. Pure beryl is colorless. However, a relatively small amount (less than 1 percent) of chromium, substituting for aluminum in the structure, is sufficient to produce a brilliant, intense green color. The substitution occurs because the ions of aluminum and chromium are both trivalent (have a net charge of +3) and are about the same size. If there is chromium present in the solution from which the beryl crystal grows an occasional chromium atom is incorporated in the structure in the site normally occupied by an aluminum atom. As few as two chromium atoms in 5,000 aluminum sites will produce a green color. Iron in the beryl structure results in yellow or blue coloration, whereas manganese produces a pink color.

Many minerals may have their color thus altered by impurities. In most cases the impurity atoms are present in sufficiently large quantities to also affect physical properties such as specific gravity and refractive index. In general, impurities do not affect cleavage or hardness. Moreover, an impurity atom in a crystal structure is usually somewhat different in size and charge from the element it replaces. The result is that the structure can tolerate the presence of only a limited amount of the impurity before the strain on the structure becomes so great that the crystal cannot grow at all. Most cases of chemical substitution involve amounts of impurities ranging from less than 1 percent to as much as 10 percent.

There are, however, numerous examples of minerals in which complete substitution is possible. An example is the mineral siderite ($FeCO_3$), a very common carbonate in ore deposits. The element manganese may substitute for iron in the siderite structure in any amount. If 49 percent of the iron is replaced by manganese, the mineral is termed a *highly manganiferous siderite*. If the manganese content exceeds the iron content, the mineral is considered a new species: rhodochrosite. Pure rhodochrosite has the formula $MnCO_3$, and we might say that iron can substitute for manganese in any amount in the rhodochrosite structure. Obviously, the structures of siderite and rhodochrosite are identical. These two minerals comprise what is known as a *solid solution series*. The physical and chemical properties vary *continuously* from one end member of the series (in this case, pure rhodochrosite or pure siderite) to the other.

In many cases the variation in properties is said to be *linear*; that is, you can make a graph showing the variation in a parameter such as refractive index as the composition changes along the series, and the graph will turn out to be a straight line. This type of relationship is very useful, because within such a solution series you can determine the chemical composition just by measuring the refractive index! A graph of specific gravity vs. composition might show a similar relationship. A major problem in using such graphs is the oversimplification of the relationship between properties and chemistry. Usually more than one element may substitute for another in a crystal structure, and one must first sort out the separate effects of each substitution before a simple graph can be used with confidence.

Gemologists sometimes have a tendency to overlook mineralogical literature in evaluating gemstones, especially in cases where solid solutions are involved. The following is an example of this oversight.

Mineralogical convention states that, in the case of a simple two-component solid solution series, the 50 percent composition marks the dividing line between the two end-member species. One of these two species may be much more familiar than the other. A good example is the case of amblygonite: (Li, Na)Al(PO₄)(F, OH). Analyses have shown that complete substitution is possible between fluorine (F) and hydroxyl (OH) in the structure. Chemical analysis for these anions is tedious and beyond the range of the gemologist. However, measurable physical properties are markedly affected by the F-OH substitution. When hydroxyl is present in greater amounts than fluorine, we have a new species, called montebrasite.

Most gems cut from members of this series are amblygonite. However, many stones have been discussed in the literature as amblygonite, when a glance at the optical data reported for the gem reveals properties belonging to montebrasite! Montebrasite is not discussed at all in standard gemological literature, whereas this may be the correct species designation for many gems now labeled amblygonite in collections. A much greater awareness of the variation of physical properties with chemistry is required in gemological work; much of the needed information is readily available in standard mineralogy texts and is reported in this book.

It is important to remember that chemical variations in minerals are seldom simple. The geological environments in which minerals form are extremely complex, and a growing crystal often has a wide variety of elements competing for space in its structure. A parameter such as refractive index is very sensitive to small variations in chemical composition. In addition, most minerals have several structural sites (positions), each of which can accommodate a variety of different atoms. For example, in the mineral diopside (CaMgSi₂O₆), sodium may substitute for calcium, titanium for magnesium, and aluminum for silicon, all at the same time and in different amounts! In such cases it is not a simple matter to correlate changes in physical properties with compositional variations.

The above discussion makes it clear that the gemologist should become accustomed to thinking about gems in terms of families or groups of minerals. Diopside, for example, is a member of a group of about eight minerals with essentially the same structure and differing in composition. The appearance of many of these species is similar, and they have many similar properties. A gemstone can be initially identified as a member of the diopside-hedenbergite series, for example, and then further testing may indicate exactly where the gem in question lies within the series. Other well-known mineral groups, in which this approach is useful, are the garnets, feldspars, spinels, humites, sodalite, and tourmaline.

A listing of the members of important groups of gem minerals is found on page 241. The group concept of relating similar gem species has been used throughout this book.

ORIGIN OF GEMSTONES

Rocks make up the crust of the Earth. They are the most familiar of geological materials and their study provides clues about the long and turbulent history of our planet.

Rocks are made up of minerals, which are the chemical building blocks of our planet. A rock can consist of one mineral, as in the case of pure limestone, which is composed entirely of the mineral calcite. Most rocks, however, are made up of several minerals. These are usually present in the form of crystals or grains. The history and origin of a rock can be deciphered from its mineral content and the way the mineral grains contact each other. This latter feature, known as *texture*, is especially important in classifying rocks.

ROCK CLASSIFICATION

Rocks are classified according to their overall chemical composition, the minerals they contain, the rock texture, the size of the mineral grains or crystals present, and obvious physical features such as lamination or banding. There are three basic types of rocks.

Igneous rocks form as a result of the cooling of molten material called *magma* that usually originates deep in the Earth, below the upper layer called the *crust*. Magma may have varying composition, and different types of magmas produce different types of igneous rocks. A magma rich in water and silica (SiO₂) may cool to yield a light-colored rock known as granite; a silica-deficient magma may produce a black, dense rock called gabbro. A given magma may produce various types of rocks, depending on the cooling history, including rate of cooling and pressure changes within the molten material.

If magma solidifies deep within the Earth and cools very slowly, crystals have a chance to grow to large size, resulting in a rock with *coarse texture*. Igneous rocks that cool more quickly, as they would nearer the Earth's surface, develop a *fine texture*. An extreme example of a fine-textured rock is volcanic glass, which cools so quickly that crystals do not have a chance to develop at all. Two different rocks may contain the same minerals in the same proportions. They are differentiated according to grain size, which is a reflection of their cooling history.

Igneous rocks formed within the Earth are called *intrusive* or *plutonic* and usually have coarse textures. *Extrusive* rocks are formed when magma is ejected at the Earth's surface, as in a volcanic eruption, and are fine grained as a result of rapid cooling.

Light-colored igneous rocks are sometimes called acidic, a misnomer relating to the time when it was believed that mineral acids such as "silicic acid" were responsible for rock formation. The chemical opposite of an acid is a base, and basic rocks are dark-colored rocks that were once presumed deficient in "silicic acid." The terms are no longer valid but are mentioned here because they are occasionally used in the literature.

Sedimentary rocks are so named because they are composed of sediments, which are either rock and mineral fragments or the mineral and chemical weathering products of these materials. About 75 percent of the rocks exposed at the Earth's surface are sedimentary, and they form by the deposition, in water or air, of rock and mineral particles or by the precipitation of mineral material in water. The most obvious and distinctive feature of sedimentary rocks is banding, or layering, known as *stratification. Mechanical* or *detrital* sediments include sand, gravel, clay, silt, and mud. These particles may become rock through the processes of cementation or compaction. The first step in the hardening process is *consolidation*, accompanied by the expulsion of water and volatile materials, and the entire process may be referred to as *lithification*. An *evaporite* is a sedimentary rock formed by the evaporation of saline water (either an ocean or lake) with the consequent precipitation of salts, such as halite, gypsum, and borates. *Coal* is a sedimentary rock composed of the remains of plants that lived millions of years ago. Chemical sedimentary rocks are formed by accumulation of marine precipitates, usually calcium carbonate. The most familiar rock formed in this way is *limestone*. Solutions containing magnesium may later alter a limestone bed, producing a massive bed of the mineral *dolomite*. Some sedimentary rocks are created by consolidation of particles laid down by winds or even glaciers.

Metamorphic rocks are created when Earth pressures and heat alter previously existing rocks. Metamorphism is a word derived from the Greek, meaning "change of form." Any kind of rock may be metamorphosed, and the major result is a reorganization of the mineral and chemical components of the previous rock. Some minerals that form in a given set of geological conditions are unstable in drastically different conditions. In the latter eventuality they actually break down, decompose, and *recrystallize* into other minerals that are more stable in the new conditions. Rocks can be metamorphosed on a wide scale as a result of the kinds of forces that produce mountain ranges. These are known as *regionally metamorphosed* rocks. Alternatively, a rock bed, such as a limestone, may be invaded by magma forced up from deep within the Earth. The heat and chemical components of the magma chemically and physically alter the limestone, resulting in the formation of a wide range of new minerals. This process is called *contact metamorphism*. Certain minerals are very characteristic of either re-

gional or contact metamorphism, and one can determine the extent of metamorphism in an area by examining the mineralogy of the rocks over a wide area. Metamorphic rocks are classified according to bulk chemistry, reflecting the composition of the original, unaltered rock and the metamorphic minerals present, which indicate the temperature and pressure reached during metamorphism.

The Earth is in a constant state of change. Rocks in some places are being melted or pulled into the interior; others are being created in spectacular volcanic episodes. Sediments are being deposited and compacted in oceans throughout the world. The earth is a closed system, with nothing added or removed (noting the negligible addition of meteoritic material). (The chemical elements of the Earth are thus repeatedly mixed and separated by geologic processes. The entire process of rock genesis, destruction, and alteration comprises a cycle. Sedimentary rocks are formed as a result of the breakdown of other rocks. Igneous rocks are created by the cooling of magma and hot solutions. Metamorphic rocks result from the transformation of igneous and sedimentary rocks by heat and pressure. All these rocks, in their turn, are worn down and become new sediments. The so-called *geologic cycle* is thus revealed as a complex mechanism of creation and destruction of rocks.

Geologic structures may be characteristic of certain rock types. For example, a volcano is clearly composed of igneous material. Large folds visible in rocks exposed on a mountain slope are evidence of the action of metamorphic forces. Terraced cliffs, such as those exposed in the Grand Canyon of Arizona, are bedded sedimentary rock layers.

It is important to remember that gems are simply minerals, albeit of a very special quality. Minerals are components of rocks. Every mineral species is characterized by a definite structure and chemical composition. The same chemical ingredients may crystallize in different structural arrangements, depending on external parameters, such as temperature and pressure. Although they may have the same composition, these different structural arrangements qualify as distinct mineral species, such as, for example, rutile, anatase and brookite, which are all composed of titanium oxide. The conditions at the time of mineral formation determine which of the three mineral species with this composition will form.

The controlling influence of physical conditions is most clearly seen in metamorphic rocks. During metamorphism the temperature and pressure conditions in a region may rise greatly over a period of time. A given assemblage of chemical ingredients may be stable in the form of a certain mineral at low pressure and temperature but when these conditions change beyond a certain point, that mineral may no longer be stable. The mineral then decomposes, and the chemical constituents arrange themselves in a way that is more stable in the new conditions.

A good example of this is the mineral quartz, the most common mineral on Earth. Quartz, in the form we see as pretty crystals or as a component of beach sand, is stable up to a temperature of 870°C. Above this temperature the framework of Si and O atoms characteristic of quartz vibrates too rapidly to hold together in the pattern of the quartz structure. An *inversion*, or change in structural arrangement, occurs and we have a new mineral called tridymite. Tridymite has the same composition as quartz (SiO_2) but a different structure that is stable at higher temperatures than the quartz structure. The tridymite structure, in fact, is more open, allowing it to accommodate the increased vibrational movement of the atoms at higher temperatures. However, even this structure is torn apart by atomic vibration at 1470°C, and a totally new mineral, known as cristobalite, forms. The cristobalite structure is capable of handling very large atomic vibrations, but only up to a temperature of 1710°C. At this temperature no structure of Si and O atoms is stable, and cristobalite melts to a very viscous liquid. The atoms in the melt are then free of the relatively rigid atomic bonds that hold a crystal structure together and can vibrate as much as is necessitated by higher temperatures within the melt.

A given rock, with a particular history of formation, therefore characterizes a very specific range of conditions in which minerals can form. The environment of formation of a mineral is thus a combination of specific conditions, such as temperature and pressure, available chemical components, and such miscellaneous factors as solution flow, metamorphic directional stresses, and rates of cooling and heating. The chemical environment is determined by local rock types and their mineral content, plus the introduction of materials by migrating waters or vapors.

Obviously, the formation of a mineral is often a complex affair. Conceptually, however, the whole subject of mineral environment and formation, collectively known as *paragenesis*, can be reduced to a simple rule: *Minerals are found where they ought to be.* This seemingly simple statement is really the first rule of mineral exploration.

For example, if you want to locate a source of peridot, you must first know that peridot is the gem form of the mineral olivine. Olivine is characteristic of basaltic rocks. A basaltic magma has the right chemical ingredients for the crystallization of olivine and also exists at the right temperature. Olivine is, in fact, the mineral with the highest melting point in a basaltic magma, and therefore is the first to crystallize when the magma cools. The olivine crystals that appear within the melt are heavier than the surrounding liquid and consequently sink. Thus,

in a large body of basalt that formed as a thick lava flow, or within an intrusive dark-colored igneous rock mass, olivine crystals of large size would most likely be found at the bottom. In fact, we do find zones of coarse-grained olivine at the lower part of lava flows or large intrusive bodies.

Gemstone occurrences are usually somewhat more complex. Gems are very special mineral oddities in that they are very pure or have formed under special conditions that allowed crystals to grow free of imperfections, inclusions, cavities, and fractures.

GEM SCARCITY

The environment of formation of a gem crystal may be the same as for any other crystal of the same species, but chance has acted in a way that produces crystals that are larger or of better color than is usually encountered in the species. In this sense, gems are actually mineralogical freaks. They are not abundant and are restricted in occurrence *only* to those localities where conditions were suitable for their formation. If the mineral in question is rare, gem-quality crystals of that species are much rarer. A particular mineral species, such as topaz, for example, may be widespread and abundant throughout the world. However, large transparent crystals of a deep pink or orange color are exceedingly uncommon. Pink and orange gem topaz, seen in a *geological* context, are so rare that it is amazing they have been found at all!

Rarity in gems is thus a function of several factors. In some cases the various requirements of composition and conditions of formation of a species are seldom fulfilled simultaneously, as in the case of proustite and manganotantalite. Such *species* are therefore rare in their own right, regardless of whether they form crystals transparent enough to cut.

Sometimes a mineral species is not rare, but transparent, cuttable crystals are very seldom encountered. This is the situation for most of the so-called *collector gems*.

Another case is rarity of color. A good example is emerald, the deep green variety of the mineral beryl. Beryl occurs throughout the world, usually in pegmatites (see page 53). Emerald owes its green color to the element chromium. Chromium, however, is *not* usually present in pegmatites. Its geochemical environment is rather in dark-colored (basic) igneous rocks. Beryl is rarely found in these latter geologic environments, largely because its primary constituent, beryllium, is rare in basic rocks. The conditions necessary for the occurrence of emerald, that is, the formation of beryl plus the availability of chromium, are mutually incompatible! This accounts for the worldwide paucity of emerald. The reasons become obvious when one understands the geologic factors.

Finally, there is scarcity in size. Topaz, for example,

occurs in crystals that weigh hundreds of pounds. These are usually colorless or very pale yellow or blue. However, topaz crystals of a fine pink color are never seen in sizes larger than a few inches. A huge faceted gem of white topaz is not especially rare, but a 10 carat pink topaz is very rare indeed.

Likewise, rubies of very fine quality (color and transparency) are extremely rare over about 10 carats, but sapphires, which are mineralogically equivalent to ruby (both are the mineral corundum), are encountered in crystals weighing hundreds of carats.

Large amethyst crystals are found in many localities. However, pieces free of inclusions weighing more than 50 carats are quite rare. In general, rarity is a combination of a number of factors, all of which depend on the basic geology of a gem species plus the status of the marketplace. Scarcity is a function of the following factors: geologic abundance of the species in question; desirable color, size, and freedom from imperfections; market availability (number of producing localities and the sizes of the deposits); demands of the market.

A gemstone occurrence is a very rare and transient geologic feature. Once exhausted, it cannot be replenished within the span of human lifetimes. Synthetics can be manufactured in the laboratory, but the value of natural gems will not be affected as long as they can be distinguished as rare *natural* objects of great beauty.

The gem market is continually faced with the threat of depletion of known gem deposits or loss of production due to political factors. This puts great pressure on other known sources to meet world demand. Depletion of supply coupled with high demand creates rising prices. Gems have had great appeal throughout history as financial products. Their main functions have been to hide, concentrate, transfer, store, and display wealth. Gems are what might be called "real value" commodities, with desirability in all cultures, throughout all the periods of human history.

Geological scarcity accounts for such rare gems as painite and taaffeite. Only one painite crystal has been found, and less than one hundred cut taaffeites are know. To be sure, more specimens of both materials may exist; painite resembles ruby and taaffeite looks like mauve spinel; misidentified cut stones may exist in various collections and inventories. Nonetheless, such rare collector gems offer a situation comparable to art. Rembrandt is dead, and no additional *original* Rembrandts can be produced. By analogy, an exhausted gem deposit can produce no more gemstones.

With this in mind, consider the future of gem prices. We may someday see rare stones command prices comparable to the levels of great art. There may be only one da Vinci "Last Supper," but there is (at least, at the time of this writing) also only one painite.

ROCK TYPES

Igneous Rocks

INTRUSIVE

Granite—core of many mountain ranges. Coarse texture, composed of potassium feldspar, quartz, plus some mica or hornblende and accessory minerals.
Syenite—similar to granite; contains little or no quartz; fine grained.
Pegmatite—very coarse-grained rock, composition like granite. Frequently contains immense crystals and rare, exotic elements. Home of many gem minerals.
Diorite—dark colored, contains plagioclase feldspar, little quartz, some biotite.
Granodiorite—like diorite, but richer in potassium feldspar.
Tonalite—like diorite, but contains some quartz.
Monzonite—intermediate between syenite and diorite.
Gabbro—diorite rich in calcic plagioclase feldspar; contains pyroxenes as opposed to amphiboles.
Anorthosite—rock composed almost entirely of anorthite feldspar.
Diabase—fine-grained gabbro typical of small intrusive bodies.
Peridotite—dark rock composed of pyroxene and olivine.
Dunite—peridotite-like rock containing chiefly olivine.
Kimberlite—an altered peridotite characterized by high-pressure minerals.

EXTRUSIVE

Rhyolite—light-colored, fine-grained rock, with composition like granite.
Obsidian—volcanic glass, with overall composition like rhyolite.
Pumice—"frothy" volcanic rock, full of gas bubbles, and will float on water!
Porphyry—igneous rock with different grain sizes, reflecting cooling history; larger crystals called *phenocrysts* lie in fine-grained *groundmass*. The phenocrysts formed by slow cooling, and then the rock was suddenly chilled.
Basalt—dark-colored, fine-grained rock, typical of lava flows. Very widespread. Also known as *traprock*.
Scoria—porous, cinderlike rock seen at tops of lava flows.
Andesite—volcanic equivalent of diorite, dark colored.
Trachyte—volcanic equivalent of syenite.

Sedimentary Rocks

Conglomerate—made of large, rounded pebbles and smaller grains, cemented together.

Sandstone—composed of sand-size (between 1/16 and 2 mm) particles. Sandstone refers to particle size, not composition; therefore, quartz sandstone is made of quartz grains.

Arkose—sandstone composed chiefly of feldspar and quartz grains.

Graywacke—dense, dark-colored sandstone with rock fragments and clay particles.

Shale—fine-grained rock composed of clay or silt-sized (microscopic) particles.

Limestone—chemical precipitate of calcium carbonate in sea water. Sometimes the fossil remains of large reefs, built by corals and other animals long ago.

Chalk—calcareous chemical precipitate, composed of tiny marine plants and animal skeletons, plus biochemically deposited calcite.

Dolomite—massive sedimentary rock composed chiefly of the mineral dolomite.

Travertine—limestone formed in caves by slow evaporation of solutions.

SEDIMENTARY FEATURES

Concretions are masses of cementing material, the same cement (such as silica or iron oxide) that caused lithification of nearby sediments. Usually spherical, they sometimes assume fantastic and grotesque shapes.

Nodules are masses of mineral material differing in composition from the rocks in which they are found.

Geodes are hollow, more or less round objects, often containing an interior lining of terminated crystals. Geodes are usually made of quartz, but may contain a wide variety of other minerals. Geodes commonly occur in shales, but also form in gas pockets in igneous rocks and accumulate in the soils resulting from the weathering of such rocks.

Metamorphic Rocks

Slate—formed by the low-grade metamorphism of shale. Pressure causes aligning of the clay particles in the shale, resulting in easy breakage of the rock into layers.

Phyllite—next step upward in metamorphism from slate. May have a shiny appearance on broken surfaces, due to parallel alignment of recrystallized mineral grains.

Schist—can be derived from various rock types by intense recrystallization; tends to break between layers to produce characteristic uneven, wavy surface. Schists are named according to the minerals they contain. Often characterized by folded, crumpled look.

Gneiss—coarse-grained, banded rock formed by intense

metamorphism. Does not show tendency to split along planes, but minerals are arranged in parallel layers.

Marble—coarse-grained calcareous rock produced by metamorphic recrystallization of limestone.

Quartzite—dense, compact rock, produced by recrystallization of quartz grains in a sedimentary quartzite or sandstone.

Skarn—complex mineral assemblage produced by contact metamorphism of an impure limestone or dolomite. Minerals of economic value in such assemblages are often called *contact deposits*.

IDENTIFICATION OF GEMSTONES

There are approximately thirty-five hundred known mineral species. A few new minerals are added every year, and occasionally an existing species is discredited when careful analysis reveals it to be a mixture of other minerals. The number of mineral species is very small in comparison to the huge list of compounds known to chemistry. This is because minerals are naturally occurring chemical elements and compounds. There are geochemical restrictions that limit the number of possible mineral species, namely, the tendency for certain elements to be restricted to specific geochemical environments. Random chance also plays a major role in terms of the temperature and pressure that happen to be prevalent in the environment where chemical reactions occur and minerals are forming.

Very rarely is a new mineral species found in large, well-formed crystals. An example of such an occurrence is the mineral brazilianite, which was described on the basis of spectacular, large, and even gemmy crystals discovered in Brazil. Usually, however, a new mineral is recognized only with great difficulty. An astute observer may be studying a complex mineral assemblage and recognize a few grains of an unfamiliar mineral. Detailed analysis may show that the material has a chemical composition slightly different from another, well-known species; the difference may be large enough to warrant calling the unknown material a new species. In some cases there is barely enough of the new mineral even to perform a complete chemical analysis! Most of the new minerals added to the known list are in this category of obscure grains very limited in quantity. Very sophisticated analytical devices are required for this type of descriptive work.

The situation with gems is not so demanding. Usually the gemologist's major problem is to pin down the composition of a gemstone in order to locate the material within a solid solution series, as for example in the case of garnets and feldspars. In some such cases a measurable property, such as refractive index, may vary linearly with chemical composition. The composition may therefore be determined by carefully measuring refractive index and using a graph to pick off the corresponding chemistry. This type of analysis works only in simple cases, such as in the olivine series, where the only major chemical variable is the ratio of iron and magnesium. In most solid solution series, however, the chemistry is far too complex for simple correlations, and a combination of tests is needed for identification.

The most useful instrument for gemstone identification is the microscope, especially a stereoscopic type fitted with special darkfield illumination in which light enters the gemstone only from the sides. This instrument is ideal for the examination of inclusions, which are frequently diagnostic in identification. Magnification also reveals cleavage developed on a small scale as well as the degree of surface finish on a stone, which allows an estimate of hardness. Fracture may also be determined by observing small chips on the girdle of a faceted gem.

The refractometer is used to measure, with good accuracy, the refractive index and birefringence of most gems. Some gems have indices too high for measurement with a standard refractometer; the microscope can sometimes be used for direct measurement of refractive index, using a technique discussed in standard gemological texts (see Bibliography on page 236). Specific gravity may be determined with heavy liquids or with torsion balances. Gravity measurement plus refractive index usually allows for unambiguous identification of a gemstone. In some cases the spectroscope provides very rapid and unambiguous analysis, as for example in distinguishing between almandine garnet and ruby. The polariscope is useful in determining the optical character of a gemstone.

There are only about two hundred fifty mineral species that have been cut as gems, a fact that makes the gemologist's life easier than that of the mineralogist, who is concerned with more than three thousand five hundred species. It is important to remember, however, that at any time a mineral species may be encountered in a form with gem potential. If such a material is brought to a gemologist for identification, he or she may be mystified when the properties of the substance do not match anything in standard gemological reference tables. In such cases it is necessary to resort to more powerful techniques for identification.

An extremely powerful diagnostic tool, routinely used by the mineralogist, is virtually unknown to the gemological fraternity. This is the X-ray powder diffraction camera, a device that can, in most instances, provide unambiguous identification of a mineral in a period of a few hours.

The detailed principles of X-ray methods are too complex for elaboration here. A brief summary of the approach is, however, warranted. X-rays are pulses of energy, like light and heat, but with very short wavelengths. The level of energy in an X-ray beam is on the same order of magnitude as the energy associated with the electrons that spin about the nucleus of all types of atoms. Consequently, if an X-ray beam enters a crystal, it can interact with the electrons of the atoms in the crystal structure. The more electrons an atom has (that is, the heavier the atom) the greater the degree of interaction.

The incoming X-ray beam enters the crystal in one specific direction. However, the electrons in the crystal's atoms absorb the X-ray energy, and re-emit this energy almost instantaneously in *all* directions (radially). The situation is as if each electron were itself acting as a source of X-rays. All the electrons affected within a particular atom combine their radiations and the atom itself acts as an X-ray source.

Intuitively, one would expect that the X-rays emerging from the crystal would be in the form of a glow or diffuse spherical emanation of uniform intensity. However, the atoms in the crystal are arranged in rows and layers, with definite spacings between them. The spacings in a crystal structure are about the same size as the wavelength of the X-rays. This situation is analogous to an optical device known as a *diffraction grating*, the principles of which may be found in any standard physics textbook. When diffraction occurs off a grating, radiation emitted from a row of regularly spaced point sources is reinforced along certain directions and is completely cancelled out along other directions! These directions can be predicted and described mathematically, based on the wavelength of the radiation and the spacing between the point sources. The case of crystals is much more complex because the diffraction takes place in *three* directions (dimensions) simultaneously, and the exact interaction of the various beams is enormously difficult to calculate. The result of all this is that whereas a single X-ray beam enters the crystal, a divergent array of diffracted beams comes out. These diffracted beams come out in specific directions. In addition, each beam is the result of interactions with various rows of atoms and a variety of types of atoms, each type contributing radiation based on its particular electronic makeup. The intensities of all the diffracted beams therefore vary widely.

A special camera has been devised in which a crystal being irradiated with X-rays is surrounded by special photographic film. The film records the positions and (through degree of darkening) the intensities of the diffracted X-ray beams. These parameters are measured on the film and listed as a set of line spacings and intensities. Such parameters have been measured and tabulated for all the known mineral species. A rapid search of the tabulation usually allows the crystal to be quickly and unambiguously identified in a matter of a few minutes.

A major advantage of the X-ray approach is that powder analysis requires a very small amount of sample. In the case of a faceted gem, a tiny bit of material can be scraped from the girdle with a diamond stylus without materially damaging the stone.

X-ray methods can be used advantageously in cases where optical and other data acquired by normal means are ambiguous. In some cases a gem is a very rare cut example of a mineral not usually found in gem quality. In this instance the standard gemological measurements are not present in tabulations in textbooks, and the mineralogical literature must be consulted. In another case, a gemologist may encounter a synthetic gem material, such as a rare-earth garnet, the properties of which are also not tabulated in the gem literature. X-ray analysis would be definitive here because the tabulation of

X-ray measurements extends to the entire range of organic and inorganic compounds as well as minerals.

X-ray equipment is expensive and requires great care in use. The X-ray beams produced for mineral analysis are extremely potent and capable of great damage to human tissue. Many large cities do have complete analytical laboratories that may offer diffraction as a service. The active gemologist should make an effort to locate such a laboratory for those times when diffraction offers special advantages in identification.

The gemologist should always remember that the chemical composition of minerals varies widely, with corresponding variation in physical properties. There is almost always a range of values in parameters such as refractive index, specific gravity and optical spectrum (presence or absence of diagnostic lines). By maintaining a continual awareness of the principles of crystal chemistry, the gemologist can avoid confusion and increase by many times the power of his or her analytical abilities.

Sources of Data Used in Text

FORMULA

The chemical composition of a mineral is a primary aspect of its definition as a species. The reader is referred to a periodic table of the chemical elements (page 243) for standard abbreviations of the names of elements.

Many formulas contain parentheses within which are listed several elements, for example (Fe,Mg). This indicates that there is a specific position in the crystal structure that may be occupied by either iron, or magnesium, or both. The element listed first within the parentheses is the one present in greater amount on the structural site. In some cases this determines the species! For example, amblygonite is $(Li,Na)Al(PO_4)(F,OH)$. However, if the formula reads $(Li,Na)Al(PO_4)(OH,F)$, we have a new species in which hydroxyl exceeds fluorine, and the species is now called montebrasite. Furthermore, if the formula is $(Na,Li)Al(PO_4)(OH,F)$, sodium exceeds lithium and the mineral is classed as yet another species, natromontebrasite. Obviously, the degree of complexity associated with solid solution can be very great. Any substitution of elements on a crystallographic structural site may (or may not) have an effect on physical properties.

Impurities also affect properties. A good example is beryl, $Be_3Al_2Si_6O_{18}$, but often containing such elements as Fe, Mn, Cr, V, and Cs. These elements are usually present in such small quantities that they are not written into the formula. However, the mineralogist understands that Cr, for example, which makes beryl the rich green color we know as emerald, substitutes for Al in the structure. A detailed knowledge of chemical substitutions and color changes in crystals requires a much greater sophistication in crystal chemical principles than can be expounded here.

Formulas given in this book are based on the most recent mineralogical studies. Chemical elements listed after a plus (+) sign following the formula are those most often noted as substituting for elements in the formula.

CRYSTALLOGRAPHY

The reader is referred to standard books on mineralogy or crystallography for detailed background and terminology. It will suffice here to say that crystals grow in such a way that their component atoms and molecules are locked together in periodic arrays, much like three-dimensional wallpaper patterns. These arrays have symmetry of various types that can be described and categorized. When this is done, it is discovered that all known crystals can be organized according to six major crystal systems: *isometric*, *tetragonal*, *hexagonal*, *orthorhombic*, *monoclinic*, and *triclinic*. A subclass of the hexagonal system that is sometimes (though erroneously) regarded as a seventh crystal system is known as *trigonal*. Each crystal system is defined in terms of crystal axes, which are imaginary lines in space that intersect at a common point and whose lengths may be described as equal or unequal to each other. The systems are further described in terms of the angles that these axes make with each other.

Various descriptive terms may be used in describing the crystals exhibited by various mineral species. These terms include prismatic (elongated), bladed, acicular (needlelike), filiform (hairlike), equant (roughly equal-length sides), pyramidal (looking like single or double pyramids), and tabular. Sometimes terms are used that refer to specific forms characteristic of specific crystal systems (octahedron, pyritohedron, and so forth). Other terms used to describe a mineral's appearance refer to state of aggregation: massive (solid and chunky), compact (solid and dense), cleavable (crystalline masses that can be cleaved), granular (masses of compact grains), stalactitic (resembling the form of stalactites), oolitic (masses of spherical grains), earthy (masses of densely packed powder).

The appearance of a mineral is largely a function of the growth process and the environment of formation. Minerals deposited in sedimentary environments tend to be earthy, stalactitic, oolitic, and sometimes massive. Igneous minerals tend to be crystalline or massive, sometimes cleavable. All these terms are somewhat subjective but are useful in getting a mental image of the appearance of a mineral as it occurs in the Earth.

COLOR

The color of a mineral or gemstone is one of the primary attributes used for identification, but it is, unfortunately, one of the least diagnostic and useful (except in a handful of cases). The colors reported include all those mentioned in the mineralogical or gemological literature. These are useful to gemologists primarily as a guide as to what could be expected in the future, that is, the *potential* color of a gemstone. A mineral may, at any time, be found in gem quality in a new or unfamiliar color. A good example is zoisite, found in Africa in a striking blue variety in the 1960s and given the trade name *tanzanite*.

The streak (color of a mineral powder) is listed where it is useful for identification. This characteristic applies almost exclusively to opaque, metallic minerals, because the powder of most transparent minerals is colorless (white).

The color names applied to gems and minerals have become familiar through long usage. Some gem color names, such as "pigeon's-blood" (ruby) or "padparadschah" (sapphire), are vague, but have remained in the marketplace because no useful alternatives existed. However, accurate color measurement instrumentation is now available and is about to revolutionize the gemstone industry. Color specification systems for most colored materials (paints, dyes, etc.) have long been employed, and standards and procedures for measurement have been established by international professional societies in the color field. A gemstone colorimeter was used to measure a large array of gemstone color varieties and species for this book. The chapter on color measurement represents the first appearance in the gemological literature of objective gemstone color data, reported in terms considered standard by the color measurement and standardization field.

The future of gemology clearly lies in the direction of greater objectivity and standardization in measurement and terminology. Reference books on color technology should rapidly start to appear on the shelves of any competent gemologist's working library. It is vital that the field of gemology start moving toward color designations (CIE, CIELAB, Munsell, OSA-UCS, etc.) that are in daily use in all other color measurement fields.

LUSTER

Luster is considered a basic descriptive parameter for minerals but varies somewhat even within a single crystal, and its usefulness is therefore limited. Lusters include: vitreous (the luster of glass—characteristic of most gem minerals); pearly (iridescent, pearl-like); resinous (luster of resin); greasy (appears covered by oil layer); adamantine (hard, steely brilliance like the reflection from a diamond); silky (fibrous reflection of silk); dull.

Luster is a phenomenon of reflected light and is mostly due to the state of aggregation of the mineral. For example, gypsum may have a vitreous luster on some crystal faces; the luster is pearly on surfaces parallel to the excellent cleavage of this mineral; and if the mineral occurs in aggregates of long fibers (satin spar), it has a silky luster. Luster can hardly be a useful diagnostic property in identifying gypsum under these circumstances!

Luster is primarily divided into two types: *metallic* and *nonmetallic*. There are also intermediate types, called *submetallic*. Any mineral that does not have a metallic appearance is described as nonmetallic, and the above descriptive terms are applied.

HARDNESS

Hardness is the resistance to scratching of a smooth surface. Hardness has little use to the gemologist, since gems are not normally scratched as a part of gem testing. A hardness is sometimes taken on the back of a statue, as for example to differentiate between jade and serpentine. But even using the girdle of a gem to perform a hardness test results in chipping on occasion.

Hardness depends on the bonding that holds the atoms together within a crystal structure. This bonding is reflected in the ease with which the layers of atoms at a surface can be separated, by applying pressure with a sample of another material. If the second material is harder than the first, it will leave a furrow, or scratch, which represents the breaking of millions of atomic bonds on a microscopic scale. The hardness of a mineral is, specifically, its "scratchability," and all minerals can be ranked in order of which one will scratch which other ones.

Mineralogist Friedrich Mohs established a reference scale of ten common minerals, ranked in order of increasing hardness, as follows:

1. Talc
2. Gypsum
3. Calcite
4. Fluorite
5. Apatite
6. Feldspar
7. Quartz
8. Topaz
9. Corundum
10. Diamond

In reality, diamond is very much harder than corundum, even though the scale says they are only one division apart. The Mohs scale is approximately linear from 1 through 9; the curve climbs sharply upward at corundum, however.

A mineral may be both hard and brittle, as in the case of diamond. Diamond will scratch any other known material, but a strong hammer blow can shatter a diamond into thousands of pieces. The perfect cleavage of diamond, in fact, allows it to be more expeditiously cut. Cleavage may be an initial diamond cutting operation, as opposed to the long and tedious process of sawing.

Hardness in a gemstone will determine the degree to which it will show wear. An opal, for example, which is quite soft for a ringstone, rapidly becomes covered with fine scratches in daily use, and the polish is quickly lost. A ruby, on the other hand, will remain bright and lustrous for years, because the material is harder than most of the abrasive particles in the atmosphere that contribute to gem wear.

The hardness of a material may vary slightly with composition and also with state of aggregation. The measurement of hardness is very tricky and often a mark that looks like a scratch is actually a trail of powder left by the supposedly harder material! It is really not critical whether the hardness of a mineral is 5 or 5 1/2. Fractional hardnesses are reported where the literature has indicated an intermediate value. A range in hardness is much more meaningful, and the values reported in this book represent all values encountered in the literature. In only one case (kyanite) does the hardness of a mineral vary very widely even within a single crystal. In most cases the hardness range reported is very small (one unit).

DENSITY

Density, or specific gravity, is a bulk property of a material that is independent of direction and is uniform within a mass of material under ideal circumstances.

In actuality, the density of a mineral varies widely, even within a single crystal, due to the presence of impurities, cracks, and bubbles. Density is a useful parameter in gem identification, so the problems in its determination should be well understood.

Specific gravity is the ratio expressing the weight of a given material compared to that of an equal volume of water at 4°C. Thus, a specific gravity of 3 means that, at 4°C, one cubic centimeter of the material in question weighs 3 times as much as one cubic centimeter of water.

The density of a compound is a function of several factors, including chemical composition and crystal structure. For example, consider diamond and graphite, both of which are crystalline forms of the element carbon. Diamond has a density of 3.5 because the carbon atoms are tightly packed together in the structure; graphite, with a much more loose, open structure, has a density of only 2.2.

The density of minerals within a solid solution series may vary linearly with change in composition. The effect of chemical substitution is seen dramatically in the case of the orthorhombic carbonate minerals aragonite and cerussite. Aragonite is $CaCO_3$ and has a specific gravity of 2.95; cerussite, with the same structure, is composed of $PbCO_3$ and has a specific gravity of 6.55! This clearly shows the role of lead versus calcium in the structure.

Specific gravities are usually measured with heavy liquids. A liquid is prepared, such as a mixture of bromoform and toluene, to have a specific density value. An unknown material dropped into the liquid may sink, float, or remain suspended in one place within the liquid. If the material sinks, it is denser than the liquid, and if it floats it is less dense. If it remains at one level it has the same density as the liquid. Very accurate measurements of specific gravity can be made by changing the density of a column of liquid through temperature variations and suspending density standards in the column.

An alternative method of measurement is the use of so-called torsion balances, such as the Hanneman balance and the Berman balance used by mineralogists. These devices are designed to weigh a sample first in air and then suspended in a liquid, such as water or toluene. The weights in both media can be measured quite accurately and specific gravities can sometimes be reported to two decimal places.

A major problem in all density measurements is the presence of impurities within the crystal being studied. These impurities hardly ever have the same specific gravity as the host material, and their presence results in measurements that are of limited use for identification purposes. Surface tension may also "float" a mineral grain in both heavy liquids and a torsion balance, resulting in an erroneously low specific gravity measurement. Accurate density measurement involves absolute cleanliness, great care in specimen preparation, accurate temperature control, and replicate measurements.

The specific gravity measurements reported in this book represent values taken from both the mineralogical and gemological literature. In most cases a range is reported, as well as a typical value or (where reported) the value of the pure material.

CLEAVAGE

Hardness, as discussed earlier, is the scratchability of a material. Cleavage and the related property, *fracture*, are both manifestations of the tendency of certain crystals to break along definite plane surfaces. As in the case of hardness, the underlying principle is that of relative bond strengths. If there are planes in a crystal structure along which the atomic bonds are relatively weak, the crystal may tend to break along such planes. Under ideal circumstances, a cleavage plane might be smooth and flat, virtually on an atomic scale.

The atomic arrangement within a crystal is symmetrical; consequently, the planes of specific bonds are symmetrically disposed within the crystal. Cleavage planes are therefore as symmetrical as crystal faces. By the same reasoning, glass can have no cleavage whatever. Glass is not crystalline but is rather a supercooled liquid, in which the atoms are not arranged in a long-range periodic array. There can therefore be no uniform bond layers and hence no cleavage.

Cleavage is usually described with reference to crystallographic axes and directions. However, this nomenclature is beyond the scope of this book, so in all cases only the number of cleavage directions in a gem species has been indicated and whether the cleavage is perfect (eminent), good, fair, or poor. Sometimes there are different degrees of cleavage perfection in different directions within the same crystal, and these have been so indicated in the text.

The term *parting* refers to breakage of minerals along directions of structural weakness. Unlike the situation in cleavage, parting is not present in all specimens of a given species.

Fracture is the way a mineral breaks other than along cleavage directions. The descriptive terms for this property are: conchoidal (shell-like, distinguished by concentric curved lines; this is the way glass breaks); fibrous; splintery; hackly (consisting of sharp-edged and jagged fracture surfaces); uneven.

Gems with perfect cleavage must be set carefully and worn carefully, as a sharp blow to the stone along a cleavage direction may easily split the gem. Spodumene is well known for its difficulty in cutting. Even topaz offers occasional problems to the cutter who is not aware of the cleavage direction, because it is virtually impossible to polish a gemstone surface that is parallel to a cleavage plane.

OPTICS

Accurate measurements of the optical properties of gems are very useful because optical properties are extremely sensitive to minute changes in composition and strain in the crystal structure.

The basis of crystal optics is the premise that light travels in the form of waves, like ripples on a pond. The distance between successive crests or troughs of such a wave is known as the *wavelength*, and the *amplitude* of the wave is the height of the wave above the median (middle position between crest and trough). In familiar terms, different colors are different wavelengths, and the amplitude is the intensity of the light. Light vibrates at right angles to its direction of motion, and the vibration takes place in all directions perpendicular to the light path.

When light passes from one medium (such as air) into another (such as water) the light is actually slowed down. In addition, the light path is bent. The deviation is always referred to a line perpendicular to the interface between the two media, which is known as the *normal* to the interface. The light is always bent toward the normal in the medium in which the light travels slower.

The ratio between the velocity of light in the two media is called the index of refraction or *refractive index*; the first medium is usually taken to be air, in which the light velocity is considered unity (1). The refractive index then becomes $1/v$, where v is the velocity of light in the denser medium. Refractive index (usually abbreviated n) is also frequently described in terms of the angle to the normal made by the incoming light beam (incident ray) and that made by the refracted beam (traveling within the denser medium). Index of refraction in these terms equals the sine of the angle of incidence divided by the sine of the angle of refraction.

It is possible for light traveling from a given medium into a less dense medium, as, for example from a crystal into air, to strike the interface at such an angle that the light is totally reflected at the interface, back into the denser medium. The incidence angle at which this takes place is known as the *critical angle*. This angle has great significance in terms of gem cutting. If the angles at which the gemstone are cut are incorrectly matched to the refractive index of the material, light entering the stone may "leak out" the bottom, causing a loss of brilliance. If the angles are correct at the bottom of the stone, light is totally reflected internally and returns to the eye of the viewer, creating brilliance that is most pleasing and is, in fact, the whole reason for cutting facets on gemstones.

The optical properties of gemstones and minerals are determined by the crystallographic symmetry of these materials. For example, isometric crystals have crystal structures that are highly symmetrical in all directions; the result is that light traveling in an isometric crystal, or a glass (which is amorphous and has no crystal structure) travels at the same speed in any direction and is not slowed down measurably in any one direction within the material. Such a material is termed *isotropic* and is characterized by a single refractive index, abbreviated in this book as *N*.

However, in all other crystals light is separated into two components. These two rays are *polarized*, that is, they each vibrate in a single plane rather than in all directions perpendicular to the direction of travel of the light. The two rays arising in such crystals are known as the *ordinary ray* and the *extraordinary ray*. All crystals other than isometric ones cause this splitting of incident light and are termed *anisotropic*.

The existence of polarized light can be demonstrated by means of a special prism known after its inventor as the *Nicol prism*. This contains specially cut pieces of the mineral calcite that are oriented in such a way as to allow only light polarized in a single plane to pass through. If two Nicol prisms are lined up and turned with their polarization directions at right angles to each other, no light may pass at all. Similarly, a Nicol prism (or similar device) can be used to test for the polarization directions of light that has traveled through a crystal specimen or gemstone. This is the basic function of such devices as the *polariscope* and *polarizing microscope*. The polarizing microscope is not generally used with gemstones, but instead with tiny mineral grains. Gemologists prefer to work with larger polarizing devices, usually 1-3 inch diameter discs of polaroid plastic, mounted in a device called a *polariscope*.

In tetragonal and hexagonal crystals there is a unique crystal axis, which is either longer or shorter than the other two axes in the crystal. Light traveling in a direction parallel to this axis vibrates in the plane of the other two axes. Since the other two axes are equivalent, this vibration is uniform and resembles the light vibration in an isotropic crystal. If a pair of Nicol prisms is placed in line with light traveling in this direction in such a crystal, and the prisms are rotated so that the polarization directions are crossed (perpendicular), no light will be seen emerging from the crystal. As a result of the presence of this unique optical direction in tetragonal and hexagonal crystals, substances crystallizing in these crystal systems are termed *uniaxial*.

All other crystals contain *two* directions in which light vibrates uniformly perpendicular to the direction of travel. Consequently, crystals in the orthorhombic, monoclinic, and triclinic systems are termed *biaxial*. The complete description of the behavior of light in such crystals is very complex and beyond the scope of this book. The interested reader is referred to standard works on optical crystallography indicated in the Bibliography on page 237.

The ray in uniaxial crystals that travels along the optic axis, and which vibrates equally in a plane at right angles to this direction, is the ordinary ray. The other ray, which vibrates in a plane that includes the unique crystal axis

direction, is the extraordinary ray. The refractive indices for these rays (directions) are the basic optical parameters for a uniaxial mineral, and are listed in this book as *o* and *e*. If the *o* ray has a velocity in the crystal greater than the *e* ray, such a crystal is termed *positive* (+); the crystal is considered *negative* (−) if the *e* ray has a greater velocity. The *birefringence* in a uniaxial crystal is the difference between the refractive indices for *o* and *e*.

In biaxial crystals there are three different crystallographic axes, and in addition there are two unique directions within the crystal that resemble the unique optic axis in a uniaxial crystal. The refractive indices of a biaxial crystal are designated by the Greek letters α (alpha), β (beta), and γ (gamma). Alpha is the lowest index, is referred to a direction in the crystal known as *X*, and is associated with the fastest light speed within the crystal. Beta is an intermediate index, corresponds to the *Y* crystallographic direction, and represents an intermediate ray velocity. Gamma is the highest refractive index, corresponds to the *Z* crystallographic direction, and is associated with the lowest ray velocity.

The birefringence in a biaxial crystal is the difference between the alpha and gamma index. The acute angle between the two optic axes within the crystal is designated $2V$ and is a useful parameter to the mineralogist. It turns out that if the beta index is exactly halfway between alpha and gamma, the $2V$ angle is exactly 90°. Finally, if beta is closer in value to gamma than to alpha, the crystal is considered optically *negative*. If the value of beta is closer to that of alpha, the crystal is termed optically *positive*.

Both refractive indices and birefringence are useful parameters in characterizing and identifying crystals, and both change with composition, the presence of impurities, and may vary even within a single crystal.

It should always be remembered that the refractive index is basically a measure of relative light velocity. Every wavelength of light travels through a given medium (other than air) at a *different* velocity, and consequently every wavelength has its own refractive index. The difference in refractive index with variation in wavelength is known as *dispersion*.

Dispersion is what makes a diamond sparkle with colors. The difference in refractive index for red vs. blue light in a diamond is quite large. As light travels through a cut gemstone, the various wavelengths (colors) therefore diverge, and when the light finally emerges from the stone the various color portions of the spectrum have been completely separated.

Dispersion is reported as a dimensionless number (that is, no units), but there is some degree of choice in selecting the wavelengths to use as reference points. By convention, the dispersion of a gemstone is taken as the difference in refractive index as measured using the Fraunhofer *B* and *G* lines. These are spectral lines observed in the spectrum of the sun, respectively at 6870 and 4308 Å (Ångstrom units: one Ångstrom is equal to one ten-billionth of a meter. This unit of length is used to describe light wavelengths).

In some cases, no dispersion information exists for a mineral or gemstone in the gemological literature; however, the mineralogical literature may have data for the refractive index measured at certain different wavelengths (not including the *B* and *G* wavelengths). In such cases it is possible to calculate the dispersion, by means of a special type of graph paper known as a *Hartman Dispersion Net*. This is a logarithmic-type paper on which one can plot refractive indices at specific wavelengths covering the entire useful range. Such plots are linear and can be extrapolated to the positions of the *B* and *G* lines. The *B-G* dispersion is then simply picked off the graph. Approximately 20 gemstone dispersions never before reported and based on calculations such as are included in this book.

In some cases, as with opaque or translucent materials, the gemologist using only a refractometer cannot measure accurate refractive indices; rather the instrument gives only a vague line representing a mean index for the material. Since this number is useful, in that it indicates what can be expected in routine work, it has sometimes been included in the text of this book. Also, the refractometer effectively measures *all* indices of refraction (that is, for all light wavelengths) simultaneously; more accurate measurements can be made if only a single wavelength is selected. This is universally taken to be the spectral (yellow) line known as *D*, which is characteristic of the emission spectrum of sodium.

Light may be absorbed differently as it passes through a crystal in different directions. Sometimes the differences are only in degree of absorption or intensity. In other cases, however, different wavelength portions of the transmitted light are absorbed in different directions, resulting in colors. This phenomenon is termed *pleochroism*. In the case of uniaxial materials, there are only two distinct optical directions and the phenomenon is termed *dichroism*. Other materials may be *trichroic*, and the pleochroic colors are sometimes very distinct and strong and are useful in identification. The pleochroic colors reported for various gems are presented in this book in the order *X*/*Y*/*Z*, separated by slashes.

Since isotropic materials (including glasses) do not affect the velocity or properties of light passing through them in different directions, isotropic materials never display pleochroism. Occasionally, however, an isotropic material may display anomalous colors in polarized light. These effects are generally attributed to strain. However, there is abundant evidence that a more likely cause is the ordered arrangement of atoms on specific crystallographic sites.

SPECTRAL

The optical spectrum of a gemstone may be extremely useful in identification or in rapidly distinguishing between two similar gemstones with similar optical properties.

The principle of the spectroscope is fairly straightforward. Light we call white actually consists of a mixture of all the wavelengths in the visible range combined in specific proportions. When such light passes through a colorless material, none of the light is absorbed, and the white light emerges unchanged. However, some materials absorb various portions of the white light, allowing other portions to emerge and reach our eyes. The remaining portions consist of white light from which certain wavelengths have been subtracted. Consequently, if a material absorbs red, orange, and most of the yellow from the original white light, all that remains is blue and green and the material appears to us as a blue-green color. A ruby appears red to us because it absorbs nearly all the violet and green light passing through it.

The optical spectroscope is a device that separates white light into a spectrum of component colors, using either a prism or a diffraction grating. The spectrum consists of either an infinite (in the case of a prism) or finite (diffraction-grating type) assemblage of images of a very narrow slit, each representing a different wavelength. A gemstone placed between the light source and the slit will absorb certain wavelengths. The slit images of these wavelengths are consequently missing from the observed spectrum, and therefore show up as dark lines. The width of the lines depends on the diameter of the slit (which is usually adjustable). Often entire segments of the spectrum are absorbed, and the result is a dark band rather than a line. The light source itself may not produce all visible wavelengths. If a spectroscope is aimed at the sun, for example, the observed spectrum contains dark lines even though there is no absorbing material in front of the slit. These are known as Fraunhofer lines, named after Joseph von Fraunhofer (1787-1826) who showed them to represent absorptions by elements within the gaseous outer layers of the sun's atmosphere.

Certain gemstones have very distinctive spectra. In general, an optical spectrum is created through the agency of certain atoms in the crystal structure, which are, in the final analysis, responsible for the light absorption. Emerald, for example, contains chromium; the spectrum of emerald contains very distinctive absorption lines representing chromium, located in the far red portion of the spectrum. Such minerals as apatite, zircon, olivine, sinhalite, and idocrase have characteristic lines that are frequently used in identification. A glance through a spectroscope, for example, is instantly sufficient to distinguish between a garnet and a ruby.

The absorption spectra of many gemstones have not yet been reported in the gem literature. In other instances the spectrum has no distinctive or useful features. In both cases the abbreviation N.D. (No Data) has been used. It is hoped that the next edition of this book will contain complete spectral information on all the rare gems for which data are currently not available.

INCLUSIONS

Inclusions are crystals of minerals, cracks, healing fissures, bubbles, hoses, and other internal features of minerals that are useful in identification. Inclusions represent minerals that were floating in solutions from which other minerals formed; they are bits of liquid and gas bubbles trapped in a mineral as it grew; they are fractures surrounding radioactive minerals contained within a host mineral. The world of gemstone inclusions is beautiful, vast, and exciting, and one to which data are continually being added.

The instrument for study of inclusions in gems is the microscope, preferably one with darkfield illumination. Sometimes inclusions are too small to be resolved with the 30-60X usually reached by stereoscopic microscopes, and magnifications of 200X or more are required.

An expert in the field of mineral and gemstone inclusions may be able not only to identify a gemstone and pronounce unambiguously whether it is natural or synthetic but also to indicate the very mine from which it came! Inclusions are the most powerful means of distinguishing the bewildering variety of manufactured stones from the much more valuable natural gems they attempt to imitate. Inclusion information in this book represents a summary of what is in the available literature; information is lacking for many of the rarer gemstones, which will, it is hoped, be provided for future editions of this book.

LUMINESCENCE

Certain electrons in atoms within the crystal structure of a mineral may be able to absorb energy and release the energy at a later time. This creates a phenomenon known as *luminescence*. If the absorbed energy is released almost immediately, the effect is called *fluorescence*; if there is a delay (ranging from seconds to hours) in the release of the energy the effect is called *phosphorescence*. The excitation energy may be X-rays, visible light, or even heat, but the most widely used energy source is ultraviolet light. Ultraviolet (UV) light is generated by several different kinds of lamps, basically of two types: longwave

(LW) UV at 3660 Å, which is generated by fluorescent-type lamps, and shortwave (SW) UV, at 2587 Å, generated by special quartz tubes.

Some minerals react in LW, some in SW, some in both, and some in neither. In many cases a mineral is not excited by UV light unless it contains an impurity element that acts as an activator. The element manganese plays such a role in many minerals. Conversely, the element iron quenches fluorescence in most minerals. The detailed reasons for this behavior are beyond the scope of this book.

Luminescence effects are useful in gemstone identification, especially in certain cases in distinguishing synthetics. However, luminescence is best used in conjunction with other gemological tests.

OCCURRENCE

The occurrences reported in this book are condensed from both the mineralogical and gemological literature. Where possible an attempt has been made to indicate the general rock types and geological environments in which a mineral occurs. Following this is a listing of specific localities that have been reported, noting, where possible, whether the material found is of major gemological significance.

It should be remembered that a mineral may be reported from a locality, and none of it is of gem quality (that is, attractive in color, transparent, and so forth). However, an occasional piece may be encountered that is suitable for cutting, and this is sufficient to establish the material in the literature as occurring in gem quality in that locality. Such possibilities are always open. The main emphasis of this section in the book is to indicate how widespread the material is and from what parts of the world it is best known.

STONE SIZES

This section of the book will, perhaps, never actually be completed but rather will continually focus on adding information as obtained.

The objective is to indicate what constitutes a "large one" for a given species in question, with respect to cut gems. In some cases catalog information for major museums exists. Much information has been compiled from verbal sources, information in the minds of expert cutters, museum curators, and collectors. In some cases I have seen no cut examples of a gem in question but have seen references to such gems in the literature or in private communications. Here only an indication can be provided of expectable gem sizes. I freely acknowledge major omissions in the information presented in this portion of the text and hope that interested readers will make the next edition more useful by providing corrections and additions.

Gemstones of major importance exist in museum collections throughout the world. Some museums have especially complete collections of rare gems, and these institutions have been mentioned frequently in the text. Abbreviations used for some of these museums are as follows:

BM: British Museum (Natural History) (London, England)
SI: Smithsonian Institution (Washington, D.C.)
DG: Devonian Group (Calgary, Alberta, Canada)
AMNH: American Museum of Natural History (New York)
ROM: Royal Ontario Museum (Toronto, Ontario, Canada)

PC: Private Collection
LA: Los Angeles County Museum (Los Angeles)
CA: California Academy of Sciences (San Francisco)
NMC: National Museums of Canada (Ottawa, Ontario)
HU: Harvard University
GIA: Gemological Institute of America

The metric carat is a unit of weight equal to one-fifth of a gram. It is the standard measure of gemstones. Where sizes are given in this book without a unit of measurement, the weight in carats is intended. Lower-cost cabochons are measured in millimeter size.

COMMENTS

This section contains general comments on wearing characteristics of gemstones, miscellaneous notes on occurrence, what constitutes high or low quality in the stone, general availability, and scarcity.

Thermal Properties

Gemologists are severely handicapped in analyzing and identifying gemstones because of necessity (and rather obviously) their testing methods must be nondestructive. This limits the measuring process to the areas of optics, including spectroscopy, luminescence, and so forth, density, and microscopic inclusions. Hardness is not routinely measured on cut gems. Moreover, the instrumentation used in this field must be simple enough to be learned by people with no real scientific training (which is the case with the vast majority of gemologists) and must be affordable. Much of the literature of gemology these days reports measurements on gems made with various kinds of advanced instrumentation, including ultraviolet absorption spectroscopy, X-ray fluorescence analysis, and even electron paramagnetic resonance. This is well and good for the literature but is of little practical value for the working gemologist and/or appraiser.

Therefore, it is important to explore the potential of any possibly diagnostic, inexpensive, simple, and nontechnical method of gemstone analysis. One such method is the measurement of thermal properties.

Heat energy may be transferred by radiation (for example, sunlight), convection (the creation of currents in a pot of boiling water), and conduction. The latter method of heat transfer is the most relevant to solid materials at room temperature, that is, gemstones. There are four thermal properties of potential interest, three of which are mathematically interrelated. However, the best one for gem testing is the one that can most easily be measured with simple instrumentation; this turns out to be thermal inertia. The others are not as useful, as outlined below:

Specific heat is the amount of heat required to raise one gram of a substance one degree Celsius. This is a constant for a given substance but one that varies little in different gem materials and therefore is not especially useful for identification purposes.

Thermal diffusivity is a measure of the velocity of heat flow in a material. If heat is applied to a substance, some of the heat energy (to a degree that depends on the specific heat of the material) goes into raising the temperature of the substance. The rest of the heat energy diffuses away from the point where the heat is being applied. The higher the thermal diffusivity of a material, the faster it will pass heat energy from one point to another.

Thermal conductivity on the other hand, is a ratio and relates the flow of heat through a given thickness of material to the temperature difference across this thickness. It turns out that thermal conductivity is directional, just like refractive index, in all but isotropic (isometric or amorphous) materials. The symmetry of optical and thermal properties is usually the same, but very few measurements on the variation of conductivity with direction have been made on gem materials.

Thermal inertia is a measure of how quickly the surface temperature of a material can be changed by a flow of heat into the material. The higher the thermal inertia, the slower the surface temperature will rise when heat is applied. This is why materials, such as plastics, that have a low thermal inertia feel warm to the touch—body heat rapidly raises the surface temperature of such materials—while stone objects feel cold.

Thermal inertia is a directional property but lends itself to simple instrumentation for measuring a mean value. The various *diamond probes* (such as those made by the GIA, Rayner, Kashan and Ceres Corp.) on the market take advantage of this fact. Such probes consist of a temperature-difference sensor (a thermocouple) and an adjacent thermal source (resistance heater) surrounded by an insulated probe housing. Care must be taken in using such instruments to prevent drafts from affecting the readings. The probe tip is placed against the material being measured (that is, a gemstone facet) and a meter reading is obtained in about one second. This reading can be related to thermal inertia. The commer-cial probes were developed specifically to distinguish diamond (with a very high thermal inertia) from its imitations, such as cubic zirconia (with much lower thermal inertia). Difficulties may be encountered with very small stones, but the instrument can be calibrated against small gems to avoid this problem.

TABLE 1.   Thermal Properties of Gem Materials, Synthetics, and Simulants as well as Some Metals at Room Temperature

Material	Thermal Conductivity (cal/cm °C sec)	Specific Heat (cal/gm °C)	Density (gm/cm³)	Thermal Diffusivity (cm²/sec)	Thermal Inertia (cal/cm² °C sec½)
Gem Materials, Synthetics, and Simulants					
Diamond	1.6-4.8	0.12	3.52[a]	3.79–11.4	0.822–1.42
Silicon carbide (synthetic)	0.215[b]	0.2*	3.17[a]	0.339	0.369
Periclase (synthetic)	0.110[b]	0.2*	3.575[a]	0.154	0.281
Corundum: c axis	0.0834[b]	0.206	4.0[a]	0.101	0.262
a axis	0.0772	0.206	4.0[a]	0.0937	0.252
c axis	0.060[c]	0.206	4.0[a]	0.0728	0.222
Topaz: a axis	0.0446	0.2*	3.53[a]	0.0632	0.177
mean, Gunnison, Colorado	0.0269	0.2*	3.531	0.0381	0.138
Pyrite: Colorado	0.0459	0.136	4.915	0.0684	0.176
Kyanite: c axis	0.0413[b]	0.201	3.66[a]	0.0562	0.174
b axis	0.0396[b]	0.201	3.66[a]	0.0539	0.171
mean, Minas Gerais, Brazil	0.0338	0.201	3.102	0.0461	0.158
Hematite: Itabira, Brazil	0.0270	0.169	5.143	0.0310	0.153
Spinel: locality unknown	0.0281	0.216	3.63[a]	0.0358	0.148
Madagascar	0.0227	0.216	3.633	0.0288	0.133
Fluorite: locality unknown	0.0219	0.220	3.18[a]	0.0313	0.124
Rosiclare, Illinois	0.0227	0.220	3.186	0.0324	0.126
Sphalerite: Chihuahua, Mexico	0.0304	0.115	4.103	0.0646	0.120
Sillimanite: Williamstown, Australia	0.0217	0.203	3.162	0.0339	0.118
Andalusite: Minas Gerais, Brazil	0.0181	0.202	3.102	0.0289	0.107
Pyrophyllite: North Carolina	0.0194	0.2*	2.829	0.0343	0.105
Jadeite: Japan	0.0159	0.206	3.196	0.0242	0.102
San Benito County, California	0.0110	0.206	3.350	0.0160	0.0873
Gahnite: Colorado	0.0103	0.2*	4.163	0.0100	0.102
Magnesite: Transvaal	0.0139	0.236	2.993	0.0198	0.0992
Rutile: c axis	0.0231[b]	0.189	4.2[a]	0.0291	0.135
a axis	0.0132[b]	0.189	4.2[a]	0.0166	0.102
mean, Virginia	0.0122	0.189	4.244	0.0153	0.0990
Grossular: Connecticut	0.0135	0.196	3.617	0.0188	0.0979
Chihuahua, Mexico	0.0134	0.196	3.548	0.0193	0.0967
Crestmore, California	0.0124	0.196	3.318	0.0190	0.0898
Quartz: c axis	0.0264[b]	0.196	2.65[a]	0.0578	0.125
c axis	0.0264[c]	0.196	2.65[a]	0.0509	0.117
a axis	0.0140[b]	0.196	2.65[a]	0.0270	0.0854
a axis	0.0160[c]	0.196	2.65[a]	0.0308	0.0912
mean, Jessieville, Arkansas	0.0184	0.196	2.647	0.0354	0.0978
Spodumene: Maine	0.0135	0.2*	3.155	0.0214	0.0923
Diopside: New York	0.0133	0.196	3.270	0.0208	0.0923
Madagascar	0.00969	0.196	3.394	0.0146	0.0802
Dolomite	0.0132	0.221	2.857	0.0209	0.0911
Olivine (peridot, Fo₈₆Fa₁₄)	0.0115	0.2*	3.469	0.0166	0.0893
Elbaite: Keystone, South Dakota	0.0126	0.2*	3.134	0.0202	0.0889
Talc, Quebec	0.0124	0.221	2.804	0.0200	0.0878
Tremolite: Balmat, New York	0.0117	0.210	2.981	0.0186	0.0854
Ontario, Canada	0.0112	0.210	3.008	0.0177	0.0839
Amblygonite: South Dakota	0.0119	0.2*	3.025	0.0197	0.0850
Zircon: Australia	0.0109	0.140	4.633	0.0167	0.0839
Enstatite(En₉₈Fs₂): California	0.0105	0.2*	3.209	0.0334	0.0821
Bronzite (En₇₈Fs₂₂): Quebec	0.00994	0.2*	3.365	0.0148	0.0818

Material	Thermal Conductivity (cal/cm °C sec)	Specific Heat (cal/gm °C)	Density (gm/cm³)	Thermal Diffusivity (cm²/sec)	Thermal Inertia (cal/cm² °C sec½)
Spessartine: Haddam, Connecticut	0.00811	0.2*	3.987	0.0102	0.0804
Datolite: Paterson, New Jersey	0.0106	0.2*	2.996	0.0177	0.0798
Anhydrite: Ontario, Canada	0.0114	0.187	2.978	0.0204	0.0796
Almandine: Gore Mountain, New York	0.00791	0.2*	3.932	0.0101	0.0789
Staurolite: Georgia	0.00828	0.2*	3.689	0.0112	0.0782
Augite: Ontario	0.00913	0.2*	3.275	0.0140	0.0773
Pyrope: Navajo Reservation, Arizona	0.00759	0.2*	3.746	0.0101	0.0754
Andradite: Ontario, Canada	0.00738	0.2*	3.746	0.00984	0.0744
Smithsonite: Kelly, New Mexico	0.00612	0.2*	4.362	0.00701	0.0731
Beryl: c axis	0.0131[b]	0.2*	2.70[a]	0.0243	0.0842
a axis	0.0104[b]	0.2*	2.70[a]	0.0193	0.0750
mean, Minas Gerais, Brazil	0.00953	0.2*	2.701	0.0176	0.0718
Calcite: Chihuahua, Mexico	0.00858	0.218	2.721	0.0145	0.0713
Axinite: Baja California	0.00767	0.2*	3.306	0.0116	0.0712
Prehnite: Paterson, New Jersey	0.00854	0.2*	2.953	0.0145	0.0710
Rhodochrosite: Argentina	0.00731	0.184	3.584	0.0111	0.0695
Flint: Brownsville, Ohio	0.00886	0.2*	2.618	0.0169	0.0681
Epidote: Calumet, Colorado	0.00627	0.2*	3.413	0.00919	0.0654
Petalite: Rhodesia	0.00856	0.2*	2.391	0.0179	0.0640
Clinozoisite: Baja California	0.00574	0.2*	3.360	0.00854	0.0621
Idocrase: Chihuahua, Mexico	0.00576	0.2*	3.342	0.00863	0.0620
Sphene: Ontario, Canada	0.00558	0.188	3.525	0.00845	0.0607
Iolite: Madagascar	0.00650	0.2*	2.592	0.0126	0.0580
Zoisite: Liksviken, Norway	0.00513	0.2*	3.267	0.00785	0.0579
Aragonite: Somerset, England	0.00535	0.209	2.827	0.00906	0.0562
Microcline: Amelia, Virginia	0.00621	0.194	2.556	0.0126	0.0554
Ontario, Canada	0.00590	0.194	2.558	0.0119	0.0541
Albite (Ab99An1): Amelia, Virginia	0.00553	0.202	2.606	0.0105	0.0540
Serpentine (lizardite): Cornwall, England	0.00558	0.2*	2.601	0.0107	0.0539
Orthoclase: Goodspring, Nevada	0.00553	0.2*	2.583	0.0107	0.0534
Sodalite: Ontario, Canada	0.00600	0.2*	2.326	0.0129	0.0528
Lepidolite: Dixon, New Mexico	0.00460	0.2*	2.844	0.00807	0.0512
Anorthite (Ab4An96): Japan	0.00401	0.196	2.769	0.00737	0.0467
Fluor-apatite: Ontario, Canada	0.00328	0.195	3.215	0.00522	0.0454
Chlor-apatite: Snarum, Norway	0.00331	0.195	3.152	0.00539	0.0451
Labradorite (Ab46An54): Nain, Labrador	0.00365	0.2*	2.701	0.00676	0.0444
Barite: Georgia	0.00319	0.113	4.411	0.00639	0.0399
Apophyllite: Poona, India	0.00331	0.2*	2.364	0.00699	0.0396
Leucite: Rome, Italy	0.00274	0.2*	2.483	0.00551	0.0369
Vitreous silica (General Electric)	0.00325	0.201	2.205	0.0074	0.0379
Hyalite: Spruce Pine, North Carolina	0.00290	0.2*	2.080	0.0070	0.0347
Glass: obsidian	0.00330[b]	0.2*	2.4[a]	0.00688	0.0398
ordinary flint (lead)	0.0018[b]	0.117[a]	3.5[c]	0.00440	0.0272
very heavy flint (lead)	0.0012[b]	0.117	4.5[a]	0.00228	0.0251
Metals					
Copper	0.927	0.092	8.89	1.13	0.871
Silver 100%	1.00	0.056	10.5	1.70	0.767
Silver 69%, gold 31% (weight)	0.237	0.048*	12.3	0.401	0.374
Silver 34%, gold 66% (weight)	0.152	0.040*	15.5	0.245	0.307
Gold 100%	0.707	0.031	19.3	1.18	0.650
Aluminum	0.485	0.214	2.7	0.839	0.529
Platinum	0.166	0.032	21.4	0.242	0.337
Platinum, 10% iridium	0.074	0.032*	21.6	0.107	0.226

Source: From D. B. Hoover, The gem diamondmaster and the thermal properties of gems, *Gems & Gemology,* Summer 1983: 77–86. © 1983 Gemological Institute of America. Reprinted with permission.

Note: Unless another reference is indicated by a superscript letter, the values for conductivity and density were taken from K. Horai, 1971, Thermal conductivity of rock forming minerals, Journal of Geophysical Research 76(5); for specific heat from R. A. Robie and D. R. Waldbaum, 1968, Thermodynamic properties of minerals and related substances at 298.15 degrees K and one atmosphere pressure and at higher temperatures, *U.S. Geological Survey Bulletin* 1259. * = assumed value; not found in the literature.

[a] R. Webster, 1982, *Gems,* 3rd ed. Hamden, Conn.: Butterworth & Archon.

[b] Chemical Rubber Company, 1966, *Handbook of Chemistry and Physics,* 47th ed. Boca Raton, Fla.: Chemical Rubber Company.

[c] S. P. Clark, 1966, *Handbook of Physical Constants,* Memoir 97. Boulder, Colo.: Geological Society of America.

Table 1 was compiled by Dr. Donald Hoover of the U.S. Geological Survey and is generally arranged in order of decreasing thermal inertia. If accurate, quantitative probes become widely used, thermal inertia could become a very useful, easily measured parameter for gemstone analysis.

Note: Quantitative measurement of thermal inertia may be difficult using instruments that were designed specifi-cally to separate diamond from other stones. New devices specifically designed for such measurements will represent the next generation of thermal meters. Surface quality (degree of flatness and polish) affects readings, as well as degree of crystallinity and chemical composition (especially in solid solution series).

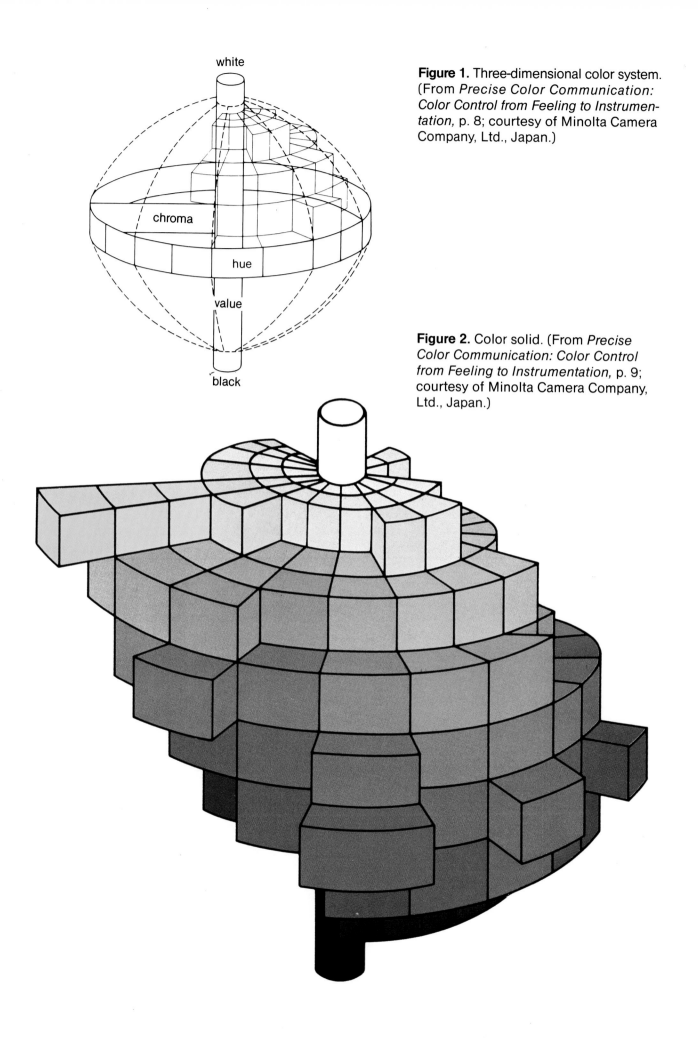

Figure 1. Three-dimensional color system. (From *Precise Color Communication: Color Control from Feeling to Instrumentation,* p. 8; courtesy of Minolta Camera Company, Ltd., Japan.)

white

chroma

hue

value

black

Figure 2. Color solid. (From *Precise Color Communication: Color Control from Feeling to Instrumentation,* p. 9; courtesy of Minolta Camera Company, Ltd., Japan.)

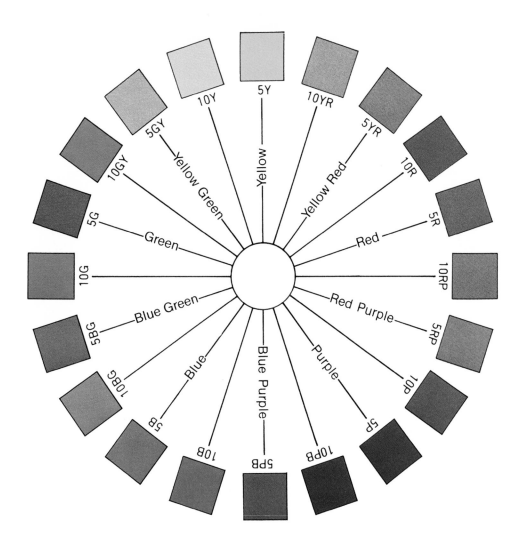

Figure 3. Munsell color wheel. (From *Precise Color Communication: Color Control from Feeling to Instrumentation,* p. 19; courtesy of Minolta Camera Company, Ltd., Japan.)

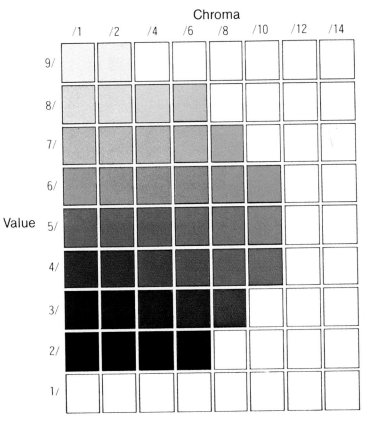

Figure 4. Munsell value and chroma for hue 5G. (From *Precise Color Communication: Color Control from Feeling to Instrumentation,* p. 17; courtesy of Minolta Camera Company, Ltd., Japan.)

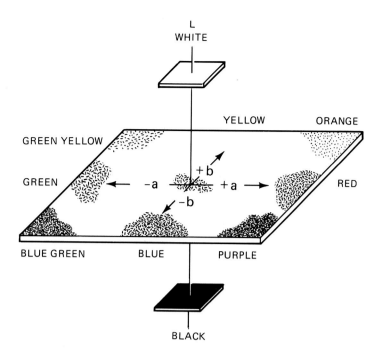

Figure 5A. Lab color space as conceived by Richard S. Hunter.

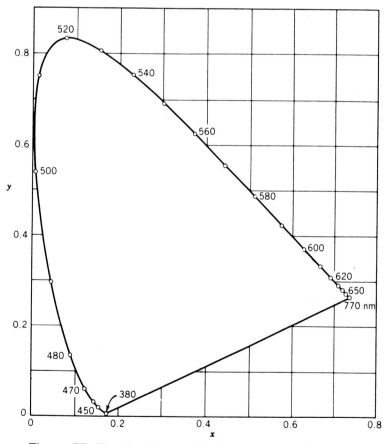

Figure 5B. The CIE chromaticity diagram (1931). All the spectral colors fall on a horseshoe-shaped line called the *spectrum locus.* These colors are indicated by their wavelengths (in nm). (After F. W. Billmeyer, Jr., and M. Saltzman, *Principles of Color Technology,* Wiley, New York, 1981, p. 125.)

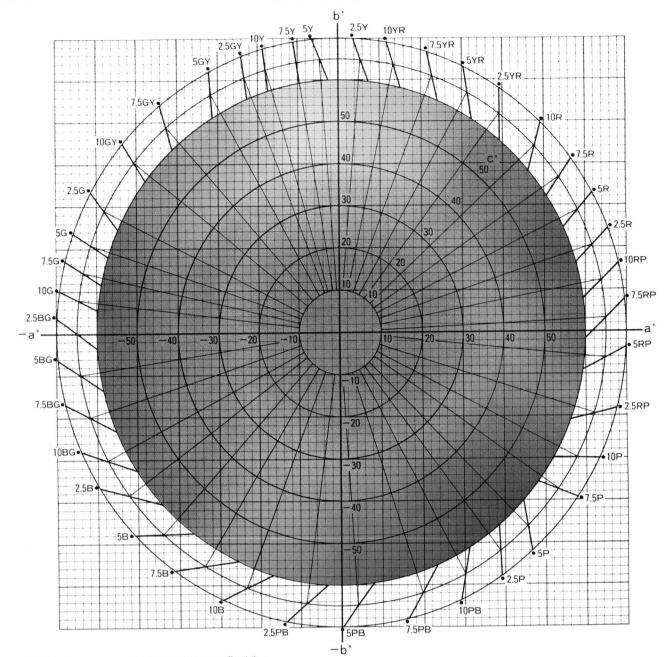

TABLE 3. Munsell (chroma C) and L*a*b* (chroma c*) notations

Munsell hue notation / L*a*b* chroma / Munsell chroma	R	YR	Y	GY	G	BG	B	PB	P	RP
1	5	7	8	7	6	5	4	4	4	4
2	9	12	15	13	11	10	9	9	9	9
3	15	17	22	22|19	16	15	13	13	13	13
4	19	22|25	29	29|25	22	20	17	17	18	18
6	27|30	34|38	42|45	43|39	34|31	28	26	26	27	26
8	37|41	46|50	56|59	58|51	45|42	38	.34	34	36	35
10	46|51	57|63	70|74	73|65	56|53	51|47	44|40	41|44	45	44
12	55|62	68|76	84|88	87|77				48|55	53	51
14	64|73	79|90	98					66	62	60
16	84	94|101	109					75		

Figure 6. L*a*b* and Munsell notations (hue, value). For extremely small or large a*b* values, multiply or divide them by an appropriate amount before plotting and reading the hue values. (From *Precise Color Communication: Color Control from Feeling to Instrumentation,* p. 19; courtesy of Minolta Camera Company, Ltd., Japan.)

Source: From *Precise Color Communication: Color Control from Feeling to Instrumentation,* p. 19; courtesy of Minolta Camera Company, Ltd. Japan.
Note: In columns with two digits, left figures are for hues 1–5 and right figures are for hues 6–10.

Color Measurement and Specification

One of the great challenges of gemology is the development of an accurate, simple, consistent, and reproducible technique for measuring and specifying gemstone colors. Until the mid-1980s little progress in this direction was made, despite the appearance and widespread promotion of various color-chart systems. None of these systems work, chiefly because they do not adequately cover the total range of gem colors, do not have enough detail in the areas they do cover, and the color-chart materials (whether printed colors or transparencies) are not of sufficiently high quality to prevent variations in production runs. The ideal solution is a gemstone colorimeter; however, such an instrument must deal with the unique optical properties of gems, including such factors as brilliancy and pleochroism, which make gemstones extremely difficult specimens for instrumental measurement.

The science of colorimetry is well established in almost all areas of endeavor where color is important, such as paint, plastics, textiles, and other industrial and consumer materials. Objective instrumentation is now routinely used in these fields, but before such instruments were available people had to rely on visual systems for specifying color, namely, color charts. These charts are sections of what we may refer to as three-dimensional color space. These three color dimensions are termed hue, lightness, and saturation.

Hue is the attribute we are describing when we speak of red, yellow, green, blue, purple, and other hues intermediate to adjacent pairs in this series. These hues can be readily visualized in terms of a color wheel (see Figure 3).*

Substantial portions of this text were provided by W. N. Hale, Jr.,[1] private color consultant and 22-year veteran of Munsell Color Co., Inc. (as both president and technical director), to whom the writer is deeply indebted.

*Figures 1-6 and Table 3 will be found in the preceding insert.

Lightness (also called **value**) is a scale with white and black as endpoints and shades of gray in between. Note, however, that *all* chromatic colors can also be scaled as to lightness as a function of their total reflectance. Lightness can be visualized in terms of a vertical axis with white at the top and black at the bottom (see Figure. 1).

Saturation (or **chroma**) is a measure of the amount of hue in a color, that is, its vividness, or how much it differs from a gray of the same lightness. Chroma can be seen in vertical sections of three-dimensional color space (Figure 2). A section along a specific radial direction of the color circle is designated as a specific hue. Lighter shades of this hue are near the top of the section, darker shades at the bottom. The chroma (vividness) of the hue increases moving outward from the central axis. Figure 2 shows that the range of chroma varies with both hue and lightness; this makes the color solid an irregular shape, rather than a simple ovoid or sphere.

Color specification can be achieved by subdividing the color solid into smaller units and giving each a name or set of numerical coordinates. This results in a classification known as a *color-order system*. There are many ways to subdivide the color solid, and, not surprisingly, there are also many color-order systems.

Some of the color-order systems created during the early decades of this century (including those of Munsell, Ostwald, Ridgway, and others) were represented by charts made of paint colors coated on paper. These were used by architects and designers for selecting and specifying colors, by industry for color selection and quality control, and by biological scientists for color classification of thousands of specimens of flora and fauna. Thus the need for accurate color measurement and specification was firmly established before instruments and related color-order systems were available. Some of these older systems (Ridgway in biology, Ostwald in architecture) are still in use today.

Perhaps the most popular and widespread of the chart-type color-order systems is the one devised by A. H. Munsell and extensively revised by the Optical Society of America (OSA) in 1943. The Munsell hue scale is based on five hues equally spaced around the hue circle (red, yellow, green, blue, purple) and intermediate hues (yellow-red, green-yellow, blue-green, purple-blue, red-purple). The major hues are abbreviated R, Y, G, B, P and the intermediate hues YR, GY, BG, PB, RP (Figure 3). Further subdivision results in forty hue charts in the *Munsell Book of Color.* Colors appear on these charts at value (lightness) intervals of one unit from 2 to 9. Chroma is represented in whole units ranging from 2 (near-gray) in two-step intervals up to as high as 14 and 16 for the most vivid colors (Figure 4). The notation system is decimal, allowing colors to be specified as accurately as required. Munsell color books are available in both matte and high gloss finish, with the latter having about fifteen hundred colors.

All these color-order systems (including the more recent German standard DIN 6164 and the Swedish Standard Natural Colour System) have certain similarities. Color sampling is along lines of constant hue (or a similar metric). Thus corresponding colors on adjacent hue charts become visually farther apart as they become progressively more saturated (that is, move further away, radially, from the center of the color circle). This means that the most vivid colors are more distant from each other than less vivid ones, often by a factor of five or more. The color charts for use with gemstones are inadequate because they do not have sufficient colors in the vivid color regions to which they extend, and they do not extend far enough. Opaque colors on paper simply cannot be produced to the color ranges of vivid, transparent gemstones. In addition, opaque paint colors do not look like transparent gemstones, even when they are, in fact, the same colors.

A major step forward came in 1931 with the international adoption of the Commission International d'Eclairage (CIE) system, resulting in greater interest in color measurement and specification, especially by colorimetry. The CIE system included standard illuminants (incandescent, sunlight, north daylight) a standard observer, and standard response functions of the human visual system. The CIE continues as the principal international organization in the field of color research and standardization and since 1931 has made important improvements and additions to the original concept.

The color industry was built around research and development of spectrophotometers and colorimeters capable of making measurements and reporting data in CIE terms. However, this created a problem with existing color-order systems. Such systems are necessarily spaced visually for their appearance under a specific light source; visual spacings and overall appearance will be accordingly altered if other sources are used. If CIE data are published for such colors, the numbers are valid only for the light source for which the measurement data were computed.

CIE color space is visually nonuniform. A more uniform color space makes specification of tolerances and small color differences more meaningful and is therefore more useful to science and industry. Extensive research has been done to produce mathematical transformations of CIE data into a more visually uniform color space.

In 1942 Richard S. Hunter designed a filter colorimeter for the measurement of opaque surface colors and with it the Hunter color-order system. This is a transformation of CIE data using simple equations that were incorporated into the computational elements of the instrument. Hunter space was of the "opposite-hue" or "opponent-hue" type as shown in Figure 5. When Hunter *a* attribute is positive, the color has redness; when negative, greenness. Similarly when *b* is positive the color has yellowness, when negative, blueness, The third Hunter attribute was *L* for lightness. Equal steps along the three scales (*L,a,b*) were intended to represent equal visual steps in the several color directions, permitting color differences to be simply computed by the formula:

$$\Delta E = \sqrt{\Delta L^2 + \Delta a^2 + \Delta b^2},$$

Where the Greek letter delta (Δ) + *E* denotes color difference.

It is common practice today for color-measuring instruments to include Hunter color notations as a readout option for expression of measurement results. Although material color samples were never produced to illustrate Hunter color space, the nearly uniform visual spacing became very useful for describing color specifications and tolerances in industry and contributed importantly to the sale and use of these instruments.

Work continued in the CIE and elsewhere to provide a color space with even better visual color spacing, resulting in the 1976 recommendation for the use of CIELAB space. This is similar to Hunter space, is a mathematical transform of CIE data, and is plotted on rectangular coordinates (see Figure 6). CIELAB color attributes are designated *L** (*L*-star), *a** (*a*-star) and *b** (*b*-star) to distinguish them from Hunter and have the same nominal meanings. As with Hunter, CIELAB is a standard readout on current instruments.[2]

An even newer opponent-hue system, developed by the Optical Society of America and called Optical Society of America-Uniform Color Spacing (OSA-UCS), is not only an improvement over Munsell spacing but is also a direct CIE transform. The OSA-UCS colors (at this writing 558 colors, available as 2 × 2 inch samples) are in scales with intervals of two units in chromaticity and one in lightness; a prototype OSA color collection produced in Denmark shows chromaticity scale intervals of only one unit, with lightness increments of 0.5

and over two thousand colors. The OSA-UCS colors are the best example of uniform color spacing produced to date and will probably appear soon as a readout option on instruments.

Some gemologists have tried, without success, to use existing color instrumentation to characterize gemstones. Instrument makers have not perceived the gem field to warrant the costly research and development necessary to devise specifically applicable instruments. The existing color charts and simplistic optical devices currently in use by gemologists are severely limited in accuracy and usefulness.

The recent marketing by Minolta Camera Co. of a lower-cost portable colorimeter motivated several researchers to modify this instrument for gemstone colorimetry. A first attempt by Dr. Richard Pettijohn adapted the Minolta sensor unit for specific use with gemstones by reducing the beam size and adding a glass plate to hold the sensor and a small mirror to reflect light passing through the stone to the sensor. However, this arrangement has proven insufficiently accurate and repeatable to be a viable solution. Moreover, the mirror arrangement dictates the "standard" illuminant for measurement to be the xenon flashlamp built into the unit rather than an independently measured white standard.

An improved version of this instrument, also using the Minolta colorimeter, was devised by W. N. Hale and J. J. Rennilson. This replaces the glass and mirror with a small white-lined integrating sphere. A gemstone mounted on a clear plate centered within the sphere is irradiated by a 2-mm light beam from below. Light reflected from the gem is mixed with that transmitted through it and picked up by a detector outlet in the sphere wall. This colorimeter, with patented illuminating and collection geometry is sufficiently accurate and repeatable for gemstone work. The data readout is in CIE data (Y,x,y) and CIELAB (L^*,a^*,b^*), for CIE standard illuminant D65 or C (both representative of standard daylight in slightly different form). It is likely that this kind of instrumentation will totally revolutionize the gemstone field, bringing order and objective reality to a chaotic system of vague and often obsolete terminology.

The Rennilson-Hale instrument was not yet available when the table of gemstone measurements (Table 2) was prepared for this book; the Pettijohn instrument was therefore used. The illuminating and viewing geometry produces results that are neither as accurate nor consistent as the integrating sphere/fiber optic system of Rennilson and Hale. Also, the conversion of CIELAB data to Munsell notation (see Figure 6 and Table 3) was done by the Minolta DP-100 microcomputer;[3] errors in conversion may arise due to the limited data storage capacity of this device.[4] Further errors are inevitable when trying to illustrate gemstones by photography and printed reproduction on paper.[5] The tabulated numerical color data must therefore not be considered accurate enough to establish benchmark points for specific gemstone species, but this degree of error is small compared to the actual variation in color exhibited by most species. The real purpose of this chapter and these measurements is to establish, for the first time in the gemological literature, the nomenclature, direction and methodology for scientific, accurate, reproducible, and objective color characterization of gemstones. The numbers themselves are considered less important in this context than an understanding of how they were obtained and the implications of this new technology for gemology and the gemstone marketplace.

NOTES

1. Hale Color Consultants, Inc., 1505 Phoenix Road, Phoenix, MD. 21131.
2. In CIELAB terminology, chroma is calculated from a^* and b^* as follows:

$$\text{Chroma} = C^* = \sqrt{a^{*2} + b^{*2}}.$$

3. Invaluable assistance in converting measured L*a*b* values to Munsell numbers, along with many valuable suggestions, was provided by Richard E. McCarty of Silver Spring, Maryland.
4. Color data on gemstones reported herein are in the form of CIELAB readout and corresponding Munsell notation. The conversion to Munsell numbers are direct CIELAB conversions. No attempt has been made to simplify the resulting Munsell values in accordance with the limited range of actual Munsell color samples. This approximation is left to the reader.
5. As many as possible of the gemstones photographed in this book were measured with the Pettijohn-Minolta colorimeter; these gems are cross-referenced by notation in the section of color plates at the back of the book, and the tabulated color information herein refers to specific gemstone colors, shapes, and weights, facilitating easy correlation with the photographs.

TABLE 2. *Color Measurements*

Gemstone	Color	Weight	Shape	Location		L*a*b*		Munsell
Actinolite	dark green	0.63	—	Tanzania	56	−7.7	9.1	7.6GY 5.5/1.7
Adamite	light green	0.86	—	Mapimi, Mexico	82	−0.6	26.0	3.2Y 8.2/3.8
Andalusite	brown-green	9.55	emerald cut	Brazil	58	−3.5	49.0	5.7Y 5.7/6.9
	light brown-green	4.72	antique	Brazil	60	1.0	14.1	1.9Y 5.9/2.1
	medium brown-green	2.92	round	Brazil	38	1.6	20.0	2.8Y 3.7/2.9
Anglesite	yellow	6.99	fancy	Morocco	75	2.7	50.0	2.1Y 7.4/7.4
Amblygonite	light yellow	10.10	round	Brazil	80	5.3	11.4	5.3YR 7.9/2.1
	light yellow	24.6	antique	Brazil	95	−3.5	20.0	6.0Y 9.4/2.8
Apatite	violet	0.59	emerald cut	Maine	71	10.3	−15.0	3.1P 7.0/4.0
	violet	1.02	hexagon	Maine	75	6.0	−7.2	4.9P 7.5/2.0
	yellow-green	8.05	rhomboid	Canada	68	−11.3	32.1	1.9GY 6.7/4.5
	yellow	8.70	antique	Mexico	83	−6.2	36.0	6.7Y 8.2/5.0
	dark blue	0.55	round	Brazil	34	−10.2	−40.6	9.7B 3.3/10.4
	medium blue	0.86	oval	Brazil	52	−22.8	−25.9	4.6B 5.1/7.8
	gray-blue	0.77	round	Burma	50	−7.5	−1.0	4.6BG 4.9/1.5
	light green	12.40	round	?	42	−6.2	9.8	5.3GY 4.1/1.6
	dark green	2.87	round	Brazil	31	−16.4	12.3	0.1G 3.0/3.2
	medium green	1.09	round	Brazil	61	−11.2	11.9	8.5GY 6.0/2.4
	light blue	1.07	emerald cut	Madagascar	76	−20.2	−4.1	7.0BG 7.5/4.2
Axinite	medium brown	1.45	round	Baja, Mexico	42	10.7	9.3	10.0R 4.1/2.6
	dark brown	8.0	pear	Baja, Mexico	21	14.2	20.6	4.8YR 2.0/4.2
Benitoite	pale blue	0.66	round	California	85	5.6	−7.6	4.4P 8.4/2.0
	medium blue	1.07	round	California	68	4.5	−27.0	6.6PB 6.7/6.3
	dark blue	1.19	round	California	46	8.4	−29.1	7.1PB 4.5/7.0
Beryl								
Aquamarine	dark blue	2.40	oval	Coronel Murta Mine, Brazil	61	−2.7	−17.5	2.8PB 6.0/4.3
	dark blue	66.53	antique	Brazil	38	−6.0	−8.0	5.8B 3.7/2.3
	dark blue	45.40	emerald cut	Brazil	54	−4.0	−11.0	0.5PB 5.3/2.8
	medium light blue	18.08	emerald cut	Brazil	80	−6.9	−9.0	8.2B 7.9/2.7
	medium blue	21.80	pear	Africa	65	−3.5	−18.0	2.6PB 6.4/4.4
Emerald	pale green	0.32	round	Colombia	85	−12.0	2.6	8.9G 8.4/2.2
	light yellow-green	—	emerald cut	Colombia	55	−55.0	15.0	6.0G 5.4/10.1
	medium green	0.88	emerald cut	Chivor Mine, Colombia	70	−41.7	2.5	2.0BG 6.9/8.0
	dark blue-green	1.35	emerald cut	Muzo Mine, Colombia	46	−73.2	9.1	8.3G 4.5/13.6
	dark green	—	emerald cut	Zambia	40	−60.0	15.0	6.0G 3.9/11.0
	light blue-green	1.96	emerald cut	Nigeria	68	−23.5	0.5	2.7BG 6.7/4.6
Green beryl	light green	11.25	round	Brazil	65	−3.5	6.5	4.3GY 6.4/1.0
	light yellow-green	18.42	triangle	Brazil	75	−5.1	13.2	2.0GY 7.4/1.9
	greenish-yellow	19.09	antique	Brazil	70	−9.3	21.1	3.2GY 6.9/3.2
	blue-green	4.54	emerald cut	Brazil	68	−5.2	3.1	2.0G 6.7/1.0
Golden beryl	dark yellow	20.00	emerald cut	Brazil	63	−8.2	39.0	8.3Y 6.2/5.4
	medium yellow	32.79	antique	Brazil	74	−6.0	34.2	7.0Y 7.3/4.8
	dark orange	18.60	antique	Brazil	45	17.4	71.7	9.9YR 4.4/11.5
	golden orange	18.98	pear	Brazil	61	−1.0	42.0	4.3Y 6.0/6.0
	golden orange	40.98	oval	Brazil	50	−0.5	41.0	4.5Y 4.9/5.9
	medium dark golden orange	3.90	emerald cut	Africa	70	10.2	70.0	0.2Y 6.9/10.7
Morganite	pink	17.33	square	Brazil	81	4.6	−0.9	2.8RP 8.0/1.1
	peach	6.92	square	Brazil	80	10.4	10.0	9.7R 7.9/2.7
	peach	9.06	oval	Brazil	90	8.9	11.8	1.3YR 8.9/2.6
Brazilianite	yellow-green	2.00	oval	Brazil	74	−1.9	17.0	5.2Y 7.3/2.4
Cassiterite	light brown	14.25	round	Bolivia	47	7.5	26.6	9.3YR 4.6/4.3
	yellow	2.88	round	Bolivia	82	1.3	33.0	1.8Y 8.1/4.9
Calcite	dark brown-orange	12.55	round	Baja, Mexico	41	23.2	58.4	7.3YR 4.0/10.1

Gemstone	Color	Weight	Shape	Location		L*a*b*		Munsell
Calcite-Co	dark rose pink	3.40	cushion	Spain	20	47.4	−16.4	3.1RP 1.9/11.9
Childrenite	peach	1.37	round	Brazil	74	19.0	9.3	3.8R 7.3/4.5
Chrysoberyl								
	brownish-green	7.80	oval	Sri Lanka	47	−3.6	28.8	6.7Y 4.6/4.0
	medium brown	6.19	oval	Sri Lanka	38	5.8	36.3	1.3Y 3.7/5.4
	brownish-yellow	7.51	round	Sri Lanka	54	2.6	27.7	1.9Y 5.3/4.1
	green-yellow	7.04	round	Sri Lanka	54	−0.4	40.4	4.2Y 5.3/5.8
	yellow-brown	11.84	oval	Brazil	67	2.8	48.1	2.3Y 6.6/7.1
	dark greenish-yellow	13.25	antique	Brazil	49	−6.0	36.3	7.7Y 4.8/5.1
	brown	9.30	emerald cut	Sri Lanka	43	6.7	42.5	1.2Y 4.2/6.5
	dark greenish-yellow	21.30	oval	Sri Lanka	59	−4.9	31.3	7.0Y 5.8/4.4
	lemon yellow	11.49	oval	Brazil	72	−9.4	30.8	0.9GY 7.1/4.2
	greenish-yellow	12.02	round	Sri Lanka	50	−7.1	41.3	8.0Y 4.9/5.7
Chrysocolla	medium blue	13.59	free form	Arizona	39	−36.0	−9.5	5.9BG 3.8/7.4
Cinnabar	red	1.37	fancy	Charcas, Mexico	11	37.4	36.5	1.1YR 1.0/9.4
Clinohumite	orange	1.52	emerald cut	USSR	36	24.8	59.0	7.3YR 3.5/10.3
Corundum								
Ruby	pink-violetish red	3.66	antique	Thailand	23	40.9	−0.8	7.5RP 2.2/9.5
	dark pinkish-red	3.56	oval	Burma	24	48.0	−19.3	2.2RP 2.3/12.3
	dark red	2.23	oval	Thailand	19	44.0	−1.3	7.6RP 1.8/10.2
	medium pinkish-red	2.30	oval	Burma	49	45.8	−21.9	0.6RP 4.8/12.0
	pink-orangy red	2.11	antique	Thailand	26	46.2	2.4	8.5RP 2.5/10.7
	medium red	2.07	antique	Thailand	24	45.9	0.2	7.9RP 2.3/10.6
	violetish-red	3.56	antique	Thailand	18	42.5	−7.2	5.4RP 1.7/10.2
	violet	1.02	pear	Thailand	38	38.8	−19.3	0.6RP 3.7/10.3
	pinkish-red	0.98	oval	Thailand	37	50.5	−19.1	2.2RP 3.6/12.8
Sapphire	light pink	2.12	oval	Sri Lanka	23	19.6	−12.1	9.1P 2.2/5.1
	medium purple-blue	3.76	antique	Sri Lanka	38	21.7	−40.7	8.9PB 3.7/10.2
	dark green	4.25	oval	Sri Lanka	20	−11.6	11.5	8.2GY 1.9/2.4
	fine medium dark blue	5.21	oval	Sri Lanka	21	23.0	−48.2	7.6PB 2.0/12.1
	medium blue	6.05	oval	Sri Lanka	47	9.7	−30.9	7.4PB 4.6/7.3
	dark blue	2.60	oval	Sri Lanka	17	15.5	−39.0	7.0PB 1.6/9.7
	violetish-pink	4.02	oval	Sri Lanka	37	33.7	−21.8	8.5P 3.6/8.9
	dark lemon yellow	16.12	oval	Sri Lanka	70	−0.3	56.8	3.8Y 6.9/8.2
	medium green	1.98	antique	Umba Valley, Tanzania	52	−5.4	19.8	9.3Y 5.1/2.7
	very pale yellow	1.40	antique	Umba Valley, Tanzania	79	4.7	5.4	1.0YR 7.8/1.3
	red-violet	1.86	emerald cut	Umba Valley, Tanzania	34	7.2	−8.9	3.1P 3.3/2.5
	orangy-yellow	3.41	antique	Umba Valley, Tanzania	55	8.3	38.2	0.1Y 5.4/6.0
	brown-pink	3.28	emerald cut	Umba Valley, Tanzania	36	15.4	12.3	9.5R 3.5/3.7
	orangy-red	0.96	antique	Umba Valley, Tanzania	40	44.7	15.6	2.8R 3.9/10.5
	blue-violet	3.77	antique	Umba Valley, Tanzania	42	8.4	−19.3	8.7PB 4.1/4.6
	green	1.46	round	Umba Valley, Tanzania	55	−9.1	19.2	3.5GY 5.4/2.9
	powder-blue	2.56	round	Umba Valley, Tanzania	54	5.4	−23.3	6.9PB 5.3/5.5
	brownish-orange	4.64	antique	Umba Valley, Tanzania	30	33.7	35.6	1.1YR 2.9/8.9

(continued)

TABLE 2.   *(Continued)*

Gemstone	Color	Weight	Shape	Location		L*a*b*		Munsell
Heated Geuda	dark golden yellow	6.13	oval	Sri Lanka	81	11.6	78.3	0.1Y 8.0/12.1
	medium orange	3.89	oval	Sri Lanka	42	11.2	54.6	0.4Y 4.1/8.4
	dark orange	4.00	oval	Sri Lanka	53	31.5	92.3	7.3YR 5.2/15.7
	yellow	2.21	oval	Sri Lanka	80	8.0	78.3	1.0Y 7.9/11.9
	orangy-yellow	3.60	oval	Sri Lanka	58	11.4	70.0	0.7Y 5.7/10.7
Miscellaneous	dark blue	3.87	emerald cut	Australia	15	8.7	−32.0	5.7PB 1.4/7.8
	dark blue-green	5.75	emerald cut	Australia	18	−7.1	−7.3	2.5B 1.7/2.2
	dark pink	6.20	oval	Sri Lanka	52	25.8	−18.1	7.7P 5.1/7.0
	dark blue	—	—	Kashmir	25	5.0	−25.0	5.4PB 2.4/6.0
	beige-yellow	5.55	oval	Sri Lanka	60	13.7	29.9	6.0YR 5.9/5.4
	dark blue	2.30	pear	Montana	28	−7.3	−8.4	4.0B 2.7/2.5
	medium blue	1.35	octagon	Montana	40	−6.0	−13.5	8.8B 3.9/3.6
	medium light blue	1.19	pear	Montana	52	0.9	−17.0	4.8PB 5.1/4.1
	light blue	1.40	shield	Montana	77	2.0	−13.5	7.0PB 7.6/3.1
	blue-green	1.47	pear	Montana	48	−8.2	0.7	1.1BG 4.7/1.5
	light yellow-green	1.77	pear	Montana	75	−8.6	13.3	6.1GY 7.4/2.2
	light greenish-yellow	1.66	shield	Montana	70	−11.9	25.3	4.0GY 6.9/3.8
	light green	1.10	octagon	Montana	64	−4.0	13.3	0.1GY 6.3/1.8
	yellow	0.95	shield	Montana	70	−2.0	26.7	4.8Y 6.9/3.8
	orange-mauve	0.96	shield	Montana	58	5.8	5.8	0.6YR 5.7/1.5
	beige	1.03	pear	Montana	60	8.1	9.5	1.7YR 5.9/2.2
Creedite	violet	0.96	emerald cut	Mexico	60	15.7	−12.6	6.6P 5.9/4.4
Crocoite	orangy-red	1.87	emerald cut	Tasmania	33	50.0	75.0	3.0YR 3.2/15.8
Cuprite	dark red	11.62	round	South Africa	6	48.5	27.7	6.9R 0.9/11.1
Diaspore	pale gray-yellow	2.10	emerald cut	Turkey	69	−0.8	13.8	4.2Y 6.8/2.0
Diopside	medium green	2.23	round	New York	72	−3.5	15.6	7.6Y 7.1/2.2
chrome	dark green	0.75	round	Kenya	36	−26.2	51.0	4.7GY 3.5/8.0
chrome	dark green	4.95	antique	USSR	10	−18.0	35.7	3.5GY 0.9/5.5
Dioptase	green	0.41	emerald cut	Tsumeb, Namibia	28	−62.6	−1.2	1.5BG 2.7/12.0
Enstatite	brown	0.52	round	Burma	52	3.3	32.5	1.9Y 5.1/4.8
	green	2.43	pear	Africa	32	−20.2	54.0	2.4GY 3.1/7.8
	light brown	4.38	emerald cut	Africa	50	14.8	40.0	7.7YR 4.9/6.8
Epidote	dark brown	3.43	cushion	Africa	2	7.3	21.7	0.1Y 0.9/3.5
Euclase	light blue-green	1.33	emerald cut	Brazil	77	−4.6	0.0	3.6BG 7.6/0.9
	dark blue	0.24	emerald cut	Zimbabwe	35	−4.5	−20.4	0.8PB 3.4/5.0
Fluorite	emerald-green	3.05	pear	Colombia	59	−27.0	19.1	0.9G 5.8/5.3
	pink	0.92	round	Switzerland	70	18.4	6.8	2.0R 6.9/4.4
	violet	5.75	round	Illinois	17	20.3	−25.1	1.8P 1.6/7.1
	blue-green	6.05	oval	England	44	−19.8	7.6	4.5G 4.3/3.6
	yellow	8.80	round	Illinois	62	0.1	49.8	3.8Y 6.1/7.2
	blue	75.77	marquise	Illinois	36	−2.8	31.3	2.2PB 3.5/7.6
Garnets								
Andradite	medium green	0.47	round	Korea	50	−13.2	33.2	2.5GY 4.9/4.8
	olive green	0.51	round	Korea	47	0.3	40.3	4.2Y 4.6/5.8
	brown	0.33	round	East Siberia, USSR	29	15.6	44.3	8.9YR 2.8/7.4
Demantoid	medium green	0.68	emerald cut	USSR	51	−38.8	54.6	7.2GY 5.0/9.8
Grossular	medium orange	9.81	round	Asbestos, Quebec	44	14.4	28.0	5.9YR 4.3/5.2
	light mint green	4.15	antique	Tanzania	70	−11.9	19.6	5.8GY 6.9/3.2
	light brownish-yellow	5.01	triangle	Tanzania	55	6.3	32.9	0.1Y 5.4/5.1
	light brownish-yellow	2.59	emerald cut	Tanzania	84	9.4	38.9	8.2YR 8.3/6.3
	cinnamon brown	4.48	antique	Tanzania	51	19.6	17.9	10.0R 5.0/5.0

Gemstone	Color	Weight	Shape	Location		L*a*b*		Munsell
	near colorless	2.18	round	Tanzania	92	0.9	8.4	0.1Y 9.1/1.3
	medium mint green	3.88	antique	Tanzania	58	−16.8	23.0	6.9GY 5.7/4.1
	dark green	2.47	emerald cut	Tanzania (tsavorite)	50	−46.6	34.6	0.5G 4.9/9.2
	dark orange	4.82	antique	Tanzania	88	44.4	66.0	0.3YR 8.7/14.7
	very pale green	4.14	antique	Tanzania	77	2.9	4.6	3.5YR 7.6/0.9
Malaya	medium brownish-orange	12.80	triangle	Tanzania	30	25.6	24.6	0.6YR 2.9/6.5
	brownish-pink	11.39	antique	Tanzania	44	17.3	5.6	9.1R 4.3/1.7
	orange	6.38	triangle	Tanzania	45	16.9	30.7	5.3YR 4.4/5.9
	gray-brown	8.23	antique	Tanzania	39	8.0	20.6	8.0YR 3.8/3.5
	pinkish-orange	8.56	antique	Tanzania	48	19.1	21.3	1.3YR 4.7/5.2
	dark orange	14.46	antique	Tanzania	25	35.9	48.9	3.3YR 2.4/10.6
Pyrope-Almandine	medium rose-pink	3.09	round	Sri Lanka	28	36.7	1.8	8.3RP 2.7/8.5
	light rose-pink	0.74	round	North Carolina	54	−24.8	−5.7	3.4RP 5.3/6.0
	dark red	0.58	round	Arizona	23	33.5	38.4	2.1YR 2.2/9.0
	brown-orange	1.27	round	Mozambique	30	38.1	22.0	6.5R 2.9/8.9
	brownish	6.48	emerald cut	?	26	38.6	28.4	8.5R 2.5/9.3
Rhodolite	red-violet	10.88	oval	Tanzania	12	22.5	−9.1	2.3RP 1.1/5.7
	brownish-violet	13.10	round	Tanzania	10	31.7	7.3	2.0R 0.9/7.3
	fine dark violet	24.46	antique	Tanzania	16	37.6	−4.8	6.0RP 1.5/9.0
Spessartine	light orange	3.61	round	Orissa, India	55	18.1	38.3	5.9YR 5.4/7.0
	medium orange	3.81	round	Orissa, India	45	29.1	55.8	5.2YR 4.4/10.6
	dark orange	5.65	oval	Orissa, India	22	34.2	54.2	4.7YR 2.1/10.8
Spessartine	dark brownish-orange	4.05	pear	Brazil	25	31.1	31.8	1.2YR 2.4/8.0
	dark brownish-orange	15.40	emerald cut	Madagascar	14	30.3	41.4	4.1YR 1.3/8.8
	light orange	4.65	oval	Amelia, Virginia	40	28.3	37.9	2.8YR 3.9/8.2
	medium brownish-orange	6.41	antique	?	31	37.2	58.6	4.1YR 3.0/11.9
	dark orange	1.27	round	Africa	38	27.5	29.6	1.2YR 3.7/7.3
	very dark brownish-orange	16.80	antique	Brazil	4	26.5	26.7	2.0YR 0.9/6.7
	light orange	1.75	round	Ramona, California	74	34.5	62.4	3.1YR 7.3/12.5
Tsavorite	medium dark green	4.11	oval	Tanzania	40	−49.0	32.4	1.0G 3.9/9.4
	fine medium green	2.47	emerald cut	Tanzania	50	−46.6	34.6	0.5G 4.9/9.2
	medium green	1.25	emerald cut	Tanzania	44	−47.2	27.8	1.6G 4.3/8.9
	dark green	4.01	oval	Tanzania	32	−51.8	32.6	1.1G 3.1/9.8
Haüyne	blue	0.04	fancy	Germany	52	1.0	−40.0	4.1PB 5.1/9.7
Hypersthene	dark bottle green	2.52	pear	Arizona	25	−6.0	41.7	8.1Y 2.4/5.7
Idocrase	brown	2.30	round	Africa	46	14.9	52.6	9.2YR 4.5/8.5
	green	1.05	round	Africa	52	−14.4	51.5	1.0GY 5.1/7.1
	brown	3.82	emerald cut	Switzerland	35	15.9	42.6	8.3YR 3.4/7.2
	brown	1.40	cushion	Italy	51	6.6	67.0	2.4Y 5.0/9.9
Iolite	blue	1.56	round	India	28	10.7	−24.0	8.2PB 2.7/5.9
	blue	3.00	emerald cut	India	26	10.1	−25.3	7.6PB 2.5/6.1
Kornerupine (chrome)	light green	0.40	round	Africa	65	−32.1	28.6	0.1G 6.4/6.7
	light brown	12.07	round	Sri Lanka	50	5.4	30.5	0.3Y 4.9/4.6
	olivy-brown	2.62	oval	Sri Lanka	34	−1.0	19.7	5.5Y 3.3/2.8
Kyanite	medium blue	8.30	cushion	Brazil	48	−11.6	−21.7	7.9B 4.7/5.8
	dark blue	4.01	cushion	Brazil	40	1.0	−33.0	3.8PB 3.9/8.0
Lazulite	blue	0.70	round	Brazil	47	−6.1	−31.5	1.5PB 4.6/7.8
Microlite	green	0.14	oval	Brazil	59	−24.0	23.3	9.4GY 5.8/5.1
Manganotantalite	red	4.85	cushion	Mozambique	11	37.2	36.5	1.2YR 10./9.4
Opal	yellow	11.74	emerald cut	Idaho	49	5.5	59.3	2.5Y 4.8/8.7
	brown-gray	5.15	round	Mexico	35	0.7	12.7	3.2Y 3.4/1.8

(continued)

TABLE 2.   *(Continued)*

Gemstone		Color	Weight	Shape	Location		L*a*b*		Munsell
Peridot		orangy-red	0.76	round	Mexico	46	50.9	95.4	4.0YR 4.5/18.6
		light orange	8.04	oval	Mexico	46	19.3	55.7	8.1YR 4.5/9.5
		medium green	8.25	antique	Arizona	47	−20.9	52.3	3.2GY 4.6/7.7
		medium green	9.20	triangle	Arizona	34	−11.9	48.5	0.1GY 3.3/6.6
		light green	4.51	pear	Norway	66	−19.0	31.7	5.9GY 6.5/5.2
		light green	8.22	oval	Egypt	58	−13.3	31.9	3.0GY 5.7/4.7
Phosphophyllite		light blue-green	0.81	emerald cut	Bolivia	85	−4.2	−1.4	9.8BG 8.4/0.9
Proustite		dark red	2.58	round	Germany	18	51.6	50.0	10.0R 1.7/13.5
Quartz									
Amethyst		lilac	6.22	emerald cut	Brazil	57	19.4	−12.0	8.6P 5.6/5.0
		light violet	9.18	oval	Brazil	37	18.5	−14.5	7.1P 3.6/5.2
		dark violet	8.52	fancy oval	Zambia	6	25.5	−26.0	3.0P 0.9/8.0
		medium dark violet	4.40	oval	Brazil	6	22.8	−21.1	3.9P 0.9/6.9
		medium dark violet	3.61	round	Brazil	12	29.8	−29.0	3.3P 1.1/9.2
		medium dark purple	6.41	round	Brazil	14	20.1	−23.2	2.3P 1.3/6.8
		dark purple	6.38	fancy emerald cut	Brazil	12	25.9	−25.3	3.5P 1.1/8.0
		"Siberian"	14.91	oval	Para, Brazil	8	30.8	−23.4	7.8P 0.9/8.5
Citrine		medium yellow-orange	7.55	round	Brazil	52	13.5	43.1	8.4YR 5.1/7.1
		brownish-orange	4.20	round	Brazil	38	7.9	34.8	0.1Y 3.7/5.4
		dark straw-yellow	8.81	oval	Brazil	55	5.4	23.9	9.8YR 5.4/3.8
		pale straw-yellow	12.64	oval	Brazil	61	0.7	19.3	2.7Y 6.0/2.8
		light orange	16.90	antique	Brazil	56	12.1	61.0	0.1Y 5.5/9.5
		medium orange	19.72	oval	Brazil	53	19.2	66.5	8.7YR 5.2/10.9
		dark orange	15.76	oval	Brazil	33	21.7	51.1	7.4YR 3.2/8.9
		dark orange ("Madeira")	15.33	oval	Brazil	29	30.5	61.1	6.3YR 2.7/11.3
Green quartz		apple green	4.48	oval	Brazil	52	−9.5	13.0	6.5GY 5.1/2.3
Rose quartz		medium pink	14.20	emerald cut	Brazil	51	13.1	4.2	2.0R 5.0/3.1
		pale pink	18.79	antique	Brazil	71	6.0	6.1	0.2YR 7.0/1.5
Smoky quartz		medium brown	23.78	round	Brazil	26	7.6	12.3	5.6YR 2.5/2.4
		light brown	15.61	emerald cut	Brazil	63	4.5	23.7	0.1Y 6.2/3.7
		medium yellow-brown	9.37	emerald cut	Brazil	43	5.6	22.5	0.1Y 4.2/3.5
		dark brown	13.57	emerald cut	Brazil	20	8.6	15.1	6.5YR 1.9/2.8
		very dark brown	7.49	emerald cut	Brazil	1	6.8	11.6	6.6YR 0.9/2.2
Rhodochrosite		pink	11.88	antique	Colorado	39	40.2	11.4	1.8R 3.8/9.4
		pink	7.15	rhomboid	Peru	51	42.1	11.9	1.3R 5.0/9.9
		orangy-red	9.42	round	South Africa	30	52.7	52.3	10.0R 2.9/14.0
		pink	3.95	round	Argentina	49	37.6	15.6	3.5R 4.8/8.8
		red	24.60	antique	South Africa	16	43.6	44.9	1.2YR 1.5/11.4
Scapolite		gold-yellow	32.44	oval	Tanzania	67	3.0	55.4	2.5Y 6.6/8.1
		gold-yellow	32.00	antique	Tanzania	53	3.2	53.7	3.0Y 5.2/7.9
		very pale yellow	5.77	antique	Brazil	76	−1.8	11.8	5.9Y 7.5/1.6
		lemon yellow	9.03	antique	Burma	61	1.0	37.0	3.1Y 6.0/5.4
		violet	4.36	oval	Tanzania	30	16.1	−16.2	4.2P 2.9/5.0
Scheelite		straw yellow	2.85	pear	Korea	84	0.0	30.3	2.5Y 8.3/4.4
Scorodite		violet-blue	1.15	fancy	Namibia	23	5.7	−13.4	8.0PB 2.2/3.3
		violet-blue	1.50	pear	Namibia	15	5.3	−26.8	4.9PB 1.4/6.6
Sinhalite		dark straw-yellow	4.58	antique	Sri Lanka	50	6.6	32.5	0.1Y 4.9/5.1
		brown	7.07	oval	Sri Lanka	16	16.7	37.6	8.1YR 1.5/6.5
		green	4.18	oval	Sri Lanka	47	1.0	25.6	3.2Y 4.6/3.7
		yellow	9.18	oval	Sri Lanka	65	8.9	37.0	9.1YR 6.4/5.9
Smithsonite		pale yellow	8.00	round	Namibia	75	4.2	9.0	5.6YR 7.4/1.6
		beige	10.40	oval	Namibia	73	1.3	6.0	9.3YR 7.2/0.9

Gemstone	Color	Weight	Shape	Location		L*a*b*		Munsell
Sodalite	intense dark blue	0.85	emerald cut	Namibia	23	20.0	−43.2	7.7PB 2.2/10.8
Sphalerite	light green	1.93	round	Colorado	68	−2.8	73.4	5.1Y 6.7/10.4
	yellow-orange	3.30	round	Spain	72	6.9	100	2.7Y 7.1/14.7
	dark green	4.65	round	Mexico	43	0.6	55.0	4.6Y 4.2/7.9
	dark orange	14.48	round	Spain	39	38.1	86.6	6.3YR 3.8/15.5
	light orange	5.57	round	Spain	55	26.6	10.3	2.9R 5.4/6.3
Sphene	brownish yellow-green	6.22	emerald cut	Madagascar	49	2.3	66.9	4.0Y 4.8/9.7
	light yellow-green	1.55	round	Baja, Mexico	73	−10.8	56.2	8.1Y 7.2/7.8
	light brown	1.76	round	Baja, Mexico	28	21.2	51.0	7.9YR 2.7/8.9
	medium green	7.01	emerald cut	India	34	−17.5	47.5	2.3GY 3.3/6.9
	emerald green	1.01	round	Baja, Mexico	24	−33.3	34.2	8.5GY 2.3/7.2
	brown	1.44	round	Baja, Mexico	60	11.9	80.4	1.0Y 5.9/12.3
	yellow-green	4.22	round	India	51	−1.3	67.8	5.2Y 5.0/9.6
	yellow	2.65	antique	India	79	−5.8	74.9	5.7Y 7.8/10.5
Spinel								
Blues	dark blue	8.35	oval	Sri Lanka	12	−0.6	−12.7	2.1PB 1.1/3.1
	medium dark blue	9.20	oval	Sri Lanka	15	−6.9	−12.7	6.2B 1.4/3.3
	light blue	9.30	oval	Sri Lanka	31	−6.6	−11.9	7.2B 3.0/3.2
	lavender-blue	15.22	oval	Sri Lanka	50	4.8	−16.8	7.5PB 4.9/3.9
	greenish-blue	4.78	round	Sri Lanka	21	−13.6	−11.1	0.7B 2.0/3.8
	cobalt-blue	11.23	emerald cut	Sri Lanka	6	−2.3	−19.7	0.8PB 0.9/4.8
	slightly violetish-blue	7.27	round	Sri Lanka	29	2.8	−20.8	4.8PB 2.8/5.1
	dark violet	5.46	antique	Sri Lanka	13	5.2	−13.7	7.2PB 1.2/3.4
	magenta	3.96	oval	Sri Lanka	19	44.4	−4.5	6.3RP 1.8/10.6
	medium purple	11.98	antique	Sri Lanka	14	7.2	−9.2	2.0P 1.3/2.5
	blue-violet	8.53	oval	Sri Lanka	25	6.0	−12.6	8.6PB 2.4/3.1
	light purple	7.98	oval	Sri Lanka	27	14.4	−9.0	9.0P 2.6/3.7
	gray-blue	14.96	antique	Sri Lanka	30	−5.1	−8.5	6.9B 2.9/2.3
Pinks	dark rose-red	8.21	round	Sri Lanka	14	27.0	2.4	9.3RP 1.3/6.3
	light rose-red	7.65	oval	Sri Lanka	30	25.3	−0.7	7.1RP 2.9/5.8
	dark pink	5.23	oval	Burma	24	−24.8	−4.8	4.7RP 2.3/6.0
	dark violetish-red	9.02	oval	Sri Lanka	21	19.3	−2.2	5.9RP 2.0/4.6
	medium reddish-purple	7.07	oval	Sri Lanka	26	27.1	−6.8	3.9RP 2.5/6.6
	grayish-pink	5.89	oval	Sri Lanka	47	21.4	2.0	8.1RP 4.6/4.9
	medium pink	6.56	oval	USSR	68	41.6	3.8	7.4RP 6.7/9.7
	slightly bluish-pink	8.87	oval	Sri Lanka	42	15.4	−2.5	4.5RP 4.1/3.7
	light dusty-pink	11.40	antique	Burma	54	16.2	−2.8	4.1RP 5.3/3.9
Reds	dark orangy-red	5.30	round	Burma	27	24.7	20.7	10.0R 2.6/6.0
	medium pinkish-orange	2.98	oval	Burma	41	43.5	10.4	0.9R 4.0/10.3
	medium brownish-pink	3.07	round	Burma	42	34.5	7.8	0.7R 4.1/8.2
	medium brown	2.34	round	Burma	45	26.4	14.4	5.7R 4.4/6.2
	light brownish-pink	10.98	oval	Burma	48	23.6	8.1	2.4R 4.7/5.5
	dark grayish-pink	3.95	round	Burma	31	14.7	4.1	2.0R 3.0/3.4
	dark red	8.89	oval	Burma	8	36.8	31.8	0.2YR 0.9/9.1
	medium red	2.68	oval	Burma	30	41.5	25.1	6.8R 2.9/9.7
	medium pinkish-red	3.21	round	Burma	27	47.5	7.4	0.1R 2.5/11.1
Spodumene	blue	29.85	oval	Brazil	53	−2.7	−3.4	6.7B 5.2/1.0
	medium pink	16.06	emerald cut	Afghanistan	59	−17.7	−12.9	2.3B 5.8/4.8
	medium pink	17.76	oval	California	58	19.1	−10.9	9.1P 5.7/4.8
	yellow-green	17.01	emerald cut	Afghanistan	63	−5.3	28.0	7.5Y 6.2/3.9
	dark pink	47.33	oval	Brazil	65	32.2	−19.0	8.7P 6.4/8.3

(continued)

TABLE 2. *(Continued)*

Gemstone	Color	Weight	Shape	Location		L*a*b*		Munsell
Taaffeite	gray-mauve	1.60	rhomboid	Sri Lanka	50	4.5	0.8	9.0RP 4.9/1.0
Topaz	yellow-brown	6.72	round	USSR	38	13.0	37.2	8.6YR 3.7/6.2
	red-orange	12.59	emerald cut	Brazil	49	38.6	37.5	9.9R 4.8/10.1
	dark beige	5.29	round	Mexico	56	12.0	26.3	6.2YR 5.5/4.8
	yellow	4.65	oval	Brazil	59	8.6	27.7	8.3YR 5.8/4.6
	dark orange	25.25	oval	Brazil	61	23.9	61.5	6.6YR 6.0/10.8
	brownish-pink	8.76	antique	Brazil	63	35.0	5.7	8.6RP 6.2/8.2
	medium blue	7.20	oval	Brazil	60	−14.3	−17.6	6.1B 5.9/5.2
	red-orange	8.45	antique	Brazil	65	34.4	26.8	7.6R 6.4/8.7
	medium pink	17.84	oval	USSR	73	25.2	−16.9	7.7P 7.2/6.7
Tourmaline								
Rubellite	pinkish-orange	36.85	emerald cut	Madagascar	25	38.3	21.2	6.4R 2.4/8.9
	dark red-violet	13.16	oval	Brazil	24	47.8	−0.9	7.6RP 2.3/11.1
	very dark violet-red	17.13	emerald cut	Brazil	5	28.0	2.8	9.6RP 0.9/6.5
	medium violet	16.73	antique	Brazil	20	38.1	−5.0	5.8RP 1.9/9.1
	dark red	10.26	antique	Ouro Fino, Brazil	12	39.5	7.4	0.1R 1.1/9.1
	dark pinkish-red	36.56	emerald cut	Brazil	19	41.8	10.4	2.0R 1.8/9.7
Blues and Greens	intense smalt blue	9.84	emerald cut	Brazil	41	−21.0	18.8	9.6GY 4.0/4.3
	blue-green	15.96	emerald cut	Brazil	50	−40.1	−0.1	2.3BG 4.9/7.7
	fine green (chrome)	10.05	triangle	Africa	30	−30.7	23.9	0.1G 2.9/6.0
	slightly yellowish-green	9.68	emerald cut	Brazil	52	−39.7	15.9	3.9G 5.1/7.3
	dark green	14.75	emerald cut	Brazil	32	−38.8	31.1	0.1G 3.1/7.7
Orangy Colors	peachy-orange	10.90	round	Mozambique	42	31.1	20.5	7.2R 4.1/7.4
	medium brownish-orange	5.74	antique	Tanzania	43	18.6	56.6	8.5YR 4.2/9.4
	dark brownish-orange	4.84	round	Tanzania	48	20.9	70.4	8.7YR 4.7/11.6
	medium orangy-brown	10.39	oval	Tanzania	28	10.7	46.0	0.4Y 2.7/7.1
	medium pinkish-brown	46.84	oval	Tanzania	31	24.0	26.4	1.8YR 3.0/6.4
Pinks	medium pink	32.32	oval	Afghanistan	57	34.7	0.0	6.5RP 5.6/8.2
	medium dark rose-pink	10.95	round	Brazil	28	34.0	−4.2	5.6RP 2.7/8.1
	slightly brownish-pink	11.13	antique	Mozambique	44	28.7	12.5	4.1R 4.3/6.6
	brown-pink	21.22	emerald cut	Stewart Mine, Pala, California	38	18.7	20.6	1.7YR 3.7/5.0
Mozambique Color Suite	medium pinkish-beige	2.51	round	Mozambique	66	23.7	7.7	1.4R 6.5/5.6
	light pinkish-beige	2.37	round	Mozambique	78	19.1	5.5	0.4R 7.7/5.6
	near colorless	2.59	round	Mozambique	85	7.9	3.9	3.5R 8.4/1.9
	light pink	2.19	round	Mozambique	56	33.2	−5.7	4.1RP 5.5/8.0
	dark rose-pink	2.15	round	Mozambique	35	47.0	−11.6	3.9RP 3.4/11.5
	dark green	2.16	round	Mozambique	24	−12.8	22.0	4.6GY 2.3/3/5
	dark brownish-green	2.34	round	Mozambique	34	−14.7	37.0	2.4GY 3.3/5.4
	medium green	2.68	round	Mozambique	52	−8.3	41.4	8.5Y 5.1/5.7
	lime green	2.10	round	Mozambique	64	−8.6	26.0	1.2GY 6.3/3.7
	very pale green	3.08	round	Mozambique	69	0.1	12.8	2.9Y 6.8/1.8
	colorless	2.22	round	Mozambique	84	1.5	2.1	2.3YR 8.3/0.4
	beige-yellow	2.04	round	Mozambique	87	3.8	21.6	9.3YR 8.6/3.4
	light brown	2.33	round	Mozambique	37	9.0	51.1	1.2Y 3.6/7.8
	dark brown	1.81	round	Mozambique	36	18.9	33.8	5.6YR 3.5/6.4
	blue	2.30	round	Mozambique	45	−8.4	−2.1	6.2BG 4.4/1.7

Gemstone	Color	Weight	Shape	Location		L*a*b*		Munsell
Willemite	golden yellow	2.35	pear	Franklin, New Jersey	85	−7.4	63.0	6.2Y 8.4/8.9
Wulfenite	yellow	6.11	oval	Namibia	63	1.0	29.0	2.8Y 6.2/4.2
	orangy-red	2.54	emerald cut	Red Cloud Mine, Arizona	45	43.8	96.1	5.4YR 4.4/17.6
Zircon	reddish-brown	19.03	oval	Sri Lanka	17	16.2	16.7	2.2YR 1.6/4.1
	brownish-yellow	17.43	oval	Sri Lanka	37	12.2	49.6	0.1Y 3.6/7.8
	violet-rose	14.20	round	Sri Lanka	20	30.9	3.4	9.4RP 1.9/7.2
	dark orange	9.26	oval	Sri Lanka	33	25.5	66.0	7.9YR 3.2/11.4
	green	4.36	oval	Sri Lanka	48	−15.4	25.8	5.4GY 4.7/4.2
	rose-red	11.26	emerald cut	Sri Lanka	19	26.2	8.3	3.1R 1.8/5.9
	lemon yellow	15.70	oval	Sri Lanka	50	−0.3	31.6	4.2Y 4.9/4.5
	medium blue	5.56	oval	Cambodia	46	−12.3	−14.1	4.9B 4.5/4.2
	yellow	8.92	oval	Sri Lanka	65	10.8	58.1	0.1Y 6.4/9.0
	pale gray-green	16.63	antique	Sri Lanka	55	7.8	14.6	5.4YR 5.4/2.7
	reddish-brown	7.77	oval	Sri Lanka	26	23.0	29.1	3.2YR 2.5/6.5
	light olive green	5.34	round	Sri Lanka	47	−0.3	19.2	4.3Y 4.6/2.7
	dark blue	2.87	round	Cambodia	56	−8.4	−11.1	6.8B 5.5/3.3
	light pink	1.36	round	Sri Lanka	71	−11.9	−5.8	0.7B 7.0/2.8
	light orange	1.44	round	Sri Lanka	59	26.2	58.1	5.7YR 5.8/10.6
	medium orange	2.59	round	Sri Lanka	52	39.4	70.9	4.0YR 5.1/13.9
	pale blue-green	2.67	round	Cambodia	77	−6.9	−1.4	7.2BG 7.6/1.4
Zoisite	violet-blue	26.54	pear	Tanzania	20	55.0	−76.3	8.6PB 1.9/20.9
	light blue-gray	1.06	round	Tanzania	75	0.7	0.6	9.5R 7.4/0.1
	medium blue	2.30	round	Tanzania	60	3.5	−20.7	6.4PB 5.9/4.8
	violet-blue	0.96	emerald cut	Tanzania	47	16.8	−35.7	8.8PB 4.6/8.7
	brown-blue	0.92	emerald cut	Tanzania	61	7.1	−11.7	2.0P 6.0/3.0

A

ACHROITE   See: Tourmaline.

ACTINOLITE   See also: Tremolite; Nephrite; Pargasite.

Formula: $Ca_2(Mg, Fe)_5Si_8O_{22}(OH)_2$.

Crystallography: Monoclinic; bladed crystals, usually elongated; fibrous, columnar aggregates. Also massive, granular. Often twinned.

Colors: Pale to dark green, blackish green, black.

Luster: Vitreous, sometimes dull.

Hardness: 5.5

Density: Usually 3.05; Tanzania: 3.03–3.07; Max.: 3.44.

Cleavage: 2 directions good, often fibrous nature. Brittle. Compact variety tough.

Optics: $\alpha = 1.619$–1.622; $\beta = 1.632$–1.634; $\gamma = 1.642$–1.644 (Tanzanian material). See diagram on p. 38. Biaxial $(-)$; $2V = 78°$.

Birefringence: 0.022–0.026.

Pleochroism: Yellow to dark green. Material transparent to nearly opaque.

α: pale yellow/yellowish-green.
β: pale yellow-green/green.
γ: pale green/deep greenish blue.

Spectral: Faint line at 5030.

Luminescence: None (due to presence of Fe).

Occurrence: Contact metamorphic limestones and dolomites; magnesium-rich limestones and ultrabasic rocks; regionally metamorphosed rocks.

Tremolite–Actinolite Data

Locality	Pleochroic Colors	α	β	γ	Birefringence	S.G.	Comments
Fowler, New York	red-violet	1.602	—	1.630	0.028	3.03	Hexagonite
Kenya	bright green	1.602	1.613	1.628	0.026	2.99	Tremolite
		1.607	1.618	1.632	0.025	3.01	
Tanzania (Lelatema)	yellow green/green	1.608	1.616	1.631	0.023	3.01	Tremolite
Tanzania	emerald green	1.611	1.623	1.639	0.028	3.30	Tremolite + Cr
Tanzania (Merelani)	yellow-green/emerald green	1.608	1.618	1.630	0.022		Smaragdite
Taiwan	yellow-green/green tones, also brownish	1.607–1.609	—	1.630–1.633	0.023–0.024	3.01	Tremolite
		1.615–1.619	—	1.631–1.633	0.014–0.016	3.01	Catseye tremolite
Uganda	yellow-green/green	1.619–1.622	1.632–1.634	1.642–1.644	0.021–0.024	3.04–3.07	Tremolite–Actinolite
	green/brown	1.633	—	1.653	0.020	3.15	Actinolite

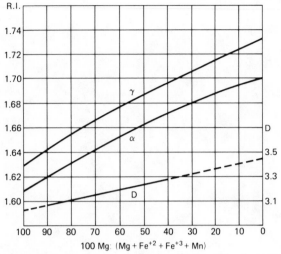

Chemical composition vs. optics and density of common hornblendes.

Adapted from W. A. Deere, R. A. Howie, and J. Zussman, 1962, *The Rock Forming Minerals,* vol. 2 (New York: Wiley), p. 296.

Chester, Vermont.
Madagascar: small, dark green crystals. Many of these are clean and suitable for faceting.
Tanzania: transparent crystals.
(See also localities for nephrite.)

Stone Sizes: Actinolite is rarely facetable and usually in small fragments. Material from Chester, Vermont, could provide stones to about 10 carats.
DG: 2.06 (greenish, step cut, Africa).

Comments: Actinolite is a member of a series that contains varying amounts of iron and magnesium. Tremolite is the Mg end, and ferroactinolite the Fe end, with actinolite in the middle. Actinolites with more than 50% Fe are very rare. *Catseye* actinolite exists (S.G. 3.0, R.I. 1.63); when chatoyant material is cut, it exhibits a fine eye. Actinolite is easy to cleave and hard to cut and would make a poor jewelry stone. Actinolite is the chief constituent of nephrite (jade). *Smaragdite* is a chrome-rich tremolite from Tanzania.

Name: Greek *aktis,* meaning *ray,* due to the fibrous nature.

ADAMITE

Formula: $Zn_2(AsO_4)OH + Co, Cu.$

Crystallography: Orthorhombic; crystals elongated or equant; druses, radial aggregates, and spheroids on matrix.

Colors: Colorless, pale green, yellowish green, yellow (various shades), bluish green, green (contains Cu); rose and violet shades (color zoned, contains Co).

Luster: Vitreous.

Hardness: 3.5

Density: 4.32-4.68 (red-violet).

Cleavage: Good 1 direction. Fracture subconchoidal to uneven.

Optics:

Locality	α	β	γ	Birefringence
Mapimi, Mexico (reddish)	1.712	1.736	1.760	0.048
Mapimi, Mexico (rose)	1.710	1.735	1.759	0.049
Mapimi, Mexico (violet)	1.710	1.735	1.758	0.048
Mapimi, Mexico (green)	1.722	1.742	1.763	0.041
Tsumeb, Namibia (Cu)	1.742	1.768	1.773	0.031
Tsumeb, Namibia (Co)	1.722	1.738	1.761	0.039
Laurium, Greece	1.708	1.734	1.758	0.050

Biaxial (+); $2V = 15°$ (Cu var.) to 88°.
Large variations in composition lead to wide variations in optical properties.

Dispersion: Strong.

Pleochroism:

Colorless/blue-green/yellow-green.
Pale rose/pale rose/pale purple.
Pink/pale rose/colorless.

Spectral: Not diagnostic.

Luminescence: Intense green in SW, LW; also lemon yellow in SW.

Occurrence: Secondary mineral in the oxidized zone of ore deposits.
Utah (various localities); California; Nevada.
Laurium, Greece: often containing copper, in lovely blue and green shades.
Mapimi, Mexico: fine sprays of crystals in limonite matrix, from the Ojuela Mine.
Tsumeb, Namibia: fine crystals, sometimes colored purple by cobalt.
Cap Garonne, France.
Also *Chile, Italy, Germany, Turkey, Algeria.*

Stone Sizes: Violet crystals noted up to 1 cm long and transparent, would yield stones up to about 1-2 carats. Green material usually not clean, would provide only small faceted gems (1-3 carats).

PC: 4.38 (pink, Mexico).

Comments: Exceedingly rare as a cut gem, although the mineral occurs in many localities. Much too soft and fragile for jewelry; strictly a collector item.

Name: After Mr. Gilbert Adam, mineralogist, of Paris, who supplied the first specimens for study.

ADULARIA See: Feldspar.

AGALMATOLITE See: Pyrophyllite.

AGATE See: Quartz.

ALABASTER See: Calcite, Gypsum.

ALBITE See: Feldspar.

ALGODONITE Also: Domeykite, Mohawkite.

Formula: Cu₆As (Domeykite = Cu₃As).

Crystallography: Hexagonal crystals rare; usually massive, granular, reniform. Domeykite is isometric.

Colors: Silver white to steel gray; tarnishes rapidly to a dull brown.

Luster: Metallic; opaque.

Hardness: 3–4 (Domeykite: 3–3.5).

Density: 8.38 (Domeykite: 7.92–8.10).

Cleavage: None. Fracture uneven in domeykite, subconchoidal in algodonite.

Occurrence: Localities that produce copper arsenide minerals.
Algodonite from *Painsdale, Michigan,* in fine crystals. In masses from the *Algodones Mines, Coquimbo, Chile,* and *Cerro de Los Aeguas, Rancagua, Chile.*
Mohawkite is a mixture of algodonite and other copper arsenides, from the *Mohawk Mine, Keweenaw Peninsula, Michigan.*
Domeykite is from the *Mohawk Mine, Michigan; Lake Superior district, Ontario, Canada; Guererro, Mexico;* also from *Chile, Germany, Sweden,* and from *Cornwall, England.* Related minerals are found at *Beloves, Czechoslovakia,* and *Mesanki, Iran.*

Stone Sizes: Cabochons could be cut to almost any size, depending on the availability of large masses of metallic rough.

Comments: Cabochons of these arsenides are bright, silvery, and metallic and are both attractive and unusual. However, they tarnish rather quickly and the surfaces turn a drab brown and lose their luster. Cut stones are rarely seen even in collections, although they are strikingly beautiful when cut and polished to a high luster. They must be sprayed with lacquer to prevent tarnishing. Algodonite and domeykite are heat sensitive, and care must be exercised in cutting.

Name: After the Algodones Mines, Coquimbo, Chile.

ALLANITE See: Epidote.

ALMANDINE See: Garnet.

AMAZONITE See: Feldspar.

AMBER Also: Succinite.

Formula: Approximately C₁₀H₁₆O + H₂S.
A mixture of hydrocarbons, plus resins, succinic acid, and oils.
Amber is the hardened resin of pine trees, sp. *Pinus succinifera,* age ∼30 million years.

Crystallography: Amorphous.

Colors: Yellow, brown, whitish yellow, reddish, cream color, orange shades. Rarely blue, greenish, violetish.

Luster: Greasy.

Hardness: 2–2.5.

Density: 1.05–1.096 (usually ∼1.08).

Cleavage: None. Fracture conchoidal.

Optics: R.I. ∼1.54.

Spectral: Not diagnostic.

Luminescence: Yellow in SW (Texas); bluish white or greenish in LW. Baltic amber may fluoresce grayish blue in SW. Inert in X-rays.
Sicilian amber is noted for its fluorescence.

Occurrence: In sedimentary deposits and on shorelines, due to the action of waves and currents in bringing material up from offshore beds.
East Prussia (now U.S.S.R.): Succinite
Entire Baltic Sea region, including *Poland, East Germany, Norway, Denmark;* also *Rumania* and *Sicily.* Sicilian material may be opalescent blue or green.
Rarely found in *England.* Southern *Mexico* (Chiapas) produces golden yellow material.
Burma: brownish yellow and brown amber; also colorless, pale yellow, and orange.
Lebanon: scarce, from very old deposits.
Dominican Republic: mined from sedimentary rocks, yellow, orange, and red colors; this amber often contains well-preserved insects and sometimes displays a strong bluish tone in reflected light.
Cedar Lake, Manitoba, Canada.
Point Barrow, Alaska.

Stone Sizes: The normal size of amber fragments is less than half a pound, but pieces weighing several pounds have been found. Amber is used often in making pipestems, as beads (tumble polished or faceted), pendants, earrings, and rings. It is also carved, sometimes ornately; used as inlay material, umbrella handles, and so forth.

Inclusions: Amber is noted for its inclusions, which are chiefly insects and pollen as well as leaves and other organic debris. These were trapped in the sticky fluid that oozed from pine trees millions of years ago and provide an intimate look at plant and insect life of that time period.

Comments: Amber is classed in various types: sea amber (found in the sea), pit amber (dug up, especially from the Baltic area), clear, massive, fancy, cloudy, frothy, fatty, and bone amber.

Frequently seen in amber are flattened starburst shapes known as *sun spangles*. These are internal feathers and are caused by stress. Amber softens at about 150°C and melts at 250-300°C. *Pressed amber,* or *ambroid,* is made by melting small pieces of amber together under great pressure. This is usually detectable by careful microscopic investigation. Amber often darkens with age to a fine red-brown color. Pressed amber, however, may turn white with age.

Copal is a fossil resin of more recent origin than true amber. Principal localities are *South America, Africa,* and *New Zealand.* Copals fluorescence whiter in SW-UV than amber and are easier to dissolve in solvents. Optical and physical properties are otherwise similar to amber. "Kauri Gum" is a copal from the kauri pine tree of New Zealand.

Amber is in great demand today, as it has been for centuries, and very large material is extremely rare, as are the more unusual colored varieties (blue, green). Good quality material is seldom used for anything but jewelry.

Name: Arabic *anbar,* which the Spanish converted to *ambar,* then later to *amber.* Succinite is from *succinum,* the Latin word for amber, meaning *juice.*

AMBLYGONITE   Also: Montebrasite (OH exceeds F); Natromontebrasite (Na exceeds Li).

Formula: (Li, Na)Al(PO$_4$)(F, OH). Usually Li greatly exceeds Na.

Crystallography: Triclinic; crystals equant to short prismatic, rough faces. Twinning common. Usually in cleavable masses.

Colors: Colorless, white, grayish white, yellow, pinkish, tan, greenish, bluish.

Luster: Vitreous to greasy; pearly on cleavages.

Hardness: 5.5-6.

Density: Approximately 2.98-3.11. amblygonite = 3.11; montebrasite = 2.98; natromontebrasite = 3.04-3.1.

Cleavage: Perfect 1 direction, good 1 direction.

Optics:

Species	Locality	α	β	γ	Birefringence	Density
Amblygonite	Chursdorf, Germany	1.578	—	1.598	.020	3.101
Amblygonite	Uto, Sweden	1.591	1.605	1.612	.021	3.065
Montebrasite	Karibib, Namibia	1.594	1.608	1.616	.022	3.085
Montebrasite	Kimito, Finland	1.611	1.619	1.633	.022	3.00
Natromontebrasite	Fremont County, Colorado	1.594	1.603	1.615	.021	3.04

Note that refractive indices and optic angle decrease as Na and F content increase. Montebrasite is optically (+) and amblygonite is (−). The change in optic sign (where $2V = 90°$) occurs at ~60% (OH). There appears to be a complete series of (OH, F) substitutions.

Pleochroism: None.

Spectral: Not diagnostic.

Luminescence: Pale blue in SW (Keystone, South Dakota). Weak orange or bright green in LW, or pale brown in LW (Pala, California).

Inclusions: Commonly veil-type inclusions, usually clouds in parallel bands.

Occurrence: Granite pegmatites.

Brazil: origin of most gem material, in crystals and masses, fine yellow color.

Custer County, South Dakota: masses up to 200 tons (nongem) and at *Tinton, South Dakota,* in masses.

Also from *Arizona; New Mexico; New Hampshire; Pala, California;* and *Newry, Maine,* in crystals up to more than 3 × 4 inches. These were found in 1940-41; they were heavily included and provided only small gems. *Germany; Varutrask, Sweden.*
Montebras, France: Montebrasite.
Karibib, Namibia: Montebrasite.
Sakangyi, Burma.

Stone Sizes: The largest cut amblygonite is ~70 carats, cut from Brazilian material. The normal size is 1-15 carats. Facetable material is known from Maine, Brazil, and Burma, but cut gems over 10 carats are scarce. *SI:* 62.5 (yellow, Brazil), 19.7 (yellow, Burma).

ROM: 15.6.
AMNH: 3 (colorless, Maine).
DG: 47 (yellow, Brazil).

Comments: Gems are usually pale straw yellow and are highly prized if the color is darker. Large stones have been cut but are extremely rare. Amblygonite is too soft and cleavable to make a good ringstone. The material from Karibib, Namibia, is lilac in color and quite beautiful when faceted, as well as being extremely rare. It should be noted that many of the so-called amblygonites reported in the literature are optically (+) and are therefore really montebrasites. Many gems in collections probably should be reexamined and relabeled, if necessary. Most yellow gems in collections and on the market are amblygonites from Brazil; however, stones from Mogi dãs Cruzes, Sao Paulo, Brazil, are montebrasite.

Names: *Amblygonite* is from the Greek words for *blunt* and *angle,* in allusion to the shapes of crystals. *Montebrasite* is from the French locality where found.

AMETHYST   See: Quartz.

AMMOLITE   See: Korite.

ANALCIME   Zeolite Group. See also: Pollucite.

Formula: $NaAlSi_2O_6 \cdot H_2O$.

Crystallography: Isometric; good crystals are common, usually trapezohedra. Massive, granular.

Colors: Colorless, white, gray, yellowish, pink, greenish.

Luster: Vitreous.

Hardness: 5-5.5.

Density: 2.22-2.29.

Cleavage: Indistinct. Fracture subconchoidal. Brittle.

Birefringence: Anomalous in polarized light.

Optics: Isotropic; $N = 1.479\text{-}1.493$.

Pleochroism: None.

Spectral: Not diagnostic.

Luminescence: Cream white in LW (Golden, Colorado).

Occurrence: Secondary mineral in basic igneous rocks; also in sedimentary rocks such as siltstones and sandstones.
Washington, Oregon, and *California* (Columbia Plateau area).
Houghton County, Michigan.
New Jersey: Watchung basalt flows.
India: Deccan Plateau.
Nova Scotia: Bay of Fundy area.
Mt. Ste. Hilaire, Quebec, Canada.
Also *Scotland, Ireland, Iceland, Norway, Italy, Czechoslovakia, Germany, Australia.*

Stone Sizes: Gems are nearly always colorless and less than 1-2 carats when faceted. Large crystals from Mt. Ste. Hilaire are white but may have small facetable areas. Crystals in basaltic cavities in general do not exceed ¼ inch in size and are transparent.

Comments: Large colorless crystals of analcime are a great rarity although small transparent crystals are abundant. Faceted gems are extremely rare and seldom seen even in large collections. The hardness is marginal for wear, but the mineral has no cleavage and should present no difficulties in cutting.

Name: From the Greek *analkis,* meaning *weak,* because of the weak electric charge analcime develops when it is rubbed.

ANATASE   Also called Octahedrite. See: Brookite, Rutile.

Formula: TiO_2.

Crystallography: Tetragonal; crystals pyramidal, striated; also tabular and prismatic.

Colors: Black, red-brown, brown, deep indigo-blue; colorless to grayish, greenish, blue-green, lavender. Banding due to zonal growth often visible.

Luster: Adamantine, sometimes slightly metallic.

Hardness: 5.5-6.

Density: 3.82-3.97.

Cleavage: Perfect 2 directions. Fracture subconchoidal. Brittle.

Birefringence: 0.046-0.067.

Optics: $o = 2.534\text{-}2.564$; $e = 2.488\text{-}2.497$.
Refractive indices are extremely variable, depending on temperature and wavelength.
Anatase is sometimes biaxial with small $2V$ (dark-colored crystals).

Dispersion: 0.213 (o); 0.259 (e).

Pleochroism: Strong in deeply colored crystals: brown/yellow-brown/greenish-blue.

Spectral: Not diagnostic.

Luminescence: None.

Occurrence: Gneisses, schists, and other metamorphic rocks; as detrital grains, as an accessory mineral in granites, and in various other igneous rocks.
California; Gunnison County, Colorado; Arkansas; Massachusetts; Virginia; North Carolina.
Canada; Brazil; Cornwall, England; Wales; Norway; France; Italy; USSR.
Switzerland: gem material from the Alpine regions.
Brazil: found in diamondiferous gravels.

Stone Sizes: Faceted gems are exceedingly rare and always very small (less than 1-2 carats). Usually the material is very dark and unappealing. Cut gems are known as large as ~6 carats.

Comments: Anatase is usually found in very small crystals, seldom transparent, and even then very dark-colored. Gems have been cut as curiosities, but are almost never seen for sale on the market because of scarcity.

Name: Greek *anatasis,* meaning *erection* because the "octahedron" of anatase is really a tetragonal bipyramid and elongated with respect to the octahedron of the isometric system.

ANDALUSITE   Varieties: Chiastolite, Viridine. See: Kyanite, Sillimanite.

Formula: Al_2SiO_5 + Fe.

Crystallography: Orthorhombic. Crystals prismatic, striated, square in cross section. Massive, compact.

Colors: Pinkish, reddish-brown, rose-red, whitish, grayish, yellowish, violet, greenish.
Chiastolite: gray crystals with black, carbonaceous cruciform pattern in interior.

Luster: Vitreous to subvitreous.

Hardness: 6.5-7.5.

Density: 3.13-3.17.

Cleavage: Distinct 1 direction. Fracture even to subconchoidal. Brittle.

Optics: $\alpha = 1.629$-1.640; $\beta = 1.633$-1.644; $\gamma = 1.638$-1.650. Near-colorless andalusite reported at low end of this range; green material at upper end.
Viridine: 1.66-1.69.
Biaxial (−), $2V = 73$-$86°$.

Birefringence: 0.007-0.011. (Viridine: 0.029.)

Dispersion: 0.016.

Pleochroism: Strongly pleochroic; olive green to flesh-red (Brazil).
Usually yellow/green/red.
Blue andalusite from Belgium: blue/colorless/colorless.

Spectral: Deep green varieties from Brazil display Mn spectrum: knife-edge shadow at 5535, fine lines at 5505 and 5475; faint lines at 5180, 4950, and 4550.

Inclusions: Veil inclusions are common. Carbon inclusions in chiastolite. Hematite flakes in Brazilian material.

Luminescence: None in LW. Brown fluorescence in SW (Lancaster, Massachusetts). Dark green or yellow-green fluorescence in SW (brown-green gems from Brazil).

Occurrence: Metamorphic rocks, usually slates and schists as a contact mineral, or developed within mica schist or gneiss. Also as a detrital mineral and very rarely in pegmatites and granites.
California; South Dakota (Black Hills); *Colorado; New Mexico; Pennsylvania; Maine; Massachusetts.*
East Africa; Spain.
Brazil: main gem source today; found as pebbles in stream beds or on hillsides under layers of clay.
Sri Lanka: gem material found as waterworn pebbles, sometimes large size.
Burma: dull green material in gem gravels.
Belgium: blue crystals.

Stone Sizes: Gems from Brazil reach 75-100 carats. Usually gems are 1-5 carats; stones in the 5-10 carat range are available at several times the cost of the smaller ones. Stones over 10 carats are quite rare and extremely rare over 20 carats.
SI: 28.3 (brown, Brazil), 13.5 (green/brown, Brazil).
ROM: 12.44 (Brazil).

Comments: Andalusite is a slightly brittle material and care is required if it is set as a ringstone. The pleochroism of andalusite is distinctive and extremely attractive. Sometimes gems are cut to show the pink and almost colorless shades; others display green in the center with brown tips or various other combinations, depending on how the rough was oriented before cutting. Catseye andalusites can be cut when fibrous inclusions are present but are extremely rare.
    Viridine is a deep green variety containing manganese.
    The blue color in material from Ottré, Western Belgium, has been attributed to an Fe^{+2}-Fe^{+3} charge transfer mechanism.
    Chiastolite is cut more or less as a curiosity, since it is always opaque; cross sections showing a well-formed black cross on a gray background are quite attractive. Chiastolite, because of the impurities it contains, has a lower hardness and density than other varieties of andalusite.

Names: After the first noted locality, Andalusia (Spain). Chiastolite is from the Greek *chiastos, arranged diagonally,* because the pattern of carbon inclusions resembles the Greek letter *Chi,* which is written χ.

ANDESINE   See: Feldspar.

ANDRADITE   See: Garnet.

ANGEL STONE   See: Palygorskite.

ANGLESITE

Formula: $PbSO_4$.

Crystallography: Orthorhombic. Crystals usually tabular, prismatic; granular; massive; stalactitic.

Colors: Colorless, white, yellowish gray, lemon to golden yellow, brownish orange, pale green, and bluish shades.

Luster: Adamantine to vitreous.

Hardness: 2.5-3.

Density: 6.30-6.39; usually 6.38.

Cleavage: Good 1 direction. Fracture conchoidal. Brittle.

Optics: $\alpha = 1.877$; $\beta = 1.883$; $\gamma = 1.894$. Biaxial (+), $2V \sim 75°$.

Birefringence: 0.017.

Dispersion: 0.044.

Pleochroism: None.

Spectral: Not diagnostic.

Luminescence: Weak yellowish fluorescence in SW and LW.

Occurrence: Secondary mineral in lead deposits, formed by oxidation of galena (PbS). There are many localities, and many have the potential of yielding gemmy crystals. *Chester County, Pennsylvania; Tintic, Utah; Arizona; New Mexico; Coeur d'Alene district, Idaho. Chihuahua, Mexico; England; Scotland; Wales; USSR; Germany; Sardinia; Broken Hill, N.S.W., Australia; Dundas, Tasmania. Morocco:* gem crystals from *Touissit,* in immense sizes for the species. *Tsumeb, Namibia:* large transparent yellowish crystals, sometimes colorless, gemmy. *Tunisia:* gemmy crystals.

Stone Sizes: The usual range is 1-6 carats for faceted gems. Anglesites very rarely are large enough to cut bigger stones than this, but some rough has yielded 100+ carat gems, notably the material from Tsumeb (*note:* A 300-carat stone broke during cutting!) and Morocco.
DG: 88.75 (yellow, coffin-shaped triangle, Tsumeb, Namibia).
ROM: 23.62 (colorless, step cut, Tsumeb).
NMC: 25.90 (yellow, scissors-cut, Morocco).
PC: 126 (light golden brown, Morocco).
    73 (yellow-orange, cushion cut, Morocco).
    63 (lemon yellow emerald cut, Morocco).
    171.12 (medium orange, Morocco).
    169 (oval, Morocco).

Comments: Anglesite gems are colorless to pale brown and are available from only a few localities. The dispersion is equal to that of diamond, and properly faceted gems are truly magnificent and bright. Low hardness and cleavage indicate great care is required in cutting, and wear is not recommended. Cut anglesites are true rarities and seldom seen except in very complete collections.

Name: Anglesey, the English locality where first found.

ANHYDRITE

Formula: $CaSO_4$.

Crystallography: Orthorhombic. Crystals equant, thick, tabular or (rarely) prismatic; massive, cleavable.

Colors: Colorless, white-gray, bluish, violet, pinkish, reddish, brownish.

Luster: Greasy; pearly on cleavage; vitreous in massive varieties.

Hardness: 3-3.5.

Density: 2.9-2.98.

Cleavage: Perfect 1 direction, nearly perfect 1 direction.

Optics: $\alpha = 1.570$; $\beta = 1.575$; $\gamma = 1.614$. Biaxial (+), $2V \sim 43°$.

Birefringence: 0.044.

Dispersion: 0.013.

Pleochroism: In violet crystals: colorless-pale yellow/pale violet-rose/violet.

Spectral: Not diagnostic.

Luminescence: Red color in LW (Germany).

Occurrence: A rock-forming mineral, associated with gypsum beds, halite, and limestones. Also occurs in hydrothermal veins, cavities in basalts, and other traprocks. *South Dakota, New Mexico, New Jersey, Texas. Nova Scotia. France, India, Germany, Austria, Poland. Faraday Mine, Bancroft, Ontario, Canada:* large purplish masses, some facetable. *Simplon Tunnel, Switzerland:* pale purple cleavages, facetable. *Mexico:* large blue masses, very lovely color. *Volpino, Italy:* a white-gray, marblelike textured material known as *vulpinite* and locally used as a decorative stone and made into cabochons.

Stone Sizes: Faceted gems are quite unusual, usually small (1-5 carats), but potentially much larger. Gems up to 9 carats have been cut, but cleavage masses could provide larger rough. Faceted gems are usually purplish or pale pink, from the Swiss and Canadian localities.
PC: 2.86 (pink-blue bicolor, Bancroft).

Comments: The blue or violet color disappears on heating and can be restored by gamma ray bombardment.

The natural color may therefore be caused by natural radiation. Gemstones are very fragile due to excellent cleavages and must be cut and handled with great care.

Name: Greek *without water,* in allusion to composition.

ANKERITE   See: Dolomite.

ANORTHITE   See: Feldspar.

ANORTHOCLASE   See: Feldspar.

ANTIGORITE   See: Serpentine.

APACHE TEARS   See: Obsidian.

APATITE   Group name. Also called Asparagus Stone.

Formula: $Ca_5(PO_4)_3(F, OH, Cl)_3$.
Ca often replaced by Sr, Mn.
Also contains: Ce, rare earths, U, Th.
PO_4 replaced by SO_4 + SiO_2.
Carbonate apatites contain CO_2. F is also present in the variety *francolite.*

Crystallography: Hexagonal. Crystals usually prismatic or stubby; massive, granular, compact; oolitic, earthy.

Colors: Colorless, green, white, blue, brown, yellow, purple, violet, gray, pink, and various shades of most of these colors.

Luster: Vitreous in crystals.

Hardness: 5 (some massive varieties 3-4).

Density: 3.10-3.35 (massive varieties 2.5-2.9).

Cleavage: Poor. Fracture conchoidal to uneven. Brittle.

Optics: $e = 1.598-1.666$; $o = 1.603-1.667$. Very variable with composition.
Gem varieties: $o = 1.632-1.649$, $e = 1.628-1.642$.
Uniaxial (−); francolite may be biaxial, $2V = 25-40°$.

Birefringence: 0.001-0.013.
Chlorapatites have the lowest birefringence (~0.001); fluorapatites medium (0.004); hydroxylapatites higher (0.007); carbonate apatites as high as 0.008; and francolite as high as 0.013.

Dispersion: 0.013.

Pleochroism: Distinct in blue-green varieties; otherwise weak. Yellow stones may give yellowish/greenish or brownish/greenish.
Gem blue apatite shows strong dichroism: blue/yellow.

Spectral: Blue and yellow apatites display a rare earth ("didymium," i.e. praseodymium + neodymium) spectrum. Yellow gems have 7-line group at 5800 and 5 lines at 5200. Blue gems give broad bands at 5120, 4910, and 4640.

Luminescence: Yellow gems fluoresce lilac-pink in SW and LW (stronger in LW). Blue apatite fluoresces violet-

Refractive Indices

Type	Locality	Color	o	e	Brirefrin-gence	S.G.
Chlorapatite	Japan	yellow	1.658	1.653	.005	—
Hydroxylapatite	Holly Springs, Georgia	—	1.651	1.644	.007	3.21
Fluorapatite	Finland	blue-green	1.633	1.629	.004	3.2
Hydroxylapatite	Sweden (with Mn)	blue-green	1.646	1.641	.005	3.22
Fluorapatite	Sweden	colorless	1.634	1.631	.003	3.27
Carbonate apatite with fluorine	Devonshire, England (francolite)	—	1.629	1.624	.005	3.14
Hydroxylapatite	Mexico	yellow	1.634	1.630	.004	—
Fluorapatite	Canada	green	1.632	1.629	.003	—
Fluorapatite	Maine	purple	1.633	1.630	.003	—
Carbonate apatite	St. Paul's Rocks, Atlantic Ocean	—	1.603	1.598	.005	—
Cut gemstone	Kenya	dark green	1.641	1.637	.004	—
Cut gemstone	Zimbabwe	yellow-green	1.643	1.638	.005	—
Cut gemstone	Mexico	yellow	1.637	1.633	.004	—
Cut gemstone	Madagascar	dark green	1.637	1.632	.005	—
Cut gemstone	Burma	green	1.636	1.632	.004	—
Cut gemstone	Brazil	deep blue	1.638	1.632	.006	—
Cut gemstone	Canada	green	1.632	1.628	.004	—
Cut gemstone	Sri Lanka (catseye)	brown	1.647-1.649	1.640-1.642	.007	—
Cut gemstone	Tanzania (catseye)	yellow	1.636-1.640	1.632-1.637	0.004	3.22-3.35

blue to sky blue, and violet material fluoresces greenish-yellow (LW) or pale mauve (SW). Green apatite fluoresces a greenish mustard color, LW stronger than SW. Manganapatite fluoresces pink in SW.

Occurrence: Apatite is found in a wide variety of rock types. Igneous rocks are usually characterized by F and OH varieties, some containing Mn. Apatite occurs in pegmatites, hydrothermal veins and cavities, metamorphic rocks, and as detrital grains in sedimentary rocks and phosphate beds.
Blue: *Burma; Sri Lanka; Brazil.*
Blue-green: *Arendal, Norway* (variety called *moroxite*); also: *Gravelotte, East Transvaal, South Africa.*
Violet: *Germany; Maine; California.*
Yellow: *Durango, Mexico; Murcia, Spain; Canada; Brazil.*
Green: *India; Canada* (trade-named *Trilliumite*); *Mozambique; Madagascar; Spain; Burma.*
Brown: *Canada.*
Colorless: *Burma; Italy; Germany.*
Catseye: Blue green and green from *Sri Lanka* and *Burma.* Green catseyes also occur in *Brazil,* and yellow stones in *Sri Lanka* and *Tanzania.*

Stone Sizes: Cut apatites are not common in museum collections. Blue gems (Brazil) are almost always small (1-2 carats). Burma produces 10 carat blue gems, but this color is very scarce in larger sizes. Yellow gems up to 15-20 carats are known from Mexico, but larger ones are quite rare. Violet stones are the rarest and smallest in general, usually under 2 carats. However, the Roebling purple apatite in *SI* is ~100 grams, a superb crystal. Blue-green clean stones are usually less than 5 carats, rare if larger. Green apatite occurs in large crystals; Canadian material has yielded 100 carat flawless stones. The world's largest golden green gem may be a 147 carat stone from Kenya. Yellowish catseyes range up to about 15 carats, and green catseyes a bit larger (20 carats).

Comments: Fluorapatite is the commonest apatite variety. Apatite is abundant throughout the world, and is, in fact, the main constituent of bones and teeth. It is also the most abundant phosphorus-bearing mineral, especially *collophane,* the massive type that makes up large beds in some localities. Apatite is brittle and heat sensitive, and must be cut and worn with care. Properly cut stones are truly magnificent, however, since they are both bright and richly colored. It is possible to assemble suites of as many as 20 gems, all different colors.

Mexican yellow apatite is perhaps the most abundant material available, and thousands of crystals exist that would cut stones up to 5 carats. Larger pieces are rare, however, even from this locality. The Mexican material may be turned colorless by careful heating.

The catseye in Tanzanian stones may be so intense that the material resembles catseye chrysoberyl.

Lazurapatite is a mixture of lapis and apatite that is found in Siberia.

Name: From the Greek, meaning *to deceive* because mineralogists had confused apatite with other species.

APOPHYLLITE

Formula: $KCa_4Si_8O_{20}(F, OH) \cdot 8H_2O$.

Crystallography: Tetragonal. Crystals pseudocubic; tabular, prismatic, sometimes pyramidal.

Colors: Colorless, white, grayish, pale yellow, pale green, dark green, reddish.

Luster: Vitreous, pearly on cleavage.

Hardness: 4.5-5.

Density: 2.3-2.5.

Cleavage: Perfect 1 direction. Fracture uneven. Brittle.

Optics: $o = 1.53\text{-}1.54$; $e = 1.53\text{-}1.54$ (variable). Optically $(+)$ or $(-)$; uniaxial.

Birefringence: 0.001 or less. May appear isotropic.

Pleochroism: None.

Spectral: Not diagnostic.

Luminescence: None.

Occurrence: Secondary mineral in basic igneous rocks, such as basalts and traprocks.
New Jersey; Oregon; Washington; Colorado; Michigan; Virginia; Pennsylvania.
Guanajuato, Mexico; Brazil; Canada; Sweden; Scotland; Germany; Ireland; Faroe Islands, Iceland; Bay of Fundy, Nova Scotia.
Bombay, India: colorless crystals and also intense apple green color, due to Fe (*Poona, India:* $o = 1.530, e = 1.533$, birefringence 0.003, S.G. = 2.37).

Stone Sizes: Apophyllites are seldom faceted, and rough to cut greater than 10 carats is very rare. Stones are usually colorless, though green Indian material is also cut.
SI: 15.4 (colorless, step-cut).
DG: 7.05 (colorless, Poona, India).
PC: 24.92 (free-form, Poona, India).

Comments: Apophyllite is very brittle and fragile, with an extremely perfect and easy cleavage. It is unsuited for jewelry, but colorless apophyllite is perhaps the whitest of all gems. The cut stones are so devoid of any trace of color that they almost appear silvery. The perfect cleavage dictates an orientation with the table of a faceted stone not perpendicular to the long axis of the crystals. The green, iron-rich apophyllite from India occurs in magnificent crystal groups, but facetable material is quite scarce and usually smaller than the colorless variety.

Name: From Greek words describing the tendency of apophyllite to exfoliate when strongly heated.

AQUAMARINE   See: Beryl.

ARAGONITE   See also: Korite.
Dimorphous with Calcite.

Formula: $CaCO_3 + Pb$, Sr, rarely Zn.

Crystallography: Orthorhombic. Pseudohexagonal, crystals often acicular, chisel-shaped, prismatic; also massive, columnar, fibrous, stalactitic, coralloidal. Frequently twinned.

Colors: Colorless, white, yellow, gray, green, blue-green, lavender, reddish, brown.

Luster: Vitreous to resinous.

Hardness: 3.5-4.

Density: 2.947 (pure). Usually 2.93-2.95; up to 3.0 if Pb present.

Cleavage: Distinct 1 direction. Fracture subconchoidal. Brittle.

Optics: $\alpha = 1.530$; $\beta = 1.681$; $\gamma = 1.685$. Biaxial (−), $2V = 18°$. Sector twinning observed.

Birefringence: 0.155.

Pleochroism: None.

Spectral: Not diagnostic.

Inclusion: Usually veil-type inclusions observed.

Luminescence: Pale rose, yellow, tan, green, rarely bluish in LW; may phosphoresce green in LW (Sicily). Yellowish, pinkish-red, tan, white in SW, also pink (Sicily).

Occurrence: Worldwide occurrences, especially in limestone caverns, hot springs, and in the oxidized zone of ore deposits.
Molina de Aragon, Spain: type locality, in stubby twinned crystals.
Bilin, Czechoslovakia.
Austria; England; Peru; Namibia; Germany.
Agrigento, Sicily: with sulfur crystals.
Chile: blue material.
Guanajuato, Mexico; Laurium, Greece: blue aragonite.
Many localities in the United States, including *New Mexico, South Dakota, Virginia, Colorado.*
Fibrous aragonite from *Wyoming, California, Iowa.*

Stone Sizes: Faceted gems are usually only a few carats. Potential exists for much larger stones. Most faceted gems are colorless, since colored material is usually massive. Straw yellow crystals from Horschenz, Germany, have yielded stones to 10 carats. The largest known cut specimen is from Bilin and weighs 110 carats.
DG: 7.85 (Germany).
PC: 110 (emerald cut, straw yellow, Bilin, Czechoslovakia).

Comments: The hardness of aragonite is too low to allow for safe wear. Aragonite is not as abundant or widespread as calcite, except (in gem use) insofar as it is the major constituent of pearls. Faceted gems are almost always very small as opposed to calcite, which occurs in huge transparent masses or crystals. Faceted aragonite gems are thus truly rare collector items.

Name: Locality, Molina de Aragon, Spain.

AUGELITE

Formula: $Al_2PO_4(OH)_3$.

Crystallography: Monoclinic. Crystals tabular and thick; prismatic; acicular. Also massive.

Colors: White, yellowish, pale blue, pale rose.

Luster: Vitreous. Pearly on cleavage surfaces.

Hardness: 4.5-5.

Density: 2.696-2.75.

Cleavage: Perfect 1 direction, good 1 direction.

Optics: $\alpha = 1.574$; $\beta = 1.576$; $\gamma = 1.588$.
White Mountain, California, material: $\alpha = 1.570$; $\beta = 1.574$; $\gamma = 1.590$.
Biaxial (+), $2V \sim 50°$.

Birefringence: 0.014-0.020.

Pleochroism: None.

Spectral: Not diagnostic.

Luminescence: None.

Occurrence: Crystals from the *Champion Mine, Mono County, California,* reach a size of about one inch; this locality is now depleted. It furnished cuttable gem material.
Masses occur at *Keystone, South Dakota* (nongem).
Palermo Mine, New Hampshire.
Potosi, Bolivia: in crystals.
Sweden: massive.
Uganda.

Stone Sizes: Most gems in existence, from the California material, are less than 1 carat up to about 3 carats. Larger stones are exceedingly rare in the case of what is already a rare mineral.

Comments: Augelite is soft and brittle, unsuited for wear. However, the gems cut from rare transparent crystals are true collector items and are seen only in very complete collections.

Name: From a Greek word meaning *luster,* because of the glassy appearance of the mineral.

AVENTURINE See: Quartz.

AXINITE Group name.

Formula: $(Ca, Mn, Fe, Mg)_3Al_2BSi_4O_{15}(OH)$.
$$+Mg = magnesioaxinite.$$
$$If\ Fe > Mn = ferroaxinite.$$
$$If\ Mn > Fe = manganaxinite.$$
$$If\ Mn > Fe\ and\ Ca < 1.5 = tinzenite.$$

Crystallography: Triclinic. Distinctive wedge-shaped crystals; also tabular.

Colors: Violet-brown, colorless, yellowish (Mn), pale violet to reddish (Mn), blue (Mg).

Luster: Vitreous.

Hardness: 6.5-7; variable with direction.

Density: 3.26-3.36; magnesioaxinite = 3.18.

Cleavage: Good 1 direction. Fracture uneven to conchoidal. Brittle.

Optics: $\alpha = 1.674\text{-}1.693; \beta = 1.681\text{-}1.701; \gamma = 1.684\text{-}1.704$.
Magnesioaxinite: $\alpha = 1.656; \beta = 1.660; \gamma = 1.668$.
Biaxial (−), $2V = 63\text{-}80°$ or more.
May turn (+) if high in Mg.

Birefringence: 0.010-0.012.

Dispersion: Large.

Pleochroism: Intense in all colored varieties: cinnamon brown/violet-blue/olive green, yellow, or colorless. Luning, Nevada: pale brown to colorless/deep brown/brownish red.
Pale blue/pale violet/pale gray (magnesioaxinite).
Sri Lanka: reddish-brown/dark violet/colorless-yellowish.

Spectral: Narrow line at 5120, broad lines at 4920 and 4660, also at 4150. Sometimes lines visible at 5320, 4440, and 4150 (latter may be strong).

Luminescence: Red in SW (Franklin, New Jersey). Dull red in SW, orange-red in LW (Tanzania: magnesioaxinite).

Occurrence: Axinite is found in areas of contact metamorphism and metasomatism.
Yuba County, California: gemmy crystals. Also gem material from *Coarse Gold, Madera County, California; New Melones, Calaveras County, California; Sri Lanka:* ferroaxinite, cinnamon-brown (indices = 1.675/1.681/1.685, birefringence = 0.010, S.G. = 3.31).
Luning, Nevada: masses.
Pennsylvania; New Jersey.
Cornwall, England; Germany; Norway; Finland; USSR; Japan; Baja California, Mexico, Tasmania.

Bourg d'Oisans, France: S.G. 3.28, R.I. = 1.68-1.69, in pockets in schist.
Switzerland: tinzenite.
Tanzania: magnesioaxinite.

Stone Sizes: Axinite is rare in faceted gems over 10 carats. Material from Baja California will yield gems to about 25 carats, but most stones, if clean, are less than 5 carats.
SI: 23.6 (brown, Mexico).
PC: 16.5 (Baja California).
Geol. Mus., London: 0.78 (magnesioaxinite, Tanzania).

Comments: Cut axinites are usually intensely trichroic, with the brown and purple colors dominating. The material is exquisite but is almost never completely free of flaws and feathers. Axinite is actually an extremely rare cut gem and could be one of the most magnificent because of its rich colors and brilliance. Clean stones over 5 carats are difficult to find and worthy of museum display. Axinite is hard enough to be worn in jewelry, though it is a bit brittle.

Name: From a Greek word meaning *axe,* in allusion to characteristic crystal shape.

AZURITE

Formula: $Cu_3(CO_3)_2(OH)_2$.

Crystallography: Monoclinic. Crystals may be large and perfect, tabular, prismatic; also massive, earthy, banded, stalactitic.

Colors: Light and dark azure blue.

Luster: Vitreous (crystals) to earthy or dull.

Hardness: 3.5-4.

Density: 3.77.

Cleavage: Perfect 1 direction. Fracture conchoidal. Brittle.

Optics: $\alpha = 1.730; \beta = 1.758; \gamma = 1.836$.
Biaxial (+), $2V \sim 67°$.

Birefringence: 0.110.

Pleochroism: Strong, in shades of blue.

Spectral: Not diagnostic.

Luminescence: None.

Occurrence: Secondary mineral in copper deposits.
Chessy, France: chessylite, fine crystals in large groups.
Morenci and *Bisbee, Arizona:* banded and massive material, also crystals.
Eclipse Mine, Muldiva-Chillagoe area, Queensland, Australia: gemmy crystals up to about 9 grams.
Kelly, New Mexico and other localities in that state.

Italy; Greece; USSR.
Tsumeb, Namibia: fine, tabular crystals, some facetable in small bits.
Zacatecas, Mexico: fine crystals (small).

Stone Sizes: Facetable crystals are always tiny, and cut gems are all less than 1 carat. It is pointless to cut larger stones, as they would be so dark as to be opaque. Dark blue crystalline material is sometimes cabbed, and cabochons may be several inches across.

Comments: Faceted azurite is a great rarity, but even small stones are extremely dark, virtually black. *Azurmalachite* is a mixture of azurite and another copper carbonate, malachite. *Burnite* is a mixture of azurite and cuprite (copper oxide). Azurite occurs in fine crystals in many localities, but in massive form is almost always mixed with malachite. In this form it is cut as very attractive cabochons and large decorative items, such as boxes. The intense blue color is distinctive and makes azurite very desirable among mineral collectors and gem hobbyists.

Name: In allusion to the color, derived from the Persian word *lazhward,* meaning *blue.*

AZURMALACHITE See: Azurite.

B

BALAS RUBY   See: Spinel.

BARBERTONITE   See: Stichtite.

BARITE

Formula: $BaSO_4$ + Ca, Sr.

Crystallography: Orthorhombic. Tabular crystals, aggregates and rosettes; massive, granular, fibrous, earthy, stalactitic.

Colors: White, grayish, yellowish to brown, blue, green, reddish. May be color zoned.

Luster: Vitreous to resinous; pearly on cleavage.

Hardness: 3-3.5.

Density: 4.50 (pure); usually 4.3-4.6.

Cleavage: Perfect 1 direction. Fracture even. Brittle.

Optics: $\alpha = 1.636$; $\beta = 1.637$; $\gamma = 1.648$.
Biaxial (+), $2V = 37°$.

Birefringence: 0.012.

Dispersion: 0.016.

Pleochroism: Weak if crystal is colored.
Brown crystal: straw yellow/wine yellow/violet.
Yellow crystal: pale yellow/yellow-brown/brown.
Green crystal: colorless/pale green/violet.

Luminescence: In SW: white (Germany, Ohio), blue-green (Germany, England), gray (Germany). In LW: greenish white, yellow-green (Germany), pinkish white (Ohio), cream-white (South Dakota).

Occurrence: Barite is common in low temperature hydrothermal vein deposits; also as a component of sedimentary rocks, sometimes in large beds; as concretions, in clay deposits, and rarely in cavities in igneous rocks. Good crystals abundant worldwide.
Meade County, South Dakota: fine brown crystals, facetable.
Colorado: exquisite blue crystals, some facetable (Sterling area).
Illinois.
Thunder Bay District, Ontario, Canada: colorless crystals suitable for cutting.
Rock Candy Mine, British Columbia, Canada: facetable yellow crystals, up to 4 inches long.
Cumberland, England: fine crystals, sometimes very large, facetable areas.
Many other localities worldwide, many with potential for clean material.

Stone Sizes: Large crystals are known, usually flawed, but many have facetable areas. English material will yield stones up to about 50 carats; one is known over 300 carats. Yellow-brown crystals from France have been cut into gems as large as 65 carats. Colorado gems are usually 1-5 carats.
PC: 42 (golden-orange, cushion cut, British Columbia).
     108 (dark brown oval, South Dakota).

Comments: Massive white barite looks like marble and could be used for decorative purposes. Faceted gems are hard to cut, and facet junctions tend to be rounded. The perfect cleavage makes wear very risky, and the low hardness would also prevent use in jewelry. In spite of the abundance of good crystals, cut barites are not commonly seen, especially in rich colors. With very few exceptions, large stones could be obtained in almost any desired color.

Name: Greek *baros,* heavy, because of the high specific gravity.

BASTITE   See: Enstatite.

BAYLDONITE

Formula: $(Pb, Cu)_3(AsO_4)_2(OH)_2$.

Crystallography: Monoclinic. Fibrous concretions; massive, granular.

Colors: Various shades of yellowish green.

Luster: Resinous.

Hardness: 4.5.

Density: 5.5.

Cleavage: Not observed.

Optics: $\alpha = 1.95$; $\beta = 1.97$; $\gamma = 1.99$.
Biaxial $(+)$, $2V$ large.

Birefringence: 0.04.

Dispersion: No data.

Pleochroism: No data.

Spectral: Not diagnostic.

Luminescence: None.

Occurrence: Secondary mineral in Pb-Cu deposits.
England; France.
Tsumeb, Namibia: only major occurrence.

Stone Sizes: Cabochons only from massive, fibrous material from Tsumeb.

Comments: Bayldonite is a nondescript greenish material that has been cut into cabochons by enterprising collectors of the unusual. Cut bayldonites are a rarity, nonetheless, and are seldom seen in collections. The luster of cabochons is sometimes almost metallic and provides a curious appearance to the cut stones. Bayldonite is compact but too soft for rings; it could be worn in bola ties and pendants.

Name: After Mr. John Bayldon.

BENITOITE

Formula: $BaTiSi_3O_9$.

Crystallography: Hexagonal. Crystals triangular in shape, flattened, very distinctive.

Colors: Blue (various shades), purple, pink, white, colorless. Sometimes zoned.

Luster: Vitreous.

Hardness: 6-6.5.

Density: 3.64-3.68.

Cleavage: Indistinct. Fracture conchoidal to uneven. Brittle.

Optics: $o = 1.757$; $e = 1.804$.
Uniaxial $(+)$.

Birefringence: 0.047.

Dispersion: 0.046.

Pleochroism: Strong: o = colorless, e = blue.

Luminescence: Intense blue in SW only, no reaction to LW.

Occurrence: *Rush Creek, Fresno County, California; Texas.*
Belgium.
Only gem locality is in *San Benito County, California,* as superb crystals in a massive, fine-grained, white natrolite. The crystals reach a size of ~2 inches across, colored white and various shades of blue, rarely pinkish or colorless, zoned. Though crystals are large, facetable areas are always very small.

Stone Sizes: Always small because crystals are badly flawed. Also, best color (along e) is seen in an unadvantageous direction in terms of the flattening of the crystals, giving smaller gems with good color. The largest stone on record is in *SI,* 7.8 carats. A large gem of 6.52 carats was cut for a private collector but stolen in transit. Most gems are under 1 carat, up to about 2-3 carats. Larger stones are exceedingly rare. The deposit has been largely worked out and available gems sold, so benitoite is becoming very difficult to obtain in cut form. However, some new material is mined and marketed every year.
AMNH: 3.57.

Comments: Benitoite is one of the most beautiful of all the rare gems, with the color of fine sapphire and the dispersion of diamond! It was discovered in 1906 and first thought to be sapphire. The dispersion is usually masked by the intense blue color. Benitoite is one of the most desirable, attractive, and scarce of all gemstones.

Name: After the occurrence in San Benito County, California.

BERYL

Formula: $Be_3Al_2Si_6O_{18}$ + Fe, Mn, Cr, V, Cs.

Crystallography: Hexagonal. Crystals prismatic, elongated or flattened, equant; often striated or etched; rolled pebbles; massive.

Colors: Colorless, white, light green, olive green, blue-green to blue (aquamarine), deep green (emerald), pink or peachy pink (morganite), greenish yellow, yellow (heliodor), pinkish orange, red (bixbite).
Beryl is one of the most familiar minerals because of the many famous gem varieties it offers. These specific gem types are named according to color and chemistry. The colorless variety, pure beryl, is termed *goshenite*. A trace of manganese adds a pink or salmon-peachy-pink

color, and we have the variety known as *morganite*. *Heliodor* or *golden beryl* derives its color from ferric iron, and the color ranges from pale yellow to deep yellowish-orange. *Aquamarine* also gets its color from iron, but in the ferrous (reduced) state, and the range is from blue-green to deep blue. *Emerald* is the best known

color variety, the color of which, a fine, intense green, is due to a trace of chromium replacing aluminum in the beryl structure. Emerald is, by definition, the green beryl colored by chromium. Other green beryls of various shades exist, which are simply termed *green beryl*, where Cr is not present and does not reveal a chromium spec-

Emerald Locality	Occurrence	o	e	Birefringence	S.G.	Comments
Austria (Habachthal)	biotite schist	1.591	1.584	0.007	2.74	
		1.582	1.576	0.006	2.73	
Australia (Poona)	schists	1.578–1.579	1.572	0.005–0.007	2.69–2.70	
(Emmaville)	pegmatite	1.575	1.570	0.005	2.68	
Brazil						
Bahia: Anagé		1.584	1.576	0.008	2.80	
Brumado		1.579	1.573	0.005–0.006	2.68	
Carnaiba	mica schist	1.588	1.583	0.006–0.007	2.72	
Salininha		1.589	1.583	0.006	2.71	
Minas Gerais (var.)		1.578–1.581	1.572–1.576	0.006–0.009	2.71–2.73	
Goias (Sta. Terezinha)	in talc and biotite schist	1.588–1.593	1.580–1.586	0.007–0.008	2.70–2.76	bluish-green
Colombia						
Chivor Mine,	cracks in dark schist	1.577–1.579	1.570–1.571	0.005–0.006	2.69	blue-green
Muzo Mine	calcite veins in dark shale	1.580–1.584	1.570–1.578	0.005–0.006	2.70–2.71	yellow-green
Gachala Mine		1.576	1.570	0.006	2.70	
Burbar Mine		1.576	1.569	0.007	2.70	
trapiche emerald	in biotite	1.583	1.577	0.006	2.70	
Ghana	poor quality	1.589	1.582	0.007	2.70	
India						
Ajmer		1.595	1.585	0.007–0.010	2.74	
(unspecified)	in biotite schist	1.593	1.585	0.007	2.73	
Mozambique (Morrua)		1.593	1.585	0.008	2.73	
Madagascar						
Ankadilalana Mine	mica schist	1.589–1.591	1.581–1.585	0.007	2.73	
North Carolina	in albite matrix	1.588	1.581	0.007	2.73	fluoresces in LW–UV
Norway (Eidsvoll)	in granite	1.590–1.591	1.583–1.584	0.007	2.68–2.76	
Pakistan						
Mingora		1.596	1.588	0.007	2.78	
Bucha	talc-quartz-carbonate enclosed in ultramafics	1.600	1.590	0.010		
Swat (general)	in metamorphics	1.595–1.600	1.588–1.593	0.007	2.75–2.78	
Zimbabwe	granite pegmatites					
Victoria Province	cutting schists, also	1.576–1.591	1.572–1.585	0.004–0.007	2.67–2.74	with alexandrite also
Bubera Province	serpentines and	1.585	1.580	0.005	–	not gemmy
Shamva Province	fine mica	1.591	1.584	0.007	–	not gemmy
Filabusi Province	aggregates	1.587–1.594	1.583–1.588	0.004	–	
Belingwe Province		1.593–1.594	1.586–1.588	0.005–0.007	–	
Sandawana		1.590–1.596	1.583–1.588	0.004–0.006	2.74–2.75	
South Africa						
Transvaal, Gravelotte (Cobra Mine, etc.)	acid pegmatites and contacting schists	1.593–1.594	1.583–1.586	0.006–0.007	2.75–2.76	
Tanzania (Lake Manyara)	in pegmatites and mica schists	1.585	1.578–1.580	0.005–0.006	2.72–2.73	with alexandrite
USSR (Urals)	biotite–chlorite schists	1.588	1.581	0.006–0.007	2.74	
Zambia						
Miku	in schists	1.589–1.590	1.581–1.582	0.007–0.009	2.74	
Mufulira		1.588	1.581	0.007	2.68	
Kitwe	in schists	1.586	1.580	0.006	2.79	
Kafubu		1.602	1.592	0.010	2.77	

trum; this also includes a deep green beryl colored by vanadium, which is technically speaking *not* emerald. A deep rose-red colored beryl, in small crystals from the Wah Wah Mountains of Utah, has been named *bixbite;* this color is also due to manganese; the material also contains Ti, Zn, Sn, Cs, Li, Rb, B, Zr, Nb, Pb, and traces of other elements.

Luster: Vitreous.

Hardness: 7.5–8.

Cleavage: Indistinct. Fracture conchoidal to uneven. Brittle.

Density:
goshenite: 2.6–2.9;
morganite: 2.71–2.90;
aquamarine: 2.66–2.80;
emerald: 2.68–2.78;
red beryl: 2.66–2.70.

Inclusions: Beryl inclusions typically are long, hollow tubes, sometimes filled with liquid; the tubes are parallel and run the length of prismatic crystals, sometimes have a brownish color and may contain gas bubbles. *Negative crystals* are also seen, as well as flat inclusions that resemble snowflakes and have a metallic look, known as *chrysanthemum* inclusions. Aquamarines contain, in addition to the above, crystals of biotite, phlogopite, rutile, pyrite, hematite, and ilmenite in skeletal crystals that sometimes allow the cutting of *star beryls.* Some aquamarines contain *snow-stars:* irregular liquid droplets in starlike patterns. These were especially noted in the Martha Rocha, a famous and large aquamarine. Red beryls from Utah display healed and unhealed fractures, growth banding, two-phase inclusions, quartz, and bixbyite.

Inclusions in Emeralds
Habachthal, Austria: Straight, broad-stemmed tremolite rods; biotite, rounded mica plates; tourmaline; epidote; sphene; apatite; rutile.
Colombia:
    Chivor Mine, 3-phase inclusions; pyrite; albite.
    Muzo Mine, 3-phase inclusions; parisite crystals (*only* known from Muzo mine), in yellow-brown prisms; calcite rhombs.
    Borur Mine, 3-phase inclusions.
    Gachala Mine, parallel growth bands, needlelike growth tubes; 3-phase inclusions: albite, pyrite; 6-sided cleavage cracks.
    Coscuez Mine, 2- and 3-phase inclusions, pyrite, albite, quartz, partially-healed fractures.
Bahia, Brazil: 2-phase inclusions; biotite; talc; dolomite crystals; liquid films.
Goiás, Brazil: Pyrite, chromite, talc, calcite, hematite; notable also = dolomite.
USSR: Actinolite crystals, singly or in groups, resembling bamboo-cane; mica plates.

Australia: Biotite (abundantly); actinolite; calcite; some 3-phase inclusions seen, tubes, "daggers," fluorite.
Transvaal, Namibia: Brown mica (makes gems dark in color); curved molybdenite crystals.
Zimbabwe: Fine long-curving tremolite needles; also 2-3 phase inclusions, short rods or fine curved fibers; color zoning; garnets; hematite; feldspar; brown mica; negative crystals.
India: Oblong cavities parallel to long crystal axis, with gas bubbles; biotite crystals parallel to basal plane; fuchsite, 2-phase inclusions; apatite crystals; groups of negative twin crystals with comma shape.
South Africa (Cobra Mine): Mica plates and 3-phase inclusions.
West Pakistan: 2-phase inclusions; thin films; some liquid inclusions, few mineral crystals.
Tanzania: 2-phase and 3-phase inclusions; square-shaped cavities and tubes; actinolite, mica.
Zambia: Biotite (black crystals) as small specks or dots; pinpoints, breadcrumb inclusions; also tourmaline (dravite) and magnetite. Material from *Kitwe* contains: rutile, chrysoberyl, muscovite, apatite, quartz; paragenesis indicates metamorphic origin.
Madagascar: brown biotite, muscovite, apatite, hematite, goethite, quartz, ilmenite, tourmaline, color zoning, 2-phase inclusions.
Norway: Mossy inclusions; also interconnected tubes (make crystals turbid).
North Carolina: Quartz crystals sometimes seen.

Optics: Beryl is uniaxial ($-$), and refractive indices vary with composition.
Goshenite: o = 1.566–1.602; e = 1.562–1.594; Birefringence = 0.004–0.008.
Morganite: o = 1.572–1.592; e = 1.578–1.600; Birefringence = 0.008–0.009.
Aquamarine: o = 1.567–1.583; e = 1.572–1.590; Birefringence = 0.005–0.007.
Maxixe beryl, rich in cesium: o = 1.584, e = 1.592, Birefringence 0.008.
Emerald: see table.
Red beryl: o = 1.568–1.572; e = 1.567–1.568; Birefringence = 0.004–0.008.

Dispersion: 0.014 (low).

Pleochroism: Distinct in strongly colored varieties:
Aquamarine: blue/colorless (sometimes greenish).
Maxixe-type aquamarine = blue/blue.
Morganite: deep bluish-pink/pale pink.
Heliodor: brownish-yellow/lemon yellow.
Emerald: blue-green/yellowish-green; rarely blue/yellowish green.
Red beryl: purplish-red/orange-red.

Spectral: Aquamarine spectrum due to ferrous iron; broad band at 4270, weak and diffuse band at 4560. Also weak line may be seen at 5370 (absent if stone has been heated).

Maxixe beryl has narrow line at 6950, strong line at 6540, and weak lines at 6280, 6150, 5500, and 5810.

Emerald spectrum very diagnostic: there are fine lines in the red, weak ones in the blue and broad absorption in the violet; *e* and *o* have different characteristics:

o: 6830/6800 doublet plus 6370 line; broad band 6250–5800; narrow lines 4775 and 4725.

e: 6830/6800 doublet, very strong; no 6370 line, but see diffuse 6620 and 6460 lines; broad absorption band is weaker, no lines visible in the blue at all.

Some Zambian emeralds contain Fe and display the spectral lines of aquamarine as well as emerald. Pleochroism in these gems is also distinctive: blue/yellowish-green.

Red beryl: Bands at 4250, 4800, 5300, and 5600–5800.

Luminescence: Emerald sometimes green in SW; very seldom weak red, orange in LW. If red fluorescence is seen, the color is visible in the Chelsea filter. Fluorescence is quenched by Fe, as in the South African and Indian emeralds. Morganite may fluoresce weak lilac.

Occurrence: Beryl occurs in granitic rocks, especially granite pegmatites; also in schists (emerald), metamorphic limestones (emerald) and hydrothermal veins. The occurrence of red beryl in rhyolitic volcanic rocks in the mountains of Utah is unique. The chemistry and mineralogy of this material is also singular. Beryl occurrences are worldwide.

Goshenite:

California; Maine; South Dakota; Utah; Colorado; North Carolina; Connecticut; Idaho; New Hampshire. Canada; Mexico; Brazil; USSR.

Morganite:

California: San Diego County, in several localities—fine crystals and gem material.

Thomas Range, Utah: deep rose-red bixbite variety.

Madagascar: in pegmatites and as alluvial material.

Minas Gerais, Brazil: fine crystals and gem material.

Heliodor:

Madagascar: gemmy crystals.

Brazil: greenish yellow to fine deep orange colored material, much of it gemmy.

Namibia: in pegmatites.

Connecticut: small but fine colored crystals, some gemmy.

Aquamarine:

Maine; North Carolina; Mt. Antero, Colorado.

Connecticut: some gem.

San Diego County, California: not much gem material.

Zimbabwe.

Minas Gerais, Brazil, also *Rio Grande do Norte, Ceara,* other localities; Brazil is the world's major source of fine aquamarine gems.

Mursinsk, USSR: also other localities.

Madagascar: fine blue gem material, more than 50 specific localities.

Jos, Nigeria: abundant material, some fine color.

Australia: Mt. Surprise, North Queensland (small).

Burma and Sri Lanka: aquamarine has been found, not common there.

Rossing, Namibia: in pegmatites.

India: at *Madras* and *Kashmir,* medium blue color.

Emerald:

Hiddenite, North Carolina.

Habachthal, Austria; Brazil; USSR; Sandawana, Zimbabwe; Poona, Australia; Cobra Mine, Transvaal, South Africa; Arusha, Tanzania; Lake Manyara, Tanzania; Ghana; Madagascar.

Colombia: at Chivor, Muzo, Gachala, Coscuez, and Borur Mines.

Swat area, *West Pakistan.*

Zambia: at Miku and Mifulira, also other locations.

Eidsvoll, Norway: in granite.

Red beryl:

Utah, especially *Wah Wah Mountains.*

Stone Sizes: Beryl crystals weighing many tons have been found in pegmatites, but these are never of gem quality. Aquamarines and green beryls, however, may be completely transparent and still be very large. A crystal weighing 243 pounds was found in Brazil in 1910 that was completely transparent; another in 1956 weighed about 135 pounds. Some very large gems have been cut from this type of material. Morganites are usually smaller, up to about 6 inches in diameter, and the largest emeralds known are less than 10 pounds. Bixbite occurs in crystals up to about 2 inches in length, and these are seldom transparent, even in small areas. The very few stones known are less than 3 carats.

Goshenite:

SI: 61.9 (colorless, Brazil).

Morganite:

SI: 287 (pink, Brazil) and 235 (pink, Brazil); 178 (pink, California); 113 (peach, California); 56 (pale pink, Madagascar); 330 (dark orange, Brazil).

Leningrad Museum: 598.7 (Rose-pink, step cut, Madagascar).

Natural Hist. Museum, Paris: 250 (pink, Madagascar).

ROM: 118.6 (pink, catseye).

BM: rose-red crystal from California weighing 9 pounds.

AMNH: 58.8 (heart-shape, Madagascar).

PC: three very large cut gems with carved tables, total weight ~1500 carats, tables carved in religious motifs.

Heliodor:

BM: 82.25 (yellow).

ROM: 78.8 (yellow, step cut, Brazil).

SI: 133.5 (yellow, Madagascar); 43.5 (golden catseye, Madagascar); 17.5 (yellow, USSR).

Aquamarine:

A crystal was found in Marambaia, Teofilo Otoni,

Brazil, blue-green, an irregular prism 19 inches long and 16 inches across and weighing 110.2 kg. It was transparent end to end. The famous Martha Rocha aquamarine, found in Brazil, weighed 134 pounds and yielded more than 300,000 carats of superb blue gems. An even larger crystal found in 1910 weighed 229 pounds but yielded only 200,000 carats of cut gems.

BM: 67.35 (blue) and 60.90 (greenish); 879 (sea-green, oval).

AMNH: 272, 215, and 160; also 355 (Sri Lanka), 144.5 (Brazil).

Hyde Park Museum, New York: 1847 carats.

SI: 1000 (blue-green, fine color, Brazil); 911 (blue, Brazil); 263.5 (blue, USSR); 71.2 (pale blue, Sri Lanka); 66.3 (pale blue-green, Maine); 20.7 (pale blue, Madagascar); 15.3 (blue-green, Idaho); 14.3 (blue, Connecticut).

Other Colors:

SI: 2054 (green-gold, Brazil); 1363, 578, and 914 (green, Brazil); 133.5 (golden yellow, Madagascar); 98.4 (pale green, Brazil); 40.4 (pale green, Connecticut); 23 (green, Maine); 19.8 (brown, star, Brazil).

Emerald:

The largest emerald crystal extant weighs 16,020 carats and is from the Muzo Mine in Colombia. Many museums around the world display fine and large emeralds, both crystals and faceted gems, as well as some carvings and tumble-polished stones.

SI: 117 (green, Colombia); 10.6 (North Carolina); 4.6 (green catseye, Colombia); 858 carat crystal—"the Gachala."

Moscow: 136 (nearly flawless, deep blue-green, step cut) (in the Diamond Fund).

Kunsthistorisches Museum, Vienna: 2681 carat vase, carved.

Topkapi Museum, Istanbul: 6-cm hexagonal crystal; fine 8-cm crystal; 3 other large crystals.

Banque Markazi, Teheran: Many cabochons between 100 and 300 carats; one is 175 carats, another 225. There are also faceted gems of 100 and 110 carats; unmounted cabochons of 320, 303, 144.4, and two others over 250 carats.

BM: "Devonshire emerald," a crystal 51 mm. long, weighs 1384 carats, fine color.

AMNH: Crystal 1200 carats, fine color, the *Patricia emerald;* 630 carat crystal—"the St. Patrick Emerald."

Banco de la República, Bogota, Colombia: collection of superb crystals from 220 to 1796 carats.

PC: Atahuallpa emerald, 45 carats, set in *Crown of the Andes,* a magnificent gold headpiece with 453 emeralds totaling 1521 carats. *Emilia crystal* from Las Cruces Mine (near Gachala) weighs 7025 carats.

Comments: The beryls are among the most popular, and also the most expensive, of all gems. A wide range of color is represented, from colorless to black. Beryls can be large and flawless, but these are best displayed in museums rather than worn. Emerald is acknowledged as one of the most desirable gemstones, and aquamarine has recently sustained an unprecedented rise in price. Morganite has similarly risen in both demand and value. Goshenite has never achieved great popularity and colorless beryls are easy to obtain at modest cost. The same general comment applies to yellow beryls, although darker-colored gems over 10-15 carats are in greater demand. Green beryls and olive-colored stones are not well known to the gem-buying public and therefore are in slight demand. Aquamarine of large size (15-25 carats and very deep blue color has become extremely scarce and very expensive. Large gems continue to be available but at ever higher prices. A major problem in aquamarine is the so-called Maxixe-type beryl, which can be irradiated to improve the color. The deeper blue is not stable, however, and such gems may rapidly fade in sunlight. The dichroscope reveals the Maxixe beryl, both windows remaining blue whereas in normal aquamarine one window would be colorless or pale yellowish.

Some controversy exists as to the definition of emerald. The type of definition involving a shade of green or depth of color is totally inadequate because it is completely subjective. A rigorous, adequate, and objective definition involves simply the presence or absence of chromium and the corresponding presence of the chromium absorption spectrum, plus (usually) a red color in the Chelsea filter. The deep green beryls colored by vanadium are therefore not emeralds, despite potentially high prices.

Emeralds from Zambia may display an unusual blue tone, with pleochroism blue-green/yellow green. Studies showed that this is due to a high content of iron (0.73%), also revealed as iron bands in the absorption spectrum. Zambian crystals may be intensely color zoned, with near colorless cores and dark green rims, almost like watermelon tourmaline. Recently discovered emeralds from Itabira, Minas Gerais, Brazil, rival the best Colombian stones in quality. They are typically light bluish-green down the *c*-axis.

Bixbite is a very rare, raspberry-red beryl from Utah, seldom seen as a cut gem and then only in very small size (1-2 carats).

Catseye and star beryls are strange curiosities. Catseye aquamarine and emerald are known, sometimes rather large. Oriented ilmenite inclusions in pale green aquamarine from Gouvernador Valadares, Brazil, create a brown body color and cause a sheen or Schiller effect that, when included in a cabochon, creates a star. Black star beryls have no fluorescence or distinctive absorption spectrum and are also known from Alta Ligonha, Mozambique. They strongly resemble black star sapphire and are often confused with the latter.

Most aquamarine is heated at 400-450°C to reduce any ferric iron present and eliminate the accompanying yellowish color. This has the effect of making blue-green material pure blue, which is considered a more desirable color in the marketplace. This heating is done just after cutting and does not affect the value of the cut stone, since virtually all aquamarine is heated in this manner.

Emeralds from Muzo and Chivor can be distinguished in a general way, because Muzo material is yellowish green, whereas that from Chivor is blue-green. It sometimes takes a trained eye to see the distinction in color, however. The inclusions in emerald may weaken the material, and hence cut gems are fragile and brittle and may be easily chipped. Care should always be taken in wearing an emerald, especially a ringstone.

Names: *Beryl* is of Greek origin but uncertain derivation. *Aquamarine* comes from Latin for *sea water,* in allusion to the color. *Morganite* is named after J. P. Morgan, the investment banker and financier. *Goshenite* is named after Goshen Massachusetts. *Heliodor* is from the Greek *helios (sun),* in allusion to the yellow color. *Emerald* is from the Greek *smaragdos (green),* through the Latin *"smaragdus"* to Middle English *esmeralde. Bixbite* is named after Maynard Bixby of Utah.

BERYLLONITE

Formula: $NaBePO_4$.

Crystallography: Monoclinic. Crystals tabular or prismatic, usually etched. Twinning common. May be pseudo-orthorhombic.

Colors: Colorless, white, pale yellow.

Luster: Vitreous; pearly on cleavage.

Hardness: 5.5-6.

Density: 2.84 (pure); usually 2.80-2.85.

Cleavage: Perfect 1 direction, good 1 direction. Fracture conchoidal. Brittle.

Optics: $\alpha = 1.552$; $\beta = 1.558$; $\gamma = 1.561$. Biaxial (−), $2V = 68°$.

Birefringence: 0.009.

Dispersion: 0.010.

Pleochroism: None.

Spectral: Not diagnostic.

Luminescence: None.

Inclusions: Hollow canals and fluid cavities arranged parallel to crystal axis. Material from Stoneham, Maine, has tubes, gas bubbles, and acicular crystals.

Occurrence: Granite pegmatites.
Newry, Maine: opaque white crystals, not really possible to cut.

Stoneham, Maine: only cuttable crystals ever found; also crystalline masses up to 1-2 inches, but only small clean areas within such masses could be cut.

Stone Sizes: All gems less than 5 carats. The mineral itself is very rare, and gems are only known from Maine localities. Stones up to 10 carats have been cut, but they are not clean.
SI: 2.5, 3.3, 3.9, 5.10 (all Maine).
DG: 5.70 (colorless, Maine).
PC: 7.82, 8.77, 4.32 (colorless, Maine).
HU: 6.22 (colorless, Maine).

Comments: Beryllonite is really not suited for wear, and since it is available only as small colorless stones, there is not much incentive to make jewelry out of it. However, beryllonite is one of the truly rare collector gems and should be greatly prized as a cut stone. The cleavage makes gems hard to cut.

Name: In allusion to the composition.

BISMUTOTANTALITE See also: Tantalite, Stibiotantalite.

Formula: $(Bi, Sb) (Ta, Nb)O_4$.

Crystallography: Orthorhombic. Crystals sometimes large; massive; stream pebbles.

Colors: Light brown to black.

Luster: Adamantine to submetallic.

Streak: Yellow-brown to black.

Hardness: 5.

Density: 8.84 (Brazil).

Cleavage: Perfect 1 direction. Fracture subconchoidal. Brittle.

Optics: $\alpha = 2.388$; $\beta = 2.403$; $\gamma = 2.428$. Biaxial (+), $2V = 80°$.

Birefringence: 0.040.

Dispersion: No data.

Pleochroism: No data.

Spectral: Not diagnostic.

Luminescence: None.

Occurrence: Pegmatites.
Gamba Hill, Uganda; Acari, Brazil.

Stone Sizes: Cut gems always small, less than 5 carats.

Comments: Extremely rare as a cut gem, even in very complete collections. Many of the minerals in the tantalite group have been faceted; bismutotantalite is perhaps the rarest of them all. The color is attractive, but low hardness and good cleavage make use in jewelry unadvisable.

Name: On account of the composition.

BIXBITE See: Beryl.

BLENDE See: Sphalerite.

BLOODSTONE See: Quartz.

BOEHMITE See: Diaspore.

BOLEITE

Formula: $Pb_9Ag_3Cu_8Cl_{21}(OH)_{16} \cdot H_2O$.

Crystallography: Tetragonal. Pseudocubic. Crystals usually cube shaped, sometimes modified by other faces, and in parallel growths.

Colors: Indigo blue to Prussian blue, blackish blue.

Streak: Blue with a greenish tinge.

Luster: Vitreous, pearly on cleavage.

Hardness: 3-3.5.

Density: 5.05.

Cleavage: Perfect 1 direction, good 1 direction.

Optics: $o = 2.05$; $e = 2.03$. Uniaxial (−).

Birefringence: 0.020.

Pleochroism: None.

Spectral: Not diagnostic.

Luminescence: None.

Occurrence: Secondary mineral in Cu and Pb deposits. *Chile; Broken Hill, N.S.W., Australia.*
Boleo, Baja California: magnificent single crystals and groups on matrix, with single crystals up to nearly ½ inch.

Stone Sizes: Crystals up to 2 cm on an edge have been found. Crystals, however, are usually nearly opaque, and facetable material is exceedingly rare. Stones up to about 1 carat have been cut, and even these are not entirely clean.

Comments: Cut boleite is strictly for collectors, since it is soft and very rare. Faceted gems of any transparency should be considered among the rarest of all gemstones. The color is so attractive that any available stones would be quickly snapped up by collectors.

Name: Boleo, Santa Rosalia, Baja California, Mexico.

BORACITE

Formula: $Mg_3B_7O_{13}Cl$.

Crystallography: Orthorhombic. Pseudo-tetragonal. Crystals small and equant.

Colors: Colorless, white, gray, yellow, pale to dark green, bluish-green.

Luster: Vitreous.

Hardness: 7-7.5.

Density: 2.95.

Cleavage: None. Fracture conchoidal to uneven.

Optics: $\alpha = 1.658\text{-}1.662$; $\beta = 1.662\text{-}1.667$; $\gamma = 1.668\text{-}1.673$. Biaxial (+), $2V = 82°$.

Birefringence: 0.011.

Dispersion: 0.024.

Pleochroism: None.

Spectral: Not diagnostic.

Luminescence: Weak greenish (SW).

Occurrence: Sedimentary deposits formed in evaporite sequences (sea water).
Choctaw Salt Dome, Louisiana; Otis, California.
Aislaby, England; Luneville, France.
Stassfurt and *Hanover* districts, *Germany:* source of the only cuttable crystals. Crystals usually small, pale colored.

Stone Sizes: Boracite crystals are very small and yield stones up to 1-2 carats. Gems over 2 carats would be considered an extreme rarity.

Comments: Boracite is not a common mineral; its occurrence is restricted to salt deposits and similar environments, resulting from the evaporation of sea water in enclosed basins. However, the mineral has no cleavage and a high hardness, so it is a shame it is not larger or more abundant. The colors of cut gems are usually delicate shades of light blue and green, and the dispersion is moderate. Cut boracite is one of the rarer of collector gems.

Name: In allusion to the borax in the composition.

BORNITE

Formula: Cu_5FeS_4.

Crystallography: Tetragonal. Crystals rare, twinned; usually massive, compact.

Colors: Copper red to bronze. Tarnishes to an iridescent purple color.

Streak: Light grayish black.

Luster: Metallic; opaque.

Hardness: 3.

Density: 5.08.

Cleavage: Traces. Fracture uneven to conchoidal. Brittle.

Occurrence: Low temperature copper deposits.
Bristol, Connecticut; Virginia; North Carolina; Montana; Arizona; Colorado; California.
Canada; Chile; Peru; England; Italy; Germany; South Africa; Madagascar.

Stone Sizes: Cabochons could be very large, several inches long, because the massive material from ore veins is available in large pieces.

Comments: Bornite is suitable only for cabochons. The bronzy color rapidly tarnishes in air to a magnificent iridescent color display, mostly purple, but also with blue and green tones. Bornite is too soft and brittle for anything but a collector curiosity, although cabochons are quite attractive when they tarnish. The material is not rare, so cabochons have no great value beyond the effort of cutting.

Name: After Ignatius von Born, eighteenth-century mineralogist.

BOWENITE   See: Serpentine.

BRAZILIANITE

Formula: $NaAl_3(PO_4)_2(OH)_4$.

Crystallography: Monoclinic. Crystals equant, prismatic, spear-shaped; also striated.

Colors: Colorless, pale yellow, yellowish-green, greenish.

Luster: Vitreous. .

Hardness: 5.5.

Density: 2.980-2.995.

Cleavage: Good 1 direction. Fracture conchoidal. Brittle.

Optics: $\alpha = 1.602$; $\beta = 1.609$; $\gamma = 1.621-1.623$.
Biaxial (+), $2V = 71°$.

Birefringence: 0.019-0.021.

Dispersion: 0.014.

Pleochroism: Weak—merely a change in shade of color.

Spectral: Not diagnostic.

Luminescence: None.

Occurrence: Hydrothermal mineral in pegmatitic cavities.
Palermo Mine, Grafton, New Hampshire.
Conselheira Pena, Minas Gerais, Brazil: only source of gem material, in crystals up to large size.

Stone Sizes: Crystals from Brazil are up to 12×8 cm. Some large gems have been cut.
AMNH: 23 (emerald cut, Brazil), 19 (round, yellow).
SI: 41.9 and 17.0 (yellow, Brazil).
PC: 24 (yellow, Brazil).
   Most gems are 1-10 carats, or even smaller. Cut stones over 5 carats are scarce today.

Comments: Brazilianite was discovered in 1944. Gems are suitable only for collections, but the color is lovely. Faceted stones are often flawed in large sizes, so a clean gem over 15 carats is a great rarity. Many crystals that are in museums would yield very large gems, but these are retained as crystal specimens and it is unlikely that they will ever be cut.

Name: After occurrence in Brazil.

BREITHAUPTITE

Formula: NiSb.

Crystallography: Hexagonal. Crystals are rare, usually massive, compact.

Colors: Light copper-red, violetish.

Streak: Reddish brown.

Luster: Metallic; opaque.

Hardness: 5.5.

Density: 7.59-8.23.

Cleavage: None. Fracture subconchoidal to uneven. Brittle.

Pleochroism: Strong in reflected light.

Luminescence: None.

Occurrence: In massive Ni sulfide ore bodies.
Cobalt district, Ontario, Canada; Sarrabus, Sardinia; Adreasburg, Harz, Germany.

Stone Sizes: Massive material could cut gems to hundreds of carats but only as cabochons.

Comments: Breithauptite is a curiosity cut for collectors, although it could be worn with care in jewelry. The color is extremely lovely, a delicate reddish or violet with metallic luster that is both unique and attractive. Sometimes the reddish sulfide is veined with streaks of native silver or colorless gangue minerals, providing interesting patterning to the color. The material is not very rare but is seldom encountered in cut form.

Name: After G. W. A. Breithaupt, a German mineralogist.

BRONZITE   See: Enstatite.

BROOKITE

Formula: TiO_2.

Crystallography: Orthorhombic. Occurs only in crystals; tabular, prismatic, pyramidal; often striated.

Colors: Brown, yellowish brown, reddish brown, dark brown to black; rarely blue.

Luster: Adamantine to submetallic.

Hardness: 5.5-6.

Density: 4.14 normal; range 3.87-4.14.

Cleavage: Indistinct.

Optics: $\alpha = 2.583$; $\beta = 2.584$; $\gamma = 2.700$-2.740. Biaxial (+).

Birefringence: 0.122-0.157.

Dispersion: Strong, ~0.131.

Pleochroism: Strong: yellow-brown/reddish-brown/orange to golden brown. An hourglass-shaped zonal coloration is sometimes seen in bluish crystals.

Spectral: Not diagnostic.

Luminescence: None.

Occurrence: In gneisses, schists and sometimes in igneous rocks; contact deposits.
North Carolina; Somerville, Massachusetts; Maine: California.
Magnet Cove, Arkansas: contact metamorphic rocks.
Ellenville, New York: hydrothermal deposits.
Tirol, Switzerland: typical Alpine deposits.
Minas Gerais, Brazil; Dartmoor, England; France; USSR.

Stone Sizes: Always less than 1-2 carats; larger stones are opaque.

Comments: Brookite is a very dark-colored mineral, transparent only in small fragments. Cuttable crystals are exceedingly rare, and attractive-looking cut stones are among the rarest of all gems. Most stones are in private collections.

Name: After the English mineralogist and crystallographer J. H. Brooke.

BRUCITE

Formula: $Mg(OH)_2$.

Crystallography: Hexagonal; tabular crystals, platy aggregates. Manganoan variety sometimes acicular. Also foliated, massive, fibrous, scaly.

Colors: White, pale green, gray, bluish. Manganoan variety yellow to brownish-red, brown.

Luster: Waxy to vitreous; pearly on cleavages.

Hardness: 2.5.

Density: 2.39.

Cleavage: Perfect basal cleavage. Sectile, plates flexible.

Optics: $o = 1.559$-1.590; $e = 1.580$-1.600. Uniaxial (+); sometimes biaxial with small $2V$.

Birefringence: 0.010-0.020.

Pleochroism: None; colorless in transmitted light.

Spectral: Not diagnostic.

Luminescence: None.

Occurrence: In low temperature hydrothermal veins in serpentine, chloritic and dolomitic schists, and metamorphic limestones.
Asbestos, Quebec, Canada: Fibrous masses up to several feet in length; also cuttable pale blue masses.
Hoboken, New Jersey: Fibrous aggregates.
Lancaster County, Pennsylvania: Plates nearly 20 cm across.
Brewster, New York: Small crystals.
California; Italy; Scotland; Sweden (manganoan var.), USSR.

Stone Sizes: Brucite is very rarely facetable. The major source for cuttable material is Asbestos, Quebec, which has yielded pale blue gems up to 1+ carats.

Comments: Brucite is extremely difficult to cut, and only a few faceted stones in the ½-1 carat size range are known.

Name: After Archibald Bruce, an early American mineralogist who first described the species.

BUERGERITE   See Tourmaline.

BURNITE   See: Azurite.

BUSTAMITE

Formula: $(Mn, Ca)_3Si_3O_9$.

Crystallography: Triclinic. Crystals tabular, usually rounded and rough; massive.

Colors: Pale flesh pink to brownish red.

Luster: Vitreous.

Hardness: 5.5-6.5.

Density: 3.32-3.43.

Cleavage: Perfect 1 direction, good 1 direction.

Optics: $\alpha = 1.662$-1.692; $\beta = 1.674$-1.705; $\gamma = 1.676$-1.707. Biaxial (−), $2V = 30$-$44°$.

Birefringence: 0.014-0.015.

Pleochroism: Weak: rose red/orange/orange.

Spectral: Not diagnostic.

Luminescence: None.

Occurrence: Manganese ore bodies, usually of metasomatic origin.
Cornwall, England; Långban, Sweden.
Franklin and *Sterling Hill, New Jersey:* in fine crystals.
Iwate and *Yamagata* prefectures, *Japan:* gemmy crystals.
Broken Hill, N.S.W., Australia: this material has high Mn content, in crystals up to 2×10 cm; S.G. = 3.41, $2V = 39°$, $\alpha = 1.688$, $\beta = 1.699$, $\gamma = 1.703$, Birefringence 0.015.

Stone Sizes: Faceted gems are usually small, less than 5 carats, and mostly in the 1-2 carat range. Catseyes are also known, up to about 5 carats.

Comments: Bustamite is very similar in appearance and properties to rhodonite. The Japanese crystals are very rich in Mn. The color, when fresh, is paler than rhodonite. Bustamite may also be fibrous, and then yields fine catseye gems, but these are extremely rare. Faceted bustamites are very attractive, especially in the pinkish shades, but stones over 1-2 carats are very rare collector items. The cleavage makes cutting difficult and wear ill advised.

Name: After the discoverer of the mineral, M. Bustamente.

BYTOWNITE See: Feldspar.

C

CAIRNGORM See: Quartz.

CALAMINE See: Hemimorphite.

CALCENTINE See: Korite.

CALCITE Dimorph of ARAGONITE. Also Cobalto-calcite = Sphaerocobaltite = CoCO$_3$; Onyx = Travertine = Flowstone (found in caves); Iceland spar; Alabaster; Marble.

Formula: CaCO$_3$.

Crystallography: Hexagonal (R). Crystals common in a huge array of forms; massive; stalactitic; chalky.

Colors: Colorless (Iceland spar), white, gray, yellow, shades of pink, green, blue, purplish red (Co).

Luster: Vitreous to pearly.

Hardness: 3.

Density: 2.71 (pure) to 2.94.

Cleavage: Perfect rhombohedral (3 directions).

Optics: $e = 1.486$-1.550; $o = 1.658$-1.740. Uniaxial ($-$).

Birefringence: 0.172-0.190.

Dispersion: Strong.

Pleochroism: None.

Spectral: Any lines seen are due to specific elements as impurities.

Luminescence: Common and from many localities around the world.

SW: red, orange, lemon yellow, shades of green, shades of blue, pink, white.
LW: orange, dull pink, tan, yellow, blue, gray.

Occurrence: Occurs in all types of rocks as the most abundant carbonate mineral on Earth. Found in veins, ore deposits, and as a constituent of rock limestone and marble. Crystals often large (many inches) and transparent. *Onyx* is the material of most limestone caves, usually banded in shades of tan and brown. *Iceland spar* is colorless calcite, transparent, sometimes in large masses. The name *alabaster* refers to gypsum and is incorrect when applied to calcite. Gem material is commonly seen from the following localities: **Missouri** (colorless), **Baja California** (brown), **Canada, New York, Montana, England, Mexico, Iceland** (colorless), and the **USSR** (pale yellow).

Stone Sizes: Rough material can be very large (hundreds of carats). Colorless material is usually step-cut or emerald-cut. Brown material from Baja is usually seen up to 50 carats, normal range 5-25 carats. Purplish red material from Paramca, Spain (cobaltian) is not transparent, usually cut 1-5 carat size. Onyx is opaque and yields cabochons and carvings of any desired size.
SI: 75.8 and 45.8 (golden-brown, Baja).
DG: 7.5 (cobaltocalcite, Spain).
PC: 4,440 (colorless); 1156 carats (colorless, twinned); 474 (yellowish, USSR).
NMC: 606 (light yellow cushion cut, with sulfide inclusions; Bancroft, Ontario, Canada); 168.2 (colorless, Portuguese cut).
HU: 1260 (Bancroft, Ontario, Canada).
ROM: 183 (colorless, Balmat, New York).
GIA: 48 (yellow, USSR).

Comments: Calcite is common and abundant throughout the world. The material has little intrinsic value since it is not scarce. However, calcite is one of the most difficult of all minerals to cut because of perfect cleavage in 3 directions. The cost of a faceted stone is therefore mostly in the labor of cutting. Normally, a faceted stone breaks during cutting, and the finished gem is much smaller than the originally intended size. Therefore, a cut calcite over 50 carats is extremely rare. Faceted stones cut from material from many localities might turn up, but the lack of scarcity value is not encouraging to potential calcite cutters.

Onyx is usually cut into slabs, made into vases, lamps, ashtrays, bookends, and many other decorative objects. It is usually banded in shades of brown, green, and buff. Marble is a metamorphic rock often used in construction and in making decorative carved objects. Coloration in the form of banding and streaks is due to impurities.

Name: *Calcite* is derived from the Latin *calx,* meaning *lime.*

CALIFORNITE   See: Garnet.

CANASITE

Formula: $(Na,K)_5(Ca, Mn, Mg)_4(Si_2O_5)_5(OH,F)_3$.

Crystallography: Monoclinic. Occurs in tiny grains, usually twinned.

Colors: Greenish yellow.

Luster: Vitreous.

Hardness: 5-6.

Density: 2.707.

Cleavage: Perfect 1 direction, good 1 direction. Brittle; grinds to feltlike powder.

Optics: $\alpha = 1.534; \beta = 1.538; \gamma = 1.543$.
Biaxial (−), $2V, \sim 53°$.

Birefringence: 0.009.

Spectral: Not diagnostic.

Occurrence: Occurs in pegmatite in the *Khibina Tundra, USSR.*

Stone Sizes: Massive blocks up to several inches have been found. Material is cut as cabochons and decorative objects.

Comments: The material usually seen on the market as "canasite" is purplish in color. It is frequently confused with another purplish material, a member of the serpentine family known as *stichtite.* However, stichtite occurs in elongated fibers that have a kind of lustrous sheen, almost asbestiform, whereas canasite is granular. Recent research seems to indicate that, in fact, the mate-

rial being called "canasite" has no canasite in it but is a new, distinct species.

Name: From the composition: Ca, Na, and Si.

CANCRINITE

Formula: $(Na,K,Ca)_{6-8}(Al,Si)_{12}O_{24}(CO_3,SO_4,Cl)_{1-2} \cdot nH_2O$.
Note: If $SO_4 > CO_3$, the species is called *Vishnevite*. The Cl-rich variety is called *microsommite*.

Crystallography: Hexagonal. Crystals prismatic, but rare; usually massive.

Colors: Colorless, white, yellow, orange, pink to reddish, pale blue, bluish gray.

Luster: Vitreous; pearly on cleavage; greasy.

Hardness: 5-6.

Density: 2.42-2.51; Vishnevite: 2.3.

Cleavage: Perfect 1 direction. Fracture uneven. Brittle.

Optics:
$o = 1.507\text{-}1.528; e = 1.495\text{-}1.503$. (cancrinite).
$o = 1.490\text{-}1.507; e = 1.488\text{-}1.495$ (vishnevite).
Uniaxial (−); chlorine-rich variety (microsommite) is optically (+).

Birefringence: 0.022 (cancrinite); 0.002-0.012 (vishnevite).

Dispersion: Weak.

Spectral: Not diagnostic.

Luminescence: None in UV.

Occurrence: Primarily in alkali-rich rocks; also as an alternation product of nepheline.
Iron Hill, Colorado; Kennebec County, Maine.
Norway; Rumania; Finland; USSR; Korea; China; Zaire; India; Uganda; Kenya.
Bancroft District, Ontario, Canada: fine gemmy material.

Stone Sizes: Masses occur up to several pounds, but cancrinite is usually in veins a few inches across. It is usually cut as cabochons and beads. The Canadian material is orangy yellow in color, with a greasy luster. Faceted stones are exceedingly rare and always less than 1-2 carats.

Comments: Cancrinite is one of the most attractive of all opaque or translucent gem materials. It is a bit too soft for average wear, but its distinctive color is worthy of jewelry. Cancrinite may be tricky to cut because it often contains numerous hard inclusions. Faceted gems even as small as 1 carat are considered great rarities.

Name: After Count Cancrin, Finance Minister of Russia.

CARNELIAN   See: Quartz.

CASSITERITE

Formula: SnO_2 + Fe,Ta,Nb.

Crystallography: Tetragonal. Crystals prismatic, pyramidal; also botryoidal, reniform with a radial fibrous structure. Twinning common.

Colors: Brown, brownish black, black, colorless, gray, yellowish, greenish, red.

Streak: White, grayish, brown.

Luster: Adamantine to vitreous; greasy on fracture surfaces.

Hardness: 6-7.

Density: 6.7-7.1; pure material 6.99.

Cleavage: Imperfect. Fracture subconchoidal to uneven. Brittle.

Optics: $o = 2.006$; $e = 2.097$-2.101.
Uniaxial (+); anomalously biaxial, $2V = 0$-$38°$, usually in zoned crystals.

Birefringence: 0.098.

Dispersion: 0.071 (nearly twice that of diamond).

Pleochroism: Weak to strong; greenish yellow or yellow-brown/red-brown. Most visible in strongly colored crystals.

Spectral: Not diagnostic.

Luminescence: None.

Occurrence: Prinicipal ore of tin; occurs in medium to high temperature veins; metasomatic deposits; granite pegmatites; rhyolites; alluvial deposits.
Alaska; Washington; California; Nevada; South Dakota; South Carolina; Virginia.
Canada; Mexico; Cornwall, England; Portugal; Japan; China; New South Wales, Australia.
Araca Mine, Bolivia: source of most of the gem material known: yellow, gray, colorless and light yellowish brown to reddish brown.
Spain: gem material in yellowish to red cuttable pieces.
Erongo tinfields, Namibia: gem material.

Stone Sizes: Clean cassiterite gems over 1 carat are quite rare. Masses occur up to several pounds in weight, but these are opaque and are sometimes cut into cabochons. Pale brown to dark brown gems up to 15 carats have been cut; slightly flawed stones up to 25 carats are known, mostly Bolivian material.
PC: 9.6 (brownish, Tasmania); 11.83 (brown, England); 28.16 (brownish).
SI: 10 (yellow-brown, Bolivia).
DG: 14.85, 9.51 (brownish, Bolivia).

Comments: Cassiterite has tremendous dispersive fire, much more than diamond, that is visible in properly cut pale-colored gems. This lighter-colored material is, however, very rare except in small fragments. Cassiterite is a fine gemstone—it is rather hard, and there is no cleavage problem. It is unfortunate that cuttable rough is so scarce. Cassiterites under 5 carats are not among the rarest of rare stones, but large clean gems definitely are.

Name: The Greek word for *tin* is *kassiteros*.

CATAPLEIITE

Formula: $Na_2ZrSi_3O_9 \cdot 2H_2O$; Dimorphous with Gaidonnayite.

Crystallography: Hexagonal; crystals thin hexagonal plates. Also lamellar masses; twinned. Gaidonnayite is orthorhombic.

Colors: Light yellow, yellowish brown, brown, salmon-pink, yellowish red. Rarely pale blue or colorless.

Luster: Vitreous, greasy, or dull.

Hardness: 5-6.

Density: 2.65-2.8.

Cleavage: Perfect 1 direction, imperfect 2 directions; also parting.

Optics: $o = 1.596$; $e = 1.624$.
Uniaxial (+).

Birefringence: 0.280.

Pleochroism: None in colorless gems.

Spectral: Not diagnostic.

Luminescence: None reported.

Occurrence: Alkalic rocks and pegmatites.
Langesundfjord District, Norway; Magnet Cove, Arkansas. Greenland; USSR; Madagascar.
Mt. Ste. Hilaire, Quebec, Canada: cuttable crystals.

Stone Sizes: Gems under 1 carat have been cut from Canadian material.

Comments: The only reported cut catapleiite is from Mt. Ste. Hilaire, Quebec, Canada, in the form of tiny colorless gems.

Name: From Greek words meaning *rare minerals* because catapleiite is usually associated with other rare minerals.

CELESTITE

Formula: $SrSO_4$.

Crystallography: Orthorhombic. Crystals common, usually tabular; also nodules, earthy, massive.

Colors: Colorless, white, gray, blue, green, yellow, orange, and red shades.

Luster: Vitreous; pearly on cleavage.

Hardness: 3-3.5.

Density: 3.97-4.00.

Cleavage: Perfect 1 direction, good 1 direction. Fracture uneven. Brittle.

Optics: $\alpha = 1.622\text{-}1.625$; $\beta = 1.624$; $\gamma = 1.631\text{-}1.635$.
Madagascar gems: $\alpha = 1.619$; $\gamma = 1.631$.
Biaxial (+), $2V = 50°$.

Birefringence: 0.009-0.012.

Dispersion: 0.014.

Pleochroism: Weak, in shades of indigo blue, bluish green, and violet.

Spectral: Not diagnostic.

Luminescence: Blue in SW. Blue or dull yellow in LW. May phosphoresce blue-white.

Occurrence: Celestite occurs in sedimentary rocks, especially limestones; it is also found in hydrothermal vein deposits, sometimes in igneous rocks.
Clay Center, Ohio; Colorado; Chittenango Falls, New York; many localities in *California.*
San Luis Potosi, Mexico; Bristol, England; Girgenti, Sicily; Madagascar; Germany; France; Austria; Italy; Switzerland; USSR; Egypt; Tunisia.
Lampasas, Texas: gemmy material (blue).
Put-in-Bay, Strontian Islands, Lake Erie: gemmy material.
Tsumeb, Namibia: gem material.
Canada: orange crystals.

Stone Sizes: Celestite gems are usually under 3 carats and are generally colorless or pale blue, often step-cut. However, some gems are known in the 30 carat range, and there is no reason why large transparent crystals cannot be found and cut.
DG: 20.1 (blue, Madagascar).
NMC: 3.11 (orange step-cut, Ontario, Canada).
PC: 2.98 (blue, New York).

Comments: Celestite is seldom seen in collections, perhaps because faceted gems have little fire and are usually colorless or pale blue, rarely orange. Gems are soft and fragile, hard to cut, and cannot be worn with safety. Celestite is strictly for collectors; large, clean faceted gems are indeed rare, whereas transparent crystals per se are not.

Name: Latin *coelestis* means *celestial,* in allusion to the delicate and lovely pale blue color often displayed by this mineral.

CERULEITE

Formula: $Cu_2Al_7(AsO_4)_4(OH)_{13}$.

Crystallography: Usually massive, compact, earthy.

Colors: Turquoise-blue shades, cerulean blue.

Luster: Earthy, dull.

Hardness: 6.5 (conflicting data, may be softer).

Density: 2.7-2.8.

Optics: Mean index ~1.60. Very fine grained.

Occurrence: Sedimentary material formed in the vicinity of copper deposits, like turquoise.
Cornwall, England.
Huanaco, Chile: original material.
Southern Bolivia: cabbing material of fine color.

Stone Sizes: Nodules are usually small, less than 1 inch and up to several inches in size. The material yields cabochons only.

Comments: Ceruleite is a little-known gem material of truly exquisite color. It takes a very high polish easily and quickly, and the color of the polished gems is far deeper than that of the rough nodules. It is extremely rare in fine, solid, cuttable pieces and consequently is rather expensive. Few cut stones are to be seen in museum collections, and the total amount of fine Bolivian material may not exceed several hundred pounds. A major problem with ceruleite is porosity, rendering the material too soft and fragile for cutting and wear. This problem can be solved by plastic impregnation. Such impregnated ceruleite has a density of 2.58.

Name: In allusion to its color; the Latin *caerulea* means *sky blue.*

CERUSSITE

Formula: $PbCO_3$.

Crystallography: Orthorhombic. Crystals common, elongated, tabular, often twinned and striated; acicular, massive.

Colors: Colorless, white, gray, "smoky," greenish (Cu inclusions), yellowish. Dark gray or black material is due to inclusions.

Luster: Adamantine to submetallic; vitreous; resinous; pearly.

Hardness: 3-3.5.

Density: 6.55.

Cleavage: Distinct 1 direction. Fracture conchoidal. Extremely brittle.

Optics: $\alpha = 1.804$; $\beta = 2.076$; $\gamma = 2.079$.
Biaxial (−), $2V = 9°$.

Birefringence: 0.274.

Dispersion: 0.055 (greater than diamond).

Pleochroism: None.

Spectral: Not diagnostic.

Luminescence: Pinkish orange (Utah) or yellow shades in LW. Pale blue or shades of green in SW.

Occurrence: Secondary mineral in the oxidized zones of lead deposits. Many localities known:
Tiger, Arizona; Colorado; Idaho; South Dakota; Utah; New Mexico; Montana; Nevada; California.
Broken Hill Mine, Zambia; Dundas, Tasmania; Broken Hill, N.S.W., Australia; Monte Poni, Sardinia; Leadhills, Scotland.
Tsumeb, Namibia: source of the largest and finest gem material; colorless, gray and yellowish, in masses up to several pounds (completely transparent).

Stone Sizes: Large masses of transparent rough are known from Tsumeb, Namibia, that could cut stones of several thousand carats. The real problem is cohesion of large stones.
Catseyes are known from 2-6 carats; the material is from Tiger, Arizona, and Tsumeb, Namibia.
SI: 4.7 (pale yellow, Tsumeb, Namibia); 109.9 (smoky, Tsumeb, Namibia).
NMC: 71.25 (colorless octagon, Tsumeb, Namibia).
PC: 408 (brownish-gray oval, Tsumeb, Namibia); 262 (emerald cut, colorless, Tsumeb, Namibia).

Comments: Cut cerussite is as beautiful as diamond since it has higher dispersion, is usually free of any body color, and has an adamantine luster. However, cerussite is extremely soft and one of the most brittle and heat sensitive of all minerals. Cutting a gem is a major chore, and cutting a very large one without breaking it is almost impossible. Consequently, faceted cerussite is one of the rarest of all gems. Abundant rough material is available among the thousands of crystals and crystal fragments recovered from Tsumeb, Namibia. Few cutters, however, have the skill and knowledge required to successfully fashion a gem from this rough. The cost of a cut stone will therefore largely reflect the cutting cost. Time, patience skill, and tender loving care are essential.

Name: From the Latin *cerussa,* the name of an artificial lead carbonate.

CEYLONITE   See: Spinel.

CHABAZITE

Formula: $CaAl_2Si_4O_{12} \cdot 6H_2O$.

Crystallography: Hexagonal. Crystals rhomb-shaped, tabular; frequently twinned.

Colors: Colorless, white, yellowish, pinkish, reddish white, salmon color, greenish.

Luster: Vitreous.

Hardness: 4-5.

Density: 2.05-2.16.

Cleavage: Distinct 1 direction. Fracture uneven. Brittle.

Optics: Variable; R.I. = 1.470-1.494.
Uniaxial (+) or (−).

Spectral: Not diagnostic.

Luminescence: None.

Occurrence: Cavities in basalt and other basic igneous rocks; also hot spring deposits.
Nevada; California; Oregon; Colorado; New Jersey; Hawaii.
Bay of Fundy district, Nova Scotia, Canada; Greenland; Scotland; Ireland; Italy; Germany; Hungary; USSR; India; Australia; Czechoslovakia.

Stone Sizes: Cut chabazites are always very small, usually less than 1-2 carats. Crystals are never entirely transparent, and often only one corner of a pinkish or colorless crystal can be cut. Very few chabazites have been cut at all, and they are seldom seen in museum collections.

Comments: Chabazite is too soft for wear. The colors are pale but attractive. Unfortunately, clean material is extremely scarce. Chabazite is not a terribly difficult material to facet, but finding suitable material is not easy. This is one of the rare gems that are seldom discussed or heard about. There may be only a handful of cut gems in existence.

Name: From the Greek *chabazios,* an ancient name applied to certain materials.

CHALCEDONY   See: Quartz.

CHALCOSIDERITE   See: Turquoise.

CHAMBERSITE

Formula: $Mn_3B_7O_{13}Cl$.

Crystallography: Orthorhombic. Crystals shaped like tetrahedra, up to 1 cm on edge.

Colors: Colorless, brownish, lilac, purple.

Luster: Vitreous.

Hardness: 7.

Density: 3.49.

Cleavage: None.

Optics: $\alpha = 1.732$; $\beta = 1.737$; $\gamma = 1.744$.
Biaxial (+), $2V \sim 83°$.

Birefringence: 0.012.

Spectral: Not diagnostic.

Luminescence: None.

Occurrence: Occurs in brines in storage well at *Barber's Hill salt dome, Chambers County, Texas.*

Stone Sizes: Cut stones are not really transparent and are usually under 2 carats. Gems are generally triangular in shape and are cut by beveling and polishing off part of the tetrahedron of a crystal to save weight. Cut stones are, in a sense, truncated crystals with their surfaces polished.

Comments: Chambersite is an exceedingly rare mineral, as might be gathered from the locality information. Crystals are generally tiny and are recovered by skin diving to a depth of as much as 70 feet in brine. Cut stones are merely curiosities and very few exist.

Name: From the Texas locality.

CHAROITE

Formula: $K(Ca,Na)_2Si_4O_{10}(OH,F) \cdot H_2O$.

Crystallography: Monoclinic; crystals thin, acicular (i.e., fibrous).

Colors: Lilac to violet, in various shades.

Luster: Vitreous.

Hardness: 5-6.

Density: 2.54-2.68.

Cleavage: Indistinct; fracture splintery.

Optics: $\alpha = 1.550$; $\beta = 1.553$; $\gamma = 1.559$. Biaxial (+).

Birefringence: 0.009.

Pleochroism: Distinct; colorless/rose-pink.

Luminescence: None reported.

Spectral: Not diagnostic.

Occurrence: This unique and striking material comes only from the *Chary River* area in the *Murun Massif, Northwest Aldan, Yakutsk, ASSR, USSR.* The material is intimately mixed with prismatic orange crystals of tinaksite, pale greenish gray microcline, and greenish black crystals of aegirine-augite. This makes a unique, distinctive, and highly ornamental rock. The geology is that of nepheline and aegirine-bearing syenites contacting limestones; the charoite rock occurs in metasomatic bodies at the contact. It is a massive material suitable for making bookends, vases, goblets and cabochons. It has been widely marketed since its original description in 1978.

Stone Sizes: Large blocks suitable for making objects a foot or more in size are available. Charoite also produces scenic stones due to the admixed minerals. Some is chatoyant.

Name: For the locality.

CHERT See: Quartz.

CHIASTOLITE See: Andalusite.

CHILDRENITE Series to Eosphorite if Mn exceeds Fe.

Formula: $(Fe,Mn)AlPO_4(OH)_2 \cdot H_2O$.

Crystallography: Orthorhombic. Crystals equant, pyramidal, platy, often doubly terminated.

Colors: Brown to yellowish brown, golden yellow.

Luster: Vitreous to resinous.

Hardness: 5.

Density: 3.2 (pure Fe end member).

Cleavage: Poor. Fracture uneven to subconchoidal.

Optics: $\alpha = 1.63$-1.645; $\beta = 1.65$-1.68; $\gamma = 1.66$-1.685. Biaxial (−), $2V = 40$-45°.

Birefringence: 0.030-0.040.

Pleochroism: Distinct: yellow/pink/colorless to pale pink.

Luminescence: None.

Spectral: May show lines of iron spectrum.

Occurrence: In granite pegmatites and hydrothermal vein deposits.
Cornwall, England; Greifenstein, Germany; Custer, South Dakota.
Minas Gerais, Brazil: gemmy crystals. These are found to be Fe:Mn = 1:1 and could be called *childro-eosphorite.*

Stone Sizes: Childrenite occurs in brown, opaque crystals up to several inches long. Transparent material is much smaller, and facetable crystals yield stones up to about 3-4 carats. In general, cuttable material in this series is closer to the eosphorite end.
DG: 3.58 (Brazil).

Comments: Cut childrenite is a great rarity, and all gems are small. Cut eosphorite is more abundantly available, though both materials are very scarce.

Name: J. G. Children, English mineralogist.

CHIOLITE

Formula: $Na_5Al_3F_{14}$.

Crystallography: Tetragonal; minute dipyramidal crystals, commonly in masses.

Colors: Colorless, white.

Luster: Vitreous.

Hardness: 3.5-4.

Density: 2.998.

Cleavage: Perfect 1 direction.

Optics: $o = 1.349$; $e = 1.342$. Uniaxial (−).

Birefringence: 0.007.

Pleochroism: None.

Spectral: Not diagnostic.

Luminescence: None.

Occurrence: *Ivigtut, Greenland:* associated with cryolite. *Miask, Urals, USSR:* in a cryolite pegmatite.

Stone Sizes: Always tiny, 1-2 carat range, if clean. Large, clean fragments do not exist for cutting. The mineral itself is quite rare.

Comments: Chiolite has nothing much to offer in the way of a gem. It is very soft, has perfect cleavage, has no appealing colors, and is usually small and nondescript. However, it has joined the ranks of minerals that have been cut by facetors who must try their hand at everything clean enough to cut. There may be less than one or two dozen cut stones in existence. Chiolite exists solely as a curiosity in the gem world.

Name: From the Greek words for *snow* and *stone* because in its white appearance it is similar to cryolite, whose name means *ice-stone.*

CHLORASTROLITE See: Pumpellyite.

CHLOROMELANITE See Jadeite.

CHONDRODITE See: Humite Group.

CHROMITE Chromite group, extensive solid-solution series.
Note: Magnesiochromite $= MgCr_2O_4$; Hercynite $= FeAl_2O_4$.

Formula: $FeCr_2O_4$.

Crystallography: Isometric. Octahedral crystals up to 1 cm on edge; massive.

Colors: Black, reddish brown.

Streak: Brown.

Luster: Submetallic; opaque, translucent in thin splinters.

Hardness: 5.5.

Density: 4.5-4.8.

Cleavage: None. Fracture uneven. Brittle. Sometimes weakly magnetic.

Optics: R.I. = 2.08-2.16. Isotropic.

Spectral: Not diagnostic.

Luminescence: None.

Occurrence: In igneous rocks rich in olivine; in serpentines; in stream and beach sands. Sometimes in massive deposits of large size.
California; Oregon; Washington; Wyoming; Maryland; North Carolina; Pennsylvania.
Canada; Cuba; Norway; USSR; France; Zimbabwe; India.

Stone Sizes: Any size could be cut from massive material. The possibility exists for some deep reddish crystals to contain very tiny facetable areas, but thus far none have been discovered.

Comments: Chromite is shiny and black, and makes a curious-looking cabochon with no special attraction. Occasionally, a cabochon has a reddish color. The stones have little value because the material is extremely abundant but are cut as curiosities only.

Name: In allusion to the composition.

CHRYSOBERYL Also called Catseye, Alexandrite.

Formula: $BeAl_2O_4$ + Fe,Ti.

Crystallography: Orthorhombic. Crystals tabular or prismatic, sixling-twins common; also massive and as waterworn pebbles.

Colors: Yellowish green, yellow, gray, brown, blue-green, deep green, red, violet. Rarely colorless. *Alexandrite* varies in color with incident light: green, blue-green, or pale green in daylight; mauve, violet to red, purplish in incandescent light. *Catseye* is usually dark yellowish brown to pale yellow, honey yellow, greenish.

Luster: Vitreous.

Hardness: 8.5.

Density: 3.68-3.80; colorless 3.70; gems usually higher, alexandrite highest.

Cleavage: Distinct 1 direction, seldom observed, varies to poor. Fracture conchoidal. Brittle.

Optics: $\alpha = 1.740\text{-}1.759$; $\beta = 1.747\text{-}1.764$; $\gamma = 1.745\text{-}1.770$. Biaxial (+), may also be (−), $2V = 70°$. Indices vary with Fe content.
Colorless (Sri Lanka): $\alpha = 1.740$; $\beta = 1.745$; $\gamma = 1.750$.
Australia: $\alpha = 1.756\text{-}1.765$; $\beta = 1.761\text{-}1.772$; $\gamma = 1.768\text{-}1.777$; SG $= 3.72\text{-}3.74$.

Birefringence: 0.008-0.012.

Properties of Alexandrite from Various Localities

	Urals	Sri Lanka	Burma	Brazil	Zimbabwe
Density	–	–	3.71	3.68	3.64–3.80
Optics					
α	1.749	1.745	1.746	1.747	1.749
β	1.753	1.749	1.748	1.748	1.752
γ	1.759	1.755	1.755	1.756	1.758
Birefringence	0.009	0.010	0.009	0.009	0.009

Dispersion: 0.015.

Pleochroism: Distinct, in shades of yellow and brown. Alexandrite: deep red/orange-yellow/green. (*Note:* Burma gem anomalous: purple/grass-green/blue-green.)

Spectral: Yellowish and brown gems have strong band at 4440 due to Fe, especially Sri Lankan gems. Also may be bands visible at 5040 and 4860. Alexandrite has narrow doublet at 6805/6875, with weak, narrow lines at 6650, 6550, and 6490 and broad band at 6400-5550. Total absorption below 4700.

Luminescence: Alexandrite fluoresces weak red in SW and LW; pale green chrysoberyl from Connecticut noted yellow-green in SW.

Inclusions: In catseye, there are short needles and tubes parallel to the long axis of the crystal. Liquid-filled cavities with 2-phase inclusions; stepped twin planes.

Occurrence: Occurs in pegmatites, gneiss, mica schist, dolomitic marbles; also found as stream pebbles and detrital grains.
South Dakota; Colorado; Maine; New Hampshire; Connecticut; New York; Finland; Zaire; Madagascar; Japan.
USSR: alexandrite of finest quality in mica schist, near *Sverdlovsk.*
India: catseyes with sillimanite fibers, from *Kerala.*
Brazil (especially *Jacuda, Bahia*): fine facetable material; also catseyes, alexandrite.
Zimbabwe: fine alexandrite, intense color change.
Sri Lanka: all types, some of the world's finest catseyes, also alexandrite; faceting material all colors, rarely colorless.
Burma: some alexandrite; rarely colorless facetable chrysoberyl.
Anakie, Queensland, Australia: yellow-green chrysoberyl.

Stone Sizes: The largest alexandrites from the classic Russian locality are in the 30-carat range. Facetable chrysoberyl is known up to several hundred carats, and catseyes of similar size have been found. Star chrysoberyls are known but are very rare.
BM: 29.4 (Sri Lanka, yellow-green); 45(*Hope Chrysoberyl,* flawless oval catseye); 43, 27.5 (Sri Lanka, alexandrites).
ROM: 42.72 (Sri Lanka, chartreuse green).

AMNH: 74.4 (emerald-cut, yellowish green)—may be world's finest of this color).
SI: catseyes: 171.5 (Sri Lanka, gray-green); 47.8 (Sri Lanka); 58.2 (*The Maharan,* Sri Lanka); faceted: 114.3 (Sri Lanka, yellow-green); 120.5 (Sri Lanka, green); 46.3 (Brazil, yellow-green); 31.7 (Sri Lanka, brown); 6.7 (Brazil, dark green star); alexandrites: 65.7, 16.7 (Sri Lanka).
Iranian Crown Jewels: 147.7 (Sri Lanka, chartreuse); 25 (gray-green catseye).
Institute of Mines, Leningrad (St. Petersburg): Urals crystal cluster, alexandrite, 6×3 cm, consisting of 3 crystals.
Fersman Museum (Moscow): Alexandrite crystal cluster 25×15 cm, with crystals up to 6×3 cm, from Urals.
PC: U.S. dealers have reported alexandrites up to about 50 carats. Catseyes up to 300 carats are in private collections. Faceted gems over 40-50 carats are very rare. Stones reported include a flawed yellow Brazilian gem of 185 carats; a superb 120 carat yellow Brazilian gem in a Japanese collection, and a 79.30 carat brown Sri Lankan oval and a 66.98 carat flawless yellow Brazilian stone in a U.S. collection. The world's largest faceted chrysoberyl is a 245 carat flawless oval, slightly yellowish green, from Sri Lanka.

Comments: Transparent chrysoberyl makes a handsome faceted gem and is one of the hardest and toughest for jewelry purposes. Cleavage is not distinct, and the hardness is near that of sapphire and ruby. In general, the bright yellow and yellow-green shades are the most desirable, but some of the browns are also striking and handsome. Properly cut gems are very brilliant, although they lack fire due to low dispersion. The chrysoberyls from Australia have unusually high refractive indices and could possibly be misidentified as yellow-brown sapphires.

Catseye gems of such minerals as apatite, tourmaline, and diopside are well known, but when the term *catseye* is used alone it always refers to chrysoberyl. The eye in a chrysoberyl catseye often has a shimmering blue tone. The silk in such a gem, which creates the chatoyancy, is so fine that a microscope is needed to resolve the fibers. Consequently, the eye is the sharpest of any catseye gemstone. The optimum color is a honey brown, and light striking the stone obliquely usually creates a shadow effect within the gem, such that the side away from the light is a rich brown, while the side facing the light is yellowish white, creating the so-called milk and honey look characteristic of the finest chrysoberyls. This appearance in a large (over 20 carats) stone results in very high value.

Alexandrite is well known today as a scarce and costly gem. Stones over 5 carats are very rare, especially if the color change is good. The quality of the color change with illumination conditions is the primary basis of alexandrite quality and value. Optimum colors are intense blue-green to green (daylight) vs. purple-red (in incandescent light). Brazilian gems tend to have pale colors, pale mauve to pale blue-green, but finer gems have been found recently in limited quantity. Substantial amounts (1200 ppm) of the element gallium (replacing Al) have been detected in some Brazilian alexandrite. Sri Lanka alexandrite is often deep olive green in sunlight, whereas Russian stones are bluish green in daylight. Zimbabwean gems are a fine emerald green color in sunlight but are usually tiny (under 1 carat) if clean. The color change in Zimbabwean gems is among the best known, and it is a shame that large clean stones are virtually unobtainable from the rough from this locality.

Names: *Catseye* is named from the resemblance of the eye in the stone to the narrow iris in the eye of a cat. Another name for this gem, *cymophane,* is from Greek words meaning *appearing like a wave* because of the opalescent appearance of some crystals. *Alexandrite* is named after Czar Alexander II of Russia, on whose birthday the gem was found. Chrysoberyl is derived from the Greek *chrysos,* meaning *golden,* in allusion to the usual yellowish color of this mineral.

CHRYSOCOLLA

Formula: $(Cu,Al)_2H_2Si_2O_5(OH)_4 \cdot nH_2O$.

Crystallography: Monoclinic. Crystals are microscopic, in aggregates; cryptocrystalline, opalline.

Colors: Blue, green, and blue-green in various shades. Mixed with matrix of quartz and oxides of Cu, Fe, and Mn, adding brown and black colors.

Luster: Vitreous (if silicified), waxy, dull.

Hardness: 2-4 (as high as 7 if heavily silicified, or inclusions in quartz).

Cleavage: None. Fracture uneven to conchoidal. Very brittle.

Optics: $\alpha = 1.575\text{-}1.585$; $\beta = 1.597$; $\gamma = 1.598\text{-}1.635$. Biaxial ($-$).
Note: If material is silicified or is included in quartz, readings may be those of quartz.

Birefringence: 0.023-0.040.

Luminescence: None.

Spectral: Not diagnostic.

Occurrence: In the oxidized zone of copper deposits. May be mixed with copper carbonates such as malachite and turquoise.
Western United States, especially *Arizona, New Mexico, Nevada, Utah, Idaho.*
Mexico; Chile; USSR; Katanga, Zaire; Israel.

Stone Sizes: Large masses of material, weighing several pounds, have been found.

Comments: Chrysocolla often forms as a gel mixed with silica and hardens to a blue material that is basically a chrysocolla-saturated quartz. This material is very hard (7), wears well, and is often seen in jewelry. Chrysocolla mixed with malachite is often sold as *Eilat Stone* and comes from many localities; the color is blue to blue-green, S.G. = 2.8-3.2. Material of fine blue color but very little silica tends to be brittle and crumbles easily, making it impossible to cut stones for jewelry purposes. *Stellarite* is the trade name for a light blue mixture of chrysocolla and quartz. *Parrot-wing* is a mixture of chrysocolla and jasper, with a brownish green appearance.

Name: In Greek *Chrysos* means *golden* and *kolla* means *glue.* This name was applied to a material used by the Greeks in soldering metals, a function now fulfilled by borax. *Eilat Stone* takes its name from Eilat, Gulf of Aqaba, Red Sea.

CHRYSOLITE See: Olivine.

CHRYSOPRASE See: Quartz.

CHRYSOTILE See: Serpentine.

CINNABAR

Formula: HgS.

Crystallography: Hexagonal. Usually massive, fine grained; crystals are prismatic or rhombohedral and characteristically twinned, especially those from China.

Colors: Scarlet red, brownish red, brown, black, gray.

Luster: Adamantine to submetallic; massive varieties dull, earthy.

Hardness: 2-2.5.

Density: 8.09.

Cleavage: Perfect 1 direction. Fracture conchoidal to uneven. Brittle.

Optics: $o = 2.905$; $e = 3.256$.
Uniaxial ($+$).

Birefringence: 0.351 (very large).

Dispersion: Strong, over 0.40.

Spectral: Not diagnostic.

Luminescence: None.

Occurrence: Cinnabar is a mineral of low temperature ore deposits; also in veins, igneous rocks, and around hot springs. Crystals are very rare.
Utah; Nevada; California; Texas; Arkansas.
Mexico; Peru; Yugoslavia; Italy; Spain; USSR; Germany.
Hunan Province, China: source of the world's finest crystals.

Stone Sizes: Cut cinnabars are extremely small, normally less than 3 carats, and very rare. Some rough exists that might cut up to 50 carats; it is unlikely that fine Chinese crystals that might be transparent would ever be cut since they are extremely valuable as mineral specimens. Cabochons of almost any size up to several inches could be cut from massive cinnabar.
DG: 2.68 (red, Mexico).
PC: 22.15, 13.91 (red, China); 19.87 (red pear shape, China).

Comments: Faceted cinnabar is extremely rare and only a handful of stones exist. It is cut primarily for collectors and is extremely soft and fragile. This is unfortunate since it is a magnificent red color. Cinnabar carved in China appears regularly on the market, but it is not abundant. Note that cinnabar is used by the Chinese to make a red pigment, which is applied to wood in the form of lacquer, and this is the nature of most "cinnabar" carvings sold.

Name: The name is very old and lost in antiquity but is believed to be derived from an Indian word, since India was the country of origin.

CINNAMON STONE   See: Garnet.

CITRINE   See: Quartz.

CLEAVELANDITE   See: Feldspar.

CLINOCHRYSOTILE   See: Serpentine.

CLINOHUMITE   See: Humite Group.

CLINOZOISITE   See: Epidote.

COBALTITE

Formula: CoAsS.

Crystallography: Isometric. Crystals usually cubes and pyritohedra or combinations of forms; also massive; granular.

Colors: Silvery white to reddish, steel gray with a violet tinge; blackish gray.

Streak: Grayish black.

Luster: Metallic; opaque.

Hardness: 5.5.

Density: 6.3.

Cleavage: Perfect 1 direction. Fracture uneven. Brittle.

Spectral: Not diagnostic.

Luminescence: None.

Occurrence: High temperature deposits, in metamorphosed rocks, and in vein deposits.
Colorado; Idaho; California.
Dashkesan, Ajerbaijan, USSR; India; Sonora, Mexico; Tunaberg, Sweden; Norway; Germany; Cornwall, England; Western Australia.
Cobalt, Ontario: in masses and fine crystals.

Stone Sizes: Massive material would cut stones of any desired size.

Comments: Cabochons are interesting because of the lovely reddish metallic appearance of this mineral. Cut stones are infrequently seen and are cut only as a curiosity by the collector who wants to have one of everything.

Name: From the composition.

COLEMANITE

Formula: $Ca_2B_6O_{11} \cdot 5H_2O$.

Crystallography: Monoclinic. Crystals are equant, prismatic, pseudorhombohedral; massive, cleavable; granular, and as aggregates.

Colors: Colorless, white, grayish, yellowish white.

Luster: Vitreous to adamantine.

Hardness: 4.5.

Density: 2.42.

Cleavage: Perfect 1 direction. Fracture subconchoidal to uneven. Brittle.

Optics: $\alpha = 1.586; \beta = 1.592; \gamma = 1.614$.
Biaxial (+), $2V \sim 55°$.

Birefringence: 0.028.

Pleochroism: None.

Spectral: Not diagnostic.

Luminescence: May fluoresce and phosphoresce strong yellowish white or greenish white in SW.

Occurrence: In saline lake deposits in arid regions. Widespread at localities in *California,* especially *Boron* and *Death Valley.*
Argentina; USSR; Turkey.

Stone Sizes: Could be as much as 50-100 carats from large crystals or masses. Crystals are normally up to about 1 inch in size.
SI: 14.9 (California).

Comments: Colemanite is cut only as a curiosity, since it has no attractive colors. Faceted gems are normally colorless, have a low dispersion (no fire), and are brittle and fragile as well as difficult to cut. They have no appeal except to collectors of the unusual, and material for cutting is potentially abundantly available, since transparent material is not extremely rare.

Name: After William T. Coleman, owner of the mine where the mineral was first found.

COPAL See: Amber.

CORAL

Formula: $CaCO_3$. (Composed primarily of the mineral Calcite.)

Crystallography: Hexagonal (R).

Colors: White, flesh pink, pale to deep rose red, salmon pink, red to dark red, blue (rarely), black. May be banded or zoned and show a cellular structure.

Luster: Dull to vitreous.

Hardness: 3.5-4.

Density: 2.6-2.7. *Note:* Black coral, composed of conchiolin, is 1.34.

Cleavage: None.

Optics: 1.69 and 1.49 (calcite indices), not usually measurable. Black coral (conchiolin) has R.I. of 1.56.

Birefringence: 0.160.

Spectral: Not diagnostic.

Luminescence: Pale violet or dull purplish red.

Occurrence: Throughout the *Mediterranean Sea* and *Red Sea* areas; *Southern Ireland; Spain; Mauritius, Malaysia; Japan; Australia; Hawaii; Taiwan.*

Stone Sizes: Branches may be several inches to several feet long but are not always thick. Coral is usually fashioned into beads, cabochons, and cameos, and is also carved. Large fine carvings of rich-colored material are very rare and costly. Most of the Mediterranean coral is worked in Italy but much is also sent to Hong Kong for cutting. Conversely, Italy is also a major buyer of Taiwanese coral.

Comments: Coral is the axial skeleton of an animal called the *coral polyp,* a tiny (1 mm), almost plantlike animal that lives in warm oceans (13-16°C). The solid material we know as coral is the colony in which these tiny animals live. Coral is often branched and treelike.

Japanese coral is pink, white, and red. Hawaii produces black coral. Black and blue corals also come from the coast off Cameroon. The best red coral comes from the Mediterranean. The darkest color is called *oxblood* and the light pink variety, *angel skin.* Some black coral is composed of conchiolin, a horny organic material, which looks like coral but is much tougher and less brittle. Large amounts of white, pink, mottled, and oxblood coral from the South China Sea are cut in China and Taiwan.

Akori coral from Cameroon was highly prized before the eighteenth century. Similar coral, in shades of red, pink, violet and yellow-orange, was found along the South African coast in 1978 and marketed as *African Star Coral.* The natural coral is nonluminiscent, but addition of dye produces a bright scarlet fluorescence in LW. The African coral is stabilized, bleached, and dyed before marketing.

Name: Latin *corallium,* from the Greek *korallion.*

CORDIERITE Gem names: Iolite; Water Sapphire. *Dimorph of* Indialite.

Formula: $(Mg,Fe)_2 Al_4Si_5O_{18}$.

Crystallography: Orthorhombic. Crystals prismatic with rectangular cross section; also massive, granular; may be pseudohexagonal. *Note:* Indialite is hexagonal.

Colors: Blue, bluish violet, smoky blue; rarely greenish, gray, yellowish, brown.

Luster: Vitreous.

Hardness: 7-7.5.

Density: 2.53-2.78. Most gems are 2.57-2.61 (higher with higher Fe content).

Cleavage: Distinct 1 direction. Fracture conchoidal. Brittle.

Optics: $\alpha = 1.522-1.558; \beta = 1.524-1.574; \gamma = 1.527-1.578$. (Sri Lanka: $\alpha = 1.530; \beta = 1.534; \gamma = 1.539$; birefringence $= 0.009$; S.G. $= 2.58$).
Biaxial (+), $2V = 65-104°$. Frequently optically (−).

Birefringence: 0.005-0.018.

Dispersion: 0.017.

Pleochroism: Intense and distinctive. Fe-rich crystals: α = colorless; γ = violet.
Mg-rich crystals: pale yellow to green/pale blue/violet, violet-blue.

Spectral: Iron spectrum. Weak bands at 6451, 5930, 5850, 5350, 4920, 4560, 4360, and 4260. Spectrum observed varies with direction of crystal.

Luminescence: None (quenched by Fe).

Inclusions: Crystals of apatite and zircon, the latter with pleochroic haloes, the outer edges of which are deep yellow. Frequently dustlike masses of tiny crystals. Also hematite plates in parallel orientation (from Sri Lanka) impart a red color, and gems are sometimes called *bloodshot iolite.*

Occurrence: In altered aluminous rocks; igneous rocks; alluvial gravels.
California; Idaho; Wyoming; South Dakota; New York; New Hampshire.

Great Slave Lake, Canada; Greenland; Scotland; England; Norway; Germany; Finland.
Connecticut: gemmy material that cuts up to 2 carats.
Madras, India: gem iolite in abundance.
Sri Lanka and Burma: gemmy material from the gem gravels.
Paraiba, Brazil: some gemmy material from *Virgolandia,* in nodules.
Babati, Tanzania: gem material.
Karasburg, Namibia: gem material.
Madagascar; Japan; Australia.

Stone Sizes: Iolites are frequently in the 1-10 carat range, dichroic with blue to violet color. Large clean stones free of inclusions are not common at all, but gems over 30 carats have been reported.
BM: worked crystal fragment of 177 grams.
NMC: 2.20, 3.93, 2.60 (Canadian localities).
PC: 17.
SI: 15.6, 9.4 (blue, Sri Lanka); 10.2 (indigo, Sri Lanka).

Comments: The crystal structure of cordierite has many similarities to that of beryl; indialite, the dimorph, in fact has the same structure as beryl. Iolite with hematite inclusions (bloodshot iolite) comes from Sri Lanka. The inclusions sometimes yield a gem showing a 4-rayed star (quite rare). The blue color of iolite along one optical direction strongly resembles sapphire, and such gems, correctly oriented in settings, are often confused with sapphires. Iolite is not a very rare material, but stones that are completely clean over 10 carats are quite uncommon, and clean 15-20 carat gems are worthy of museum display.

Name: After Mr. Cordier, a French geologist who first studied its crystals. *Iolite* is from Greek *ios (violet)* and *lithos (stone).*

CORUNDUM   (= Ruby, Sapphire)

Formula: Al_2O_3 + Fe,Ti,Cr.

Crystallography: Hexagonal (trigonal). Crystals common, often barrel-shaped, prisms with flat ends, sometimes bipyramidal; also massive, granular, in rolled pebbles.

Colors: Pinkish red, medium to dark red varieties are called *ruby.* All other colors are called *sapphire,* including colorless, white, gray, blue, blue-green, green, violet, purple, orange, yellow, yellow-green, brown, golden amber, peachy pink, pink, and black.

Luster: Vitreous to adamantine.

Hardness: 9.

Density: 3.99-4.1; usually near 4.0.

Cleavage: None. Fracture conchoidal; frequent parting. Slightly brittle, usually tough.

Optics: $o = 1.757\text{-}1.770$; $e = 1.765\text{-}1.779$ (usually 1.760, 1.768).
Uniaxial (−).
See table.

Birefringence: 0.008-0.009.

Dispersion: 0.018 (low).

Pleochroism: Very pronounced.
Ruby: strong purplish red/orangy red.
Blue sapphire: strong violet-blue/blue-green.
Green sapphire: intense green/yellow-green.
Orange sapphire: yellow-brown or orange/colorless.
Yellow sapphire: medium yellow/pale yellow.
Purple sapphire: violet/orange.
Brownish orange sapphire: brownish orange/greenish.
Padparadscha: orange-yellow/yellowish orange.

Luminescence: The luminescence of corundum is intense and distinctive in identification.
Ruby: Burma stones fluoresce intensely, red, in SW, LW, and X-rays. Red fluorescence is, however, *not* diagnostic of country of origin or natural origin. Thai ruby fluoresces weak red in LW, weak or none in SW. Sri Lankan ruby fluoresces strong orange-red in LW, pink (moderate) in SW.
Sapphire: Blue stones give no reaction, except some blue Thai gems, which fluoresce weak greenish white in SW. Sri Lankan blue sapphire may fluoresce red to orange in LW, light blue in SW. Green gems are inert. Sri Lankan yellow sapphire fluoresces a distinctive apricot color in LW and X-rays, and weak yellow-orange in SW. The fluorescence in LW is proportional to depth of color of gem.
Pink sapphire: Strong orange-red in LW, weaker color in SW.
Violet or alexandritelike sapphire: strong red in LW, weak light red in SW.
Colorless: moderate light red-orange in LW.
Orange: strong orange-red in LW.
Some sapphires from Sri Lanka, Montana, and Kashmir glow dull red or yellow-orange in X-rays.

Spectral: The spectrum of ruby and sapphire can be used diagnostically.
Ruby: A distinctive spectrum; a strong red doublet at 6942/6928 is notable, and this may reverse and become fluorescent. Weaker lines at 6680 and 6592. Broad absorption of yellow, green, and violet. Additional lines seen at 4765, 4750, and, 4685. (The reversible fluorescent doublet is a sensitive test for the presence of chromium in a corundum. Even mauve and purple sapphires have a trace of Cr and show these lines.)
Sapphire: The ferric iron spectrum dominates these stones. In green and blue-green gems, rich in iron, there are lines at 4710, 4600, and 4500 in the blue-green region. Also lines at 4500 and 4600 may seem to merge and

become a broad band. The three bands described are generally known as the 4500 complex and are very distinctive in sapphires. Some blue Sri Lanka sapphires also show a 6935 red fluorescent line and the 4500 line is very weak in these gems. Intermediate sapphire colors are a mixture of the various spectra discussed.

Occurrence: Corundum is a mineral of metamorphosed crystalline limestones and dolomites, as well as other metamorphic rock types such as gneiss and schist; also in igneous rocks such as granite and nepheline syenite. Gem corundums are often found in placer deposits. Non-gem corundum is abundant throughout the world, but gem material is more restricted in occurrence.

Burma: Ruby historically comes from the Mogok stone tract. The history of the mines here is long, complex, and turbulent. Gems occur in a gravel layer called *byon* at a depth of 20 to 100 feet and are recovered by washing and screening with broad screens and then hand-picking encouraging-looking pebbles. Corundum originates in metamorphic marbles that have largely weathered away. This is the source of the world's finest rubies.

Thailand: The areas of major importance here are Chantabun and Battambang. The corundum deposits have only been worked in a major way in modern times. Gems are found in a sandy layer within 6 to 20 feet of the surface and are recovered by washing. Thai rubies are important on the current market because of the scarcity of Burmese gems.

Cambodia: Pailin in Cambodia is a source of some of the world's finest sapphires, but the country is not significant as a ruby producer.

Kashmir: Fine sapphires occur in northern India in the NW Himalayas at an elevation of nearly 15,000 feet. The deposit is snowed under most of the year. Gems occur in a pegmatite and in the valley below, in surface debris. Kashmir sapphires have a cloudiness due to inclusions and an extremely good blue color, making them greatly desired, but they are extremely scarce.

Pakistan: Ruby and spinel of fine quality occur in the

Characteristics of Ruby and Sapphire from Various Localities

Locality	Variety	Color	e	o	Birefrin-gence	S.G.	Comments
Australia	Sapphire	light blue	1.761	1.769	0.008	4.02	
		dark blue	1.763	1.772	0.009	3.99	
		green	1.763	1.772	0.009	4.00	
		yellow	1.765	1.774	0.009	3.97	
		yellow-green	1.767	1.775	0.008	3.99	
		golden yellow	1.763	1.772	0.008	4.01	
Brazil							
Jauru, Matto Grosso	Sapphire	dark blue	1.762	1.770	0.008	3.95–4.05	
Burma	Ruby	finest red	1.760–1.769	1.768–1.778	0.008–0.009	3.996	
	Sapphire	dark blue	1.762	1.770	0.008	4.00	
India							
Kashmir	Sapphire	fine blue	1.762	1.770	0.008	3.99	
Colombia	Sapphire	blue, violet	1.762	1.770	0.008	3.99–4.02	
Japan	Ruby	purplish-red to pink	1.761	1.769	0.008	3.89	
Malawi	Sapphire	various	1.760–1.761	1.770	0.009	—	
	Ruby	red	1.762–1.763	1.771–1.772	0.009	—	
Nepal (Taplejung district)	Ruby	red	1.760	1.768	0.008	3.98	
Pakistan Hunza Valley	Ruby	red	1.762	1.770	0.008	3.99	
Sri Lanka	Ruby	red	1.761–1.763	1.769–1.772	0.008	3.99–4.00	
	Sapphire	blue	1.757–1.760	1.765–1.768	0.008	4.00	
		yellow	1.760–1.761	1.768–1.769	0.008	3.99–4.01	
		green	1.765–1.770	1.773–1.779	0.008–0.009	4.00–4.01	
Tanzania	Ruby	red	1.764	1.772	0.008	3.99	
Longido	Sapphire	orange	1.760–1.763	1.768–1.772	0.008–0.009	3.99	
Umba River Valley	Sapphire	red-brown	1.763–1.765	1.771–1.773	0.008	3.99–4.06	
Thailand	Ruby	red	1.760–1.764	1.768–1.772	0.008	4.01	
	Ruby	dark red	1.768	1.776	0.008	4.00	
Yugoslavia Prilip	Ruby	red	—	~1.765	—	3.80–3.98	

Note: Colorless: $e = 1.759–1.761$; $o = 1.768–1.769$; blue and green: $e = 1.762–1.770$; $o = 1.770–1.779$. Among sapphires the green gems, more iron-rich, have higher indices.

Hunza Valley on the Pakistan side of the Kashmir Valley. The color is comparable to Burma ruby but the material is heavily flawed.

Sri Lanka: Sri Lanka is a source of many colors of sapphire, as well as ruby and star gems. Gems occur here in a gravel layer known as *illam* at a depth of up to 50 feet. The material is washed and screened, and gems are recovered by hand-picking. Sri Lanka ruby is not as good as Burma material, and the sapphires are often pale in color but can be very large.

Australia: Anakie, Queensland, is a source of sapphire in blue, green, and yellow shades, as well as some ruby. All are in alluvial deposits; some fine green gems are known, as well as an occasional excellent blue gem. Other occurrences are noted in New South Wales, especially the Inverell district (often referred to as the New England fields). Victoria is a location for green sapphire. Ruby has been found in the Harts Range, Northern Territory.

Montana: Yogo Gulch is a well-known locality for fine blue sapphire of very good color that occurs in igneous dikes. The crystals are very flattened and waferlike, so it is difficult to cut large, full-cut gems from them. Crystals occur in many different colors and are usually quite small, but the blue stones are extremely fine. This material is often zoned and may have a curious metalliclike luster. Ruby is uncommon here.

North Carolina: At Cowee Creek, in Macon County, small rubies and sapphires are found in stream gravels and soil. The quality is usually poor, but an occasional fine, small ruby is found.

Namibia: At Namaqualand opaque ruby is found that is suitable for cabochons.

Colombia: Blue and violet sapphires, many showing a distinct color change, are being mined near Mercaderes, Cauca, Colombia, probably originating in alkalic basalts. Crystals are prismatic and rounded, up to 3 cm in size. Colors are typically blue, green-brown, and violetish, but some yellow, pink, and red crystals have also been found. The blues are somewhat pale; some asteriated material also exists. The stones are rich in iron and poor in titanium. Metallic rutile crystal inclusions are typical.

Japan: Transparent crystals to 5 cm in amphibole-zoisite rock on *Mt. Gongen, Hodono Valley, Ehime Prefecture.*

Scotland: Blue sapphire crystals (cuttable) up to about 45 mm in diameter have been found at *Loch Roag, Isle of Lewis, Outer Hebrides.* Colors are variable, sector zoning observed. Paragenesis similar to that of Pailin, Cambodia. Cut stones are small (maximum 2-3 carats).

Tanzania: Large ruby of fine color and quality is found in green, massive chromiferous zoisite. The crystals are usually opaque, and the rock as a whole is cut as a decorative material, but occasionally some small areas of this ruby are transparent enough to facet. Many colors of sapphire are found in the vicinity of Morogoro, Tanga Province, along with some ruby. The Umba River Valley is a source of fine sapphires in a wide range of colors.

Zimbabwe: Sapphires of various colors are found, often zoned with a creamy-white core and blue outer zone, or vice versa. The crystals are well formed and usually up to 3 inches in diameter. At the Baruta Mine, in Northeast Zimbabwe a deep blue crystal of 3100 carats was found. Zimbabwe is also a source of black star sapphire. Sapphires from here are not well known on the market.

Malawi: Sapphires were found about 1958 at Chimwadzulu Hill.

Kenya: Excellent ruby is known from a small ruby mine. The ruby is pinkish but of fine color and is usually in small sizes.

Afghanistan: Ruby of fine color has come from Jagdalek, near Kabul. This is an ancient source of many of the fine stones of ancient times.

India: Mysore produces poor quality rubies but a significant amount of star ruby. Some of the stones from this area are of excellent quality but are not common.

Brazil: The Matto Grosso area has produced sapphires. Gem corundum is occasionally found in *Norway; Finland; Greenland; USSR; Czechoslovakia; Pakistan; Nepal.*

Inclusions: In general, Burmese, Thai, and Australian blue sapphires contain crystals of plagioclase feldspars, orthoclase, niobite, columbite, calcite, monazite, zircon, apatite, fergusonite, and thorite. Tanzanian sapphires contain crystals of chlorapatite, pyrite, magnetite, biotite, graphite, phlogopite, zircon, and spinel.

Brazil (Jauru, Matto Grosso): rounded gas-filled discs that resemble bubbles.

Burma (Mogok): short rutile needles at 60° angles; silk consisting of hollow tubes plus crystals of rutile, spinel, calcite, mica, garnet; zircon crystals with haloes; color swirls known as *treacle.*

Thailand: feathers = canals and tubelike liquid inclusions; flat, brownish cavities; twin planes; crystals of niobite, almandine, apatite, pyrrhotite; plagioclase crystals in sapphires. Rutile is absent.

Sri Lanka: long rutile needles; healing cracks; zircon crystals with haloes; flakes of biotite and phlogopite mica; feathers with irregular liquid hoses inside; color zoning is frequent; crystals of spinel, graphite, ilmenite, apatite.

Pakistan (Hunza Valley): phlogopite; chlorite; monazite; spinel; rutile; magnetite; pyrite, calcite.

Cambodia (Pailin): specks of uranian pyrochlore (ruby red color, very small).

Kashmir: yellow and brown feathers and thin films; liquid-filled canals; veil-like lines at 60° and 120°; cloudy haziness; negative crystals, flat films; rods and tubes.

Tanzania (Umba River Valley): apatite; graphite; pyrrhotite.

Tanzania (Longido): pargasite, spinel, zoisite.

Australia: Discoloration and twin lamellae; rutile crystals; liquid-filled feathers, flat cavities; color zoning is frequent.

Nepal: Undulating veils, strong color zoning, prismatic crystals, margarite.

Malawi (Chimwadzulu Hill): fine tubes; small black crystals and short rods; healed fissures; color zoning.

Stone Sizes: Sapphires, in general, reach a far greater size than do rubies. A ruby of 30 carats is a great rarity, whereas sapphires in museum collections weighing hundreds of carats are not uncommon. The largest rubies come from the chrome-zoisite matrix in Tanzania, but these are not really of gem quality. Fine gem rubies of large size occur in the Sri Lankan gravels, with smaller ones from Burma and Thailand. Enormous sapphires of fine color and transparency have been found in the gem gravels of Sri Lanka and Burma, but most are from Sri Lanka. A 1400-gram ruby was found in Yugoslavia (Prilip) but was not gemmy. Malawi material reaches a size of about 12 carats (sapphire). Large sapphires have been found in Australia; Montana sapphires over 1 carat are very rare, but the blue ones are magnificent in this size range. In general, a fine blue sapphire over 5-10 carats is very rare, as is a fine ruby over 3-4 carats on the current market.

Ruby:

Crown Jewels of England: Edwardes Ruby, 167 carats.
Cathedrale St.-Guy, Prague: 250 carats.
Narodni Museum, Prague: 27.11 (Burma).
AMNH: 100 (de Long star ruby).
BM: ruby crystal of 690 grams (Burma).
PC:
Historical rubies include a 400 carat Burmese rough that yielded 70 and 45 carat gems. A rough of 304 carats was found about 1890. Also famous are the Chhatrapati Manick and the 43-carat Peace Ruby.
Iranian Crown Jewels: fine buckle of 84 Burma ruby cabs, up to 11 carat size.
SI: 138.7 Rosser Reeves star ruby (red, Sri Lanka); 50.3 (violet-red star ruby, Sri Lanka); 33.8 (red star, Sri Lanka).
LA: Burma crystal 196.1 carats.

Sapphire:

SI: 423 (blue Sri Lanka, "Logan sapphire"); 330 (blue star, Burma, "star of Asia"); 316 (blue, Sri Lanka, "Star of Artaban"); 98.6 (deep blue, "Bismarck sapphire"); 92.6 (yellow, Burma); 67 (black star, Thailand); 62 (black star, Australia); 42.2 (purple, Sri Lanka); 35.4 (yellow-brown, Sri Lanka); 31 (orange, Sri Lanka); 25.3 (colorless, Sri Lanka); 19.9 (pink, Sri Lanka); 16.8 (green, Burma).
PC: Black Star of Queensland, oval, found in 1948, 733 carats, world's largest black star. A yellow crystal of 217.5 carats was found in Queensland in 1946.

Natural History Museum, Paris: le Raspoli, 135 carat brown, lozenge-shaped rough, clean.
Tested by GIA: 5600 carat sapphire cabochon; also Mysore (India) ruby cab of 1795 carats; Montana blue sapphire, cushion-cut, 12.54 carats, believed largest stone from this locality.
Diamond Fund, Moscow: 258.8 (blue), fine, lively gem.
ROM: 179.4 (golden yellow, Sri Lanka); 28.6 (padparadscha, Sri Lanka); 43.95 (greenish yellow, Sri Lanka); 193.3 (blue star sapphire).
British mission to Burma, in 1929, saw 951 carat sapphire, which may be the largest ever found there.
AMNH: 536 (blue, "Star of India"); 116 (blue, "Midnight Star"); 100 (yellow, Sri Lanka); 100 (padparadscha, very fine, Sri Lanka); 163 (blue, Sri Lanka); 34 (violet, Thailand).
Iranian Crown Jewels: Hollow rectangular cabochon of 191.6 carats; oval, yellow gem of 119 carats. Also fine Kashmir blue oval, nearly clean, ~75 carats.

Comments: Ruby is the most valuable of all gemstones, and sapphire is one of the most popular. Despite the enormous size of these gems as seen in museum and Royal collections, corundums available on the market are usually of more modest size. A 3-4 carat ruby, if of fine quality, is a rare and very expensive gem today. Sapphires of good blue color over 5 carats, if clean, are similarly rare and also valuable. There is an abundance of good quality small sapphires but not of rubies.

Star corundum is created by the inclusion of rutile needles within the host corundum crystal. The rutile needles orient themselves according to the hexagonal symmetry of the corundum, and reflections from these needles provide a chatoyancy. When such material is cut into a cabochon the sheen is concentrated along the top of the stone into three white lines crossing at 120° angles, creating a six-rayed star. Very rarely there are two distinct sets of needles oriented according to the first and second order prisms of the corundum (30° apart), resulting in a strong, 12-rayed star.

Next to diamond, corundum is the hardest mineral known and is very compact and dense, with no cleavage. As a result, corundum is one of the best of all jewelry stones, especially star corundum, which is tough as well as scratch-resistant. Faceted gems are slightly brittle and can be chipped, though much less easily than other gems. Very few ruby deposits are known that can be actively worked, which creates ever greater strain on ruby supply in the marketplace. Many more sapphire deposits are in operation, so the situation here is not as critical.

Name: *Corundum* is from the Sanskrit word *kurivinda.* *Ruby* and *sapphire* come from the Latin words meaning *red* and *blue,* respectively. *Padparadscha* is a Sinhalese word meaning *lotus blossom.*

COVELLITE

Formula: CuS.

Crystallography: Hexagonal. Crystals are tabular; also massive and cleavages.

Colors: Light to dark indigo blue; purplish; commonly iridescent, yellow and red.

Streak: Shining gray-black.

Luster: Submetallic to resinous; opaque, except in thin slivers.

Hardness: 1.5-2.

Density: 4.68.

Cleavage: Perfect and easy 1 direction. Facture uneven. Brittle. Thin sheets flexible.

Optics: $o = 1.45$.
Uniaxial (+).

Pleochroism: Strong, but visible only in very thin sheets.

Luminescence: None.

Occurrence: Secondary enrichment zones of copper mines.
Butte, Montana; Wyoming; South Dakota; Colorado; Utah; California; Alaska.
Sardinia, Italy; Argentina; New Zealand; Philippines; Germany; Australia; Yugoslavia.

Stone Sizes: Cabochons are generally cut from massive or foliated material. The stones can be very large, up to several inches long.

Comments: Covellite is cut strictly as a collector curiosity. Cut gems have no great value, but the blue or iridescent colors can be very attractive. Covellite is much too soft to wear and difficult to cut—it can be scratched with a fingernail!

Name: After N. Covelli who discovered the mineral on Mt. Vesuvius, Italy.

CREEDITE

Formula: $Ca_3Al_2(SO_4)(F,OH)_{10} \cdot 2H_2O$.

Crystallography: Monoclinic. Crystals short, prismatic; also radial clusters.

Colors: Colorless, white, rose to lilac or purple.

Luster: Vitreous.

Hardness: 4.

Density: 2.71-2.73.

Cleavage: Perfect 1 direction. Fracture conchoidal. Brittle.

Optics: $\alpha = 1.461; \beta = 1.478; \gamma = 1.485$.
Biaxial (−), $2V = 64°$.

Birefringence: 0.024.

Dispersion: Moderate.

Spectral: Not diagnostic.

Luminescence: Medium white to cream color (SW); bright white to cream (LW).

Occurrence:
Darwin, California; Granite, Nevada.
Colquiri, Bolivia.
Creede, Colorado: in cavities in rock with fluorite and barite.
Wagon Wheel Gap, Colorado: in a fluorite-barite mine.
Santa Eulalia, Chihuahua, Mexico: in crystals up to 1 inch long, gemmy.

Stone Sizes: Faceted gems very small, usually less than 1-2 carats.
PC: 0.96 (purple, Chihuahua).

Comments: Creedite is one of the very rare minerals known to collectors. It may well be that less than a dozen creedite gems have ever been cut. The mineral itself is rare, cuttable crystals even more so. These would be colorless or purple and from the Mexican occurrence. The hardness is too low for wear—strictly a collector gem.

Name: Occurrence in the Creede Quadrangle, Colorado.

CRISTOBALITE   See: Quartz.

CROCOITE

Formula: $PbCrO_4$.

Crystallography: Monoclinic. Crystals prismatic, sometimes hollow.

Colors: Red-orange, cherry red, orange, yellowish.

Streak: Orange-yellow.

Luster: Adamantine to vitreous.

Hardness: 2.5-3.

Density: 5.9-6.1.

Cleavage: Indistinct. Brittle.

Optics: $\alpha = 2.29\text{-}2.31; \beta = 2.36; \gamma = 2.66$.
Biaxial (+), $2V = 57°$.

Birefringence: 0.270.

Dispersion: Strong.

Pleochroism: Orange-red to blood red.

Spectral: Distinct band at 5550 but seen only in thin fragments. Transmits mainly in the yellow-red region of the spectrum.

Luminescence: Weak reddish to dark brown (SW); weaker effect in LW.

Occurrence: Secondary mineral in oxidized zones of lead deposits.
Dundas, Tasmania: best crystals found in the world, some gemmy; large clusters.
Beresov District, USSR: red crystals.
Tiger, Arizona: very tiny crystals.
California; Minas Gerais, Brazil.

Stone Sizes: Gems can be up to about 10 carats, but these are usually not transparent. Clean stones up to 1-2 carats are available in deep red-orange color from Tasmania.
DG: 14.5 (orange, Tasmania).
SI: 5.7 (orange-red, Tasmania).

Comments: Crocoite is one of the loveliest of all collector stones. It's too soft and brittle for wear, but it is quite a rare mineral and relatively few stones have been cut. The dispersion is high but completely masked by the intense body color.

Name: From the Greek *krokos,* meaning *saffron,* in allusion to the color.

CRYOLITE

Formula: Na_3AlF_6.

Crystallography: Monoclinic. Crystals cuboidal and prismatic; usually massive.

Colors: Colorless, white, brownish, reddish; rarely gray to black.

Luster: Vitreous to greasy.

Hardness: 2.5.

Density: 2.97.

Cleavage: None. Fracture uneven. Brittle.

Optics: $\alpha = 1.338$; $\beta = 1.338$; $\gamma = 1.339$.
Biaxial (+), $2V = 43°$.

Birefringence: 0.001; almost isotropic.

Dispersion: 0.024 (approximately).

Pleochroism: None.

Spectral: Not diagnostic.

Luminescence: None observed.

Occurrence: Occurs in alkalic rocks at *Ivigtut, Green-land.*
Also *Spain; USSR; Colorado* (small amounts).

Stone Sizes: Large cabochons could be cut from the abundant material in Greenland. Facetable material is quite rare, however, and only tiny gems can be obtained.

Comments: Cut cryolite is somewhat translucent, and has a "sleepy" look. The cuttable material has a very low birefringence, is colorless, and very soft—not exactly an exciting-looking gem. However, there are very few cut stones in existence because of the extreme scarcity of suitable rough. In addition, cryolite is only found abundantly at one locality (Ivigtut).

Name: From the Greek *kryos (frost)* and *lithos (stone),* hence *ice-stone,* in allusion to its appearance.

CRYSTAL   See: Quartz.

CUPRITE

Formula: Cu_2O.

Crystallography: Isometric. Crystals, cubes, and octahedra, or combinations; also needlelike, in densely packed mats called *chalcotrichite* with no gem significance.

Colors: Brownish red, red, purplish red, nearly black.

Streak: Brownish red.

Luster: Adamantine to submetallic; earthy.

Hardness: 3.5-4.

Density: 6.14; Namibia = 6.0-6.07.

Cleavage: Poor. Fracture conchoidal to uneven. Brittle.

Optics: $N = 2.848$.

Pleochroism: Sometimes anomalously pleochroic.

Luminescence: None.

Occurrence: Secondary mineral in copper deposits. Usually microscopic crystals.
Arizona; New Mexico; Pennsylvania; Colorado; Utah; Idaho.
Mexico; Bolivia; Chile; France; USSR; Zaire; Japan; other locations.
Onganja, Namibia: unique occurrence, with crystals up to more than 6 inches across, blood red and transparent; often coated with green malachite.

Stone Size: Largest mass of cuttable cuprite (*PC*) is completely transparent and weighs 2 kg. Before the amazing Onganja discovery, the largest stones were less than 1 carat, as only tiny crystals had ever been found. Onganja stones have been cut up to 300 carats, are flawless, and potentially could be much larger.
SI: 203.75 (octagon, Namibia); 172, 125.5, 110 (red, Namibia).
ROM: 66.34 (oval, Namibia).
PC: 299.5 (oval, Namibia).
DG: 48.6 (red, Namibia).

Comments: Cuprite is one of the rarest of all gems. For all practical purposes, cuttable material comes from only one locality. Only good crystals or pieces of crystals are cuttable, however, as other material from this mine is opaque. Mineral collectors do not wish to see their fine crystals cut, limiting the supply of available faceting material. Cut gems have a metallic appearance and magnificent deep red color. There are unwearable, but among the most beautiful of all gems and someday may be extremely rare in the marketplace.

Name: From the Latin *cuprum (copper),* in allusion to the composition.

CYPRINE   See: Idocrase.

D

DANBURITE

Formula: $CaB_2Si_2O_8$.

Crystallography: Orthorhombic. Crystals prismatic with wedge-shaped terminations, like topaz.

Colors: Colorless, white, pink, light to dark yellow, yellowish brown, brown.

Luster: Vitreous to greasy.

Hardness: 7.

Density: 2.97-3.03 usually 3.00.

Cleavage: Indistinct. Fracture subconchoidal to uneven. Brittle.

Optics: $\alpha = 1.630$-1.633; $\beta = 1.633$-1.637; $\gamma = 1.636$-1.641. Biaxial (−); $2V = 88°$ in red to green light; optically (+) at lower wavelengths.

Birefringence: 0.006-0.008.

Dispersion: 0.017.

Pleochroism: None.

Spectral: Sometimes shows rare earth spectrum, so-called didymium lines.

Luminescence: Sky blue to bright blue-green in LW. Also thermoluminescent (red).

Occurrence: In dolomites; in carbonate veins in granitic rocks.
Danbury, Connecticut: type locality.
Charcas, San Luis Potosi, Mexico: colorless, yellow, light pink (gemmy).
Mogok, Burma: yellow and colorless, sometimes large crystals (rolled pebbles).
Obira, Bungo, Kyushu, Japan: colorless crystals, sometimes gemmy.

Madagascar: yellow crystals at Mt. Bity, often gemmy.
USSR: colorless, gemmy material.

Stone Sizes: Danburite is not a very rare mineral, but it is scarce in large facetable pieces. The usual range is 1-5 carats, especially for colorless material from Mexico. The yellow Burmese gems are rare today, especially in the 7-10 carat range.
BM: Burma gem, step-cut, flawless, wine-yellow color, 138.61 carats.
PC: 20 (Burma, peach color); 22.76 (yellow, Madagascar); 37 (USSR).
SI: 18.4 (yellow, Burma) 12.4, 10.5 (colorless, Mexico); 7.9 (colorless, Japan).
LA: 115 (brownish emerald cut, Madagascar).
ROM: 12.72 (colorless step cut, USSR).

Comments: Danburite is a hard and durable stone with poor cleavage—an excellent choice for wear. The dispersion is quite low, so gems have no fire but are very bright when properly cut. Large ones are very rare, but sufficient material exists to allow almost every collector to have a colorless gem.

Name: After the type locality, Danbury, Connecticut.

DATOLITE

Formula: $CaBSiO_4(OH)$.

Crystallography: Monoclinic. Crystals prismatic or stubby; massive, granular.

Colors: Colorless, white, pale yellow, green, also pink, reddish, and brownish due to impurities; massive varieties can be white to orange-brown or pink.

Luster: Vitreous.

Hardness: 5-5.5.

Density: 2.8-3.0.

Cleavage: None; fracture uneven to conchoidal; brittle.

Optics: $\alpha = 1.622$-1.626; $\beta = 1.649$-1.658; $\gamma = 1.666$-1.670. Biaxial (−), $2V = 75°$.

Birefringence: 0.044-0.047.

Dispersion: 0.016.

Pleochroism: None.

Spectral: Not diagnostic.

Luminescence: Blue in SW (attributed to the presence of Eu).

Occurrence: A secondary mineral in basic igneous rocks and traprocks.
Springfield, Massachusetts; Lane's Quarry, Westfield, Massachusetts; Paterson, New Jersey (and other localities in the state).
Faraday Mine, Ontario, Canada: colorless material.
Tyrol, Austria; Habach, Austria; Cornwall, England.
Lake Superior Copper district, Michigan: nodules of massive datolite.

Stone Sizes: Brown or white massive material will cut cabochons up to several ounces. The colors in the Michigan material are due to copper staining. Cabochons are seldom seen in collections—collectors prefer to polish the faces of sliced-open nodules. These can be up to about 6 inches in diameter. The best faceting material comes from Massachusetts, with fine pale green material from New Jersey. The largest gems cut from this are in the 5-carat range. Larger stones are very rare.
SI: 5.4 and 5.0 (colorless, Massachusetts).
HU: 13.21 (flawless triangle, Massachusetts).
NMC: 0.45 (colorless, Canada).

Comments: Datolite is a rather soft gemstone if wear is considered. The nodules come in very attractive colors. Faceted stones are extremely brilliant, though their dispersion (fire) is low. Most faceted gems are colorless, pale yellowish or pale green.

Name: From a Greek word meaning *to divide* because of the granular nature of the massive variety.

DEMANTOID See: Garnet.

DIAMOND

Diamond is the best known gemstone. Its history of use and great value extends thousands of years into the past. Diamond has been the center of intrigue, warfare, romance, and tradition on a scale unequaled by any other gem.

The history and lore of diamonds, diamond technology, and cutting are subjects so vast in themselves that they are far beyond the scope of this book. Several excellent books on these topics are listed in the Bibliography on page 237.

Formula: C (carbon).
Essentially pure with only minor traces of impurities.

Crystallography: Isometric. Crystals sometimes sharp octahedra, dodecahedra, and combinations with other forms. Crystals modified, often rounded and distinguished by the presence of triangular-shaped pits on octahedral faces (once believed to be due to etching, these "trigons" are currently believed to be a result of the growth process).

Colors: Colorless, gray, shades of yellow, brown, pink, green, orange, lavender, blue, black; rarely red.

Luster: Adamantine.

Hardness: 10. Diamond is the hardest natural substance and easily scratches any other mineral. The difference in hardness between diamond and corundum (9) is very much greater than that between any other two minerals on the Mohs scale.

Density: 3.515; Carbonado 2.9-3.5.

Cleavage: Perfect 1 direction (octahedral). Brittle. In spite of its great hardness, diamond can be split easily along octahedral planes. This feature is useful in cutting, since cleaving a large diamond saves weeks of laborious sawing. The cleavage also makes it possible for diamonds to be chipped in wear.

Optics: Isotropic, index very constant; $N = 2.417$.

Dispersion: 0.044. This high dispersion in a colorless diamond creates the "fire" that is the source of the diamond's attractiveness.

Pleochroism: None.

Spectral: The absorption spectra of various colored diamonds are quite distinctive and useful, especially in distinguishing irradiation-colored diamond from natural colored stones. The colored diamonds can be grouped into several series:
Cape Series: Colorless to yellow diamonds that fluoresce blue. Strong lines at 4155, 4785, 4650, 4520, 4350, and 4230. Most lines are hard to see.
Brown Series: Brown, green, and greenish yellow diamonds that fluoresce green. Strong line at 5040 plus weak lines at 5320 and 4980.
Yellow Series: Colorless, brownish yellow or yellow and yellow-fluorescing. This series includes the true "canary" yellow diamonds. No discrete spectrum but sometimes a weak line at 4155.
Type II-B Blue: No absorption spectrum.
Pink diamonds show the so-called "cape" absorption line at 4150 and a broad, diffuse band centered at 5500. The strength of this band correlates with the intensity of color of the diamond.

Luminescence: Many diamonds fluoresce blue to violet, with fluorescence sometimes in zones (often a result of twinning). The effect is sometimes strong enough to be visible in daylight. Yellow stones sometimes fluoresce yellow-green. Some pink diamonds from India fluoresce and phosphoresce orange. The famous Hope diamond, deep blue in color, phosphoresces deep red. Most fluorescence occurs in LW; the SW reaction is weaker and the same as LW. Many diamonds fluoresce bluish white in SW. Blue-fluorescing diamonds may phosphoresce yellow (an "afterglow" reaction). The various diamonds have been organized into types, with varying UV transparency.

Type I: Transparent to all wavelengths down to about 3000 Å; this type contains nitrogen and is further subdivided into Types Ia and Ib. Type Ia represents the majority of all diamond, and the nitrogen is in the form of platelets. About 0.1% of Type I diamonds are Type Ib, in which the nitrogen is dispersed throughout the crystal.

Type II: Transparent all the way to 2250 Å; this type contains aluminum. Type IIa does not phosphoresce in SW and contains little nitrogen. Type IIb has bluish phosphorescence in SW and is also electrically conductive. Nitrogen in these diamonds is absent or very scarce.

Inclusions: Diamond crystals frequently contain crystals of other minerals.

Olivine may look like bubbles (rounded crystals), present in single crystals or clusters, often on octahedral faces and aligned parallel to octahedral edges. These are pale green or colorless.

Garnet is present in single crystals or clusters; brown, orange, yellow, pink, violet-red, lilac, and purple colors have been observed. These are usually pyrope garnets and sometimes reach large size. They are seen frequently in South African diamonds.

Graphite is present as black inclusions.

Pyrrhotite, pyrite, pentlandite, ilmenite, and *rutile* (dark-colored ore minerals) may resemble graphite inclusions; these are typical of diamond from Ghana.

Diamond crystals are often seen as inclusions in other diamonds, usually in perfect crystal forms.

Chrome diopside is present as emerald-green, well-formed crystals. Also seen in South African diamonds is *chrome enstatite.*

Chrome spinel in octahedra, sometimes distorted, usually reddish-brown or black; these are commonly seen in Russian diamonds.

Ruby has also been observed in an eclogitic diamond.

Cloudlike inclusions are sometimes in the shape of a Maltese cross, and are diagnostic of diamonds from India.

Occurrence: Diamond is a mineral formed at very high temperatures and pressures, deep within the earth. Synthetic diamond is produced at pressures as high as 100,000 atmospheres (equivalent to 200 miles of rock!) and temperatures around 5000°C; these conditions may approximate those of natural diamond formation. Diamond formed at depth is apparently "exploded" to the surface in fissures that become circular near the surface and are known as "pipes." The mineralogy of the rocks in these pipes, known as *kimberlite,* is unusual and unique and reflects high pressure of formation. Diamond is found in kimberlites and also in alluvial deposits (streams, river channels, beaches, deltas, and former stream beds) derived from kimberlite weathering and erosion.

South Africa: Diamonds were first discovered on the shores of the Orange River. After several "rushes," abundant "diamond fever," and a turbulent period of changing ownership, nearly all the deposits were under control of De Beers Consolidated Mines, Ltd, by 1888. De Beers is now part of Anglo American, a huge conglomerate that also owns the rich gold mines of the Rand in South Africa. South African diamonds are among the world's most famous, and such mines as Premier, Jagersfontein, Bultfontein, Dutoitspan, and Wesselton are famous for their output. South Africa is still a world leader in diamond production, but large stones are becoming very scarce.

Other African countries: Diamonds are found in many parts of Africa. *Zimbabwe* is noted for alluvial deposits. The huge production of very fine stones from *Angola* has been interrupted by political problems. *Ghana* produces diamond from gravel beds, mostly industrial; some are gem quality. The *Ivory Coast* and *Republic of Guinea* produce alluvial diamonds. A large deposit is known in *Namibia* where the Orange River enters the Atlantic Ocean. Huge machines work enormous beach deposits in *Namaqualand,* and other spots along this coast. *Central African Republic* produces diamonds associated with gravel beds. Alluvial diamonds occur in *Zaire* and especially in *Sierra Leone.* The Sierra Leone diamonds are among the world's finest. They occur in river gravels, are often very large, and are of top gem quality. Occasional stones are found in *Tanzania;* John Williamson found a large pipe in 1935, and some fine diamond has been recovered from this deposit. Other African sources include *Lesotho* and *Botswana.*

India: The first major historical source of diamonds, and also the source of many of the largest and most famous gems (including the Hope diamond). Mines are in Golconda, Andhra Pradesh (Hyderabad), Kollur, and other localities. Indian diamonds are primarily alluvial, found in sandstones and conglomerates or gravel deposits.

Brazil: Produces a large quantity of diamond, but little of good gem quality. The Diamantina district was opened in 1725, and diamond also comes from Bahia, Minas Gerais, Matto Grosso, and other states. Diamond in Brazil occurs in a variety of rock types and also alluvial deposits. Most of the stones are small in size but an occasional large, fine gemstone is found. Bahia produces black microcrystalline diamond known as *carbonado*. The largest of these found weighed 3078 carats.

Borneo and *Indonesia:* Small alluvial deposits. Most stones are small (less than 1 carat). Diamonds from Borneo have been reported to be harder than those from other deposits.

Venezuela: A substantial alluvial production, mostly of small, yellowish crystals.

USSR: Russia is one of the leading world suppliers of diamonds. The country is rich in pipes (several hundred have been found), some of very large size (such as the famous "Mir" pipe). However, most Russian diamonds are very small, severely limiting the value of the production. A high percentage of crystals is of good color and transparency, and the production is substantial enough to be a major factor in the world diamond market. All the pipes are located in Siberia, where weather conditions make mining both difficult and expensive.

Australia: As long ago as 1972 it was realized that the geology of northwestern Australia was strikingly similar to that of South Africa's diamond region. A group called the Ashton Joint Venture Partners started to explore this region and found kimberlite pipes in 1976. A diamondiferous pipe was then found at Ellendale in 1977 and a rich field of alluvial diamonds at Smoke Creek in 1979. An immense pipe known as AK-1, south of Lake Argyle, is being developed; this pipe is complex with an elongated surface outcrop. AK-1, discovered in 1979, contains more than 100 million tons of kimberlite, much of it with an unusually high grade of 7 carats per ton. It was estimated that Smoky Creek plus AK-1 could add as much as 50% to the world's known diamond reserves. However, Argyle diamonds tend to be small and low in quality (5% gem, 40% low-grade gem, 55% industrial). South African diamond will therefore continue to dominate the world gemstone market. However, Australia (in carat production) is expected to become the world's largest diamond producer.

United States: The only significant diamond deposit in North America is at Murfreesboro, Arkansas. This is a very large pipe, which has never been systematically developed and might be extremely rich. It is on government-owned land and has been worked surficially only by tourists who pay a small fee for the privilege of digging. The largest crystal found here weighed 40.23 carats and was named the "Uncle Sam" diamond.

Alluvial diamonds have been found throughout the United States, presumably carried south by waters flowing from Canadian glaciers thousands of years ago. The Canadian source pipes have never been discovered, however. Large diamonds found in Virginia include the "Dewey" (1885, 23.75 carats) and the "Punch Jones" (34.46 carats).

Stone Sizes: The largest rough diamonds ever found include the Cullinan (3106 carats, white, South Africa, 1905); the Excelsior (995.2 carats, white, South Africa, 1893), the Star of Sierra Leone (968.8 carats, white, Sierra Leone, 1972), and the Great Mogul (787.5 carats, white, India, 1650). A fine yellowish octahedron of 616 carats is on display at the Mine Museum in Kimberley, South Africa, found in 1975.

The world's largest uncut diamond, an 890 carat "fancy intense golden yellow" is owned by the Zale Corp. The stone is African in origin, but from an undisclosed source. If cut, it could yield a finished stone of 600 carats, which would then become the world's largest polished diamond. The Zale diamond is the fourth largest rough ever found.

The largest cut stones include: Cullinan I (530.2, white, pear shape, in the British Crown Jewels), Cullinan II (317.4, white, cushion, British Crown Jewels), Great Mogul (280.0, white, dome-shape, location unknown), Nizam (277.0, white, table-cut, was in India in 1934), Jubilee (245.35, white, cushion, privately owned, Paris), and the Orloff 189.6, white, rose-cut, Russian Diamond Fund in the Kremlin).

Comments: Diamond is the most romanticized and heavily marketed of all gemstones. Nearly every jewelry establishment handles diamonds, even if it has no other gemstones in stock. The annual world production of diamonds is on the order of 10 tons. Of course, only a small percentage of this is gem quality, but diamond of very fine quality is nowhere near as scarce as equivalently high quality ruby or emerald.

Name: From the Greek word *adamas,* meaning the *hardest steel,* and hence the hardest gemstone.

DIASPORE   *Dimorph of* Boehmite.

Formula: AlO(OH) + Mn.

Crystallography: Orthorhombic; crystals are elongated plates, acicular needles; also massive, foliated.

Colors: Colorless, white, yellowish, pink, rose red to dark red (due to Mn), lilac, greenish, brownish.

Luster: Vitreous; pearly on cleavage.

Hardness: 6.5-7.

Density: 3.3-3.5; Turkish material 3.39.

Cleavage: Perfect 1 direction. Fracture conchoidal.

Optics: $\alpha = 1.702$; $\beta = 1.722$; $\gamma = 1.750$. Biaxial (+), 2V = 85°.

Birefringence: 0.048.

Pleochroism: Strong in manganiferous variety: violet-blue/pale green/rose to dark red.

Spectral: Not diagnostic; Turkish stones show broad bands at 4710, 4630, 4540, and a sharp line at 7010.

Luminescence: Dull pale yellow in SW (Chester, Massachusetts); Turkish stones fluoresce green in SW.

Occurrence: In metamorphosed limestones, chloritic schists, and altered igneous rocks. Also in bauxite deposits.
Mamaris, Yagatan, Mugla Province, Turkey: gemmy, pale-brown crystals of very large size.
Chester, Massachusetts: with corundum in emery deposit; some fragments cuttable.
Chester County, Pennsylvania: fine transparent crystals up to 2 inches long and ¼ inch thick, colorless to brown; some cuttable.
Hungary: good crystals.
Postmasburg district, South Africa: manganiferous variety.
Cornwall, England; Greenland; Norway; Sweden; France; Switzerland; Germany; Greece; USSR; Japan; China.

Stone Sizes: Diaspore crystals from Massachusetts were, when found, apparently suitable for cutting, and a few gems may have been cut from the Pennsylvania material. However, cut disapore was, at best, an extremely unlikely gemstone until the find of crystals in Turkey. This locality has produced the vast majority of cut diaspore now in existence. Moreover, the locality produced cuttable pieces enormously larger than had ever been known previously in the mineral.
PC: some of the larger Turkish stones include: 157.66 (brown, emerald-cut—world's largest); 26.97 (light brown, oval); 10.63 (light brown).

Comments: Diaspore is hard enough to make a durable jewelry stone, but the typical light brownish color is not easy to sell. Despite the large Turkish material, this is a *very* rare gemstone indeed.

Name: From the Greek *diaspeirein,* meaning *to scatter,* because it falls apart in the hot flame of a blowpipe.

DICKINSONITE

Formula: $H_2Na_6(Mn,Fe,Ca,Mg)_{14}(PO_4)_{12} \cdot H_2O$.

Crystallography: Monoclinic. Crystals tabular, pseudo-rhombohedral; foliated, micaceous, radiating.

Colors: Oil green, olive green, yellowish green, brownish green, brownish.

Luster: Vitreous; pearly on cleavage.

Hardness: 3.5-4.

Density: 3.38-3.41.

Cleavage: Perfect and easy, 1 direction. Fracture uneven.

Optics: $\alpha = 1.648\text{-}1.658$; $\beta = 1.655\text{-}1.662$; $\gamma = 1.662\text{-}1.671$.
Biaxial (+), $2V \sim 90°$.

Birefringence: 0.013-0.014.

Dispersion: Strong.

Pleochroism: Pale olive green to pale yellowish green.

Spectral: Not diagnostic.

Luminescence: None observed.

Occurrence: A secondary phosphate mineral in granite pegmatites.
Branchville, Connecticut; Portland, Connecticut; Poland, Maine.

Stone Sizes: Very tiny green gems, less than 1-2 carats, have been cut from Connecticut material.

Comments: This mineral is seldom even mentioned in the gem literature because it is so rare and has been so seldom cut. Faceted gems are practically nonexistent, and would be among the rarest of all cut stones.

Name: After the Rev. William Dickinson in recognition of his interest in the locality where first found.

DINOSAUR BONE   See: Quartz.

DIOPSIDE

Formula: $CaMgSi_2O_6$.
Complete series to $CaFeSi_2O_6 = Hedenbergite$
Intermediate members = *Salite, Ferrosalite*
Ferrosalite rich in Mn and Zn = *Jeffersonite*
Diopside rich in Mn = *Schefferite*
Diopside rich in Mn and Zn = *Zinc Schefferite* (variety)
Diopside rich in Cr = *Chrome Diopside* (variety)
Diopside color varieties include *baikalite, alalite* and *malacolite* (pale green) and *violane* (purple).

Crystallography: Monoclinic. Crystals often well formed, prismatic, stubby, also massive.

Colors: Colorless, white, gray, pale green, dark green, blackish green, brown, yellowish to reddish brown, bright green (Cr variety); rarely blue.
Schefferite is light to dark brown.
Hedenbergite always dark green, brownish green, or black.

Luster: Vitreous.

Hardness: 5.5-6.5.

Density: Usually 3.29; range 3.22-3.38 for diopside, higher if more Fe present.

Cleavage: Perfect 1 direction. Fracture uneven to conchoidal. Brittle.

	Diopside	Hendenbergite	Jeffersonite	Schefferite	Chrome Diopside
Optics					
α	1.664–1.695	1.716–1.726	1.713	1.676	1.668–1.674
β	1.672–1.701	1.723–1.730	1.722	1.683	1.680
γ	1.695–1.721	1.741–1.751	1.745	1.705	1.698–1.702
2V	50–60°	52–62°	74°	60°	55°
Density	3.22–3.38	3.50–3.56	3.55	3.39	3.17–3.32
Birefringence	0.024–0.031	0.025–0.029	0.032	0.031	0.028
Pleochroism	none	pale green/green-brown	dark/light brown	dark/light brown	yellow/green

Intermediate compositions have intermediate properties in the diopside-hedenbergite series; increasing iron content results in higher properties. The pleochroism of salite is: pale green/blue-green/yellow-green.

Spectral: Chrome diopside has lines at 5080, 5050, 4900, plus fuzzy bands at 6350, 6550, 6700 and a doublet at 6900.
Pale green diopside gives lines at 5050, 4930, and 4460.

Luminescence: Blue or cream white in SW, also orange-yellow; sometimes mauve in LW. May phosphoresce a peach color.

Occurrence: In Ca-rich metamorphic rocks; in kimberlite (Cr-diopside).
Burma: yellow faceted gems; also catseyes and pale green faceting material.
Madagascar: very dark green cutting material.
Sri Lanka: cuttable pebbles.
Ontario, Canada: green faceting material.
Quebec, Canada: red-brown material that cuts gems to 2 carats.
Ala, Piedmont, Italy: fine green diopside (*alalite* is local name).
St. Marcel, Piedmont, Italy: violet variety of diopside (*violane*).
Zillerthal, Austria: fine green crystals, some transparent.
Georgetown, California: green diopside. *Crestmore, California:* large crystals (non-gem).
DeKalb, New York: fine transparent green crystals up to several inches in length.
Slyudyanka, USSR: green crystals (*baikalite* or *malacolite*); and chrome diopside.
Outokumpu, Finland: fine deep green Cr-diopside.
Nammakal, India: star stones and catseyes, also dark green facetable material.
Franklin, New Jersey: jeffersonite, schefferite, and Zn-schefferite.
Långban, Sweden: jeffersonite, schefferite, and Zn-schefferite.
Kenya: chrome diopside.

Stone Sizes: New York material provides cutting rough of fine quality and large size. The Italian, Swiss, and Austrian diopsides are usually smaller but of fine color. Diopside from Madagascar is very dark green and less attractive, up to about 20 carats. Chrome diopsides are known up to about 10-15 carats. Most diopside localities provide material that cuts 2-10 carat gems.
AMNH: 38.0 (green, New York).
SI: 133.0 (black, star, India); 24.1 (black, catseye, India); 19.2 (green, Madagascar); 6.8 (yellow, Italy); 4.6 (yellow, Burma).

Comments: Violane has been used for beads and inlay—transparent material is always very tiny. The color of this material is deep violet or blue and is very rare. Catseye material cuts extremely sharp eyes, the best being from Burma. Faceted diopside is not extremely rare, but large (over 15 carats) clean stones are. Colors are usually dark, so a bright and attractive gem is most desirable. Hedenbergite and the intermediate varieties tend always to be opaque except in very thin splinters. Chrome diopside, quite rare in sizes over 3-4 carats, has become available in commercial quantities from the USSR. The color is excellent, with Cr content about 0.5% by weight.

Name: Greek words meaning *appearing double*.

DIOPTASE

Formula: $CuSiO_2(OH)_2$.

Crystallography: Hexagonal. Fine crystals are common in certain localities; stubby, elongated.

Colors: Rich emerald green, bluish green.

Streak: Pale blue-green.

Luster: Vitreous; greasy on fractures.

Hardness: 5.

Density: 3.28-3.35.

Cleavage: Perfect 1 direction. Fracture conchoidal to uneven. Brittle.

Optics: $o = 1.644$-1.658; $e = 1.697$-1.709.
Uniaxial (+).

Birefringence: 0.053.

Dispersion: 0.036.

Spectral: Broad band at about 5500; strong absorption of blue and violet.

Luminescence: None.

Occurrence: Oxidized zone of copper deposits.
Zaire; Chile; USSR.
Arizona: microscopic crystals.
Guchab and *Tsumeb, Namibia:* world's finest crystals, some transparent but mostly filled with cleavage planes and fractures. These crystals are a superb color, on matrix, and up to 2 inches long.

Stone Sizes: Crystals may be fairly large, but clean areas within such crystals are always very small, and stones are never larger than 1-2 carats. Cabochons up to about 15 carats are sometimes cut from translucent masses.

Comments: Dioptase is abundant in mineral collections throughout the world and is not considered a great rarity, but faceted gems are extremely rare due to a paucity of clean fragments. Clean stones over 1 carat are virtually nonexistent, and few collections have stones at all. Cabochons are blue-green, translucent, and quite attractive but are much too soft for wear.

Name: From Greek words meaning *to see through* because the cleavage directions can be determined just by looking into the crystals.

DOLOMITE

Formula: $CaMg(CO_3)_2$ + Fe, Mn, Zu, Pb, Co.
Note: $CaFe(CO_3)_2$ = Ankerite. $CaMn(CO_3)_2$ = Kutnahorite. There is a complete series from dolomite, through ferroan dolomite, to ankerite.

Crystallography: Hexagonal (R). Crystals rhomb-shaped, sometimes with curved faces; saddle-shaped; massive or granular; twinning common.

Colors: Colorless, white, gray, green, pale brown, pink (Mn present). Ankerite is tan to brown, and kutnahorite is pink. Dolomite may also be pink due to Co.

Luster: Vitreous to pearly.

Hardness: 3.5-4; varies with direction in crystal.

Density: 2.85, as high as 2.93; ankerite, 2.93-3.10.

Cleavage: Perfect 1 direction. Fracture subconchoidal. Brittle.

Optics:
dolomite: o = 1.679-1.703; e = 1.500-1.520.
Uniaxial (−).
ankerite: o = 1.690-1.750; e = 1.510-1.548.
Uniaxial (−).

Indices increase from dolomite values with increasing substitution of iron.

Birefringence: 0.179-0.185. (Ankerite, 0.182-0.202).

Spectral: Not diagnostic.

Luminescence: Orange, blue, pale green, creamy white, weak brown in SW. Orange, blue, pale green, creamy white in LW.

Occurrence: In sedimentary rocks; in Mg-rich igneous rocks that have been altered; geodes.
Quebec, Cananda; Mexico; Brazil; Germany; Austria; Switzerland.
Missouri, Oklahoma, Kansas: so-called Tri-State Mineral Region.
Keokuk, Iowa: in geodes.
New Mexico: transparent material, cuttable.
Eugua, Navarra, Spain: magnificent crystals and clusters, often large size, perfectly formed and completely transparent.
Pribram, Czechoslovakia: cobaltian dolomite (pink).
Czechoslovakia and Hungary: kutnahorite.
Ankerite is a mineral of veins and hydrothermal or low-temperature deposits.

Stone Sizes: Massive material is generally carved; often it is stained pretty colors and may be naturally color-banded. Faceted dolomite from New Mexico reaches a size of about 5 carats. Spanish material can provide stones over 100 carats.
PC: 18.38 (Spain).

Comments: Dolomite is a rarely seen gem with distinctive birefringence (as a carbonate) but is too soft and fragile for wear. Spanish crystals are widely sold to collectors so transparent material is fairly abundant.

Name: After Deodat Dolomieu, French engineer and mineralogist.

DOMEYKITE   See: Algodonite.

DRAVITE   See: Tourmaline.

DUMORTIERITE   See also: Holtite.

Formula: $Al_7O_3(BO_3)(SiO_4)_3$.

Crystallography: Orthorhombic. Crystals prismatic and very rare; usually massive, fibrous, granular.

Colors: Blue, violet, brown, pinkish, blue-green, greenish.

Luster: Vitreous to dull.

Hardness: 8-8.5; massive varieties 7.

Density: 3.26-3.41.

Cleavage: Good 1 direction, not observed in massive material; fracture splintery or uneven.

Optics: $\alpha = 1.686$; $\beta = 1.722$; $\gamma = 1.723$.
Brazil: $\alpha = 1.668$-1.673; $\beta = 1.682$-1.684; $\gamma = 1.685$-1.688.
SG = 3.31-3.35.
Uniaxial (−), $2V = 13$-$56°$.

Birefringence: 0.15-0.37.

Pleochroism: Black/brown/red-brown; also: blue-black/blue/colorless.

Luminescence: Blue (France) in SW; also blue-white to violet (California) in SW.

Spectral: Not diagnostic.

Occurrence: In aluminous metamorphic rocks; in pegmatites.
Pershing County, Nevada: violet gem material.
Arizona.

France; Madagascar; Brazil (Minas Gerais): facetable bluish-green material.
Sri Lanka: transparent, reddish-brown stones.

Stone Sizes: Massive blue and violet material occurs in pieces weighing several pounds. Only a small amount of facetable material has ever been discovered (Brazil, Sri Lanka), and these gems tend to be very small (under 1-2 carats). Only a few faceted dumortierites exist. Arizona dumortierite is actually a quartz-impregnated variety.

Comments: Dumortierite is a beautiful and very hard material, eminently suitable for jewelry. The cabochon material is the only generally known form, since faceted stones are so rare. Fibrous inclusions have been noted in the transparent Brazilian stones.

Name: After M. Eugene Dumortier, a paleontologist.

E

EILAT STONE See Chrysocolla.

EKANITE

Formula: $(Th,U)(Ca,Fe,Pb)_2Si_8O_{20}$.

Crystallography: Tetragonal. Crystals elongated parallel to long crystal axis; massive pebbles.

Colors: Green, dark brown, light brown, emerald green.

Luster: Vitreous.

Hardness: 5-6.5.

Density: 3.28-3.32.

Cleavage: None.

Optics: $o = 1.573$; $e = 1.572$.
Uniaxial ($-$). Gems usually $\simeq$ 1.590-1.596.

Birefringence: 0.001.

Spectral: May show lines at 6300 and 6580.

Luminescence: Not diagnostic.

Occurrence: Discovered in 1953 as waterworn, translucent green pebbles at *Eheliyagoda*, near *Ratnapura*, Sri Lanka. Occurs in the gem gravels. Some cut Sri Lankan stones have 4-rayed stars. *Mt. Ste. Hilaire, Quebec, Canada.*
Central Asia.

Stone Sizes: A stone was tested by the London Gem Labs in 1975: 43.8 carats, blackish color, S.G. = 3.288, R.I. = 1.595 (average); radioactive; 2 spectral lines seen. A 351 carat rough has also been reported.

Comments: Ekanite is metamict as a result of the U and Th content. The properties vary, depending on the degree of breakdown of the structure. Ekanite is one of the very rarest of all gems, and only a few are known. More un-doubtedly exist that have been sold as other Sri Lankan gems, but the total number of gems is a mere handful.

Name: After F. L. D. Ekanayake who first found it in a Sri Lankan gravel pit.

ELAEOLITE See: Nepheline.

ELBAITE See: Tourmaline.

EMERALD See: Beryl.

ENSTATITE *Orthopyroxene Group:* Bronzite; Hypersthene; Ferrohypersthene; Eulite; Orthoferrosilite.

Composition: This is a complex solid-solution series involving Fe and Mg silicates. The series extends from enstatite: $MgSiO_3$, through bronzite: $(Mg,Fe)SiO_3$, hypersthene$(Fe,Mg)SiO_3$, to orthoferrosilite: $FeSiO_3$. Like the plagioclase feldspars, the series is arbitrarily broken into six regions of composition (numbers refer to percentage of orthoferrosilite molecule in formula):

0	10	30	50	70	90	100
Enstatite	Bronzite	Hypersthene	Ferrohypersthene	Eulite	Orthoferrosilite	

Crystallography: Orthorhombic. Crystals are prismatic and not common for most members of the series. Twinning is common, visible as lamellae in crystals; often crystals have interleaved lamellae of ortho- and clino-pyroxenes.

Colors: *Enstatite* is colorless, gray, green, yellow, and brown. The same range applies to *bronzite. Hypersthene* is green, brown, and grayish black. *Orthoferrosilite* tends to be green or dark brown, generally somber tones.

Luster: *Enstatite* is vitreous. *Bronzite* is vitreous to submetallic. *Hypersthene* is vitreous, pearly, or silky. *Orthoferrosilite* is vitreous.

Hardness: 5-6 for the whole series.

Density: See table.

Cleavage: Good in 1 direction for all species in series.

Optic Sign: The optic sign changes along the series, from (+) to (−) and back to (+). The break points are at 12% and 88% orthoferrosilite:

```
0  (+) 12                       (−)                88  (+)  100
+---+-----------------------------------------------+---+
Enstatite                                          Orthoferrosilite
```

Dispersion: Generally low and becomes zero when $2V = 90°$ and $2V = 50°$.

Birefringence: In general, lower than that for the clinopyroxenes (see table).

Pleochroism: The entire series has a characteristic pleochroism: pink to green.
α: pale red-brown/purplish/brown pink.
β: pale greenish brown/pale reddish yellow/pale brown-yellow.
γ: pale green/smoky green/green.

Spectral: All gems in this series show a strong line at 5060 and often at 5475.
Tanzanian gems: also diffuse lines at 4550, 4880, and 5550.
Arizona gems: diffuse line at 4880.
Sri Lankan gems: diffuse line at 5550.
Brazilian and Indian gems: diffuse lines at 4880 and 5550.
Other lines noted: 5090, 5025, 4830, 4590, and 4490.

Luminescence: None.

Occurrence: Mg-rich members of the series are common in basic and ultrabasic rocks; also in layered intrusions; volcanic rocks: high-grade metamorphic rocks; regionally metamorphosed rocks and hornfels; meteorites. Gem enstatite occurs in *Burma, Tanzania,* and *Arizona*. Also noted from Mairimba Hill, Kenya (yellowish green; $\alpha = 1.652$; $\gamma = 1.662$; birefringence $= 0.010$; S.G. $= 3.23$). Other noteworthy localities are *Norway, California,* and *Germany.*
India produces 4-rayed star enstatites.
Rare green gems come from *Kimberley, South Africa.*
Bronzite comes from *Mysore, India,* and *Styria, Austria;* 6-rayed bronzite stars have been found.

Hypersthene is noted from *Norway, Greenland, Germany,* and *California,* with gem material from *Baja California, Mexico.*
Bastite is an altered enstatite (S.G. = 2.6, hardness = 3.5-4, opaque) from which cabochons are cut. Localities: *Burma* and *Harz Mountains, Germany.*
Embilipitiya, Sri Lanka: colorless enstatite (cut gems up to $\simeq$ 20 carats!) with R.I. = 1.658-1.668; birefringence = 0.010; S.G. = 3.25; quartz inclusions.
Ratnapura, Sri Lanka: green and brown enstatite with R.I. = 1.665-1.675; birefringence = 0.010; S.G. = 3.23.

Stone Sizes: In general, gems from this series are small (large ones are too dark in color to be attractive), and crystals tend to be small. The exception is star stones, of which large examples exist. Enstatites and hypersthenes of 5-10 carats, if clean and lively in color, are very rare stones. Indian star enstatites over 50 carats are frequently encountered, but Indian faceted gems over 10 carats are rare.
ROM: 12.97 (enstatite, Burma).
SI: 11.0, 8.1, 7.8 (enstatite, brown, Sri Lanka); 3.9 (enstatite, brown, Austria).
PC: 4.5 (hypersthene, brown, Africa); 26.6 (enstatite, green, India).
LA: 80 (dark brown cushion-cut, Africa).

Inclusions: Tabular scales of hematite and goethite have been noted in hypersthene.

Comments: Most gem enstatites have indices in the range 1.663-1.673. The brown and green gems from Tanzania are enstatites, as are the brownish-green stones from Sri Lanka. Green and brown gems from India and Brazil tend to be in the bronzite composition range. The gems of the orthopyroxene series are usually very dark, slightly brittle because of cleavage, and generally not appealing for jewelry purposes. The 4-rayed star gems are widely sold at a very low price, and the material is extremely plentiful. However, clean gems of hypersthene and enstatite are not abundant, except in very small (1-2 carat) sizes. Even in this size the colors tend to be dark and muddy. These are all true collector gemstones. Orthoferrosilite is included for completeness and has no gem significance.

Names: *Enstatite* from the Greek for *an opponent* because of its high melting point. *Bronzite* is named for

	Enstatite	Bronzite	Hypersthene	Orthoferrosilite
Density	3.20–3.30	3.30–3.43	3.43–3.90	3.90–3.96
Optics				
α	1.650–1.665	1.665–1.686	1.686–1.755	1.755–1.768
β	1.653–1.671	(intermediate)		1.763–1.770
γ	1.658–1.680	1.680–1.703	1.703–1.772	1.772–1.788
sign	(+)	(−)	(−) (+)	(+)
Birefringence	0.010	0.015	0.017	0.018

its bronzy color and luster. *Hypersthene* is from the Greek words for *very strong* or *tough*. *Orthoferrosilite* is named for its crystallography and composition. *Bastite* is also named for its composition: Ba, Si, Ti.

EOSPHORITE   Series to Childrenite if Fe exceeds Mn.

Formula: $(Mn,Fe)AlPO_4(OH)_2 \cdot H_2O$.

Crystallography: Monoclinic (pseudo-orthorhombic). Crystals prismatic, often twinned.

Colors: Colorless, pale pink, pale yellow, light brown, reddish brown, black.

Luster: Vitreous to resinous.

Hardness: 5.

Density: 3.05 (pure Mn end member); 3.08 (Brazil).

Cleavage: Poor; fracture uneven to subconchoidal.

Optics: $\alpha = 1.638\text{-}1.639; \beta = 1.660\text{-}1.664; \gamma = 1.667\text{-}1.671$. Biaxial (−), $2V = 50°$.

Birefringence: 0.029-0.035. (*Note:* less than childrenite.)

Pleochroism: Distinct: yellow/pink/pale pink to colorless.

Spectral: Strong line at 4100, moderate at 4900 (in brownish-pink material).

Luminescence: None observed.

Occurrence: In granite pegmatites, usually associated with Mn phosphates.
Branchville, Connecticut; Maine; Keystone, South Dakota; North Groton, New Hampshire.
Hagendorf, Germany.
Minas Gerais, Brazil: excellent, flat, pink crystals up to 4×1 cm, at *Itinga*.

Stone Sizes: Cut eosphorites are always small, usually less than 3-4 carats. Cuttable crystals are usually very small and badly flawed, only from the Brazil localities.

Comments: Pink gems are extremely attractive when cut, especially as round brilliants. The hardness makes wear unrecommended; cutting presents no great problems. This is a very rare gemstone, seen only in a few collections.

Name: From Greek *eosphoros,* meaning *dawn-bearing,* in allusion to the pink color.

EPIDOTE GROUP
The epidote group consists of three related minerals that are fairly well known to collectors and hobbyists, plus one popular gem mineral and three less common species.

Formula: The general formula of the epidote group is $X_2Y_3Z_3(O,OH,F)_{13}$, where X = Ca, Ce, La, Y, Th, Fe, Mn; Y = Al, Fe, Mn, Ti; Z = Si, Be.
Zoisite and *Clinozoisite:* $Ca_2Al_3Si_3O_{12}(OH)$.
Epidote: $Ca_2(Al,Fe)_3Si_3O_{12}(OH)$.
Piedmontite: $Ca_2(Mn,Fe,Al)_3Si_3O_{12}(OH)$ (also called *piemontite*).
Allanite: $(Ca,Ce,La,Y)_2(Mn,Fe,Al)_3Si_3O_{12}(OH)$.
Mukhinite: $Ca_2(Al_2V)Si_3O_{12}(OH)$.
Hancockite: $(Pb,Ca,Sr)_2(Al,Fe)_3Si_3O_{12}(OH)$.

Crystallography: All are monoclinic, except zoisite which is orthorhombic. Crystals prismatic and tabular; also granular, massive, fibrous; sometimes twinned, often striated.

Colors:
Clinozoisite is colorless, pale yellow, gray, green, pink; often zoned.
Epidote shows shades of green, yellow, gray, grayish white, greenish black, black.
Piedmontite is reddish brown, black, rose red, pink.
Hancockite is brownish or black.
Allanite is light brown to black.
Zoisite is gray, green, brown, pink *(thulite),* yellowish, blue to violet *(tanzanite).*

Luster: Vitreous; pearly on cleavages; massive materials dull. Allanite resinous, pitchy.

Hardness: 6-7. Epidote sometimes slightly harder, piedmontite softer.

Luminescence: Usually none. Thulite (pink zoisite) from Nevada sometimes medium pale brown in SW. Also thulite from North Carolina is orangy-yellow in LW.

Cleavage: Perfect 1 direction in all (different orientation in zoisite). Fracture conchoidal to uneven. Brittle.

Dispersion: For tanzanite: 0.019. Values for other epidote group minerals are in the same range.

Pleochroism: None in *clinozoisite.* Distinct red to yellowish brown in *hancockite.*
Allanite: reddish brown/brownish yellow/greenish brown; light brown/brown/dark red-brown; colorless/pale green/green.
Epidote: colorless, pale yellow or yellow-green/greenish yellow/yellow-green.
Zoisite: deep blue/purple/green (tanzanite); reddish-purple/blue/yellowish brown *(tanzanite);* pale pink/colorless/yellow; dark pink/pink/yellow *(thulite).*
Piedmontite: yellow/amethystine violet/red.

Spectral: Most members of the group have nondiagnostic spectrum; epidote has a very strong line at 4550, weak line is sometimes seen at 4750. This spectrum is very sensitive to direction within the material and is not visible in certain orientations. Tanzanite has a broad absorption in the yellow-green centered at 5950, with faint bands also at 5280 and 4550 and a few weak lines in the red.

Occurrence: The minerals of the epidote group form at low temperatures in low- to medium-grade metamorphic rocks. Allanite is more commonly found in igneous rocks such as pegmatites. Clinozoisite and epidote are also found in igneous rocks, and piedmontite is found in schists and manganese ore deposits. Zoisite occurs in calcareous rocks such as metamorphosed dolomites and calcareous shales subjected to regional metamorphism.

Epidote:

McFall Mine, Ramona, California; Idaho; Colorado; Michigan; Connecticut; Massachusetts; New Hampshire. Baja California, Mexico; Arendal, Norway; Czechoslovakia; USSR; Japan; Korea; Australia; Kenya; Madagascar. Switzerland: many localities.
Bourg d'Oisans, France: fine crystals.
Italy: Piedmont, other localities.
Untersulzbachthal, Austria: main source of faceting rough.
Burma: at *Tawmaw,* a chrome-rich material, fine deep green color *(tawmawite).*
Sri Lanka: yellow-brown (pleochroism = yellow-green/brown/greenish-yellow); $\alpha = 1.718$; $\beta = 1.734$; $\gamma = 1.738$; birefringence = 0.020; S.G. = 3.33.
Outokumpu, Finland: chromiferous epidote (tawmawite).
Minas Gerais, Brazil: cuttable, yellowish-green crystals (these are trichroic, low in iron; indices 1.722/1.737/1.743; birefringence 0.021; density 3.3-3.5).
Blue Ridge, Unaka Range, North Carolina (also in *Virginia, Georgia*): *unakite,* a granite consisting of pink feldspar and green epidote. A similar rock is also known from Zimbabwe.

Clinozoisite:

Nevada; Colorado.
Timmons, Ontario, Canada; Ireland; Iceland; India; Italy; Switzerland; Austria; Czechoslovakia.
Kenya: gray-green crystals.
Gavilanes, Baja, Mexico: brownish, facetable crystals.

Piedmontite:

Pennsylvania; Missouri.
Scotland; Vermland, Sweden; Morbihan, France; Japan; Otago, New Zealand.
California and Arizona: many localities.

Piemonte, Italy: in sericite schists.
Egypt: in a porphyry, colored red by piedmontite.

Hancockite:
Franklin, New Jersey: only notable locality, in small crystals.

Allanite:
Various localities throughout the *United States.*
Canada; Norway; Sweden; Greenland; USSR; Madagascar.

Zoisite:
South Dakota; Massachusetts.
Wyoming: greenish-gray material, sometimes tumble-polished for jewelry.
Washington: thulite.
California and Nevada: thulite.
North Carolina: thulite.
Baja, Mexico; Scotland; Austria; Finland; USSR; Japan; Germany.
Longido, Tanzania: deep green crystals, colored by chromium, with ruby crystals.
Lelatema, Tanzania: fine blue-violet crystals, up to large size, often gemmy (tanzanite).
Norway: thulite.
Greenland: thulite.

Stone Sizes: Unakite occurs in huge blocks weighing many pounds and is often cut into spheres as well as cabochons. Facetable epidote is rare over 5 carat sizes, and cut clinozoisite tends to be even smaller. Allanite is hardly ever cut except as cabochons: piedmontite is opaque and massive, also cut only as cabochons. Tanzanite is the only member of the epidote group that reaches large sizes in faceted gems. Rough tanzanite crystals weighing hundreds of carats have been found.
SI: 122.7 (blue, tanzanite, Tanzania); 18.2 (blue catseye tanzanite, Tanzania); 3.9 (epidote, brown, Austria).
DG: 7.30 (clinozoisite, brownish, Iran); 6.90 (epidote, brown).
PC: 220 (blue, tanzanite, Tanzania); 15 (clinozoisite, light brown-green, Baja).

Comments: The epidote minerals are very interesting and span a wide range of the gem market.

Hancockite, from New Jersey is very rare, and if a faceted gem exists it would be extremely small (under 1-2 carats).

	Clinozoisite	Epidote	Piedmontite	Hancockite	Allanite	Tanzanite	Zoisite	Thulite
Density	3.21-3.38	3.38-3.49	3.45-3.52	4.03	3.4-4.2	3.35	3.15-3.38	3.09
Optics								
α	1.670-1.715	1.715-1.751	1.732-1.794	1.788	1.640-1.791	1.692	1.685-1.705	1.695
β	1.675-1.725	1.725-1.784	1.750-1.807	1.810	1.650-1.815	1.693	1.688-1.710	—
γ	1.690-1.734	1.734-1.797	1.762-1.829	1.830	1.660-1.828	1.700	1.697-1.725	1.701
2V	(+)14-90°	(−)90-116°	(+)2-9°	(−)50°	(+−)40-123°	(+)	(+)0-60°	(−)
Bire-fringence	0.005-0.015	0.015-0.049	0.025-0.073	0.042	0.013-0.036	0.009	0.004-0.008	0.006

Epidote is usually so dark in color that a large faceted gem is nearly black, lifeless, and uninteresting; small stones, under 3-4 carats, are often bright and lively, however.

Clinozoisite would be a better-looking gem, but is very rare in sizes over 5 carats. The only well-known gem source is Baja, Mexico, though an occasional crystal from another locality yields a fine gem.

Allanite is very dark in color and seldom cut. The content of rare earth and radioactive elements causes it to become metamict with severe damage to the internal crystalline structure.

Unakite is a widely used and popular cabochon material that is exported throughout the world. It is best known from the United States, but Ireland, Zimbabwe, and probably other countries have similar rocks.

Mukhinite is a very rare mineral, in small grains from Gornaya Shoriya, USSR, and has never been cut.

Piedmontite is a distinct species but is often confused with thulite, which is a pink manganiferous variety of the species zoisite; piedmontite is dark brown or reddish in color, seldom in large masses, whereas thulite can occur in large pieces and is often bright pink in color. Both materials make lovely cabochons.

Pure clinozoisite is very rare; it usually contains some iron, and there is a complete solid-solution series from it to epidote.

Tawmawite is a deep emerald-green epidote from Burma, the color of which is due to chromium. This material is very rare.

Tanzanite is the best known member of the epidote group and is a variety of zoisite. The name was given by Tiffany & Co. in connection with a trade promotion, and has stuck although it has no mineralogical significance. Tanzanite occurs in a variety of colors at the Tanzanian locality, but most crystals are heated to about 700°F to create a deep, intense blue with violet dichroism. Tanzanite is soft and brittle, considering it is a popular ringstone, and great care should be exercised in wearing it. Inclusions that have been noted in tanzanite include actinolite, graphite, and staurolite.

Epidote group materials often contain fibrous inclusions that create a chatoyancy and yield catseye gems when cut into cabochons. Catseye clinozoisite and epidote are known. Catseye tanzanites are very rare but have been found.

Names: *Epidote* is derived from Greek for *increase* because the base of the prism has one side longer than the other. *Zoisite* is named after Baron von Zois, who presented Werner, the great mineralogist, with the first specimens of the material. *Thulite* is after Thule, the ancient name for Norway. *Tanzanite* is the Tiffany & Co. tradename for blue zoisite, named after the country of origin, Tanzania. *Clinozoisite* is the monoclinic dimorph of *zoisite*. *Piedmontite (piemontite)* is after the locality

in Italy, Piemonte (Piedmont). *Unakite* is named after the Unaka range of mountains in the United States. *Allanite* is named after mineralogist T. Allan. *Tawmawite* is named after the Burmese locality. *Mukhinite* for A. S. Mukhin, Soviet geologist.

ETTRINGITE   Series to Sturmanite.

Formula: $Ca_6Al_2(SO_4)_3(OH)_{12} \cdot 24H_2O$.

Crystallography: Hexagonal; usually flattened hexagonal dipyramids; sometimes prismatic, fibrous.

Colors: Colorless; transparent to translucent, milky.

Luster: Vitreous.

Hardness: 2-2.5.

Density: 1.77.

Cleavage: Perfect, rhombohedral.

Optics: $o = 1.491$; $e = 1.470$.

Uniaxial (−).

Birefringence: 0.021.

Pleochroism: None; colorless in transmitted light; dehydrates and turns white.

Spectral: Not diagnostic.

Luminescence: None.

Occurrence: At type locality *(Ettringen, Rhine Province, Germany)* in cavities of metamorphosed limestone inclusions in alkaline igneous rocks. Also in metamorphosed limestones.
Ettringen, Germany: In tiny crystals.
Franklin, New Jersey: Minute crystals.
South Africa: Associated with sturmanite at the *Jwaneng mine,* near *Hotazel.* The sturmanite forms yellowish coatings, with ettringite cores.

Stone Sizes: Material from Ettringen and Franklin is microscopic. A 2.5 carat pale yellow ettringite was faceted from material found in the center of a mass of sturmanite from South Africa. This may be the largest known for the species.

Comments: Ettringite is not generally facetable; any cut stone would be considered an extreme rarity. South African material has yielded minute stones, some of which may have been labeled sturmanite.

Name: After the locality in Germany.

EUCLASE

Formula: $BeAlSiO_4(OH)$.

Crystallography: Crystals tabular or prismatic, often well developed.

Colors: Colorless, white, pale blue, pale green, violet, dark blue, yellow.

Luster: Vitreous.

Hardness: 6.5-7.5. May be variable within a single crystal.

Density: 2.99-3.10 (colorless = 3.08).

Cleavage: Perfect 1 direction; fracture conchoidal. Brittle.

Optics: $\alpha = 1.650$-1.652; $\beta = 1.655$-1.658; $\gamma = 1.671$-1.676. Biaxial (+), $2V = 50°$.
Dark blue (Zimbabwe): $\alpha = 1.652$; $\beta = 1.656$; $\gamma = 1.671$; birefringence = 0.019; S.G. = 3.06-3.13.

Birefringence: 0.019-0.025.

Pleiochroism: Zimbabwe dark blue material displays intense pleiochroic colors: azure blue/Prussian blue/greenish-blue.

Dispersion: 0.016.

Spectral: There are two vague bands at 4680 and 4550; if Cr is present, it may display a characteristic spectrum in the red with a doublet at 7050.

Luminescence: Feeble or none.

Occurrence: Euclase is a mineral of granite pegmatites.
Minas Gerais, Brazil: Ouro Preto (fine gem material in good crystals up to a length of about 6 cm); *Santana de Encoberto* (material with high birefringence and included crystals of apatite, hematite, rutile, and zircon); *Bôa Vista* (cuttable crystals).
Orenburg District, South Urals, USSR: cuttable crystals.
Miami, Zimbabwe: cuttable crystals in shades of intense blue, cobaltian hue, some like fine sapphire.
Morogoro District, Tanzania; Colorado; Ireland; Austria; Norway.

Stone Sizes: Crystals are more commonly found in small sizes, about 1 inch for colorless material. Most euclase, in fact, is colorless, and strongly colored material is very rare. Blue and green gems are scarce over 2-3 carats, with violet being the most unusual. Colorless gems are also rare over 5-6 carats, although stones up to about 20 carats have been cut. Gems reported over 50 carats are museum pieces.
SI: 144 (lime green, Brazil); 48.7 (green): 12.5 green, Brazil; 8.9 (yellow, Brazil); 3.7 (blue-green, Brazil).
DG: 15.45 (colorless, Brazil); 14.0 (mint green, Brazil).
PC: 18.29 (blue-green oval, Brazil); 7.43 (blue, Brazil); Brazilian violet crystals reported that would yield stones up to 10 carats.

Comments: Euclase is a hard enough gem to be worn safely in jewelry. It may not be terribly exciting to look at (if colorless), but the colored gems are truly beautiful and exceedingly rare over a few carats in size. These gems can be very brilliant. The cleavage makes cutting a bit tricky.

Name: From the Greek *eu (easy)* and *klasis (fracture),* because of the easy cleavage.

EUDIALYTE

Formula: $Na_4(Ca,Fe,Ce,Mn)_2ZrSi_6O_{17}(OH,Cl)_2$. (*Note: Eucolite* = calcium-rich variety.)

Crystallography: Hexagonal (trigonal); tabular crystals, may be hexagonal or trigonal; also prismatic, rhombohedral, massive.

Colors: Shades of brownish red, yellowish brown, pink, red. Often translucent.

Luster: Vitreous; greasy; may be dull.

Hardness: 5-5.5.

Density: 2.74-2.98.

Cleavage: Basal, indistinct; fracture uneven; brittle.

Optics: $o = 1.591$-1.623; $e = 1.594$-1.633.
Uniaxial (+) but sign variable (eucolite reported to be (−) with higher indices and S.G.).

Birefringence: 0.003-0.010.

Pleochroism: Varies with body color.

Spectral: Not diagnostic.

Luminescence: Not reported.

Occurrence: Nepheline syenites and associated pegmatites:
Julienhaab District, Greenland: crystals up to 1 inch in length.
Kola Peninsula, USSR; Pilansberg, South Africa.
Ampasibitika, Madagascar.
Magnet Cove, Arkansas: rich red color, in feldspar.
Mt. Ste. Hilaire, Quebec, Canada: facetable ($o = 1.596$; $e = 1.600$; birefringence = 0.004).
Kipawa Complex, Sheffield Lake, Temiscamingue County, Quebec, Canada: red, facetable.
Sweden: $o = 1.598$; $e = 1.604$; birefringence = 0.004; S.G. = 2.88.

Stone Sizes: Faceted gems well under 1 carat in size have been cut from Quebec material. These are deep red and extremely rare.
NMC: 0.30, 0.40 (intense red, Sheffield Lake, Quebec, Canada).

Comments: Although cabochons could be cut from massive eudialite or translucent crystals, transparent material suitable for faceting is elusive and always small.

Name: From Greek words meaning *easy to dissolve* because of its easy solubility in acids.

EULITE   See: Enstatite.

EUXENITE   *Series to* Polycrase.

Formula: $(Y,Ca,Ce,U,Th)(Nb,Ta,Ti)_2O_6$;
Polycrase: $(Y,Ca,Ce,U,Th)(Ti,Nb,Ta)_2O_6$.

Crystallography: Orthorhombic. Crystals prismatic, stubby; as aggregates; massive.

Colors: Black, sometimes with a tinge of brown or green.

Streak: Grayish, yellow-brown.

Luster: Submetallic; vitreous to resinous.

Hardness: 5.5-6.5.

Density: 4.30-5.87 depending on the Ta content and hydration.

Cleavage: None. Fracture conchoidal. Brittle.

Optics: Isotropic due to metamictization. $N = 2.06\text{-}2.24$.

Luminescence: None.

Occurrence: In granite pegmatites; also as detrital grains. *California; Colorado; Pennsylvania; Maine. Norway; Canada; Greenland; Brazil; Finland; Zaire; Madagascar; Australia. Wyoming:* large crystals.

Stone Sizes: Gems cut from euxenite are almost always small, as the material is seldom transparent.

Comments: Euxenite is seldom seen in collections. Most collectors would not regard the mineral as facetable, but transparent fragments and areas of crystals have been noted that could cut small gems. Sometimes cabochons are cut by collectors, but these are not very striking. The colors of faceted stones would be too dark to make them appealing.

Name: From the Greek *euxenos (hospitable)* because of the many useful elements it contains. *Polycrase* is from the Greek, meaning *mixture of many,* also in allusion to the composition.

F

FAYALITE   See: Olivine.

FELDSPARS

Feldspars are the most common minerals at the Earth's surface. In fact, if the entire composition of the Earth's crust were regarded as a single mineral, it would calculate out almost exactly as a feldspar.

The feldspars are complex aluminosilicate minerals containing K, Na, and Ca, with some rarer types rich in Ba. The structures of these species are very similar. However, most feldspars crystallize from a melt in igneous rocks. The structures at high temperatures are different from those at low temperatures. In addition, the various compositions that may exist at high temperatures may not be stable at low temperatures. When a feldspar cools, it may segregate internally into separate mineral crystals, one type oriented within the other according to the symmetry of the host crystal. The specific type of intergrowth, composition of the minerals involved, and the size of the included crystals all depend on the original high-temperature composition and the cooling history of the feldspar, which may be very complex. It is easy to see why it may take years for a mineralogist simply to understand the complexities of the feldspar group, let alone contribute new data.

These complications, while both troublesome and intriguing to mineralogists, are not critical to gemological discussions. We may therefore simplify the discussion to a summary of the basic feldspar species and their properties, insofar as these are relevant to gemstones.

Potassium Feldspars: These all have the composition $KAlSi_3O_8$ but differ in structure. *Orthoclase* is monoclinic; *Sanidine* and *Anorthoclase* are also monoclinic, but the distributions of atoms within the structures are distinctive and different from each other and orthoclase. *Microcline* is triclinic. The properties are summarized in

Properties of the Potassium Feldspars

	Microcline	Orthoclase	Sanidine/Anorthoclase
Crystallography	Triclinic	Monoclinic	Monoclinic
Twinning	Lamellar twinning is not seen in the potassium feldspars		
Hardness	6–6.5	6–6.5	6
Density	2.54–2.63	2.55–2.63	2.56–2.62
Optics			
α	1.514–1.529	1.518–1.529	1.518–1.527
β	1.518–1.533	1.522–1.533	1.522–1.533
γ	1.521–1.539	1.522–1.539	1.522–1.534
sign	(−)	(−)	(−)
2V	66–103°	33–103°	18–54°
Dispersion	—	0.012	—
Spectral	none distinct	strong 4200 line; bands at 4450, 4200	none distinct
Luminescence	yellow-green in LW; inert SW; green in X-rays.	weak blue in LW or orange in SW; white to violet in X-rays.	not reported

the table below. Sanidine and Anorthoclase contain appreciable sodium.

Plagioclase Feldspars: The term plagioclase indicates a solid-solution series, ranging in composition from *albite* ($NaAlSi_3O_8$) to *anorthite* ($CaAl_2Si_2O_8$); for convenience the series was long ago arbitrarily divided into six distinct species as follows: *albite* (Ab); *oligoclase* (Og); *andesine* (Ad); *labradorite* (La); *bytownite* (By); *anorthite* (An). The series is divided according to the relative percentages of albite vs. anorthite:

Ab	Og	Ad	La	By	An
Ab 100	90 70	50	30	10	0

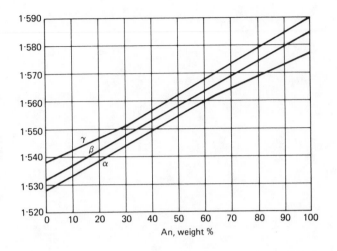

The optical parameters vary nearly linearly with composition, but because of the structural complexities, X-ray diffraction work is usually advised in identification of a plagioclase feldspar. Most plagioclase crystals are twinned according to various laws related to the crystal structures and also the distribution of atoms in the structures. Zoning is common and is due to variation in the growth history of the crystals and to the fact that, in a magma, the composition of the melt changes as crystallization proceeds and minerals are extracted from the molten mass. The properties of a plagioclase crystal may therefore vary widely within a small grain. Plagioclases also are often clouded, that is, contain dustlike particles of other minerals, including spinel, rutile, garnet, magnetite, clinozoisite, muscovite.

Compositions within the feldspar group are complicated by the fact that K may enter the plagioclase structure or Na the orthoclase structure. The resulting compositions are know as ternary (three-component) feldspars. In addition, as in the plagioclase series itself, high-temperature mixed feldspar compositions are stable, but at low temperatures unmixing occurs, that is, a segregation of the potassic and sodic molecules into separate feldspar phases, one distributed within the other. This creates such oddities as *perthites* (mixtures of albite with oligoclase or orthoclase), *sunstone, moonstone,* and *peristerites,* which are albite–oligoclase mixtures. The presence of feldspar lamellae in another feldspar gives rise to the *Schiller effect,* an iridescence due to light refraction. Schiller is best developed in labradorites, creating a lovely color play in shades of green, blue, gold and yellow. The color may be uniform or vary within a single feldspar crystal.

Most feldspar crystals are tabular and flattened and (in the case of plagioclase) usually complexly twinned. All the plagioclases are triclinic, and all the feldspars have excellent cleavage in two directions. The luster is vitreous, inclining to pearly on the cleavages. Feldspars are sometimes massive, cleavable, or granular.

Microcline may be colorless, white, pink, yellow, red, gray, or green to blue-green. The latter color is popular in gem circles, and the blue-green variety known as *amazonite* is widely cut into cabochons, beads, and carvings. Orthoclase is usually colorless, white, gray, yellow, reddish, and greenish, whereas sanidine is colorless, pinkish, or brownish. The plagioclases are all colorless, white, or gray, although the drabness is often broken by spectacular Schiller effects. Moonstones may be colored by impurities such as goethite (brown).

Microcline
Occurrence: Microcline occurs in acidic alkali-rich plutonic rocks; also in rocks such as pegmatites, granites, syenites, and schists.

Properties of Plagioclase Feldspars

	Albite	Oligoclase	Andesine	Labradorite	Bytownite	Anorthite
Hardness of all species = 6–6.5						
Density	2.57–2.69	2.62–2.67	2.65–2.69	2.69–2.72	2.72–2.75	2.75–2.77
Optics						
α	1.527	1.542	1.543	1.560	1.561	1.577
β	1.531	1.546	1.548	1.563	1.565	1.585
γ	1.538	1.549	1.551	1.572	1.570	1.590
sign	(+)	(−)	(+/−)	(+)	(−)	(−)
2V	77°	82°	76–86°	85°	86°	70°
Birefringence	0.011	0.007	0.008	0.012	0.009	0.013

Pala, California; Maine; New York; North Carolina.
USSR; Norway; Sweden; Germany; Italy; Japan; South
Africa.
Colorado (Pike's Peak area): amazonite.
Amelia Courthouse, Virginia: finest amazonite in the
United States.
South Dakota: perthite.
Canada: perthite, especially Ontario and Quebec.
Brazil: fine amazonite.
India (Kashmir District): amazonite.
Australia (Harts Range).

Stone Sizes: Amazonite cabochons up to almost any size are available; the material is usually sold by the pound to hobbyists. The same applies to perthite. The Amelia material has fine color and translucency, but perfect cleavage adds fragility.

Comments: Microcline crystals, associated with smoky quartz, are popular mineral specimens from the Pike's Peak area of Colorado. The color of amazonite ranges from pale green to dark green and blue-green. Pinkish orthoclase is also often present as an intergrowth.

Orthoclase

Occurrence: A component of many rocks, especially alkalic and plutonic acid rocks, also granites, pegmatites, syenites.
Many localities in the United States.
Canada.
Switzerland: fine crystals, known as adularia (S.G. = 2.56), from the St. Gotthard Region; the material contains some Na.
Itrongahy, Madagascar: fine, transparent yellow orthoclase in large crystals, usually with rounded faces. (Indices 1.522/1.527; birefringence 0.005; S.G. 2.56.) Faceted gems may be very large and deep in color.
Greenland: brownish transparent crystals to more than 2 inches.
Tvedestrand, Norway: orthoclase sunstone, deep red-orange, in masses up to a few inches in size.
Sri Lanka: in the gem gravels.
Burma: gravels.

Stones Sizes: Madagascar produces by far the largest cuttable orthoclase known.
SI: 249.6 (yellow, Madagascar); 104.5 (pale green catseye, Sri Lanka); 22.7 (white star, Sri Lanka); 6.0 (colorless, North Carolina).

Comments: Yellow and colorless catseye gems are known from Burma and Sri Lanka. Some of these (Sri Lankan) stones are also asteriated. Yellow faceted orthoclase is a handsome gemstone. Unfortunately, the cleavage makes it less advantageous for wear. Also, fine rough is hard to find, but large stones are displayed in museums. Ortho-clase moonstone is also found and will be discussed with plagioclase moonstones.

Sanidine

Occurrence: A component of acid igneous rocks.
Oregon; California.
Near Koblenz, Germany: brown transparent gems; S.G. 2.57-2.58; birefringence 0.007; indices: 1.516-1.520/1.520-1.525/1.522-1.526.
Ashton, Idaho: sanidine crystals in volcanic tuff, up to 1 cm, colorless, well formed. Indices: 1.516-1.519/1.520-1.522/1.521-1.523; $2V = 8-19°$; birefringence 0.003-0.005.

Stone Sizes: Sanidine is not a common mineral and is hardly ever seen as a gemstone. Crystals tend to be colorless and nondescript and are rare in cuttable sizes.

Comments: Sanidine is a mineral of volcanic rocks, with little gem significance.

Perthite

Occurrence: Perthite is an intergrowth of albite, oligoclase, plus orthoclase or microcline. The characteristic texture is produced by unmixing from high temperature. The appearance of the material depends on the cooling history, and hence the relative crystal sizes of the different feldspars in the mixture. Usually perthite consists of brown and white lamellae; the white feldspar often has a golden yellow or white Schiller. Perthitic intergrowths are very typical of the whole range of plagioclase compositions and therefore must be considered one of the most abundant mineral associations in nature.

Fine perthite that is suitable for cutting comes from Dungannon Township, Ontario, Canada, in large pieces, and from various localities in Quebec, as well as from other countries.

Peristerite

Occurrence: Peristerite is well known from Ontario, Canada, where it is very abundant. It is also found at Kioo Hill, Kenya: S.G. 2.63; $\alpha = 1.531$; $\beta = 1.535$; $\gamma = 1.539$.

Comments: Compositions in the calcic oligoclase range (Ab_{76}) cool and unmix to an inhomogeneous mixture of two feldspars, producing a Schiller, which in the case of peristerites is white or bluish. The effect seems to emanate within the body of the feldspar as a kind of glow.

Albite

Composition: $Ab_{100}-Ab_{90}$.

Crystallography: Triclinic. Twinned; platy crystals.

Colors: Colorless, white, yellow, pink, gray, reddish, greenish.

Luster: Vitreous to pearly.

Luminescence: Usually none; may be whitish in LW, lime green in X-rays (Kenya).

Spectral: Not diagnostic.

Occurrence: Albite usually forms at low temperatures; it is common in pegmatites, granite, and other igneous rocks, various metamorphic rocks, also marbles.
Essex County, New York.
Ontario, Canada; Quebec, Canada; Madagascar; Austria.
Rutherford Mine, Amelia, Virginia: fine colorless albite, facetable, large; crystals are platy variety known as *cleavelandite.*
Upson County, Georgia: moonstone.
South Dakota: cleavelandite.
Brazil: cleavelandite.
Kenya: colorless crystals, some with blue or yellow tinge. (Indices: 1.535/1.539/1.544; S.G. 2.63).
Many other localities worldwide.

Stone Sizes: Clean gems are usually in the 1-3 carat range, from cleavelandite crystals. Catseye gems up to about 50 carats are known.
ROM: 12.25 (catseye, Burma).
DG: 11.13 (cateye, white).

Comments: Translucent albite is sometimes found that is colored a rich green by inclusions of chrome-rich jadeite. Albite is sometimes intergrown with emerald, especially in the strange hexagonal skeletal crystals known as *trapiche emeralds.* Facetable albite from Madagascar has indices: $\alpha = 1.530\text{-}1.531$; $\beta = 1.532\text{-}1.533$; $\gamma = 1.539\text{-}1.540$; birefringence 0.009-0.010; density 2.62. Small faceted gems are fairly rare, almost always from the tips of cleavelandite crystals. Albite gems are colorless in most cases and not exciting to look at. Albite moonstones are known from many localities (discussed below).

Moonstone

Moonstone refers to feldspar of widely varying composition and from a wide variety of localities. The basic attribute is the presence of finely dispersed plates of one feldspar within another as a result of unmixing on cooling.

Orthoclase moonstone consists of albite within an orthoclase matrix. A blue color is produced if the albite crystals are very fine; the sheen is white if the albite plates are thick. The color of the orthoclase may be white, beige, brown, red-brown, greenish, or yellowish. Red coloration is due to goethite (iron oxide) inclusions. Some of this material cuts fine catseyes, where the sheen is concentrated into a narrow band. The sheen in moonstone is referred to as *adularescence.*

The density of such material is 2.56-2.59; material from Sri Lanka tends to be at the low end of this range, material from India at the higher end. The refractive index is usually 1.520-1.525; birefringence 0.005.

The moonstone from Burma and Sri Lanka is adularia and displays a white to blue sheen. The body colors may be white, blue, or reddish brown. The blue-sheen material, especially when the body of the moonstone is colorless and transparent, is very rare and greatly prized in large sizes (over 15 carats).

Grant County, New Mexico produces a very fine quality sanidine moonstone with a blue sheen. Orthoclase moonstone from Virginia is of a quality comparable to the Sri Lankan material: indices 1.518-1.524; birefringence 0.006. Moonstone also comes from Tanzania and several localities in the United States.

Inclusions: Moonstones are characterized by fissure systems along incipient cleavages in the body of the material created by exsolution pressures. Such fissure systems are short parallel cracks with shorter cracks emanating perpendicularly along the length of the parallel fissures. These resemble many-legged insects under the microscope and are known as *centipedes.* Moonstones also have rectangular dark areas due to stress cracking or negative crystals. Sometimes a cavity extends from such a rectangular dark area that creates an inclusion with a comma shape. Burmese moonstones are characterized by oriented needle inclusions.

Stone Sizes: Moonstone is rare in both large size and fine quality, but Indian material with strong body color is abundant and very inexpensive. This is fortunate because the material is well cut and very attractive. Moonstone with a blue sheen is the most valuable and is rare in stones over 15-20 carats. Stones with a silvery or white adularescence are abundant and available in sizes up to hundreds of carats.

Oligoclase, Andesine, Bytownite, Anorthite

These feldspars are rarely encountered in gem form. Their occurrence is widespread throughout the world, in a great variety of rock types and environments, but in most cases transparent crystals are rare.

In many cases faceted gems are identified as a feldspar in the plagioclase series, but the finder does not have the instrumentation needed to pin down the species. This is accomplished by a combination of optical and X-ray analysis. A few plagioclase gems have been well characterized, however, and reported in the literature.

Occurrence:
Oligoclase is reported from the *Hawk Mine, Bakersville, North Carolina,* in colorless to pale green facetable crystals. The indices are 1.537-1.547; density 2.651. Oligoclase is also reported from *Kenya,* colorless grains, with indices as follows: $\alpha = 1.538\text{-}1.540$, $\beta = 1.542\text{-}1.544$, $\gamma = 1.549\text{-}1.550$; birefringence 0.010-0.011; S.G. 2.64. North Carolina gems up to about 1-5 carats, colorless to pale green, are reported. Oligoclase from *Baffin Island, N.W.T., Canada* has yielded cut gems up to about 5 carats.

Andesine is known from many localities, including

California; Utah; Colorado; South Dakota; Minnesota; New York; North Carolina; Colombia; Argentina; Greenland; Norway; France; Italy; Germany; South Africa; India; and Japan.

Bytownite is found in basic plutonic rocks, some metamorphic rocks, and meteorites. Localities include *Montana; South Dakota; Oklahoma; Minnesota; Wisconsin; Scotland; England; Sweden; Japan; and South Africa.* Bytownite is sometimes reddish in color and pebbles from *Arizona* and *New Mexico* have been faceted into small gems. Bytownite is also reported from *Plush, Oregon,* but this is a well-known locality for labradorite in facetable crystals; it may be that some of the feldspar has a borderline composition and crosses over into the bytownite range.

Anorthite is the most calcic of the plagioclases, and sometimes makes up a distinctive rock known as *anorthosite,* which has been extensively studied. Localities for the mineral include *Pala, California; Grass Valley, Nevada; Italian Mountains, Colorado; Greenland; England; Sweden; Finland; Italy; Sicily; India; and Japan.* Anorthite has been cut for collectors but very rarely, and faceted gems are always small. However, a locality on *Great Sitkin Island, Alaska* has yielded cut gems as large as 8 carats. This pale yellow anorthite may be the largest known.

Labradorite

Of all the feldspars, none besides orthoclase is as frequently encountered as a faceted gem as is labradorite. The material ranges in color from colorless to yellow, but inclusions of minerals such as hematite and copper create a wide range of other body colors. These are best known from localities in Oregon. In addition, the phenomenon of Schiller is best developed in the labradorite range of plagioclase compositions. Translucent to opaque labradorite that shows blue, green, and golden Schiller colors is widely cut by hobbyists. Labradorite with Schiller is also a component of many dark-colored igneous rocks that are used in building and construction as facing materials. Such rocks are very attractive when polished because the blue sheen of the labradorite grains flashes out at many different angles.

Inclusions: Zircon and magnetite; also ilmenite and rutile tablets (Madagascar). Hematite inclusions create an *aventurescence* or sparkly effect due to reflection off of parallel included flakes. This reflection creates a rolling sheen of golden red spangles, leading to the name *sunstone.* Sunstone is also characteristic of oligoclase and is discussed below. Microscopic particles of metallic copper and lead account for some of the unusual colors observed in Oregon labradorite.

Pleochroism: Usually absent in feldspars but most notable in labradorite from Oregon. It is better developed in darker-colored stones:

Stone Color	Pleochroism
Yellow	colorless/light yellow
Red-orange and blue-green (multicolored)	bluish green/light red-violet/reddish orange
Bluish green	bluish green/light orange/colorless
Red orange	orange/light reddish purple
Orange	orange/reddish orange
Yellowish green	bluish green/light orange
Blue-green and violet	red-violet/reddish orange/bluish green

Other Effects: A labradorite moonstone is known from Madagascar. It has a blue sheen and the indices are: $\alpha =$ 1.550-1.553; $\gamma =$ 1.560-1.561; birefringence 0.008-0.010; S.G. 2.70.

Occurrence: Labradorite is best known from *Nain, Labrador:* crystals here are up to 2 feet long, but are badly cracked.
New York; Texas.
Modoc County, California: facetable crystals to 1 inch.
Finland: fine Schiller, very intense; cut stones called *spectrolite.*
Clear Lake, Millard County, Utah: facetable crystals.
Nevada: facetable crystals.
Madagascar: moonstone effect.
Australia: pale yellow, transparent material; indices $\alpha =$ 1.556, $\gamma =$ 1.564; S.G. 2.695.
Oregon: facetable; labradorite has the following properties: $\alpha =$ 1.559-1.563; $\gamma =$ 1.569-1.573; birefringence 0.008; S.G. 2.71-2.73; material is $Ab_{32}An_{68}$.

Stone Sizes: Labradorite rocks are available in very large sizes, suitable for facings of office buildings. This material is also sometimes cut into cabochons. Labradorite in larger crystals, with uniform Schiller (rather than in smaller, randomly oriented grains) is frequently cut into cabochons by hobbyists. The best material for this purpose comes from Finland, but the material is not common and is fairly expensive compared to other feldspars.

Faceted gems up to about 130 carats are known. It is likely that somewhat larger material exists, but fracturing of rough prevents the cutting of larger stones.
SI: 11.1 (yellow, Utah); 5.8 (yellow, Nevada); 30 (pale yellow, Idaho); 23.8 (yellow, Oregon); 39 (yellow, Oregon); 23.43 (yellow, Mexico).
PC: 62.5 (yellow, Mexico).
LA: 129 (yellow, Mexico).

Comments: The Schiller in labradorite is similar to that in peristerite, but the color range includes blue, green, blue-green, gold, yellow, and purple. The color play is iridescent like the feathers of a peacock.

Faceted labradorite makes a handsome, although unusual jewelry stone. It is as hard as moonstone or any of the other feldspars that are worn regularly in jewelry, but the cleavage is always worth minding. Gems larger than 20 carats can be considered exceptional. Oregon material is abundantly available in the 2-10 carat range. Oregon gems are colorless to pale yellow but often are green or red-orange with a pink Schiller. These odd colors are due to copper and lead, and the Schiller is due to colloidal copper.

Sunstone

This material contains hematite or goethite inclusions, which reflect light in parallel orientation and create a sparkling sheen in gold to brown color shades. Sunstone may be oligoclase or labradorite in composition and is much admired as a cabochon material among hobbyists. Very fine material is not abundant and is hard to obtain.

Occurrence:
New Mexico; New York; North Carolina; Maine; Pennsylvania; Virginia.
Lake Baikal, USSR; Bancroft area, Ontario, Canada.
Tvedestrand and Hitterö, Norway; as masses in quartz veins.
Lake Huron (Canada side): brownish to pink color.
Kangayam, India.
Harts Range, N.T., Australia: an untwinned microcline microperthite with aventurine-type reflections due to inclusions of thin, brownish-red hexagonal inclusions, in two sets at 90° angles. Properties are: $\alpha = 1.520$; $\beta = 1.525$; $\gamma = 1.527$; birefringence = 0.007; S.G. = 2.57; hardness = 6-6.5; no UV fluorescence.

Stone Sizes: Cabochons from Norwegian and Indian material may reach 100 carats or more. Most available material cuts smaller stones, however, This is because the rough is usually badly shattered and cracked.

Names: Microcline is from Greek words meaning small and inclined because the cleavage is close to but not quite 90°. Amazonite is named after the Amazon River basin in South America. Orthoclase is from Greek words meaning break straight because the cleavages are at 90°. Sanidine is also from the Greek, sanis, meaning board, in reference to the tabular crystals. Anorthoclase is from Greek words for not upright because the cleavage is not 90°.

Feldspar is from the Swedish feldt + spat because it was found in fields overlying granite. Plagioclase is from the Greek, meaning oblique cleavage.

Albite comes from the Latin albus, meaning white, because the mineral is usually white, Perthite is named for the locality, Perth, Ontario, Canada. Adularia is also a locality-derived name from Adular-Bergstock, Switzerland, where the variety occurs. Peristerite is from the Greek word peristera, meaning pigeon. The name moonstone alludes to the lustrous sheen of this material, in the same way that sunstone derives its name.

Oligoclase comes from Greek words meaning little break because the cleavage was believed to be less perfect than in albite. Andesine is named after the Andes Mountains of South America. Bytown, Canada, gave its name to bytownite. Anorthite is from the Greek words an plus orthos, meaning not straight, because the crystal faces meet at an oblique angle. Labradorite was, of course, named for its occurrence in Labrador.

FERGUSONITE   Series to Formanite: $YTaO_4$.

Formula: $YNbO_4$ + Er, Ce, Fe, Ti.

Crystallography: Tetragonal Crystals prismatic, pyramidal; usually masses.

Colors: Black, brownish black; surface altered brown, gray, or yellow.

Streak: Greenish gray, yellowish brown, brown.

Luster: Vitreous; submetallic; alters to dull surface.

Hardness: 5.5-6.5.

Density: 5.6-5.8. Formanite: 7.03 (calculated).

Cleavage: Traces. Fracture subconchoidal. Brittle.

Optics: Isotropic due to metamictization. $N = 2.05$-2.19 (mean), variable.

Pleochroism: Weak.

Occurrence: Granite pegmatites rich in rare earths.
California; North Carolina; Virginia; Texas; Massachusetts.
Norway; USSR; Ytterby, Sweden; East Africa; Zimbabwe; Madagascar.
Formanite is from Western Australia.

Stone Sizes: Cabochons are cut to several inches from massive material. Faceted stones are extremely tiny (less than 1 carat).

Comments: This mineral is not abundant and is known from various localities. Cabochons are cut merely as curiosities, as they have no special features that would recommend them except rarity. There are reports of transparent grains or parts of crystals that have been cut by collectors, but these are merely curiosities and are seldom encountered.

Name: After Robert Ferguson, a Scottish physician.

FERROHYPERSTHENE   See: Enstatite.

FERROSALITE   See: Diopside.

FERROSILITE   See: Enstatite.

FERROTANTALITE   See: Manganotantalite.

FIBROLITE   See: Sillimanite.

FIRE AGATE   See: Quartz.

FLINT   See: Quartz.

FLOWSTONE   See: Calcite.

FLUORITE

Formula: CaF_2.

Crystallography: Isometric. Usually in good crystals, cubes, octahedra, and other forms, often twinned; also massive, granular.

Colors: An extremely wide range is represented: colorless, purple (various shades), green (various shades), blue-green, blue, yellow to orange, brown (various shades), white, pink, red, brownish red, pinkish red, brownish black, black. Crystals are frequently color-zoned.

Luster: Vitreous.

Hardness: 4.

Density: 3.180; massive material with impurities 3.0–3.25.

Cleavage: Perfect 4 directions. Quite brittle. Cleavage is octahedral, very easy.

Optics: Isotropic; $N = 1.432$–1.434.

Dispersion: 0.007 (very low).

Spectral: U and rare earths are often present; spectrum reflects their presence. Spectra usually vague, however. Green material has lines at 6340, 6100, 5820, and 4450 and a broad band at 4270.

Luminescence: Yellow, blue, white, reddish, violet, green in LW. Fluorescence likely due to U and rare earths, sometimes to organic inclusions (hydrocarbons). Some material is thermoluminescent; some is phosphorescent. Phosphoresces in X-rays. Subject of luminescence and fluorescence began with studies of fluorite.

Occurrence: In hydrothermal deposits; sedimentary rocks; hot springs; rarely in pegmatites; usually associated with sulfide ore deposits, There are many localities worldwide.
New Mexico; Colorado; Michigan.
Italy; South Africa; Austria; Czechoslovakia; Germany; Korea; Africa; USSR.
England: Blue John or *Derbyshire Spar* used for more than fifteen hundred years as decorative material in vases, carvings, bowls, and so forth. It is banded in white and shades of blue, violet, and reddish brown. *Derbyshire* deposits now exhausted. Also from *Cumberland* and *Cornwall.*
Chamonix, Switzerland: octahedral pink crystals, on quartz, very rare.
Illinois: best known, especially violet material from

Rosiclare. Occurs in many colors in Illinois, also *Missouri* (purple, blue, yellow, brown, colorless).
Westmoreland, New Hampshire: bright green fluorite in crystals up to 8 inches across.
Ontario, Canada: banded, violet material in calcite.
Colombia: (green).
Huanzala, Peru: pink crystals.

Stone Sizes: Fluorites can be very large because of the availability of suitable rough from a wide range of localities. Many fluorite crystals are transparent.
SI: 729 (green, Colombia); 492, 354 (pink, Korea); 348 (pale blue, Korea); 263, 234 (light brown, Africa); 118 (purple, England); 354 (pale yellow, Illinois); 229, 124.5 (green, New Hampshire); 117 (green, Africa); 111.2 (violet, Illinois); 118.5, 85.4 (blue, Illinois); 32.7 (colorless, Illinois); 13 (pink, Switzerland).
DG: 68 (deep blue, Namibia); 23.7 (pink, Africa); 72.4 (green).
HU: 180 (green, New Hampshire).
LA: 1031 (yellow, triangle, Cave-in-Rock, Illinois, world's largest yellow fluorite); 100 (chrome fluorite, Colombia); 30 (chrome fluorite, Azusa Canyon, Los Angeles County, California).
PC: 100+ (pink, South Africa); 203.5 (yellow, Illinois); 17.92 (brown, Michigan); 3969 (Kashmir-sapphire blue, Illinois).

Comments: Fluorite is too fragile for wear because of its cleavage and brittleness. It is also on the soft side for jewelry use. Fluorite does, however, occur in a very wide range of attractive colors. Faceted gems can be extremely bright, despite the low index of refraction, since the material takes a high polish. Most of the available stones are in the blue-violet-green range; pinks are rare as is the fine chrome-green material from Colombia. Bicolor gems are sometimes cut from zoned crystals. An English fluorite with an alexandritelike color change (pink-blue) has been reported, as has similar material from Cherbadung, Switzerland. Large fluorites totally free of internal flaws are extremely rare.

Name: From the Latin *fluere (to flow)* because it melts easily and is used as a flux in smelting.

FORMANITE   See: Fergusonite.

FORSTERITE   See: Olivine.

FRIEDELITE

Formula: $(Mn,Fe)_8Si_6O_{18}(OH,Cl)_4 \cdot 3H_2O$.

Crystallography: Hexagonal (R). Crystals are tabular, needlelike, hemimorphic, and very rare. Usually massive, fibrous aggregates, cryptocrystalline.

Colors: Pale pink to dark brownish red, red, brown, orange-red.

Luster: Vitreous.

Hardness: 4-5.

Density: 3.04-3.07.

Cleavage: Perfect 1 direction. Fracture uneven. Brittle.

Optics: $o = 1.654-1.664$; $e = 1.625-1.629$.
Uniaxial (−).
Usually refractometer shows shadow edge at about 1.645.

Birefringence: 0.030.

Spectral: Broad band at 5560 and also 4560 (indistinct); spectrum not diagnostic.

Luminescence: May be reddish in LW and SW. Some material green (SW) and yellow (LW).

Occurrence: In manganese deposits.
Örebro, Sweden; Adervielle, France; USSR; Austria.
Franklin, New Jersey: source of gem material. Usually brownish, cryptocrystalline and looks like a fibrous chalcedony. Seams of the material at this deposit were up to 2 inches wide.
Kuruman, South Africa: massive dark rose red.

Stone Sizes: Translucent stones up to 1-5 carats normal; cabochons to about 30×40 mm. The larger stones lose any transparency.

Comments: Friedelite is not abundant, and little material has been faceted. The cabochons cut from Franklin material are lovely, rich colored, and usually translucent. The faceted gems are exceedingly rare and true collector items. Such stones are seldom seen even in large collections. Cabochons of material from the deep manganese mine at Kuruman, South Africa are rose-red and translucent.

Name: After the French chemist and mineralogist, Charles Friedel.

G

GADOLINITE

Formula: $Be_2FeY_2Si_2O_{10}$.

Crystallography: Monoclinic. Crystals rough and coarse, often terminated; massive.

Colors: Black, greenish black, brown, very rarely light green.

Streak: Greenish gray.

Luster: Vitreous to greasy.

Hardness: 6.5-7.

Density: 4.0-4.65 (usually 4.4); metamict material ~ 4.2.

Cleavage: None. Fracture conchoidal. Brittle.

Optics: $\alpha = 1.77$-1.78; $\gamma = 1.78$-1.82.
Biaxial (+), $2V = 85°$. Usually metamict and amorphous, hence isotropic.

Birefringence: High, and variable 0.01-0.04.

Occurrence: Granites and granite pegmatites.
Colorado; Texas; Arizona.
Greenland; Sweden; Norway; USSR; Japan; Switzerland; Australia.

Stone Sizes: Norwegian crystals have been found up to 4 inches across and nodules up to 60 pounds have been unearthed in Texas. This massive material cuts cabochons up to several pounds. Faceted gems, however, would be very tiny and very rare since the mineral is rarely transparent, even in thin splinters.

Comments: This is not a terribly attractive gemstone, but faceted gems would be a tremendous rarity. The material is quite brittle, but there is no cleavage to cause problems in cutting. I do not know of the existence of a faceted gem at this writing.

Name: After the Swedish chemist, J. Gadolin.

GAHNITE   See: Spinel.

GALAXITE   See: Spinel.

GARNET FAMILY

Formula: $A_3B_2Si_3O_{12}$. A = Fe, Ca, Mn, Mg; B = Al, Fe, Ti, Cr.

The garnets are a complex family of minerals, all having very similar structures but varying enormously in chemical composition and properties.

Garnets, for convenience, have in the past been grouped according to composition. Garnets containing Al in the B position in the formula are widely called *pyralspites* (acronym: PYRope, ALmandine, SPessartine) and garnets with Ca in the A position are called *ugrandites* (Uvarovite, GRossular, ANDradite).

There is complete solid solution between certain garnet species, but not between others, due to specific differences in internal structure. Uvarovite is a fairly rare garnet with restricted occurrence; the other five garnets may be thought of as comprising a five-component system (see diagram illustrating the general scheme of chemical substitutions).

The formulas of the garnet species are listed here to show similarities.

Uvarovite: $Ca_3Cr_2Si_3O_{12}$ *Pyrope:* $Mg_3Al_2Si_3O_{12}$
Grossular: $Ca_3Al_2Si_3O_{12}$ *Almandine:* $Fe_3Al_2Si_3O_{12}$
Andradite: $Ca_3Fe_2Si_3O_{12}$ *Spessartine:* $Mn_3Al_2Si_3O_{12}$
Also note:
   Goldmanite: $Ca_3V_2Si_3O_{12}$. Tiny, dark green crystals.

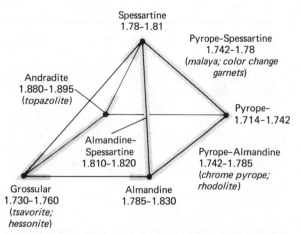

Spessartine
1.78-1.81

Pyrope-Spessartine
1.742-1.78
(*malaya; color change garnets*)

Andradite
1.880-1.895
(*topazolite*)

Pyrope-
1.714-1.742

Almandine-
Spessartine
1.810-1.820

Pyrope-Almandine
1.742-1.785
(*chrome pyrope;
rhodolite*)

Grossular
1.730-1.760
(*tsavorite;
hessonite*)

Almandine
1.785-1.830

Garnet species and varieties; shaded lines indicate chemical substitutions; varieties are in italics; refractive indices as shown.

Hydrogrossular: $Ca_3Al_2(SiO_4)_{3-x}(OH)_{4x}$. May be a component of grossular.

Henritermierite: $Ca_3(Mn,Al)(SiO_4)_2(OH)_4$. Tetragonal, very garnetlike, often twinned.

Kimzeyite: $Ca_3(Zr,Ti)_2(Al,Si)_3O_{12}$.

Knorringite: $Mg_3Cr_2Si_3O_{12}$. Like a "chromiferous pyrope."

Majorite: $Mg_3(Fe,Al,Si)_2Si_3O_{12}$. Purple; found in a meteorite!

Schorlomite: $Ca_3Ti_2Fe_3O_{12}$.

Yamatoite: $Mn_3V_2Si_3O_{12}$.

These are mostly rare species, but the fact that the garnet structure type can accommodate such a wide variation in composition indicates the range of substitutions possible in natural garnets. This accounts for the huge range of colors seen in the family as a whole.

Optical properties of garnets are very dependent on chemistry. Sometimes straight-line graphs are used to relate composition with refractive index or density. This type of graph assumes a simple additive relationship in chemical substitution and is inadequate when several substitutions occur simultaneously. In many instances a chemical analysis is needed to positively identify a garnet.

Physical Properties

The garnets have no cleavage but display a conchoidal fracture and are somewhat brittle and tend to chip easily. The luster is vitreous, inclining to resinous in grossular, andradite, and some almandines. The hardness is 6.5-7.5 in grossular and uvarovite; 6.5-7 in andradite; and 7-7.5 in the pyralspite series.

Garnets are all isometric, and crystals show the common forms in this crystal system, such as the trapezohedron and dodecahedron. Interestingly, the most common isometric forms, the cube and octahedron, are extremely rare in garnet crystals. Garnets may also be massive, granular, and in tumbled pebbles.

Colors:

Uvarovite: dark green.

Grossular: colorless, white, gray, yellow, yellowish green, green (various shades: pale apple green, medium apple green, emerald green, dark green), brown, pink, reddish, black.

Andradite: yellow-green, green, greenish brown, orangy yellow, brown, grayish black, black. The color is related to the content of Ti and Mn. If there is little of either element, the color is light and may resemble grossular.

Pyrope: purplish red, pinkish red, orangy red, crimson, dark red. *Note:* Pure pyrope would be colorless; the red colors are derived from Fe + Cr.

Almandine: deep red, brownish red, brownish black, violet red.

Spessartine: red, reddish orange, orange, yellow-brown, reddish brown, blackish brown. *Malaya* is a pyrope-spessartine from the Umba River Valley of Tanzania; the colors include various shades of orange, red-orange, peach, and pink.

A well-known commercial garnet is intermediate between pyrope and almandine. It is often said that such a garnet is a mixture of "molecules" of these garnets, whereas this really means its structure contains both Fe and Al. The intermediate garnet, known as *rhodolite,* usually has a distinctive purplish color.

The above variations make it easy to see why it is foolish to try to guess the identity of a garnet on the basis of color alone!

Stone Sizes: Garnet crystals are usually small, microscopic up to about 6 inches in the case of grossular. Garnets in rock, with poor external forms, may be much larger, such as the almandine from Gore Mountain, New York, which reaches a diameter of 60 cm. A few spessartines in Brazil have weighed several pounds and have retained great transparency and fine color, but these are very rare. A typical garnet crystal is about half an inch to an inch in diameter.

Optics: These are very dependent on chemistry, as indicated previously; the pyralspites are generally isotropic, but the presence of the large Ca atom in the structure of the ugrandites makes them birefringent. Grossular and andradite are almost always zoned, often twinned, and are distinctly *not* isotropic in the microscope. Recent X-ray data, in fact, clearly show that ugrandites can be orthorhombic and some may even be monoclinic, perhaps as a result of cation ordering on certain crystallographic sites.

Uvarovite

Density: 3.4-3.8 (usually 3.71-3.77).

Optics: $N = 1.74-1.87$.

Occurrence: Chromites and serpentines, that is, metamorphic environments where both Ca and Cr are present.

Oregon.
Thetford, Quebec, Canada.
Outokumpu, Finland: best known locality, in large, fine, green crystals.
Norway.
USSR: fine crystals.
South Africa.
Northern California: in chromite deposits.

Stone Sizes: Faceted uvarovites are extremely rare because crystals are always opaque. An occasional crystal may have a transparent corner that could yield a stone of less than 1 carat, even though crystals may reach a size of 1-2 inches.

Comments: The color of uvarovite is like that of emerald (deep, rich green), so it is a shame that crystals cannot be cut. Uvarovite is a rare mineral, prized by collectors. It is not generally regarded as a gem garnet.

Name: After Count S. S. Uvarov of Russia, one-time president of the St. Petersburg (Leningrad) Academy.

Grossular

Also known as *hessonite, essonite, cinnamon stone; rosolite* is a pinkish variety from Mexico.

Density: 3.4-3.71; usually near 3.65.

Optics: $N = 1.72$-1.80; usually 1.73-1.76 (with $V = 1.743$-1.759).

Dispersion: 0.027.

Spectral: None in pale-colored, faceted gems; a trace of almandine may produce a faint iron spectrum. A trace of Cr may produce a chrome spectrum in green varieties. Massive grossular may show a weak line at 4610 or a band at 6300. Green, massive grossular from Pakistan shows a line at 6970 (weak) with weak lines in the orange, plus a strong band at 6300 and diffuse lines at 6050 and 5050. Orange stones may have bands at 4070 and 4030.

Luminescence: Usually none in UV. All massive material glows orange in X-rays, as do many faceted gems.

Occurrence: In metamorphosed, impure calcareous rocks, especially contact zones; also in schists and serpentines; worldwide occurrence, widespread.
Eden Mills, Vermont: fine orange crystals, some gemmy, with green diopside.
California: many localities.
New England: many localities.
Asbestos, Quebec, Canada: fine orange to pinkish crystals at the Jeffrey Mine, up to 2 inches across, gemmy. Also colorless ($N = 1.733$).
Lake Jaco, Chihuahua, Mexico: large pinkish, white, and greenish crystals; color zoned concentrically, usually opaque; crystals up to about 5 inches in diameter.

Sri Lanka: grossulars are found in the gem gravels (hessonite).
Wilui River, USSR: opaque green crystals with idocrase.
China: massive white grossular.
Australia (Harts Range, Northern Territory): hessonite.
New Zealand: hydrogrossular.
Kenya and Tanzania: fine grossular in various colors, especially the dark green material being marketed as *tsavorite,* containing V and Cr.
South Africa: massive green material that resembles jade.
Pakistan: some faceted green gems; also massive green grossular, various shades.
Brazil; Switzerland.

Stone Sizes: Hydrogrossular and massive varieties are cut as cabochons of large size, including green shades and also pink, translucent grossular. Massive white material from China has been carved. Orange and brown grossulars up to several hundred carats from the Sri Lankan gem gravels have been found; the fine cinnamon-colored stones from Quebec are clean only in small sizes, but good gems up to about 25 carats have been cut. Tsavorite is rare in clean gems over 1 carat; the largest known are in the 10-20 carat range.
SI: 64.2 (orange-brown, Sri Lanka).
PC: 13.89 (yellow, oval).
AMNH: 61.5 (cameo head of Christ, hessonite).
NMC: 23.94, 13.40, 8.50 (brownish-orange hessonite, Asbestos, Quebec); 4.68, 2.94 (colorless, Asbestos, Quebec).

Comments: Grossular has a granular appearance under the microscope, sometimes referred to as *treacle,* a swirled look due to included diopside crystals and irregular streaks at grain boundaries. Zircon crystals are included in some grossulars, as well as actinolite and apatite (Tanzania material). So-called *Transvaal jade* is the green massive material from South Africa. The color of grossular depends on the content of Fe and Mn. If there is less than 2% Fe, grossular is pale or colorless. Greater amounts of Fe produce brown and green colors, and a rich green shade is due to Cr. *Californite* is a mixture of idocrase and grossular, usually pale to medium green in color. It comes from California, Pakistan, and South Africa.

Hydrogrossular is a component of the massive grossulars. Material from New Zealand is known as *rodingite* ($N = 1.702$, density 3.35). Transvaal jade occurs in green, gray-green, bluish, and pink colors, is compact and homogeneous, may have a splintery fracture and waxy luster. The gray material contains zoisite. Pink material, containing Mn, has $N = 1.675$-1.705, density 3.27. The green, jadelike material has $N = 1.728$, density 3.488. Pakistan massive grossular has $N = 1.738$-1.742, density 3.63, with a Cr absorption spectrum. Similar material from Tanzania has $N = 1.742$-1.744, density 3.68.

Colorless grossular from Georgetown, California, has

$N = 1.737$, density 3.506. Yellow garnet from Tanzania fluoresces orange in X-rays and also UV, $N = 1.734$, density 3.604. *Tsavorite* from Lualenyi, Kenya, has $N = 1.743$, density = 3.61 (mean). It is inert in UV light, contains a trace of Cr and a significant amount of vanadium. The color of these tsavorites is therefore due to vanadium, not chromium as originally suspected.

The pinkish grossular in marble from Lake Jaco and Morelos, Mexico, is variously known as *xalostocite*, *landerite*, and *rosolite*.

Andradite
Melanite has 1-5% Ti oxide; *schorlomite* is rich in Ti also; *topazolite* from Italy is yellowish-green; *demantoid* is rich green, colored by Cr.

Density: 3.7-4.1; melanite about 3.9; demantoid 3.82-3.88.

Optics: $N = 1.88-1.94$; melanite: ~ 1.89; demantoid: 1.881-1.888; schorlomite: 1.935; topazolite (yellow): 1.887.

Dispersion: 0.057 (large).

Spectral: A strong band is visible at 4430, cutoff at the violet end of the spectrum. Sometimes (in demantoids) the Cr spectrum is visible, with a doublet at 7010, sharp line at 6930, and 2 bands in the orange at 6400 and 6220. Demantoid is red in the Chelsea filter.

Luminescence: None.

Inclusions: Demantoid is distinguished by so-called horse-tail inclusions of byssolite (fibrous amphibole); these are diagnostic for this gem. These inclusions also occasionally produce catseye gems.

Occurrence: Andradite occurs in schists and serpentine rocks (demantoid and topazolite); also in alkali-rich igneous rocks (melanite and schorlomite); and in metamorphosed limestones and contact zones (brown and green colors).
San Benito County, California: topazolite ($N = 1.855-1.877$, S.G. = 3.77-3.81), demantoid ($N = 1.882$, S.G. = 3.81), and unusual catseye material.
Arizona; New Jersey; Pennsylvania.
Greenland; Norway; Sweden; Uganda; Sri Lanka.
Colorado: melanite.
Arkansas: schorlomite.
New Mexico: in metamorphic limestones and ore deposits.
USSR: fine demantoid from the Urals. Also some (small) brown andradite.
Zaire: brown and green andradite, also some demantoid.
Ala, Piedmont, Italy: dark apple green demantoid garnet; also topazolite (yellow).
Korea: andradite, some fine green with Cr.
Monte Somma, Vesuvius, and Trentino, Italy: melanite (black).

Stone Sizes: Andradite is seldom faceted, but brownish stones up to a few carats are known. Demantoid, however, is a rare but well-known gem, and is probably the most valuable of all the garnets.
SI: 10.4 (USSR); also 4.1, 3.4, and 2.3.
PC: 18 (sold in New York City); a California collector owns a huge topazolite (green color) that would yield faceted gems over 20 carats. This crystal weighs ~ 1 ounce.
USSR: many fine demantoids in museum collections.

Comments: Demantoid was once reasonably available in jewelry, but since there is no current production it now is seen primarily in antique jewelry. Stones larger than 10 carats are very rare. Topazolite of fine yellow color is usually very small, and a cut gem over 2-3 carats would be rare. Black garnets have occasionally been used in mourning jewelry. Brown andradite is not a well-known gem garnet. The dispersion of andradite is the highest of any garnet, and gems have tremendous fire, but this is usually masked by the body color. The fire is eminently visible in some paler demantoids, which makes them distinctive and much more attractive than comparably colored grossulars, which have much lower dispersion. The horse-tail inclusions are proof positive in identification.

Pyrope
Density: 3.65-3.87.

Optics: $N = 1.730-1.766$.

Dispersion: 0.022.

Spectral: The chromium spectrum of emission lines in the far red is absent in pyrope; however, the almandine (iron) spectrum is often visible. Otherwise, Cr masks the almandine spectrum and we see a narrow, weak doublet at 6870/6850, with possible weak lines at 6710 and 6500. A broad band, about 1000 Å wide, may be visible at 5700.

Luminescence: None.

Inclusions: Pyrope contains small rounded crystals, circular snowballs of quartz crystals, and (from Arizona) octahedra and minute needles.

Occurrence: In peridotites, kimberlites, and serpentine rocks, and sands and gravels derived from their weathering; also in eclogite and other basic igneous rocks.
Utah; New Mexico; Arkansas; North Carolina.
Czechoslovakia; Brazil; Argentina; Tanzania; Transbaikalia, USSR; Bingara, N.S.W., Australia; Anakie, Queensland, Australia; Ottery, Norway.
Arizona: a component of ant hills.
Umba Valley, East Africa: shows color change (see below).
South Africa: in kimberlite and eclogite associated with diamond; fine color.
The best known pyrope is from near *Trebnitz, Czechoslovakia*, the so-called Bohemian garnets. The garnets

occur in volcanic breccia and tuffs and conglomerates. These garnets provided a major local industry in the nineteenth Century, but the deposits are exhausted. An enormous quantity of pyrope from these mines was sold.

Stone Sizes: Pyropes of large size are extremely rare. Stones over 1-2 carats are usually very dark. Many large gems are in the Kunsthistorisches Museum in Vienna. There are stories about hen's-egg-sized gems in the former Imperial Treasury in Vienna. The Green Vaults of Dresden contain a huge gem said to be the size of a pigeon's egg. Reports of a 468.5 carat gem also appear in the literature.

Comments: A pure pyrope (end member in the series) is unknown in nature. Pyropes always contain some almandine and spessartine components. The almandine component can easily be detected spectroscopically. Large, clean pyropes of lively color are very rare and would be very expensive. Some pyropes show an interesting color change. Material from Norway ($N = 1.747$, S.G. $= 3.715$) is wine red in incandescent light, violet in daylight, but these stones are very small (about half a carat). Pyrope from the Umba Valley in East Africa ($N = 1.757$, S.G. $= 3.816$) are pyrope-spessartines (with some Ca and Ti); they are greenish blue in daylight and magenta in tungsten light. They have inclusions of plates of hematite and rutile needles. All these color-change pyrope-spessartines have absorption bands at 4100, 4210, and 4300 that may merge to form a cutoff at 4350. In stones with a strong change of color, a band at 5730 is broad and strong. Gems sold as pyrope are usually almandines with a pyrope component, especially if they are of large size. The pyropes from South Africa occur with diamonds, and sometimes pyrope crystals are inclusions within diamonds. The color of these is superb, blood red, but the sizes are always very small. *Malaya* is a variety of pyrope-spessartine that varies in color from red, through shades of orange and brownish orange to peach and pink. Absorption bands are always visible at 4100, 4210, and 4300 that may merge to form a cutoff at 4350. There may also be absorption bands at 4600, 4800, 5040, 5200, and 5370. These stones are only known from Tanzania.

Almandine
Density: 3.95-4.3.

Optics: $N = 1.75$-1.83; usually above 1.78.

Dispersion: 0.027.

Spectral: The spectrum of almandine is distinctive and diagnostic: there is a band 200 Å wide at 5760 (strong) and also strong bands at 5260 and 5050. Lines may appear at 6170 and 4260. This pattern of 3 (or sometimes 5) bands is seen in all almandines, and most garnets with a significant almandine component.

Luminescence: None.

Inclusions: Almandine is usually included with a variety of minerals. There are zircon crystals with haloes due to radioactivity; irregular, dotlike crystals, and lumpy crystals; rutile needles, usually short fibers, crossed at 110° and 70°; there are dense hornblende rods (especially from Sri Lanka); asbestiform needles of augite or hornblende that run parallel to the dodecahedral edges; also apatite; ilmenite; spinel; monazite; biotite; quartz.

Occurrence: Almandine is a widespread constituent of metamorphic rocks; also in igneous rocks, in contact metamorphic zones, and as an alluvial mineral.
Colorado; South Dakota; Michigan; New York; Pennsylvania; Connecticut; Maine.
Canada; Uruguay; Greenland; Norway; Sweden; Austria; Japan; Tanzania; Zambia.
Fort Wrangell, Alaska: fine, well-formed crystals in slate.
California; Idaho: star garnets.
Major gem almandine sources are as follows:
India: Jaipur (in mica schist); also *Rajasthan* and *Hyderabad;* some stars also.
Sri Lanka: at *Trincomalee,* fine color and large size.
Brazil: Minas Gerais; Bahia.
Idaho: star garnets.
Madagascar: large sizes.

Stone Sizes: Almandines of large size are known, such as the 60-cm crystals in rock at the Barton Mine, New York. This material is so badly shattered that stones up to only 1-2 carats can be cut from the fragments. Indian and Brazilian almandine constitutes the bulk of material on the marketplace.
SI: 174 and 67.3 (stars, red-brown, Idaho); 40.6 (red-brown, Madagascar).

Comments: Almandine is perhaps the commonest garnet. Gemstones always have some spessartine and pyrope components, and this creates a wide range of colors, including brown, red-brown, purplish red, wine red, purple, and deep red. Inclusions of asbestiform minerals (pyroxene or amphibole) create a chatoyancy that yields, in cabochons, a 4-rayed star. Star gems come primarily from Idaho and India. The Idaho material has $N = 1.808$, density 4.07 (up to 4.76 due to inclusions). Inclusions in faceted gems vary widely, but are usually not too obtrusive. This is especially true of the silk, which is often visible only under magnification.

Rhodolite
Rhodolite is intermediate in composition between almandine and pyrope, with a ratio of Al to Fe of 2 to 1 (that is, 2 pyrope + 1 almandine). The distinctiveness of rhodolite is in its color, which is nearly always a purplish red.

The absorption spectrum always shows almandine lines. Inclusions include apatite crystals (North Carolina) and any of the other inclusions found in almandine. The color of a garnet is misleading, and a chemical analysis is required to show whether a garnet is an almandine or pyrope, or a mixed crystal.

Density: 3.79-3.80 (Tanzania); 3.83-3.89 (Zimbabwe); 3.84-3.89 (North Carolina).

Optics: $N = 1.750$-1.760 (Zimbabwe); 1.760-1.761 (North Carolina); 1.745-1.760 (Tanzania).

Dispersion: 0.026.

Occurrence:
North Carolina: rhododendron red, lilac, pinkish.
Sri Lanka; Madagascar; India; Tanzania; Zimbabwe.

Stone Sizes:
SI: 74.3, 22.1 (Tanzania); 16.5 (North Carolina).

Comments: The original locality for rhodolite was Cowee Creek, Macon County, North Carolina. Stones from this locality are usually very small (under 1-2 carats), but new finds in Africa have yielded gems over 75 carats. Material from the North Pare Mountains, Tanzania, may show a color change, blue in daylight to purplish red in incandescent light, similar to alexandrite ($N = 1.765$, S.G. = 3.88).

Spessartine
Density: 3.8-4.25; gems usually 4.12-4.20.

Optics: $N = 1.79$-1.81; 1.803-1.805 (Brazil). 1.795 (Amelia, Virginia).

Dispersion: 0.027.

Spectral: The Mn spectrum is evident: lines at 4950, 4850, 4620 (all weak) and strong lines at 4320, 4240 (weaker), and 4120 (intense). Almandine may be present, contributing lines at 4320 and 4120.

Luminscence: None.

Inclusions: Wavy feathers, due to liquid drops that have a shredded look, especially in gems from Sri Lanka and Brazil.

Occurrence: In granite pegmatites; also gneiss, quartzite and rhyolite, and sometimes as a component in skarns.
Nevada; Colorado; New Mexico; Pennsylvania; North Carolina.
San Diego County, California: good crystals, especially at Ramona (fine orange gems).
Amelia Court House, Virginia: fine orange to deep brownish material, gemmy.
Norway; Tsializina, Madagascar.
Sri Lanka and Burma: in the gem gravels.
Brazil (Arassuahy and Ceara): large crystals (up to several pounds), gemmy, fine color.

Stone Sizes: Gems weighing more than 100 carats have been cut from Brazilian and Madagascar rough. Amelia stones are fine color (orange) but small, up to about 15-20 carats, although crystals weighing several pounds have been found there.
SI: 109 (red, Brazil); 53.8 (red, Brazil); 40.1 (orange, Virginia).
AMNH: 96 (reddish, Brazil—not clean).

Comments: Spessartine is fairly rare as a gem garnet, and one of the most beautiful. Large stones are very rare, and usually quite dark. The finest color is an orangy red, as exemplified by the material from Ramona, California, and Amelia, Virginia. A red-brown tint indicates a higher content of almandine, accompanied by higher refractive index; pale orange colors are closer to pure spessartine. Spessartine as a component of almandine tends to add a lively reddish tinge of color.

Unusual color-change garnets with large amounts of V and Cr have been reported from East Africa. These are primarily spessartine, with an unusually large component of grossular. The color change may be as follows:
1. greenish yellow-brown (transmitted fluorescent light) to purplish red (reflected fluorescent); reddish orange to red (incandescent light) $N = 1.773$, S.G. = 3.98; spessartine/grossular/almandine.
2. light bluish green (transmitted fluorescent) to purple (reflected); light red to purplish red (incandescent) $N = 1.763$, S.G. = 3.89; spessartine/grossular/pyrope.

So-called alexandritelike garnets have also been noted, changing from violet-red to blue-green. These are usually small, but a stone of 24.87 carats was sold in 1979.

Names: *Garnet* comes from the Latin word *granatus,* meaning *grain.* This originated in the comparison of garnet grains in rock with the scattered dark seeds of the pomegranate fruit.
Uvarovite is named after Count S. S. Uvarov, one-time president of the St. Petersburg (Leningrad) Academy.
Grossular is named after *R. grossularia,* the botanical name for the gooseberry, because of the resemblance of the color (pale green) to that of the plant.
Hessonite is from a Greek word meaning *inferior* because of its lower hardness.
Tsavorite is named after the Tsavo National Park in Kenya.
Californite is named after the original occurrence in California.
Andradite is named after the Portugese mineralogist d'Andrade, who described one of the subvarieties of this species. *Topazolite* is named after its resemblance to yellow topaz.
Demantoid comes from the French *demant (diamond)* because of the brilliance and luster.
Melanite comes from the Greek *melanos* (black).

Pyrope comes from the Greek word for *firelike,* in allusion to the red color.

Almandine is a corruption of the locality name Alabanda, in Asia Minor, from which place came the red garnets described by Pliny.

Rhodolite is from the Greek *rhodon, rose,* in allusion to its color.

Spessartine is named after the locality Spessart, in Northwest Bavaria (Germany).

Malaya is a Bantu word meaning "out of the family," sometimes said to mean "deceiver."

GAYLUSSITE

Formula: $Na_2Ca(CO_3)_2 \cdot 5H_2O$.

Crystallography: Monoclinic. Crystals elongated, flattened, and wedge-shaped.

Colors: Colorless, white, grayish, yellowish.

Luster: Vitreous.

Hardness: 2.5-3.

Density: 1.995.

Cleavage: Perfect 1 direction. Fracture conchoidal. Brittle.

Optics: $\alpha = 1.445; \beta = 1.516; \gamma = 1.522$.
Biaxial (−), $2V = 34°$.

Birefringence: 0.077.

Pleochroism: None.

Spectral: Not diagnostic.

Luminescence: Weak cream white in SW (Nevada). May be triboluminescent.

Occurrence: In alkaline lakes or evaporite deposits rich in borax.
California: Searles Lake, Owens Lake, China Lake, Borax Lake.
Wyoming; Nevada.
Mongolia, China.
Venezuela: in clay beds.
Kenya: in transparent crystals, from Lake Amboseli.

Stone Sizes: Crystals from Searles Lake have been found up to 2 inches long. Gems cut from such crystals could be up to about 20-30 carats.

Comments: This mineral is very hard to cut because of extreme softness and cleavage. Gaylussite dries out slowly in air and the surfaces may turn white. Stones in collections are therefore best stored in sealed containers to prevent dehydration. Gaylussite is seen only in very comprehensive collections, and relatively few stones have

been cut. Transparent crystals are not terribly rare, but faceted gems are relatively uninteresting.

Name: After the eminent French chemist, Professor L. J. Gay-Lussac.

GLASS: See: Obsidian.

GOLDMANITE   See: Garnet.

GOSHENITE   See: Beryl.

GRANDIDIERITE

Formula: $(Mg,Fe)Al_3BSiO_9$.

Crystallography: Orthorhombic. Crystals elongated and not well formed; massive.

Colors: Blue-green; translucent.

Luster: Vitreous.

Hardness: 7.5.

Density: 2.85-3.0.

Cleavage: Perfect 1 direction, good 1 direction.

Optics: $\alpha = 1.583\text{-}1.602; \beta = 1.618\text{-}1.636; \gamma = 1.622\text{-}1.639$.
Biaxial (−), $2V = 30°$.
(Madagascar stone: $\alpha = 1.583; \gamma = 1.622$; S.G. = 2.85).

Birefringence: 0.039.

Pleochroism: Strong: dark blue-green/colorless/dark green.

Spectral: Not diagnostic.

Luminescence: None.

Occurrence: Generally in pegmatites.
Andrahomana, South Madagascar: only well-known locality.

Stone Sizes: Cut as cabochons up to about 1 inch (1-10 carats). At best, the material is translucent, and generally is opaque.

Comments: Grandidierite is a rather rare mineral, with a lovely blue-green color. It is never transparent enough to facet, but attractive, sometimes even jadelike cabochons are cuttable from the translucent material. The high hardness makes it suitable for wear, although cutters have to pay close attention to the cleavage. Cut grandidierite is seldom seen in collections because few collectors have even heard of it or know it exists in cuttable form.

Name: After Alfred Grandidier, a French explorer, who described the natural history and geography of Madagascar.

GROSSULAR   See: Garnet.

GYPSUM   Also known as *Alabaster;* variety *Satin Spar.*

Formula: $CaSO_4 \cdot 2H_2O$.

Crystallography: Monoclinic. Crystals often perfect and large; tabular; rosettes; lenticular; *helictites* are grotesque shapes found in caves; often twinned; massive; granular.

Colors: Colorless, white, gray; impurities make it yellowish, reddish, brownish, greenish. Sometimes banded and patterned like marble.

Luster: Subvitreous; pearly on cleavages.

Hardness: 2.

Density: 2.32 (range 2.30–2.33).

Cleavage: Perfect and easy, 1 direction; distinct 2 other directions.

Optics: $\alpha = 1.520; \beta = 1.523; \gamma = 1.530$. Biaxial (+), $2V = 58°$.

Birefringence: 0.010.

Dispersion: 0.033.

Pleochroism: None.

Spectral: Not diagnostic.

Luminescence: Sometimes indistinct brownish or greenish white in UV. Inert in X-rays.

Occurrence: In sedimentary rocks and deposits; saline lakes; oxidized parts of ore deposits; volcanic deposits. *Utah; Michigan; Colorado; South Dakota; New Mexico; New York; Kansas;* other states.
California: many locations.

Mexico: at *Naica, Chihuahua,* in enormous crystals to 6 feet long.
Braden, Chile: crystals reported up to 10 feet long.
Alabaster from *England; Tuscany, Italy.*

Stone Sizes: Massive gypsum in any desired size (for cabochons and carvings). Fibrous material cut into large carvings, up to several pounds. Faceted gypsum could be up to hundreds of carats, as large transparent crystals exist.

Comments: Gypsum is one of the most abundant minerals and is found especially in evaporite environments. Alabaster, the massive, granular variety, has been used for thousands of years, made into vases, bowls, and other useful and decorative objects. Today it is used in ashtrays, clock housings, paperweights, and so forth.

Gypsum can be scratched by the fingernail, so it is much too soft for hard use. Care must be taken in handling carvings and useful objects, but scratches can be polished out rather easily.

Selenite is the term applied to colorless, transparent crystals. *Satin spar* is used to describe massive fibrous varieties that are often cut into cabochons or carved into animal shapes. This material has a great chatoyancy, and brown-colored satin spar makes lovely decorative items. Faceted gypsum is not often seen since cut stones are unattractive and very difficult to fashion, due to the exceptionally perfect cleavage and low hardness of the material.

Name: *Gypsum* from the Greek *gypsos,* a name applied to what we now call plaster. *Satin spar* in allusion to the satiny luster of the fibrous material. *Selenite* from the Greek word for *moon,* due to the pearly luster on cleavage surfaces. *Alabaster* from the Greek word *alabastros,* a stone from which ointment vases were made.

H

HACKMANITE See: Sodalite.

HAMBERGITE

Formula: $Be_2BO_3(OH,F)$.

Crystallography: Orthorhombic. Crystals prismmatic, flattened.

Colors: Colorless, white, grayish white, yellowish white.

Luster: Vitreous to dull.

Hardness: 7.5.

Density: 2.35-2.37.

Cleavage: Perfect 1 direction. Fracture conchoidal to uneven. Brittle.

Optics: $\alpha = 1.55; \beta = 1.59; \gamma = 1.63$.
Biaxial (+), $2V = 87°$.

Birefringence: 0.072.

Dispersion: 0.015.

Spectral: Not diagnostic.

Inclusions: Tubes.

Luminescence: None in most specimens; sometimes weak pink-orange in LW (Norway).

Occurrence: In syenite pegmatites and alkali pegmatites, in crystals up to 2×1 inch.

Anjanabanoana, Madagascar: large gemmy crystals. Non-gem material from *Kashmir, India; Czechoslovakia; Ramona, California; Langesundsfjord, Norway.*

Stone Sizes: Hambergite is a fairly rare mineral, seldom transparent enough to facet. Cut gems over 5 carats are very rare. In 1968 a dealer offered a white stone of 28.86 carats, however.
PC: 40.20 (largest reported); also 7.6, 5.93.

Comments: Hambergite is a gem for collectors of the unusual, although it is hard enough for wear. The remarkable properties of this material are noteworthy—it has the lowest known density for any gem of such high birefringence. This combination of properties makes identification fairly easy. Stones have little fire and may resemble quartz, but the birefringence is much larger than that of similar-appearing gemstones. Usually cut stones are not clean, but filled with cleavage traces.

Name: After Axel Hamberg, Swedish mineralogist, who called attention to the mineral.

HANCOCKITE See: Epidote.

HAÜYNE Sodalite Group: See Lazurite.

Formula: $(Na,Ca)_{4-8}(Al_6Si_6)O_{24}(SO_4,S)_{1-2}$.

Crystallography: Isometric. Crystals dodecahedral or octahedral; usually rounded grains.

Colors: Blue; also white, shades of gray, green, yellow, and red. Translucent to semitransparent.

Luster: Vitreous to greasy.

Streak: Slightly bluish to colorless.

Hardness: 5.5-6.

Density: 2.40-2.50. (Eifel = 2.40.)

Cleavage: Distinct 1 direction. Fracture conchoidal to uneven. Brittle.

Optics: $N = 1.496-1.505$. (Eifel = 1.502.)

Spectral: Not diagnostic.

Luminescence: Usually none; sometimes orange-red in LW (Germany).

Occurrence: Alkaline igneous rocks, associated with leucite and nepheline.
Montana; South Dakota; Colorado.
Quebec, Canada; France; Laacher See, Germany; Italy; Morocco.

Stone Sizes: Opaque material is cut into cabochons up to an inch or two, but faceted gems are exceedingly rare and always small (under 1-2 carats), chiefly from the Eifel region of West Germany.

Comments: Haüyne is one of the major constituents of lapis lazuli, a well-known and ancient gem material. It is, however, rarely seen as a distinct gem species. It is cut for collectors mainly as a curiosity, but faceted gems that are deep blue in color are extremely beautiful. Blue is the most sought after color in this material.

Name: After René Just Haüy, one of the great early mineralogists.

HAWK'S EYE   See: Quartz.

HEDENBERGITE   See: Diopside.

HELIODOR   See: Beryl.

HELIOTROPE   See: Quartz.

HEMATINE   See: Hematite.

HEMATITE

Formula: Fe_2O_3.

Crystallography: Hexagonal (R). Crystals in wide variety of forms, often lustrous or tarnished. Massive; compact; fibrous; reniform (kidney ore); micaceous; stalactitic; earthy.

Colors: Steel gray to black; blood red in thin slivers or crystals. Massive material is brownish red.

Streak: Deep red or brownish red.

Luster: Metallic, submetallic, dull; glistening in micaceous variety.

Hardness: 5-6.5.

Density: 4.95-5.26.

Cleavage: None. Fracture even to subconchoidal. Brittle.

Optics: $o = 3.22$; $e = 2.94$.
Uniaxial ($-$).

Birefringence: 0.280.

Occurrence: A major ore of iron; usually in sedimentary deposits in thick beds; also in igneous rocks, metamorphic rocks, and lavas (deposited from vapor).
Lake Superior region, *Minnesota; Michigan; Wisconsin; New York; Alaska; Tennessee; Pennsylvania; Missouri; South Dakota; Wyoming; Arizona.*
Elba, Italy; Canada; Mexico; Cuba; most European countries.
Brazil: fine crystals, also massive material from a locality near *Ouro Preto.*
England: kidney ore from *Cumberland* area.

Stone Sizes: Hematite is almost always opaque, usually cut into beads, cameos, intaglios, and carvings of any desired size. Massive material is available in very large pieces, solid, and good for cutting. Opaque submetallic gems are also sometimes faceted in the nature of marcasite, with a flat base and a few facets.

Comments: Hematite was used by the American Indians and others as a face paint (so-called red ochre). The polishing compound known as *rouge,* used widely on silver and gold, is powdered hematite. The streak is characteristic and diagnostic. Hematite is a weak electrical conductor, as opposed to *psilomelane,* a similar-appearing manganese oxide. Much hematite is cut in Idar-Oberstein, Germany, but the material comes from England. Hematite is simulated by a variety of materials. One of these, known as *hematine,* is a mixture of stainless steel with sulfides of Cr and Ni. It has a red streak but is quite magnetic, whereas hematite is not. Hematine is made into intaglios and cameos. Hematite crystals that may be transparent are far too thin to cut, so faceted stones are unknown. A massive material consisting of a mixture of hematite, martite, and gangue minerals occurs near Ouro Preto, Brazil. The material is granular and has a dark brown, rather than a red, streak.

Name: From the Greek *hema (blood),* due to the red streak (powder) and appearance of some specimens.

HEMIMORPHITE

Formula: $Zn_4Si_2O_7(OH)_2 \cdot H_2O$.

Crystallography: Orthorhombic. Crystals tabular and thin, striated; fan-shaped aggregates.

Colors: White, colorless, pale blue, greenish, gray, yellowish, brown.

Luster: Vitreous, silky; dull.

Hardness: 4.5-5.

Density: 3.4-3.5.

Cleavage: Perfect 1 direction. Fracture even to subconchoidal. Brittle.

Optics: $\alpha = 1.614$; $\beta = 1.617$; $\gamma = 1.636$.
Biaxial (+), $2V = 46°$.

Birefringence: 0.022.

Pleochroism: None.

Spectral: Not diagnostic.

Luminescence: None observed.

Occurrence: A secondary mineral in the oxide zones of ore deposits.
Found throughout the southwestern *United States* and *Mexico;* various localities worldwide.
Mexico: crystals up to several inches in length are found at *Mapimi, Durango,* and *Santa Eulalia, Chihuahua;* some of these are transparent and will yield stones up to ~ 7-10 carats. Also found as blue crusts.

Stone Sizes: Blue massive material cut as cabochons to several inches in length. Colorless material from Mexico in faceted gems 1-3 carats; larger stones are very rare.
DG: 1.90 (colorless, Mexico).

Comments: Hemimorphite is very rare as a faceted gemstone. Suitable material is known only from Mexico thus far. The massive blue material is a very delicate color, but is seldom cut because not very much has appeared on the market.

Name: In allusion to crystal forms.

HENRITERMIERITE See: Garnet.

HERCYNITE See: Chromite, Spinel.

HERDERITE

Formula: $CaBePO_4(F,OH)$.

Crystallography: Monoclinic. Crystals stout or prismatic; tabular; crusts.

Colors: Colorless, pale yellow, greenish white, pink, green, violet.

Luster: Vitreous.

Hardness: 5-5.5.

Density: 2.95-3.02.

Cleavage: Interrupted. Fracture conchoidal. Brittle.

Optics: $\alpha = 1.591$-1.594; $\beta = 1.611$-1.613; $\gamma = 1.619$-1.624. Biaxial (−), $2V = 67$-$75°$. Can be (+). In general: herderite with (OH) is (+), with F is (−).
Note: Green gem from Brazil: $\alpha = 1.581$; $\beta = 1.601$; $\gamma = 1.610$; birefringence 0.029; S.G. 3.02; contains 7% F.

Birefringence: 0.029-0.030.

Dispersion: 0.017.

Pleochroism: None or weak.

Spectral: Not diagnostic.

Luminescence: Pale green in LW and SW; also pale violet in SW (Brazil, green gem) and stronger violet in LW. Orange fluorescence in X-rays with persistent phosphorescence.

Occurrence: Late stage hydrothermal mineral in granite pegmatites.
New Hampshire.
Germany; Austria; USSR.
Maine: colorless and pale yellow crystals.
Minas Gerais, Brazil: crystals up to nearly fist size, colorless and pink; some green, violetish.

Stone Sizes: Faceted gems from Maine are usually small (1-5 carats) and pale colored or colorless. Brazil gems, however, have stronger color and may be up to 25-30 carats from larger crystals.
SI: 5.9 (green, Brazil).
DG: 3.65 (blue, Brazil).
NMC: 4.65 (light violet octagon, Brazil).

Comments: Herderite is a rare collector gem, especially in larger sizes. It is too soft for wear but is attractive when cut. Clean stones are very hard to find. There is always the possibility of new and larger material coming on the market from Brazilian sources.

Name: After S. A. W. von Herder, a mining official in Freiburg, Germany.

HESSONITE See: Garnet.

HETEROSITE See: Purpurite.

HIDDENITE See: Spodumene.

HODGKINSONITE

Formula: $MnZn_2SiO_5 \cdot H_2O$.

Crystallography: Monoclinic. Crystals pyramidal or prismatic; massive; granular.

Colors: Bright pink to reddish brown, purplish pink.

Luster: Vitreous.

Hardness: 4.5-5.

Density: 3.91-3.99.

Cleavage: Perfect 1 direction. Fracture conchoidal. Brittle.

Optics: $\alpha = 1.720$; $\beta = 1.741$; $\gamma = 1.746$.
Biaxial (−), $2V = 52°$.

Birefringence: 0.026.

Pleochroism: Distinct: lavender/colorless/lavender.

Spectral: Not diagnostic.

Luminescence: Dull red in LW.

Occurrence: In metamorphosed limestone at *Franklin, New Jersey* with various other Zn and Mn minerals. Individual crystals reached ¾ inch in diameter, in veins up to several inches thick. The material was mined out years ago.

Stone Sizes: Cut gems are very small, less than 2 carats. This is an exceedingly rare material, available from only one locality and only from older specimens.
PC: 0.89.

Comments: Hodgkinsonite is one of the rarest of all collector gems. Cut stones are bright and richly colored, but the crystals were never abundant and still fewer had transparent areas. Fewer than 10 cut stones may exist.

Name: After H. H. Hodgkinson of Franklin, New Jersey, who discovered the mineral.

HOLTITE

Formula: $Al_6(Ta,Sb,Li)[(Si,As)O_4]_3(BO_3)(O,OH)_3$ + Fe, Be, Ti, Mn, and Nb. Related to *dumortierite*.

Crystallography: Orthorhombic. Compact pebbles of acicular crystals, 2-15 mm diameter. Needles often in parallel arrangement.

Colors: Cream white, buff, olive green, brownish.

Luster: Dull to resinous.

Hardness: 8.5.

Density: 3.90.

Cleavage: Good 1 direction.

Optics: $\alpha = 1.743-1.746$; $\beta = 1.756-1.759$; $\gamma = 1.758-1.761$. Biaxial (−), $2V = 49-55°$.

Birefringence: 0.015.

Pleochroism: Distinct: yellow/colorless/colorless.

Luminescence: Dull orange in SW, bright yellow in LW.

Occurrence: Alluvial tin deposit near *Greenbushes, Western Australia,* associated with cassiterite.

Stone Sizes: Could yield cabochons up to about 1 inch.

Comments: This mineral was first noted in 1937 but was not described in detail until 1971. It has not yet been seen as a gem, but the high hardness would allow it be worn with no risk of scratching. Holtite is now considered to be a variety of dumortierite. The mineral comes from the one locality, and a cut stone would have to be considered a great rarity.

Name: After Harold E. Holt, prime minister of Australia from 1966 to 1967.

HORNBLENDE   See: Actinolite, Pargasite, Amphibole.

HOWLITE

Formula: $Ca_2B_5SiO_9(OH)_5$.

Crystallography: Monoclinic. Crystals tiny; usually nodular masses, chalky or porcellaneous.

Colors: White, opaque except in tiny grains.

Luster: Subvitreous.

Hardness: 3.5 or less.

Density: 2.45-2.58.

Cleavage: Smooth and even fracture.

Optics: $\alpha = 1.583-1.586$; $\beta = 1.596-1.598$; $\gamma = 1.605$. Biaxial (−), $2V$ large.

Birefringence: 0.022.

Pleochroism: None.

Spectral: Not diagnostic.

Luminescence: Brownish yellow in SW; some California material deep orange in LW.

Occurrence: Microscopic crystals or nodules occur in arid regions or borate deposits.
California: abundant nodules, up to a weight of several hundred pounds, as at *Lang* in *Los Angeles County.* Also occurs in the *Mohave Desert, California.*
Nova Scotia: small nodules.

Stone Sizes: Spheres up to about 8 inches in diameter have been cut; also seen as cabochons and tumble-polished stones.

Comments: Howlite is always opaque in nodules; it is an abundant material and easy to acquire. Sometimes it contains black, threadlike impurities resembling the veining in turquoise. Howlite is frequently dyed blue to resemble turquoise, and it makes a most convincing simulant. The white material is relatively unexciting in appearance.

Name: After H. How who described a mineral of approximately the same composition.

HUEBNERITE

Formula: $MnWO_4$ Series to Ferberite: $FeWO_4$.

Crystallography: Monoclinic; crystals prismatic; flattened; tabular, often striated in direction of elongation. Often in crystal groups, radiating or parallel aggregates. Commonly twinned.

Colors: Brownish black, yellowish to reddish brown, red. Streak yellowish, reddish brown, blackish to greenish gray. Sometimes color banded; sometimes tarnished iridescent.

Luster: Submetallic to resinous.

Hardness: 4-4.5 (increases with iron content).

Density: 7.12-7.18 (increases with iron content).

Cleavage: Perfect in 1 direction; fracture uneven; brittle.

Optics: $\alpha = 2.17\text{-}2.20$; $\beta = 2.22$; $\gamma = 2.30\text{-}2.32$. Biaxial (+).

Birefringence: 0.13.

Pleochroism: Varies with locality and iron content: bright yellow/orange-red/orange-red; greenish-yellow/orange-red/bright red; olive green/brick-red/dark red.

Spectral: Not diagnostic.

Luminescence: None.

Occurrence: High-temperature hydrothermal ore veins; quartz veins in or near granitic rocks; Many localities in western *United States (Colorado; Idaho; Nevada; New Mexico; Arizona; South Dakota).*
France; Czechoslovakia; Australia.
Pasto Bueno, Peru: transparent crystals.

Stone Sizes: Huebnerite is transparent, and opacity increases with iron content. Material suitable for faceting occurs in Peru, and stones of several carats in weight may be cut but tend to be dark.

Comments: It should not be difficult to find numerous small faceted huebnerites among larger gemstone collections. Certainly ample material exists to cut a number of such gems, although they are rarely offered for sale.

Name: After Adolph Hübner, a metallurgist from Freiburg, Saxony (Germany). Ferberite was named after Rudolph Ferber, of Gera, Germany.

HUMITE GROUP Members of this group include Humite, Clinohumite, Norbergite, and Chondrobite.

These minerals are easily confused with each other as they have similar properties. The compositions are related in a very distinctive way:

$$\text{Norbergite: } Mg(OH,F)_2 \cdot Mg_2(SiO_4)$$
$$\text{Chondrodite: } Mg(OH,F)_2 \cdot 2Mg_2(SiO_4)$$
$$\text{Humite: } Mg(OH,F)_2 \cdot 3Mg_2(SiO_4)$$
$$\text{Clinohumite: } Mg(OH,F)_2 \cdot 4Mg_2(SiO_4)$$

TiO_2 present in humite and clinohumite strongly affects their optical properties. All members of this group have poor cleavage and vitreous luster. All are biaxial (+) and generally yellowish brown in color.

Luminescence: Usually inert in SW, sometimes golden yellow; dull orange to brownish orange in LW.

Occurrence: In contact zones in limestone or dolomite. Rarely in alkaline rocks of igneous origin. This paragenesis is true for all members of the humite group. *Wiberforce, Ontario, Canada.*
Tilly Foster Mine, Brewster, New York: fine crystals of chondrodite, reddish brown, some rather gemmy, associated with humite and clinohumite. This locality is the source of most gem chondrodite.
Kafveltorp, Orebro, Sweden: yellowish material.
Pargas, Finland: yellowish material.
Loolekop, East Transvaal: in a carbonatite.
Norbergite from: *Franklin, New Jersey; Orange County, New York; Norberg, Sweden.*
Clinohumite from: *California; Ala, Italy; Malaga, Spain; Lake Baikal, USSR.*

Stone Sizes: Cut humites are always small, generally in the 1-3 carat range. Crystals tend to be dark and filled with inclusions and fractures. Larger cut gems would be extremely rare.

Comments: Faceted chondrodite is almost unknown, a

	Norbergite	Chondrodite	Humite	Clinohumite ———	(USSR)
Crystallography	orthorhombic	monoclinic	orthorhombic	monoclinic	
Colors	yellowish tan	yellow, brown, red	yellow, deep orange	yellow, brown, white	
Hardness	6.5	6.5	6	6	
Density	3.15-3.18	3.16-3.26	3.20-3.32	3.17-3.35	
Optics					
α	1.563-1.567	1.592-1.615	1.607-1.643	1.629-1.638	1.631
β	1.567-1.579	1.602-1.627	1.639-1.675	1.662-1.643	1.639-1.647
γ	1.590-1.593	1.621-1.646	1.639-1.675	1.662-1.674	1.668
2V	44-50°	71-85°	65-84°	73-76°	
Birefringence	0.026-0.027	0.028-0.034	0.029-0.031	0.028-0.041	0.037
Pleochroism					
α	pale yellow	very pale yellow/ brownish yellow	yellow	golden yellow/ deep reddish yellow	
β	very pale yellow	colorless/ yellowish green	colorless/ pale yellow	pale yellow/ orange yellow	
γ	colorless	colorless/ pale green	colorless/ pale yellow	pale yellow/ orange yellow	

pity since the color is very rich and the material is hard and durable enough for wear. Cutting presents no great difficulty, but rough is virtually unobtainable, and only tiny stones could be produced. The same is true for norbergite and humite. The exception seems to be clinohumite from the Pamir Mountains in the USSR. Crystals occur there in sizes allowing the production of small (1-3 carats), slightly brownish yellow but flawless gems. This material fluoresces slightly orangy yellow in SW. Only a handful of gems have been cut.

Names: Chondrodite from the Greek *chondros,* a grain, in allusion to the mineral's granular nature. Humite is named after Sir Abraham Hume, an English collector of gems and minerals of the nineteenth century. Norbergite is named after the locality at Norberg, Sweden, where it is found. Clinohumite is the monoclinic end of the humite--clinohumite series.

HUREAULITE

Formula: $Mn_5(PO_4)_2[(PO_3)(OH)]_2 \cdot 4H_2O$.

Crystallography: Monoclinic. Crystals prismatic up to 3 cm, tabular; massive; compact.

Colors: Pale rose, violet-rose, yellowish, red-orange, orange-red, brownish orange, yellowish to reddish brown, gray, colorless.

Luster: Vitreous to greasy.

Hardness: 3.5.

Density: 3.19.

Cleavage: Good 1 direction. Fracture uneven. Brittle.

Optics: $\alpha = 1.637\text{-}1.652$; $\beta = 1.645\text{-}1.658$; $\gamma = 1.649\text{-}1.663$. Biaxial (−), $2V = 75°$.

Birefringence: 0.012.

Pleochroism: colorless/pale rose to yellow/reddish yellow-brown.

Spectral: Not diagnostic.

Luminescence: None.

Occurrence: In phosphate masses in granite pegmatites. *Branchville, Connecticut; North Groton, New Hampshire; South Dakota.*
Haute Vienne, France; Portugal; Germany; Poland.
Pala, California: orange masses.

Stone Sizes: Massive material suited only for cabochons. No faceted gems have been reported to date, but facetable material likely exists and one day will be cut.

Comments: The colors are rich and lively, but the mineral is too soft for wear. Hureaulite is a collector gem and is very rare even in cabochon form.

Name: After the locality, Hureaux, France.

HURLBUTITE

Formula: $CaBe_2(PO_4)_2$.

Crystallography: Orthorhombic; crystals prismatic, chunky, with etched surfaces and striations.

Colors: Colorless to greenish white; may be stained yellow. Streak: white.

Luster: Vitreous to greasy.

Hardness: 6.

Density: 2.88.

Cleavage: None; fracture conchoidal; brittle.

Optics: $\alpha = 1.595$; $\beta = 1.601$; $\gamma = 1.604$. Biaxial (−).

Birefringence: 0.009.

Pleochroism: None.

Spectral: Not diagnostic.

Luminescence: None reported.

Occurrence: In pegmatite with muscovite, albite, and other minerals at the *Smith Mine, Chandler's Mill, Newport, New Hampshire.*

Stone Sizes: This is an extremely rare mineral, and small clean cuttable fragments have yielded minute faceted stones. They are transparent and colorless, all under 1 carat in size.

Name: After Cornelius Hurlbut, well-known professor of mineralogy at Harvard University.

HYALITE   See: Opal.

HYDROGROSSULAR   See: Garnet.

HYPERSTHENE   See: Enstatite.

I

ICELAND SPAR   See: Calcite.

IDOCRASE   Alternative name: Vesuvianite.

Formula: $Ca_{19}Al_4Fe(Al,Mg,Fe)_8Si_{18}O_7(O,OH,F)_8$ + Be, Cu, Cr, Mn, Na, K, Ti, B, H_2O, U, Th, Zn, Sn, Sb, rare earths.

Density: 3.32-3.47.

Cleavage: None. Fracture conchoidal.

Optics: Variable depending on paragenesis and mineral associations.
Uniaxial (+) or (−); sometimes anomalously biaxial (−) or (+); twinned.

Environment	e	o	Birefringence
Serpentinites	1.705–1.750	1.702–1.761	0.018
Contact metamorphic rocks	1.655–1.733	1.674–1.737	0.015
Alkalic rocks	1.655–1.727	1.715–1.731	0.004
Regionally metamorphosed rocks	1.697–1.698	1.705–1.707	0.008

Locality	Color	e	o	Birefringence	Comments
Asbestos, Quebec, Canada	green	1.704	1.708	0.004	
	emerald green	1.717	1.721	0.004	
	brown	1.711	1.714	0.003	
	mauve	1.703	1.704	0.001	contains Mn
Laurel, Quebec, Canada	brownish yellow	1.705	1.710	0.005	

Incredible array of elements substitute in the idocrase structure.

Crystallography: Tetragonal. Crystals often well formed, prismatic, pyramidal, often with complex modifications; granular, massive. Often intergrown with grossular.

Colors: Colorless, green (various shades), brown (various shades), white, yellow (various shades), red, brownish red, blue, blue-green, pink, violet. Sometimes color zoned.

Luster: Vitreous to resinous.

Hardness: 6-7.

Note: Antimonian idocrase from contact metamorphic rocks, greenish-yellow grains, $e = 1.758$-1.775, $o = 1.775$-1.795; birefringence 0.017-0.025; Sb_2O_3 >15%.

Dispersion: 0.019-0.025.

Pleochroism: Usually weak in same colors as crystal. Also green/orange and green/yellow-green (from Quebec).

Spectral: Strong line at 4610, weak at 5285.

Luminescence: None.

Occurrence: Serpentines and related rocks; contact metamorphic deposits, especially in limestones and dolomites; alkalic rocks; regionally metamorphosed rocks.

Finland; Japan; Korea; Tanzania.
Arkansas.
California: californite; also crystals at Pulga.
Ala, Piedmont, Italy: fine brown and green crystals.
Zillerthal, Tyrol, Switzerland: brown crystals; also at Zermatt, other locations.
Laurel, Quebec, Canada: bright yellow grains and masses.
Amity, New York (xanthite): brown crystals, large; seldom cut.
Telemark, Norway (cyprine): fine blue masses with pink thulite.
Asbestos, Quebec, Canada: superb crystal groups and masses, apple green, sometimes colored deep green by Cr or pink by Mn.
Kenya: green and brown crystal fragments suitable for faceting.
Sanford, Maine: brown and green crystals and masses.
Wilui River, USSR: green crystals (known as wiluite).
Morelos, Mexico: green crystals associated with pink grossular in lake bed.
Quetta, Pakistan: fine green crystals; some transparent.

Stone Sizes: Crystals up to several inches in length occur at a few localities, but these are seldom transparent except in small areas. The maximum expectable size for a faceted idocrase is on the order of 10 carats (for brown material from Italy and Africa), perhaps 15 carats in green material.
SI: 3.5 (brown, Italy); 7.1 (brown, Tanzania).
DG: 8.50 (brown, Africa).
NMC: 3.15, 2.95, 2.28 (Laurel, Quebec).

Comments: Idocrase is one of the lesser known and more beautiful collector gems. When properly cut it is as bright and attractive as the grossular garnets, which it so strongly resembles. The complexities of its chemistry lead to a huge range in properties and colors. Cuttable material is known from Italy (brown and green), Quebec (pale green, bright yellow), New York (brown), Pakistan (green), Kenya (brown and green).

Californite is a massive idocrase-grossular mixture reported first from California and later found in various other localities, such as Africa and Pakistan. The density is 3.25-3.32 and there is a strong 4610 band in its spectrum, which is easily distinguished from the chrome spectrum of jadeite.

Name: From the Greek words idos and krasis, meaning mixed appearance, because idocrase crystal forms resemble those seen on other species. Vesuvianite from Mt. Vesuvius, where the mineral occurs in small, perfect crystals.

INDERITE   Also known as Lesserite; dimorph of Kurnakovite.

Formula: $Mg_2B_6O_{11} \cdot 15H_2O$.

Crystallography: Monoclinic. Crystals prismatic, up to 10×1 cm; nodular; acicular crystals also.

Colors: Colorless; massive varieties white to pink.

Luster: Vitreous; pearly on cleavage.

Hardness: 2.5.

Density: 1.78-1.86.

Cleavage: Perfect 1 direction. Fracture uneven. Brittle.

Optics: $\alpha = 1.486\text{-}1.489; \beta = 1.488\text{-}1.493; \gamma = 1.504\text{-}1.507$. Biaxial (+), $2V = 37\text{-}52°$.

Birefringence: 0.017-0.020.

Spectral: Not diagnostic.

Luminescence: None.

Occurrence: Borate deposits in arid regions.
Kern County, California: large crystals, often transparent.
Inder borate deposit, Kazakhstan, USSR: as nodules in red clay.

Stone Sizes: Gems over 50 carats or more could be cut from large transparent crystals.

Comments: Inderite is very soft and difficult to cut, and only a few stones have been cut by hobbyists. There is plenty of cuttable material in existence, and although the material comes from only a few localities, it is not considered a great rarity. The surface of cut stones may become white and cloudy after cutting; care must be taken in storage and to dry the stones after cutting.

Name: After the locality, Inder Lake, Kazakhstan, USSR.

INDICOLITE   See Tourmaline.

IOLITE   See: Cordierite.

J

JADE See: Jadeite, Nephrite.

JADEITE (= JADE) Pyroxene Group.

Formula: $NaAlSi_2O_6$.

Crystallography: Monoclinic. Crystals very rare and tiny, usually granular with tough, interlocked crystals; fibrous; as alluvial boulders and pebbles.

Colors: Colorless, white, all shades of green, yellow-green, yellowish brown, brown, red, orange, violet (mauve), gray, black.

Green Jadeite Color Terminology

United States	Orient
Imperial	Old Mine
Glassy	Canary
Apple Green	New Mine
Spinach	Oily
Moss-in-Snow	Pea Green
Apple Green	Flower Green

Luster: Vitreous.

Hardness: 6.5-7.

Density: 3.25-3.36; usually 3.34+.

Cleavage: None (massive). Fracture splintery. Very tough.

Optics: $\alpha = 1.640$; $\beta = 1.645$; $\gamma = 1.652\text{-}1.667$. Shadow edge usually 1.66. Biaxial (+), $2V = 67°$.

Birefringence: 0.012-0.020.

Pleochroism: None.

Spectral: Jadeite has a distinctive spectrum useful in identification.

There is a strong line at 4375, weak bands at 4500 and 4330. The 4375 line is diagnostic for jadeite but may not be seen in rich, deep green material, which has a Cr spectrum: strong line at 6915, weak at 6550 and 6300.

Luminescence: Pale colors may show dim white glow in LW. No reaction in SW. X-rays may give intense blue-violet glow in pale yellow and mauve stones.

Occurrence: Jadeite occurs chiefly in serpentine derived from olivine rocks. Also as alluvial boulders. The finest jade comes from *Burma.*

Hmaw-Sit-Sit, Upper Burma: once thought to be jadeite mixed with albite, showing dark spots and green vein pattern, later identified as ureyite (a different pyroxene mineral) in natrolite.

USSR: apple green-colored jadeite at some localities; also fine translucent, Cr-rich jadeite at the *Kantegir River,* West Sayan.

New Zealand; Japan; Mexico; Guatemala; San Benito County, California: lenses and nodules in chert, various colors; also mixed with nephrite.

Comments: *Jadeite* is usually marketed through Yunan Province, China. Green boulders may have a brown skin due to weathering, which is often utilized in carving. The best jade known is Burmese in origin and occurs in a wide range of colors. There are many simulants and imitations. *Imperial jade* is exceedingly rare and very costly. Another popular color is a fine apple green shade, as well as lavender (mauve). The rich green material from Burma is sometimes called *Yunan jade* and is extremely beautiful when light passes through it. *Chloromelanite* is opaque, dark green to black jade that is seldom seen in jewelry but is occasionally carved.

The value of a jade item is as much a function of the artistry of the carving or workmanship and the antiquity value as the color and quality of the jade itself. The complexities of evaluation caused by these factors make jade a very specialized gemstone and the market largely a collector market.

Name: *Jade* from the Spanish *piedras de ijada, (stone of the loins);* this is due to the healing powers for kidney ailments ascribed to jade, doubtless as a result of sympathetic magic because of the kidney or organ shapes of tumbled pebbles. Translated into French this was *pierre de l'éjade;* a printer's error when the name first appeared in French made it *pierre de le jade,* which the English people quickly chopped down to simply *jade.*
See also: Nephrite.

JASPER   See: Quartz.

JEFFERSONITE   See: Diopside.

JEREMEJEVITE

Formula: $Al_6B_5O_{15}(OH,F)_3$.

Crystallography: Hexagonal; crystals elongated and tapering; also small grains.

Colors: Colorless, pale blue-green, pale yellow-brown.

Luster: Vitreous.

Hardness: 6.5-7.5.

Density: 3.28-3.31.

Cleavage: None; fracture conchoidal.

Optics: $e = 1.637-1.644$; $o = 1.644-1.653$.
Uniaxial (−).
Cores of crystals sometimes biaxial (from USSR), $2V = 0-50°$.
Biaxial rims also sometimes observed in Namibian material.

Birefringence: 0.007-0.013.

Pleochroism: Light cornflower blue/colorless to light yellow (Namibian material).

Spectral: Vague absorption band at about 5000.

Luminescence: None.

Occurrence: *Cape Cross,* near *Swakopmund, Namibia:* very long pyramidal crystals (up to 2 cm), blue-green color: $e = 1.639$; $o = 1.648$; birefringence 0.007.
A few single crystals were found on *Mt. Soktuj, Nerchinsk district, East Siberia, USSR,* in loose granitic debris under the turf.

Stone Sizes: No gems have been reported from the USSR material. However, the Swakopmund crystals have been cut, with gems up to about 5 carats possible. These are a lovely blue-green color, are relatively easy to cut, and are hard enough for wear. Typical faceted stone sizes are from under 1 carat up to about 2 carats.

Comments: Until the Namibian material was found, jeremejevite was an exceedingly rare mineral available only in microscopic grains. The African crystals are amazing in being both large and gemmy. Few gems have been cut from the material since the crystals are prized by collectors and the extent of the find is unknown. The crystals are not abundant at the locality, so jeremejevite will remain an extremely rare collector gemstone.

Name: After Pavel V. Jeremejev, Russian mineralogist and engineer.

JET

Formula: C.
Carbon, plus impurities; *not a mineral.*

Crystallography: Amorphous. Usually in coal seams as black masses and lumps.

Colors: Black, brownish.

Luster: Dull; vitreous when polished.

Hardness: 2.4-4.

Density: 1.19-1.35.

Cleavage: None. Conchoidal fracture. Brittle.

Optics: Blurred shadow edge on refractometer at 1.66.

Other Tests: Burns like coal and gives burning coal odor with hot needle.

Occurrence: Jet is fossilized wood, actually lignite, a form of brown coal.
Henry Mountains, Utah; Colorado; New Mexico.
Spain; Aude, France; Germany; USSR; Poland; India; Turkey.
Whitby, England: jet in seams; classic locality.

Stone Sizes: Carvings and cabochons of any desired size could be cut.

Comments: Jet has been known since Neolithic times and has been the most popular of all black gems. It has been used for many years in mourning jewelry. It is less popular and widely used in modern times. It takes a very good polish and is less brittle than the harder anthracite coal that it resembles. Jet is often faceted (the stones have a flat bottom) to add sparkle to the somber tones of jet jewelry.

Name: Originally from Gagates, the name of a town and river (Gagae) in Asia Minor.

JULGOLDITE   See: Pumpellyite.

K

KÄMMERERITE

Formula: $(Mg,Cr)_6(AlSi_3)O_{10}(OH)_8$. (Chlorite Group).

Crystallography: Triclinic; crystals hexagonal shape, bounded by steep sided pyramids.

Colors: Red to purplish red, cranberry red.

Luster: Vitreous; pearly on cleavages.

Hardness: 2-2.5.

Density: 2.64.

Cleavage: Perfect basal cleavage; micaceous; laminae flexible.

Optics: $\alpha = 1.597$; $\beta = 1.598$; $\gamma = 1.599$-1.600. Biaxial; optic sign variable.

Birefringence: 0.003.

Pleochroism: Strong; violet/hyacinth-red.

Spectral: Not diagnostic.

Luminescence: None reported.

Occurrence: In chromite deposits, associated with clinochlore and uvarovite.
Erzincan, Turkey: distinct crystals.
Lake Itkul, near Miask, USSR.
California; Texas; Pennsylvania.

Stone Sizes: Facetable material is quite rare and always small. Minute gems, 1-2 carats, have been cut from Turkish material.

Comments: Kämmererite is a beautiful but rare mineral. It is micaceous; consequently, it is extraordinarily difficult to facet, which has severely limited the availability of cut gems. It would have to be handled with great care to avoid cleaving. A few clean, well-cut gems do exist, nonetheless, a testimony to the perseverence of hobbyists!

Name: After A. Kämmerer, the mining director at St. Petersburg.

KIMZEYITE   See: Garnet.

KNORRINGITE   See: Garnet.

KORITE   Also known as Ammolite; Calcentine.

Formula: $CaCO_3$.

Crystallography: Orthorhombic (aragonite).

Colors: White, highly iridescent, especially shades of red and green.

Luster: Vitreous to resinous.

Hardness: 4.

Density: 2.80 (pure aragonite = 2.95).

Cleavage: Several directions; brittle.

Optics: $\alpha = 1.520$; $\gamma = 1.670$.

Birefringence: 0.150.

Occurrence: Korite is fossil ammonite shell, most notably from *Alberta, Canada.* The material is classified (class/genus/species) as Cephalopoda/*Ammonoidea/placenticeras meeki.* These shells are approximately 71 million years old and vary in diameter up to approximately 25 cm. The iridescent aragonite outer layer may be 6 mm thick. This is usually too thin to support itself in jewelry, so korite (or ammolite) is often fabricated into triplets with quartz tops and shale or synthetic spinel as backing material. Only about 5% of the ammonites found at the locality have any suitable gem material, and of these only about 20% of the shell can be used.

KORNERUPINE

Formula: $Mg_3Al_6(Si,Al,B)_5O_{21}(OH)$.

Crystallography: Orthorhombic; crystals prismatic; also fibrous, columnar.

Colors: Colorless, white, pink, greenish yellow, blue-green, sea green, dark green, brown, black.

Luster: Vitreous.

Hardness: 6-7.

Cleavage: Perfect 2 directions; fracture conchoidal; brittle.

Density: 3.27-3.45; gems are 3.28-3.35.

Optics: varies with locality:

Locality	α	β	γ	Birefrin-gence	Density
Madagascar	1.661	1.673	1.674	0.013	3.28
Sri Lanka	1.669	1.681	1.682	0.013	3.35
catseye	1.673	1.686	1.690	0.017	—
Germany	1.675	1.687	1.687	0.014	3.37
Natal	1.682	1.696	1.699	0.017	3.45
Greenland	1.667	1.679	1.682	0.015	3.30
East Africa	1.662	1.675	1.677	0.015	—

Biaxial ($-$), $2V = 3$-$48°$; gems sometimes pseudo-uniaxial.

Dispersion: 0.018.

Pleochroism: Pronounced and visible to the naked eye: Sri Lanka; Madagascar: yellowish brown/brown/greenish. Kwale District, Kenya: intense green/light green/greenish yellow.
Kenya; Tanzania: emerald green/bluish gray/reddish purple.
Greenland: dark green/reddish blue/light blue.

Spectral: Weak band seen at 5030.

Inclusions: Zircon, apatite crystals.

Luminescence: None (Sri Lanka) or yellowish (Burmese green gems, stronger in East African stones) in LW and SW.

Occurrence: First found in Greenland in radiating crystals (not gemmy), later in cuttable fragments.
Finskenaesset, Southwest Greenland: giant crystals up to 23 cm, yielding cabochons and small (up to ~2 carats) faceted gems of dark green color.
Weligama gem gravels, Matara district, Sri Lanka: greenish to dark yellowish-green catseyes. The eye effect is intense. Stones tend to be small, but cabochons over 7

carats have been reported. Also from *Matale,* yellow-brown and reddish pebbles, in gravels.
Mogok, Burma: greenish-brown material in gem gravels.
Kwale district, Kenya: light green material, some large clean pieces; colored green by vanadium.
Tanzania: chrome variety with green color, cuttable.
Gatineau County, Quebec, Canada: large crystals, dark green to greenish yellow.
Itrongahy, Madagascar: large gemmy dark green crystals, also pale aquamarine-blue.
Betroka and Inanakafy, Madagascar: gray to brown prismatic crystals.

Stone Sizes: Most gems are under 5 carats, but occasional large material from Sri Lanka, Burma, or East Africa yields a gem in the 25-30 carat range. Canadian crystals are large (up to 2 inches across) but are not generally cuttable. The largest crystals of all, from Greenland, yield only small cut stones.
SI: 21.6 (brown, Sri Lanka); 10.8 (brown, Madagascar); 8.1 (green, Sri Lanka).
DG: 6.4 (Sri Lanka).
PC: 16.50 (golden, Sri Lanka); 7.57 (catseye, Sri Lanka).

Comments: Star kornerupine also has been found (Mogok, Burma) but is *very* rare. Kornerupine is generally dark brown or green and not very attractive due to the somber colors. The light green material from Kenya is much more appealing, but the sizes are always small (under 3 carats as a rule). The color is caused by traces of Fe, Cr, and V. Despite the fact that many stones are in museums and private collections, kornerupine is a rather rare gemstone and, for the collector, worth acquiring when available.

Name: After the Danish geologist Kornerup.

KUNZITE   See: Spodumene.

KURNAKOVITE   Dimorph of Inderite.

Formula: $Mg_2B_6O_{11} \cdot 15H_2O$.

Crystallography: Triclinic. Crystals large and blocky, often in clusters; large cleavable masses; aggregates.

Colors: Colorless, with a white surface coating.

Luster: 2.5-3.

Density: 1.78-1.85.

Cleavage: Good 1 direction. Fracture conchoidal. Brittle.

Optics: $\alpha = 1.488$-1.491; $\beta = 1.508$-1.511; $\gamma = 1.515$-1.525. Biaxial ($+$), $2V = 80°$.

Birefringence: 0.027-0.036.

Pleochroism: None.

Spectral: Not diagnostic.

Luminescence: None.

Occurrence: Borate deposits in arid areas.
Inder Lake, Kazakhstan, USSR.
Boron, Kern County, California: crystals to 24 inches across and large masses.

Stone Sizes: California material could yield stones of several hundred carats from large transparent masses or cleavages.

Comments: Kurnakovite is similar to inderite. Both are colorless and very uninteresting as faceted gems, which is why very few have been cut. The material is obtainable in large size, but softness and cleavage make cutting a real chore.

Name: After N. S. Kurnakov, Russian mineralogist and chemist.

KUTNAHORITE See: Dolomite.

KYANITE Trimorphous with Andalusite, Sillimanite.

Formula: Al_2SiO_5.

Crystallography: Triclinic. Crystals bladed, flattened and elongated; fibrous, massive.

Colors: Blue, blue-green, green; also white, gray, yellow, pink, nearly black. Color zoned in individual crystals.

Luster: Vitreous; pearly on cleavage.

Hardness: 4-7.5; varies with direction in single crystals.

Cleavage: Perfect 1 direction.

Density: 3.53-3.68; gems usually upper end of range. Cr-kyanite = 3.67-3.70.

Optics: $\alpha = 1.710$-1.718; $\beta = 1.721$-1.723; $\gamma = 1.727$-1.734.
Cr-kyanite: $\alpha = 1.714$; $\beta = 1.724$; $\gamma = 1.731$; birefringence = 0.017; S.G. = 3.67.
$\alpha = 1.720$; $\beta = 1.730$; $\gamma = 1.753$; birefringence = 0.033; S.G. = 3.70.
Biaxial (−), $2V = 82$-$83°$.

Birefringence: 0.017 (Cr-kyanite up to 0.033).

Dispersion: 0.020.

Pleochroism: Pronounced: violet-blue/colorless/cobalt-blue.
Also pleochroic in all shades of yellow-green and green.

Spectral: One line observed in deep red at 7100 and 2 lines in deep blue, with dark edge at about 6000.

Luminescence: Variable fluorescence, mostly dim red in LW.

Occurrence: In schists, gneiss, and granite pegmatites. Many localities are known.
Various places in the *United States*, especially *Yancy County, North Carolina:* deep blue or green crystals, up to 2 inches long, some facetable.
Vermont; Connecticut; Virginia; Georgia; Massachusetts.
Mozambique: dark blue, with Cr and Ti.
India; Italy.
Brazil: large blue and blue-green crystals.
Machakos District, Kenya: large blue crystals, banded with green; also colorless!
Switzerland: with staurolite in schist.
Kenya: fine blue color, facetable.

Stone Sizes: Gems have been cut up to about 20 carats; they are seldom completely clean over 5 carats, however. Many of these stones are Brazilian; some are African.
SI: 10.7 (blue, Brazil); 9.1 (green, Brazil); 4.9 (blue, Tanzania).
PC: 6.57 (blue-green, North Carolina).
DG: 14.0 (blue, Africa); 8.55 (bluish, Africa).
ROM: 40.26, 12.38 (rectangular step-cut, Brazil).

Comments: Kyanite is very rare as a faceted gem, especially if free from inclusions and flaws. The material is extremely difficult to cut because of its perfect cleavage and the extreme variability in hardness in different directions in the same crystal. A few catseye kyanites are known to exist.

Name: From the Greek *kyanos,* meaning *blue.*

L

LABRADORITE See: Feldspar.

LANDERITE See: Garnet.

LANGBEINITE

Formula: $K_2Mg_2(SO_4)_3$.

Crystallography: Isometric. Crystals are rare; usually massive, bedded; in nodules.

Colors: Colorless, white, gray, yellowish, greenish, pinkish, violet.

Luster: Vitreous.

Hardness: 3.5-4.

Density: 2.83.

Cleavage: None. Fracture conchoidal. Brittle.

Optics: $N = 1.536$.

Luminescence: Faint greenish white in LW (New Mexico).

Occurrence: Evaporite deposits from marine waters. *Saskatchewan, Canada; North Germany; Austria; India. Carlsbad, New Mexico:* beds up to 7 feet thick.

Stone Sizes: Colorless stones potentially up to 10-15 carats. Cabochons of any size.

Comments: This material is nondescript and is cut solely as a curiosity. The gems are soft, pale colored, or colorless, with no fire. Few cut stones have been reported, but this may be due to a lack of interest rather than a lack of suitable rough.

Name: After A. Langbein of Leopoldshall, Austria.

LAPIS LAZULI See: Lazurite.

LAWSONITE

Formula: $CaAl_2Si_2O_7(OH)_2 \cdot H_2O$.

Crystallography: Orthorhombic. Crystals prismatic; massive, granular.

Colors: Colorless, white, gray, blue, pinkish.

Luster: Vitreous to greasy.

Hardness: 6+.

Density: 3.05-3.12.

Cleavage: Perfect in 2 directions.

Optics: $\alpha = 1.665$; $\beta = 1.674\text{-}1.675$; $\gamma = 1.684\text{-}1.686$. Biaxial (+), $2V = 84°$.

Birefringence: 0.019.

Dispersion: High.

Pleochroism: Blue/yellow-green/colorless *or* pale brownish yellow/deep blue-green/yellowish.

Spectral: Not diagnostic.

Luminescence: None.

Occurrence: Low-temperature metamorphic rocks; metamorphic schists; glaucophane schists.
Santa Clara, Cuba; Italy; Japan; New Caledonia; France; Italy; other locations.
Tiburon Peninsula, California: original material.
Covelo, Mendocino County, California: 2-inch crystals.

Stone Sizes: The maximum likely is 2-3 carats. Gems are pale blue in color.

Comments: Lawsonite is extremely rare as a faceted stone, seldom reported and generally unavailable.

Name: After Professor A. C. Lawson of the University of California.

LAZULITE Series to Scorzalite: (Fe,Mg)Al₂(PO₄)₂(OH)₂.

Formula: $(Mg,Fe)Al_2(PO_4)_2(OH)_2$.

Crystallography: Monoclinic; crystals acute pyramidal; massive, compact, granular.

Colors: Blue, blue-green, light blue, deep azure blue.

Luster: Vitreous to dull.

Hardness: 5.5-6.

Cleavage: Indistinct to good, 1 direction; fracture uneven; brittle.

Table of Properties in Lazulaite–Scorzalite Series

Property	Lazulite (Mg)	Mg½Fe½	Scorzalite (Fe)
Density	3.08	3.22	3.38
Optics:			
α	1.604–1.625	1.626	1.627–1.639
β	1.633–1.653	1.654	1.655–1.670
γ	1.642–1.662	1.663	1.664–1.680
Sign	(−)	(−)	(−)
2V	69°	—	62°
Birefringence	0.031–0.036	0.037	0.038–0.040

Pleochroism: Strong: colorless/blue/dark blue.

Luminescence: None.

Spectral: Not diagnostic.

Occurrence: Quartz veins; granite pegmatites; metamorphic rocks, especially quartzites. Scorzalite is a relatively rare mineral; lazulite is more abundant, and the localities are better known, as follows:
Palermo Quarry, North Groton, New Hampshire; Graves Mountain, Georgia; South Dakota.
Potosi, Bolivia; Lobito Bay, Angola; Horrsjoberg, Sweden; Madagascar.
Yukon, Alaska: fine gemmy crystals.
Champion Mine, Mono County, California: masses to 6 inches across.
Bhandara district, India: gemmy crystals (indices 1.615/1.635/1.645; S.G. = 3.17).
Minas Gerais, Brazil: fine blue gemmy crystals; α = 1.604-1.629; β = 1.628-1.655; γ = 1.638-1.666; birefringence = 0.031-0.037; S.G. = 3.07-3.24.

Stone Sizes: Faceted gems are usually in the 0.5-2 carat range, with clean stones over 5 carats extremely rare. Even the small gems tend to be badly flawed. The large masses from California are not clean enough to facet.

Comments: Lazulite makes a magnificent, deep blue gemstone. The supply of rough is limited, although the mineral itself has widespread occurrence. Faceted lazulite strongly resembles blue apatite. The hardness is marginal for use in jewelry. Cabochons have been cut from massive lazulite, such as the material from New Hampshire and California.

Both color and pleochroism are the same for lazulite and scorzalite, but the optical properties and density are quite different, varying with the Fe/Mg ratio, and therefore are useful in distinguishing the two species.

Name: *Lazulite* is from the German *lazurstein,* meaning *blue stone. Scorzalite* is named after E. P. Scorza, a mineralogist at the Brazilian Department of Mines.

LAZURAPATITE See: Apatite.

LAZURITE (= LAPIS LAZULI) Sodalite Group.

Formula: $(Na,Ca)_8(Al,Si)_{12}O_{24}(S,SO_4)$.

Crystallography: Isometric. Crystals very rare, dodecahedral, up to about 2 inches in size. Also massive, compact, disseminated, in veins.

Colors: Deep blue, azure blue, violet-blue, greenish blue.

Streak: Light blue.

Luster: Dull.

Hardness: 5-6 (depending on impurity content).

Density: Pure: 2.38-2.45.
gem lapis: 2.7-2.9 or higher if much pyrite present.

Cleavage: Imperfect; none in massive material. Fracture uneven.

Optics: Isotropic. $N \sim 1.50$.

Inclusions: Pyrite (brassy yellow) and white calcite in massive material.

Luminescence: Orange spots or streaks in LW (Afghanistan and Chile), dimmer and more pink in SW. X-rays cause yellowish glow in streaks. May fluoresce whitish in SW.

Chemical Test: A drop of HCl on lapis releases H_2S gas (rotten egg odor).

Occurrence: Contact metamorphic mineral in limestone, formed by recrystallization of impurities; also in granites.
Italy: Labrador; Mogok, Burma; Pakistan.
California: blue-gray with white spots.
Colorado: stringers in limestone, dark color, much pyrite, from *Italian Mountain* in the western part of the state.
Badakshan, Afghanistan: among the oldest operating mines in the world (7,000 years). Lapis occurs in large blocks and crystals in white matrix. Source of the world's finest lapis.
Sludyanka River, Mongolia: light blue lapis, with pyrite.
Chilean Andes: gray and blue mixture, color inferior to Afghan material.

Stone Sizes: Rough blocks from Afghanistan, of fine color, are known up to 100 kg. One block of Chilean material, found in a Peruvian grave, was 24 × 12 × 8 inches. A 40.5 cm tall vase of fine blue material is in the Pitti Palace, Florence, Italy.

Comments: The gem known as lapis lazuli, or simply lapis, is actually a rock, composed of lazurite, haüyne, sodalite, and nosean, all members of the sodalite group of minerals. Lazurite itself may be considered a sulfur-rich haüyne. Calcite and pyrite in various percentages are also present in the rock. The finest lapis is considered to be a solid, deep blue with no white calcite spots and just a sprinkling of brassy yellow pyrite. Such material is found only in Afghanistan and Pakistan, in commercially interesting quantities. The Colorado material is quite fine but of limited availability.

Lapis is very well suited to men's jewelry because it has a rich blue color and does not show wear easily. It is fairly tough, takes an excellent polish, and is dark enough not to be a problem in color coordination with clothes.

Name: From a Persian word, *lazhward,* meaning *blue.*

LEGRANDITE

Formula: $Zn_2(OH)AsO_4 \cdot H_2O$.

Crystallography: Monoclinic. Crystals prismatic, also in sprays and fans.

Colors: Yellow, colorless.

Luster: Vitreous.

Hardness: 4.5.

Density: 3.98-4.04.

Cleavage: Poor. Fracture uneven. Brittle.

Optics: $\alpha = 1.675$-$1.702; \beta = 1.690$-$1.709; \gamma = 1.735$-1.740. Biaxial (+), $2V = 50°$.

Birefringence: 0.060.

Pleochroism: Colorless to yellow.

Spectral: Not diagnostic.

Luminescence: None.

Occurrence: In vugs in limonite. Only occurrence is in Mexico.
Flor de Pena Mine, Nuevo León, Mexico: first discovered locality.
Ojuela Mine, Mapimi, Mexico: best-known locality, from which come magnificent crystal clusters, single crystals up to 6 cm long and 7.5 mm thick. This is the source of the only cuttable material.

Stone Sizes: The maximum to expect in a cut legrandite is about 2-4 carats, although a 10-carat stone has been reported! A larger stone would be a great rarity, and even

1 carat gems are very hard to find. Many mineral specimens exist, but transparent crystals are extremely rare even in the source locality.

Comments: This mineral was first described in 1932, and it has become a very popular specimen mineral with collectors because of its intense yellow color and esthetic crystal groupings. It is too soft for wear, but the yellow color is unique among gems and very distinctive. This is one of the loveliest of all the rare collector gemstones.

Name: After a Belgian mine manager, Mr. Legrand, who collected the first specimens.

LEPIDOLITE   Mica family.

Formula: $K(Li,Al)_3(Si,Al)_4O_{10}(F,OH)_2$.

Crystallography: Monoclinic. Crystals tabular; also masses of plates, spheroidal masses.
Colorless: Yellow, pink, purplish, white, grayish.

Luster: Pearly on cleavage.

Hardness: 2.5-4.

Density: 2.8-3.3.

Cleavage: Perfect and easy 1 direction.

Optics: $\alpha = 1.525$-$1.548; \beta = 1.551$-$1.585; \gamma = 1.554$-1.587. Biaxial (−), $2V = 0$-$58°$.

Birefringence: 0.018-0.038.

Pleochroism: Absorption stronger in the plane of the cleavage.

Spectral: Not diagnostic.

Luminescence: None.

Occurrence: Almost exclusively in granite pegmatites; also in tin veins.
San Diego County, California; Gunnison, Colorado; Black Hills, South Dakota; Wyoming; Arizona; New Mexico; New England, especially *Maine.*
Sweden; Germany; Finland; Czechoslovakia; USSR; Madagascar; Japan; Bikita, Zimbabwe.
Brazil: fine pink and reddish crystals.

Stone Sizes: Large nodules from California are up to 6 inches or more across. Lepidolite, like the other micas, is rarely transparent enough to facet, and then it is so difficult to cut that few people ever attempt the feat! Facetable lepidolite does exist, notably from Brazil.

Comments: Reddish granular or massive lepidolite is usually slabbed for ornamental purposes, such as ashtrays, paperweights, and bookends. Faceted micas are virtually nonexistent because of the perfection of the cleavage and the variable hardness within crystals.

Name: From the Greek *lepis, (scale)* because of the scaly nature of the massive material.

LESSERITE   See: Inderite.

LEUCITE

Formula: $KAlSi_2O_6$.

Crystallography: Tetragonal (pseudo-cubic). Crystals trapezohedral; granular.

Colors: Colorless, white, gray, yellowish.

Luster: Vitreous; dull on some crystals.

Hardness: 5.5-6.

Density: 2.47-2.50.

Cleavage: Poor. Fracture conchoidal. Brittle.

Optics: Isotropic; $N \sim 1.50$. Optically (+) if uniaxial.

Birefringence: Low to zero.

Luminescence: Medium-bright orange in LW (Italy) or none. Bluish glow in X-rays.

Occurrence: In potassium-rich basic lavas.
Wyoming; Montana; Arkansas; New Jersey.
British Columbia; France; Germany; Zaire; Uganda; Australia.
Alban Hills, near *Rome, Italy:* source of the world's only transparent leucite crystals. These are colorless, up to about 1 cm.

Stone Sizes: Italian material has been cut to about 3 carats. There is very little of this material, always small, and clean only in very tiny stones.

Comments: Leucite is abundant in various lava rocks but is extremely rare in facetable crystals. The material has little appeal except for its extreme scarcity. Stones often have a slight milky or cloudy look, and anything over 3 carats is likely to be included.

Name: From the Greek *leukos,* meaning *white.*

LIDDICOATITE   See: Tourmaline.

LINARITE

Formula: $PbCu(SO_4)(OH)_2$.

Crystallography: Monoclinic. Crystals prismatic; also in druses and crusts.

Colors: Dark azure blue.

Streak: Pale blue.

Luster: Vitreous to subadamantine.

Hardness: 2.5.

Density: 5.30.

Cleavage: Perfect 1 direction. Fracture conchoidal. Brittle.

Optics: $\alpha = 1.809; \beta = 1.838, \gamma = 1.859$. Biaxial (−), $2V = 80°$.

Birefringence: 0.050.

Pleochroism: Pale blue/medium blue/Prussian blue.

Spectral: Not diagnostic.

Luminescence: None.

Occurrence: Secondary mineral in the oxidized zones of lead-copper deposits.
Blanchard Mine, Socorro County, New Mexico; California; Montana; Utah; Idaho; Nevada.
England; Scotland; Spain; Germany; Sardinia; USSR; Canada; Argentina; Peru; Chile; Japan; Australia; Tsumeb, Namibia.
Mammoth Mine, Tiger, Arizona: large crystals of fine color.
Grand Reef, Arizona: large crystals, some cuttable.

Stone Sizes: Faceted gems over 1 carat are very rare. Anything over ½ carat is remarkably large for linarite. Crystals tend to be filled with fractures or are translucent and are usually very thin blades on rock. Grand Reef material has yielded cut gems in the 2-carat range.

Comments: The blue color of linarite is magnificent, and it is a pity that large facetable rough has not been found. Clean areas of crystals are usually very small, and breakage in cutting due to the softness and cleavage of the mineral further complicates the salvaging of a large gem. This is a lovely collector item and an extremely rare one.

Name: After the locality, Linares, Spain.

LIZARDITE   See: Serpentine.

LUDLAMITE

Formula: $Fe_3(PO_4)_2 \cdot 4H_2O$.

Crystallography: Monoclinic. Crystals tabular, wedge-shaped; also granular.

Colors: Apple green, dark green, pale green, greenish white, colorless.

Streak: Pale greenish white.

Luster: Vitreous.

Hardness: 3.5.

Density: 3.19.

Cleavage: Perfect 1 direction. Fracture conchoidal. Brittle.

Optics: $\alpha = 1.650\text{-}1.653; \beta = 1.667\text{-}1.675; \gamma = 1.688\text{-}1.697$. Biaxial (+), $2V = 82°$.

Birefringence: 0.038-0.044.

Spectral: Not diagnostic.

Luminescence: None.

Occurrence: A secondary mineral in the oxidized zone of ore deposits; also due to the alteration of primary phosphates in granite pegmatites.
New Hampshire.
Cornwall, England; Hagendorf, Germany.
Blackbird Mine, Lemhi County, Idaho: fine crystals up to ½ inch across.
South Dakota: crystalline masses to 12 inches in diameter with 7 mm crystals at *Keystone.*

Stone Sizes: Ludlamite is seldom cut, and transparent material is always small. The potential may exist for 5-10 carat gems, but most are in the 1-2 carat or smaller range.

Comments: Ludlamite has a lovely green color but is too soft for wear. Large crystals are known from only a few localities, and cut stones are extremely rare.

Name: After Henry Ludlam, of London, English mineralogist and collector.

LUSAKITE   See: Staurolite.

M

MAGNESIOCHROMITE See: Chromite.

MAGNESITE

Formula: $MgCO_3$.

Crystallography: Hexagonal (R). Crystals very rare (rhombs); massive, compact, fibrous.

Colors: Colorless, white, gray, yellowish to brown.

Luster: Vitreous to dull.

Hardness: 3.5-4.5.

Density: 3.0-3.12.

Cleavage: Perfect rhombohedral; brittle.

Optics: $o = 1.700\text{-}1.717$; $e = 1.509\text{-}1.515$.
Uniaxial (−).

Birefringence: 0.022.

Luminescence: Blue, green, white in SW, often with greenish phosphorescence.

Other Tests: Effervesces in warm acids.

Occurrence: Alteration product of magnesium-rich rocks; sedimentary deposits; as a gangue mineral in hydrothermal ore deposits.
Norway; Austria; India; Algeria; Korea; Zaire; South Africa.
Brumado, Bahia, Brazil: magnificent and large rhomb-shaped crystals, often transparent, colorless.

Stone Sizes: Largest known cut magnesite is 134.5 carats *(SI)* from Brazil material. Most other gems are under 10-15 carats.

Comments: Gems of completely transparent magnesite are both rare and beautiful. The huge birefringence is obvious even in small stones, and larger gems have a sleepy look, or fuzziness, due to the doubling of back facets as seen through the table. Faceted magnesite is rarely seen, and the material is relatively difficult to cut. Facetable crystals come only from Brazil.

Name: In allusion to the composition.

MAJORITE See: Garnet.

MALACHITE

Formula: $CuCO_3(OH)_2$.

Crystallography: Monoclinic. Crystals are prismatic, usually small; also massive, sometimes banded; stalactitic; as crusts.

Colors: Green (various shades due to admixed clay in massive material), dark green.

Streak: Pale green.

Luster: Adamantine in crystals; vitreous; fibrous; dull.

Hardness: 3.5-4.5.

Density: 4.05 (as low as 3.6 in admixtures or when fibrous.).

Cleavage: Perfect 1 direction. Fracture uneven. Brittle.

Optics: $\alpha = 1.655$; $\beta = 1.875$; $\gamma = 1.909$.
Biaxial (−), $2V = 43°$.
Mean index reading of 1.85 on massive material.

Birefringence: 0.254.

Pleochroism: Colorless/yellow-green/deep green.

Luminescence: None.

Other Tests: Effervesces in warm acids.

Occurrence: In the oxidized portions of copper ore bodies, with azurite and cuprite.
Arizona, at *Bisbee* and *Gila,* other localities; *New Mexico; Utah; Tennessee.*
Zambia; Broken Hill, N.S.W., Australia.
Tsumeb, Namibia: magnificent large crystals.
Mednorudyansk, USSR: immense masses, some up to 50 tons! Much good for cutting. Also mine at *Nizhne-Tagilsk.*
Zaire: banded material, also stalactitic, most familiar on marketplace.

Stone Sizes: Cabochons and carvings can be virtually any size from banded material. Stalactites have been found several feet long. In the USSR place settings, including dinner plates and goblets, have been carved from fine malachite. Exquisite inlay work has also been done, and malachite slabs have been used as paneling in palace rooms. Facetable crystals are virtually nonexistent. Any cut gem would be very small, less than 2 carats.

Comments: Malachite is one of the most popular and beautiful of decorative stones. Its rich, patterned coloration in shades of green is unique among gems. Malachite can (with great care) be turned on a lathe to make goblets and candlesticks. It is extensively used to make cabochons, beads, boxes, and carvings of all kinds. Fibrous aggregates are packed masses of crystals, and these also take a high polish. Facetable crystals are microscopic in size since larger ones are too opaque to let light through. A faceted gem larger than ½ carat would be opaque.

Name: From a Greek word meaning *mallow* (an herb plant), in allusion to the color.

MANGANOCOLUMBITE   See: Manganotantalite.

MANGANOTANTALITE   Series to Manganocolumbite; Ferrotantalite; Columbotantalite.

Formula: $(Mn,Fe)(Ta,Nb)_2O_6$; Mn: Fe = 3:1.

Crystallography: Orthorhombic. Crystals short prismatic; massive.

Colors: Brownish black, reddish brown, scarlet red.

Streak: Dark red.

Luster: Vitreous to resinous.

Hardness: 5.5-6.5.

Density: Mozambique material = 7.73-7.97.

Cleavage: Distinct 1 direction. Fracture subconchoidal to uneven. Brittle.

Optics: $\alpha = 2.19$; $\beta = 2.25$; $\gamma = 2.34$. Biaxial (+), 2V large.

Birefringence: 0.150.

Dispersion: High.

Pleochroism: Shades of brown and red-brown. Also deep red/pale pink.

Luminescence: None.

Spectral: Not diagnostic.

Occurrence: In granite pegmatites; sometimes in placer deposits.
Pala, California; Portland, Connecticut; Amelia, Virginia.
Andilana, Madagascar; Sanarka River, Urals, USSR; Sweden; Wodgina, Western Australia.
Minas Gerais, Brazil: facetable crystals.
Alta Ligonha, Mozambique: gem quality crystals. Also from the *Morrua Mine, Zambesia.*

Stone Sizes: Cuttable crystals seldom reach 1 inch in size, and gems over 10 carats are rarities. However, the material is so dense that even a small stone is relatively heavy.
DG: 3.05 (red-brown, Brazil).

Comments: Manganotantalite makes a spectacular red-brown gem that is a very rare collector's item. Transparent material is light enough in color to allow lots of light to enter and leave a cut gem, and properly cut stones are lively and brilliant. Cutting is difficult because of the cleavage.

Name: After the composition, a manganiferous tantalite.

MANGANPECTOLITE   See: Pectolite.

MANSFIELDITE   See: Scorodite.

MARBLE   See: Calcite.

MARCASITE   Dimorph of Pyrite.

Formula: FeS_2.

Crystallography: Orthorhombic. Crystals abundant, tabular, pyramidal, often with curved faces; also massive; granular; radial; globular; cockscomb-shaped aggregates.

Colors: Pale brassy yellow to whitish; may be iridescent.

Streak: Greenish black.

Luster: Metallic; opaque.

Hardness: 6-6.5.

Density: 4.85-4.92.

Cleavage: Distinct 1 direction. Fracture uneven. Brittle.

Occurrence: Marcasite forms at low temperatures, especially in sedimentary environments such as clays, shale, coal beds, and in low temperature veins. Marcasite is abundant and widespread throughout the world.
Illinois; Oklahoma; Missouri; Kansas; Wisconsin.
Germany; Austria; Bolivia; France; Czechoslovakia.

England: in the chalk deposits along the coast and at *Folkstone.*

Stone Sizes: Massive material exists that could cut cabochons of any desired size. Marcasite is often faceted, the stones having flat backs. This type of jewelry was very popular in the Victorian era. The cutting style is known as the *flattened rose-cut.* Such gems were set in white-metal settings such as rhodium-plated silver.

Comments: Marcasite was used by the ancient Greeks, and it was also polished in large slabs by the Incas of Central America. There were surges of popularity for marcasite jewelry in the eighteenth century and the Victorian era, but marcasite is seldom seen in modern jewelry. It is quite brittle, and a sharp blow can easily crack a stone and loosen it in its setting. Much of the "marcasite" in antique jewelry is actually the dimorph of marcasite, *pyrite* (see page 154). Steel is also used as an imitation marcasite but is magnetic, whereas marcasite is not.

Name: Of Arabic or Moorish origin; it was applied to common crystallized pyrite by miners until about 1800.

MARIALITE See: Scapolite.

MEIONITE See: Scapolite.

MELANITE See: Garnet.

MELINOPHANE See: Meliphanite.

MELIPHANITE (= MELINOPHANE)

Formula: $(Ca,Na)_2Be(Si,Al)_2(O,OH,F)_7$.

Crystallography: Tetragonal. Crystals thin and tabular; also aggregates.

Colors: Colorless, shades of yellow, reddish.

Luster: Vitreous.

Hardness: 5-5.5.

Density: 3.0-3.03.

Cleavage: Perfect 1 direction. Fracture uneven. Brittle.

Optics: $o = 1.612$; $e = 1.593$.
Uniaxial (−).

Birefringence: 0.019.

Pleochroism: Distinct in shades of yellow and red.

Spectral: Not diagnostic.

Luminescence: None.

Occurrence: Nepheline syenites and skarns.
Julienhaab district, Greenland; Langesundsfjord, Norway; Gugiya, China.

Stone Sizes: Crystal clusters have been found up to several inches long. Clean, facetable material is very rare, however; the material is sometimes cut into small cabochons.

Comments: Meliphanite is an extremely rare gemstone, and perhaps fewer than 5-10 faceted stones have ever been cut.

Name: From Greek words meaning *appearing as honey,* in allusion to the color.

MELLITE

Formula: $Al_2C_6(COO)_6 \cdot 18H_2O$ (aluminum mellitate).

Crystallography: Tetragonal. Crystals prismatic, pyramidal; granular, nodular, massive.

Colors: Honey yellow, reddish, brownish, rarely white.

Streak: White.

Luster: Resinous to vitreous.

Hardness: 2-2.5.

Density: 1.58-1.64.

Cleavage: Indistinct. Fracture conchoidal. Sectile.

Optics: $o = 1.539$-1.541; $e = 1.509$-1.511.
Uniaxial (−).
Sometimes anomalously biaxial.

Birefringence: 0.028-0.032.

Pleochroism: Weak; yellow/yellow-brown.

Spectral: Not diagnostic.

Luminescence: Dull white in SW, or medium light blue. Medium light blue in LW (Germany) or lemon yellow. May be weak brown in SW (USSR).

Occurrence: A secondary mineral in brown coals and lignites.
Artern and *Bitterfeld, Germany; Paris Basin, France; Czechoslovakia; Tula, USSR.*

Stone Sizes: Mellites are always small (1-3 carats) and may be quite transparent.

Comments: Mellite is one of the most unusual of all gems, being an organic material formed by inorganic processes, just the reverse of the situation with pearls and coral. Crystals are additionally unusual in being pyroelectric (they generate an electric current when heated). Mellite is soft and very fragile, but is quite beautiful when cut. Truly this is one of the most interesting of the rare gemstones.

Name: From the Latin word *mel,* meaning *honey,* in allusion to the color.

MESOLITE   See: Natrolite.

MICA   See: Lepidolite.

MICROCLINE   See: Feldspar.

MICROLITE   Pyrochlore Group.

Formula: $(Na,Ca)_2Ta_2O_6(O,OH,F)$.

Crystallography: Isometric. Crystals octahedral; also grains and masses.

Colors: Pale yellow to brown, reddish, green.

Streak: Pale yellow to brown.

Luster: Vitreous to resinous.

Hardness: 5-5.5.

Density: 4.3-5.7; usually 5.5.

Cleavage: Octahedral (not always evident). Fracture subconchoidal to uneven. Brittle.

Optics: $N = 1.93$-1.94 if slightly metamict; also 1.98-2.02. Metamictization may cause anomalous birefringence.

Spectral: Not diagnostic.

Luminescence: None.

Occurrence: Primary mineral in granite pegmatites.
Connecticut; Maine; Massachusetts; South Dakota; Colorado; New Hampshire.
Greenland; Norway; Sweden; Finland; France; Madagascar; Western Australia.
Amelia, Virginia (Rutherford Mines): green and brown crystals, some gemmy ones up to a few inches in length.
Brazil: fine green crystals, some gemmy.

Stone Sizes: Cabochons can be cut to several inches in length (brownish or reddish massive material). Faceted gems are generally under 3-4 carats in weight; larger would be extremely rare. A crystal found in 1885 was garnet red in color, weighed 4.4 carats in the rough, and was cut into a stone that looked like a red zircon.
SI: 3.7 (brown, Virginia).

Comments: Microlite is usually opaque to translucent and is cut into cabochons by collectors. Faceted gems are very beautiful and extremely rare. Green Brazilian gems weighing less than 1 carat have appeared on the market and the potential exists there for larger stones.

Name: From the Greek *mikros (small),* due to the small size of the crystals found at the original locality.

MICROSOMMITE   See: Cancrinite.

MILARITE   Osumilite Group.

Formula: $K_2Ca_4Be_4Al_2Si_{24}O_{60} \cdot H_2O$.

Crystallography: Hexagonal. Crystals prismatic and tabular; in grains.

Colors: Colorless, pale green, yellowish, yellowish green.

Luster: Vitreous.

Hardness: 5.5-6.

Density: 2.46-2.61.

Cleavage: None. Fracture conchoidal to uneven. Brittle.

Optics: $o = 1.532$-1.551; $e = 1.529$-1.548.
Uniaxial $(-)$.

Birefringence: 0.003.

Spectral: Not diagnostic.

Luminescence: None.

Occurrence: In vugs in granites and syenites; hydrothermal veins.
St. Gotthard, Switzerland: green crystals.
Guanajuato, Mexico: yellow and yellow green crystals on matrix, flat, platelike.
Africa: occasional small facetable crystals found.

Stone Sizes: Crystals occur up to about 4 cm across, but facetable areas in such crystals are very small. Stones over 1 carat could be considered large for the species.

Comments: Milarite was originally known as a green mineral, until fine yellow crystals were discovered in Mexico in 1968. Larger Mexican crystals have transparent areas and have been faceted into small gems of pleasant appearance but great rarity.

Name: After the Val Milar, Switzerland, because the mineral was (mistakenly) thought to have occurred there.

MILLERITE

Formula: NiS.

Crystallography: Hexagonal. Crystals capillary or acicular; tufted; fibrous; also massive and cleavable.

Colors: Brassy and bronze yellow; tarnishes greenish gray.

Streak: Greenish black.

Luster: Metallic; opaque.

Hardness: 3-3.5.

Density: 5.3-5.6.

Cleavage: Perfect 2 directions. Fracture uneven. Brittle.

Occurrence: A low-temperature mineral in limestones and dolomites, serpentines, and ore deposits in carbonate rocks.
Illinois; Wisconsin; Iowa.
Wales; Czechoslovakia; Germany.

Antwerp, New York: fine sprays of acicular crystals.
Gap Mine, Lancaster County, Pennsylvania: acicular tufts.
Missouri: in geodes.
Hall's Gap, Kentucky: tufts of fibers in geodes.
Timagami, Ontario, Canada: large cleavable masses.

Stone Sizes: Cabochons of any size could be cut from massive material.

Comments: Massive millerite is sometimes cut into a cabochon by a collector or sliced into slabs for decorative purposes. The yellow color is very rich and attractive, and the cut gems are indeed curiosities. The mineral is too soft for wear. Massive millerite is of no great interest to mineral collectors and therefore might be difficult to obtain in the marketplace, although it is abundant at certain localities.

Name: After mineralogist W. H. Miller, who first studied the crystals.

MIMETITE Apatite Group, Pyromorphite series.

Formula: $Pb_5(AsO_4)_3Cl$.

Crystallography: Monoclinic (pseudo-hexagonal). Crystals acicular; globular; botryoidal.

Colors: Sulfur yellow, yellowish brown, orange-yellow, orange, white, colorless.

Luster: Subadamantine to resinous.

Hardness: 3.5-4.

Density: 7.24, lower if Ca replaces Pb.

Cleavage: None. Fracture subconchoidal to uneven. Brittle.

Optics: $o = 2.147$; $e = 2.128$.
Biaxial (−); may sometimes be uniaxial.

Birefringence: 0.019.

Pleochroism: Weak in yellow shades.

Spectral: Not diagnostic.

Luminescence: Orange-red in LW (Tsumeb, Namibia).

Occurrence: A secondary mineral in the oxidized zone of lead deposits.
Pennsylvania.
Scotland; Sweden; France; Germany; USSR; Czechoslovakia; Australia.
Southwestern United States: many localities.
Chihuahua, Mexico: fine globular orange and yellow masses.
Mapimi, Durango, Mexico: yellowish globular masses.
Cornwall and *Cumberland, England:* a variety called *campylite.*

Tsumeb, Namibia: fine yellow transparent crystals, up to 1 inch long.

Stone Sizes: Cabochons up to an inch or two can be cut from globular orange and yellow masses from Mexico, and these make unusual and interesting stones. Tsumeb crystals are extremely rare (one pocket found), and most of the crystals are being preserved as specimens and will not be cut. Small broken crystals were cut, yielding some stones up to a few carats in weight, with a maximum of 5-7 carats.

Comments: Faceted mimetite is one of the rarest of all gems since only one pocket of transparent crystals has ever been found (at Tsumeb), and few of these crystals have been cut. Orange and yellow cabochons are richly colored but are too soft for wear.

Name: From a Greek word meaning *imitator,* because of the resemblance to pyromorphite.

MOHAWKITE See: Algodonite.

MONAZITE

Formula: $(Ce,La,Y,Th)PO_4$.

Crystallography: Monoclinic. Crystals small, tabular, wedge-shaped; faces often rough or uneven; also massive, granular; detrital.

Colors: Brown, reddish brown, yellowish brown, pink, yellow, greenish, grayish white, white.

Luster: Vitreous to subadamantine; resinous; waxy.

Hardness: 5-5.5.

Density: 4.6-5.4.

Cleavage: Distinct 1 direction, sometimes perfect. Fracture conchoidal to uneven. Brittle.

Optics: $\alpha = 1.774$-1.800; $\beta = 1.777$-1.801; $\gamma = 1.828$-1.849.
Biaxial (+), $2V = 11$-15°.
Higher refractive index is accompanied by lower birefringence.

Birefringence: 0.049-0.055.

Pleochroism: Faint or none (yellowish shades). Sri Lanka material = reddish orange/golden yellow.

Spectral: Extremely complex spectra observed, mostly rare earth types.

Luminescence: None.

Occurrence: An accessory mineral in igneous rocks and gneisses; sometimes in large crystals in granite pegmatites; as a detrital mineral in sands.
Petaca district, New Mexico; Amelia, Virginia.
Norway; Finland.
Colorado: fine crystals.

Wyoming: crystals to several pounds.
Madagascar: in fine crystals.
Switzerland: excellent crystals in alpine vein deposits.
Sri Lanka: orange pebbles.
Callipampa, Bolivia: good crystals.
Deposits of alluvial material in *Australia, India, Brazil, Malaya, Nigeria.*

Stone Sizes: Faceted gems would normally be under 5 carats, either from Swiss crystals or from portions of crystals from other localities. Facetable material is very rare and cut stones are absent from all but a few private collections. Large cabochons could be cut from various large crystals that have been found.

Comments: Monazite may be partially metamict, with $N = 1.79$. Stones can be an attractive yellow or brown color but are usually small.

Name: From the Greek *monazein, to be solitary,* because of the rarity of the mineral.

MONTEBRASITE   See: Amblygonite.

MOONSTONE   See: Feldspar.

MORDENITE   Zeolite Group.

Formula: $(Ca,Na_2,K_2)(Al_2Si_{10})O_{24} \cdot 7H_2O$.

Crystallography: Orthorhombic. Crystals prismatic; fibrous, cottony, compact.

Colors: Colorless, white; stained yellowish, pinkish.

Luster: Vitreous to silky.

Hardness: 4-5.

Density: 2.12-2.15.

Cleavage: Perfect 1 direction. Fracture conchoidal. Brittle.

Optics: $\alpha = 1.472\text{-}1.483; \beta = 1.475\text{-}1.485; \gamma = 1.477\text{-}1.487$. Biaxial (+), $2V = 76\text{-}104°$. Also optically (−).

Birefringence: 0.005.

Pleochroism: None.

Spectral: Not diagnostic.

Luminescence: None.

Occurrence: In veins and cavities in igneous rocks; also forms as hydration product of natural glasses. *California; Idaho; Utah; Colorado; Wyoming. Nova Scotia, Canada; Scotland; Yugoslavia; USSR; Japan; New Zealand.*

Stone Sizes: Cabochons can be cut from nodules that reach a size of about 1 inch. Faceted gems have not been reported.

Comments: Compact, fibrous material is cabbed because the fibers provide a chatoyancy that sometimes yields weak catseyes. Coloration in the material is due to staining. This is a relatively unexciting mineral, and gems are equally uninspiring. Nevertheless, it has been reported as being cut for collectors.

Name: From the locality at Morden, King's County, Nova Scotia, where first found.

MORGANITE   See: Beryl.

MORION   See: Quartz.

MOSS AGATE   See: Quartz.

MUKHINITE   See: Epidote.

N

NAMBULITE

Formula: $NaLiMn_8Si_{10}O_{28}(OH)_2$.

Crystallography: Triclinic. Crystals prismatic, flattened, and wedge shaped.

Colors: Reddish brown, orange-brown, orange.

Streak: Pale yellow.

Luster: Vitreous.

Hardness: 6.5.

Density: 3.51.

Cleavage: Perfect 1 direction, distinct 1 direction.

Optics: $\alpha = 1.707; \beta = 1.710; \gamma = 1.730$. Biaxial (+), $2V = 30°$.

Birefringence: 0.023.

Dispersion: Weak.

Pleochroism: Weak.

Spectral: Not diagnostic.

Luminescence: No data.

Occurrence: Nambulite is a rare mineral reported in crystals up to 8 mm long at the *Tunakozawa Mine, Northeast Japan*. These crystals are found in veins cutting manganese oxide ores. Much larger crystals, up to approximately 3 cm across, have more recently been found in *Namibia*, at the *Kombat Mine*, near *Tsumeb*. I have seen a completely transparent crystal in a private collection that would yield about 20-25 carats of flawless faceted gems, the largest of these perhaps 10 carats in weight.

Stone Sizes: Gems up to about 10 carats could potentially be cut from Namibian crystals.

Comments: The color of Namibian nambulite is a striking orange-red, very intense, and not really like any other gem I have seen. Cut stones would be both extremely rare and quite magnificent, perhaps bearing some similarities to rhodonite.

Name: After Professor Matsuo Nambu of Tohoku University, Japan, for his studies of manganese minerals.

NATROLITE; MESOLITE; SCOLECITE   Solid-solution series, Zeolite Group.

Formula: *Natrolite:* $Na_2(AlSi_3O_{10}) \cdot 2H_2O$. *Mesolite:* $Na_2Ca_2(Al_2Si_3O_{10}) \cdot 8H_2O$ (intermediate in series). *Scolecite:* $Ca(Al_2Si_3O_{10}) \cdot 3H_2O$.

All three minerals are fibrous or elongated zeolite minerals that occur in single crystals or radial aggregates. Mesolite crystals are always twinned.

Colors: Colorless, white (natrolite sometimes gray, yellowish, reddish).

Luster: Vitreous; silky in fibrous varieties.

Cleavage: Perfect 2 directions. Fracture uneven. Brittle.

Luminescence: Some natrolite fluoresces yellow-orange in LW (Germany). Indian mesolite may fluoresce pink (LW); mesolite may fluoresce cream white to green in LW (Colorado). None observed in scolecite.

Occurrence: Cavities in basalts and other dark igneous rocks. Scolecite occasionally forms in schists and contact zones at limestones.
Colorado; New Jersey; Oregon; Washington.
Nova Scotia, Canada; Greenland; Scotland; Iceland.
Ice River, British Columbia, Canada.
California: natrolite in *San Benito County;* scolecite at *Crestmore, Riverside County.*

	Natrolite	Mesolite	Scolecite
Crystallography	Orthorhombic, pseudo-tetragonal	Monoclinic, pseudo-orthorhombic	Monoclinic, pseudo-orthorhombic
Hardness	5	5	5
Density	2.2–2.26	2.26	2.21–2.29
Optics			
α	1.473–1.483	1.505	1.507–1.513
β	1.476–1.486	1.504–1.508	1.516–1.520
γ	1.485–1.496	1.506	1.517–1.523
sign	(+)	(+)	(−)
2V	58–64°	~ 80°	36–56°
Birefringence	0.012	0.001	0.007

Poona, India: large crystals of scolecite and natrolite, some facetable.

Brevig, Norway: natrolite.

USSR: huge natrolite crystals.

Australia: mesolite.

Sicily: mesolite.

France: natrolite.

Germany: natrolite.

Rio Grande do Sul, Brazil: immense crystals of scolecite. Brazilian scolecite reported: $\alpha = 1.512$; $\beta = 1.518$; $\gamma = 1.523$; birefringence = 0.011; S.G. = 2.21.

Mt. Ste. Hilaire, Quebec, Canada: large natrolite crystals (white, opaque).

Southern Quebec: in asbestos mines, natrolite crystals to 3 feet long and 4 inches across (not of gem quality).

Bound Brook, New Jersey: one find of natrolite crystals, thousands of single crystals well terminated, up to 6 inches long, many transparent.

Stone Sizes: Natrolites were known only in stones under 1 carat until the Bound Brook, New Jersey, find. Some of these crystals cut flawless gems over 20 carats.

SI: 9.31, 7.9 (colorless, New Jersey).

DG: 7.95 (colorless, New Jersey); also scolecite, 0.98 (India).

PC: 15 (Ice River, British Columbia).

Mesolite is never found in large transparent crystals. Faceted gems are thus very rare, although the possibility exists that larger crystals could be found one day. Fibrous material cuts fine catseye gems, but these also are small and fragile.

Scolecite is also rare in facetable crystals; areas of some of the large Indian and Brazilian material might cut gems in the 5-10 carat range, but these specimens are in museums and will not be cut. Other stones would likely be in the 1-3 carat range and colorless.

Comments: All three zeolites form elongated crystals; faceted gems are almost always, therefore, elongated emerald- or step-cuts. The New Jersey natrolites are by far the largest known faceted gems in this group. All three minerals are relatively fragile and soft, have good cleavage, and are white and more or less uninteresting, except for rarity. Compact masses, cut into cabochons, might be more durable due to interlocking of the fibers. The minerals can readily be distinguished on the basis of optical properties.

Names: *Natrolite* from the Latin *natron (soda)* because of the presence of sodium. *Mesolite* from the Greek *mesos*, an intermediate position, because of its position between natrolite and scolecite in chemistry and properties. *Scolecite* is from the Greek *skolex (worm)* because a borax bead of the mineral sometimes curls up like a worm.

NATROMONTEBRASITE See: Amblygonite.

NEPHELINE

Formula: $(Na,K)AlSiO_4$.

Crystallography: Hexagonal. Crystals stumpy, sometimes very large; massive, compact; in grains.

Colors: Colorless, white, gray, yellowish, greenish, bluish, dark green, brick red, brownish red.

Luster: Vitreous to greasy.

Hardness: 5.5-6.

Density: 2.55-2.66

Cleavage: Indistinct. Fracture subconchoidal. Brittle.

Optics: $o = 1.529\text{-}1.546$; $e = 1.526\text{-}1.542$. Uniaxial (−).

Birefringence: 0.004.

Dispersion: Low.

Spectral: Not diagnostic.

Luminescence: Medium light blue (Germany) or medium dull orange (Ontario) in LW.

Occurrence: Plutonic and volcanic rocks; pegmatites associated with nepheline syenites.

Julienhaab district, Greenland; Langesundsfjord, Norway;

Germany; Finland; USSR; Burma; Korea.
Various localities in the *United States,* especially *Maine* and *Arkansas.*
Ontario, Canada: crystals up to 15 inches long (non-gemmy).
Vesuvius, Italy: small, glassy transparent grains.

Stone Sizes: Cabochons of nepheline have been cut in various sizes; crystals, especially those from Canada, can reach enormous size but are not attractive. Faceting material is extremely rare and very small.

Comments: A variety called *elaeolite* is red, green, brown, or gray, massive or in crystals filled with minute inclusions. These inclusions produce a sheen that yields a catseye effect in cabochons. Facetable nepheline is a great rarity, and very few gems have been cut, always in the 1-2 carat range or smaller.

Name: From a Latin word meaning *cloud* because it becomes cloudy when immersed in acid. *Elaeolite* is from a Latin word for *oil* because of its greasy luster.

NEPHRITE (= JADE) Fibrous variety of Actinolite.

Formula: $Ca_2(Mg,Fe)_5(Si_4O_{11})_2(OH)_2$.

Crystallography: Monoclinic. Masses of fibrous crystals, densely packed and very tough.

Colors: Creamy beige (mutton fat jade) when rich in Mg. Green colors, due to Fe. Brown (oxidized Fe); sometimes a surface skin is dark brown. Also yellowish, grayish brown, yellow-green, black.

Luster: Vitreous to greasy; dull.

Hardness: 6-6.5.

Density: 2.90-3.02; usually 2.95.

Cleavage: None. Fracture splintery. Very tough.

Optics: $\alpha = 1.600$-1.627; $\gamma = 1.614$-1.641. Biaxial (−). Usually refractometer shows a shadow edge at about 1.62.

Birefringence: 0.027.

Pleochroism: Strong dichroism, masked due to the fibrous nature of the material.

Spectral: Doublet at 6890, two vague bands at 4980 and 4600; sharp line at 5090.

Luminescence: None.

Occurrence: Nephrite is most frequently encountered in the form of rolled boulders.
Wisconsin: gray-green color, not too attractive.
Alaska: green colors, in very large masses, sometimes fibrous (chatoyant).

California: alluvial material, various green shades, in boulders up to 1000 pounds.
Lander, Wyoming: boulders mottled green with white —very distinctive material.
New Zealand: Maori Greenstone, in situ and in boulders, usually dark green to black.
Fraser River, British Columbia, Canada: dark-colored nephrite, little of which is very fine quality.
USSR (at *Lake Baikal*): dark spinach-green color with abundant graphitic black inclusions or spots—very distinctive jade, fine color.
China (Sinkiang Province): generally light in color.
Poland: creamy white to gray-green, with green patches (near *Jordansmuhl*).
Fengtien, Taiwan: spinach green to pea green, in seams in rock; despite abundance of material on market in former years, large pieces are very scarce. Also catseyes noted.
Cowell, South Australia: material similar to New Zealand; large amounts potentially available.
Mashaba district, Zimbabwe; Germany; Mexico.

Stone Sizes: Alluvial boulders of several tons are not uncommon in certain localities. Large fine pieces are always carved, for example, the sculpture *Thunder,* by Donald Hord, in Wyoming jade (145 pounds).
AMNH displays a huge block of nephrite from Poland weighing 4718 pounds.
SI displays a boulder of several hundred pounds, sliced open, with a thin slab backlit to show the color.

Comments: Nephrite colors do not match in either variety or intensity the colors of jadeite. With few exceptions, nephrite shades are usually dark and somber, and nephrite never attains the fine green of Imperial jade (jadeite). The Chinese long ago mastered the art of carving nephrite, and immense brush pots and statues grace many museums around the world. Of special note is the M. M. Vetleson jade collection that occupies an entire room at *SI.* Carvings have been done using only one side of a jade boulder, leaving the rough shape as a background. Fine use is also made of the weathering skin (brownish) of green nephrite, creating a cameo effect, sometimes displaying great detail and fine workmanship.

Catseye nephrite from Taiwan has also been reported. The catseyes are due to parallel arrangement of fibers (ferroactinolite content = 10%). The colors found include greenish to honey yellow, dark green, dark brown and black. The properties are as follows: $\alpha = 1.613$-1.616; $\beta = 1.626$; $\gamma = 1.632$-1.637; birefringence = 0.016; S.G. = 3.01-3.05.

Name: From the Greek word *nephros,* meaning *kidney;* the rounded, organlike shape of nephrite boulders and pebbles undoubtedly stimulated people to regard these stones as magical cures for the organs they resembled, through sympathetic magic. See also: Jadeite.

NEPTUNITE

Formula: $(Na,K)_2(Fe^{+2},Mn)TiSi_4O_{12}$; (mangan-neptunite has Mn,Fe^{+2}).

Crystallography: Monoclinic; crystals prismatic, usually square in cross section, lustrous and very well formed.

Colors: Extremely dark red, appearing microscopically black. Transparent in small fragments, otherwise opaque.

Streak: reddish brown.

Luster: Vitreous.

Hardness: 5-6.

Density: 3.19-3.23.

Cleavage: Perfect 1 direction; fracture conchoidal; brittle.

Optics: $\alpha = 1.690\text{-}1.691$; $\beta = 1.693\text{-}1.700$; $\gamma = 1.719\text{-}1.736$. Biaxial (+).

Birefringence: 0.029-0.045.

Pleochroism: yellow/deep red.

Spectral: Not diagnostic.

Luminescence: None.

Occurrence: In alkaline rocks and carbonatites but most especially embedded in natrolite in San Benito County, California, where it occurs in spectacular crystals associated with benitoite and joaquinite.
Narsarsuk, Julianhaab district, Greenland.
Mt. Ste. Hilaire, Quebec, Canada.
Kola Peninsula, USSR: mangan-neptunite.
San Benito County, California.

Stone Sizes: Neptunite is opaque except in minute fragments, from which tiny faceted stones (under 1 carat) of deep red color have been cut. The color intensity limits the practical size of gemstones; opaque blackish stones in the 20-30 carat range could be cut but would not display the lovely red color neptunite displays in smaller fragments.

Name: For Neptune, god of the sea in mythology, because it was found associated with aegirine, named after Aegir, Scandinavian god of the sea.

NICCOLITE

Formula: NiAs.

Crystallography: Hexagonal. Crystals very rare; massive.

Colors: Pale coppery red; tarnishes black.

Streak: Pale brownish black.

Luster: Metallic; opaque.

Hardness: 5-5.5.

Density: 7.78.

Cleavage: None. Fracture uneven. Brittle.

Luminescence: None.

Occurrence: In vein deposits in basic igneous rocks, usually associated with ores of Ag, Co, and Ni.
Sonora, Mexico; Germany; France; Austria; Czechoslovakia; Japan.
California; Colorado; New Jersey.
Sudbury district, Ontario, Canada: in large masses; also at *Cobalt, Thunder Bay,* and the *Gowganda district, Ontario.*

Stone Sizes: Cabochons of any desired size could be cut from massive pieces.

Comments: Niccolite is always cut as cabochons. The color is a delicate peachy red and is extremely beautiful, especially in polished material. The metallic luster combined with this unusual color is very distinctive. Niccolite is hard enough to be worn on bola ties and pendants. It sometimes tarnishes to a darker color, but a coat of clear nail polish may prevent this.

Name: From *niccolum,* the Latin word for *nickel.*

NORBERGITE   See: Humite Group.

NOSEAN   See: Lazurite.

O

OBSIDIAN (= **VOLCANIC GLASS**)

Formula: Variable composition: SiO_2 approximately 66-72% + oxides of Ca, Na, K, and so forth. Basaltic glass is ~50% SiO_2.

Crystallography: Amorphous; usually as rounded masses ejected in volcanic eruptions, as small broken pieces, fine, hairlike filaments (for example, Pelee's Hair), and as flows.

Colors: Black; gray, banded with brown streaks; rarely green, blue, red.
Basaltic glass is black, brown, gray, blue, and blue-green. Iridescence noted: gold, silver, blue, violet, green, and combinations of these colors, due to inclusions of minute bubbles that reflect light.

Luster: Vitreous.

Hardness: 5; 6 for basalt glass.

Density: 2.33-2.42; 2.70-3.0 for basalt glass.

Cleavage: None. Fracture conchoidal (best example of this type of fracture). Very brittle. Basalt glass may be splintery, brittle.

Optics: Isotropic. $N = 1.48$-1.51; usually 1.49.
Crystals included in the glass may be birefringent.

Inclusions: Elongated, torpedo-shaped bubbles, round bubbles, teardrop-shaped bubbles. Bubbles are often in parallel arrangement. Needlelike inclusions may give a silvery sheen. Protogenic silica minerals crystallizing in obsidian may be white and resemble snowflakes, hence the term *snowflake obsidian*.

Luminescence: None.

Occurrence: Most occurrences of obsidian used in gems are in the *United States*. Obsidian is found in areas of present and former volcanic activity. *Nevada; Hawaii. Iceland; Japan.*
Oregon: some iridescent material is known.
Wyoming: notably at Yellowstone National Park.
New Mexico: Apache tears, small rounded obsidian lumps in white perlite shells.
Arizona; Colorado; California: several localities.
Utah: major source of snowflake obsidian.
Mexico: obsidian abundant, especially banded and sheen varieties.

Stone Sizes: Fragments range from microscopic to many inches across. Carvings up to 8-10 inches could be made. Larger pieces of obsidian are available in place in certain localities.

Comments: Obsidian is an attractive material and displays a wide variety of appearances. *Snowflake obsidian,* with spherulites of cristobalite, is widely used in jewelry as beads and cabochons. *Apache tears,* which are cores of unaltered glass in nodular shells of decomposed obsidian, are popular among beginning hobbyists. Some of these have been faceted. Green, blue, and reddish (transparent) obsidians are quite rare, these sometimes faceted by hobbyists. Obsidian is heat-sensitive, so care must be used in cutting; it is also rather brittle, so is delicate in jewelry. Faceted gems tend to be very dark and unattractive, except in small sizes or in the blue and green varieties.

Name: The material was supposed to have been discovered in Ethiopia by a man named Obsius.

ODONTOLITE See: Vivianite.

OLIGOCLASE See: Feldspar

OLIVINE (= **PERIDOT**) Solid-solution series: Forsterite (Mg) to Fayalite (Fe).

Properties of Gem Olivines

	%MgO	%FeO	α	β	γ	Birefringence	Density	2V-sign
Forsterite	64.65	0	1.635	1.651	1.670	0.035	3.22	82°(+)
Mogok, Burma	57.8	1.11	1.654	1.671	1.689	0.036	3.22	86°
Zabargad, Egypt	54	8–10	1.652	1.669	1.688	0.036	3.34	—
Norway	51.86	8.5	1.650	1.665	1.686	0.036	3.30	—
Tanzania	51.2	7.7	1.650	1.658	1.684	0.034	3.25	—
Arizona (light green)	49.8	8.2	1.649	1.665	1.686	0.037	3.28	—
Arizona	49.5	10.4	1.652	1.671	1.689	0.037	3.34	—
Mexico (light green)	49.8	8.6	1.651	1.669	1.684	0.033	3.33	—
Mexico (brown)	48.2	11.0	1.655	1.673	1.690	0.035	—	—
New Mexico	49.4	8.7	1.652	1.671	1.688	0.036	3.33	—
Sri Lanka (olive)	48.1	10.8	1.651	1.660	1.690	0.039	3.36	—
Sri Lanka (almost colorless)	—	3.6	1.640	1.657	1.675	0.035	3.20	—
Kenya (yellowish)	—	—	1.650	—	1.686	0.036	3.45	—
Kenya (brownish)	—	—	1.651	—	1.681	0.038	3.35	—
Fayalite	0	70.51	1.827	1.869	1.879	0.052	4.39	134°(−)

(Greenish peridots generally have a density of 3.3–3.4; brownish stones about 3.5.)

Formula: Mg_2SiO_4-Fe_2SiO_4. Rarely Mn also present.

Crystallography: Orthorhombic. Crystals rare, usually striated prisms, corroded grains; often as rolled pebbles, or in nodules called *bombs* in volcanic areas.

Colors: *Forsterite:* green, pale lemon yellow.
Fayalite: green, yellowish, amber brown, brown, olive green.

The color of olivine is due to ferrous iron. The best green gemstones have an iron content of about 12–15%. More Fe than this results in an unattractive, muddy color. Very bright green colors may result from a trace of Cr.

Luster: Oily to vitreous.

Hardness: 6.5 (fayalite) to 7 (forsterite).

Cleavage: Imperfect to weak. Fracture conchoidal. Brittle.

Optics; Density: vary with composition.

Dispersion: 0.020.

Pleochroism: None in *forsterite.*
Peridots: weak, green to yellow-green.
Fayalite: greenish yellow/orange-yellow/greenish yellow.

Luminescence: None.

Inclusions: Glass balls that look like bubbles in Hawaiian material; some U.S. localities contain inclusions of Cr-spinel (not magnetite as previously thought); also noted are biotite grains, and *lotus leaves,* which are petal-like liquid inclusions around Cr-spinel crystals.

Occurrence: *Forsterite* occurs in magnesian limestones that have been altered by heat and pressure from igneous intrusion; *fayalite* is rare, occasionally seen in lithophysae (balls of cristobalite) in obsidian. Intermediate olivines are a main constituent of basic igneous rocks, and concentrations in basalts and ultrabasic rocks can be mined for gem content.

Riverside, San Bernardino County, California; Bolton, Massachusetts.

Hawaii: in volcanic bombs.

New Mexico and *Arizona:* peridot occurs as grains, which are used by ants to build large hills; these grains are erosional fragments from a parent rock, now eroded away. Peridot is mined on the Navajo Indian Reservation, and stones cut from these fragments are usually small (under 5 carats), with an occasional larger gem.

Kenya: brown crystals.

Zabargad (Zebirget), Egypt (Isle of St. John): this is the most ancient source for peridot as well as a source of some of the most confusing name mixups in gem literature. Zabargad (Zebirget, Zebirged) is an island in the Red Sea that is often shrouded in fog, making it difficult for ancient navigators to find. The location had been lost, in fact, for centuries and was rediscovered about 1905. The island is located 35 miles off the Egyptian coastal port of Berenica. Crystals of peridot are found in veins of nickel ore in an altered peridotite rock. The color of the gem material is a medium green, not too dark, and very rich.

Burma: peridot is found in masses on the slopes of *Kyaukpon,* near *Mogok.* The material yields dark green, oily gems of fine color, transparent, some of several hundred carats in size. This is the world's only major source of very large peridot.

Norway: peridot is found at *Ameklovdalen, Sondmore.* The gems are paler than from other localities and are of a lovely lime-green hue because the material contains less Fe. Cuttable pieces are very rare in large size and seldom yield cut stones over 5 carats.

Mexico: one of the world's largest deposits of olivine is located in the state of *Chihuahua.* The material is similar to Arizona peridot but also occurs in brown grains.
Emali, Kenya: gem quality.
Ratnapura, Sri Lanka: olive-green gems; also nearly colorless material that is the closest in composition to forsterite of any gem olivine known.
Mt. Batchelor, North Queensland, Australia: yellow-green, dark green, gemmy; potential for stones up to about 20 carats.
Umba district, Tanzania; Minas Gerais, Brazil; Ross Island, Antarctica: some cuttable material.
USSR; Finland; Italy; Germany; Greenland; New Caledonia.

Spectral: Peridot shows a strong iron spectrum, with three main bands: strong at 4930, narrow at 4730, broad at 4530; there are also some vague bands at 6530 and 5290, but the set of three evenly spaced bands is distinctive.

Stone Sizes: Burmese material cuts the largest gems, followed by Egyptian material. Peridot from Antarctica is limited to a few stones under 2 carats. Arizona material over 10 carats is very rare in cut form.
SI: 310 (Egypt); 287 (Burma); 22.9 (Arizona).
ROM: 108, 87.1, 83.3 (Burma).
DG: 82.4, 24.7 (Burma).
PC: 284.85 (Egypt); 34.65 (Arizona).
Geological Museum, London: 136 (Burma).
Topkapi Museum, Istanbul: many large and fine cabochons. An immense clean crystal of more than 100 carats from Norway (by far the largest known) is in a European collection.

Comments: Catseye and star peridots are known but are very rare. The low hardness of peridot means that ringstones will show scratches rather rapidly and may become badly chipped. The cleavage may allow an occasional stone to split if it is struck a sharp blow. Peridot is an ancient gem, often referred to as *chrysolite,* a term still used in referring to intermediate members of the olivine series. There is considerable variation in shade of green depending on the locality of origin. Brown gems rich in iron are not commonly seen but can be very beautiful, especially when the color is more golden than brown.

Names: *Chrysolite* from the Greek, meaning *yellow stone. Forsterite* after J. Forster, a mineralogist. *Fayalite* is named after the Fayal Islands in the Azores because it was believed to occur there in volcanic rocks. *Olivine* from the Latin *oliva (olive)* because of the similarity in color. *Peridot* is from the thirteenth-century English *peridota.*

ONYX   See: Calcite, Quartz.

OPAL

Formula: $SiO_2 \cdot nH_2O$. Water = 1-21% in opal, usually 6-10% in precious opal.

Crystallography: Amorphous. Recent work shows that opal is composed of an aggregate of tiny spherical particles, that is, a solidified gel; often forms concretions; botryoidal; reniform; stalactitic.

Colors: Colorless, white, yellow, orange, and red (various shades), yellowish brown, greenish, blue, gray, black, violet.

Luster: Vitreous, waxy, pearly.

Hardness: 5.5-6.5.

Density: 1.99-2.25; orange-red variety ~2.00; black and white opal, 2.10; green opal, 2.12.

Cleavage: None. Fracture conchoidal. Brittle.

Optics: Isotropic; $N = 1.44$-1.47.
Mexican opal as low as 1.37, usually 1.42-1.43.

Dispersion: Very low.

Spectral: None.

Luminescence: Green fluorescence in opal often due to included U minerals. Much opal fluoresces strong white in SW, LW, sometimes with persistent phosphorescence. (See table below.)

Fluorescence in Opal

Locality	SW	LW
White Cliffs, Australia	–	medium blue; phosphorescent
Park, Wyoming	dull white; phosphorescent	strong white; phosphorescent
Queretaro, Mexico	dull white; phosphorescent	bright blue; phosphorescent
Virgin Valley, Nevada	bright green	medium green, blue-white; phosphorescent
Quartzite, Arizona	pale yellow	bright pale yellow

Opal may also fluoresce brownish. Black opal is generally inert. Fire opal luminesces greenish brown. Common opal often fluoresces green.

OPAL TERMINOLOGY

Siliceous sinter; geyserite: massive, glassy opal that forms around hot springs and geysers; no gem significance.

Diatomaceous earth; tripoli: fine-grained, powdery masses of opal or the siliceous remains of microscopic marine animals called diatoms. Often used as polishing agents, fillers.

Pseudomorphs: opal may, in percolating through the ground, replace (on a microscopic or even cellular basis) wood, bone, and shells.

Hyalite: transparent, colorless, or white to gray opal, glassy, occasionally faceted but generally no gem significance.

Common opal: opaque or glassy opal, in a wide range of colors, sometimes with a waxy luster; often fluorescent; seldom cut into gems.

Water opal: transparent, colorless opal that may have fire in it.

Note: The term *fire* refers to the magnificent play of color displayed by opal, which is due to light diffraction from neatly stacked layers of the microscopic spheres of which opal is composed. Common opal is a jumble of spheres of random sizes, but in precious opal the spheres are the same size, and they are layered in neat rows. The particular color seen depends on the size of the spheres and the angle of viewing.

Fire opal: transparent to translucent red or orange opal, which may or may not have fire in it! The term fire opal refers to a *body color,* not to *play of color.*

Precious opal: opal of any color with fire or play of colors displayed.

White opal: white body-color opal, usually with play of color.

Gray opal: light to dark body color, with play of color superimposed.

Black opal: black body color with fire, often spectacular against dark background. Body color also very dark bluish, greenish, or brownish.

Semiblack opal: another way of describing *gray opal.*

Milk opal: milk white, translucent, also yellowish or greenish in color.

Crystal opal: water opal or milk opal, generally rich in fire; transparent to translucent in transmitted light; colors seen by reflected light.

Contra-luz opal: very rare type, usually from Mexico, with color play in *both* transmitted and reflected light.

Hydrophane: light colored, opaque, becomes iridescent and transparent when soaked in water.

Jasper opal: reddish-brown opal, opaque, resembles jasper.

Cachalong: porcelaniferous, often bluish-white, very porous—adheres to the tongue.

Prase opal: translucent or opaque green opal; a common opal resembling prase.

Moss opal: white to brownish opaque opal that contains dendritic inclusions.

Menilite: opaque gray to brown opal with a concretionary structure.

Tabasheer: opaline silica occurring in the joints of bamboo.

Girasol: opal that is almost transparent and has a billowy light effect within it, resembling moonstone.

Chrysocolla in opal: blue material, with finely disseminated chrysocolla that gives the color.

Liver opal: term sometimes used for brown common opal.

Resin opal: yellowish brown common opal with a waxy luster.

TERMS FOR COLOR AND COLOR DISTRIBUTION IN OPAL

Onyx opal and *agate opal:* alternating layers of precious and common opal. In *catseye opal* the color play is concentrated in the form of an eye or band. *Matrix opal* consists of specks of precious opal in a rock matrix, usually sandstone; this type of opal is often dyed black to enhance the color play. *Ironstone opal* is in a brown, hard, compact type of sandstone. Matrix opal may also be layers or stringers of opal in a rock matrix.

Flame opal: sweeping reddish streaks and bands move across the gem, resembling flickering flames.

Flash opal: as the gem is moved back and forth, flashes of color appear and disappear at various spots.

Harlequin opal: the color display is in the form of angular or quiltlike patches, all in contact with each other, like a mosaic.

Pinfire opal: the color is in the form of tiny dots or speckles, set close together.

Peacock opal: many colors appear in the same gem, resembling the display of the tail of the male peacock.

Also *gold opal* (gold fire), *blue opal* (bluish fire), *lechosos opal* (green colors).

Occurrence: In sedimentary rocks or where low-temperature solutions bearing silica can percolate through rocks.

Honduras: deposits known since before 1843, perhaps much older than that. Occurs as veins in dark reddish to black trachyte rock. White opal contrasts strongly with the dark-colored matrix. Pieces not large, seldom very spectacular.

Czechoslovakia: source of opal known in Roman times, near the village of *Czerwenitza* (formerly in Hungary). Opal occurs as seams in grayish brown andesite rock. The opal is a mosaic of strong colors and is very attractive, against a milky-white background color. Much of this is harlequin opal.

Indonesia: very little known material, as thin seams in dark rock. Much of it is water opal and resembles material from Mexico. The white opal resembles poor-grade Australian. Some black opal is produced that is very unusual and consists of reddish flecks of color swimming in a translucent but very dark brown body. Most gems are very small (less than 10 carats) from this locality, and production is very small.

Mexico: Mexican opal occurs in siliceous volcanic lavas, in cavities, and in many localities. Yellow and red fire opal comes from a trachyte porphyry at *Zimapan* in *Hidalgo*. Hyalite and precious opal that is completely transparent, colorless, and rich in fire occurs at *San Luis Potosí, Chihuahua*. *Queretaro* is a well-known opal-producing locality. Fine Mexican opal is very rare in large sizes (over 50 carats) but is among the most beautiful.

Virgin Valley, Nevada: opal occurs in *Humboldt County* as cracks and seams in opalized wood. This was discovered about 1900. The opal is magnificent, but is very hydrous and has a strong tendency to crack due to loss of water when exposed to the air. This behavior is known as *crazing*, or, when on the surface, *checking*. Whole skeletons of extinct animals have been replaced by fine precious opal at this locality. Similar opal is found in *Idaho*.

Brazil: opal occurs in sandstone in *Piaui State*, northern Brazil, and also near *Manaus*, northern Brazil. The material is white and fiery and sometimes resembles good-quality Australian white opal. It is perhaps the most durable opal, low in water and not heat sensitive—I have seen a cut gem held for a half a minute over a candle flame with no adverse effects. The material seems to be abundant and much of it is shipped to Hong Kong where it is cut and sold, often as Australian opal.

Poland: green prase opal, colored by nickel.

Tanzania: nickeliferous opal resembling chrysoprase occurs in Tanzania, associated with brown limonite. The R.I. (1.452) is lower than that of chrysoprase (1.535), as is the gravity (2.125 versus 2.620). Stone sizes tend to be small.

Australia: the first discoveries were probably about 1850, but major finds were made in Queensland about 1872. Australian opal is in various types:

Boulder opal: shells of coarse, hardened, sandy clay with layers of opal in between.

Yowah nuts: walnut-sized concretions, in a regular layer, like a conglomerate. The opal is the central kernel and never reaches the outer edge.

Seam opal: thin to thick seams of white or black opal in sandstone matrix. Also known as sandstone opal. Large stones are very rare in this material.

Major finds of Australian opal are best known from specific localities:

Lightning Ridge: black opal in nodules, world's finest of this material; first mined commercially about 1905.

Coober Pedy, South Australia: discovered about 1915; only white opals found here, in sandstone and claystone matrix, but some very fine.

Andamooka, South Australia: opals found here about 1930; very distinctive opal, white and also brownish in color; may be artificially blackened to enhance the appearance of the fire in the matrix.

White Cliffs area: started about 1889, but the opal is usually small, with veinlets of precious opal within common opal.

Gabanintha (Murchison Goldfield): bright green opal, colored by copper, is found in quartz.

Mintabie: mined since 1931, about 350 km northwest of Coober Pedy. This area has now been extensively prospected.

Australia is the best known opal-producing area in the world, but the deposits have been worked so intensely that they are becoming depleted. Many fewer miners are now working the opal fields than 10 years ago, and new discoveries are rare. This factor, plus worldwide demand, is putting tremendous pressure on opal prices.

Stone Sizes: Like diamonds, many large and fine opals have been given individual names. Only a few are included here; others are described in books specifically about opal.

Olympic Australis: Coober Pedy; uncut was 127 ounces.

Noolinga Nera: Andamooka; 86 ounces rough, cut 205 carat oval.

Roebling Opal: Rainbow Ridge, Nevada, 2610 (in *SI*).

Light of the World: Lightning Ridge, Australia, 252, partly cut.

Red Admiral or *Butterfly:* Lightning Ridge, possible 40-50 carats in rough. Many regard this gem as the world's most beautiful opal.

Pride of Australia: Lightning Ridge, 226, partly cut.

Pandora: Lightning Ridge, 711, cut.

SI: Australian gems; 345, 155, and 83 (all white); black opals of 58.8, 54.3, and 44. Also 355 (black, Nevada); 143.2 (orange, precious, Mexico); 55.9 (colorless, precious, Mexico); 39 (pale yellow-orange, precious, Brazil). Virgin Valley opals at *SI* include the Roebling Opal (19 ounces).

ROM: 69.58 (Contra-luz, Mexico).

Comments: Opal is one of the most popular of all gems. It is very rare in large sizes (over 30-40 carats); especially rare is black opal, which is the loveliest and most expensive of all opal varieties. The value of opal lies in the size of the stone, the colors it displays, and the pattern of the color. Opal prices may also vary according to advertising and the fashion of the time.

Opal is hydrous, and when it dehydrates, it tends to crack spontaneously. It may crack or craze immediately upon being taken from the ground or at any time thereafter, even after a period of many years! Opals kept in jewel cases and drawers may suddenly develop minute, threadlike cracks. The only way to prevent this is to keep opals perpetually in a jar of water, which is inconvenient. Much of the value of an opal is lost when cracking occurs since the cracks seriously impair the strength of the gem and may allow it to fall out of the setting.

The hardness of opal is only about 5.5, which is very low for a gem used in jewelry; opal is *not* a good ringstone, but people persist in wearing it as such. Many opals in rings are damaged beyond repair, or crack and fall out and are lost. Frequently an opal in a ring is found to be chalk white and lifeless; this may be due solely to a network of scratches on the surface that destroys the polish and reduces the color play. The opal can be fixed by simple repolishing. Opal is usually very brittle and heat sensitive, so great care must be used in cutting to prevent cracking. Opals (or any other gems, for that matter) should not be worn while washing dishes because of the thermal shock of the hot water.

Opal may have excellent color play but occur as very thin seams in rock or in white opal without fire. These seams can be utilized by cementing them to a backing material such as potch opal (without fire), obsidian, or a ceramic, using a black epoxy cement. The black cement makes the colors appear stronger. Such a composite stone is known as a *doublet*. If a quartz cabochon is cemented on top of the opal layer, the stone is called a *triplet* and is a three-layer sandwich with opal in the middle. Triplets are good ringstones because the quartz is hard and protects the opal from scratching.

Bits of precious opal are sometimes suspended in tiny glass or plastic spheres or tear-shaped vials in water or (usually) glycerine so they float slowly and gently. These jewels are known as *floating opals*.

Many types of opal can be treated to enhance their appearance. A common technique is to immerse white or gray opal (especially from Andamooka) in sugar solution and then in strong sulfuric acid. The acid carbonizes the sugar and leaves microscopic carbon specks in the opal, which effectively blacken the body color and make the spots of fire stand out better. Opal has been synthesized by Pierre Gilson of France and Inamori of Japan, and is imitated by a variety of other materials, including plastics and glass.

Name: *Opalus* was the ancient Latin name of this gem, probably derived from Sanskrit *upala,* meaning *precious stone.* The Greek *opallios* literally means "to see a change of color."

ORBICULAR JASPER   See: Quartz.

ORTHOCLASE   See: Feldspar.

ORTHOFERROSILITE   See: Enstatite.

P

PAINITE

Formula: $Ca_4Al_{20}BSiO_{38}$.

Crystallography: Hexagonal, pseudo-orthorhombic.

Color: Dark red, garnetlike in hue.

Luster: Vitreous.

Hardness: 8.

Density: 4.0.

Cleavage: Not determined.

Optics: $o = 1.816$; $e = 1.787$.
Uniaxial (−).

Birefringence: 0.029.

Pleochroism: o = deep ruby red; e = pale brownish orange.

Spectral: Faint Cr spectrum.

Inclusions: Minute cavities in thin sheets; inclusions of tabular hexagonal crystals (phlogopite).

Luminescence: Weak red in LW, strong red in SW.

Occurrence: *Burma*, in the gem gravels of *Mogok*. One red crystal was discovered in 1951 and identified in 1957 as a new mineral.

Comments: No cut gems are known. The first discovered specimen is the red crystal in the British Museum in London, weighing 1.7 grams. The color resembles garnet, and the density is that of garnet or ruby. This means that there might be cut gems in existence that have been misidentified as ruby or garnet. The refractive indices are unlike those for ruby, and the material is so clearly birefringent that it could not be confused with garnet, if

tested. Also, a garnet of this color would display the almandine spectrum, a very definitive test.

This is perhaps the rarest of all gem species—not a single cut stone is known to exist, and only a few crystals have ever been identified!

Name: After the discoverer, A. C. D. Pain.

PALYGORSKITE (Angel Stone) = **ATTAPULGITE.**

Formula: $(Mg,Al)_2Si_4O_{10}(OH) \cdot 4H_2O$.

Crystallography: Monoclinic and orthorhombic, with many polytypes. Crystals very elongated, in bundles; usually thin flexible sheets made up of complexly intergrown fibers, resembling parchment or leather.

Colors: White, gray, rose pink, pale pink, yellowish.

Luster: Dull; translucent.

Hardness: Pure material very soft (around 2); angel skin is impregnated with silica and hardness = 4.5.

Density: 2.21 (pure); angel stone is 2.1-2.2.

Cleavage: Easy; not observed on impregnated material; tough.

Optics: Around 1.55 (probably reading values for quartz impregnation) for angel stone.

Occurrence: Palygorskite is a product of alteration and occurs in hydrothermal veins, serpentines, and granitic rocks.
Attapulgas, Georgia; Metalline Falls, Washington.
Scotland; England; France; USSR; Morocco.
Peru; Mexico: angel stone.

Comments: This material has been marketed as *angelskin opal*, but this is a misnomer as the material is altogether different from opal. Angel stone is a microcrystaline quartz impregnating manganiferous, pale pink palygorskite. The silica impregnation makes the material hard and durable enough to cut. Palygorskite is related to sepiolite (meerschaum) and structurally contains amphibolelike silicate chains. The parchmentlike, matted aggregates of fibrous crystals typical of palygorskite have led to the fanciful designations *rock-wood* and *mountain-wood* or *mountain-leather.* The color of angel skin is very attractive and the material is suitable for both cabochons and carvings.

Name: Palygorskite after a locality in the Urals, USSR; attapulgite after the locality in Georgia.

PAPAGOITE

Formula: $CaCuAlSi_2O_6(OH)_3$.

Crystallography: Monoclinic; crystals tiny, flattened; usually microcrystalline coatings and aggregates, sometimes mixed with quartz.

Colors: Cerulean blue; leaves no streak.

Luster: Vitreous.

Hardness: 5-5.5; may be approximately 7 if silicified.

Density: 3.25 if pure; may be lower (for example, 2.42 on Arizona material) if mixed with quartz.

Cleavage: Distinct on crystals; not observed on microcrystalline material; pure mineral is brittle, tough if mixed with quartz.

Optics: $\alpha = 1.607$; $\beta = 1.641$; $\gamma = 1.672$. Biaxial (−).

Birefringence: 0.065.

Pleochroism: None reported.

Spectral: Bands centered at 4480, 5150, and 5550.

Luminescence: None reported; inert in LW and SW.

Occurrence: Orignally found as tiny crystals associated with ajoite at *Ajo, Pima County, Arizona.* This was not cuttable. Material mixed with quartz was reported from a locality near *Elko, Nevada.* This is hard, tough, and takes a high polish making it suitable for cabochons. A regular interlocking structure is visible under magnification, and tiny metallic copper crystals may also be noted. The material is similar in appearance to chrysocolla or turquoise. Cabochons are translucent to opaque with a vitreous luster.

Stone Sizes: Cabochons up to several inches in length can be cut from the massive material.

Name: For the Papago Indian tribe that lived in the region around Ajo, Arizona.

PARGASITE   See also: Actinolite; Hornblende; Amphibole; Series to Ferropargasite if Fe exceeds Mg. Amphibole Group; closely related to Hornblende.

Formula: $NaCa_2(Mg,Fe)_4Al(Si_6Al_2)O_{22}(OH)_2$.

Crystallography: Monoclinic; crystals prismatic, also massive, compact or granular.

Colors: Light brown to brown, grayish black, bluish green, dark green.

Luster: Vitreous.

Hardness: 5-6.

Density: 3.069-3.181.

Cleavage: Perfect 1 direction; parting 2 directions.

Optics: $\alpha = 1.613$; $\beta = 1.618$; $\gamma = 1.635$. Biaxial (+), $2V = 120°$.

Birefringence: 0.022.

Pleochroism: Colorless/very light brown/light brown; colorless/bluish green/bluish green; greenish yellow/green/bluish green.

Spectral: Not diagnostic.

Luminsecence: None.

Occurrence: A widespread component of igneous and metamorphic rocks.
Pargas, Finland.
Fresno, California; Burlington, Pennsylvania.
Scotland; Sweden; USSR; Austria; Venezuela.
Baffin Island, Nova Scotia, Canada.

Stone Sizes: Pargasite from Nova Scotia has yielded faceted gems in the 2-3 carat range. The mineral, though abundant and widespread, seldom occurs in crystals transparent enough for cutting stones over ½ carat.

Comments: The amphibole group is very large and extremely complex and contains numerous distinct species that vary subtly in chemistry and physical properties. Pargasite and ferropargasite are calcic amphiboles that generally are lumped together as *hornblende,* even though up to 16 distinct minerals belong to this group, including actinolite (see page 37). The identity of a specific amphibole is determined (ideally) by a chemical analysis or by detailed measurements of density, color, and optical data. There are undoubtedly a great many localities that could potentially yield cuttable crystals.

Name: After the locality, Pargas, Finland.

PARISITE

Formula: $Ca(Ce,La)_2(CO_3)_3F_2$.

Crystallography: Hexagonal; crystals double hexagonal pyramids, often steep, sometimes prismatic, striated; sometimes rhombohedral.

Colors: Brownish yellow, brown, grayish yellow.

Luster: Vitreous to resinous; pearly on basal cleavage surfaces.

Hardness: 4.5.

Density: 4.36.

Cleavage: Distinct basal parting or cleavage; perhaps due to alteration. Fracture subconchoidal to splintery; brittle.

Optics: $o = 1.676$; $e = 1.757$. Uniaxial (+).

Birefringence: 0.081.

Pleochroism: Weak.

Spectral: Not diagnostic.

Luminescence: Not reported.

Occurrence: In carbonaceous shale beds in the emerald deposits of *Muzo, Colombia;* also as typical inclusions in emerald crystals. Also in alkali pegmatites in *Norway.*
Muzo, Colombia.
Langesundsfjord, Norway.
Italy; Madagascar; Manchuria.
Quincy, Massachusetts; Ravalli County, Montana.

Stone Sizes: Parisite is a rare mineral, and crystals are usually very small. Tiny faceted stones (all under 1 carat) have been cut from Montana material.

Name: After J. J. Paris, proprietor of the mine at Muzo where the mineral was first discovered.

PEARL

Formula: $CaCO_3$(aragonite), about 82-86%; conchiolin, 10-14%; water, 2%.
These proportions are variable.

Crystallography: Orthorhombic (aragonite), with the minute crystals radially oriented and a concentric structure.

Colors: The color of a pearl is a result of a *body color* and an *overtone color* (known as *orient*) present (due to surface effects) as a lustrous sheen. The orient is the color seen as *reflected* by a diffuse light source. The rest of the color observed is due to the body color. There are sometimes two overtone colors, one seen on the surface in full view, the other at the edge.

Luster: Pearly, dull.

Hardness: 2.5-4.5.

Density: 2.6-2.78; conch pearls, 2.85; cultured pearls, 2.72-2.78, that is, heavier than most natural pearls, but this is *not* a diagnostic test.

Cleavage: None. Fracture uneven. Roughness is variable.

Birefringence: 0.156 (aragonite).

Optics: $N = 1.53-1.69$, but not observed; usually vague shadow edge in this range.

Acids: Pearls will dissolve in all acids.

Luminescence: Natural pearls may be light blue, yellowish, greenish, or pinkish in LW, SW. Cultured pearls no reaction, or same as natural in LW. Freshwater pearls always glow yellowish white in X-rays.

Pearl Colors: The surface tone or orient is due to diffraction at the edges of overlapping plates of aragonite crystals at the surface. These edges cause a feeling of roughness when a pearl is rubbed across the teeth.

Body Colors:
White, as follows: white (no overtone); cream (no overtone); light cream to light yellow; light rose (pinkish overtone on white background); cream rosé (cream background with deep rose overtone); fancy pearls (cream background, with overtone of rose; blue or green secondary overtone seen at edges of pearl).
Black: includes gray, bronze, dark blue, blue-green, green. Some have metallic overtones.
Colored Pearls: neither black nor white, usually with a blue background color, plus red, purple, yellowish, violet, blue, green. More frequently seen in freshwater pearls.

Darker colors are apparently due to dark conchiolin in the core of a pearl showing through the thin layers of aragonite crystals.

Shapes of Pearls: Round; pear-shaped (squat = egg shape, elongated pear = drop shape); button (flat back); half pearls (flat back); three-quarter pearls (¾ round with flat area); seed pearls (unsymmetrical, less than ¼ grain); dust pearls (almost microscopic); blister pearls (attached to shell); baroque pearls (any irregular shape not mentioned); slugs (baroque pearls with a poor luster).

Occurrence: Salt-water pearls are the most important on the market. These come principally from the species of oyster known as *Pinctada*.
Persian Gulf: the world's major pearl-producing area, especially close to the coasts of Iran, Oman, and Saudi Arabia. These waters have produced pearls for more than 2000 years.
Persian Gulf pearls are usually small (less than 12 grains). The diving season is roughly May-September, and the waters are worked by hundreds of small boats. The diving depth is about 30-90 feet but usually less than

60 feet. Pearls are recovered from oysters, washed, and then sold to merchants in Bombay, India. Then follows a bleaching operation (using hydrogen peroxide and sunlight), sorting, grading, and drilling. Poor-quality pearls go the Far East, in general. Better pearls go mostly to Paris and from there many reach the United States. Bombay is chiefly a brokerage center.

Persian Gulf pearls are creamy white. Density is 2.68-2.74.

Gulf of Manaar: an arm of the Indian Ocean, between Sri Lanka and India. The waters have been fished for pearls for more than 2500 years, but fishing now is sporadic. The government of Sri Lanka controls the fishing and auctions the oysters that are caught. The oysters are opened by leaving them on the ground to rot, and the decomposition products are searched for pearls, which then go to Bombay. Gulf of Manaar pearls are pale cream white, sometimes with fancy overtones of blue, green, and violet. Density is 2.68-2.74.

Red Sea: not a major pearl producer today. The pearls are reputed to be whiter than those from other sources.

Australia: pearl oysters are fished off the west, northwest, and north coasts. Armored diving suits are now used. Recovery of the shells is as important as recovery of the pearls since the shells provide a major industry. Australian pearls are silvery white to yellow. Density is 2.67-2.78.

South Seas: native fisheries operate around Micronesia and Polynesia. The pearls may be large (up to 7100 grains!) and are generally round. Tahiti is the major pearl center. The colors are usually white with little orient but also can be yellow, gray, and black. A metallic, grayish cast is characteristic.

Japan: Japanese waters are rapidly becoming too polluted for the existence of *Pinctada*. Cultured pearls now constitute a much bigger industry. Japanese pearls are white, often with a greenish tinge. Density is 2.66-2.76.

Venezuela: Venezuelan oysters are usually small varieties, and the pearls vary in color from white to bronze, also black. White pearls from here may be very iridescent and almost glassy. Density 2.65-2.75.

Mexico; Panama: fisheries here are small and not important commercially.

Florida; Gulf of California: occasionally pearls are found, especially conch pearls, which are pink (from conch shells). Pearls are also found in abalone, and colors may be green, yellow, blue, and other tones. California has produced black pearls. Density of Florida pearls (pink) is about 2.85; California, 2.61-2.69. Abalone shells are often hollow inside with bright iridescent colors that make them very distinctive. Conch shells are often used to make cameos. Conch pearls are usually pink, with a very distinctive flamelike surface pattern.

Freshwater Pearls: come from a mussel called *Unio*, rather than from oysters. Freshwater pearls are found in rivers throughout the world, including Europe, South America and the United States. Notable occurrences are in:

Scotland; Wales; England; Ireland.
France: Germany; Austria.
Mississippi River and its tributaries.
Amazon River Basin.
Nova Scotia.
East Pakistan.

Cultured Pearls: Patents for processes to produce cultured pearls were granted in Japan about 1910. The basic work was down by Otokichi Kuwabara, Tatsuhei Mise, Tokichi Nishikawa, and Kokichi Mikimoto. The process developed involves the insertion of a bead of mother-of-pearl (shell) up to about 13 mm in diameter, along with a piece of tissue from a part of the oyster known as the mantle, into the body of the oyster. The oysters upon which the surgery has been performed are allowed to convalesce in sheltered waters for 4-6 weeks. They are then allowed to grow, in cages, for a period of 3-6 years at a depth of 7-10 feet. Nacre accumulates around the inserted bead to form a pearly layer. Japan is the world leader in cultured pearl production.

Cultured *blister pearls* are half-pearls formed by accumulation on a half-bead stuck to the shell of the oyster. Large-diameter beads can be used. After pearl growth, the nacrous (pearly) dome is removed and cemented onto a mother-of-pearl bead. This product is called a *Mabe pearl.*

Some cultured pearls are grown in fresh water in Lake Biwa, Japan, using clams. As many as 30 insertions per clam can be tolerated without killing the animal. Growth requires about 3 years, and the pearls have excellent color and luster.

Externally, cultured and natural pearls are virtually identical. Identification *requires* skilled use of special tools, such as the pearl endoscope or X-ray apparatus. X-radiography offers the only positive proof of the origin of a pearl. Other tests are helpful but not conclusive.

Stone Sizes: One metric carat = 4 pearl grains The *Hope Pearl* in the *BM* is 2 inches long, 4.5 inches in circumference at the broad end, and weighs 1800 grains. This is a salt-water pearl, perhaps of Burmese origin.

The *Queen Pearl* is of freshwater origin, pink, round, translucent, weighs 93 grains, and was found near Paterson, New Jersey!

Miracle of the Sea is pear-shaped and weighs 1191 grains.

La Pellegrina, a very famous pearl from the Orient, weighs 111.5 grains. Other notable pearls include:

La Peregrina (Panama), 203 grains.
The Gogibus (West Indies), 504 grains.
La Regente, 337 grains.
Pearl of Asia, 2420 grains.

The following table gives the approximate weights (in grains) of pearls of mm sizes:

Diameter in mm	Weight
1	0.02
2	0.25
3	0.75
4	1.75
5	3.50
6	6.0
7	9.75
8	14.5
9	19.5
10	28.0
11	38.0
12	48.0
13	61.0
14	81.0
15	101.0

Comments: Maximum beauty is not usually found in large pearls. They form, basically, by encapsulation of an irritant by tissues of a mollusc. The value of pearls is a function of color, luster, orient, translucency, texture, shape, and especially size. Groups of pearls, such as beads, create complex valuation problems because degree of matching becomes an issue. The price of a group of pearls or a single pearl is determined by a complex formula involving a base price multiplied by the *square* of the weight in grains. The base rate is higher for higher-quality and for matched pearls. In addition, there are ways of averaging sizes to determine the overall size to use in the formula for groups of pearls. The base rate is a fluctuating market factor, determined by experience.

The introduction of cultured pearls early in this century caused a major depression in the prices of pearls since high-priced, rare, natural pearls could not initially be distinguished from cultured ones. The market took many years to recover, and with unambiguous laboratory tests now available, fine pearls have recovered their original esteem. Cultured pearls are fully accepted and occupy a larger share of the market than natural pearls. Large (over 12 mm) pearls of fine color and orient are very rare and costly, and even more so if available in matched groups.

Name: From the Latin word *perula,* meaning *pearl.*

PECTOLITE   Series to Serandite (through Manganpectolite).

Formula: $NaCa_2Si_3O_8(OH) + Mn$.

Crystallography: Triclinic. Crystals acicular, radial or globular masses; often terminated.

Colors: Colorless, white, gray.

Luster: Vitreous to silky.

Hardness: 4.5-5.

Density: 2.74-2.88.

Cleavage: Perfect 1 direction. Fracture splintery.

Optics: $\alpha = 1.595\text{-}1.610; \beta = 1.605\text{-}1.615; \gamma = 1.632\text{-}1.645$. Biaxial (+), $2V = 50\text{-}63°$. Refractometer spot reading at about 1.60.

Birefringence: 0.036.

Spectral: Not diagnostic.

Luminescence: In LW, orange-pink (Bergen Hill, New Jersey), cream white (Lendalfoot, Scotland). In SW, greenish yellow (Scotland), yellowish, orange with green areas (Magnet Cove, Arkansas, and Lake County, California), faint yellow with phosphorescence (Paterson, New Jersey).

Occurrence: In cavities in basaltic rocks, associated with zeolites; in lime-rich metamorphic rocks. *Scotland; Sweden; Czechoslovakia; USSR; Morocco; South Africa; Japan.*
New Jersey: Paterson area, in fine radial sprays; also at *Franklin* and *Sterling Hill.*
Alaska: massive, jadelike (used as jade substitute); also fine-grained, pale blue-green.
Lake County, California: dense material suited for cabochons.
Magnet Cove, Arkansas: pinkish manganiferous material.
Canada: Thetford Mines, Quebec; Asbestos, Quebec: magnificent prismatic crystals, some facetable, also twinned, up to 5 inches long; pale blue-green color, white.
Greenland: manganiferous.
Dominican Republic: compact, white, and various shades of blue (sometimes dark) material capable of cutting cabochons with high polish *(larimar).*

Stone Sizes: Cabochons up to a few inches have been cut from dense, massive, or fibrous material. A few small

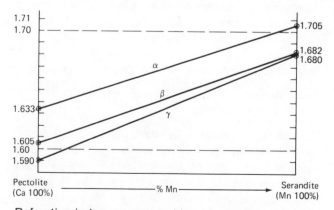

Refractive index vs. composition in pectolite-serandite series.

faceted gems have been cut from material found at Asbestos, Quebec, about 1973. These are the only known faceted pectolite gems; they range in size up to about 3 carats.

Comments: Fibrous material has a chatoyancy that gives a catseye effect to cabochons. Pectolite is a curiosity for collectors. The fibrous agregates are seldom cohesive enough to cut, and the material is too soft and fragile for wear, unless the fibers are intergrown. Such material could be jadelike in toughness as well as appearance. When sufficiently compact, cabochons take an excellent polish. The material from Quebec is extremely rare, and transparent crystals are usually tiny.

Dominican pectolite is the loveliest in the world; it is compact and takes a very high polish. It is colored in various shades of blue, and the finest is dark and translucent. The local trade name for the material is *Larimar;* it and, though locally abundant, this is a *rare* gem material. The blue color is due to copper.

Name: From the Greek *pektos,* meaning *congealed* because of the translucent appearance the mineral sometimes has.

PENTLANDITE

Formula: $(Fe,Ni)_9S_8$.

Crystallography: Isometric. Crystals extremely rare; massive, granular.

Color: Light bronze yellow.

Streak: Bronze brown.

Luster: Metallic; opaque.

Hardness: 3.5-4.

Cleavage: None. Fracture conchoidal. Brittle.

Luminescence: None. Nonmagnetic.

Occurrence: Associated with pyrrhotite and other nickel ores in basic rocks.
Norway; Transvaal, South Africa; Alaska; California; Nevada.
Sudbury, Ontario, Canada: major ore mineral, huge masses.

Stone Sizes: Cabochons of any desired size can be cut from massive material.

Comments: Pentlandite resembles other yellowish metallic minerals and is cut by collectors as a curiosity. The cut stones are quite attractive but too soft for hard wear. Pentlandite is usually intimately intermixed with pyrrhotite and chalcopyrite in Canadian ore bodies, creating an interesting, multicolored metallic appearance.

Name: After J. B. Pentland who first noted the mineral.

PERICLASE

Formula: MgO.

Crystallography: Isometric. Crystals octahedral, cubic; commonly as rounded grains.

Colors: Colorless, white, gray, yellow, brownish yellow, green, black.

Luster: Vitreous.

Hardness: 5.5.

Density: 3.56.

Cleavage: Perfect 1 direction. Fracture uneven. Brittle.

Optics: Isotropic; $N = 1.736$.

Luminescence: Pale yellow in LW (Terlingua, Texas).

Occurrence: Occurs in marbles, due to high-temperature contact metamorphism.
Texas; New Mexico.
Spain; Sardinia; Czechoslovakia.
Crestmore, Riverside County, California: embedded grains.
Vesuvius, Italy: as glassy grains in the lava rocks.
Nordmark, Sweden: in the Mn mines.

Stone Sizes: I have not seen any faceted gems, but if such gems existed, they would be very small. Transparent grains from Vesuvius might be cuttable, but in general periclase is not known in transparent, large crystals.

Comments: Periclase has been synthesized in large masses in the laboratory, but these have no market significance. A faceted natural periclase would be a great rarity due to the extreme scarcity of suitable faceting rough. The expected size would be less than 1 carat.

Name: From the Greek *peri* plus *klastos,* to *break around,* in allusion to the cleavage.

PERIDOT   See: Olivine.

PERISTERITE   See: Feldspar.

PERTHITE   See: Feldspar.

PETALITE

Formula: $LiAlSi_4O_{10}$.

Crystallography: Monoclinic. Crystals rare, tabular; usually massive, cleavable.

Colors: Colorless, white, gray, yellow, sometimes reddish or greenish white, pink.

Luster: Vitreous to pearly.

Hardness: 6-6.5.

Density: 2.3–2.5.

Cleavage: Perfect 1 direction. Brittle.

Optics: $\alpha = 1.503\text{–}1.510$; $\beta = 1.510\text{–}1.521$; $\gamma = 1.516\text{–}1.523$. Biaxial (+), $2V = 83°$.

Birefringence: 0.012–0.014.

Spectral: Not diagnostic; may be a vague band at 4540 in some stones.

Luminescence: In LW pale orange (Wyoming) or buff (Maine). May be orange in X-rays.

Occurrence: In granite pegmatites, in crystals and masses. *North Bonneville, Wyoming; Greenwood, Maine; San Diego County, California; Bolton, Massachusetts. Uto, Sweden; Elba, Italy; USSR. Londonderry, Western Australia:* facetable material. *Arassuahy, Brazil:* large, clean masses. *Bikita, Zimbabwe:* considerable material mined for Li content. *Karibib, Namibia:* colorless, transparent, and pinkish material.

Stone Sizes: Petalites are usually small, up to about 20 carats from Brazilian crystals and smaller from other localities. Some Brazilian and Namibian rough has yielded somewhat larger stones in the 50 carat range. *SI:* 55 (colorless, Namibia); 48.3, 45.9, 26.6 (colorless, Brazil). *DG:* 14.8 (colorless, Australia). *PC:* 48.25 (colorless).

Comments: Most faceted petalites are colorless and glassy looking. They are desirable because of their rarity and if they are free of inclusions, especially in large sizes. A considerable number of 1–10 carat faceted gems from Brazil have been available on the market. Massive pink material from Namibia is occasionally cabbed.

Name: From the Greek *petalos, (leaf)*, in allusion to the cleavage. *Castorite*, the name applied to crystals, is after Castor, one of the heavenly twins in Greek mythology (see Pollucite).

PETRIFIED WOOD See Quartz.

PHENAKITE

Formula: Be_2SiO_4.

Crystallography: Hexagonal. Crystals rhombohedral, prismatic, acicular; also granular, and in fibrous spherulites.

Colors: Colorless; also yellow, pink, brown, pinkish red, all due to surface stains; some crystals are colored by impurities.

Luster: Vitreous.

Hardness: 7.5–8.

Density: 2.93–3.00.

Cleavage: Indistinct, 1 direction. Fracture conchodial. Brittle.

Optics: $o = 1.654$; $e = 1.670$. Uniaxial (+).

Birefringence: 0.016.

Dispersion: 0.005.

Pleochroism: Observed in strongly colored crystals; for example, in a greenish-blue stone: violet-red/intense blue.

Spectral: Not diagnostic.

Luminescence: Pale greenish or blue in UV light, occasionally pale rose. Sometimes fluoresces blue in X-rays.

Inclusions: Crystals of aikinite; also mica (Brazil).

Occurrence: In granite pegmatites, often in good crystals. *Pala County, California; Colorado (Pike's Peak* area); *New Hampshire; Lord's Hill, Maine. Kragero, Norway; France; Switzerland; Czechoslovakia; Usugara district, Tanzania; Klein Spitzkopje, Namibia. Habachtal, Austria:* small gemmy colorless or yellowish crystals. *Virginia:* crystals up to 2 inches across. *USSR:* reddish color. *San Miguel de Paracicaba, Brazil:* large colorless crystals, often clean and cuttable.

Stone Sizes: Crystals up to $5 \times 10 \times 18$ cm have been found, though these are usually heavily flawed. The largest known rough was a pebble found in Sri Lanka that weighed 1470 carats and cut a 569 carat clean gem and several smaller stones. The large stone has many needlelike inclusions. *SI:* 22.2 (colorless, USSR); 21.9 (colorless, Brazil). *NMC:* 23.41 (colorless, Brazil). *PC:* 21.21, 19.17 (colorless, USSR).

Comments: Phenakite is very hard and suited for wear in jewelry, but it is colorless and not exciting to look at. Cut gems have little fire but are very bright. Red gems cut from material from the USSR are seldom seen and are very rare. The normal faceted gemstone is in the 1–5 carat range.

Name: From the Greek for *deceiver* because it was mistaken for quartz.

PHOSGENITE

Formula: $Pb_2CO_3Cl_2$.

Crystallography: Tetragonal. Crystals prismatic, thick and tabular; massive, granular.

Colors: Colorless, white, yellowish white, gray, shades of brown, greenish, pinkish.

Luster: Adamantine.

Hardness: 2-3.

Density: 6.13.

Cleavage: Distinct 1 direction. Fracture conchodial. Somewhat sectile.

Optics: $o = 2.114$-2.118; $e = 2.140$-2.145. Uniaxial (+).

Birefringence: 0.028.

Pleochroism: Very weak, reddish/greenish, only in thick pieces.

Luminescence: Strong yellowish fluorescence in UV and X-rays.

Occurrence: A secondary mineral in lead ore deposits.
California; Colorado; Arizona; New Mexico; Massachusetts.
Matlocks, England; Tarnow, Poland; USSR; Tasmania; Australia; Tunisia.
Monte Poni, Sardinia: fine yellow-brown crystals up to 5 inches across; some have facetable areas.
Tsumeb, Namibia: some cuttable.

Stone Sizes: Phosgenite is very rare as a faceted gem, almost always less than 2 carats, and usually yellowish brown in color (Sardinia). A few larger stones, up to about 10 carats, are known.

Comments: Massive material can be cut into interesting cabochons of various colors, up to the size of the rough (several inches). Phosgenite is too soft to wear. The strong fluorescence is of interest to specialists in fluorescent minerals.

Name: From *phosgene*, a name for the compound $COCl_2$ (carbonyl chloride) because the mineral contains C, O, and Cl.

PHOSPHOPHYLLITE

Formula: $Zn_2(Fe,Mn)(PO_4)_2 \cdot 4H_2O$.

Crystallography: Monoclinic. Crystals prismatic to tabular, well developed.

Colors: Colorless to blue-green.

Luster: Vitreous.

Hardness: 3-3.5.

Density: 3.08-3.13.

Cleavage: Perfect 1 direction. Fracture uneven. Brittle.

Optics: $\alpha = 1.595$-1.599; $\beta = 1.614$-1.616; $\gamma = 1.616$-1.621. Biaxial (−), $2V = 45°$.

Birefringence: 0.021-0.033.

Pleochroism: None.

Spectral: Not diagnostic.

Luminescence: Fluoresces violet in SW.

Occurrence: In massive sulfide deposits *(Bolivia)* and in granite pegmatites *(Germany)*.
Potosi, Bolivia: magnificent single crystals up to about 3 × 2 inches; refractive indices of this material 1.597-1.621, density 3.08, fine blue-green color, transparent.
Hagendorf, Germany: small crystals associated with secondary phosphate minerals.

Stone Sizes: Only Bolivian material has been cut, but some crystals have been found that could yield stones of about 75 carats or more. These are superb and very rare crystal specimens and will undoubtedly never be cut. Most stones are in the 1-10 carat range, cut from crystal fragments and broken crystals.
SI: 26.9 (Bolivia).
PC: 74, flawless (Bolivia).
DG: 5.25 (Bolivia).

Comments: Phosphophyllite possesses a color almost unique in gems, a lovely blue-green shade enhanced by cutting. This is a *very* rare mineral. Stones are seldom available because of lack of incentive to cut up good crystals. Few large stones exist; the material is quite brittle and fragile and very difficult to cut, with an easily developed cleavage. This is one of the more desirable of the collector gems as well as one of the more expensive ones. Analysis has shown the Bolivian material to be almost Mn-free, unlike the German material that contains Mn.

Name: After Greek words for *phosphorus-bearing* and *cleavable*.

PICOTITE   See: Spinel.

PICTURE JASPER   See: Quartz.

PIEDMONTITE   See: Epidote.

PLAGIOCLASE   See: Feldspar.

PLANCHEITE   See: Shattuckite.

PLASMA   See: Quartz.

PLEONASTE   See: Spinel.

POLLUCITE   Series to Analcime; Zeolite Group.

Formula: $Cs_{1-x}Na_xAlSi_2O_6 \cdot xH_2O$; $x \sim 0.3$. Also written: $(Cs,Na)_2(Al_2Si_4)O_{12} \cdot H_2O$.

Crystallography: Isometric. Crystals cubic, very rare; massive, fine-grained.

Colors: Colorless, white, gray; tinted pale pink, blue, violet.

Luster: Vitreous, slightly greasy.

Hardness: 6.5-7.

Density: 2.85-2.94.

Cleavage: None. Fracture conchoidal. Brittle.

Optics: Isotropic; $N = 1.518-1.525$.

Dispersion: 0.012.

Luminescence: Orange to pink fluorescence in UV and X-rays.

Inclusions: Usually whitish, resembling spikes or balls, very small; also very tiny snowflakes, bulging at the centers.

Occurrence: In granite pegmatites.
San Diego County, California; Middletown, Connecticut. Bernic Lake, Manitoba, Canada; Elba, Italy; Finland; Kazakhstan, USSR; Karibib, Namibia.
Custer County, South Dakota: massive material in thick seams.
Newry, Maine: gem material.
Various localities in *Maine* and *Massachusetts.*
Varutrask, Sweden: massive lilac to white material ($N = 1.518$, S.G. 2.90).

Stone Sizes: Masses in South Dakota reach 3-4 feet in thickness, opaque, whitish. Gems are usually colorless and very small; Maine material cuts stones from masses that reach a size of 10 inches.
SI: 8.5 (colorless, Maine); 7.0 (colorless, Connecticut).
PC: 3.85 (pinkish, Maine).

Comments: Pollucite is a very rare cesium mineral. In fact, it is the only mineral in which Cs is an essential constituent. Gems are always very small, under 10 carats, despite the existence of large beds at some localities. It is colorless and lacks fire when cut but is of interest for its great rarity.

Name: Pollux was, along with Castor, a brother of Helen of Troy in Greek mythology. This mineral was found in Italy in 1846, and named *pollux;* it was associated with another mineral, named *castor,* which was later studied and renamed *petalite.*

POLYCRASE See: Euxenite.

POWELLITE

Formula: $Ca(Mo,W)O_4$. Isostructural with Scheelite.

Crystallography: Tetragonal; crystals usually pyrami-

dal (faces often striated), also tabular; massive, foliated, pulvurent, ocherous.

Colors: Straw yellow, greenish yellow, pale greenish blue, blue, blackish blue, dirty white (grayish) to gray, brown, blackish.

Luster: Subadamantine to greasy (on fracture surfaces).

Hardness: 3.5-4.

Density: 4.23 (varies with tungsten content); Indian material 4.26 (colorless) to 4.28 (brown).

Cleavage: Indistinct; fracture uneven; brittle and fragile.

Optics: $o = 1.967-1.974$; $e = 1.978-1.985$. Uniaxial (+).

Birefringence: 0.011.

Dispersion: 0.058.

Pleochroism: Blue material is blue/green (Michigan); yellow material is yellow/light yellow (India).

Spectral: Not diagnostic.

Luminescence: Fluoresces yellowish white-golden yellow in both LW and SW.

Occurrence: A secondary mineral in the oxidation zone of ore deposits.
Houghton County, Michigan: blue cuttable material.
Utah; Nevada; California; Arizona; New Mexico.
Pandulena Hill, Nasik, India: unique occurrence, scattered crystals associated with zeolite minerals in basalt cavities.
Turkey; USSR; Morocco.

Stone Sizes: The Michigan material is cuttable only to yield extremely minute stones, and until the Indian material was found powellite was essentially unknown as a gem material. The Indian crystals are quite transparent and cuttable, and gems up to about 3 carats have been cut. These are among the rarest of collector gems.

Name: After the American explorer and geologist, John Wesley Powell.

PRASE See: Quartz.

PREHNITE

Formula: $Ca_2Al_2Si_3O_{10}(OH)_2 + Fe$.

Crystallography: Orthorhombic. Crystals prismatic and tapering, rare; massive, in druses and crusts, stalactitic.

Colors: Pale green, dark green, yellow, yellowish green, gray, white, colorless.

Luster: Vitreous to pearly.

Hardness: 6-6.5.

Density: 2.80-3.00; gem material usually 2.88-2.94.

Cleavage: Distinct 1 direction. Fracture uneven. Brittle.

Optics: $\alpha = 1.611$-1.632; $\beta = 1.615$-1.642; $\gamma = 1.632$-1.665. Biaxial (+), $2V = 65$-$69°$. Usually refractometer gives shadow edge about 1.63.
Note: Faceted material from Australia, indices 1.618/1.625/1.648; birefringence 0.030. Values for optical constants increase with increasing iron content.

Birefringence: 0.021-0.033.

Pleochroism: None.

Spectral: Not diagnostic.

Luminescence: May be dull brownish yellow in UV and X-rays.

Occurrence: A low-temperature mineral occurring by deposition from goundwaters in basaltic rocks associated with zeolites; hydrothermal crystals, in cavities in acid igneous rocks; in serpentine rocks due to late-stage mineralization.
California; Colorado; Michigan; Massachusetts; Connecticut.
France; Italy; Austria; Germany; USSR; Czechoslovakia; South Africa; Pakistan; New Zealand.
New Jersey: in basalts, associated with zeolites.
Fairfax Quarry, Centreville, Virginia: fine green material.
Asbestos, Quebec, Canada: in acidic dikes, in crystals up to 3 inches long (colorless).
Scotland: facetable.
Australia: facetable.

Stone Sizes: Large masses, up to several tons in size have been encountered in New Jersey traprocks. Single masses weighing 400 pounds have been collected. Australia and other localities produce translucent material that yields interesting faceted gems up to about 30 carats.
DG: 38.20 (yellow, Australia).
SI: 4.4 (yellow-green, Scotland).

Comments: Prehnite is popular as a cabochon material among hobbyists because of its lovely green and blue-green to yellow colors. Completely transparent material is extremely rare but might be found in crystals from Asbestos, Quebec. Yellowish to greenish translucent material from Australia has been faceted and makes a striking cut gemstone with a rich color and interesting appearance, with a soft, velvety look. Some catseye stones have also been reported. Material from Scotland has yielded cuttable fragments, but such faceted gems are rather small (under 5 carats).

Name: After Colonel Hendrik von Prehn, who first found the material on the Cape of Good Hope.

PROSOPITE

Formula: $CaAl_2(F,OH)_8$.

Crystallography: Monoclinic; crystals minute, tabular; commonly massive, granular.

Colors: Colorless, white, gray.

Luster: Vitreous.

Hardness: 4.5.

Density: 2.88.

Cleavage: Perfect; not seen on massive material; fracture conchoidal.

Optics: $\alpha = 1.501$; $\beta = 1.503$; $\gamma = 1.510$. Biaxial (+).

Birefringence: 0.009.

Pleochroism: None.

Spectral: Not diagnostic.

Luminescence: None reported.

Occurrence: In tin veins, alkalic pegmatites, and as an alteration product of topaz in volcanic rocks.
St. Peters Dome, El Paso County, Colorado: cryolite deposit.
Dugway district, Tooele County, Utah: greenish color due to a trace of copper.
Santa Rosa, Zacatecas, Mexico: associated with azurite; blue material.
Germany; Tasmania.

Stone Sizes: Prosopite is a nondescript mineral of no gem significance, except for the beautiful blue material from Zacatecas, Mexico. This material is turquoise-blue, with density variable from 2.69-2.85. Distinction from turquoise is chiefly based on the lower refractive index (1.50 vs. 1.62 for turquoise). Mexican prosopite is evenly colored due to approximately 1.4% copper content. It makes an effective and attractive turquoise substitute.

Name: From a Greek word meaning *a mask,* in allusion to the deceptive nature of the material when found as pseudomorphs.

PROUSTITE   Dimorph of Xanthoconite.

Formula: Ag_3AsS_3.

Crystallography: Hexagonal (R). Crystals prismatic, rhombohedral; massive, compact.

Colors: Deep red, scarlet to vermilion red.

Streak: Bright red.

Luster: Adamantine to submetallic.

Hardness: 2-2.5.

Cleavage: Distinct 1 direction. Fracture conchoidal to uneven. Brittle.

Optics: $o = 3.088$; $e = 2.792$. Uniaxial (−).

Birefringence: 0.296.

Pleochroism: Strong in shades of red.

Spectral: Not diagnostic.

Luminescence: None.

Occurrence: Low-temperature ore deposits or the upper portions of vein deposits.
Idaho; Colorado; Nevada; California.
Sarrabus, Sardinia.
Cobalt district, Ontario, Canada: small crystals.
Batopilas, Chihuahua, Mexico: small crystals.
Freiberg, Germany: fine crystals; other German localities, sometimes in very fine and large crystals, some cuttable.
Dolores Mine, Chanarcillo, Chile: world's finest proustite occurs here, in crystals of deep red color, often transparent, up to 6 inches long and very thick. The occurrence here is unique.

Stone Sizes: Most cuttable proustite is from Chile, but cuttable crystals in private collections and museums are not about to be cut up. Occasional fragments from Germany are transparent. Gems weighing several hundred carats could be cut from crystals on display in various museums. The finest proustites known are in the collection of the British Museum of Natural History, London.
SI: 9.9 (red, Germany).

Comments: Proustite is one of the most sought-after of all collector minerals because of its magnificient color and the brilliance of good crystals. It is far too soft for wear, and exposure to light causes it to turn black (a photochromic effect due to the silver present) so the material should not be displayed in strong light. Faceted gems are deep red with a metallic surface that is both beautiful and distinctive. One of the rarest of all the better-looking collector gems.

Name: After J. L. Proust, a French chemist.

PSEUDOPHITE See: Serpentine.

PUMPELLYITE (= CHLORASTROLITE) Also note: Ferropumpellyite: contains ferrous iron. Julgoldite: contains both ferric and ferrous iron.

Formula: $Ca_2MgAl_2(SiO_4)(Si_2O_7)(OH)_2 \cdot H_2O$.

Crystallography: Monoclinic. Crystals fibrous, flattened plates, in clusters or dense mats of random fibers.

Colors: Green, bluish green, brown.

Luster: Vitreous; silky when fibrous.

Hardness: 6; chlorastrolite: 5-6.

Density: 3.18-3.33; chlorastrolite: 3.1-3.5.

Cleavage: Distinct in 2 directions. Fracture splintery. No cleavage in massive material.

Optics: $\alpha = 1.674\text{-}1.702$; $\beta = 1.675\text{-}1.715$; $\gamma = 1.688\text{-}1.722$. Biaxial (+) and (−), $2V = 26\text{-}85°$. May show anomalous birefringent colors. Mean index ~ 1.7.

Birefringence: Moderate.

Dispersion: Moderate.

Pleochroism: Distinct, as follows:
α: colorless/pale greenish yellow/pale yellowish green.
β: bluish green/pale green/brownish yellow.
γ: colorless/pale yellowish brown/brownish yellow.
Note: Pale-colored pumpellyite has low birefringence, weak dispersion, and lower indices. Dark-colored pumpellyite has higher values for all these properties.

Luminescence: None.

Spectral: Not diagnostic.

Occurrence: Pumpellyite occurs in a wide variety of igneous and metamorphic rocks and environments.
Scotland; Austria; Finland; USSR; New Zealand; South Africa; other localities.
Calumet, Michigan: in copper ores; also at *Isle Royale, Lake Superior, Michigan* (non-gem) and on the *Keweenaw Peninsula, Michigan* (non-gem).
Lake Superior: basic igneous rocks on the periphery of the lake contain spherical aggregates of green fibers of chlorastrolite, in masses. This material is sometimes cut but is not homogeneous.
California: in glaucophane schists.
New Jersey: in basalts (traprocks).

Stone Sizes: Chlorastrolite is cut as cabochons up to 1 to 2 inches long. Very fine deep green material occurs in small sizes, yielding stones less than 1 inch long.

Comments: The gem variety of pumpellyite, chlorastrolite, is best known from the Lake Superior district of the United States. It typically forms aggregates of packed fibers that are mixed with other minerals, resulting in a green and white pattern reminiscent of tortoise shell. The effect is best observed when the fibers are in radial clusters that yield circular markings. The turtle-back pattern is considered most desirable and, because of the chatoyancy of the fibers, seems to move within the stone as the lighting is changed. Pumpellyite is a common mineral in many parts of the world, but fine green material is scarce and greatly prized by collectors. The best color is a very intense green resembling the color of fine emerald or Imperial jade. Good-quality chlorastrolite with strong pattern and color is now difficult to obtain.

Name: *Pumpellyite* after Raphael Pumpelly, Michigan geologist who did pioneering studies of the Keweenaw Peninsula copper district of Michigan. *Chlorastrolite* is from Greek words meaning *green star stone*.

PURPURITE   Series to Heterosite.

Formula: $(Mn,Fe)PO_4$.

Crystallography: Orthorhombic. Crystals rare, in small masses and cleavages.

Colors: Deep rose to reddish purple; alters on outside to brown or black.

Streak: Reddish purple.

Luster: Dull, satiny.

Hardness: 4-4.5.

Density: 3.69.

Cleavage: Good 1 direction. Fracture uneven. Brittle.

Optics: $\alpha = 1.85$; $\beta = 1.86$; $\gamma = 1.92$.
Biaxial (+), 2V moderate.

Birefringence: 0.007.

Dispersion: Very strong.

Pleochroism: Strong: gray/rose-red or deep red/purplish red.

Spectral: Not diagnostic.

Luminescence: None.

Occurrence: A secondary mineral, due to the oxidation of phosphates in granite pegmatites.
South Dakota; California; North Carolina.
France; Portugal; Western Australia.
Usakos, Namibia: rich purplish masses.

Stone Sizes: Cabochons up to several inches long can be cut from cleavages.

Comments: This material is never transparent and is too soft for wear. However, cabochons are a magnificent purplish rose hue that have essentially no counterpart in the gem world. The material is available from Namibia in abundance and at low cost.

Name: After the Latin *purpura (purple),* in allusion to the color.

PYRARGYRITE

Formula: Ag_3SbS_3. Related to *proustite*.

Crystallography: Hexagonal (R); crystals prismatic, often hemimorphic. Usually massive, compact, disseminated.

Colors: Dark red.

Streak: Purplish red.

Luster: Adamantine.

Hardness: 2.5.

Density: 5.85.

Cleavage: Distinct 1 direction. Fracture conchoidal to uneven, brittle.

Optics: $o = 3.08$; $e = 2.88$.
(*Note*-these reported measurements were made using the Li line at 6710 rather than the customary Na line at 5890)
Uniaxial (−).

Birefringence: 0.200.

Pleochroism: None observed.

Spectral: Not diagnostic.

Luminsecence: None reported.

Occurrence: In low temperature hydrothermal vein deposits, as an important ore of silver.
Freiburg, Germany; Guadalajara, Spain.
Mexico: Guanajuato and *Durango.*
Colorado; Idaho; Nevada; California.
Ontario, Canada; Czechoslovakia; Chile.
Colquechaca, Bolivia: fine crystals, gemmy.

Comments: Pyrargyrite is found in a number of localities in well-formed crystals, but these are usually small. However, larger, transparent crystals from Bolivia and Chile have provided a limited amount of cuttable rough. Stones approaching 50 carats have been cut, but these tend to be too dark to be really attractive. They are exceedingly rare, however, since pyrargyrite is seldom transparent, usually even less so than the related sulfide, proustite.
PC: 40 (shield-cut, Bolivia)

Name: From Greek words meaning *fire* and *silver,* in allusion to the color and composition.

PYRITE   Dimorph of Marcasite.

Formula: FeS_2.

Crystallography: Isometric. Crystals abundant and widespread, sometimes very large and displaying an immense variety of forms; also massive, granular.

Color: Brassy yellow, sometimes with iridescent tarnish.

Streak: Greenish black.

Luster: Metallic; opaque.

Hardness: 6-6.5.

Density: 5.0-5.03.

Cleavage: Indistinct. Fracture conchoidal to uneven. Brittle.

Other Tests: Nonmagnetic; insoluble in HCl.

Occurrence: The most abundant of all sulfide minerals; occurs in nearly all rock types and most geological environments. Localities too numerous to list in detail. Fine crystals are known from the following localities: *Leadville, Colorado; French Creek, Pennsylvania; Bingham, Utah.*
Elba, Italy; Ambassaguas, Spain; England; Austria; Germany; Switzerland; Sweden; Peru; Bolivia.

Stone Sizes: Cabochons of any size could be cut from the large crystals that have been found. Pyrite is usually seen in inexpensive jewelry, faceted in rose-cut fashion with flat backs, similar to the older marcasite jewelry popular during the Victorian era.

Comments: Pyrite is more commonly known as *fool's gold* and is familiar to nearly every mineral collector. It has been used for centuries both in jewelry and as an ore of iron. "Marcasite" stones in jewelry are frequently pyrite, since the latter is more stable. The material is very brittle and heat sensitive and requires some care in cutting. Cabochons are sometimes cut, but they have no special appeal.

Name: From the Greek word for *fire,* because pyrite emits sparks when struck like a flint.

PYROCHLORE See: Microlite.

PYROPE See: Garnet.

PYROPHYLLITE

Formula: $Al_2Si_4O_{10}(OH)_2$.

Crystallography: Monoclinic. Crystals tabular, often curved and deformed; foliated, radial, granular, compact.

Colors: White, yellow, pale blue, grayish green, brownish green.

Luster: Pearly to dull, greasy.

Hardness: 1-2.

Density: 2.65-2.90.

Cleavage: Perfect 1 direction. Sectile.

Optics: $\alpha = 1.534$-1.556, $\beta = 1.586$-1.589; $\gamma = 1.596$-1.601. Biaxial ($-$), $2V = 53$-$62°$.
Vague shadow edge on refractometer at about 1.6.

Birefringence: 0.050.

Spectral: Not diagnostic.

Luminescence: Weak cream white in LW (China)—variety called *agalmatolite.*

Occurrence: In schistose metamorphic rocks; also in hydrothermal veins with micas, quartz.

California; Arizona; Deep River, North Carolina; Pennsylvania; Georgia.
Minas Gerais, Brazil; Mexico; Sweden; Belgium; Switzerland; Japan; USSR; Korea.
Transvaal, South Africa: so-called *koranna stone,* which is dark gray and is about 86% pyrophyllite; R.I. ~ 1.58, S.G. 2.72; also called *South African Wonderstone.*

Stone Sizes: Cabochons and carvings are cut from massive material, any practical size.

Comments: Pyrophyllite resembles talc in many ways and is indistinguishable by eye from soapstone. Chemical tests are needed to distinguish them. North Carolina material is often used in carvings, as is the material from China known as *agalmatolite.*

Name: From the Greek words for *fire* and *leaf* because of the sheetlike nature and thermal properties of the mineral. *Agalmatolite* means *figure stone,* in allusion to its use in carvings.

PYROXMANGITE

Formula: $(Mn,Fe)SiO_3$.

Crystallography: Triclinic. Crystals tabular; usually massive, in grains, cleavable.

Colors: Reddish brown, dark brown, pale to rose pink, purplish pink. The darker colors are due to alteration.

Luster: Vitreous to pearly.

Hardness: 5.5-6.

Density: 3.61-3.80.

Cleavage: Perfect 2 directions. Fracture uneven. Brittle.

Optics: $\alpha = 1.726$-1.748; $\beta = 1.728$-1.750; $\gamma = 1.744$-1.764. Biaxial (+), $2V = 35$-$46°$.

Birefringence: 0.016-0.020.

Pleochroism: Slight in shades of pink and red.

Spectral: Not diagnostic.

Luminescence: None.

Occurrence: In metamorphosed rocks rich in *manganese.*
Kern County, California; Iva, South Carolina; Boise, Idaho: pale pink.
Broken Hill, New South Wales, Australia: in fine crystals and grains, with rhodonite.
Scotland; Sweden: red-brown.
Finland: brown.
Honshu, Japan: gemmy material.

Stone Sizes: Faceted gems are always small since the material is extremely scarce and available only as small transparent grains. Large cabochons could be cut from cleavages and massive material. Collectors should expect to see stones up to about 2 carats.

Comments: Pyroxmangite is a very rare gemstone; grains are seldom clean enough to facet. The material resembles rhodonite and bustamite to a certain degree but can be distinguished on the basis of optic sign and birefringence. Faceted gems are hard to cut because of the cleavages, but once completed they are extremely beautiful and rich in color.

Name: Originally thought to be manganiferous pyroxene, based on studies of the material from South Carolina.

PYRRHOTITE

Formula: $Fe_{1-x}S$.

Crystallography: Hexagonal; also orthorhombic, monoclinic, depending on stoichiometry. Crystals tabular, platy, pyramidal, sometimes in clusters (rosettes); usually massive or granular.

Colors: Bronze-yellow to bronze-red or brownish; tarnishes readily, becomes iridescent.

Streak: grayish black.

Luster: Metallic; opaque.

Hardness: 3.5-4.5.

Density: 4.58-4.65.

Cleavage: None; sometimes basal parting observed; fracture subconchoidal to uneven; brittle.

Other Tests: Magnetic, varying in intensity, lost on heating. Decomposed by HCl.

Occurrence: Associated with pyrite and other sulfides throughout the world, often as a magmatic segregation in basic igneous rocks. Occasionally in pegmatites and contact metamorphic rocks, fumaroles, and basalts. Also occurs in meteorites.
Sudbury, Ontario, Canada.
Morro Velho, Brazil.
Rumania; Italy; Germany; Norway; Sweden.
Potosi Mine, Santa Eulalia, Chihuahua, Mexico.
Pennsylvania; Tennessee; New York; Maine; Connecticut.

Stone Sizes: Cabochons of almost any size could be cut from the massive material. Such stones are always opaque and metallic and can be attractive.

Name: From a Greek word meaning *reddish.*

Q

QUARTZ (= SILICA)

Formula: SiO_2.

Crystallography: Hexagonal (R). Occurs in a wide variety of crystal forms, up to large size; also as crystalline masses, cryptocrystalline, granular, in veins and stringers.

Colors: Colorless, white, gray (various shades) and many shades of yellow, orange, brown, purple, violet, pink, green, and black.

Luster: Vitreous (crystalline varieties); greasy, waxy (cryptocrystalline varieties).

Hardness: 7.

Density: 2.651 (very constant); in chalcedonies, up to 2.91.

Cleavage: None or indistinct. Fracture conchoidal to uneven. Brittle. Cryptocrystalline varieties tough.

Optics: $o = 1.544$; $e = 1.553$ (very constant). Uniaxial (+).

Birefringence: 0.009 (some chalcedonies 0.004).

Dispersion: 0.013.

Pleochroism: None; weak in amethyst and citrine; strong (pink shades) in rose quartz.

Luminescence: Varies widely due to traces of impurities, usually in the cryptocrystalline varieties. Fluorescent colors include browns, greens, white, orange (LW, SW). Some material shows phosphorescence. X-rays produce faint blue glow in rose quartz.

Occurrence: Quartz is one of the most common minerals on Earth; it occurs in a wide variety of rock types and geological environments. Localities are too numerous to list but are given in standard mineralogy texts.

Inclusions: More than forty types of minerals have been found as inclusions in crystalline quartz. Rock crystal frequently contains cavities or negative crystals with bubbles, creating what are known as two-phase inclusions. A network of cracks creates iridescent effects to produce what is called *iris quartz*. The minerals noted include:

Rutile: red, golden, silvery color.
Sagenite: any type of acicular (needlelike) crystals.
Tourmaline: black, other colors.
Actinolite: green; fibrous variety known as *byssolite*.
Chlorite: mossy, greenish inclusions.
Goethite: yellow and orange wisps, fibers, and crystals.
Hematite: blood-red platelets.
Chrysocolla: blue-green, finely disseminated.
Dumortierite: blue and violet colors.
Also: scapolite; hornblende; epidote; anatase; brookite; chlorite; micas; ilmenite; calcite; gold; dufrenoysite; oil droplets.

Quartz catseyes have been found. The catseye effect is due to inclusions of fine asbestos. The colors are usually yellowish, brownish, or pale green. This material is always cut into cabochons to bring out the effect. Occurrence: *India; Sri Lanka; Fichtelgebirge, Germany.*

Crocidolite (blue asbestos) may decompose and alter to quartz, retaining the fibrous structure. This can be further cemented by quartz and stained by iron oxides to yield a dense, siliceous, fibrous material called *tigereye*. The original blue crocidolite, if present, may add a blue tone and this is called *zebra tigereye*. If the material is unstained by iron and therefore solid blue, it is called *hawk's-eye*. Occurrence: *South Africa.*

Crystalline Quartz

Crystalline quartz is separated here from cryptocrystalline or microcrystalline quartz. The crystalline varieties are those that occur in distinct, visible crystals: *amethyst, smoky quartz, citrine, rose quartz,* and *milky quartz.* The color origins in crystalline quartz are complex and are only now beginning to be fully understood.

The stable form of quartz below a temperature of 573°C is known as α-quartz. Between 573° and 870° another silica mineral, *tridymite,* forms. At 1470°, tridymite undergoes a structural rearrangement, resulting in the appearance of a new silica type called *cristobalite,* which is isometric. Finally, at 1710°, cristobalite melts to an extremely viscous liquid. If this liquid is chilled quickly, a glass forms *(silica glass)* that has many useful properties but no regular internal structure.

Cristobalite has no gem significance but appears in some types of volcanic glass (see *obsidian,* page 137) as white globules and crystals resembling snowflakes. These form as a result of rapid cooling from high temperature.

The colored, crystalline quartz varieties generally occur in pegmatites and veins, having been deposited from water solutions over a long period of time. As a result of slow crystal growth, many such crystals achieve great internal perfection and yield enormous pieces of faceting rough. The only color varieties that do not form such large crystals are amethyst and rose quartz.

Rock Crystal: Used in faceted gems, beads, carving, decorative objects, and lamps. The material is common and has little intrinsic value, except in very large, flawless pieces. There are many types of mineral inclusions known. Occurrence: *Hot Springs, Arkansas; Herkimer, New York; Swiss Alps; Minas Gerais, Brazil; Japan; Madagascar; New South Wales, Australia; Upper Burma; Canada.*

Milky Quartz: The milkiness is due to myriad tiny cavities and bubbles filled with CO_2 or water. Vein quartz is often white and frequently contains gold. This quartz is little used in gems, except cabs with milky quartz and yellow gold specks. Occurrence: *California; Colorado.*

Brown Quartz: The variety called *smoky quartz* is pale beige, tan, brown, or deep brown in color. Very dark brown material is known as either *morion* or *cairngorm,* the latter from the locality in the Cairngorm Mountains, Scotland. The color appears to be caused by natural radioactivity. Occurrence: *Minas Gerais, Brazil; Scotland; Madagascar; Switzerland; Korea; California; North Carolina.*

Yellow Quartz: This variety is known as *citrine* and ranges in color from pale yellow through yellow-orange to rich golden orange, to very dark orange. A deep brown color is produced by heating certain types of amethyst. The name is from the old French *citrin* meaning *yellow,* and the color is due to ferric iron. Occurrence: *Minas Gerais, Brazil; Madagascar.*

Amethyst: Amethyst is violet or purple quartz. The lightest color, a pale lilac shade, is known as *Rose of France.* The deepest color, especially with flashes of red against a purple background, is referred to as *Siberian.* The term today usually implies a color rather than a locality. The name *amethyst* is from the Greek *amethystos,* meaning *not drunken* because the Greeks believed imbibing from an amethyst cup would prevent intoxication. Occurrence: *Brazil; Zambia; USSR; Namibia; Australia; Nigeria; India; Uruguay; Mexico; Arizona; North Carolina.*

Inclusions: Prismatic crystals and negative cavities, thumbprint marks, so-called rippled fractures, and twinning lines.

Transparent *green quartz* is produced by heating certain types of amethyst.

Amethyst-citrine: This material, also known as *ametrine, trystine,* and so forth, was originally reported from Rio Grande do Sul, Brazil, but later was shown to occur in Bolivia. Cut gems display both violet and yellow colors, sometimes in a striking zonal pattern, corresponding to rhombohedral growth regions. Heat treatment of both natural and synthetic amethyst can produce similarly colored material, and such stones are indistinguishable from natural ones.

Rose Quartz: The color of rose quartz is due to Ti. The material is nearly always cloudy or translucent, rarely transparent. The color is pale pink to deep pink, rarely rose-red. It is mainly used in cabochons, carvings, and decorative objects. Microscopic rutile needles may create a star effect. Occurrence: *Maine; South Dakota; New York; Brazil; Madagascar; India; Japan; Namibia; USSR.*

Quartzite: A rock made up of tightly packed quartz grains, formed at high temperature and pressure, due to metamorphism. Sometimes it contains small crystals that reflect light, and this material is called *aventurine.* Usually the included crystals are a green, chrome-rich mica called *fuchsite.* Other micas that may form aventurine include gray varieties or brown types (from Chile). The density is usually 2.64-2.69. Occurrence: *Spain; USSR; India; Chile.*

Dumortierite Quartz: A dense, deep blue to violet material made up of crystalline quartz colored by dumortierite, a complex borosilicate.

Cryptocrystalline Quartz

Cryptocrystalline quartz varieties are colored chiefly by mineral impurities in the growth environment, including oxides of Fe, Mn, Ti, Cr, Ni, and other elements. They form either as gelatinous masses that slowly dehydrate and crystallize or by deposition from slowly percolating groundwaters, depositing silica over a long period of time. This latter type of deposition results in banding that is seen in certain types of agate. Deposition within a spherical cavity, such as a gas pocket in basalt or other volcanic rock, results in concentric banding also seen in agates.

Cryptocrystalline quartz varieties offer a huge diversity of patterns and colors. The most generally widespread of these materials is composed of tiny fibers of silica and is known as *chalcedony*. Names within the cryptocrystalline quartz family are generally based on colors and patterns. The solid-colored materials are mostly chalcedony stained by oxides and are referred to as *jaspers*. Banded varieties, or materials with mosslike inclusions, are known as *agate*.

Chalcedony: Unstained material often grayish blue, compact form of silica. Occurrence: *India; USSR; Iceland; Mexico; California.*

A purple-colored chalcedony from Arizona has been marketed under the trade name *damsonite*. The material occurs in veins and blocks up to 1 m thick, with masses over 100 kg recovered. Properties are normal for chalcedony (R.I. = 1.54, S.G. = 2.61), and coloration appears to be the same as that for amethyst.

Carnelian: Translucent to semiopaque, red, orange-red, or brownish chalcedony. The color is due to iron oxide. Almost any chalcedony can be turned red by heating in an oven since it contains finely disseminated iron compounds that are oxidized by heating. Occurrence: *Brazil; Uruguay; Egypt; India.*

Sard: Similar to carnelian, sard is more brownish in color and more opaque. Occurrence: *Brazil; Uruguay.*

Plasma: Deep green; opaque due to densely packed actinolite crystals.

Prase: Green or yellowish green chalcedony.

Bloodstone: Also known as *heliotrope,* consists of dark green plasma with blood-red and orange spots of iron oxides. Occurrence: *India; Brazil; Australia; United States.*

Onyx: Banded black and white chalcedony.

Sardonyx: Banded onyx, with red and white layers.

Chrysoprase: Translucent green chalcedony colored by nickel. May resemble fine jade. Occurrence: *Western Australia (Yandramindra, Wingelina, Kalgoorlie); USSR; Brazil; California.*

Flint and Chert: Opaque, dull gray, or whitish chalcedony, very compact and hard.

Patterned Chalcedony

Agate: Usually takes the form of colored layers or bands, flat or concentric. Also mossy or dendritic inclu-

sions, sometimes creating the impression of landscapes, vegetation, and so forth. *Banded agates* have regular color layers and bright colors. The *moss agates* have mossy inclusions of mineral oxides. *Scenic agates* have inclusions that look like pictures of scenery, with lakes, shorelines, trees, and shrubs. *Lace agate* is banded with intricate swirls and loops. *Fire agate* has platy crystals of iron oxide layered with chalcedony, resulting in iridescence brought out by cutting and polishing. *Shell agate* is patterned by silicified shells in the rock. *Turritella agate* is composed mostly of shells and shell fragments of the gastropod *Turritella* and certain other species.
Occurrence: Moss agates are from *India, Scotland, and the northwestern United States.* Scenic agates are from *Yellowstone National Park, Wyoming and Montana.* Banded agate is from *Brazil, Uruguay, Madagascar, Mexico, and the United States.* Lace agate is from *Mexico, Arizona, and Namibia (blue).* Fire agate is from *Mexico.*

Jasper: Usually a mass of tiny silica crystals pigmented by impurities. The colors may be very strong, especially shades of brown, yellow, red, and green. Jasper occurs worldwide. *Orbicular jasper* has spherules of banded agate in a jasper matrix. *Scenic* or *picture jaspers* have fanciful patterns that may resemble scenery, such as ocean waves, shores, and rolling hills. Occurrence: *Oregon; Idaho; Utah; Montana; Wyoming.*

Chrysocolla in Quartz: A tough, siliceous material consisting of blue chrysocolla in fine particles disseminated in silica, to produce a rich blue, hard material that takes an excellent polish. Occurrence: *Arizona; New Mexico; Mexico.*

Petrified Wood: Colorful agate that has replaced tree trunks and limbs; the woody structure is preserved in many cases and can be seen with a microscope. The colors may be very bright and strong. Occurrence: *Arizona; New Mexico; California; Washington; Oregon;* various European countries; many other localities.

Dinosaur Bone: Silicified dinosaur bone! It has a lovely brownish color and interesting pattern. Occurrence: *Colorado; Wyoming; Utah.* Other colors include red, pink, blue, purple, green, orange, etc.

Stone Sizes:

Rock crystal reaches enormous size, as illustrated by the 12.75-inch diameter, 107-pound perfect sphere of flawless Burmese material in *SI*. This is the largest fine crystal ball in the world. Faceted gems of thousands of carats have been cut, such as the 7000 carat stone in *SI* and the 625 carat star quartz from New Hampshire.

Citrines in the thousands of carats are also known. *SI* has Brazilian stones of 2258, 1180, 783, 278, 265, and 217 carats, for example, and most large museums have similar baubles.

Smoky quartz is in the same size league as citrine, but

larger stones get very dark and opaque. *SI:* 4500 (California) and 1695 (Brazil), plus others.

Rose quartz gems are seldom transparent, especially above 20-30 carats. Large spheres of rose quartz are milky at best.

Amethyst is rare in very large, transparent masses. The fine gems at *SI* are exceptional, such as the 1362-carat Brazilian stone and the 202.5-carat stone from North Carolina.

Quartzite and *milky quartz* are massive varieties available in large pieces. *Chalcedony* is usually nodular, but masses can be several pounds and many inches in diameter.

Star quartz is a rarity, but especially noted in rose quartz. *SI* has a sphere of Brazilian star material weighing 625 carats.

Chrysoprase nodules of 700 and 1470 kilos have been found near Kalgoorlie, Western Australia.

Comments: Quartz is composed of Si and O, the two most abundant elements in the crust of the Earth. It displays a vast array of colors and shapes (when in crystals), and the cryptocrystalline varieties offer an almost endless spectrum of color and pattern. The basic properties of crystalline quartz are very constant despite color variation.

Many silica varieties can be treated by heating, irradiation, and dyes to alter their color. *Chalcedony* is frequently dyed with aniline dyes to many rich colors. The quartz gems vary in scarcity, with amethyst the rarest color, especially in large clean pieces. Cryptocrystalline varieties are so abundant that they offer a rich selection of decorative stones for wear at very modest cost.

Names: *Rock crystal* is from the Greek *krystallos*, meaning *ice*, because the Greeks thought it was ice frozen forever hard by an unnatural frost created by the gods. *Amethyst* comes from the Greek *amethystos*, as mentioned. *Citrine* is in allusion to the color citron (yellow). *Chalcedony* is an ancient name, perhaps from Chalcedon, a seaport in Asia Minor. *Agate* is from the Greek *achate*, the name of a river in southwestern Sicily where the material was found. *Onyx* is from the Greek word for *nail* or *claw. Sard* is from Sardis, the ancient locality reputed to be the origin of the stone. *Carnelian* is from the Latin *carnis (flesh)*, in allusion to the red color. *Plasma* is from the Greek for *something molded or imitated* because it was used for making intaglios. *Prase* is from the Greek *prason*, meaning *leek*, in allusion to the color. *Heliotrope* is from Greek words *helios (sun)* and *tropein (turn)* because, according to Pliny, it gives a red reflection when turned to face the sun while immersed in water. *Flint* and *chert* are of uncertain origin.

QUARTZITE see: Quartz.

R

REALGAR

Formula: AsS.

Crystallography: Monoclinic. Crystals prismatic, striated; compact, powdery.

Colors: Dark red, orange-red.

Streak: Orange-yellow.

Luster: Resinous to greasy.

Hardness: 1.5-2.

Density: 3.56.

Cleavage: Good 1 direction. Fracture conchoidal. Sectile.

Optics: $\alpha = 2.538$; $\beta = 2.684$; $\gamma = 2.704$. Biaxial (−), $2V = 40°$.

Birefringence: 0.166.

Dispersion: Strong.

Pleochroism: Strong: colorless to pale yellow.

Spectral: Not diagnostic.

Luminescence: None. May decompose on strong exposure to light.

Occurrence: Low-temperature hydrothermal vein deposits, especially with ores of lead and silver.
Getchell Mine, Nevada; Manhattan, Nevada; Mercur, Utah; Boron, California.
Rumania; Czechoslovakia; Germany; Switzerland; Japan.
King County, Washington: fine crystals, up to 2 inches long, some gemmy.

Stone Sizes: Occasional fragments of Washington crystals will cut gems to about 3 carats.

Comments: Realgar is very seldom transparent, although the mineral is widespread in occurrence throughout the world. It is extremely soft and fragile, difficult to cut, and impossible to wear. It is cut only for collectors but is extremely rare in cut form. Stones are a fine red color and very lovely.

Name: From the Arabic *Rahj-al-ghar,* meaning *powder of the mine.*

RHODIZITE

Formula: $CsAl_4Be_4B_{11}O_{25}(OH)_4$.

Crystallography: Isometric. Crystals dodecahedral or tetrahedral, up to 2 cm size; massive.

Colors: Colorless, white, yellowish white, yellow, gray, rose red.

Luster: Vitreous to adamantine.

Hardness: 8.5.

Density: 3.44.

Cleavage: Difficult. Fracture conchoidal. Brittle.

Optics: Isotropic; $N = 1.694$.
Anomalously birefringent (may not be truly isotropic).

Dispersion: 0.018.

Spectral: Not diagnostic.

Luminescence: Weak yellowish glow in SW; strong greenish and yellowish, with phosphorescence, in X-rays.

Occurrence: A pegmatite mineral with few noteworthy localities.
Antandrokomby, Madagascar (and other localities in that country): yellowish and greenish crystals, some gemmy.
Near *Mursinsk, USSR:* rose red color.

Stone Sizes: Madagascar material in fragments clean enough to cut has provided stones up to about 3 carats. *SI:* 0.5 (Madagascar).

Comments: Rhodizite is quite a rare mineral, and only Madagascar has produced gem-quality crystals. Faceted gems are extremely rare and usually pale in color. The mineral is rather hard and stones would be excellent for jewelry, especially since there is no cleavage.

Name: From the Greek for *to be rose-colored* because it imparts a red color to the flame of a blowpipe.

RHODOCHROSITE   Series to Siderite (with Fe substitution); series to Calcite (with Ca substitution).

Formula: $MnCO_3$ + Fe, Ca.

Crystallography: Hexagonal (R). Crystals rhombs and elongated scalenohedra; massive, compact, stalactic.

Colors: Pale pink, rose red, deep pink, orangish red, yellowish, gray, tan, brown.

Luster: Vitreous to pearly.

Hardness: 3.5-4.

Density: 3.4-3.6 (pure = 3.7).

Cleavage: Perfect rhombohedral. Brittle.

Optics: o = 1.786-1.840; e = 1.578-1.695. Uniaxial (−).
Ca in formula reduces indices and density; Fe and Zn increase them. This also applies to the birefringence. Single crystals may be zoned and the refractive index varies up to 0.01 within a space of one inch in some material.

Birefringence: 0.201-0.220.

Pleochroism: Faint in deep red varieties.

Spectral: Band at 5510 and 4100, plus vague lines at 5350 and 5650.

Other Tests: Effervesces in warm acids.

Luminescence: Fluoresces medium pink in LW (Michigan), also dull red to violet in SW (Argentina and Colorado).

Occurrence: A gangue mineral in hydrothermal veins and a secondary mineral in ore deposits.
Colorado: spectacular crystals, pink to deep red, small to 3 inches on an edge. The world's finest rhodochrosite comes from *Alma, Colorado;* some is facetable (red) and pink faceting rough also exits from other localities.
Butte, Montana: crystal groups (non-gem).
Magdalena, Mexico: sometimes in cuttable pieces.
Hotazel, South Africa: facetable, deep reddish crystals.

San Luis, Catamarca Province, Argentina: massive and banded material, also stalactites up to 4 feet long! These have concentric structures that display interesting bullseyes when cross-sectioned. Some Argentinian material is translucent and has been faceted.
Peru: facetable, pink crystals.

Stone Sizes: Massive material from Argentina occurs in large pieces and has been carved, cut into beads, boxes, cabochons, and useful objects. Faceted, translucent pink material cuts stones up to about 20 carats. South African rhodochrosite is rich rose red in color and rare in facetable crystals. The largest cut gems are in the 60-carat range. *SI* has South African gems of 20.8, 15.2, and 9.5 carats. Colorado pink gems are perhaps the loveliest of all and have been cut up to about 15 carats flawless. Most stones are under 5 carats.
DG: 5.95 (red, South Africa).
PC: 59.65 (red oval, South Africa).
NMC: 18.05 (red oval, South Africa).

Comments: Rhodochrosite is very rare in faceted form. The specimens are in such demand among mineral collectors that it would be an outrage to most to cut up a good crystal. Hotazel gems of large size have been available, but larger clean stones are very scarce and expensive. Colorado pink rhodochrosite in clean gems is also expensive, and anything over 2-4 carats is considered very large. Argentinian material is translucent at best and much less costly, but few gems have appeared on the market. Mexican gem material resembles Colorado material but is generally quite small. Peruvian stones resemble those from Colorado also.

Name: From the Greek for *rose-colored*, in allusion to the color.

RHODOLITE   See: Garnet.

RHODONITE   Pyroxene Group.

Formula: $MnSiO_3$ (+ Ca to maximum of 20%).

Crystallography: Triclinic. Crystals tabular; massive, cleavable, granular.

Colors: Rose red, pink, brownish red; often veined by black Mn oxides.

Luster: Vitreous; massive material dull.

Hardness: 5.5-6.5.

Density: 3.57-3.76 (massive); 3.67 in crystals.

Cleavage: Perfect 1 direction. Fracture conchoidal. Brittle (crystals); tough if compact.

Optics: Biaxial (+), $2V$ = 63-76°. Shadow edge at 1.73 in massive varieties. See following table:

	α	β	γ	Birefringence	Density	2V
Honshu, Japan	1.726	1.731	1.739	0.013	3.57	64°
Pajsberg, Sweden	1.720	1.725	1.733	0.013	3.62	75°
Broken Hill, New South Wales, Australia	1.723–1.726	1.728–1.730	1.735–1.737	0.011–0.013	3.68–3.70	74°
General	1.711–1.738	1.716–1.741	1.723–1.752	0.011–0.014	3.57–3.76	63–76°

Pleochroism: Weak, but may be distinct: yellowish red/pinkish red/pale yellowish red.

Spectral: Broad band at 5480, strong narrow line at 5030, diffuse weak band at 4550. May also see lines at 4120 and 4080.

Luminescence: Medium dull red in SW (Hungary), dull deep red in LW (Langban, Sweden).

Occurrence: In manganese-bearing ore bodies or in their vicinity.
California; Colorado; Montana; Franklin, New Jersey. Cornwall, England; Mexico; South Africa.
USSR: massive pink and rose colored material, very fine and rich *(Sverdlovsk).*
Australia: fine transparent crystals and massive material at *Broken Hill, New South Wales.*
Vermland, Sweden: good color gem material.
Honshu, Japan: facetable material.
Daghazeta, Tanzania: fine-quality massive material.
Bella Koola, British Columbia, Canada: fine pink, with black patterns; some translucent.

Stone Sizes: Massive rhodonite from various localities is available in large pieces, often with attractive black veining of manganese oxides. This material is cut into cabochons, goblets, vases, and other decorative objects, including figurines and boxes. Faceted gems are extremely rare and are derived primarily from crystals found in Australia and Japan. The maximum size of such stones is in the 2-3 carat range, but a few larger stones may exist.

Comments: Rhodonite is a popular and useful decorative material, ranging in color from pink to a fine rose-red. Faceted gems have an intense and beautiful color but are delicate due to perfect cleavage. This cleavage is extremely easy to develop, and rhodonite has the reputation of being one of the most difficult of all gems to facet. Most available rough is very small. British Columbia produces fine rhodonite similar in appearance to the Russian material. The best of B.C. rhodonite, however, is deep rose-pink and translucent. The grains of gemmy rhodonite embedded in galena (lead sulfide) at Broken Hill, New South Wales, Australia, are distinctive. Rhodonite occurs at this locality with *pyroxmangite,* a related mineral, and also with *bustamite,* $(Ca,Mn)Si_2O_6$, which occurs in crystals up to 100 cm long! Cuttable bustamite does occur and may exist in many collections, labeled as rhodonite. However, the distinctly lower refractive indices of bustamite should prove diagnostic.

Name: From the Greek *rhodos,* in allusion to the color.

RICOLITE See: Serpentine.

ROCK CRYSTAL See: Quartz.

ROSOLITE See: Garnet.

ROYAL AZEL See: Sugilite.

ROYAL LAVULITE See: Sugilite.

RUBELLITE See: Tourmaline.

RUBY See: Corundum.

RUTILE

Formula: TiO_2 + Nb, Ta, Fe.

Crystallography: Tetragonal. Crystals prismatic, vertically striated, well developed, often twinned into a series of contact twins with up to eight individuals, sometimes looping to form a complete circle! Also massive; granular.

Colors: Black, deep red, brownish red. Greenish (if Nb present), also bluish and violet. A variety rich in Cr is deep green.

Streak: Pale brown to yellowish; grayish or greenish black.

Luster: Metallic to adamantine.

Hardness: 6-6.5.

Density: 4.23; ferroan variety = 4.2-4.4; with Nb and Ta = 4.2-5.6.

Cleavage: Distinct 1 direction. Fracture conchoidal to uneven. Brittle.

Optics: $o = 2.62$; $e = 2.90$.
Uniaxial (+).
Sometimes anomalously biaxial.

Birefringence: 0.287.

Dispersion: 0.280.

Pleochroism: Distinct: shades of red, brown, yellow, green.

Spectral: Not diagnostic.

Luminescence: None.

Occurrence: Commonly seen as needles in quartz *(rutillated quartz)* and in agate *(sagenite)*. Also present as fibers in corundum, creating stars in these gems. Present as needle inclusions in a wide variety of gem minerals.

Also occurs as a high-temperature mineral, in gneiss and schist, also in Alpine-type veins; found in igneous rocks, pegmatites, regionally metamorphosed rocks, including crystalline limestones, and as detrital grains.
Virginia; North Carolina; South Dakota; California.
USSR; Switzerland; France.
Graves Mountain, Georgia: in quartz veins, fine crystals, up to several pounds in size.

Magnet Cove, Arkansas: in huge rough crystals.
Brazil: large, fine crystals.

Stone Sizes: Large crystals often have transparent areas that can provide stones for faceting. However, a cut rutile above 2-3 carats is so dark it looks opaque, effectively limiting the size of cut gems.
DG: 3.70.

Comments: Rutile is often cut as a curiosity, but the finished gem is disappointing because it is so dark. The gems are usually deep red in color, but the color is so intense that it cannot be easily seen in stones larger than 1 carat. Cabochons of rutile might show reddish reflections in cracks and along imperfections. Swiss rutile seems a bit more transparent than material from other localities.

Name: From the Latin *rutilus (red),* in allusion to the color.

S

SALITE   See: Diopside.

SAMARSKITE   See also: Euxenite, Fergusonite.

Formula: $(Y,Ce,U,Ca,Pb)(Nb,Ta,Ti,Sn)_2O_6$.

Crystallography: Monoclinic. Crystals rough, tabular; massive, compact.

Colors: Velvety black, yellowish brown on exterior.

Streak: Black to reddish brown.

Luster: Dull after alteration; resinous; vitreous, submetallic.

Hardness: 5-6.

Density: 5.25-5.69 (variable)—usually near upper end of range.

Cleavage: Indistinct. Fracture conchoidal. Brittle.

Optics: Isotropic; $N = 2.20$ (variable).
Isotropic nature caused by metamictization.

Pleochroism: None.

Luminescence: None.

Occurrence: A widespread pegmatite mineral.
North Carolina; Colorado.
USSR; Norway; Madagascar; Zaire; Japan; Minas Gerais, Brazil; Madras, India.

Stone Sizes: Large cabochons can be cut from masses found at various localities. This material is essentially opaque.

Comments: Samarskite is a very heavy material from which lustrous black to brownish cabochons are sometimes cut as curiosities. The material is rather brittle and is not intended for wear. It is rarely seen or displayed since black stones are not terribly attractive. Sometimes a stone is faceted in the nature of jet or marcasite.

Name: In honor of Colonel Samarski, a Russian mining official.

SANIDINE   See: Feldspar.

SAPPHIRE   See: Corundum.

SAPPHIRINE

Formula: $Mg_{3.5}Al_{9.0}Si_{1.5}O_{20}(+ Fe)$. Complex substitution of Mg/Al/Si with charge balancing.
Two polytypes: Sapphirine-2M = $(Mg,Al)_8(Al,Si)_6O_{20}$; monoclinic. Sapphirine-1Tc = $(Mg,Al)_8(Al,Si)_6O_{20}$; triclinic.

Crystallography: Monoclinic or triclinc; crystals tabular; usually granular or as disseminated grains.

Colors: Pale blue, bluish gray, greenish gray, green; depth of blue color varies with Fe. Also (rarely) purplish pink.

Luster: Vitreous.

Hardness: 7.5.

Density: 3.4-3.5.

Cleavage: Indistinct; fracture uneven to subconchoidal.

Optics: $\alpha = 1.714\text{-}1.716; \beta = 1.719\text{-}1.721; \gamma = 1.720\text{-}1.723$.
Biaxial (−).

Birefringence: 0.006.

Pleochroism: Distinct: X = pinkish buff; yellowish; pale smoky brown; colorless; Y = sky blue; sapphire blue; greenish blue; Z = dark sky blue; sapphire blue.

Spectral: Not diagnostic.

Luminescence: None reported.

Occurrence: In mineral veins or cavities in eruptive igneous rocks.
Milford, Utah; Keweenaw Peninsula, Michigan; Lake Superior, Minnesota.
Canada; Scotland; England; Sweden; Czechoslovakia; Japan; South Africa; Greenland; Madagascar; Italy; Sri Lanka.

Stone Sizes: Facetable sapphirine is exceedingly rare, even though the material occurs in transparent grains. *GIA* noted a very unusual purplish-pink stone of 1.54 cts, oval, with an included mica "book" (phlogopite), from Sri Lanka; R.I. = 1.701-1.707; β = 1.705; birefringence = 0.006; S.G. = 3.51. The refractive indices of sapphirine are close to idocrase, but the former is biaxial. Other such gems exist but have been misidentified.

Name: In allusion to the (sapphire blue) color.

SARCOLITE

Formula: $(Ca,Na)_4Al_3(Al,Si)_3Si_6O_{24}$.

Crystallography: Tetragonal. Crystals equant, grains.

Colors: Reddish, rose red, reddish white.

Luster: Vitreous.

Hardness: 6.

Density: 2.92.

Cleavage: None. Fracture conchoidal. Very brittle.

Optics: o = 1.604-1.640; e = 1.615-1.657.
Uniaxial (+).

Birefringence: 0.011-0.017.

Occurrence: In volcanic rock at *Mt. Vesuvius, Italy—* this is the only locality *(Monte Somma).*

Comments: Tiny gems have been faceted from crystals found at the only known locality at Monte Somma. These stones are all very small (under 1-2 carats) and are extremely rare.

Name: From the Greek words for *flesh* and *stone,* in allusion to the color.

SARD See: Quartz.

SATELITE See: Serpentine.

SATIN SPAR See: Gypsum.

SCAPOLITE (= **WERNERITE**) Solid-solution series: Marialite to Meionite. Mizzonite is intermediate.

Formulas: *Marialite:* $3Na(AlSi_3)O_8 \cdot NaCl$.
Meionite: $3Ca(Al_2Si_2)O_8 \cdot CaCO_3$.

Crystallography: Tetragonal; crystals prismatic, often large and coarse; massive, granular, cleavages.

Colors: Colorless, white, bluish gray, pale greenish yellow, pink, violet, brown, orangy-brown, golden yellow, orangy-yellow.

Luster: Vitreous; resinous; pearly on cleavages.

Hardness: 6.

Density: 2.50-2.78; varies with composition.

Cleavage: Distinct 2 directions. Fracture uneven to subconchoidal; brittle.

Dispersion: 0.017.

Pleochroism: *Pink and violet stones:* dark blue/lavender blue; colorless/violet.
Colorless and pale yellow stones: colorless to pale yellow/yellow.

Table of Scapolite Group Properties

Locality	Color	o	e	Birefringence	Density
Marialite	—	1.546-1.550	1.540-1.541	0.004-0.008	2.50-2.62
Entre Rios, Mozambique	yellow	1.568	1.548	0.020	2.70
Umba River, Tanzania	yellow-gold	1.562-1.567	1.543-1.548	0.019	2.66-2.67
Umba River, Tanzania	violet	1.539-1.540	1.531-1.534	0.007	2.59
Umba River, Tanzania	yellow	1.553	1.539	0.014	2.63
Umba River, Tanzania	very pale yellow	1.579	1.553	0.026	2.74
Rio Pardo, Brazil	golden yellow	1.570-1.574	1.549-1.552	0.021	2.68-2.70
Burma	colorless	1.560	1.544	0.016	—
Burma	pink	1.558	1.545	0.013	—
Burma	light yellow	1.587	1.554	0.033	—
Burma	pale pink	1.549	1.540	0.009	2.63
Burma (catseye)	violet	1.560	1.544	0.016	2.63
Sri Lanka (catseye)	gray	1.583	1.553	0.030	—
Kenya (catseye)	brown	1.57		—	2.73
Madagascar	(colorless)	1.568-1.571	1.550-1.552	0.018-0.020	—
Meionite	—	1.590-1.600	1.556-1.562	0.024-0.037	2.78

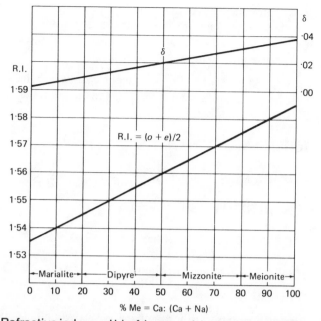

Refractive index and birefringence (δ) as related to chemical composition in the scapolite group. Chemistry is expressed as (molecular) percent meionite, which reflects the ratio Ca/(Ca + Na) in the formula. Refractive index is plotted as a mean index = (o + e)/2.

Adapted from W. A. Deer, R. A. Howie, and J. Zussman, 1962, *The Rock Forming Minerals,* vol. 4 (New York: Wiley), p. 329.

Spectral: Pink and violet stones show bands in the red at 6630 and 6520 due to Cr. Strong absorption in the yellow part of the spectrum.

Luminescence:

Burma: yellow to orange in LW (U spectrum), also pink in SW.

Tanzania: strong yellow in both LW, SW; violet stones = pink in SW, inert in LW.

Quebec: massive material fluoresces in LW (+ phosphorescence).

Some yellow faceted gems fluoresce lilac in SW, strong orange in X-rays.

Occurrence: In contact zones; regionally metamorphosed rocks; altered basic igneous rocks.

Madagascar: yellow, facetable crystals.

Espirito Santo, Brazil: pale yellow crystals, sometimes large, facetable.

Burma: white, yellow, pink to violet, all cuttable; also bluish, pinkish, white catseyes.

Kenya: brownish catseyes.

Dodoma, Tanzania: finest transparent golden yellow to orangy-yellow material, sometimes very pale to near colorless; also violetish and pink (rare) cuttable crystals.

Quebec, Canada: lemon yellow, opaque scapolite, some with silky luster.

Ontario, Canada: light yellow, pink and green material yielding tiny cut gems.

Stone Sizes: Burmese white and yellow gems have been found in large sizes. Pink Burmese step-cut gems to 70 carats have been reported. Catseyes are usually under 10 carats, but larger ones are known. Tanzania produces the finest golden yellow scapolite known in commercial quantities. Pink gems are extremely rare, violet stones very rare in sizes over 5 carats. Brazilian yellow scapolite is cuttable up to about 30 carats but is usually flawed (long thin tubes) at this size.

ROM: 28.4, 57.6 (yellow, Brazil); 7.91 (pink, Burma); 65.63 (colorless, Burma); 18.8 (gray, catseye); and 18.3 (pink, catseye).

SI: 288 (colorless, Burma); 29.9, 19.7 (catseye, colorless, Burma); 29 (yellow, Brazil); 17.3 (catseye, pink, Sri Lanka); 12.3 (pink, Burma); 103.4, 52.2 (yellow-orange, Tanzania).

DG: 3.34 (blue catseye, Burma); 21.25 (white catseye, India).

PC: 14.83 (violet, Tanzania—largest known of this color); 52.92 (green-brown catseye).

Comments: Catseye scapolites from Burma are very rare, possess an unusually sharp eye, and occur in various colors. Cabochons from opaque Quebec and Ontario material are very lovely and often fluoresce brightly. The Tanzanian golden scapolite is much darker in tone than the Brazilian material, and is also much cleaner. Moreover, there is enough available to make jewelry promotion feasible. The pink-purple Tanzanian material is extremely rare in sizes over about 5 carats. Most gems of this color are in the 1-2 carat range. Faceted Burmese scapolites are also rarely found in the marketplace.

Name: *Scapolite* from the Greek *skapos (shaft)* because of the stumpy nature of its prismatic crystals. *Marialite* is named after Maria Rosa, wife of G. vom Rath, German mineralogist. *Meionite* is from Greek *meion (less),* because its pyramidal form is smaller than that of idocrase from Vesuvius, which it resembles. *Mizzonite* is also from the Greek *meizon (greater)* because the axial ratio is larger than that of meionite.

SCHEELITE

Formula: $CaWO_4$ + Mo.

Crystallography: Tetragonal. Crystals octahedral shaped, tabular; massive, granular.

Colors: Colorless, white, gray, yellowish white, brownish, orange-yellow, greenish, violet, reddish.

Luster: Vitreous to adamantine.

Hardness: 4.5-5.

Density: 5.9-6.3.

Cleavage: Distinct 1 direction. Fracture subconchoidal to uneven. Brittle.

Optics: $o = 1.918$-1.920; $e = 1.934$-1.937. Uniaxial (+).

Birefringence: 0.016.

Dispersion: 0.038.

Spectral: Faint "didymium" lines in the yellow and green, especially 5840.

Luminescence: Brilliant bluish white in SW; inert in LW, or dull yellow (Sri Lanka).

Occurrence: In contact metamorphic deposits; hydrothermal veins; pegmatites; placer deposits.
Connecticut; South Dakota; Nevada; New Mexico. Finland; Switzerland; France; England; Italy; Czechoslovakia; Germany; Japan; Australia; Canada; Bolivia; Peru.
Arizona: brown, large crystals, sometimes gemmy.
California: colorless gemmy crystals.
Utah, near *Milford:* orange crystals, octahedral, some with clear tips.
Korea: white, grayish crystals; sometimes very large, cuttable in portions.
Sri Lanka: colorless, gray, yellow (gemmy).

Stone Sizes: Crystals from Korea, Arizona, and other localities may be very large (4 inches on an edge) and are cuttable in sections. California gems may reach 70 carats; Mexican and Arizona stones are usually up to about 10 carats, but an orange Mexican stone over 100 carats has been cut. Utah crystals rarely cut stones over 7 carats. Crystals from Korea up to 13 inches have been found, but none of these has been cuttable.
SI: 37, 18.7, and 15.8 (colorless, California); 12.4 (golden yellow, Mexico).
ROM: 14.0 (colorless, California).
AMNH: 20.65 (near Bishop, California).
PC: 17.58 (yellow, Mexico); 12.20 (Sri Lanka).
DG: 8.70 (Cohen Mine, Nevada).
NMC: 8.55 (intense orange kite step-cut, Emerald Lake, Yukon Territory, Canada).

Comments: Large scheelites are very rare but are among the most beautiful of all the collector gems. The dispersion approaches that of diamond, and properly cut gems can have tremendous fire and brilliance. Crystals in museums could yield stones over 100 carats. Smaller, clean gems are available in the marketplace.

Name: After Karl Wilhelm Scheele, Swedish chemist, who proved the existence of tungsten in scheelite in 1781.

SCHEFFERITE   See: Diopside.

SCHORL   See: Tourmaline.

SCHORLOMITE   See: Garnet.

SCOLECITE   See: Natrolite.

SCORODITE   Series to Mansfieldite: $AlAsO_4 \cdot 2H_2O$.

Formula: $FeAsO_4 \cdot 2H_2O$.

Crystallography: Orthorhombic. Crystals pyramidal, tabular, prismatic; massive, crusts.

Colors: Pale grayish green, yellowish brown to brown, colorless, bluish green, blue, violet.

Luster: Vitreous to resinous.

Hardness: 3.5-4.

Density: 3.28-3.29.

Cleavage: Imperfect. Fracture subconchoidal. Brittle.

Optics: Biaxial (+), variable $2V$.

Properties of Scorodite from Various Localities	α	β	γ	Birefringence	2V
Durango, Mexico	1.784	1.795	1.814	0.030	75°
Idaho	1.738	1.742	1.765	0.027	60°
Oregon	1.741	1.744	1.768	0.027	40°
Tsumeb, Namibia	1.785	1.796	1.816	0.031	75°

Pleochroism: Intense: purplish/bluish (Tsumeb).

Spectral: One line at 4500, broad absorption in the green (Tsumeb).

Luminescence: None. Soluble in HCl.

Occurrence: A secondary mineral resulting from the oxidation of arsenious ores.
Utah; South Dakota; California; Washington; Idaho; Nevada; Wyoming.
Ontario, Canada; Japan; England.
Durango, Mexico: fine blue crystals.
Ouro Preto, Minas Gerais, Brazil: good crystals, some gemmy.
Tsumeb, Namibia: pleochroic blue crystals, to 25 mm long, some gemmy.

Stone Sizes: Cut gems are always small, mostly from Tsumeb material. The maximum to expect is about 5 carats but even this would be very large for the species. *SI:* 2.6 (purplish, Namibia).

Comments: Gems of scorodite are extremely rare (usually Tsumeb), but cut stones have a lovely color and intense pleochroism. Too soft to wear, the stone is suited for collectors of the rare and unusual.

Name: From the Greek for *garliclike* because the material emits the typical garlic odor of arsenic when heated.

SCORZALITE See: Lazulite.

SELENITE See: Gypsum.

SELLAITE

Formula: MgF_2.

Crystallography: Tetragonal; crystals prismatic, acicular, fibrous aggregates.

Colors: Colorless, white.

Luster: Vitreous.

Hardness: 5-5.5.

Density: 3.15.

Cleavage: Poorly observed although literature indicates perfect in 2 directions. Fracture conchoidal; brittle.

Optics: $o = 1.378$; $e = 1.390$. Uniaxial (+).

Birefringence: 0.012.

Pleochroism: None.

Spectral: None.

Luminescence: None reported.

Occurrence: Sellaite occurs in a wide variety of geological environments.
Vesuvius, Italy: in volcanic fumaroles.
Harz Mountains, Germany: in evaporite beds.
Italy; France: in veins.
Nertschin, USSR: in pegmatites.
Oslo Region, Norway: cavities in a soda-granite.
Brumado Mine, Bahia, Brazil: gemmy crystals in a metamorphic magnesite deposit.

Stone Sizes: The Brazilian sellaite is the world's only extant cuttable material, and the largest crystals found thus far are only 5 cm long with small transparent areas. Thus, gems of only a few carats have or could be produced. This is an exceedingly rare gemstone, both in occurrence and number of cut stones.

Name: After the Italian mining engineer and mineralogist, Quintino Sella.

SENARMONTITE Isomorphous with Valentinite.

Formula: Sb_2O_3.

Crystallography: Isometric. Crystals octahedral, up to 3 cm on edge; massive.

Colors: Colorless to grayish white.

Luster: Resinous.

Hardness: 2-2.5.

Density: 5.5.

Cleavage: Traces. Fracture uneven. Very brittle.

Optics: Isotropic; $N = 2.087$.

Luminescence: None.

Spectral: Not diagnostic.

Occurrence: A secondary mineral formed by the alteration of stibnite (Sb_2S_3).
Inyo County, California; South Dakota.
Quebec, Canada; Algeria; France; Germany; Sardinia; Italy.

Stone Sizes: There are reports of very tiny gems having been cut from transparent crystal fragments. Stones up to 1-2 carats seem possible.

Comments: Senarmontite is a rare mineral, restricted in occurrence to the presence of antimony sulfide ores. It is much too soft to wear, and the colors are usually nondescript. However, a faceted senarmontite in any size would be a great rarity.

Name: After Henri de Senarmont, professor of mineralogy at the School of Mines in Paris, who first described the species.

SERANDITE Series to Pectolite.

Formula: $Na(Mn,Ca)_2Si_3O_8(OH)$.

Crystallography: Triclinic. Crystals prismatic in appearance, stubby, well formed.

Colors: Rose red, pinkish, salmon red.

Luster: Vitreous, pearly on cleavage.

Hardness: 4.5-5.

Density: 3.32.

Cleavage: Perfect 1 direction. Fracture uneven. Brittle.

Optics: $\alpha = 1.660$; $\beta = 1.664$; $\gamma = 1.688$. Biaxial (+), $2V = 35°$.

Birefringence: 0.028.

Spectral: Not diagnostic.

Luminescence: None.

Occurrence: In nepheline syenite rocks at *Mt. Ste. Hilaire, Quebec, Canada.* Also known from *Los Islands, Guinea.*

Stone Sizes: Cut serandite over 2-3 carats is very rare. In fact, cut gems of any size are very rare. Cutting material comes only from Quebec, and even large crystals seldom have facetable areas.
USNM: 2+ (Quebec).
PC: 5+ (flawed).
NMC: 18.65, 2.8 (translucent).

Comments: This essentially is another one-locality mineral, where very small gems have been cut from an occasional crystal fragment that is not always even transparent.

Name: For J. M. Sérand, West African mineral collector.

SERPENTINE   A group of minerals.

Serpentine is a group of four species with the same composition but different properties: *antigorite, chrysotile, clinochrysotile,* and *lizardite.* All may form rocks that are cut and polished.

Formula: $Mg_3Si_2O_5(OH)_4$ + Ni.

Crystallography: Monoclinic. Usually flaky or masses of fibers, never in crystals; fibers usually too small for good optical readings.

Colors: White, yellowish, shades of green, yellowish green, brownish green, bluish white to bluish green, brownish red.

Luster: Resinous; greasy; pearly; waxy; earthy.

Hardness: 2.5; bowenite, 4-6.

Density: Variable, 2.44-2.62 is gem range; bowenite, 2.58-2.62.

Cleavage: Perfect 1 direction. Fibrous.

Spectral: Bowenite gives bands at 4920 and 4640-not diagnostic.

Luminescence: Williamsite may glow weak whitish green in LW.

Occurrence: Serpentine forms due to the alteration of basic and ultrabasic rocks. In some instances it may be mistaken for nephrite jade.
Bowenite (a translucent green or blue-green variety of antigorite).
New Zealand: dark bluish green, S.G. 2.67.
Delaware River, Pennsylvania: dark green.
Smithfield, Rhode Island: dark green.
China: light yellowish green.
Afghanistan: green.
Transvaal, South Africa: banded in green shades.
Williamsite (a very translucent variety of antigorite): apple green color.
Rock Springs, Maryland: best-known locality; may contain Cr and be deep green in color; R.I. (mean) 1.56, S.G. 2.6-2.62, hardness 4.5.
Lizardite
Kashmir, India; Scotland: gray, green, S.G. 2.51.
Lizard Peninsula, Cornwall, England: veined various colors; S.G. 2.45.
South Africa; Austria; Anglesey, Wales.
Ireland: mixture of serpentine and carbonates, locally known as *Connemara marble;* mean R.I. 1.56, S.G. 2.48-2.77; absorbtion line at 4650.
Antigorite: Faceted gem found in material from *Pakistan,* yellowish-green, nearly transparent; indices 1.559-1.561, birefringence 0.001-0.002.
Verd Antique: a green serpentine veined with calcite and other minerals. Found in *Greece; Italy; Egypt; Vermont.*

Stone Sizes: Serpentine is always massive, and usually cut as beads, cabochons, or carved into various useful and decorative objects. Occasionally, it is translucent enough to be faceted (especially williamsite), and such gems are indeed interesting and quite lovely.

Comments: *Bowenite* is usually blue-green, yellow-green, or dark green and translucent; it is used for carving, knife handles, and so forth, and in jewelry. *Williamsite* contains dark octahedral crystals of chromite, and patches of white brucite (magnesium hydroxide). *Ricolite* is a banded serpentine from Rico, New Mexico. *Satelite* is a serpentine pseudomorph after asbestiform tremolite from Maryland and California, grayish to greenish blue. *Pseudophite* or *styrian jade* is from Austria and is an aluminous serpentine, with hardness 2.5, refractive index

	Antigorite	Chrysotile	Clinochrysotile	Lizardite
Optics				
α	1.560	1.532-1.549	1.569	1.538-1.554
β	1.566	—	—	
γ	1.571	1.545-1.556	1.570	1.546-1.560
Birefringence	0.014	0.013	0.001	0.008
Density	2.61	2.55	2.53	2.55
Hardness	2.5-3.5[a]	2.5	—	2.5

[a]Bowenite. a variety of antigorite. has S.G. 2.58-2.62: hardness 4-6.

1.57, density 2.69. *Chrysotile,* in fibrous form, is best known as *asbestos* and is widely used in industry for its physical properties.

Names: *Serpentine* from the serpentlike markings seen in a serpentine marble; *chrysotile* is from the Greek *chrysos* (golden) and *tilos* (fibrous), aptly describing the properties of this mineral. *Antigorite* and *lizardite* are named after the type localities, Antigorio Valley, Piedmont, Italy, and Lizard, Cornwall, England. *Bowenite* is after G. T. Bowen, who studied material from Rhode Island (though he misidentified the material as nephrite). *Williamsite* is named after L. W. Williams, who first found it.

SHATTUCKITE

Formula: $Cu_5(SiO_3)_4(OH)_2$.

Crystallography: Orthorhombic. Crystals slender prismatic; massive, granular; fibrous.

Color: Blue of various shades.

Luster: Vitreous to silky.

Hardness: Not determined.

Density: 3.8-4.11.

Cleavage: Very good in 2 directions. Fracture uneven to splintery.

Optics: $\alpha = 1.752\text{-}1.753$; $\beta = 1.782$; $\gamma = 1.815$. Mean refractive index 1.75.
Biaxial (+), $2V = 88°$.

Birefringence: 0.063.

Spectral: Not diagnostic.

Luminescence: None.

Occurrence: An alteration product of secondary copper minerals.
Shattuck Mine, Bisbee, Arizona: dense blue massive material; also psuedomorphous after malachite.
Ajo, Arizona: with other copper minerals.
Katanga, Zaire: masses of light blue crystals; fibrous, radial aggregates, sometimes resembling a pale blue pectolite.

Stone Sizes: Only cabochons can be cut, up to several inches in length.

Comments: Shattuckite is often mixed with quartz, and data often reported for properties may be erroneous. The cabochons are rich blue in color and very popular, but the material is not abundant and seldom seen on the market.

Name: From the Arizona locality, the Shattuck Mine. Recent studies have shown that plancheite, a mineral similar to and often confused with shattuckite, is a distinct species. The formula of plancheite is: $Cu_8(Si_4O_{11})_2(OH)_4 \cdot xH_2O$.

SHORTITE

Formula: $Na_2Ca_2(CO_3)_3$.

Crystallography: Orthorhombic. Crystals wedge-shaped, to maximum size of 155 mm.

Colors: Colorless to pale yellow.

Luster: Vitreous.

Hardness: 3.

Density: 2.60.

Cleavage: Distinct 1 direction. Fracture conchoidal. Brittle.

Optics: $\alpha = 1.531$; $\beta = 1.555$; $\gamma = 1.570$.
Biaxial (−), $2V = 75°$.

Birefringence: 0.039.

Spectral: Not diagnostic. Pyroelectric.

Luminescence: Pinkish orange to orange-brown in SW (Green River, Wyoming).

Occurrence: Occurs in clays from an oil well, 20 miles west of *Green River, Wyoming;* also in clay from an oil well in *Uintah County, Utah.*

Stone Sizes: Very small, less than 1 carat.

Comments: Shortite is an exceedingly rare, not overly attractive mineral. Cut gems are among the rarest of all faceted stones. The material is a carbonate and is therefore fragile and soft.

Name: After Maxwell N. Short, professor of mineralogy at the University of Arizona.

SIDERITE   Series to Rhodochrosite ($MnCO_3$) and Calcite ($CaCO_3$).

Formula: $FeCO_3$.

Crystallography: Hexagonal (R). Crystals rhomb shaped; also massive, granular; globular; oolitic.

Colors: Pale yellowish brown, pale yellowish, pale green, greenish gray, yellowish gray, grayish brown, reddish brown, blackish brown; rarely almost colorless.

Luster: Vitreous, pearly, silky, dull.

Hardness: 3.5-4.5.

Density: 3.83-3.96.

Cleavage: Perfect rhombohedral. Brittle.

Optics: $o = 1.873$; $e = 1.633$.
Uniaxial (−).

Birefringence: 0.240.

Spectral: Not diagnostic.

Luminescence: None.

Occurrence: A widespread mineral in sedimentary deposits; hydrothermal ore veins; also in pegmatites; basaltic rocks.
Colorado; Connecticut; Idaho.
Austria; France; Germany; Italy.
Minas Gerais, Brazil: large and fine crystals.
Mt. Ste. Hilaire, Quebec, Canada: brown rhombs up to 15 inches on edge.
Panesqueira, Portugal: fine light brown crystals, some transparent.
Ivigtut, Greenland: rich brown, gemmy-looking crystals in cryolite.
Cornwall, England: greenish crystals, some transparent, known as *chalybite.*

Stone Sizes: Siderite is not usually cut as cabochons because the massive material is not attractive, and the perfect cleavage makes cutting very difficult. Faceted siderite is rare and stones are usually small (1-5 carats).
NMC: 2.60, 2.25 (light brown, Quebec, Canada).

Comments: Siderite is a difficult stone to facet, but cut gems of great beauty have been fashioned, especially from Portugese rough.

Name: From the Greek *sideros (iron)* in reference to the composition. *Chalybite* is from the Greek *of steel,* referring to the Fe and C content.

SILICA   See: Quartz.

SILLIMANITE (= FIBROLITE)   Trimorphous with Kyanite, Andalusite.

Formula: Al_2SiO_5.

Crystallography: Orthorhombic. Crystals prismatic, rare; usually fibrous masses.

Colors: Colorless, white, gray, yellowish, brownish, greenish, bluish, violet-blue.

Luster: Vitreous to silky.

Hardness: 6.5-7.5.

Density: 3.23-3.27; compact varieties 3.14-3.18.

Cleavage: Perfect 1 direction. Fracture uneven. Brittle.

Optics: $\alpha = 1.654$-$1.661; \beta = 1.658$-$1.662; \gamma = 1.673$-$1.683.$ Biaxial (+), $2V = 21$-$30°.$

Birefringence: 0.020.

Spectral: Distinct lines (Sri Lanka) at 4620 and 4410, weak at 4100.

Dispersion: 0.015.

Pleochroism: May be strong:
α: pale brown, pale yellow to green;
β: brown or greenish;
γ: dark brown or blue, violet blue.

Luminescence: Weak reddish fluorescence in blue Burmese material. None observed in Sri Lankan stones.

Occurrence: A mineral of metamorphic rocks, such as schists and gneiss; also granites.
Idaho; South Dakota; Oklahoma; Pennsylvania; New York; Connecticut; Delaware; North Carolina; South Carolina.
Canada; Ireland; Scotland; France; Germany; Czechoslovakia; Brazil; India; Madagascar; Korea; South Africa; Tanzania.
Sri Lanka and *Burma:* green, blue, violet-blue facetable material; also from Sri Lanka, grayish green, chatoyant fibrolite.
Kenya: facetable crystals, pale bluish color to colorless, S.G. 3.27.

Stone Sizes: Faceted gems are usually small (under 5 carats) and quite rare. Catseye gems are generally in the same size range, up to 10 carats, may be black, yellow, or grayish green.
SI: 5.9 (black catseye, South Carolina).
BM: 35 (fibrolite).
Geology Museum, London: 17 (fibrolite).

Comments: The fibrolite from Burma and Sri Lanka is well known to gem collectors, and highly prized because of its great scarcity. Blue and greenish gems are lovely, although very difficult to cut. Chatoyant material sometimes yields catseye fibrolites, which are also very rare. The material from Kenya is just as attractive as Burmese fibrolite but seems to be somewhat smaller in size.

Name: After Benjamin Silliman, mineralogist, of Yale University. *Fibrolite* is in allusion to the fibrous nature of this variety.

SIMPSONITE

Formula: $Al_4Ta_3O_{13}(OH)$.

Crystallography: Hexagonal. Crystals tabular, prismatic; also in crystalline masses.

Colors: Colorless, pale yellow, cream white, light brown, orange.

Luster: Vitreous, adamantine.

Hardness: 7-7.5.

Density: 5.92-6.84.

Cleavage: None. Fracture conchoidal. Brittle.

Optics: $o = 2.034$; $e = 1.976$.
Uniaxial ($-$).

Birefringence: 0.058.

Pleochroism: None.

Spectral: Not diagnostic.

Luminescence: In SW, bright blue-white (Western Australia), bright pale yellow (Bikita, Zimbabwe), medium pale yellow (Ecuador) or light blue (Paraiba, Brazil).

Occurrence: In granite pegmatites, usually with biotite.
Bikita, Zimbabwe; Alto do Giz, Ecuador; Kola Peninsula, USSR.
Onca and *Paraiba, Brazil:* facetable material.
Tabba Tabba, Western Australia: facetable yellowish crystals.

Stone Sizes: Crystals have been found up to 5 cm, but only tiny stones have been cut from available rough. In general, stones are only seen from Brazil and Australia. A typical size is 0.5-1 carat.

Comments: Simpsonite is an extremely rare gemstone. The material from Western Australia is bright yellow-orange and very beautiful. The mineral is hard and durable, with no cleavage, and could easily become a popular gemstone if it were more abundant. Gems over 1 carat should be considered extremely rare because clean material is a very small percentage of the limited supply of simpsonite that has been found.

Name: After Dr. E. S. Simpson, former government mineralogist of Western Australia.

SINHALITE

Formula: $MgAlBO_4$.

Crystallography: Orthorhombic; found only as grains and rolled pebbles.

Colors: Yellowish, yellow-brown, dark brown, greenish brown, light pink, brownish pink.

Luster: Vitreous.

Hardness: 6.5-7.

Density: 3.475-3.50.

Cleavage: Not determined.

Optics: $\alpha = 1.665\text{-}1.676$; $\beta = 1.697$; $\gamma = 1.705\text{-}1.712$.
(Sri Lanka = 1.669/1.702/1.706).
Biaxial ($-$), $2V = 56°$.

Birefringence: 0.035-0.037.

Pleochroism: Distinct: pale brown/greenish brown/dark brown.

Spectral: Very distinctive; similar to but distinct from peridot: bands at 4930, 4750, 4630 (absent in peridot), 4520 and 4350; general absorption of the violet end of the spectrum.

Luminescence: None.

Occurrence: A contact metamorphic mineral in limestones at granite contacts; alluvial.
Warren County, New York: no gem value.
Northeast Tanzania (in a skarn): pink to brownish pink, some gemmy areas.
Burma: one rolled pebble noted.
Sri Lanka: major source of gem sinhalite, as rolled pebbles in gem gravels.

Stone Sizes: Interestingly, sinhalite, though quite rare, occurs in large sizes in the Sri Lankan gravels. The normal range is 1-20 carats, but gems over 100 carats have been found from time to time.
SI: 109.8 (brown, Sri Lanka); 43.5, 36.4 (brown, Sri Lanka).
PC: 158 (Sri Lanka)—this is the largest known sinhalite gem.
DG: 24.76 (Sri Lanka).
NMC: 21.99 (light brown, Sri Lanka).

Comments: Long thought to be brown peridot, sinhalite was investigated in 1952 and found to be a new mineral. When cut, it is richly colored, bright, and attractive, and resembles citrine, peridot, or zircon. Large gems are very rare, but smaller stones are available in the marketplace. Some people have reported that it was easier at times to find a large sinhalite for sale than a small one, however, as rough pebbles from Sri Lanka are often large.

Name: From the old Sanskrit word for Ceylon (now Sri Lanka), *sinhala*.

SKUTTERUDITE   See: Smaltite.

SMALTITE

Formula: $(Co,Ni)As_{3-x}$. Considered to be an arsenic-deficient *Skutterudite*.

Crystallography: Isometric. Crystals cubic to octahedral; massive, fine-grained.

Colors: Silver gray to tin white; may tarnish gray to iridescent.

Luster: Metallic; opaque.

Streak: Black.

Hardness: 5.5-6.

Density: ~6.1.

Cleavage: Distinct 2 directions. Fracture uneven to conchoidal. Brittle.

Luminescence: None.

Occurrence: Occurs in medium- to high-temperature veins, with Ni and Co minerals.
California; Colorado.
Cobalt district, Ontario, and *British Columbia, Canada.*
Chile; Switzerland; Germany.

Stone Sizes: Cabochons could be cut to any size from massive material.

Comments: Smaltite is a collector's oddity, cut only as cabochons. It is seldom seen in collections since it is not especially distinctive, with a color resembling other metallic sulfides and arsenides.

Name: From its use as a source of cobalt for the pigment *smalt,* which is blue.

SMITHSONITE

Formula: $ZnCO_3$ + Fe, Ca, Co, Cu, Mn, Cd, Mg, Pb.

Crystallography: Hexagonal (R). Crystals rhombohedral; massive, botryoidal, compact, stalactic.

Colors: White, gray, pale to deep yellow, yellowish brown to brown, pale green, apple green, blue-green, blue, pale to deep pink, purplish, rarely colorless.

Luster: Vitreous to pearly, earthy, dull.

Hardness: 4-4.5.

Density: 4.3-4.45.

Cleavage: Perfect rhombohedral. Brittle.

Optics: $o = 1.848$; $e = 1.621$.
Uniaxial (−).

Birefringence: 0.227.

Dispersion: 0.037.

Spectral: Not diagnostic.

Other Tests: Effervesces in warm acids.

Luminescence: In SW, medium whitish blue (Japan), blue-white (Spain), rose red (England), and brown (Georgia, Sardinia). In LW, greenish yellow (Spain) and lavender (California).

Occurrence: Smithsonite is a secondary mineral in the oxidized zone of ore deposits.
Colorado; Montana; Utah.
Germany; Austria; Belgium; France; Spain; Algeria; Tunisia.
Kelly, Socorro County, New Mexico: blue and blue-green, massive crusts, fine color.
Marion County, Arkansas: yellow, banded crusts.
Laurium, Greece: fine blue and green crystals.
Sardinia, Italy: banded yellow material.

Tsumeb, Namibia: yellowish and pinkish crystals, also green—facetable.
Broken Hill, Zambia: transparent crystals to 1 cm.
Australia: yellow.
Mexico: pink and bluish crusts; much variation in color.

Stone Sizes: Beautiful cabochons up to many inches may be cut from the massive material from New Mexico, Sardinia, and other localities. Crusts in some localities are several inches thick. The pink material from Mexico is especially lovely. Facetable crystals are rare, known only from the African localities, and stones over 10 carats could be considered exceptional.
PC: 45.1 (dark yellow, emerald-cut, Tsumeb).

Comments: The blue-green smithsonite from New Mexico has been popular with collectors for many years. Pinkish colors are due to cobalt, yellow to cadmium. The low hardness of smithsonite makes it unsuited for jewelry, but properly cut faceted gems are magnificent. The dispersion is almost as high as diamond, and faceted stones have both rich color and lots of fire. Among the most beautiful are the yellowish stones from Tsumeb, Namibia.

Name: After James Smithson, the benefactor whose bequest founded the Smithsonian Institution in Washington, D.C.

SOAPSTONE   See: Talc.

SODALITE   Variety: *Hackmanite* (rich in S); Sodalite Group.

Formula: $Na_4Al_3(SiO_4)_3Cl$.

Crystallography: Isometric. Crystals rare (dodecahedral); massive, granular.

Colors: Colorless; white, yellowish, greenish, reddish; usually light to dark blue.

Luster: Vitreous; greasy.

Hardness: 5.5-6.

Density: 2.14-2.4; massive blue ~2.28.

Cleavage: Poor. Fracture uneven to conchoidal. Brittle.

Optics: Isotropic; $N = 1.483-1.487$.

Dispersion: 0.018.

Spectral: Not diagnostic.

Luminescence: In LW, usually orangy red to violet; also dull pink in SW (Guinea).
Hackmanite, from Dungannon Township, Ontario, Canada: bright pale pink in SW, bright yellow-orange in LW. Mineral is white, may turn raspberry red after exposure

to SW; color fades rapidly in sunlight, and cycle is repeatable.

Occurrence: In nepheline syenites and related rock types.
Montana; South Dakota; Colorado; Arkansas; Maine; New Hampshire; Massachusetts.
Greenland; Langesundsfjord, Norway; Rajasthan, India; Bahia, Brazil; USSR; Scotland; Ruma, French Guinea.
Bancroft, Ontario, Canada: massive, deep blue material, reddish streaks.
Dungannon Township, Ontario, Canada: hackmanite; also sodalite from British Columbia, other locations.
Ohopoho, northern Namibia: extremely intense, solid blue material, sometimes very translucent, almost transparent (*N* = 1.486).

Stone Sizes: Massive blue material provides blocks for carvings, decorative objects, and cabochons or spheres to almost any desired size, especially from Canada and Namibia. Much sodalite is carved in Idar-Oberstein, Germany, made into boxes and beads. Faceted gems are sometimes cut from very translucent Namibian material, but these gems are very dark and not very transparent, except in tiny sizes (under 1 carat).

Comments: Sodalite is extremely rich in color, also quite tough and easy to cut, making it very desirable among hobbyists. Faceted gems are very lovely despite their lack of transparency because the color is so beautiful. Sodalite group minerals are also responsible for the fine color of lapis lazuli, another blue gem.

Name: In allusion to the sodium content.

SOGDIANITE

Formula: $(K,Na)_2Li_2(Li,Fe,Al,Ti)_2Zr_2(Si_2O_5)_6$.

Crystallography: Hexagonal; crystals not observed; massive, platy.

Color: Bright violet.

Luster: Vitreous to waxy.

Hardness: 7, if pure (South Africa = 5-6).

Density: 2.90, pure (South Africa = 2.76).

Cleavage: Perfect 1 direction.

Optics: *o* = 1.606; *e* = 1.608. Uniaxial (−).

Birefringence: 0.002.

Pleochroism: Not reported.

Spectral: Diagnostic, sharp lines at 4110, 4190, and 4370; weak bands at 4880-4930 and 6300-6450.

Luminescence: Very weak dark red in SW, weak violet in LW.

Occurrence: In the *Alai Range, Tadzhik, SSR*, platy masses up to 10 × 7 × 4 cm, in a vein pegmatoidal body compositionally like an alkalic granite.
Also occurs at the *Wessel Mine, Karuman, North Cape Province, South Africa.*

Comments: Sogdianite is an extremely rare mineral, suitable for cabochons. The color is striking and the material is hard enough to take a good polish. It is usually mixed with other minerals, so the SG and hardness are variable. Chemical analysis may be required to differentiate sogdianite from sugilite, but the latter is far more abundant.

Name: From *Sogdiana*, the name of an ancient state in Middle Asia.

SPESSARTINE   See: Garnet.

SPHAEROCOBALTITE   See: Calcite.

SPHALERITE (= BLENDE)   dimorph of Wurtzite.

Formula: ZnS + Fe.

Crystallography: Isometric. Crystals widespread, in various shapes; massive, cleavable, granular.

Colors: Colorless (very rarely); black (rich in Fe), brown, orange, yellow, green, orange-red, white gray.

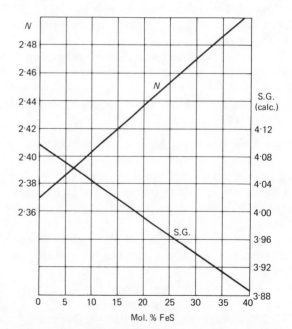

Refractive index *(N)* and specific gravity plotted against chemical composition in sphalerite, in which Fe substitutes for Zn, in the formula (Zn,Fe)S.

Adapted from W. A. Deer, R. A. Howie, and J. Zussman, 1962, *The Rock Forming Minerals,* vol. 5 (New York: Wiley), p. 174.

Streak: Pale brown to colorless.

Luster: Resinous to adamantine.

Hardness: 3.5-4.

Density: 3.9-4.1.

Cleavage: Perfect dodecahedral. Brittle.

Optics: Isotropic; $N = 2.37-2.43$ (Spanish material 2.40).

Dispersion: 0.156 (extremely high).

Spectral: Sometimes 3 bands seen in the red at 6900, 6670, and 6510 due to cadmium.

Luminescence: Bright orange-red to red in LW, SW, from many localities.
Material from Otavi, Namibia is triboluminescent.

Occurrence: Sphalerite is the chief ore of zinc, the most abundant zinc mineral, and is common in low-temperature ore deposits, especially in limestones; also in sedimentary rocks; hydrothermal ore veins.
Wisconsin; Montana; Colorado; Idaho; Arizona.
Canada; Tsumeb, Namibia; England; Scotland; Sweden; France; Germany; Czechoslovakia; Rumania; Australia.
Missouri, Oklahoma, Kansas: so-called Tri-State Region, heavily mineralized by lead and zinc, with many localities and operating mines.
Tiffin, Ohio: red.
Colorado; Utah: may be transparent.
Franklin, New Jersey: almost colorless to pale green, transparent variety known as *cleiophane.*
Santander, Spain: major gem locality, large cleavages of red-orange color.
Cananea, Sonora, Mexico: fine green transparent material, often pale colored and color zoned, sometimes yellow.
Kipushi, Zaire: dark green material containing elevated amounts of Co and Fe.

Stone Sizes: Gems of hundreds of carats could easily be cut from the large reddish material from Spain. This material is also sometimes cut as cabochons. Green cleiophane from New Jersey has yielded faceted gems as large as 15 carats. Mexican gems could be cut to 50 carats.
SI: 73.3, 68.9 (yellow-brown, Utah); 59.5 (yellow-green, New Jersey); 48 (yellow, Mexico); 61.9, 45.9 (yellow, Spain).
CA: 150.3 (dark red-brown oval, Spain).
NMC: 100.1 (dark orange, round, Spain).
PC: 24.8 (gray-green, Mt. Ste. Hilaire, Quebec).

Comments: Sphalerite is one of the most beautiful of all cut gems. It occurs in shades of green, yellow, orange, brown, and fiery red (all colors due to Fe) that are enhanced by faceting. The luster can be adamantine, like diamond, so cut gems with a good polish are very bright, and the dispersion is about four times that of diamond. Consequently, faceted gems are alive with fire and color, which is strong enough to be seen even against the rich body color. Pale-colored or colorless sphalerite is extremely rare, but gems of the other colors are easily available, as there is no shortage of facetable rough. Sphalerite, for all its beauty, is too soft and fragile to wear in jewelry. It has dodecahedral cleavage (six directions) and the material is rather brittle and easily scratched. It could be a very important gem if harder and less fragile. Larger stones (over 20 carats) usually have some inclusions, as well as veils and flaws, so a completely transparent stone is also considered rare. Cutting is all-important, and the appearance of a cut gem depends largely on the quality of the surface polish.

Black sphalerite is called *marmatite,* and the word for sphalerite in European schools is *blende.*

Name: From the Greek *sphaleros,* meaning *treacherous,* because it often resembles galena (lead sulfide) but yielded no lead when first smelted. In Europe sphalerite is called *blende,* from the German *blenden,* meaning *to dazzle. Marmatite,* the black variety, is named after the locality at *Marmato, Italy.*

SPHENE (= TITANITE)

Formula: $CaTiSiO_5$.

Crystallography: Monoclinic. Crystals often wedge shaped, well formed, flattened, prismatic; also massive, compact.

Colors: Colorless, yellow, green, gray, brown, blue, rose red, black. Often zoned. Color correlates with Fe content: green and yellow due to low Fe; brown and black due to high Fe.

Luster: Adamantine to resinous.

Hardness: 5-5.5.

Density: 3.45-3.55.

Cleavage: Distinct 1 direction. Brittle.

Optics: $\alpha = 1.843-1.950$; $\beta = 1.870-2.034$; $\gamma = 1.943-2.110$. Biaxial (+), $2V = 17-40°$; lower indices with lower Ti content.

Locality	α	γ	Birefringence	S.G.
Madagascar	1.910	2.070	0.160	3.52
Mexico	1.908	2.080	0.181	3.53
Sri Lanka	1.909	2.099	0.190	3.52
Brazil	1.911	—	—	3.53

Birefringence: 0.100-0.192.

Dispersion: 0.051 (strong).

Pleochroism: Moderate to strong: α = pale yellow; β = brownish yellow; γ = orange-brown. Sometimes (blue crystals): colorless/blue.

Spectral: Sometimes see "didymium" or rare earth spectrum. This is especially distinctive in Sri Lankan gems (sharp lines at 5860, 5820, 5300, and others).

Luminescence: None.

Occurrence: Sphene occurs as an accessory mineral in igneous rocks, and in metamorphic rocks such as schist and granite, often in fine crystals.
New York; Canada: brown and black crystals.
Madagascar: green crystals, some large.
Zillerthal, Austria; Grisons, Switzerland: both gem localities in past years.
Sri Lanka: dark brown, yellowish green, honey yellow.
Pakistan; Burma: some gemmy material found.
Mettur, India: about 30 miles from *Salem, Tamilnadu, South India*—yellow, brown, green.
Baja, Mexico: yellow-brown, brown, green, dark green (Cr-bearing) gemmy crystals. This may be one of the world's major sphene deposits, with gemmy crystals to 4 inches.
Minas Gerais, Brazil: twinned yellowish to greenish crystals, often gemmy.

Stone Sizes: Sphene is very rare in clean stones over 5-10 carats. Even a 5-carat flawless gem is considered a rare and fine stone. Indian material generally cuts to about 10 carats, Madagascar material to perhaps 15 carats, and Brazilian yellow stones over 5 carats are scarce. Sri Lankan gems are mainly under 10 carats. Burmese stones over 20 carats are known, but Baja, Mexico, has the potential for producing some of the largest faceted gems. Chrome sphene of fine color is extremely rare, especially over 2-3 carats.
SI: 9.3 (golden, Switzerland); 8.5 (brown, New York); 5.6 yellow-brown, Mexico).
PC: 63 carats (green); 106 (intense dark green, from India, square emerald-cut and near flawless with enormous dispersion—by far the world's largest cut sphene).
DG: 4.95 (red!).
NMC: 50.75 (green, Brazil, very fine).

Comments: Sphene is a magnificent gemstone, rich in fire and with superb, intense body colors. The hardness is, unfortunately, low, and gems are brittle and easily scratched. The best-looking stones are round brilliant-cut. Chrome sphene from Baja is the color of fine emerald and very rare, especially if clean and larger than 1 carat. The Brazilian yellow gem material has a sleepy look and is not as bright as that from Baja. Some of the largest and most spectacular green gems have been cut from Indian material.

Name: Sphene is from the Greek *sphenos (wedge),* in allusion to the characteristic wedge-shaped crystals. *Titanite* alludes to the dark brown to black color of the original titanium-rich specimens.

SPINEL   Spinel Group.

Formula: $MgAl_2O_4$ + many substitutional elements.

Crystallography: Isometric. Crystals octahedral; also as grains, massive.

Colors: Various shades of red, blue, green; also brown, black, gray, lilac, purple, orange, orange-red, rose, nearly colorless.

Luster: Vitreous.

Hardness: 7.5-8.

Density: 3.58-3.98; gems 3.58-3.61; see table below.

Cleavage: None. Fracture conchoidal.

Dispersion: 0.020.

The spinel group is fairly large, with widely varying chemistry and properties. All are isometric oxides of Mg, Fe, and Zn with aluminum and traces of other elements.

There is a continuous solid solution between spinel and gahnite, and refractive index and specific gravity both vary with chemistry, as might be expected.

Refractive index variation with color, as generally observed in gems:
red: 1.715-1.735;
blue: 1.715-1.747;
others: 1.712-1.717 (normal).

Spectral: Very distinctive spectra, useful in identification. *Red and pink:* chromium spectrum, has broad band at 5400, plus absorption of violet; group of fine lines in the red may be fluorescent "organpipe" lines.

	Formula	R.I.	S.G.	Color
Spinel	$MgAl_2O_4$	1.719	3.55-3.63	various (above)
Gahnite	$ZnAl_2O_4$	1.805	4.0-4.62	deep green
Gahnospinel	$(Mg,Zn)Al_2O_4$	1.725-1.753+	3.58-4.06	blue, dark blue
Hercynite	$FeAl_2O_4$	1.835	4.40	black, dark colors
Ceylonite (pleonaste)	$(Mg,Fe)Al_2O_4$	1.77-1.78	3.63-3.90 especially 3.80	very dark colors
Picotite	$Fe(Al,Cr)_2O_4$	—	4.42	dark green to black
Galaxite	$MnAl_2O_4$	1.92	4.04	deep red to black

Gahnospinels from Sri Lanka

ZnO(%)	FeO(%)	N	S.G.
0.14	2.34	1.716	3.60
7.18	1.92	1.723	3.72
10.27	2.52	1.731	3.77
12.98	1.47	1.737	3.86
18.21	1.93	1.747	3.97
24.81	1.90	1.752	4.05

Blue: iron spectrum has lines in blue especially at 4580, plus narrow line at 4780 and weak lines at 4430 and 4330; two strongest are at 6860, 6750, plus 6350, 5850, 5550 and 5080. (*Note:* This iron spectrum is distinctive vs. the cobalt blue of synthetic spinel.) Nigerian blue gahnite also has bands at 7000 and 5700 like those seen in spinel.
Mauve and pale blue: similar spectrum to blue, but weaker.

Luminescence: *Reds and pinks:* crimson in LW, also SW; red in X-rays; no phosphorescence.
Blue: inert in UV.
Deep purple: red in LW, essentially inert SW, lilac in X-rays.
Pale blue and violet: green in LW, X-rays, essentially inert in SW.

Inclusions: Spinels are generally free of inclusions, but some inclusions are distinctive. Silk, as in sapphires and ruby, is seldom seen in spinel. Angular inclusions known as *spangles* are seen; distinctive are rows and swirls of tiny octahedra of another spinel, such as magnetite ($FeFe_2O_4$). Also characteristic are iron-stained films and feathers, especially at edges of gems. Also zircon inclusions and darkened surrounding areas, *zircon haloes*, (due to radioactivity), accompanied by feather around zircon, due to stress cracking. Natural spinels also contain octahedral-shaped cavities *(negative crystals),* sometimes filled with calcite.
Mogok, Burma: calcite, apatite, dolomite, olivine.
Sri Lanka: zircon, sphene, baddeleyite, phlogopite, apatite, spinel.

Occurrence: Spinels are found in metamorphic rocks and their weathering products. Especially found in contact deposits (marbles and limestones).
California; Montana; New York; Colorado; New Jersey; Massachusetts; Virginia.
Canada; France; Italy; Germany; Finland; India.
Sweden: gahnite.
Jemaa, Nigeria: fine blue gahnite, S.G. = 4.40-4.59, R.I. = 1.793.
Madagascar: blue, gemmy gahnite.
Australia: gahnite.
Japan: galaxite.
USSR: gemmy, fine pink material from Kuchi Lal in the Pamir Mountains.
New Zealand: gahnite.

Afghanistan: fine red spinel, source of many large gems of the ancient world.
Sri Lanka: worn pebbles in wide variety of colors, especially pinks and blues; all the blue ones have a trace of Zn; many from Sri Lanka are black. The rare cobaltian variety is unique to Sri Lanka.
Burma: spinels from the gem gravels, often as perfect octahedra.
Cambodia and *Thailand:* spinels in alluvial gravels.

Stone Sizes: Spinels are known up to hundreds of carats, in various colors.
SI: 45.8 (pale purple, Sri Lanka); 36.1 (indigo blue, Burma); 34 (red, Burma); 29.7 (pink-violet, Sri Lanka).
BM: deformed red octahedron from Sri Lanka, 520; another crystal, 355.
PC: 11.25 (Sri Lanka, superb cobaltian spinel, intense blue emerald cut).
Louvre, Paris: fine red gem, 105.
AMNH: 71.5 (red, Sri Lanka).
Crown Jewels of England: Black Prince's Ruby, red spinel, estimated at 170; *Timur ruby,* red spinel, 361.
Diamond Fund, Moscow: fine red spinel, over 400.
Banque Markazi, Teheran, Iran: red stone over 500, another over 200, one about 225.

Comments: Spinel is an important gem historically because it has been confused with other gemstones, especially ruby. Large red gems such as the *Black Prince's Ruby* and the *Timur Ruby* in the Crown Jewels of England have proven to be fine large red spinels *(ruby spinel).* In ancient times this material was known as *Balas ruby.*

Star spinels have occasionally been cut, with 4-rayed stars, and colored gray or grayish-blue to black (from Burma); a 6-rayed star can be seen in such material if oriented along the 3-fold symmetry axis of the crystal, that is, parallel to the edges of an octahedral face.

Fine red spinels over 3 carats are very difficult to obtain because of the political upheaval in Southeast Asia, which has made gem dealing very difficult. Large spinels of other colors are available from time to time. The value of fine red spinels is sure to increase due to their scarcity and a general interest in colored stones among the gem-buying public.

Alexandritelike spinels are known that are grayish blue when viewed in daylight and amethystine color in incandescent light. These are quite rare and usually small. Some stones from Sri Lanka change from violet (daylight) to reddish violet, due to the presence of Fe, Cr, and V.

Remarkable blue stones containing cobalt may be difficult to distinguish from flux-grown or flame-fusion synthetics. However, flame-fusion synthetics often display chalky whitish-green fluorescence in SW-UV and strong red in LW. The synthetics also display "cross-hatched" or "snakelike" anomalous birefringent patterns in cross polarized light. Natural cobaltian spinel also shows absorption bands at 4340, 4600, and 4800Å, which are not observed in synthetic material. The band at 4600 is especially diagnostic.

Names: The name *spinel* is of doubtful origin; it may come from the Latin *spina* (little thorn), alluding to spine-shaped crystals, but this is not a common habit for spinel. *Ceylonite* is named after the locality, Ceylon (now Sri Lanka), and *gahnite* after the Swedish chemist, J. G. Gahn. *Galaxite* is named after the plant of the same name, which grows in an area where the mineral was first discovered, near Galax, Virginia.

SPODUMENE   Color varieties: Kunzite, Hiddenite. Older name: Triphane.

Formula: LiAlSi$_2$O$_6$.

Crystallography: Monoclinic. Crystals prismatic, flattened, often corroded; massive.

Colors: Colorless, gray, pale to dark yellow, pink, violet, pale green, deep green, blue-green, blue.

Luster: Vitreous.

Hardness: 6.5-7.5.

Density: 3.0-3.2; gems usually 3.18.

Cleavage: Perfect 1 direction. Fracture conchoidal. Brittle.

Optics: $\alpha = 1.653$-1.670; $\beta = 1.660$-1.669; $\gamma = 1.665$-1.682. Biaxial (+), $2V = 55$-$68°$.

Birefringence: 0.014-0.027.

Dispersion: 0.017.

Pleochroism: Pronounced:
pink crystals: purple-violet/colorless;
green crystals: green/blue-green/colorless to pale green.

Spectral: Not diagnostic in kunzite. Hiddenite shows a chromium spectrum, with doublet at 6905/6860 and weaker lines at 6690 and 6460, broad absorption at 6200. Yellow-green spodumene shows a distinct band at 4375 and a weaker band at 4330.

Luminescence: *Kunzite:* golden pink to orange in LW, weaker in SW, orange in X-rays (with phosphorescence); X-irradiated kunzites may change color to blue-green, but this color disappears in sunlight. Yellow-green *spodumene:* orange-yellow in LW, weaker in SW., strong in X-rays but no color change in body of material. *Hiddenite* gives orange glow in X-rays, with phosphorescence.

Occurrence: A mineral of granite pegmatites.
King's Mountain, North Carolina; Maine; Connecticut; Massachusetts.
Etta Mine, South Dakota: immense white to gray crystals, up to 40 feet long, embedded in rock.

Pala district, California: fine kunzite, gem quality, plus yellow-green spodumenes.
Hiddenite, North Carolina: type locality for emerald green spodumene; also at *Stony Point, North Carolina;* this material contains Cr and shows Cr spectrum.
Madagascar: kunzite, green and yellow spodumene, gem quality.
Minas Gerais, Brazil: major gem locality for kunzite, yellow spodumene, some green. Material from Brazil contains no Cr, and green varieties are *not* hiddenite.
Afghanistan: all colors, some very large crystals; gem quality.
Burma: gem quality.

Stone Sizes: Very large spodumene crystals exist, as in South Dakota, but these are not gem quality. Kunzite crystals do reach a size of many pounds while retaining fine color and transparency, and very large gems have been cut from nearly all the colors.
PC: ~137 (deep yellow, Afghanistan), also 1160, 1240 (yellow); 720 (kunzite, spectacular dark color, Brazil).
SI: 327 (yellow, Brazil); 71.1 (yellow, Madagascar); 68.8 (yellow-green, Brazil); 880 (kunzite, Brazil); 336, 297 (deep violet, Brazil); 177 (kunzite, California); 11.6 (kunzite, North Carolina).
HU: kunzite crystals from Pala, California—2200 grams.
Naturhistorisches Museum, Vienna: hiddenite crystals, 3 × 0.6 cm.
Denver Museum: 296.7 (kunzite, Brazil).
CA: 122.24 (light green cushion-cut, Brazil).
LA: 1260 (kunzite).

Comments: Spodumene is a very attractive material and occurs in some pleasing colors. The pink variety, *kunzite,* is the best known, but yellow gems from Brazil and Afghanistan are also lovely (Afghanistan produces *much* deeper yellow material than Brazil) as are the light blue-green stones from the same localities. *Hiddenite* is known only from North Carolina and is extremely rare and costly; the color is a medium-deep green, never the intense dark green of fine emerald, and crystals are always very small.

The perfect cleavage of spodumene makes cutting extremely difficult, and most hobbyists have some trouble with the material. Spodumene should be worn with some caution to prevent breakage. The pleochroism is intense, and cut stones should be oriented with the table perpendicular to the long axis of the crystal for the best effect. Kunzites of jewelry size are abundant and inexpensive.

Name: Spodumene is from the Greek *spodumenos (burnt to ashes),* in describing the common gray color of the mineral. *Kunzite* is named after G. F. Kunz, noted author and gemologist for Tiffany and Co. *Hiddenite* is named after W. E. Hidden, one-time superintendent of the mine in North Carolina where it was found.

SPURRITE

Formula: $Ca_5Si_2O_8CO_3$.

Crystallography: Monoclinic. Crystals anhedral; usually massive, granular.

Colors: Gray, lavender-gray, purple.

Luster: Vitreous. Translucent.

Hardness: 5.

Density: 3.0.

Cleavage: Distinct 1 direction.

Optics: $\alpha = 1.640$; $\beta = 1.674$; $\gamma = 1.679$.
Biaxial $(-)$, $2V = 40°$.

Birefringence: 0.039.

Dispersion: Not reported.

Pleochroism: Not reported.

Spectral: Not reported.

Luminescence: Not reported.

Occurrence: A contact mineral in limestones.
Crestmore, California; Tres Hermanes, New Mexico.
Scawt Hill, County Antrim, Ireland.
Velardena mining district, Durango, Mexico.

Comments: This attractive but rather rare mineral has seldom been cut as a gemstone. Polished slabs and rough material appeared in 1986 at a mineral show in substantial quantities, however. This material is Mexican, translucent to opaque, and medium to dark purple in color. The hardness and tenacity are adequate for use as cabochons.

Name: After the American geologist, Josiah Edward Spurr.

STAUROLITE

Formula: $(Fe,Mg,Zn)_2Al_9Si_4O_{23}(OH) + Zn$ or $+ Co$.

Crystallography: Monoclinic (pseudo-orthorhombic). Crystals prismatic, typically twinned at 60° or 90°, the latter termed *fairy crosses;* massive.

Colors: Dark brown, reddish brown, yellowish brown, brownish black.

Luster: Vitreous to resinous.

Hardness: 7-7.5.

Density: 3.65-3.83.

Cleavage: Distinct 1 direction. Fracture conchoidal. Brittle.

Optics: $\alpha = 1.739$-1.747; $\beta = 1.745$-1.753; $\gamma = 1.752$-1.761.
Biaxial $(+)$, $2V = 82$-$90°$.
Indices increase with iron content.

Birefringence: 0.011-0.015.

Dispersion: 0.023.

Pleochroism: Distinct: colorless/yellow or red/golden yellow.

Spectral: Not diagnostic. Weak band at 5780, strong at 4490.
Zincian staurolite: strong broad bands at 6100 and 6320, weaker narrow bands at 5315; spectrum absorbed beyond 4900.

Luminescence: None.

Occurrence: Staurolite is a mineral of metamorphic rocks, such as schists and gneiss.
New Hampshire; Maine; Vermont; Connecticut.
Canada; France; USSR; Zambia; Scotland.
Virginia, North Carolina, Georgia: abundant fairy crosses and twinned crystals.
New Mexico: fine twinned crystals.
Brazil: facetable crystals rarely found.
Switzerland: occasionally a facetable crystal is encountered in schists.
Lusaka, Zambia: Lusakite.

Stone Sizes: Staurolite is almost never transparent, but if it is, it is then very dark. Cut stones are always tiny, less than 2 carats in general, faceted from Brazilian or Swiss crystals.
SI: 3.0 (dark brown, Brazil).

Comments: Faceted staurolites are extremely rare and always small and dark in color. Staurolite forms very interesting crystals, but cut gems are too dark to be attractive and lack fire. Nonetheless they are true rarities and prized for their scarcity.
   Zincian staurolite, though very rare, is lighter in color and more attractive as a cut gem; S.G. 3.79, indices 1.721-1.731; trichroic: green/red/yellow. May be red-brown in incandescent light, yellow-green in daylight.
   Lusakite is a deep blue, strongly pleochroic cobaltian staurolite from Lusaka, Zambia.

Name: From the Greek *stauros + lithos,* meaning *stone cross.*

STEATITE   See Talc.

STIBIOTANTALITE   Series to Tantalite.

Formula: $Sb(Ta,Nb)O_4$.

Crystallography: Orthorhombic. Crystals prismatic, striated, often twinned, massive.

Colors: Dark brown to light yellowish brown, reddish yellow, yellowish gray, reddish brown, greenish, yellow. Often zoned.

Streak: Yellow-brown.

Luster: Vitreous to resinous.

Hardness: 5-5.5.

Density: 7.34-7.46.

Cleavage: Distinct 1 direction. Fracture subconchoidal. Brittle.

Optics: $\alpha = 2.37$; $\beta = 2.40$; $\gamma = 2.46$. Biaxial (+), $2V = 75°$.

Birefringence: 0.090.

Dispersion: 0.146.

Spectral: Not diagnostic; may show "didymium" lines.

Luminescence: None.

Occurrence: In granite pegmatites, often in good crystals.
Topsham, Maine. San Diego County, California: gemmy crystals.
Varuträsk, Sweden. Wodgina district Western Australia: as rolled pebbles.
Brazil; Mozambique: gemmy crystals.

Stone Sizes: This material is virtually unknown in cut stones over 10 carats. The material is fairly rare, but transparent specimens are extremely rare.
DG: 4.65 (Brazil).
SI: 7.3 (yellow, Brazil); 2.5 (brown, Mozambique).

Comments: Cut stibiotantalite strongly resembles sphalerite, but the luster is much less brilliant (sphalerite can be adamantine), and stibiotantalite is usually more heavily included, as well as strongly birefringent. This birefringence gives the cut gems a *sleepy* look due to doubling of back facets as seen through the table. Cut gems over 2-3 carats are among the rarest of collector items.

Name: In allusion to the composition.

STICHTITE Dimorph of Barbertonite.

Formula: $Mg_6Cr_2(CO_3)(OH)_{16} \cdot 4H_2O$.

Crystallography: Hexagonal (R). Massive, foliated, fibrous, lamellar, scaly.

Colors: Lilac to rose pink.

Streak: White to lilac.

Luster: Pearly, waxy, greasy.

Hardness: 1.5-2.5; greasy feel.

Density: 2.16 (Quebec); 2.22 (South Africa).

Cleavage: Perfect 1 direction. Friable, flexible laminae (inelastic).

Optics: $o = 1.545$; $e = 1.518$.
Uniaxial (−).
Shadow edge seen at about 1.53.

Birefringence: 0.027.

Pleochroism: Light to dark red.

Spectral: Typical Cr spectrum: 3 lines in the red at 6655 to 6300.

Luminescence: None.

Occurrence: In serpentine rocks, usually associated with chromite.
Black Lake, Quebec, Canada.
Dundas, Tasmania: mixed with green serpentine.
Transvaal, South Africa; Algeria.

Stone Sizes: Massive material is sometime cut into cabochons, but the material is usually used to carve decorative objects such as ashtrays and bookends. The color is usually lilac to purplish, often veined with green serpentine, and the color combination is quite handsome. Blocks weighing several pounds are obtainable.

Comments: Stichtite is not facetable, but the pink color is quite striking in cabochons. Cut stones are especially beautiful when there are other minerals present to add splashes of green and yellow. This material somewhat resembles a pink, granular material from the USSR referred to as *canasite.*

Name: After Robert Sticht of Tasmania, general manager of the Mt. Lyell Mining and Railway Co.

STOLZITE

Formula: $PbWO_4$. Dimorphous with Raspite.

Crystallography: Tetragonal; crystals tabular and thick, or dipyramidal. Crystal faces commonly striated.

Colors: Brown, yellowish brown, fawn beige, tan, yellow red, red, greenish.

Luster: Resinous to subadamantine.

Hardness: 2.5-3.

Density: 7.9-8.34.

Cleavage: Indistinct; fracture conchoidal to uneven; brittle.

Optics: $o = 2.27$; $e = 2.19$.
Uniaxial (−).

Birefringence: 0.08.

Pleochroism: Not reported.

Spectral: Not diagnostic.

Luminescence: None reported.

Occurrence: A secondary mineral in the oxidation zone of tungsten-bearing ore deposits.
Broken Hill, New South Wales, Australia.
Brazil; England; Sardinia; Germany; Nigeria.
Utah; Arizona; Massachusetts; Pennsylvania.

Stone Sizes: Stolzite is a rare mineral (much rarer than wulfenite) and usually occurs in very minute crystals. However, the Australian crystals may be up to 1 inch in size, and tiny transparent areas have yielded very small cut stones of a bright orange color.

Name: After Dr. Stolz of Bohemia who first called attention to the mineral.

STRENGITE See: Variscite.

STRONTIANITE Aragonite Group. Series to Aragonite (CaCO$_3$), Witherite (BaCO$_3$).

Formula: SrCO$_3$.

Crystallography: Orthorhombic. Crystals prismatic, often in tapering crystals in sprays and fans; massive, granular.

Colors: Colorless, white, gray, yellowish, yellowish brown, greenish, reddish.

Luster: Vitreous to resinous.

Hardness: 3.5.

Density: 3.63–3.785, depending on Sr content (vs. Ca).

Cleavage: Perfect 1 direction. Fracture uneven. Brittle.

Optics: $\alpha = 1.52$; $\beta = 1.66$; $\gamma = 1.67$.
Biaxial (−), $2V = 7°$.

Birefringence: 0.150.

Dispersion: 0.008–0.028.

Spectral: Not diagnostic.

Luminescence: In SW and LW, may be white, olive green, bluish green, with phosphorescence. Both fluorescent and phosphorescent in X-rays.

Occurrence: A low-temperature mineral, in veins, geodes, marls, and sulfide veins.
San Bernardino County, California; Schoharie, New York; Ohio; New Mexico; Texas; Louisiana; South Dakota; Washington.
Scotland; Mexico; India; Austria.
Carleton County, Ontario, Canada; British Columbia, Canada; Germany: major deposits.
Pennsylvania: small crystals.

Stone Sizes: Very small faceted gems have been cut from small, pale-colored crystals from various localities, especially Germany and Austria. The maximum size is about 2-4 carats, but an occasional larger stone might be encountered.

Comments: Strontianite is a collector's oddity, with no spectacular properties to recommend it. Colors are usually pale and there is little fire; in addition, the high birefringence doubles back facets and kills the brilliance of the stone. Cut strontianites are, however, decidedly uncommon and worth pursuing for their scarcity value.

Name: From the town in Scotland where the mineral was first found.

SUCCINITE See: Amber.

SUGILITE

Formula: (K,Na)(Na,Fe^{+3})$_2$(Li$_2$Fe^{+3})Si$_{12}$O$_{30}$ + Mn.

Crystallography: Hexagonal; occurs as subhedral grains; massive.

Colors: Light brownish yellow; lavender, intense reddish violet (manganiferous), purplish, dark rose-red.

Luster: Vitreous.

Hardness: 6-6.5.

Density: 2.74 (variable).

Cleavage: None; massive material tough.

Optics: $o = 1.610$; $e = 1.607$ (India: $o = 1.595$; $e = 1.590$, Africa: $o = 1.610$; $e = 1.606$).
Uniaxial (−).

Birefringence: 0.003–0.005.

Pleochroism: Not reported.

Spectral: Strong band at 4190, weak band at 4110; broad diffuse band centered at 5700.

Luminescence: None.

Occurrence: Originally reported from Iwagi Islet, Southwest Japan, in an aegirine syenite mass within a biotite granite. Later occurrences were noted in India and Africa, these with manganese content sufficient to produce a rich amethystine coloration. The mineral closely resembles sogdianite, but sugilite does not contain Ti and Zr, therefore chemical analyses will distinguish these two minerals.
Wessels Mine, Kuruman district, near *Hotazel, South Africa.*
Madhya Pradesh, India.

Comments: The Japanese material occurs as tiny yellowish crystals and was first discovered in 1944. Then, in 1955, dark pink prismatic crystals identified as sugilite were found in a few samples of manganese ore from what was then known as India's Central Province. Cuttable sugilite was not known until 1975, when a thin seam of the material was found in a core-drill sample in a manganese mine 14 miles northwest of Hotazel, in the Kuruman manganese fields of South Africa. The material occurred in low-grade ore, so mining proceeded in a different direction until 1979-1980, when the lower-grade ore was explored. A huge mass, as much as 10-12 tons, of sugilite was discovered at a depth of 3,200 feet. Only half of this material had the fine grape-jelly color associated with the gem variety, and of this, a tiny percentage (perhaps 0.1%) is translucent. The names *Royal Lavulite, Royal Azel* and *Cybeline* have been used in marketing the material. A commercial reserve sufficient for marketing exists in the Wessels Mine.

Name: After Professor Ken-ichi Sugi, the Japanese petrologist who first discovered the mineral.
Royal Lavulite is named after the lavender color, *Royal Azel* from the locality, Hotazel.

SULFUR Alpha modification.

Formula: S + Se.

Crystallography: Orthorhombic. Crystals tabular and pyramidal, often well formed; massive; powdery.

Colors: Yellow, yellowish brown, yellowish gray, reddish, greenish.

Streak: White.

Luster: Resinous to greasy.

Density: 2.05-2.09.

Hardness: 1.5-2.5.

Cleavage: Imperfect. Fracture conchoidal. Sectile. Very brittle.

Optics: $\alpha = 1.958$; $\beta = 2.038$; $\gamma = 2.245$. Biaxial (+), $2V = 68°$.

Birefringence: 0.291.

Dispersion: 0.155.

Pleochroism: Distinct in shades of yellow.

Spectral: Not diagnostic.

Luminescence: None.

Occurrence: Sulfur is usually in combination with metals as sulfides; it occurs in native form in volcanic and hot spring areas (deposited from vapor); sedimentary rocks, and in huge quantities at salt domes.
Wyoming; Nevada; California.
Chile; Mexico.
Girgenti, Sicily: fine, large crystals.
Cianciana, Sicily: good crystals.
Louisiana and *Texas:* salt domes.

Stone Sizes: Transparent crystals exist that could yield stones over 50 carats, but these are specimens and not for cutting. Broken crystals have occasionally been faceted.

Comments: Sulfur has no use as a gem. It is so heat sensitive that a crystal held in the hand may crack due to thermal shock. A crystal dropped from a height of several inches would most likely chip or crack—not ideal properties for jewelry stones! Cutting sulfur is enormously difficult, but the challenge has been met by cutters who have succeeded in fashioning stones of small size. Facetable sulfur is actually not very common, so cut gems do have some scarcity value.

Name: An ancient name for this mineral.

SUNSTONE See: Feldspar.

T

TAAFEITE

Formula: $BeMg_3Al_8O_{16}$ + Fe, Mn, Zn, V, Cr.

Crystallography: Hexagonal; crystals microscopic, prismatic; known chiefly as rounded pebbles and cut gemstones.

Colors: Colorless, greenish, pinkish, lilac to purple, bluish, bluish violet, red.

Luster: Vitreous.

Hardness: 8-8.5.

Density: 3.60-3.62; Zincian = 3.71.

Cleavage: Not reported.

Optics: o = 1.721-1.724; e = 1.717-1.720.
Uniaxial. (−).
Zincian: o = 1.730; e = 1.726; birefringence = 0.004.

Birefringence: 0.004-0.009.

Pleochroism: Not reported.

Spectral: Not diagnostic; however, the spectra of gem taaffeites are similar to those of red and blue-violet spinels containing Fe and Cr.

Luminescence: Distinct green in UV and X-rays.

Inclusions: Inclusions reported in Sri Lankan taaffeites include: phlogopite; garnet; muscovite; apatite; spinel; zircon; fingerprints of negative crystals and spinels; and partly healed liquid fractures. The apatite crystals tend to be well-formed prisms, colorless to yellow. The apatites, negative crystals, and fingerprints are commonly observed.

Occurrence: In metamorphosed limestones and skarns; also as rolled pebbles, very rarely (China) in crystals (microscopic).

China: reported in dolomitized limestone in Hunan Province (o = 1.747; e = 1.741; birefringence = 0.006).
Burma: (o = 1.720; e = 1.716; birefringence = 0.004; S.G. = 3.59).
USSR: (o = 1.735; e = 1.726; birefringence = 0.009).
Sri Lanka: assumed origin of most known cut gems.
Note: Polytype of taaffeite discovered in the Musgrave Ranges, Central Australia (o = 1.739; e = 1.735; S.G. = 3.68).

Stone Sizes: The originally discovered taaffeite came out of a lot of mauve spinels and weighed 1.419 carats; part of this stone was analyzed, and the remainder was recut into a gem of 0.55 carat. This was presented to the discoverer, Count Edward Charles Richard Taaffe, a Bohemian-Irish gemologist living in Dublin. A second stone identified as taaffeite weighed 0.86 carats and is now in the *Geological Museum, London.* A third taaffeite of 0.84 carats, identified at the Gemological Institute of America laboratory in New York, resides in the *SI* collection along with a dark brownish-purple gem of 5.34 carats. Many other stones have been identified, perhaps as many as 50. A Sri Lankan collector owns a flawless mauve oval weighing 13.22 carats. A 10.13 carat gray-mauve oval, lightly included, resides in another private collection, as well as a pink oval of 11.24 carats and numerous smaller stones. A Burmese taaffeite of 3.04 carats, also pale mauve, has been reported.

Comments: Taaffeite reacts to most gemological tests like mauve-colored spinel, but can be distinguished on the basis of its birefringence. Additional stones will undoubtedly be discovered in the future (generally misidentified as spinel) as collectors search for these rarities. Taaffeite is one of the rarest of mineral species, and surely among the very rarest and most desirable of all collector gemstones.

A zincian taaffeite with ZnO as high as 4.66% has

been reported. The material is reddish violet due to Mn and Cr and has higher refractive indices and S.G. than normal taaffeite.

A red gemstone (1.02 carats) was reported from Sri Lanka with the following properties: R.I. = 1.717-1.721, birefringence = 0.004, S.G. = 3.61, hardness = 8+, hexagonal, slight reddish luminescence, Cr present (emission line in spectrum). This was first thought to be taaffeite, later considered a new species and named *taprobanite* (after *Taprobane*, ancient name of the island of Sri Lanka). This material was eventually proven to be a taaffeite after all, and the name taprobanite has been dropped from use. However, the intense research into this problem led to a revised formula for taaffeite.

Name: After Count Taaffe, Bohemian-Irish gemologist, who discovered the first stone in 1945.

TALC (= SOAPSTONE = STEATITE)

Formula: $Mg_3Si_4O_{10}(OH)_2$.

Crystallography: Monoclinic, triclinic. Tabular crystals up to 1 cm; usually massive, foliated, fine grained, compact.

Colors: Pale green, dark green, greenish gray, white, gray, silvery white, brownish. Colors are due to impurities.

Luster: Greasy, pearly, dull.

Hardness: 1; greasy feel.

Density: 2.20-2.83.

Cleavage: Perfect 1 direction. Flexible and elastic lamellae. Sectile.

Optics: *Monoclinic:* $\alpha = 1.539\text{-}1.550$; $\beta = 1.589\text{-}1.594$; $\gamma = 1.589\text{-}1.600$.
Triclinic: $\alpha = 1.545$; $\beta = 1.584$; $\gamma = 1.584$.
Biaxial (−), $2V = 0\text{-}30°$ in monoclinic.
Shadow edge at 1.54.

Birefringence: *Monoclinic:* 0.050. *Triclinic:* 0.039.

Spectral: Not diagnostic.

Luminescence: Usually none. Some is pinkish in LW (Silver Kale, California).

Occurrence: In hydrothermally altered ultrabasic rocks and thermally altered siliceous dolomites. Worldwide occurrence, sometimes in large beds, often associated with serpentines.
Many localities in the *United States,* especially *Vermont, New Hampshire, Massachusetts, Virginia, North Carolina, Georgia, California.*
Lake Nyasa, Central Africa; India; China; Australia; Zimbabwe; Canada; USSR.
Egypt: ancient deposit.

Stone Sizes: Steatite and soapstone are known in mas-

sive pieces that will yield large carvings, up to several pounds.

Comments: Steatite may be slightly harder than talc, due to impurities. *Talc* itself is often pseudomorphous after other minerals. Massive talc is easy to carve and is widely used for this purpose.

Name: Talc is from the Arabic word *talk* or *talq,* the name of the mineral. *Steatite* is from the Latin *steatis,* a type of stone, derived from the Greek word *steatos,* meaning *fat.*

TANTALITE   Series to Columbite: $(Fe,Mn)(Nb,Ta)_2O_6$.

Formula: $(Fe,Mn)(Ta,Nb)_2O_6$.

Crystallography: Orthorhombic. Crystals tabular prismatic, in aggregates, massive, compact.

Colors: Black, brownish black, reddish brown; may tarnish iridescent.

Streak: Black, brownish black, reddish brown.

Luster: Submetallic to vitreous.

Hardness: 6-6.5.

Density: 8.2; decreases with Ta content (columbite, 5.2).

Cleavage: Distinct 1 direction. Fracture uneven. Brittle.

Optics: $\alpha = 2.26$; $\beta = 2.30\text{-}2.40$; $\gamma = 2.43$.
Biaxial (+), $2V$ Large. Usually opaque, indices measured on powders or thin splinters.

Birefringence: 0.160.

Pleochroism: Strong; brown/red-brown.

Spectral: Not diagnostic.

Luminescence: None.

Occurrence: In granite pegmatites.
Colorado; Wyoming; New England.
Canada; Brazil; Madagascar; France; Sweden; Finland; USSR; Zimbabwe; Western Australia.
South Dakota: various localities.
California: various localities.

Stone Sizes: Very large crystals weighing many pounds have been found. The material is usually dark colored, opaque, and of interest only for cabochons.

Comments: Tantalite is too dark to be of use as a faceted gem but is sometimes cut as a collector curiosity, either faceted or in cabochons. These could be of any desired size.

Name: After the mythical character Tantalus, because it is difficult to dissolve the mineral in acids prior to analysis.

TANZANITE   See: Epidote.

TEKTITE

Formula: Silica (75%) + Al, Fe, Ca, Na, K, Mg, Ti, Mn.

Crystallography: Amorphous—a glass.

Colors: Black, green, greenish brown, brown in moldavites; other tektites black, colorless to brown; usually opaque.

Luster: Vitreous.

Hardness: 5.5-6.5.

Density: 2.21-2.96 (see table).

Cleavage: None. Fracture conchoidal. Brittle.

Optics: Isotropic; $N = 1.46$-1.54.

Spectral: Not diagnostic. Moldavites may show two vague bands in the blue and orange.

Inclusions: Often see numerous rounded or torpedo-shaped bubbles; also swirl striae that are *unlike* those seen in paste (glass used to imitate gemstones).

Luminescence: None in UV. Yellow-green in X-rays.

Occurrence: Tektites occur worldwide in fields in which the glass bits are literally strewn over the ground, covering a very wide area (see table).

Stone Sizes: Faceted gems are usually cut from moldavites because the color of these tektites is lighter than most others. The color is a bottle green resembling diopside, and gems up to about 25 carats have been cut, although very large moldavites have been found. Various other tektites from the United States have been cut as curiosities, mostly small. The refractive index of a tektite seems to vary (positively) with iron content.

Comments: Tektites were first discovered in 1787 in Czechoslovakia (then Moravia) near the River Moldau, hence the name *moldavite*. It has been argued that tektites originated as a result of violent explosive activity on the Moon and were thrown all the way to the Earth's surface. Other scientists, currently in the majority, argue that tektites are of terrestrial origin. The issue is being debated in a lively way.

Name: *Moldavite* is from the River Moldau; other tektite names are from the localities where they occur.

TEPHROITE

Formula: Mn_2SiO_4.

Crystallography: Orthorhombic; crystals prismatic, elongated; commonly massive, compact, as disseminated grains.

Colors: Reddish brown, salmony pink, blue-green, olive green, gray.
Streak: pale gray.

Luster: Vitreous to greasy.

Hardness: 6.

Density: 4.11.

Cleavage: Distinct; fracture conchoidal, uneven; brittle.

Optics: $\alpha = 1.770$-1.788; $\beta = 1.807$-1.810; $\gamma = 1.817$-1.825. Biaxial ($-$).

					Tektites
Name	Locality	Maximum Size	Density	Refractive Index	Color
Moldavite[a]	Czechoslovakia	235 grams	2.27-3.40	1.48-1.54	bottle green
Australite[a]	Australia	218 grams	2.38-2.46	1.50-1.52	black, brown edge
Darwin glass	Tasmania	—	2.75-2.96	1.47-1.48	green, black
Javaite	Java	—	2.43-2.45	1.509	black
Billitonite	Billiton Island (near Borneo)	—	2.46-2.51	1.51-1.53	black
Indochinite[a]	Indochina	3200 grams	2.40-2.44	1.49-1.51	black
Philippinite (rizalite)	Philippines, especially Luzon	—	2.44-2.45	1.513	black
Ivory Coast tektite	Ivory Coast	—	2.40-2.51	1.50-1.52	black
Libyan Desert Glass[a]	Libya	4500 grams	2.21	1.462	pale greenish yellow
Bediasite[a]	Gonzales County, Texas	91.3 grams	2.33-2.43	1.48-1.51	black
Georgia tektite[a]	Georgia	—	2.33	1.485	light olive-green
Massachusetts tektite[a]	Martha's Vineyard, Massachusetts	—	2.33	1.485	light olive-green

[a]Have been faceted.

Birefringence: 0.037-0.047.

Pleochroism: Distinct: greenish blue/reddish/brownish red.

Spectral: Not reported, but Mn lines should be observed.

Occurrence: In iron-manganese ore deposits and associated skarns.
California; Colorado.
Franklin and *Sterling Hill, New Jersey:* cuttable.
England; Sweden; France; Japan.
Tamworth, N.S.W., Australia: small Mn deposits with massive tephroite streaks in rhodonite.
This material is suitable for cabochons.

Comments: Tephroite is generally reddish brown and barely translucent. However, it takes a good polish and is massive enough to make good cabochons. Only the New Jersey and Australian localities seem to have provided such material, however. Faceted gems are unknown.

Name: From the Greek *tephros,* meaning *ash colored.*

THAUMASITE

Formula: $Ca_3Si(CO_3)(SO_4)(OH)_6 \cdot 12H_2O$.

Crystallography: Hexagonal. Crystals acicular; usually massive, compact.

Colors: Colorless, white.

Luster: Vitreous, silky, greasy.

Hardness: 3.5.

Density: 1.91.

Cleavage: Indistinct. Fracture subconchoidal. Brittle.

Optics: $o = 1.500\text{-}1.507$; $e = 1.464\text{-}1.468$.
Uniaxial $(-)$.

Birefringence: 0.036.

Spectral: Not diagnostic.

Luminescence: White in SW (Paterson, New Jersey) with phosphorescence.

Occurrence: Associated with zeolites; in lime-rich metamorphic rocks.
Crestmore, California; Beaver County, Utah; Cochise County, Arizona.
Paterson, New Jersey: fine crystals.
Centreville, Virginia: in masses.
Långban, Sweden.

Stone Sizes: Found as relatively compact fibrous masses up to a few inches in size. Facetable material does not exist, but cabochons have been cut from some of the more compact material.

Comments: Massive thaumasite cuts interesting catseye cabochons, especially if it is chatoyant, but the effect is relatively weak. The mineral is rather soft but seems to harden after being exposed to air.

Name: From the Greek *thaumasein (to be surprised)* because of its rather unusual chemical composition.

THOMSONITE   Zeolite Group.

Formula: $NaCa_2Al_5Si_5O_{20} \cdot 6H_2O$.

Crystallography: Orthorhombic. Crystals prismatic or acicular, and very rare; usually compact, or in radial or fibrous aggregates.

Colors: Colorless, white yellowish, pink, greenish, grayish. A translucent green variety has been called *lintonite.*

Luster: Vitreous to pearly.

Hardness: 5-5.5.

Density: 2.25-2.40.

Cleavage: Perfect 1 direction. Fracture uneven. Brittle.

Optics: $\alpha = 1.497\text{-}1.530$; $\beta = 1.513\text{-}1.533$; $\gamma = 1.518\text{-}1.544$.
Biaxial $(+)$, $2V = 42\text{-}75°$.
Shadow edge at 1.52-1.54.

Birefringence: 0.021.

Spectral: None. Pyroelectric.

Luminescence: Patches of brown and white in LW.

Occurrence: Thomsonite is a secondary mineral in lavas and basic igneous rocks.
Oregon; California; Colorado; New Jersey.
Nova Scotia, Canada; Greenland; Ireland; Scotland; Italy; India; Czechoslovakia; Germany.
Isle Royale, Michigan: patterned pebbles.
Stockly Bay, Michigan: lintonite; also at *Grand Marais, Cook County, Minnesota* (Thomsonite Beach).

Stone Sizes: Cabochons up to several inches in length have been cut from material recovered in Michigan at Isle Royale, the best known locality. Large pieces are not abundant, especially with good patterns. Faceted gems are exceedingly rare; gems up to 5 carats from a German locality have been reported to me.

Comments: *Thomsonite* cabochons take a high polish but are somewhat brittle. These are especially lovely when a pinkish gray eyelike pattern is present, but such material is rare. *Lintonite,* from Michigan, is translucent and green and is sometimes mistaken for jade. A faceted thomsonite must be considered a great rarity.

Name: Thomsonite for Thomas Thomson, the Scottish chemist who first analyzed the material. *Lintonite* is after a Miss Linton.

TIGEREYE   See: Quartz.

TINZENITE   See: Axinite.

TITANITE   See: Sphene.

TOPAZ

Formula: $Al_2SiO_4(F,OH)_2$ + Cr.

Crystallography: Orthorhombic. Crystals prismatic, stumpy, sometimes very large, often well formed; also massive, granular, as rolled pebbles.

Colors: Colorless, white, gray, pale to medium blue, greenish, yellow, yellow-brown, orange, pale pink, deep pink, tan, beige, red.

Luster: Vitreous.

Hardness: 8.

Cleavage: Perfect basal (1 direction). Fracture conchoidal. Brittle.

Dispersion: 0.014.

Density: There is a rough correlation between color and density, as follows: *pink:* 3.50-3.53; *yellow:* 3.51-3.54; *colorless:* 3.56-3.57; *blue:* 3.56-3.57.

The refractive indices and density of topaz have been linearly correlated with the ratio of (OH) to (OH + F) in the formula.

Pleochroism: Varies with color of material:
Dark yellow: citron yellow/honey yellow/straw yellow.
Pale blue: bright blue/pale rose/colorless.
Dark rose-red: red to dark red/yellow to honey yellow/rose red.
Rose-pink: yellow/purple/lilac.
Red-brown: reddish/reddish/yellow.
"Burned" pink: rose/rose/colorless.
Brown: yellow-brown/yellow-brown/weak yellow-brown.
Green: colorless to blue-green/green to bright blue-green/colorless to bright green.

Inclusions: Usually planes of tiny liquid inclusions, each containing a gas bubble. Some three-phase inclusions have been noted also.

Spectral: Not diagnostic. Heated pink gems contain Cr, and may show a Cr spectrum with a weak line at 6820. As in ruby, this line may reverse and become fluorescent.

Luminescence: *Blue and colorless:* weak yellow-green in LW, weaker in SW, greenish white to violet-blue in X-rays, and gems turn brown due to irradiation. *Sherry brown* and *pink:* orange-yellow in LW, weaker in SW, sometimes greenish white in SW. This material fluoresces brownish yellow to orange in X-rays.

Occurrence: In pegmatites and high-temperature quartz veins; also in cavities in granite and rhyolite; in contact zones; in alluvial deposits as pebbles.
New Hampshire: crystals.
Texas: colorless and blue, some facetable to large size.
Pike's Peak area, *Colorado:* fine blue crystals in granitic rocks; also colorless, reddish, yellow, some facetable.
Thomas Range, Utah: sherry-colored terminated crystals in rhyolite; facetable.
Minas Gerais, Brazil: fine yellow to orange crystals, facetable to large size; also colorless and pale yellow crystals up to several hundred pounds in size, mostly transparent; pale blue crystals and rolled pebbles, much facetable; some orange crystals contain Cr and when heated (burned) turn pink and show a Cr spectrum. Such material may be distinctly reddish even before heating.
Mardan, Pakistan: fine pink crystals, terminated, cuttable, in limestone matrix, at *Ghundao Hill*, near *Katlang*.
San Luis Potosí, Mexico: fine brownish to sherry-colored crystals; also colorless, many excellent forms, cuttable, some yellowish; can be darkened by irradiation but color fades in sunlight.
Urals, USSR: fine blue crystals, often cuttable; also green, magenta colors (gemmy) and pinks from *Sanarka*.
Jos, Nigeria: fine blue crystals, also white, many cuttable.
Madagascar: various colors in crystals and pebbles, often cuttable.

Locality	α	β	γ	Birefringence	Density	Color	Comments
USSR	1.609	—	1.619	0.010	3.53	bluish pale yellow	F-rich
Ouro Preto, Brazil	1.629	1.631	1.637	0.008	3.53	brownish	rich in (OH), Cr
Thomas Range, Utah	1.607	1.610	1.618	0.011	3.56	sherry	
Katlang, Pakistan	1.629	1.632	1.649	0.010	3.52	rose-pink	contains Cr
Katlang, Pakistan	1.610	1.613	1.619	0.009	3.56	brownish	
Tarryall Mountains, Colorado	1.610	—	1.620	0.010	3.56	blue	
Schneckenstein, Saxony, Germany	1.619	—	1.627	0.008	3.53	faint yellow	

Sri Lanka and *Burma:* from the gem gravels, colorless, yellow, and blue gemmy masses.

Queensland and *Tasmania, Australia:* blue, colorless and brownish gem crystals.

Tingha, New South Wales, Australia: green, gemmy.

Klein Spitzkopje, Namibia: colorless and blue crystals from pegmatites, gemmy.

Zimbabwe; Cornwall, England; Scotland; Japan: crystals and pebbles.

Schneckenstein, Germany: faint yellow, gemmy.

Stone Sizes: Crystals of topaz may weigh hundreds of pounds and are often quite gemmy at this size. Gems up to 20,000 carats have been cut from material of various colors. Museums seem to delight in obtaining monster-sized topaz gems for display. Pink gems over 5 carats (Pakistan) are rare, however, and a Brazilian deep orange gem weighing more than 20 carats is considered large.

The largest known pink topaz is an oval of 79+ carats, from the USSR. The largest Brazilian topaz crystal ever found of an orange color ("precious topaz") reportedly measured 5×27 cm and weighed nearly 2 kg. A very fine lot (9 cuttable crystals) found in the 1960s weighed over 900 grams and yielded several superb gems, one weighing more than 100 carats and several over 50 carats.

The gem giants exist in blue, colorless, and pale yellow colors. Red topaz from the tips of some Brazilian crystals is exceedingly rare, the largest about 70 carats. *SI:* 7725 (yellow, Brazil); 3273 (blue, Brazil); 2680 (colorless, Brazil); 1469 (yellow-green, Brazil); 1300 (sherry, Brazil); 685 (pale blue, Brazil); 398 (pale blue, USSR); 325 (colorless, Colorado); 170.8 (champagne, Madagascar); 146.4 (pale blue, Texas); 93.6 (orange, Brazil); 50.8 (colorless, Japan); 34 (deep pink, Brazil); 24.4 (blue, New Hampshire); 17 (blue, California). *AMNH:* 71 (red, Brazil); 308 (pale blue, Brazil); 258 (deep blue, Brazil); 1463 (deep blue, egg-shaped, Brazil); 241 (pale orange-brown, Burma). *BM:* 137 pounds (crystal, Norway); 1300 (colorless, Brazil); 614 (blue, Brazil). *ROM:* 3000 (blue, Brazil); 365 (pale brown, Burma). *LA:* 1800 grams (orange crystal, Brazil). *NMC:* 498.61 (light blue, untreated, Brazil). *PC:* 173 (blue, Texas); 7,033 (dark blue, treated); 21,327 (light blue, treated, emerald-cut, reputedly the world's largest faceted gemstone called *The Brazilian Princess*); ~79 (pink oval, USSR, world's largest this color but not flawless); 58.8 (pink oval, USSR, flawless).

Comments: Topaz is a popular and durable gem, occurring in a wide range of colors. The rarest colors are natural pink, from the USSR, Pakistan, and (rarely) Brazil; red; and fine golden orange, sometimes with a pink tone. Colorless topaz can, through irradiation plus heat treatment, be turned a deep blue color unknown in natural topaz. This is often sold on the market as a substitute for the much higher-priced dark aquamarine,

and no detection test exists for the irradiation treatment. A very dark blue topaz should have its origin questioned if sold at a very high price, since this color in nature would be a great rarity. Treated blue topaz has become one of the most popular and abundant materials in the gemstone marketplace.

Name: Topaz may derive from the Sanskrit word *tapas,* meaning *fire,* in allusion to the orange color; alternatively, it comes from the name of the island in the Red Sea called *topazos,* meaning *to seek.*

TOPAZOLITE See: Garnet.

TOURMALINE GROUP

Tourmaline is a name applied to a family of related minerals, all having essentially the same crystal structure but varying widely in chemical composition, color, and properties. The nomenclature of tourmalines is complex because there are nine distinct mineral species in the group, as well as a wide variety of names that have been applied to specific color varieties. Tourmaline crystals are abundant worldwide, are sometimes large and well terminated, and often are cuttable.

Formulas:

Dravite: $NaMg_3Al_6B_3Si_6O_{27}(OH)_3(OH,F)$

Uvite: $CaMg_3(Al_5Mg)B_3Si_6O_{27}(OH)_3(OH,F)$

Schorl: $Na(Fe,Mn)_3Al_6B_3Si_6O_{27}(OH)_3(OH,F)$

Elbaite: $Na(Li,Al)_3Al_6B_3Si_6O_{27}(OH)_3(OH,F)$

Liddicoatite: $Ca(Li,Al)_3Al_6B_3Si_6O_{27}(OH)_3(OH,F)$

Buergerite: $NaFe_3Al_6B_3Si_6O_{30}F$

Chromdravite: $NaMg_3Cr_6(BO_3)_3Si_6O_{18}(OH)_4$

Tsilaisite: $Na(Mn,Al)_3Al_6(BO_3)_3Si_6O_{18}(O,OH,F)_4$

Ferridravite: $(Na,K)(Mg,Fe^{+2})_3Fe_6^{+3}(BO_3)_3Si_6O_{18}$ $(O,OH)_4$

Crystallography: Hexagonal (trigonal). Crystals common, usually long prismatic, heavily striated along length, various terminations; also equant, acicular.

Colors: Tourmalines come in all colors from colorless to black. Crystals are frequently color zoned along their length (bicolor, tricolor, particolor, and so forth) or concentrically zoned *(watermelon tourmaline). Dravite* is usually black to brown, may be colorless. *Uvite* is black, brown, and green, usually dark colors. *Schorl* tends to be black, blue, or blue-green. *Buergerite* is always dark brown to black, with a bronze-colored iridescence or Schiller under the crystal surface. The gem tourmaline, *elbaite,* occurs in a huge range of colors and shades. *Liddicoatite* is a relatively newly described species that was for years considered to be elbaite (from Madagascar) but when investigated turned out to be a calcium analog of elbaite. *Chromdravite,* as might be expected, is an intense dark green color from the USSR. Gemmy, bright yellow manganiferous elbaite, close to tsilaisite in composition, has been found in Zambia.

Properties in Tourmaline Group

Species	o	e	Birefringence	Density (range)	Density (average)
Dravite	1.627–1.675	1.604–1.643	0.016–0.032	3.90–3.29	3.10
Uvite	1.632–1.660	1.612–1.639	0.017–0.021	3.01–3.09	3.04
Schorl	1.638–1.698	1.620–1.675	0.016–0.046	2.82–3.24	3.13
Elbaite	1.619–1.655	1.603–1.634	0.013–0.024	2.84–3.10	3.05
Tsilaisite	1.645–1.648	1.622–1.623	0.023–0.028	—	3.13
Liddicoatite	1.637	1.621	0.016	—	3.02
Buergerite	1.735	1.655–1.670	0.065–0.080	3.29–3.32	3.30
Ferridravite	1.80–1.82	1.743	0.057	3.18–3.33	3.26
Chromdravite	1.778	1.772	0.006	3.39–3.41	3.40

Certain color varieties of tourmaline have widely used names. *Achroite* is colorless tourmaline; *rubellite* refers to pink and red shades, and blue tourmaline is generally referred to as *indicolite.*

Luster: Vitreous.

Hardness: 7-7.5.

Spectral: Not diagnostic; usually weak spectra observed.

Dispersion: 0.017

Pleochroism: The absorption of the o-ray in tourmaline is strong enough to plane-polarize light. Sometimes this ray is totally absorbed and a tourmaline may appear to be isotropic because it shows only one absorption edge on the refractometer. Pleochroism is especially strong in dark green and brown tourmalines. Pale colors have weak dichroism. Light traveling along the length of a prismatic crystal always shows a deeper color than at right angles to this direction.

Density: Differentiated according to tourmaline color (approximate values):
Pink and red: 3.01-3.06.
Pale green: 3.05.
Brown: 3.06.
Dark green: 3.08-3.11.
Blue: 3.05-3.11.
Yellow-orange: 3.10.
Black: 3.11-3.12.

Inclusions: Tourmaline displays elongated or threadlike cavities, sometimes with two-phase inclusions. The tubes usually run parallel to the length of crystals and, when densely packed, may produce a chatoyant effect that yields catseye gems in cabochons. There may be gas-filled fractures in red tourmalines; also flat films that reflect light and appear black. Also: hornblende; mica crystals; apatite; zircon.

Luminescence: Tourmalines are usually weak to inert.

Typical Pleochroic Colors for Tourmaline Species

Specimen	o	e
Buergerite	yellow-brown	very pale yellow
Dravite	yellow	colorless
	orange-yellow	pale yellow
	dark green	olive green
	bluish green	yellowish green
	medium to dark brown	yellowish to light brown
Elbaite	medium pink	light pink or colorless
	green	yellow to olive green
	blue-green	light green to purplish
	blue	colorless to pink to purple
Ferridravite	dark brown to dark olive green	light olive green to light brown
Liddicoatite (like *elbaite* but type specimen is dark brown		light brown)
Schorl	blue to greenish blue	yellow, yellow-brown, pale violet, or colorless
	green-brown	rose-yellow
	dark brown	yellow, light brown, or yellowish blue-green
Uvite (like *dravite*)		
Chromdravite	dark green	yellow-green
Tsilaisite	yellow-brown	intense yellow

Source: From R. V. Dietrich, *The Tourmaline Group,* Van Nostrand Reinhold, New York, 1985, p. 144; copyright © 1985 by Van Nostrand Reinhold Company Inc.

in UV light. Stones may be chalky blue to strong blue in SW (Newry, Maine). Pink gems from Brazil may be blue or lavender in SW, and gems from Tanzania (golden yellow, brown and green stones) are strong yellow in SW.

Optics: Uniaxial (−). See table.

Occurrence: Tourmaline occurs in crystalline schists; in granites and granite pegmatites (especially elbaite); in gneiss, marbles and other contact metamorphic rocks (especially dravite, uvite). Tourmaline is also found as inclusions in quartz.

Sri Lanka: Yellow and brown crystals; this is the original source of gem tourmaline, now known to be uvite rather than dravite.

Burma: The *Mogok* area produces red tourmalines, also some pink elbaites and brown uvites.

Mursinka, Urals, USSR: also at *Nerchinsk,* blue, red, and violet crystals in a decomposed granite.

Central Karelia, USSR: chromdravite (dark green).

Brazil: In *Minas Gerais* and other states, usually elbaite, in a huge variety of colors and sometimes large crystals; also bicolor, catseye, watermelon tourmaline. Especially noteworthy are the immense cranberry-red crystals from the Jonas Lima Mine and the superb dark red material from Ouro Fino.

Kashmir, India: Green elbaite crystals (refractive indices 1.643, 1.622; S.G. 3.05, birefringence 0.021).

Nuristan, Afghanistan: superb gem elbaite in shades of blue, pink, green, even emerald green.

Usakos, Namibia: Fine elbaite of rich green color (chrome tourmaline).

Klein Spitzkopje, Otavi, Namibia: Tourmaline in many shades of green and other colors (elbaite).

Zimbabwe: In the *Somabula Forest* area, fine elbaite.

Mozambique: At *Alta Ligonha,* pale-colored elbaite in various shades; bicolors.

Madagascar: Liddicoatite (previously thought to be elbaite) in a huge range of colors, shades; crystals often concentrically zoned with many color zones, triangular in outline; many crystals very large. Also fine rubellite.

Tanzania: Elbaite containing Cr and V, resulting in rich green shades.

Kenya: Fine, deep red and other colors; the red is dravite; (also yellow shades).

Indices:

e	o	Birefringence	S.G.	Color
1.623	1.654	0.031	3.07	red
1.626	1.657	0.031	3.08	red
1.619	1.642	0.022	3.04	yellow

Glenbuchat, Aberdeenshire, Scotland: color-zoned elbaite up to several cm, suitable for cutting.

California: Elbaite in abundance at *Pala* and other local-ities, in both fine crystals and gemmy material. The pink elbaite from here is a unique pastel shade.

Maine: At *Newry,* huge deposit of fine elbaite, with exquisite gem material in green, blue-green, blue, and pink to red colors.

Connecticut: At *Haddam,* elbaite in small but fine crystals, color-zoned.

Mexico: Buergerite occurs in rhyolite at *San Luis Potosí.*

New York; New Jersey: At *Franklin,* and *Hamburg, New Jersey,* and at *Gouverneur* and *DeKalb, New York,* uvite crystals, some with gem potential. This material had always been regarded as dravite.

Zambia: At *Chipata,* dark red crystals similar to Kenyan dravite. Indices 1.624-1.654; birefringence = 0.030; S.G. = 3.03-3.07 (average 3.05). Also tsilaisite, gemmy yellow material with MnO up to 9.2%, very rare.

There are many other tourmaline localities, but the above are the major gem-producing ones.

Stone Sizes: Tourmalines weighing hundreds of carats have been cut out of material from various localities. Brazil and Mozambique produce some of the largest stones, but Maine and California crystals of very large size have been discovered. Most larger museums have fine tourmaline collections and display very large gems. A representative collection of tourmaline colors would have to encompass well over 100 stones.

SI: 246 (pink, faceted egg, California); 116.2, 100 (pink, California); 172.7, 124.8 (champagne color, Mozambique); 122.9 (green, Mozambique); 117, 110 (green, Brazil); 110.8 (pink, USSR); 75 (rose-red, Brazil); 62.4 (pink, Brazil); 18.4 (pink, Maine); 103.8 (rose, Mozambique); 60 (blue-green, Brazil); 41.6 (brown, Sri Lanka); 23.5 (pale brown, Brazil); 17.9 (green, South Africa); 17.7 (yellow-green, Elba, Italy).

PC: 258.08 (green catseye); 256 (green, Maine—very large for locality).

Comments: Tourmaline is one of the most popular of gems among collectors because it is usually inexpensive and occurs in a vast array of colors. The colors are due to an almost unbelievable complexity of chemical composition, to which John Ruskin's quip (1890) still applies: "the chemistry of [tourmaline] is more like a mediaeval doctor's prescription than the making of a respectable mineral." *Schorl,* the black tourmaline, was used in mourning jewelry during the Victorian era, a practice little used today. Such material is seldom seen in jewelry at all in modern times. Tourmaline crystals are often cracked and flawed, which puts a premium on clean gemstones, especially those over about 10 carats in size. The only acceptable type of inclusions are the tubes that, when densely packed, produce a chatoyancy and catseye effect in cabochons. The eye in *catseye tourmalines* can be very strong, set against a richly colored gem. Tourmalines occur in a wide enough range of colors to satisfy just about any fashion requirement. There is no cleavage, and the slight brittleness of the material is not a major problem in wear. Small tourmalines (under 5 carats) are fairly easy to obtain at modest cost. Very large, fine-colored stones are both rare and costly, however.

Names: *Tourmaline* is from the Singhalese word *turamali*, meaning *mixed-colored stones* because tourmalines were often confused with other gems. *Dravite* is named after the Carinthian district of Drave, Austria. *Schorl* is an old German mining term for unwanted minerals associated with ore. *Elbaite* is after the Isle of Elba, Italy. *Buergerite* is named after Professor Martin J. Buerger, crystallographer and well-known research scientist. *Liddicoatite* is named after Richard T. Liddicoat, director of the Gemological Institute of America. *Chromdravite* is named for its composition. *Uvite* is named after the Sri Lankan locality.

TRANSVAAL JADE   See: Garnet.

TRAPICHE EMERALD   See: Feldspar.

TRAVERTINE   See: Calcite.

TREMOLITE   Variety: Hexagonite. Series to Actinolite. Amphibole Group. See also: Jade, Nephrite.

Formula: $Ca_2Mg_5Si_8O_{22}(OH)_2$ + Fe.

Crystallography: Monoclinic. Crystals prismatic or bladed; fibrous, massive, granular.

Colors: White, colorless, gray, pale greenish, pink, brown.

Luster: Vitreous.

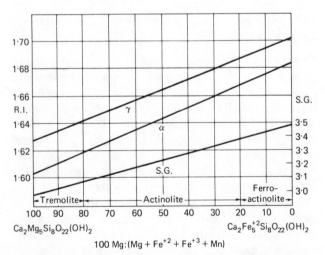

Refractive index and specific gravity variations with chemical composition in the tremolite-ferroactinolite series. Composition is expressed as $Mg/(Mg + Fe^{2+} + Fe^{3+} + Mn)$.

Adapted from W. A. Deer, R. A. Howie, and J. Zussman, 1962, *The Rock Forming Minerals*, vol. 2 (New York: Wiley), p. 257.

Hardness: 5-6.

Density: 2.9-3.2 (catseye gem, Ontario, 2.98; hexagonite, 2.98-3.03).

Cleavage: Good 2 directions. Fracture uneven. Brittle.

Optics: Variable with composition (see figure). $\alpha = 1.560$-1.562; $\beta = 1.613$; $\gamma = 1.624$-1.643. Biaxial $(-)$, $2V = 81°$. *Note:* Tanzania, green crystals: 1.608-1.631, S.G. 3.02.

Birefringence: 0.017-0.027; hexagonite 0.019-0.028.

Pleochroism: *Hexagonite:* bluish-red/deep rose/deep red-violet. *Tanzanian green crystals:* light yellowish green/light green/green.

Spectral: Not diagnostic. Some tremolite shows a line at 4370 typical of jadeite. Chromiferous material may display chromium spectrum.

Luminescence: Hexagonite shows orange, medium pink to pinkish red fluorescence in LW, SW. Also, medium greenish white in SW (Lee, Massachusetts) and dull yellowish in LW.

Occurrence: Tremolite occurs in contact and regionally metamorphosed dolomites, in magnesian limestones, and in ultrabasic rocks.
California; Arizona; Utah; Colorado; Connecticut; South Dakota; Massachusetts.
Italy; Switzerland; Austria.
Fowler, New York: hexagonite, some cuttable; also at *Edwards* and *Balmat, New York.*
Ontario and *Quebec, Canada:* gray, green and blue crystals; a chatoyant greenish variety found in *Ontario* cuts interesting catseye gems.
Burma: green catseye gems.
Lelatema, Tanzania: green facetable crystals up to 25 mm.
Sierra Leone: Cr-rich tremolite, deep green with Cr spectrum displayed.

Stone Sizes: Small colorless and transparent tremolite crystals are very rare, and cut gems are true collector items. The largest of these is in the 5-10 carat range. Larger crystals exist but are usually badly fractured. *Hexagonite* is known in facetable material only from New York and these pieces yield gems to only about 1 carat. Chrome tremolite is also very rare and cut gems are tiny. Catseye hexagonites have also been cut.
PC: 1.21 (medium purple, New York).
NMC: 1.39 (deep purple, New York); 4.55 (dark blue catseye, Ontario); 12.55 (dark brown catseye, Ontario).

Comments: It is possible to misidentify tremolite, mistaking it for other amphiboles. Hexagonite is the rarest of the gem varieties of tremolite. If tremolite occurs in very tiny fibrous crystals, densely matted and interlocked, it is then known as *nephrite (jade)*. Material containing more or less parallel fibers is somewhat chatoyant and yields weak catseyes. These are sometimes called *catseye jades*, but have been tested and are actually tremolite or (if more iron-rich) actinolite.

Name: From the Tremola Valley on the south side of St. Gotthard, Switzerland. *Hexagonite* was so named because it was thought to be a hexagonal mineral when first described.

TRIDYMITE   See: Quartz.

TRIPHANE   See: Spodumene.

TRIPHYLITE

Formula: $Li(Fe^{+2}, Mn^{+2})PO_4 + Mg$.   Series to Lithiophilite.

Crystallography: Orthorhombic; crystals prismatic, often with rounded faces, but very rare; usually massive, cleavable, compact.

Colors: Greenish gray, bluish gray; alters to brownish or blackish hues (lithiophilite is clove brown, yellowish brown, honey yellow, salmon).

Luster: Vitreous; resinous to subresinous.

Hardness: 4-5.

Density: 3.42. Pure Fe end of series = 3.58, pure Mn end (lithiophilite) = 3.34. The halfway point (Fe:Mn = 1:1) = 3.52; density is *not* linear with Fe:Mn ratio.

Cleavage: Perfect 1 direction; fracture subconchoidal to uneven.

Optics: $\alpha = 1.689-1.694$; $\beta = 1.689-1.695$; $\gamma = 1.695-1.702$. Biaxial (+).
May sometimes be observed optically (−) and uniaxial interference figures may be observed, depending on the Fe:Mn ratio. Refractive indices increase with Fe content but may be substantially decreased if Mg substitutes for (Fe,Mn).

Birefringence: 0.006-0.008.

Pleochroism: Absent or very weak; some lithiophilite may show deep pink/pale greenish yellow/pale pink.

Spectral: Not diagnostic.

Luminescence: None reported.

Occurrence: As a primary mineral in granitic pegmatites, often altered to a wide array of secondary phosphates.
Black Hills, South Dakota: as enormous crystals up to 6 feet long.
New Hampshire: excellent crystals at *Chandler's Mill, Palermo, Grafton Center, North Groton.*

Massachusetts; Maine; Pala, California. Germany; Finland; Sweden; France; Brazil.

Stone Sizes: Large stones conceivably could be cut from some of the immense crystals found in South Dakota, but these are usually opaque or altered. Tiny brown stones have been cut from Brazilian material. This is the kind of mineral that could surprise the world of gem species collectors by appearing as cuttable crystals from a newly discovered deposit at almost any time.

Name: From Greek words meaning *threefold* and *family,* in allusion to the presence of three cations.

TSAVORITE   See: Garnet.

TUGTUPITE

Formula: $Na_4AlBeSi_4O_{12}Cl$.

Crystallography: Tetragonal. Only occurs in massive and compact form.

Colors: White to pink, rose red, bluish, greenish; mottled.

Luster: Vitreous to greasy.

Hardness: 4-6.5 reported.

Density: 2.3-2.57.

Cleavage: Distinct. Fracture conchoidal. Brittle.

Optics: $o = 1.496$; $e = 1.502$.
Uniaxial (+) or (−).
May be anomalously biaxial with $2V$ from 0° to 10°.

Birefringence: 0.006-0.008.

Pleochroism: Strong: bluish-red/orange-red.

Spectral: Not diagnostic.

Luminescence: Very distinctive rose-red color. Generally redder in SW than LW.
Taseq, Greenland: SW, pastel orange-red; LW, bright orange: phosphoresces bright cream or orange-cream, better reaction in SW.
Kvanefjeld, Greenland: LW, bright orange to orange-red; SW, cerise red, and very intense; phosphoresces dull red to medium cream white.
The material darkens in color when exposed to UV light and slowly bleaches.

Occurrence: Veins in nepheline syenite pegmatite, in Greenland.
Tugtup, Illimaussaq, Greenland: from the *Taseq* and *Kvanefjeld* areas.
Also noted on the *Kola Peninsula, USSR.*

Stone Sizes: Only a few faceted gems have been cut, all very small, and not completely transparent. A typical gem size would be 1-2 carats. Translucent material can also be faceted but is usually cut into cabochons. Decorative objects were carved from some larger pieces when tugtupite was first found.

Comments: Tugtupite was discovered in 1960 and has been used sporadically in jewelry. The material has a rich color and has been sought after by collectors of fluorescent minerals because of its intense reaction in UV. Tugtupite seems to have diminished in abundance and is somewhat hard to obtain, especially in cuttable pieces, and it seems that the material was quite scarce at the source locality. Clean faceted gems are great rarities.

Name: After the locality. *Tugtup* means *reindeer,* hence, *reindeer stone.*

TURQUOISE   Series to Chalcosiderite.

Formula: $CuAl_6(PO_4)_4(OH)_8 \cdot 5H_2O + Fe$.

Crystallography: Triclinic. Crystals extremely rare and microscopic; microcrystalline, massive; concretionary; veins and crusts.

Colors: Crystals blue. Massive materials dark blue to pale blue, green, blue-green, apple green, grayish green.

Luster: Crystals vitreous; massive, waxy or dull, earthy.

Hardness: 5-6.

Density: Crystals 2.84; massive in the range 2.6-2.9.
Iran, 2.75-2.85;
United States, 2.6-2.7;
China, 2.70;
Eilat, Israel, 2.56-2.70;
Sinai Peninsula, 2.81;
Tibet, 2.72;
Bahia, Brazil, 2.40-2.65.

Cleavage: None in massive material. Fracture even, sometimes conchoidal.

Optics: Massive material gives shadow edge (mean refractive index) of 1.62.
Crystals: $\alpha = 1.61$; $\beta = 1.62$; $\gamma = 1.65$.
Biaxial (+), $2V = 40°$.

Birefringence: 0.040.

Pleochroism: Weak: colorless/pale blue or pale green.

Spectral: can be distinctive; lines at 4600 (vague) and 4320—these are usually seen in light reflected from the turquoise surface.

Luminescence: Greenish yellow to blue in LW, inert in SW and X-rays.

Occurrence: Turquoise is formed by the action of percolating groundwaters in aluminous rocks where Cu is present, as in the vicinity of copper deposits.
Lynch Station, Virginia: the only well known occurrence of crystals. These are microscopic, but an occasional

larger one could be tempting to a cutter, and some very tiny faceted gems might exist (well under 1 carat).
Iran: the district of *Nishapur,* on *Ali-mersai Mountain.* Turquoise is found in porphyry and trachyte rocks, cemented by brown limonite. The color is uniform and a lovely sky blue, sometimes veined by thin lines of limonitic matrix. The blue is often very intense. The mines have been worked for centuries, and Persian (now Iranian) turquoise is almost synonymous with material of the highest quality.
Tibet: turquoise is the national gem of this country, and green is the most prized color. Very little material is available today.
China: some mines appear to have operated there in ancient times. Archaeological finds dated as early as 1300 B.C. indicate the possibility of a centuries-old exploitation of local deposits. Fine turquoise is currently mined in the Wudang mountain area of northwestern Hubei Province and also in Shaanxi Province about 150 km to the northwest. The material occurs as compact nodules typically up to 8 cm, with much larger masses occasionally found. The color ranges from pale blue to light green.
Egypt: on the *Sinai Peninsula,* turquoise is mined at *Serâbît el Khâdim* and *Maharâh.* These mines operated as early as 1000 B.C., and the turquoise was used by the Pharaohs. The producing area extends along the *Suez Gulf,* where the material occurs in sandstone. Earth movements have brecciated the turquoise and matrix, and there is considerable limonite present. The color is blue to greenish blue; some may fade in the sun.
USSR: turquoise is reported from the *Uzbek Republic.*
Chile: at the *Chuquicamata* copper mine turquoise of very fine color is found. Not much has reached the marketplace.
Australia: dense, compact turquoise of fine color has been found in large deposits. This material is solid, takes a high polish, and is uniform in color. The nodules in which it occurs may reach a size of hundreds of pounds. The material has a slight tendency to shear along planes of weakness. The color resembles that of Persian (Iranian) turquoise.
Mexico: some turquoise has been reported from *Zacatecas.*
Pau a Pique, Bahia, Brazil: Porous and cryptocrystalline material, R.I. ~ 1.618.
United States: there are many turquoise localities in the United States. Connoisseurs can tell the actual mine of origin of many cut gemstones because of distinctive nuances in color and matrix. The variation in these characteristics is enormous. Most of the mines are in *Nevada,* some are in *Arizona,* and others are in *Colorado* and *New Mexico.* Among the better known localities are:
Fox Mine (Nevada): huge production; active since 1915.
Blue Gem Mine (Nevada): large variation in color, noted for blue and green colors in the same stone.

Stormy Mountain Mine (Nevada): dark blue, hard material with black chert matrix.

Lander Blue Mine (Nevada): finely divided spiderweb, with tiny turquoise specks; this is rare and highly valued today.

Bisbee (Arizona): intense dark blue material, wispy matrix.

Kingman (Arizona): some deep blue material has been treated to improve color.

Leadville (Colorado): small stones, deep blue with a tinge of green.

Santa Rita (New Mexico): pale to deep blue colors.

Other notable locations in Nevada are the following mines: *Papoose, Zuni, Montezuma, Crow Springs, Carlin, Red Mountain, Godber.*

Comments: Massive turquoise is always opaque, and the less porous varieties take a good polish. Turquoise is used in beads, carvings, and other jewelry. It often has a brownish matrix, which is cut along with the turquoise and provides color contrast and pattern. Turquoise is frequently simulated by other materials, both natural and artificial, and pale turquoise is extensively treated to improve the color. It is very difficult to tell that such treatments have been performed without detailed knowledge and testing equipment; some of the imitations are very realistic. *Spiderweb turquoise* is veined with black matrix, in a pattern that looks like crocheted lace. Higher values in turquoise are generally associated with darker shades and less green tint in the blue color.

Several turquoiselike materials have been discovered that may well be labeled turquoise and circulating in the marketplace. One of these is yellow-green in color, a more intense shade than that of variscite, with a density in the turquoise range. A chemical analysis showed more than 8% zinc oxide; the mineral is named *faustite* and is a zinc analog of turquoise.

Another turquoiselike material was found to have a mean R.I. of 1.50-1.51, S.G. 2.88, hardness 4-5, and bluish color. A chemical analysis of this material showed that it matches the mineral *prosopite:* $CaAl_2(F,OH)_8$; in addition, there were large amounts of Cu and yttrium.

Name: *Turquoise* is of ancient derivation and means *Turkish* because it was originally brought to Europe and Persia (Iran) via Turkey.

U

ULEXITE

Formula: $NaCaB_5O_9 \cdot 8H_2O$.

Crystallography: Triclinic. Acicular crystals, nodules of fibers, tufts *(cottonballs),* and veins of parallel fibers.

Colors: Colorless, white.

Luster: Vitreous to silky.

Hardness: 1-2.5.

Density: 1.65-1.95.

Cleavage: Perfect 1 direction. Brittle.

Optics: $\alpha = 1.496$; $\beta = 1.505$; $\gamma = 1.519$.
Biaxial (+), $2V = 78°$.

Birefringence: 0.023.

Luminescence: Blue-green in SW, some phosphorescence.

Occurrence: In playa deposits and dry lakes associated with other borates.
Nevada.
Argentina; Peru; Chile; USSR.
California: world's major source; also source of TV stone and cabochon material.

Stone Sizes: Nodules up to several pounds occur. The material is always cut as cabochons; faceting material has never been found.

Comments: The fibrous material cuts interesting catseye cabochon gems, but they are curios only since they are much too soft and fragile for wear. The eye can be very strong, however. Sometimes ulexite occurs in seams, consisting of tightly packed parallel fibers. These are transparent along their length, and the packed aggregates act like an array of parallel glass fibers, displaying the property of fiber optics. If the material is polished perpendicular to the fiber direction, a piece of ulexite will transmit an image from the bottom of the slab to the top. For this reason the material has been nicknamed *TV stone* and is popular among mineral enthusiasts.

Name: After the German chemist George L. Ulex, who first presented a correct chemical analysis of the species.

UNAKITE   See: Epidote.

UVAROVITE   See: Garnet.

UVITE   See: Tourmaline.

V

VALENTINITE   See: Senarmontite.

VANADINITE

Formula: $Pb_5(VO_4)_3Cl + P, As.$

Crystallography: Hexagonal. Crystals hexagonal prisms, also tabular, filiform, skeletal.

Colors: Red, orange, orange-red, brownish red, pale yellow, yellow, brownish. Rarely colorless; zoned.

Streak: White to yellowish.

Luster: Resinous to subadamantine.

Hardness: 2.5-3.

Density: 6.88; range 6.5-7.1.

Cleavage: None. Fracture conchoidal. Brittle.

Optics: $e = 2.350, o = 2.416$.
Uniaxial (−).

Birefringence: 0.066.

Dispersion: 0.202.

Pleochroism: Very slight, shades of orange and yellow.

Spectral: Not diagnostic.

Luminescence: None.

Occurrence: Secondary mineral in the oxidized zone of ore deposits, especially lead deposits. *Arizona (Apache Mine, Mammoth Mine,* elsewhere); *New Mexico; California; Utah; South Dakota; Colorado.*
Chihuahua, Mexico; Algeria; Scotland; Argentina; Tunisia; USSR; Austria; Sardinia.
Mibladen, Morocco: large red to brown crystals.

Stone Sizes: Faceted gems are extremely rare and always small (less than 1 carat). The material is not normally cut into cabochons because it is almost always in good crystals that are prized by collectors. Potential faceting material would most likely come from Arizona or Morocco.

Comments: A faceted vanadinite may be considered a tremendous rarity. Fewer than ten such gems may have been cut. This is unfortunate since the color is rich and beautiful. Arizona crystals tend to be very small, but the ones from Morocco reach a size of several inches.

Name: In allusion to the composition.

VARISCITE   Series to Strengite: $FePO_4 \cdot 2H_2O$.

Formula: $AlPO_4 \cdot 2H_2O$.

Crystallography: Orthorhombic. Crystals octahedral and very rare; also massive, crusts, nodules.

Colors: Colorless, pale green, dark green, yellowish green, blue-green.

Luster: Crystals vitreous; massive waxy to dull.

Hardness: 3.5-4.5.

Density: 2.2-2.57.

Cleavage: *Crystals:* good 1 direction; fracture conchoidal; brittle.
Massive: none; fracture splintery to uneven.

Optics: $\alpha = 1.563; \beta = 1.588; \gamma = 1.594$.
Shadow edge at about 1.56.
Biaxial (−), 2V moderate.

Birefringence: 0.031.

Spectral: Not diagnostic. Strong line at 6880, weaker line at 6500.

Luminescence: Dull green (Lewiston, Utah) or green (Fairfield, Utah) in SW; whitish green in LW from these localities.

Occurrence: Forms by the action of phosphate-bearing waters on aluminous rocks.
Arkansas; California; Nevada; Arizona; Pennsylvania. Germany; Czechoslovakia; Austria; Queensland, Australia; Brazil; Spain.
Fairfield County, Utah: rich-colored nodules up to 24 inches across, mixed with other massive complex phosphates.
Tooele, Utah: massive, rich green nodules, suitable for cutting.

Stone Sizes: Nodules of variscite may weigh many pounds and have been found up to a diameter of about 24 inches. The material is suitable only for cabochons, but variscite mixed with other phosphates is sometimes cut into spheres or used in decorative displays.

Comments: Variscite has occasionally been used as a turquoise imitation. It is very popular among hobbyists as a cabochon material because of the interesting patterns in the Utah material. Variscite mixed with quartz from Ely, Nevada, has been named *Amatrix* (for *American matrix*).

Name: After Variscia, the old name of the Voigtland district in Germany where it was first found.

VÄYRENENITE

Formula: $BeMnPO_4(OH,F)$.

Crystallography: Monoclinic; crystals prismatic or in druses.

Colors: Pale pink, rose-red.

Luster: Vitreous.

Hardness: 5.

Density: 3.183-3.215 (Pakistan = 3.23).

Cleavage: Distinct 1 direction; brittle.

Optics: $\alpha = 1.638-1.669$; $\beta = 1.658-1.661$; $\gamma = 1.664-1.667$. Biaxial (−), $2V = 54°$.
(Pakistan material R.I. = 1.639-1.667).

Birefringence: 0.026.

Pleochroism: (Pakistan) yellow-pink/light pink/dark pink.

Spectral: Not reported.

Luminescence: None reported.

Occurrence: In lithium pegmatites.
Viitaniemi, Finland.
Pakistan: pink, cuttable material.

Stone Sizes: Faceted gems are extremely small (approximately 0.5 carat) and exceedingly rare.

Comments: The only reported gems are of Pakistani material, reddish-pink in color, and tiny.

Name: For Heikki Allan Väyrynen, a Finnish geologist.

VERD ANTIQUE See: Serpentine.

VESUVIANITE See: Idocrase.

VILLIAUMITE

Formula: NaF.

Crystallography: Isometric; crystals tiny; usually massive, granular.

Colors: Deep carmine-red, lavender pink to light orange; becomes colorless if heated to 300°C.

Luster: Vitreous.

Hardness: 2-2.5.

Density: 2.79.

Cleavage: Perfect 1 direction; brittle.

Optics: $N = 1.327$; isotropic.

Birefringence: Sometimes anomalous.

Pleochroism: Anomalous, strong: yellow/pink to deep carmine-red.

Spectral: Not diagnostic.

Luminescence: None.

Occurrence: In alkalic rocks, such as nepheline syenites.
Kola Peninsula, USSR.
Los, Guinea: Los is an island off the Guinea coast; facetable villiaumite occurs in nepheline syenite in reddish crystals, R.I. = 1.330-1.332, S.G. 2.79.
Francon Quarry, Mt. Ste. Hilaire, Quebec.

Stone Sizes: Los material might yield faceted gems up to 1-2 carats. Gems under 2 carats have been cut from Quebec material.
SI: 1.2 (orange-red).
PC: 12.1 (red, Quebec, cabochon?).

Comments: Villiaumite is seldom discussed among collectors of rare gemstones because until recently no facetable material was known. The material from Los was reported in 1976 and has been cut into tiny gemstones of deep red color. Despite their small size, they are desirable because so few stones exist. The material from Quebec is larger but very scarce. Villiaumite is somewhat water-soluble, and cutters must use special tricks (such as using alcohol as a cutting coolant) to facet the material.

Name: After M. Villiaume, a French explorer in whose

collection of rocks from Guinea the material was first discovered.

VIRIDINE See: Andalusite.

VISHNEVITE See: Cancrinite.

VIVIANITE

Formula: $Fe_3(PO_4)_2 \cdot 8H_2O$.

Crystallography: Monoclinic. Crystals prismatic, tabular, equant; in clusters, radial groups. Also massive, bladed, fibrous; crusts, earthy masses.

Colors: Colorless (fresh); darkens to shades of green and blue, then dark green, dark bluish green, dark purplish, bluish black.

Streak: Colorless, then dark blue after a time.

Luster: Vitreous, pearly on cleavage; also dull, earthy.

Hardness: 1.5-2.

Density: 2.64-2.68.

Cleavage: Perfect 1 direction. Fracture fibrous. Thin pieces are flexible and sectile.

Optics: $\alpha = 1.569\text{-}1.616$; $\beta = 1.602\text{-}1.656$; $\gamma = 1.629\text{-}1.675$. Biaxial (+) $2V = 63\text{-}83°$.

Birefringence: 0.040-0.059.

Pleochroism: Intense: blue/pale yellowish green/pale yellowish green; or deep blue/pale bluish green/pale yellow green; or indigo/yellowish green/yellowish olive-green.

Luminescence: None.

Spectral: Not diagnostic.

Occurrence: A secondary mineral in ore veins; also occurs as an alteration product of primary phosphate minerals in granite pegmatites; forms as sedimentary concretions.

Colorado; California; New Jersey; Delaware; Maryland; Florida.

Canada; Australia; Japan; Germany; USSR; France; England.

Lemhi County, Idaho: fine crystals.

Bingham Canyon, Utah: crystals to 5 inches in length.

Richmond, Virginia: good crystals.

Black Hills, South Dakota: in pegmatites.

Llallagua and *Poopo, Bolivia:* fine cuttable crystals to 6 inches long.

N'gaoundere, Cameroon: massive crystals up to 4 feet long, dark in color, cuttable.

Stone Sizes: Faceted gems are rarely cut because the material is so soft and fragile. The cleavage is almost micaceous, making it very difficult to polish gems. The Bolivian material, for example, could cut stones up to 75-100 carats (indices are 1.585/1.603/1.639, S.G. 2.64).

Comments: Vivianite is so fragile and soft that cut gems would be difficult to handle safely, let alone wear. The material darkens spontaneously, so the color of an attractive stone might disappear after a time, making it less enticing to spend the time cutting such material. The color of vivianite is very rich, and a few stones have been cut anyway.

Odontolite is a phosphate (actually fossil bone and teeth) that has been stained by vivianite and may resemble turquoise.

Name: After J. G. Vivian, an English mineralogist who discovered the species.

W

WARDITE

Formula: $NaAl_3(PO_4)_2(OH)_4 \cdot 2H_2O$.

Crystallography: Tetragonal. Crystals pyramidal; as crusts, aggregates, fibers, spherules.

Colors: Colorless, white, pale green to bluish green.

Luster: Vitreous.

Hardness: 5.

Density: 2.81-2.87.

Cleavage: Perfect 1 direction. Fracture conchoidal. Brittle.

Optics: $o = 1.586\text{-}1.594$; $e = 1.595\text{-}1.604$.
Uniaxial (+).
Sometimes anomalously biaxial.

Birefringence: 0.009.

Pleochroism: None.

Spectral: Not diagnostic.

Luminescence: None.

Occurrence: In phosphate masses in sediments, and in pegmatites.
Keystone, South Dakota; Pala, California.
Fairfield, Utah: in large nodules with variscite and other phosphates. Also at *Amatrice Hill, Lucin, Utah.*
Montebras, France: as an alteration of amblygonite.
West Andover, New Hampshire: in crystals to 1 cm.
Piedras Lavradas, Paraiba, Brazil: greenish white crystals to about 1 inch.

Stone Sizes: Faceted gems are very rare, cut from Brazilian material. Cabochons are cut of white wardite mixed with green variscite from Utah. Faceted gems would all be under 2-3 carats in size.

Comments: Wardite is another of the many phosphates that have been cut by collectors. It is pale colored and not terribly attractive and is fairly soft and fragile. It is seen far more frequently as cabochons than as faceted stones.

Name: After Henry A. Ward, American naturalist and collector.

WATER SAPPHIRE   See: Cordierite.

WAVELLITE

Formula: $Al_3(OH)_3(PO_4)_2 \cdot 5H_2O$.

Crystallography: Orthorhombic. Crystals very tiny; usually as radial aggregates of acicular crystals; often spherical crystal clusters; crusts; stalactitic.

Colors: White, greenish white, green, yellowish green, yellow, yellow-brown, brown to brownish black. Very rarely colorless, bluish.

Luster: Vitreous; also resinous to pearly.

Hardness: 3.5-4.

Density: 2.36.

Cleavage: Perfect 1 direction. Fracture subconchoidal to uneven. Brittle.

Optics: $\alpha = 1.520\text{-}1.535$; $\beta = 1.526\text{-}1.543$; $\gamma = 1.545\text{-}1.561$.
Biaxial (+), $2V = 71°$.

Birefringence: 0.025.

Spectral: Not diagnostic.

Luminescence: Occasionally bluish in LW (various localities).

Occurrence: A secondary mineral in hydrothermal veins; also in aluminous and phosphatic rocks.

200

Chester County, Pennsylvania; Alabama; Florida; Colorado; California.
Bolivia; England; Ireland; France; Portugal; Germany; Czechoslovakia; Bulgaria; Rumania; Tasmania.
Hot Springs, Arkansas: in fine, spherical and radial groups of acicular crystals.

Stone Sizes: Cabochons up to several inches in length can be cut from Arkansas material. No faceted gems have yet been reported.

Comments: Wavellite is a very attractive mineral that is well known to collectors. It is not generally regarded as cabochon material, but its radial aggregate crystal clusters can be cut into extremely interesting stones. These gems are very difficult to cut because of splintering of the radiating crystal clusters. The individual crystals of wavellite in the clusters are very small, and a faceted gem would be a tremendous rarity.

Name: After William Wavell, a physician in England, who discovered the mineral.

WELOGANITE

Formula: $Sr_5Zr_2C_9H_8O_{31}$.

Crystallography: Hexagonal; crystals hexagonal, barrel shaped with heavy striations on prism faces, also grooved due to oscillatory growth. Crystals distinctive, terminated by pedion or pyramids. Also massive.

Colors: White, lemon yellow, amber. Crystals may be zoned.

Luster: Vitreous.

Hardness: 3.5.

Density: 3.20.

Cleavage: Perfect; fracture conchoidal.

Optics: $\alpha = 1.558$; $\beta = 1.646$; $\gamma = 1.648$. Uniaxial (−).

Birefringence: 0.090.

Pleochroism: None.

Spectral: Not diagnostic.

Luminescence: None reported.

Occurrence: In an alkalic sill intruding a limestone at St. Michel, Montreal Island, Quebec, Canada.

Stone Sizes: Clean, yellowish stones (mostly under ½ carat) have been faceted from this material.
NMC: 4.27 (light greyish-yellow); 0.52 (light yellow).

Name: For William E. Logan, first director of the Geological Survey of Canada.

WERNERITE   See: Scapolite.

WHEWELLITE

Formula: $CaC_2O_4 \cdot H_2O$ (calcium oxalate).

Crystallography: Monoclinic. Crystals prismatic or equant, also in twins.

Colors: Colorlesss, white, yellowish, brownish.

Luster: Vitreous to pearly.

Hardness: 2.5-3.

Density: 2.19-2.25.

Cleavage: Good in 1 direction, 2 others distinct. Fracture conchoidal. Brittle.

Optics: $\alpha = 1.489$; $\beta = 1.553$; $\gamma = 1.649$-1.651. Biaxial (+), $2V = 80°$.

Birefringence: 0.159-0.163.

Dispersion: 0.034.

Spectral: Not diagnostic.

Luminescence: None.

Occurrence: Coarse crystals occur in coal seams and concretions (organic origin). Also as a hydrothermal mineral in ore veins.
Elk Creek, South Dakota: fine crystals up to 6 cm in length, among the finest in the world.
Czechoslovakia; France; Hungary; USSR.
Havre, Montana: in septarian concretions.
Burgk, Germany: crystals up to several inches in length.

Stone Sizes: Crystals are usually very small, colorless. Faceted gems from these will reach a maximum of about 2 carats.

Comments: Whewellite is one of the most unusual minerals because of its chemical composition and occurrence. It is seldom seen by collectors, and even less thought of as a faceted gemstone. It is really just a curiosity, and there is nothing intriguing about it except its rarity. The dispersion is fairly high but hard to appreciate because of the usual small size of cut gems.

Name: After William Whewell, English natural scientist and philosopher.

WILKEITE   Apatite Group.

Formula: $Ca_5(SiO_4,PO_4,SO_4)_3(O,OH,F)$.

Crystallography: Hexagonal. Crystals rounded; granular; massive.

Colors: Pale pinkish, yellowish, rose red.

Luster: Vitreous to resinous.

Hardness: 5.

Density: 3.12-3.23.

Cleavage: Imperfect; very brittle.

Optics: $o = 1.640$-1.650; $e = 1.636$-1.646. Uniaxial (−).

Birefringence: 0.010.

Spectral: Not diagnostic.

Luminescence: None reported.

Occurrence: In metamorphosed marbles.
Kyshtym, Urals, USSR; Laacher See, Germany. Crestmore, California: in marble.

Stone Sizes: Cuttable crystal fragments have been encountered, but I know of no faceted gems.

Comments: Wilkeite is a rare silicate—sulfate apatite that has not been encountered as faceted gems; however, I have seen cuttable crystals that would yield stones in the 1-5 carat range. These would be extremely rare stones.

Name: After R. M. Wilke, mineral collector and dealer in Palo Alto, California.

WILLEMITE

Formula: Zn_2SiO_4.

Crystallography: Hexagonal (R). Crystals prismatic, short and stubby or long needles; massive compact; granular.

Colors: Colorless, white, gray, various shades of green, yellow, orange, red-brown.

Luster: Vitreous to resinous.

Hardness: 5.5.

Density: 3.89-4.10 (usually the latter).

Cleavage: Poor. Fracture conchoidal. Brittle.

Optics: $o = 1.691$; $e = 1.719$. Uniaxial (+).

Birefringence: 0.028.

Pleochroism: Dichroism variable.

Spectral: Weak bands at 5830, 5400, 4900, 4420, and 4320; strong band at 4210.

Luminescence: Intense green or yellow-green in SW (Franklin, New Jersey), also in LW. Sometimes intensely phosphorescent (green).

Occurrence: In zinc ore bodies or metamorphic deposits where Zn is present.
Greenland; Belgium; Algeria; Zaire; Zambia. Franklin and *Sterling Hill, New Jersey:* the foremost willemite occurrence; stubby green crystals and greenish orange masses to several inches in length. Also massive brown material and crystals to 6 inches long, called *troostite.*
Inyo County, California; Utah; Arizona: microcrystals at various localities.
Tsumeb, Namibia: small colorless crystals and bluish masses.
Mt. Ste. Hilaire, Quebec: blue, gemmy crystals.

Stone Sizes: Faceted gems are known to a maximum size of about 10 carats, mostly from the Franklin, New Jersey, occurrence. Cabochons to several inches are frequently cut from massive Franklin material.
SI: 11.7 and 11.1 (yellow-orange, Franklin, New Jersey).
NMC: 6.75, 0.30 (light blue, Quebec).
PC: 5.39 (pastel orange, New Jersey).

Comments: Cabochons of massive brown troostite from New Jersey are attractive, as are cabochons of willemite with black franklinite and red zincite in white calcite. These latter stones fluoresce vividly in UV light. Faceted willemite is extremely rare and stones larger than 1-2 carats are worthy of museums. Most such stones are pale green, yellow-orange, or brownish green, rarely blue (from the Quebec locality). Gems are difficult to polish, and the material is too soft and fragile for use in jewelry.

Name: After King William I of the Netherlands. *Troostite* after an early American mineralogist, Gerard Troost.

WILLIAMSITE   See: Serpentine.

WITHERITE   Series to Strontianite: $SrCO_3$.

Formula: $BaCO_3$.

Crystallography: Orthorhombic. Crystals twinned to yield pseudohexagonal dipyramids; prismatic; globular, botryoidal; granular; fibrous.

Colors: Colorless, white, gray with a tinge of yellow, green, or brown.

Luster: Vitreous to resinous.

Hardness: 3-3.5.

Density: 4.27-4.79.

Cleavage: Distinct 1 direction. Fracture uneven. Brittle.

Optics: $\alpha = 1.529$; $\beta = 1.676$; $\gamma = 1.677$. Biaxial (−), $2V = 16°$.

Birefringence: 0.148.

Spectral: Not diagnostic. Effervesces in acid.

Luminescence: Green and yellow in SW (England) with phosphorescence. Yellowish, with phosphorescence, in LW. Fluoresces in X-rays.

Occurrence: A low-temperature mineral in hydrothermal vein deposits.
Lockport, New York; Kentucky; Montana; Arizona; California.
Austria; Germany; Czechoslovakia; France; Japan; USSR; England.
Minerva Mine, Rosiclare, Illinois: large yellowish crystals.

Stone Sizes: Witherite is not normally cut into cabochons because the color is too pale to be attractive. Faceted gems, even those under 5 carats, are usually more translucent than transparent.

Comments: Witherite is very rarely faceted; if it is faceted, it is quite rare. Stones are not especially beautiful, and they are soft and fragile as well. Their only major attribute is rarity. Witherite is fairly easy to cut but somewhat difficult to polish.

Name: After William Withering, an English physician and mineralogist, who first noted the mineral.

WOLLASTONITE

Formula: CaSiO₃.

Crystallography: Triclinic. Crystals tabular; massive, cleavable, fibrous, granular.

Colors: White, colorless, gray, pale green.

Luster: Vitreous to pearly; silky if fibrous.

Hardness: 4.5-5.

Density: 2.8-3.09.

Cleavage: Perfect 1 direction. Fracture splintery. Brittle.

Optics: $\alpha = 1.616\text{-}1.640$; $\beta = 1.628\text{-}1.650$; $\gamma = 1.631\text{-}1.653$. Biaxial (−), $2V = 38\text{-}60°$.
Shadow edge in refractometer about 1.63.

Birefringence: 0.015.

Spectral: Not diagnostic.

Luminescence: Fluoresces blue-green and phosphoresces yellow in SW, same in LW, from California, Alaska, Pennsylvania. Material from Asbestos, Quebec, Canada, is nonluminescent.

Occurrence: Metamorphosed limestones and alkalic igneous rocks.
California (various localities); *Willsboro, New York; Alaska; Pennsylvania; New Mexico.*
Ontario and *Quebec, Canada; Chiapas, Mexico; Norway; Italy; Rumania; Finland.*
Isle Royale, Lake Superior: compact, pale red material, good for cutting cabochons.

Stone Sizes: Cabochons up to several inches in length can be cut from fibrous and massive material. Very few faceted gems have been reported.
USNM: 1.22.
NMC: 4.05.
PC: 0.75 (Asbestos, Quebec).

Comments: Interesting cabochons have been cut from wollastonite, especially from the fibrous material (which yields catseye stones) and the reddish material from Lake Superior's Isle Royale. Wollastonite is strictly a curiosity and as a mineral is not especially rare. It resembles other white fibrous minerals, however, and is sometimes difficult to identify without using X-ray techniques. Facetable wollastonite is exceedingly rare, the material from Asbestos, Quebec (Jeffrey Mine) being singularly notable. Such gems are, moreover, extremely difficult to cut because of the cleavage and fibrosity of the mineral.

Name: After W. H. Wollaston, British mineralogist and chemist.

WULFENITE

Formula: PbMoO₄.

Crystallography: Tetragonal. Crystals commonly tabular with square outline; also pyramidal; massive, granular.

Colors: Orange, (various shades), brownish orange, yellow, brownish yellow, yellow-orange, red, brown, yellowish gray, tan, greenish brown.

Luster: Resinous to adamantine.

Hardness: 2.5-3.

Density: 6.5-7.0.

Cleavage: Distinct 1 direction. Fracture uneven to subconchoidal. Brittle.

Optics: $o = 2.405$; $e = 2.283$.
Uniaxial (−).

Birefringence: 0.122.

Dispersion: 0.203.

Pleochroism: Weak, in orange to yellow tints.

Spectral: Not diagnostic.

Luminescence: None.

Occurrence: Secondary mineral in the oxidized zone of ore deposits.
Arizona (Glove Mine, Rowley Mine, Red Cloud Mine, Mammoth Mine, others); New Mexico; Nevada; Utah; Wheatley Mines, Chester, Pennsylvania; Loudville, Massachusetts.
Mexico: Los Lomentos, many other locations; *Poland; Yugoslavia; Austria; Czechoslovakia; Germany; Sardinia; Algeria; Morocco; Australia.*

Tsumeb, Namibia: yellowish tan crystals up to 5 inches on edge, some facetable.

Stone Sizes: Most wulfenite crystals, especially those from U.S. localities, are too thin for the cutting of gemstones. However, an occasional crystal is both thick and transparent enough for faceting, notably from the Red Cloud Mine, the Seventynine Mine, and others. Some of these have yielded gems up to about 5 carats. Tsumeb, Namibia, has produced wulfenite crystals several inches across, from which gems up to 50 carats have been faceted. *SI:* 46.1, 15.7, 9.6 (pale yellow, Tsumeb); 10^+ (orange, Los Lomentos, Mexico). *PC:* 54 (yellow, Tsumeb). *DG:* 15.25 (yellow, Tsumeb); 9.44 (red, Arizona).

Comments: The red of wulfenite, especially from the Red Cloud Mine in Arizona, is one of the richest colors in nature. Specimens of wulfenite are esthetically magnificent and are greatly prized by collectors. The crystal habit is tabular and the individual crystals are usually very thin, making it difficult to find a suitable cutting fragment. Gems are then difficult to cut because of the softness of the material and its sensitivity to heat and vibration. These characteristics make wulfenite totally unsuited for jewelry, but it makes a spectacular collector gem of great rarity. A red wulfenite over 1 carat is extremely scarce, likewise a yellowish or orange one over 1-2 carats. The only larger stones come from Tsumeb material, but the facetable crystals from this locality were extremely uncommon and very few stones have been cut from them.

Name: After the Austrian mineralogist, Franz Xavier Wulfen, who wrote a lengthy monograph in 1785 on the lead ores of Carinthia.

WURTZITE See: Sphalerite.

X

XALOSTOCITE   See: Garnet.

XANTHITE   See: Idocrase.

XANTHOCONITE   See: Proustite.

XONOTLITE

Formula: $Ca_6Si_6O_{17}(OH)_2$.

Crystallography: Monoclinic; crystals acicular; usually massive, fibrous or compact.

Colors: Chalky white to colorless, pink, light to medium gray.

Luster: Greasy; pearly; dull vitreous.

Hardness: 6.

Density: 2.71.

Cleavage: Good in one direction; tough.

Optics: $\alpha = 1.583$; $\beta = 1.583$; $\gamma = 1.593$. Biaxial (+).

Birefringence: 0.010.

Pleochroism: None.

Spectral: None.

Luminescence: None reported.

Occurrence: Typically as veinlets in serpentine or in contact zones. Small fragments may be translucent to transparent.
California; Michigan; Virginia; Puerto Rico.
Tetela de Xonotla, Mexico.
Laghi di Posina, Vicenza, Italy.

Stone Sizes: Translucent faceted stones (not truly transparent) up to several carats in size have been cut from Italian material. The material is strong, takes a good polish, and is extremely rare as both a species and as cut specimens.

Name: After the Mexican locality.

Y

YUGAWARALITE

Formula: $CaAl_2Si_6O_{16} \cdot 4H_2O$.

Crystallography: Monoclinic; crystals tabular and very flat.

Colors: Colorless to white.

Luster: Vitreous.

Hardness: 4.5.

Density: 2.23-2.25.

Cleavage: Imperfect; very brittle.

Optics: $\alpha = 1.495$; $\beta = 1.497$; $\gamma = 1.504$. Biaxial (+).

Birefringence: 0.009.

Pleochroism: None.

Spectral: None.

Luminescence: None reported.

Occurrence: In veins and crystals in volcanic rocks in *Japan* and in huge crystals in breccia cavities in *India*. *Yugawara Hot Spring, Kanagawa Prefecture, Japan. Khandivali Quarry*, near *Bombay, India. Alaska; Iceland; Sardinia; British Columbia*.

Stone Sizes: Superb, well-formed, colorless, transparent crystals up to 3 cm long occur at the Khandivali Quarry, Bombay, India, with physical properties close to the literature values for the mineral. A few colorless faceted gemstones have been cut from this exceptional and extremely rare material.

Name: From the original Japanese locality.

Z

ZEKTZERITE

Formula: LiNa(Zr,Ti,Hf)Si$_6$O$_{15}$.

Crystallography: Orthorhombic; crystals generally tabular, pseudohexagonal, transparent to translucent.

Colors: Colorless to pink, sometimes with color zoning.

Luster: Pearly on crystal faces, vitreous on cleavage and fracture surfaces.

Hardness: 6.

Density: 2.79.

Cleavage: Perfect in 2 directions.

Optics: $\alpha = 1.582$; $\beta = 1.584$; $\gamma = 1.584$. Biaxial (−).

Birefringence: 0.002. The material is virtually isotropic.

Pleochroism: None.

Luminescence: Fluoresces light yellow in SW, inert in LW, no phosphorescence either SW or LW.

Occurrence: In a small number of miarolitic cavities in a riebeckite granite in *Okanogan County, Washington.* This is the only known locality. Crystals up to 35 mm in size have been found, some transparent enough to yield small (less than 2 carats) faceted gems. Typical crystals are 4-15 mm in size, sometimes perched on riebeckite crystals.

Stone Sizes: Colorless faceted gems in the 1-2 carat range have been reported. The material, and hence the cut stones, are exceedingly rare.

Name: After Jack Zektzer of Seattle, Washington, who initiated the investigation of the newly discovered mineral.

ZINCITE

Formula: ZnO + Mn.

Crystallography: Hexagonal. Crystals hemimorphic and very scarce; massive, cleavable, compact, grains.

Colors: Dark red, brownish red, deep yellow, orange-yellow; colorless if pure.

Streak: Orange-yellow.

Luster: Subadamantine to adamantine.

Hardness: 4-4.5.

Density: 5.68.

Cleavage: Perfect 1 direction but difficult. Fracture conchoidal.

Optics: $o = 2.013$; $e = 2.029$. Uniaxial (+).

Birefringence: 0.016.

Dispersion: 0.127.

Pleochroism: None.

Luminescence: None.

Occurrence: In metamorphosed limestone and zinc ores.
Franklin, New Jersey: only major locality; massive red ore, also in crystals up to 4 inches long, but these were found only in secondary calcite veins.
Poland; Spain; Tasmania.

Stone Sizes: Cabochons have been cut from granular zincite in white calcite from Franklin. Faceted gems of Franklin material are very rare, maximum about 20 carats. Most of the (few) faceted zincites are in the 1-3 carat range.

SI: 20.1 and 12.3 (red, New Jersey).
AMNH: 16.27 (red, Franklin, New Jersey).
Philadelphia Academy of Natural Science: 12.7 (red, New Jersey).
PC: 3.28 (clean, superbly cut, probably world's finest).
HU: 3.08 (red, New Jersey).

Comments: Zincite is a very rare mineral, essentially restricted to one important locality. Well-terminated crystals were found only up to about 3-4 inches, but larger masses, weighing several pounds, have been encountered in the ore bodies. These are not especially interesting, but cabochons with red zincite, green willemite, and white calcite, peppered with black franklinite, are unique to the Franklin occurrence and are extremely beautiful as well as highly fluorescent. Spheres have also been cut from this material. Cut zincite is one of the rarest of all gemstones. It is seldom completely transparent; usually it is slightly cloudy or translucent.

Name: In allusion to the composition.

ZIRCON

Formula: $ZrSiO_4$ + Fe, U, Th, Hf.

Crystallography: Tetragonal. Crystals prismatic, pyramidal; often twinned; rounded pebbles.

Colors: Reddish brown, yellow, gray, green, red; various other colors induced by heating.

Luster: Vitreous to adamantine; sometimes greasy.

Cleavage: Imperfect. Fracture conchoidal. Very brittle.
   Zircon crystals usually contain traces of radioactive elements such as U and Th. These decay within the crystals, and over a period of thousands of years result in severe damage to the crystal structure of the host zircon. The damage can be severe enough to destroy the lattice itself, ultimately decomposing the zircon internally into a mixture of quartz and zirconium oxide that is essentially amorphous. This damaged, nearly isotropic zircon is called *low zircon,* whereas the undecayed material is called *high zircon.* Material slightly damaged by radia-

tion is called *intermediate zircon,* and a complete transition exists between the low and high type.

Birefringence: 0.008-0.069. Optically uniaxial (+).

Dispersion: 0.039 for all zircon types.

Spectral: Zircon spectra are very distinctive and useful in identification. The strongest pervasive line is at 6535, seen even in types where a strong spectrum is absent. There are many narrow lines and strong bands across the whole spectrum, ranging from more than 40 lines (Burma green stones) to only a few lines (orange gems from New South Wales, Australia). Heat-treated stones and low types have a weak spectrum. Colorless, blue, and golden-brown (all heat-treated) stones display one fine line at 6535, and perhaps also a line at 6590. The complex spectrum of other zircons includes lines at 6535, 6910, 6830, 6625, 6605, 6210, 6150, 5895, 5625, 5375, 5160, 4840, 4600, and 4327. Red zircons may display no spectrum at all.

Inclusions: Angular zoning and streaks are sometimes seen in the low type. Some silk is seen occasionally, as well as tension cracks and epigenetic cracks stained with iron oxides. Metamict crystals may have bright fissures known as *angles.*

Heating Effects: Heating helps to crystallize partially metamicted zircons and results in a higher specific gravity; the absorption spectrum also sharpens. Heating green Sri Lankan zircon makes it paler in color. Red-brown Sri Lankan material becomes colorless, sometimes reddish-violet. Red-brown Thai and Cambodian stones turn colorless, blue, or golden.

Luminescence: The fluorescence of zircon is variable. Some material is inert, other crystals glow intensely. Mustard yellow is a typical fluorescent color (SW), also yellow-orange. Some zircons glow dull yellow in LW and may phosphoresce. Zircon may be whitish, yellow, greenish, or violet-blue in X-rays.

Pleochroism: Distinct in *blue stones:* deep sky blue/colorless to yellowish gray. *Red:* red/clove brown. *Brown:* reddish brown/yellowish brown.

	Low Zircon	Intermediate Zircon	High Zircon
Colors	green; also brown, orange	brownish green, dark red	colorless, blue brownish orange
Optics			
o	1.78–1.85 (almost isotropic)	1.85–1.93	1.92–1.94 (often 1.925)
e	—	1.84–1.970	1.97–2.01 (often 1.984)
Birefringence	0 to 0.008	0.008–0.043	0.036–0.059 (usually the latter)
Density	3.9–4.1 (usually about 4.0)	4.1–4.65	4.65–4.8 (usually about 4.70)

Occurrence: In igneous rocks worldwide, especially granites. Also found as alluvial material.
South Dakota; Colorado; Oklahoma; Texas; Maine; Massachusetts; New York; New Jersey.
USSR; Korea; Germany; Brazil.
Sri Lanka: one of the most important zircon areas, material of all colors, in gravels.
Burma: yellowish and greenish stones found in gem gravels with ruby, complex absorption spectrum in these stones.
Thailand: one of the most important commercial sources of gem zircon.
Cambodia: chief source (although no current production) of material that heat-treats colorless and blue.
France: red crystals at *Espaly, St. Marcel.*
Quebec and *Ontario, Canada:* dark, opaque crystals up to 15 pounds, yield only tiny gems.
Arendal, Norway; New South Wales, Australia: fine gem material (orange).
Emali, Tanzania: white zircon pebbles.

Stone Sizes: The largest zircon gems are from Southeast Asian gem gravels.
SI: 118.1 (brown, Sri Lanka); 97.6 (yellow-brown, Sri Lanka); 75.8 (red-brown, Burma); 64.2 (brown, Thailand); 23.5 (green, Sri Lanka); 23.9 (colorless, Sri Lanka); 103.2 (blue, Thailand).
Geology Museum, London: 44.27 (blue); 22.67 (golden); 14.34 (red; 21.32 (white).
ROM: 23.8 (brown); 17.80 (blue); 61.69 (blue, step-cut).
AMHN: 208 (greenish-blue, Sri Lanka).

Comments: Zircon is an underrated but magnificent gemstone. When it is properly cut, it rivals diamond in beauty, but often the cutting is not correct and the gem is relatively dull and lifeless. The dispersion is very high, close to that of diamond. Zircon is very brittle and edges of stones are easily chipped and abraded. Zircon must be worn carefully to prevent damage. The range of color in the material is wide, and many additional colors are produced by heating.

High Zircon is fully crystalline and has the highest properties, whereas the low type is metamict, due to bombardment of the internal crystal structure by alpha particles released by U and Th. In cases of extreme damage to the structure, the material may appear isotropic, with lower refractive indices and less brilliance when cut. Interestingly, the dispersion is the same for both the high and low types. The popular blue color can be produced only by heating zircon; the same is true for the colorless and golden yellow shades. The crystals that yield these lovely colors are usually reddish-brown. Large, fine-colored zircons are very rare stones, and even smaller fine ones are seldom seen in jewelry today. Catseye zircon has also been reported from Sri Lanka.

Name: Zircon is from the Arabic *zargun,* from the Persian *zar (gold)* plus *gun (color).* The name is ancient.

ZOISITE See: Epidote.

ZUNYITE

Formula: $Al_{13}Si_5O_{20}(OH,F)_{18}Cl$.

Crystallography: Isometric, typically in tetrahedral crystals, rarely octahedrons; twinned.

Colors: Colorless, grayish, pale beige-brown.

Luster: Vitreous.

Hardness: 7.

Cleavage: Easy 1 direction; brittle.

Density: 2.87.

Optics: $N = 1.600$.

Pleochroism: None.

Spectral: Not diagnostic.

Luminescence: Fluoresces intense red (Quartzsite).

Occurrence: At the type locality, the Zuni mine, near *Silverton, Colorado,* enclosed in guitermanite; also as a vein mineral in Ouray County, Colorado, and as an alteration product of feldspar in a dike rock in Saguache County.
Quartzsite, Arizona: large crystals.
Postmasburg, South Africa: in aluminous shales.
Kuni village, Gumma Prefecture, Japan: transparent tetrahedral crystals.
Algeria.

Stone Sizes: Cuttable zunyite may be found in Japanese material but has never been reported. However, in 1986 enormous (up to 2 cm) crystals of zunyite were found in a prospect pit near Quartzsite, Arizona. These are perfect tetrahedra, pale beige-brown in color, in matrix. Minute areas of some of these crystals were perfectly transparent, colorless, and suitable for cutting into faceted gems up to ½ carat in size.

Name: After the type locality in Colorado.

Gemstones from the Laboratory

HISTORY

Humans have always sought to emulate nature and capture her secrets. The early alchemists, building on the dreams of antiquity, thought they could turn lead into gold. In like manner, the dream of creating valuable gemstones has inspired many attempts at the laboratory duplication of nature's crystalline masterpieces. Unfortunately, virtually all of these attempts were doomed to failure. You cannot recreate a complex feat of natural magic unless you understand the magician's trick. And a complete understanding of the structure and formation of natural crystalline solids, even with twentieth-century skills, remains elusive, although many parts of the puzzle have been solved.

However, the ultimate prize—to actually create valuable gemstones out of inexpensive chemicals, like turning base metal into precious metal—was tempting beyond imagination. In fact, as early as 1885, the first marketable gemstones were born in laboratory furnaces in France. Ruby had actually been made as early as 1837, but the material was not transparent or large enough for gemstone use. The work of Frémy and Verneuil opened the door to commercial sapphire and ruby manufacture, and by around 1902 the basic problems had been solved. An earlier gem, marketed in Switzerland and known as *Geneva ruby* has recently been shown to be a prior, successful product of the ruby-making procedure developed by August Verneuil.

Once it had been demonstrated that gemstones could be manufactured in commercial size and quality, a new era of intensive research was spawned. At this writing, the following gemstones (and approximate dates of first commercially viable production) have been manufactured: ruby (1885-1905); sapphire (1910); spinel (1910); star ruby and sapphire (1947); rutile (1948); emerald (1950,

1965); quartz (1950); diamond (1955; 1970); turquoise (1972); alexandrite (1973); opal (1974); lapis lazuli (1976); and jadeite (1984). Many other gemstones have been synthesized but await commercial exploitation.

Many of the techniques used to create gemstones in the laboratory were not developed to create misery for gemologists. The almost-magical science (some would call it an art) of crystal growth, almost exclusively a twentieth-century technology, is mainly concerned with crystals per se. Crystals are among the most important materials of civilization. In fact, nearly all of the things we take for granted today, including all forms of transportation, communication, banking, commerce, and manufacture, down to portable radios, TV sets, auto ignitions, and hearing aids, would not work at all without exotic, specially made crystalline materials. It can safely be said that the technology for growing crystals of these materials has become critical to the well-being of society. There is no aspect of daily existence in technologically advanced countries that is not influenced directly or indirectly by crystals.

Crystal growers make use of certain fundamental aspects of natural laws; these laws govern the states of matter and the interactions of atoms and molecules. One such law, known as the second law of thermodynamics, states that natural processes tend to run in a direction that produces the greatest entropy. *Entropy* is the degree of disorder, or randomness, of a system. The tendency of natural processes (that is, the direction in which things tend to go if left entirely to themselves) is to move in the direction of lowest energy. In other words, natural processes *spontaneously* go in a way that releases rather than absorbs energy. It turns out that energy is released when an atom or molecule attaches itself to an already-existing cluster of other atoms and molecules (a *nucleus*). The major focus of crystal growers is to use this principle in a controlled way. All crystal growth methods boil down to an effort to alter the energy configuration of a chemical system very carefully; this would create the spontaneous change in the system that would cause randomly moving atoms to attach themselves to a nucleus, or seed crystal, fortuitously provided by the crystal grower. If everything goes according to plan, the atoms attach themselves slowly, deliberately, and in a way that follows the structural configuration of the seed crystal. The process continues until (1) there are no suitable loose atoms left to attach, or (2) the energy configuration of the system stabilizes and the *driving force* of the process ceases to operate.

One way to provide the driving-force energy is to change the temperature of the system. Another way is to change the number of loose atoms available, that is, the saturation of these atoms within the medium in which the crystal is growing. These two general techniques—changing temperature or changing saturation—are the basic methods by which nearly all laboratory-produced crystals are grown. These are also the two chief methods of crystal growth in natural environments.

CRYSTAL GROWTH

A crystal is characterized by long-range order; that is, the atoms in a crystal are arranged in regular, periodic arrays or patterns (like wallpaper). The object of crystal growth is to add more atoms and perpetuate the pattern. A *seed* crystal is used to provide the basic template, and the *raw material* (loose atoms) remains mobile by being vaporized, melted, or dissolved in a solution. Thus, we may speak of *vapor growth, melt growth, flux growth,* or *solution growth,* depending on the medium used for crystallization. Crystal growth is achieved by forcing the unattached atoms in the growth medium to attach themselves to the seed. This is theoretically relatively simple to do. All that is required is to cause the growth medium to contain more unattached atoms than the medium can handle at a specific temperature. Unfortunately, it is not so easy to make the atoms go exactly where you want them to go. This is why some people speak of the "*art and science of crystal growing.*"

In human societies, when cities become too crowded there is an exodus to the suburbs. If a growth medium, let's say a solution, is forced to contain an excess of dissolved material at a given temperature, the energy of the system may *become* out of equilibrium at a *lower* temperature. The direction of *spontaneous* change, the one that results in a lower overall energy for the system, is that which dumps some of the dissolved material back out of solution. If the dumping tendency is strong enough (that is, a very rapid temperature drop) the atoms will actually coalesce into many small nuclei, even though the process of nucleation *absorbs* energy and is therefore

not favored by thermodynamics. The best alternative to this random, uncontrolled growth is to provide a template, or seed crystal, for the dumped atoms to join. Crystal growth is tricky; many things can go wrong.

In light of this, it is absolutely amazing that gems exist. A gemstone is a transparent and outwardly perfect crystalline mass, (ideally) free of visible imperfections or flaws, of uniform color and sometimes of immense size. It is difficult enough to grow such perfect crystals in a controlled laboratory environment. It is nothing short of miraculous that, given the randomness of natural environments, nature has been able to produce crystals large and perfect enough to yield gemstones. In some cases, humans have yet to figure out how mother nature, the magician, has even been able to pull off the trick!

Following is an abbreviated summary of the basic methods used to grow crystals. All of the gemstones being made in laboratories are made by one or more of these methods.

Vapor Growth: Substances best grown from vapor are those that pass directly from a solid to a vapor when heated or those whose components can easily be transported in vapor form. Materials that pass readily from solid to vapor are said to be *volatile.* In vapor-transport techniques, the desired substance reacts (usually at a high temperature) with another material, and the products of the reaction are even more volatile than the original substances. These newly formed products are moved to a new location, usually at a lower temperature, where they react in a reverse way to recreate the starting materials. If the procedure is done carefully, the reaction yields single crystals. Vapor-grown crystals are characteristically long needles or thin plates; in some cases crystal growth yields lacelike aggregates known as *dendrites* (for example, snowflakes).

Vapor-grown crystals include most metals, cadmium and zinc sulfides and arsenides, and various oxides. No gems are commercially grown in this way.

Melt Growth: Most natural crystals were formed in molten environments deep within the Earth. The sizes of the crystals (grains) in a rock and the way in which the grains have grown together are meaningful to geologists and tell a great deal about the cooling history of the rock. Gemstones, including olivine (peridot), feldspars and others, are occasionally cut from larger crystals in such igneous materials.

The general term for melt growth is *solidification.* Everyone grows crystals from a melt. Water, after all, is nothing more than molten ice, a crystalline solid that freezes (solidifies) at only 32°F. Snowflakes, although dendrites, are single crystals of ice. However, the ice cubes in your refrigerator are not. Uncontrolled freezing of a melt generally results in the formation of many tiny crystallites that all grow at the same general rate to fill up the available space. An ice cube is thus a *polycrystalline aggregate,* consisting of a myriad of intergrown crystals. Poured ingots of molten metals crystallize in much the same way.

Growth from the melt is very convenient and requires relatively unsophisticated equipment in many cases. This method is unsuitable, however, for growing materials that contain water or volatile components; such materials decompose at their melting point. In technical language, a "congruently melting" material is one that does not change composition at the boundary between the solid and liquid state and can therefore be grown by one of the following methods.

The *Bridgman-Stockbarger Method* (Fig. 7) was developed around the same time by P. W. Bridgman (American), D. C. Stockbarger (German), and the Russians J. Obreimov, G. Tammann, and L. Shubnikov in the period 1924-1936. A specially shaped container is used, generally a cylindrical tube that tapers to a cone with a small point at one end. The tube is fulled with powder of the desired crystalline material and lowered through a heater (radio-frequency or electrical resistance types are most common), pointed side down. The material in the tube melts, but the small conical tip is the first part of the container to emerge from the heater. In ideal circumstances (not all that difficult to achieve) the first bit of molten material to solidify forms a single crystal, rather than a polycrystalline aggregate. Further solidification continues as an extension of the pattern provided by this *induced* seed crystal, until the entire cylinder is frozen, and the container is filled with a single crystal.

There are many variations of this technique, some adapted for specialized applications such as the growth of high-purity metals. The method is extremely simple in concept and can be employed to grow truly immense crystals, the largest to date being more than 3 feet across and weighing more than a ton (sodium iodide, cesium iodide, and so forth). It is commonly used for the growth of halides, many sulfides, and a variety of oxides.

The *Verneuil Technique* (Fig. 8), or *flame fusion,* was developed in the late 1800s by August Verneuil, one of the great pioneers of gemstone synthesis. Verneuil had deposited sealed papers with the Paris Academy of Sciences in 1891 and 1892. When opened in 1910, these documents revealed the details of Verneuil's work on ruby synthesis, opening the door to large-scale production. The equipment detailed by Verneuil was so cleverly designed that modern factories still employ furnaces with essentially the same specifications as the original. Perhaps several hundred materials have been grown by the Verneuil method, and it is one of the least costly of all crystal growth techniques.

The Verneuil torch is an inverted oxyhydrogen blow-

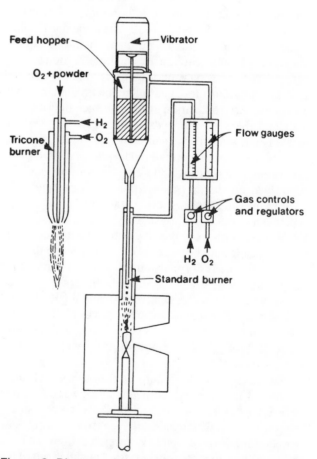

Figure 8. Diagram of the Verneuil furnace; the tricone burner (left) is used for many synthetic stones. Reprinted from Michael O'Donoghue, *A Guide to Man-made Gemstones* (New York: Van Nostrand Reinhold, 1983), p. 24.

Figure 7. In the Bridgman technique, a specially shaped crucible, filled with a powder of the desired crystal *(C),* is lowered through a furnace *(B).* The powder melts and a crystal starts to form in the pointed tip of the crucible as the crucible emerges into a cool part of the furnace. A single crystal grows *(D)* as the molten material solidifies. The entire assembly is surrounded by insulation *(A).* Reprinted from Joel E. Arem, *Man-Made Crystals* (Washington, D.C.: Smithsonian Institution Press, 1973), p. 28.

torch; a powder of the substance to be grown is dribbled through this flame, and the molten drops fall onto a rotating rod, which is slowly withdrawn. The withdrawal rate is adjusted carefully, so that the molten droplets raining onto the rod solidify in a controlled fashion and build up a single crystal. The purity of the finished crystal is a function of the starting powder and the atmosphere in which the crystal is grown. The quality of the Verneuil crystal, or *boule* (French for *ball*) depends on the purity and particle size of the feed powder, the flame temperature, rate of rotation and withdrawal of the seed rod, and the shielding of the crystal from drafts. Verneuil-type crystals have also been grown using different heat sources, such as plasma arcs and parabolically reflected carbon arcs (*arc-imaging* technique).

The popularity of the Verneuil method for crystal production is illustrated by the fact that, by the 1920s, factories in Europe were turning out hundreds of millions of carats of Verneuil crystals annually. Among the gem materials produced commercially in this way are sapphire, ruby, star corundum, spinel, rutile, strontium titanate, and a vast array of oxides and other compounds.

The *Czochralski technique* (Fig. 9), or *crystal pulling,* was originally developed to measure the speed of crystallization of metals. It is now as important as the Verneuil method in gemstone crystal growth. The technique involves the melting of a starting powder in a crucible, generally platinum, iridium, graphite, or ceramic. A rotating rod with a tiny seed crystal on the end is lowered into the crucible until it just touches the melt, and then is slowly withdrawn. Crystallization at the interface between the melt and the seed proceeds in two ways: (1) Surface tension pulls some of the melt slightly out of the crucible onto the seed. Once this material leaves the melt, it cools just enough to solidify, adding to the seed crystal. (2) Also, heat conduction allows the solid to extend very slightly into the melt, assuring that ample material is pulled out to make the growing crystal ever larger. Crystal growth continues in this way until the entire contents of the crucible have been pulled out and added to the rod.

The pull-rate is normally on the order of 1 mm to 10 cm per hour. Czochralski crystals can be enormous—the size of baseball bats! A number of technologically vital crystals, such as pure silicon, are grown by pulling, as are many materials that are cut as gems. These include ruby, sapphire, YAG, GGG, alexandrite, and a wide variety of unusual oxides.

There are several variations on the basic Czochralski method. One, the *Kyropoulos technique,* was developed by S. Kyropoulos between 1925 and 1935. It is best suited to growing crystals much wider than they are long. The temperature of the crucible is lowered downward from the seed, as opposed to the crystal being pulled out of the melt. In *zone growth* (zone refining) a movable heater actually moves the melt zone, while the container and contents remain motionless. Extremely high purities are

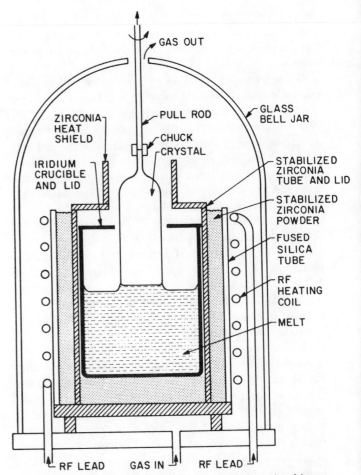

Figure 9. Apparatus for the Czochralski growth of large high-melting crystals such as synthetic ruby, YAG, and GGG; crucible diameter may be as large as 15 cm (6 in). Reprinted from Kurt Nassau, *Gems Made by Man* (Radnor, Pa.: Chilton, 1980), p. 87.

attainable in this way, as the moving melt zone acts as a kind of *impurity sweeper.*

Another variation, called *edge-defined film-fed growth,* allows crystals to be pulled through dies with shaped configurations; the growing crystal follows these outlines, resulting in continuous single crystals in the form of rods, sheets, tubes, and even more complex shapes.

A problem arises when materials are so reactive that they cannot be melted, even in such unreactive containers as platinum and iridium, or if the melting point of the material to be grown exceeds that of the available container materials. The latter is the case with cubic zirconium oxide (CZ) which melts at the fantastically high temperature of 2750°C. (4982°F.)

Single crystal growth of CZ was not managed until the 1970s, when a research group in the USSR perfected a technique (previously known) called *skull melting* (Fig. 10). The *skull* is an open-ended cup made of copper cylinders; the cup is filled with powdered zirconium oxide and heated by radio frequency induction until the powder melts. The region immediately adjacent to the

CRYSTAL GROWTH 215

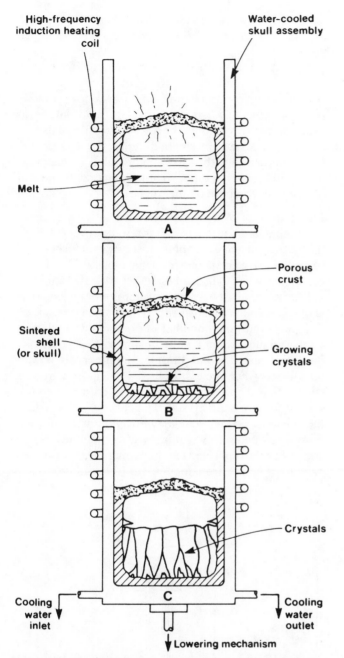

High-frequency induction heating coil

Water-cooled skull assembly

Melt

Porous crust

Sintered shell (or skull)

Growing crystals

Crystals

A

B

C

Cooling water inlet

Cooling water outlet

Lowering mechanism

Figure 10. Skull melting (cubic zirconia). *A:* formation of a porous crust. *B:* growth of parallel columns. *C:* solidified melt. Reprinted from Michael O'Donoghue, *A Guide to Man-made Gemstones* (New York: Van Nostrand Reinhold, 1983), p. 59.

copper cylinders, however, remains solid because the cylinders are hollow and water cooled. The molten zirconia is thus effectively contained within a 1-millimeter-thick shell of solid zirconia. The entire assembly is allowed to slowly cool, and crystal growth proceeds by nucleation of parallel crystal columns until the entire mass has solidified. A typical skull contains about a kilogram of material, of which half emerges as cuttable CZ. At this writing, zirconium oxide (also hafnium oxide) is the only important gemstone material grown by this method.

Solution Growth: Solutions are perhaps the most familiar crystal growth environments. Even the simple act of making a cup of instant coffee is a study in solubilities, involving different rates and degrees of solubility of such widely different substances as sugar, powdered coffee, and saccharine. If you go swimming at the beach, the slippery uncomfortable feeling you get after awhile is the result of seawater evaporation, leaving a fine crust of sodium chloride and other salts on your skin. You can even see the crystal shapes (cubes in the case of sodium chloride) with a magnifying glass.

Solution growth has major advantages, including high mobility of dissolved components, convenience, and ease of control. The apparatus for solution growth can be as simple and inexpensive as a pot of water and some mason jars; most gemstones, however, require far more elaborate and expensive apparatus!

Although 5 pounds of sugar can be dissolved in a quart of boiling water, it is unlikely that such high solubilities can be found among oxides and silicates. In addition, although pure water is an excellent solvent for many compounds, the ones of gemological interest have such low solubilities that, for practical purposes, they may be considered insoluble. As in the case of natural environments, however, a bit of *mineralizer* (for example, sodium hydroxide) dissolved in hot water *dramatically* increases its capability for dissolving silicates such as quartz, beryl, and so forth. It is also much more effective to put the water under both high pressure and high temperature. Under these conditions, called *hydrothermal growth*, many mineral crystals can be duplicated in the laboratory. Moreover, since these are the same kinds of conditions that prevail in the ground, the resulting crystals often look strikingly like those found in ore deposits.

A major difference, however, is size. Nature is relatively unconcerned about the corrosion of container walls, the rupturing of growth vessels if the pressure gets too high, or even the exact chemistry (or purity) of the growth solutions. Very high temperatures and pressures are created with impunity. The result can be spectacular indeed: spodumene crystals up to 40 feet long, feldspars the size of railroad boxcars, and people-sized quartz crystals. To date the largest hydrothermal (quartz) crystals grown in laboratories weigh less than a few hundred pounds and are only a foot or so in diameter.

The growth of sugar crystals (rock candy) and other salts can be achieved at room temperature and pressure in simple containers. Silicates cannot be grown in this way. These substances can, however, be crystallized in steel cylinders called *bombs* (Fig. 12), which are loaded with feed material, water, mineralizers, and seed crystals and placed inside a sealed unit called an autoclave (Fig. 11). A hydrothermal growth apparatus is a pressure cooker. The bomb is heated within the device, and, since it is sealed, once the water in it expands to fill the cylinder, the pressure rises as the temperature is raised. The tem-

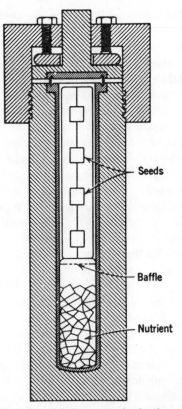

Figure 11. A silver-lined laboratory hydrothermal auto-clave, about 35 cm (14 in) long. Reprinted from Kurt Nassau, *Gems Made by Man* (Radnor, Pa.: Chilton, 1980), p. 104. *(Courtesy of A. A. Ballman and R. A Laudise, Bell Laboratories.)*

perature is carefully monitored, and the water added to the bomb exactly measured to achieve a predetermined pressure level.

Hydrothermal synthesis is not of great significance for technological applications, except in the case of quartz. It is, however, of tremendous importance for synthetic gemstones because so many natural materials form hydrothermally within the Earth. Among the gems produced in this way are emerald, amethyst, and citrine. Hydrothermal growth is especially suited to materials that contain water or other volatile components and that therefore decompose on melting.

Flux Growth: Water is an effective solvent for many substances familiar to us all. It is not, however, a powerful enough solvent to dissolve most oxides, silicates, and so forth. Ice is a crystalline solid that melts at 32°F. Other crystalline solids can also be melted at temperatures of only a few hundred degrees; if water is molten ice, what about the solution capabilities of other molten substances?

It turns out that a number of compounds, including borax, lithium oxide + molybdenum oxide, potassium fluoride, lead oxide and fluoride, and others are powerful solvents when melted; in fact, some crystal growers believe that it should be possible to find a molten-salt solvent for any given crystal. The earliest gem crystals, the rubies of Fremy, were grown from molten-salt solutions of corundum. A vast array of compounds can be grown in this way (Fig. 13), including alexandrite and emerald (Fig. 14), from molten salt (flux) solutions.

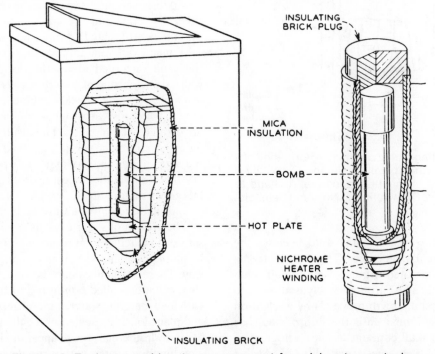

Figure 12. Enclosure and heating arrangement for a laboratory autoclave. Reprinted from Kurt Nassau, *Gems Made by Man* (Radnor, Pa.: Chilton, 1980), p. 105. *Courtesy of A. A. Ballman and R. A. Laudise, Bell Laboratories.)*

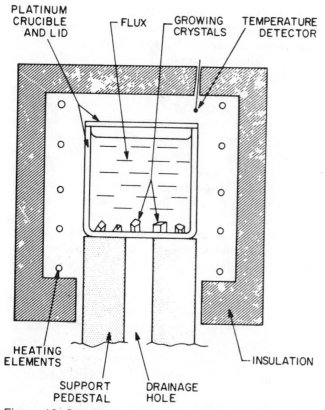

Figure 13. Crucible inside the flux-growth furnace. Reprinted from Kurt Nassau, *Gems Made by Man* (Radnor, Pa.: Chilton, 1980), p. 80.

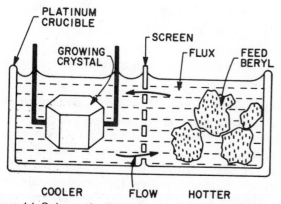

Figure 14. Schematic diagram of the flux transport growth of synthetic emerald used by Gilson. Reprinted from Kurt Nassau, *Gems Made by Man* (Radnor, Pa.: Chilton, 1980), p. 147.

Special Methods: The previous discussion encompasses the overwhelming majority of materials. However, some crystals require very unusual growth conditions (this was certainly true of cubic zirconia until skull melting became a commercial process!). Perhaps the most notable of these is diamond.

Diamond is a product of extremely high temperatures and pressures, conditions chiefly found in the Earth's mantle at a depth of 15 or more miles below the surface. The major obstacle to diamond synthesis was finding (1) equipment that could produce these conditions, and (2) materials to use in making this equipment that would allow the equipment itself to survive (and maintain) these conditions! Success was claimed often in the period 1850–1950, but never truly documented. Unquestionable proof of diamond synthesis was, in fact, not forthcoming until 1955, when scientists at General Electric Co. announced a breakthrough. A 1,000-ton press achieved a simultaneous temperature of 5,000°F and pressure of 1.5 million pounds per square inch. Diamond forms from carbon very quickly (seconds to minutes) at these conditions, and so the production of synthetic diamond for industrial purposes is now routine, with millions of carats produced annually. However, the production of large, transparent diamond crystals suitable for gemstone use remains technologically elusive, and very expensive. A major breakthrough in this area could well be the most significant development in gemstone synthesis in history. It is not pure fiction to imagine that such a breakthrough could occur within a decade, since gem quality crystals up to about 1¼ carats have already been made.

DEFINITIONS

It is important to clarify the terminology associated with laboratory-produced gemstones since some confusion exists in the literature.

The International Committee on Technical Terminology (ICTT) in 1974, after three years of meetings and deliberations, proposed the following definitions:

Synthetic (n.) A human-produced chemical compound or material formed by processes that combine separate elements or constituents so as to create a coherent whole; a product so formed.
Synthetic (adj.) Pertaining to, involving, or of the nature of synthesis; produced by synthesis; especially not of natural origin.
Homocreate (n.) A human-produced substance (solid, liquid, or gas) whose chemical and physical properties are within the range of those possessed by the specific variety of the natural substance that the *homocreate* is intended to duplicate.
Homocreate (adj.) Synthetic *and* possessing chemical and physical properties that are essentially the same as those of its natural counterpart; created the same as.

A substance such as emerald, made in the laboratory, is a *homocreate*. Its properties are specifically designed to mimic those of the equivalent substance produced by nature. However, cubic zirconia, GGG, and YAG are true *synthetics*—simply compounds made in the laboratory, put together from components. They have no natural counterparts and are used as gemstones based on their own meritorious properties. In other words, all homocreate materials are synthetic; but not all synthetics are homocreate.

These definitions were unanimously approved by the ICTT and have been adopted by most professional scientific societies. If gemology is ever to consider itself a true science, it will only do so if it begins to walk in step with other disciplines having a much longer history of empirical and theoretical evolution.

CHARACTERISTICS

Each crystal-growing method is somewhat unique and uses different equipment, chemicals, containers, and so forth. Natural crystals also grow in a wide variety of physical and chemical environments. Every crystal-growth process leaves its mark on the growing crystal in the form of color zones, inclusions, surface shapes, and so forth.

At any given moment during the growth of a crystal the surface is characteristic of both the environmental conditions and the growth process. As material is added to this surface, the newly added layer becomes the new outermost layer. We can therefore say that crystal growth is characterized by a succession of surfaces, and a crystal's history is documented by the record of its surfaces, in a way very analogous to tree rings. Moreover, crystal-growth environments are seldom absolutely pure. Contaminants may enter the growing crystal and be trapped within it; these may be chemical impurities or sometimes crystals or bits of foreign substances. Even the kinds of surfaces bounding the crystal during growth are characteristic of the growth process. Many of these features are visible, with correct illumination, under a microscope. Microscopy is therefore unquestionably the most powerful working tool for the gemologist who wishes to distinguish between natural and synthetic materials. This is especially important because most homocreate materials have properties almost identical to their natural counterparts, or properties within the range observed for the natural substances. Easily measured properties such as refractive index, specific gravity, emission spectrum, optic sign, even color, are not always definitive in identifying homocreates.

Also, the range of materials and growth methods used today is so vast that considerable experience is required to make positive identification. Crystal inclusions may be so small that magnifications up to 50× or more are required to see them properly; such inclusions may be the only proof of natural versus synthetic origin. Some gemstones, such as amethyst and citrine, are extremely difficult to distinguish, and in some cases identification is impossible. The value of a gemstone in the marketplace is largely a function of rarity, a feature not typical of synthetic stones. The marketplace has expressed great concern over the issue of nondetectable synthetics and their impact on gemstone prices. To be sure, a nondetectable homocreate would be a serious problem if no tests could be developed to recognize it. It must be realized that pecuniary interests drive *all* markets. In the past few years the emphasis has been heavily weighted toward *making* good homocreates since the monetary return for success is immense and *far* greater than the reward for developing new detection methods. In other words, you can make a lot more money fooling the marketplace with a newly created gemstone than by selling instruments to detect these gemstones. The gemological field has a lot of catching up to do.

We must recognize that a certain (it is hoped small) percentage of homocreate gemstones will escape detection and enter the marketplace as natural gemstones. If this percentage is not too great, the market will not be adversely affected. It is only when a large portion of a marketplace is affected by created gemstones that problems may arise. The pattern seems to be one of increasing awareness, not only among gemologists but also in the public sector. Awareness is the most important aspect of this problem. *Most* gems can be proven to be either natural or synthetic. The *real* danger is in not being suspicious enough to have the stone tested in the first place.

Following is a brief summary of the characteristics typical of various homocreate and synthetic gems produced in laboratories. It must be remembered that overlap in features is common, and single characteristics, with a few notable exceptions, are seldom sufficient for positive identification.

Vapor Growth: This is not of major importance for gemstones. The most obvious feature might be dendritic patterns or zoning.

Melt Growth: Some techniques, such as Bridgman-Stockbarger, would leave virtually no identifying characteristics. Czochralski and Verneuil crystals, however, have such rapid growth rates that certain features become apparent. Melt growth is typified by rounded surfaces versus the plane surfaces found in natural crystals. These are observed as faint (sometimes distinct) lines visible with correct lighting. If you want to see what these so-called *curved striae* look like, take a telephone book, bend it slightly, and look at the side with a 2× magnifying lens. The image of a stack of gently curved parallel lines is very similar to the series of parallel bands (actually the series of former surfaces of the growing crystal) seen in most Verneuil crystals. Curved striae are instantaneous proof of synthetic origin. They are never found in natural crystals. Pulled crystals do not normally display such features. Instead, we may find tiny metallic inclusions that separated from the container used to grow the material (for example, platinum) and occasional round bubbles. Round bubbles or tadpole-shaped bubbles with curved tails are also typical of melt-grown crystals and are positive identification features.

Solution Growth: This is a real gray area since natural crystals typically grow in hydrothermal solutions. The highest percentage of misidentified homocreates probably falls into this category. Experience, a good, high-powered microscope, and a suspicious nature are likely to be a gemologist's most useful tools. Multiphase inclusions (gas/liquid) are found in both natural and solution-grown crystals, although three-phase inclusions (solid/liquid/gas) have not yet been duplicated in the laboratory in sufficient numbers to create identification problems.

Flux Growth: The most commonly observed feature is flux particles trapped in the synthesized crystal; these may resemble breadcrumbs or comets, clouds of dustlike particles, twisted veils, and so forth.

No single feature may prove diagnostic in some cases. Rather, the gemologist must rely on experience and a broad pattern of features for identification. Even so, it is common for some stones to defy analysis. The best rule of thumb is when in doubt, don't buy. If you pay the price for a fine quality natural stone, be sure it can be proven so.

BERYL—EMERALD

Formula: $Be_3Al_2Si_6O_{18}$ + Cr/V (trace of Cl in hydrothermal synthetics).

Crystallography: Hexagonal; synthetic crystals (depending on growth method) prismatic, equant, very thin tabular.

Color: Green (modified by yellow/blue).

Luster: Vitreous.

Hardness: 7.5-8.

Cleavage: Indistinct; fracture conchoidal to uneven; brittle.

	Natural	Flux	Hydrothermal	Lechleitner Overgrowths
Optics				
o	1.572–1.600	1.560–1.563	1.566–1.576	1.578–1.605
e	1.570–1.593	1.563–1.566	1.571–1.576	1.570–1.599
Birefringence	0.005–0.009	0.003–0.005	0.005–0.007	0.005–0.010
Density	2.68–2.78 (usually over 2.69)	2.65–2.67	2.67–2.71	—

Dispersion: 0.014

Pleochroism: Distinct: yellow-green/blue-green.

Luminescence:
LW: Gilson = mustard-yellow; Zerfass = weak red; Regency = bright red; Biron = inert; Lennix = red; V-beryl = inert; Crystal Research = inert; Seiko = green (distinctive); Chatham = medium to strong red-brown to red (Chatham stones transmit UV to 2300 whereas natural stones are opaque below 3000).
SW: Gilson = orange; others inert.
X-rays: Gilson = dull red.

Spectral: Strong and typical of natural emeralds. V-beryl (Australia) may show a weak band at 6100. Gilson material has a diagnostic line at 4270. Biron spectrum same as natural.

Inclusions
Flux Grown:
  Gilson: Veil-like feathers.
  Lenix: Flux particles; two-phase inclusions resembling feathers.
  USSR: Flux-void fillings and healed fractures (orangy brown).
  Seiko: Flux inclusions, concentrated in a plane between color zones; strong color zoning; Starburst inclusions; dustlike flux, seemingly at surface of gem but actually inside the stone.
  I.G. Farben/Zerfass: Phenakite inclusions; profuse twisted veils.
  Chatham: Fingerprint veils; phenakite crystals; flux inclusions.

Hydrothermal:
  Regency (Linde): Portions of seed crystals; phenakite crystals; daggerlike inclusions (nail heads); flattened healed cracks, with two-phase inclusions visible (high magnification); pointed hollow tubes.
  Lechleitner: Parallel color bands; dustlike particles; wedge-shaped two-phase inclusions parallel to growth direction; octahedral gold crystals.
  Biron: Fingerprints; veils; fractures; nail heads with liquid and gas; two-phase large inclusions; white comet tails; gold particles; phenakite; growth features.
  Crystal Research: Two-phase inclusions; color banding (in early material).
  Inamori: Two-phase inclusions.

Comments: Synthetic emeralds typically have slightly lower refractive indices and birefringence than do natural stones. Flux-grown emerald does not show the infrared spectrum characteristic of water in the beryl structure. This infrared spectrum is characteristic only of natural and hydrothermal synthetic emeralds. Flux-grown emeralds typically have relatively low R.I., S.G., and show strong red fluorescence in UV. Chlorine appears to be a diagnostic trace element found *only* in hydrothermal synthetics. Other trace elements overlap with natural material and are therefore not diagnostic. Natural emeralds contain Na, Mg and Fe in significantly higher amounts

Tabulated Data on Synthetic Emerald

Source	e	o	Birefringence	S.G.
Hydrothermal				
Lechleitner				
Overgrowth	1.571–1.601	1.571–1.610	0.005–0.010	2.68–2.71
Solid	1.569	1.574	0.005	2.70
Beryl sandwich	1.566	1.570	0.004	2.68
Linde (= Regency)	1.566–1.572	1.571–1.578	0.005–0.006	2.67–2.70
Biron	1.569	1.573	0.004–0.005	2.68–2.71
Crystal Research	1.571–1.575	1.566–1.570	0.005	2.68
(V-beryl)				
Inamori	1.563	1.568	0.005	2.65–2.70
(Kyocera)				
Flux				
Gilson	1.558–1.561	1.565–1.575	0.003–0.005	2.65–2.70
Seiko	1.561	1.565	0.004	2.66
Lenix	1.562	1.566	0.004	2.62–2.65
Zerfass	1.555	1.561	0.006	2.66
USSR	1.559	1.563	0.004	2.65
Chatham	1.560	1.565	0.003–0.004	2.64–2.66

Notes: The Cr content of Lechleitner emerald is approximately 4–10% (weight), with mean R.I. varying from 1.576–1.605 as the Cr content increases. By contrast, Linde emerald has Cr = 0.3–1.2% and R.I. (mean) = 1.568–1.575. Natural emeralds usually have a maximum Cr content below 2%, but R.I. also varies with other impurities.

The properties of Seiko (flux-melt) emeralds are reported as similar to those of other synthetics.

Natural emeralds generally have contents of Na and Mg on the order of 1+ weight percent, whereas synthetic emeralds have very low concentrations of these elements.

(more than 0.1%) than synthetic emeralds but contain lower amounts (less than 18%) of silica and alumina.

Regency emerald is the material formerly made by Linde, manufactured under license by Vacuum Ventures, Inc. This material is therefore identical with the Linde product.

CHRYSOBERYL (Alexandrite)

Formula: $BeAl_2O_4$ (+ Cr/Fe).

Crystallography: Orthorhombic; synthetic crystals well formed.

Colors: Like natural alexandrite, violet-red/bluish green, depending on lighting source.

Luster: Vitreous.

Hardness: 8.5.

Density: 3.73 (flux); 3.715 (Czochralski).

Optics: Biaxial (+).
R.I. = 1.746–1.755 (flux); 1.740–1.749 (Czochralski).

Birefringence: 0.009 (flux, Czochralski).

Dispersion: 0.015.

Pleochroism: Red/orange/green as for natural material.

Spectral: Transmission in two bands at approximately 4900 and 6700; this creates the alexandrite visual color change.

Luminescence: Czochralski crystals fluoresce strong red in UV and X-rays. Seiko material also strong red under LW.

Inclusions: Layer of dustlike inclusions parallel to seed face; strong banding; wispy veils in flux-grown material. Pulled material may have tiny platinum crystals. Pulled alexandrite has been made in the USSR with crystals up to 100 × 20 × 10 mm reported; these crystals vary in color with direction: cherry-red/blue-green/yellow-green. Seiko alexandrite is made by floating-zone growth, with crystals similar in shape to Verneuil boules; internal features (tadpolelike bubbles, and so forth) are similar to Verneuil. A general overall swirled appearance is distinctive.

Comments: Large crystals of alexandrite have been pulled from the melt by Kyocera of Japan. Flux-grown material has been marketed by Creative Crystals Co. of California. The melt-grown Seiko material is made by the same company that makes synthetic quartz crystals for Seiko watches. The color change is excellent and properties are generally comparable to those of natural alexandrite. A synthetic chrysoberyl (not alexandrite) has been grown hydrothermally in Czechoslovakia.

CORAL

Formula: $CaCO_3$ (Aragonite).

Crystallography: Orthorhombic; manufactured and sold as cylindrical, massive pieces.

Colors: Oxblood red, red, bright rose, salmon, angel's skin.

Streak: Dark red.

Luster: Translucent.

Hardness: 3.5.

Density: 2.43-2.70.

Cleavage: Grainy texture.

Optics: $N = 1.468$-1.658 (spot average = 1.55-1.58).

Luminescence: Weak purplish red where dye is concentrated.

Comments: This is a Gilson product. The grainy texture is due to the presence of particles of varying size. There are no growth features similar to those seen in natural coral. This material must be considered a coral stimulant or imitation. It effervesces (leaving a small residual red pigment) in HCl.

CORUNDUM

Formula: Al_2O_3.

Crystallography: Hexagonal (trigonal); shape is a function of growth method.

Colors: Pure corundum is colorless; impurity-induced coloration is as follows: Pink/red (Cr); yellow-orange (Ni+Cr+Fe); yellow-green (Ni+Fe+Ti); green (Co+V+Ni) blue (Fe+Ti); purple/violet (Cr+Ti+Fe); alexandrite color change (V) gold (Cu); pink (Mn); gray (Fe); maroon (Co+Cr); yellow (Ni).

Luster: Vitreous to adamantine.

Hardness: 9.

Density: 3.97-4.1; typically 4.00.

Cleavage: None. Fracture conchoidal; slightly brittle; tough.

Optics: $o = 1.757$-1.768; $e = 1.765$-1.776; typically 1.762-1.770. Colorless Verneuil sapphire = 1.760-1.769. Uniaxial ($-$).

Birefringence: 0.008.

Dispersion: 0.018.

Pleochroism: As for natural corundum; dark red rubies with brownish tone (Kashan) show up very orangy.

Luminescence: May be stronger in synthetic versus natural stones. Synthetic rubies may phosphoresce after exposure to X-rays, although the Ramaura stones do not. This effect may be correlated with iron content, as synthetic rubies typically contain less iron than natural stones. SW: Rubies fluoresce, all types, weak to strong. Color may be orangy red or yellowish red (Chatham) also dull, chalky red (Ramaura, Lechleitner). Synthetic yellow sapphire is generally inert in UV light. Orangy stones colored by Mn and Cr may fluoresce deep red, and stones with Fe and V fluoresce orange. Chatham orange sapphire fluoresces weak orange or yellowish red, blue sapphire patchy, uneven reaction in shades of chalky greenish/yellowish/brownish red, orange and yellow. Ramaura ruby dull chalky red to orangy-red, moderate, also chalky bluish-white zones. Lechleitner blue sapphire very weak chalky whitish blue.
LW: Fluorescence usually stronger in rubies than with SW, dull red, orange red. Chatham sapphire fluoresces same colors LW as SW, but usually stronger. Ramaura fluoresces chalky dull red to orangy red, moderate to strong. Lechleitner blue sapphire inert in LW. Seiko *padparadscha* fluoresces strong red.

Spectral: Usually not diagnostic, as synthetic and natural stones exhibit much the same spectra. However, absorption bands at 4500, 4600, and 4700, all due to iron and visible in many natural yellow, blue and green sapphires, are not seen in synthetic stones.

Inclusions: Plato-Sandmeier effect between crossed polars (interference colors).
Verneuil: Curved striae (most characteristic), curved zones of small bubbles, swarms of gas bubbles, spherical gas bubbles, unmelted particles, strings of bubbles.
Geneva: Same as Verneuil, more bubbles, angular striations.
Frémy: Triangular inclusions, so-called coat hangers.
Early Hydrothermal: Natural seed with polysynthetic twin lamellae surrounded by synthetic coating; gas bubble trails and liquid feather fingerprints.
Chatham: Lacelike fingerprints, netlike mesh inclusions, disseminated Pt platelets. Dense white cloudlike areas; transparent crystals; fractures and healed fractures; Color zoning. Thin white needles. Flux inclusions in varying patterns.
Kashan: Flux inclusions (conclusive ID); parallel hoses and flux-drop inclusions; fine cloudlike or foglike veils.

The so-called hair-pins or comets of melt drops with long white tails are considered diagnostic for Kashan. Very tiny inclusions of cryolite also seem to be characteristic.

Ramaura: Residual unmelted flux, angular or rounded, white to orange-yellow. Flat or wispy flux fingerprints; comet-tails, growth features, color zoning with wedge-shaped zones.

Knischka: Broad, dustlike clouds; liquid feathers; negative crystals, perched on the ends of long crystalline tubes (characteristic). Unusual two-phase inclusions at high magnification. Flux inclusions, Pt particles (hexagonal black plates).

Czochralski: Very fine striations occasionally seen, normally no growth features or inclusions.

Lechleitner: Flux fingerprints and wispy veils, ranging from transparent/colorless to opaque/white; curved striae. Higher concentration of inclusions in sapphire versus ruby.

Comments: Synthetic corundum was the earliest of the mass-produced gemstone materials to come from the laboratory. The existence of a ruby in an antique setting does *not* therefore guarantee natural origin, since rubies of sufficient size for cutting were grown a full century ago. Corundum is one of the easiest gems to grow and is amenable to perhaps the widest range of growth methods.

The properties of synthetic corundum are virtually identical to those of natural material. Therefore, optical measurements, luminescence, spectral data, and the like are all of limited usefulness in identification. As with the vast majority of synthetic products, the critical diagnostic features are inclusions. The evaluation of such features is almost an art and can only be performed by a skilled gemologist who has examined many natural and synthetic stones and is thoroughly familiar with their microscopic appearance. Even assuming such skills, a certain small percentage of synthetic stones are misidentified as natural, and in some cases the laboratories cannot make a positive identification either way. This percentage, at least at this writing, is small enough not to seriously affect the market for natural gemstones.

Star corundum is made by dissolving titanium oxide in molten corundum and cooling the material at a rate that allows the dissolved oxide to exsolve as needlelike crystals of rutile; these orient themselves in accordance with the trigonal symmetry of the host corundum. Reflections from these densely packed crystals produce the effect known as a star.

Luminescence is a useful diagnostic test; natural blue sapphires do not react to UV light, whereas many Chatham blue sapphires fluoresce a distinct pale greenish color in LW and dull green in SW. Verneuil sapphires tend to fluoresce whitish to milky green in SW.

Stone Sizes: The early Frémy rubies were thin, tabular crystals that were initially a few mm in size but eventually were grown to a diameter of about 10 mm (though less than 1 mm thick). The so-called Geneva rubies marketed as natural stones between 1885 and 1903 were recently shown to be an early Verneuil-type synthetic; stones were generally only a few carats, as the boules were only about $\frac{1}{4}$ inch across. The flame-fusion boules grown by August Verneuil reached a length of only about 1 inch; however, modern factories, using updated versions of Verneuil's original equipment routinely produce boules 6 inches long and 1 inch in diameter, and ruby boules as long as 17 inches have been grown. Star corundum in a wide range of colors is also routinely grown. The stars in such material are exceedingly sharp and intense, which itself aids in distinguishing them from natural star rubies and sapphires. Internal stresses that accumulate during the growth of Verneuil crystals can be relieved only by allowing the boule to crack after it has cooled. Modern Verneuil factories contain as many as 250+ torches, and global Verneuil production capacity has been estimated at as much as a billion carats annually. Czochralski ruby crystals are true giants, reaching a size of up to nearly 10 pounds; colorless sapphire crystals grown for military purposes have reached a size of 22 pounds. Flux-grown rubies are typically an inch or two in diameter, and hydrothermal crystals seldom reach a size greater than 3-4 inches. A colorless sapphire crystal weighing more than 100 pounds was grown by controlled solidification in a crucible.

CUBIC ZIRCONIA = Phianite (+ Y) = Djevalite (+ Ca)

Formula: ZrO_2 (+ Y or Ca).

Crystallography: Isometric; crystals irregular due to growth process (skull melting).

Colors: Colorless if pure; many colors produced by dopant impurities (see table).

Cubic Zirconia Dopant Colors

Dopant	Color
Ce	yellow-orange-red
Co	lilac
Cr	olive green
Cu	yellow
Er	pink
Eu	pink
Fe	yellow
Ho	pink
Mn	brown-violet
Nd	lilac
Ni	yellow-brown
Pr	amber
Tb	brownish green
Ti	yellow-brown
Tm	pale green
V	green

Luster: Vitreous.

Hardness: 8-8.5.

Density: 5.5-6.0. C-Ox: green = 5.52; blue = 5.34.

Cleavage: None; fracture conchoidal to uneven; somewhat brittle (good wearability).

Optics: $N = 2.15$-2.18.

Birefringence: None.

Dispersion: 0.058-0.066.

Luminescence:

Y-stabilized material: weak reddish/greenish yellow in UV.
Ca-stabilized material: yellow fluorescence in UV.
Pink (Er-doped): yellow-green in LW, faint green in SW.
Lilac (Nd-doped): bright peridot green in LW, faint green in SW.
Orange (Ce-doped): red in LW.
Other doped colors inert.

Inclusions: Small gas bubbles; tiny solid inclusions, often in rows; clouds of tiny particles; striae (rarely).

Stone Sizes: Rough material is limited by the size of the growth apparatus; typical crystal fragments are on the order of 1 × 2 inches but could be made slightly larger if warranted; pieces up to 8 × 3 × 3 cm are routinely made.

Comments: Cubic zirconia (CZ) is the most realistic and popular diamond simulant ever mass produced. It is so diamondlike in appearance that, when first introduced, it fooled many gemologists and jewelers who were not yet aware of its existence in the marketplace. However, it is quickly and easily distinguished from diamond by thermal conductivity (which is much greater in diamond than in CZ). Special devices such as the Ceres Diamond Probe, distributed by the leading domestic manufacturer of CZ, were created especially for the purpose of separating diamond from its simulants.

Zirconia is the only synthetic gem material routinely made with skull-melting techniques. This method uses a water-cooled crucible heated by radio-frequency induction. Careful temperature control allows the material immediately adjacent (perhaps a 1-mm thick zone) to the crucible wall to remain frozen, while the remainder of the oxide is molten. The frozen layer prevents the molten salt from attacking the crucible, and crystallization is achieved through slow cooling. The process yields irregular masses, not euhedral crystals.

Cubic zirconium oxide is, in fact, known as a natural material. It was discovered in 1937 during a routine investigation of some metamict zircons. The monoclinic form of the same composition is known as the mineral baddeleyite. Cubic zirconia is used widely in ceramics because of its high melting point. Pure zirconium oxide

melts at 2750°C. The cubic form does not crystallize from a melt of pure composition but can be stably produced (and preserved as the cubic modification down to room temperature) by adding stabilizers such as oxides of Ca, Mg, or Y to the melt. Single crystals of cubic zirconia were first grown in 1969, but these were very small (about ½ inch). An enlarged version of the 1969 apparatus later produced much larger crystals, and when cubic zirconia gems were introduced into the marketplace in 1976, all previously used diamond imitations (YAG, GGG, and so forth) become obsolete.

DIAMOND

The properties of synthetic diamond are essentially identical to those of the natural material. Even the various types of naturally occurring diamond (Ia, Ib, IIa, IIb) that differ in composition and conductivity have all been synthesized.

Attempts to synthesize diamond were made as long ago as 150 years. A full century of experimentation proved fruitless, mainly because the pressure and temperature conditions under which diamond forms could not be attained with apparatus available during this time period. Diamond readily forms from carbon at a temperature over 4000°C and a pressure between 1 and 3 million pounds per square inch. These awesome conditions, which prevail in the Earth's lower crust or upper mantle (where diamonds form in nature) can only be duplicated in the lab using specially prepared steels and alloys and cleverly designed equipment, largely pioneered by the Harvard University scientist-philosopher, Percy Bridgman. In 1954 H. Tracy Hall, a scientist with General Electric, became the first person to verifiably produce diamonds. The G.E. team included Hall, F. P. Bundy, H. M. Strong, R. H. Wentorf, J. E. Cheny, and H. P. Bovenkerk. The initial crystals were quite small, but in 1970 G.E. made crystals up to about 1 carat in size, which yielded cut stones from about ¼ to ½ carat, in various colors including yellow and blue. Some of these cut stones and crystals were donated in 1971 to the Smithsonian Institution for its permanent collection.

The shape of synthetic diamond crystals depends on the temperature of formation, and may be cubes, octahedra, dodecahedra, or combinations of these forms. The addition of B, as in nature, produces a blue color, whereas nitrogen dispersed in the structure gives yellow, brown, and green hues.

Free-world production of synthetic diamond is estimated at more than 100 million carats per year.

Distinguishing Features: G.E. synthetics are inert in LW ultraviolet, but in SW colorless synthetic diamond fluoresces strong yellow with persistent phosphorescence of the same color. Grayish-blue material fluoresces and phosphoresces slight greenish yellow; yellow material is inert in SW. Blue and near-colorless material may show a cruciform pattern of fluorescence. Synthetic diamond appears to be characterized by strong short wave UV fluorescence and phosphorescence while remaining inert in LW.

Near-colorless synthetic diamond is electrically conductive; no such natural material has yet been reported. G.E. synthetic diamonds (made with iron-containing flux) also exhibit magnetic reaction, not seen in natural diamond. Inclusions in these stones include diffuse clouds of tiny pinponts, and rounded, opaque metallic platelike or rodlike flux inclusions. G.E. synthetic diamonds appear strain free in polarized light.

There seem to be fundamental differences in the magnetic properties of natural versus synthetic diamond; this may form the basis of a distinguishing test when sufficient measurements are made to reveal statistically significant results.

GARNETS (YAG and GGG)

Formula: YAG = $Y_3Al_5O_{12}$. GGG = $Gd_3Ga_5O_{12}$.

Crystallography: Isometric; pulled cylindrical crystals for both YAG and GGG.

Colors:
YAG is colorless if pure; many colors are produced with various dopants:

Color	Dopant	S.G.	R.I.
colorless	—	4.56	1.832
green	Tb	6.06	1.873
pale yellow	Tm	6.48	1.854
yellow-pink	Er	6.43	1.853
pale yellow	Yb	6.62	1.848
pale yellow	Lu	6.69	1.842
yellow-green	Dy	6.20	1.85
golden yellow	Ho	6.30	1.863
pale green	Pr	—	—
lilac	Nd	—	—
green	Cr	—	—
red	Mn	—	—
blue	Co	—	—
yellow	Ti	—	—

GGG is colorless if pure; slightly impure material turns brownish on exposure to UV. Also red, blue, green, and so forth.

Luster: Vitreous for both YAG and GGG.

Hardness: YAG = 8.5; not brittle. GGG = 6-7.

Density: YAG = 4.55-4.57 (Ga-doped = 5.06-5.08). GGG = 7.02-7.09.

Cleavage: None; fracture conchoidal to uneven for both YAG and GGG.

Optics: For YAG N = 1.83 (Ga-doped = 1.90). For GGG N = 1.92-2.03.

Birefringence: None for both YAG and GGG.

Dispersion: YAG = 0.028. GGG = 0.038-0.045.

Pleochroism: None for both YAG and GGG.

Spectral: Typical R.E. spectrum from dopants for YAG and GGG. YAG also has Cr lines if Cr-doped.

Luminescense: For both YAG and GGG, colorless material fluoresces strong yellow in LW, weaker in SW. Bright glow in X-rays.

Stone Sizes: Czochralski crystals of YAG pulled up to approximately 2×8 inches or about 4 pounds. Czochralski crystals of GGG pulled up to approximately 4×12 inches or about 35 pounds.

Comments: True synthetic analogs of natural silicate garnets are difficult to make in the laboratory, have little technological interest, and have been grown only in very small sizes. However, a huge family of technologically vital compounds with the garnet *structure* exists, and many of these are commercially manufactured on a large scale. These materials fit the general formula $A_3B_2C_3O_{12}$ (or $A_3B_5O_{12}$ if B and C are the same element). Many are compounds of rare earth elements. Variations in both the basic chemistry and dopant impurities can lead to a vast range of colored crystals with gemstone potential.

The first of these garnet-structure oxides were grown by the flux method. A very important material, $Y_3Fe_5O_{12}$ (yttrium iron garnet, = YIG) is vital to microwave devices and computer bubble memories. This compound is jet black. However, two useful laser materials, yttrium aluminum garnet (YAG) and gadolinium gallium garnet (GGG) were recognized as early as 1962 as having gemstone potential. Highly perfect YAG crystals doped with Nd were grown from the melt by Czochralski methods in the late 1960s. As a result, colorless and doped YAG became widely available at a low enough cost to stimulate gem use.

Oxides of GD and GA are much more expensive than that of yttrium. Moreover, GGG, if even slightly impure, turns brownish on exposure to ultraviolet light (for example, sunlight). These factors, plus a high specific gravity, have limited the gemstone use of GGG. YAG was the dominant diamond imitation of the 1960s and 1970s, essentially completely replacing rutile and strontium titanate in this role. All such simulants were supplanted by cubic zirconia by 1976, so the popularity of both YAG and GGG were short lived. YAGG (Ga-doped YAG) resembles tsavorite and is also grown from flux. These gems have natural-looking feathers and crystals. Pulled crystals tend to have twisted, droplike inclusions as well as black crystals with square and triangular shapes.

JADE

Formula: $NaAlSi_2O_6$.

Crystallography: Monoclinic.

Colors: Colorless, green (Cr), lavender (Mn), greenish gray, yellow, black (excess Cr). Addition of TiO_2 aids whiteness and translucency.

Luster: Vitreous.

Hardness: 6.5-7.

Comments: Researchers at General Electric produced jadeite discs, in various colors, within a high-pressure cell. The starting material was a mixture of oxides first melted to a glass, then reground and recrystallized within the jadeite P-T stability field. An alternative method was to grind up and recrystallize (with chemicals added to produce the desired color) natural jadeite. Times involved ranged up to 24 hours, Discs up to ½ inch diameter and ⅛ inch thickness were produced, but the size could be increased by using larger apparatus. The researchers projected that *Imperial* quality jade could be produced with this method. The details were published in 1984.

A little-known patent dating back to 1951, however, detailed a process for making synthetic materials to serve as an ideal jadeite simulant. Insufficient information is presented to know whether a true homocreate product was made. The S.G. of this material was given as 3.2-3.8, hardness 6-7, soapy-waxy feel, and colors included white, brown, green, yellow, black, and blue.

An amorphous material called *Siberian jade* or *reformed jade,* manufactured in Japan, is dark green with a hardness of 5-5.5, S.G. = 2.67, and N = 1.523 (anomalously anisotropic), with absorption bands at 4000-4600 and 6000-7000. Inclusions observed in this material include needles of apatite and dendrites.

The G.E. jadeite could pose serious detection problems if made in larger sizes. The look of the finished product is strikingly like that of natural jade; microstructures are slightly different, with the synthetic having a glassy-looking second phase present at grain boundaries, visible under very high magnification (300-500×). Apparently the composition of the mixture must be precisely controlled to prevent the formation of this glassy phase, a problem that may also account for the extreme rarity of translucent or transparent natural jadeite.

LAPIS LAZULI

Formula: $Na_8(AlSiO_4)_6S_2$ (= synthetic ultramarine).

Crystallography: Cubic; cryptocrystalline—granular texture.

Colors: Dark blue, violet-blue—comparable to the finest natural lapis.

Hardness: 5.5-6 (natural lapis = 5.5).

Density: 2.46 (average); material is somewhat porous (natural lapis = 2.81). Range 2.40-3.0.

Cleavage: None; fracture uneven.

Optics: N = 1.50-1.55 (spot).

Birefringence: None.

Spectral: Not diagnostic.

Luminescence: Inert; calcite inclusions, if present, may fluoresce pink in LW.

Comments: The Gilson product reacts much more readily to sulfuric acid than natural lapis, with effervescence and sulfurous fumes evident. It is also decomposed by HCl. The material is quite porous (as much as 5.7% porosity) and the density is consequently much lower than natural lapis. Natural, crushed pyrite is added to the Gilson product to make it more natural looking. The pyrite in natural lapis, however, is far more irregular in shape than the rounded grains in Gilson material and is not as evenly distributed in the rock. Pyrite in Gilson lapis also tends to pull out of the matrix during polishing, a characteristic almost never observed with natural material. Gilson makes lapis both with and without pyrite.

The Gilson material consists of synthetic ultramarine plus two hydrous zinc phosphates. It has therefore been suggested that this material be termed an *imitation lapis* rather than a homocreate material.

OPAL

Formula: $SiO_2 \cdot nH_2O$.

Crystallography: Noncrystalline (amorphous); aggregate of submicroscopic silica particles.

Colors: Colorless, white, as made in the laboratory, with variable play of colors produced by diffraction effect. Body colors produced also include gray, black, yellow-brown.

Luster: Vitreous, pearly.

Hardness: 4.5-6+ (natural opal generally 5.5).

Density: 1.91-2.24 (Gilson); 2.20 (Inamori).

Cleavage: None; fracture conchoidal; brittle.

Optics: Isotropic; N = 1.41-1.45 (Gilson); N = 1.46 (Inamori).

Birefringence: None.

Luminescence:
SW: strong chalky yellow-green diagnostic for Gilson. Faint yellow fluorescence in Inamori. Gilson orange opal fluoresces bluish white.
LW: Faint or no reaction, except Gilson orange *fire opal* may be dull blue or green.

Inclusions: Occasional gas bubbles. Distinctive cellular chicken-wire or snakeskin pattern is diagnostic of Gilson opal; also seen in Inamori.

Comments: An opal-like material with good color play has also been made in Japan, consisting of plastic spheres about 220 nm in diameter, and bonded with plastic. The color play of this material arises in the same way as in natural opal, that is, diffraction from layers of uniformly packed spheres of constant size; in the case of the plastic opal, however, the spheres are not silica but polystyrene. The R.I. is 1.485 (corresponding to that of an acrylic coating on the polystyrene matrix), sometimes with anomalous birefringence, and the S.G. = 1.19. Both LW and SW give a whitish fluorescence. Tradenames such as *Pastoral Opal* and *neo-noble opal* have been used in conjunction with these plastic imitation opals.

Gilson material contains distinctly less water than natural opals; white Gilson synthetic also contains measurable amounts of ZrO_2 and in some cases organic materials. Gilson opal is like natural opal to the unaided eye, but differences are apparent under magnification.

QUARTZ

Synthetic quartz has virtually identical properties to natural material. In fact, it is perhaps the one synthetic for which no really satisfactory diagnostic test exists to separate it from natural material. Inclusions that are clearly natural in origin, or some kinds of twinning, are the only proof of a natural stone.

Quartz is a vital electronic material because of its characteristic *piezoelectricity,* that is, pressure applied to a slice of quartz crystal produces an electric current, depending on the orientation and thickness of the slice. Conversely, an alternating voltage applied to such a quartz slice causes it to vibrate. This effect is valuable in communications equipment and oscillators, such as the ones used in crystal watches.

Production of synthetic quartz was deemed vital to U.S. security during World War II, but perfection of the required technology escaped American researchers. Following the war, notes and equipment seized from the German laboratory of Dr. Richard Nacken provided the missing clues, and by 1950 quartz manufacture, centered in Ohio, was a commercial reality.

All synthetic quartz is manufactured using hydrothermal transport techniques. The feed material is natural quartz, and the transport medium is an alkali-rich water solution superheated under pressure in an autoclave. Crystals weighing about 15 pounds are routinely produced, but giants as large as 40 pounds have also been made with production equipment.

Colored Quartz: Colorless quartz of high purity, although technologically valuable, has minimal value as a faceted gemstone. However, colored quartz gems are a staple of the commercial marketplace and are extremely popular due to widespread availability and low cost. Colorless quartz is amazingly pure. Colors are created by minor amounts of impurities, coupled with the effects of irradiation, typically using cobalt-60. The following treatment processes are widely understood and used commercially:

Q + Fe = brown/yellow;

Q + Fe + heat = green;
Q + Fe + irradiation = violet (amethyst);
Q + Co + heat = blue;
Q + Al + irradiation = dark brown;
Q + irradiation + heat = yellow-green;
where Q = colorless quartz.

Large amounts of synthetic citrine and amethyst are made commercially in the USSR and Japan; the chief U.S. manufacturer is Sawyer Research Products Co. of Cleveland, Ohio. However, the most important synthetic amethyst and citrine in the marketplace today is that from Japan. It is hydrothermal and very difficult to distinguish from natural material. Japanese synthetic quartz has liquid-filled feathers and two-phase inclusions, sharp growth zoning parallel to one rhombohedral face, and unique twin structures that are different in appearance from the polysynthetic lamellae seen in natural amethyst. The chief distinguishing test for natural vs. synthetic amethyst is the appearance of twinning in crossed polarized light.

RUTILE

Formula: TiO_2.

Crystallography: Tetragonal.

Colors: Near colorless (slightly yellowish); orange, brown, red, blue, green, black. Rutile boules slightly deficient in oxygen are blue-black as grown, but turn slightly yellowish when annealed in oxygen. Light blue colors are the result of oxidation after growth. Yellow-red-amber colors are produced by adding Co or Ni (no oxidation necessary); V and Cr yield red colors, and Be gives bluish white. Mo, W, and U give bluish white and light to dark blue shades.

Luster: Subadamantine.

Hardness: 6-7.

Density: 4.25.

Cleavage: Distinct; fracture conchoidal to uneven; extremely brittle.

Optics: $o = 2.61\text{-}2.62$; $e = 2.87\text{-}2.90$.

Birefringence: 0.287.

Dispersion: 0.28-0.30 (about six times that of diamond).

Pleochroism: None.

Spectral: Absorption band at 4250, cuts off violet end of spectrum.

Luminescence: None; blue stones are slightly electrically conductive.

Comments: The major period of manufacture and marketing of rutile was 1948-1955; this was the first of the long series of diamond imitation gemstones. It is truly a homocreate, but the colors of the manufactured material are not duplicated in nature. The softness, extreme brittleness, slightly yellowish cast, and unrealistically high dispersion prevented rutile from achieving the incredible market popularity of later diamond simulants such as cubic zirconia. Rutile has been grown by many techniques, including vapor transport, plasma-arc, Verneuil, hydrothermal, flux, and chemical transport. The majority of commercial crystals were made by Verneuil methods. Asteriated rutile can be made by adding approximately 0.5% Mg oxide and annealing the finished boule in oxygen. Commercial Verneuil production uses a modified flame-fusion torch that allows added oxygen to be supplied to the growing boule, preventing it from becoming oxygen deficient and therefore black. The modified equipment with the added oxygen tube is known as a *tricone torch.*

The color of rutile boules can be improved (that is, made nearly colorless) by adding a small amount of aluminum oxide.

SCHEELITE

Formula: $CaWO_4$.

Crystallography: Tetragonal; crystals usually pulled.

Colors: Wide variety with rare earth dopants, including purple; red-brown; pale green; pale yellow; colorless (pure); yellow-brown; dark red; dark yellow-green.

Luster: Vitreous.

Hardness: 4.5-5.

Density: 5.9-6.1.

Cleavage: None.

Optics: $o = 1.920$; $e = 1.937$.

Birefringence: 0.017.

Dispersion: 0.026.

Pleochroism: A purple stone (Nd-doped) had a distinctive spectrum with strong lines at 6670 and 4340 and a distinct band at 5690-5590; other colors also have distinctive absorption spectra.

Luminescence: Pale green = pink in SW; other colors fluoresce mostly shades of blue/blue-white in SW.

Comments: Scheelite is also grown from vapor and flux. Pulled crystals display gas bubbles, occasionally Rh or Ir inclusions (metallic).

SILICON CARBIDE

Formula: SiC.

Crystallography: Hexagonal; crystals platy, thin.

Colors: Green, blue-green, light green, colorless.

Luster: Adamantine.

Hardness: 9.5.

Density: 3.17-3.20.

Cleavage: None.

Optics: $o = 2.65$; $e = 2.69$. Uniaxial (+).

Birefringence: 0.043.

Dispersion: Approximately 0.09 (about double that of diamond).

Luminescence: Fluoresces mustard-yellow in LW.

Comments: Silicon carbide is an important industrial abrasive material. It is made in large quantities, inexpensively, by fusing sand and coke in an electric furnace. It can also be made in an arc furnace or by flux growth or vapor-phase decomposition. The crystals tend to be platy and well formed, usually very thin, but sometimes thick enough to cut gemstones. The luster, hardness, and dispersion are all excellent for gem use, but the material tends to have a greenish cast. It has never appeared in quantity on the market as a diamond simulant or as a synthetic sold on its own merits.

Inclusions observed include platy, hexagonal-shaped negative crystals, oriented parallel to crystal faces, and scattered small needles.

"SLOCUM STONE"

Formula: A silicate glass with Na, Mg, Al, and Ti.

Crystallography: Amorphous.

Colors: Colorless, white, black, amber, green.

Luster: Vitreous.

Hardness: 5.5-6.5.

Density: 2.41-2.51 (typically 2.48).

Cleavage: None; fracture conchoidal, tough.

Optics: $N = 1.49$-1.53; kaleidoscopic effect in crossed polars.

Birefringence: None.

Luminescence: Inert in UV.

Comments: This curious opal imitation made by John Slocum of Michigan can be manufactured in sizes up to several centimeters. Magnification reveals thin, irregular splintery inclusions that create a color play. These inclusions are thin pieces of heated and metallicized silica gel. The colors change with the viewing angle.

Bubbles with very unusual shapes are observed in Slocum Stone. The best color play is seen when viewing the included flakes on their large surfaces, rather than edge-on. This material has achieved an amazingly high degree of acceptance and popularity for an imitation material.

SPINEL

Formula: $MgAl_2O_4$ (+ impurity dopants).

Crystallography: Isometric; crystals are boules made by flame fusion.

Colors: Pure mateial is colorless. Impurity dopants produce red, brown, green (Cr); blue, green, brown, pink (Fe); yellow, brown, red (Mn); blue (Co); pink (Cu); green (Cr + Mn); blue (Co + Cr); turquoise-blue (Ni). Perhaps as many as 30 distinct colors are produced commercially.

Luster: Vitreous.

Hardness: 7.5-8.

Density: Verneuil = 3.64; Blue Verneuil = 3.63-3.67; Red Verneuil = 3.60-3.66; Red-flux = 3.59+; Blue-flux = 3.63; natural 3.60 (3.59-3.67).

Optics: Verneuil N = 2.728; Blue Verneuil N = 1.723-1.729; Red Verneuil N = 1.720-1.722; Blue-flux N = 1.715; natural N = 1.718 (1.711-1.719). Synthetic spinel, Verneuil-grown and stabilized with aluminum oxide, typically shows R.I. of 1.728 as compared to the characteristic natural reading of 1.718. However, R.I. and S.G. values for flux-grown stones are within the range of natural spinels.

Cleavage: None; fracture conchoidal.

Dispersion: 0.020.

Pleochroism: None.

Spectral: Typical of dopant. Natural blue spinel characterized by 4600 band due to iron, not seen in (current) synthetics. Stoichiometric red Verneuil spinel has one strong line, not at all like the organ-pipe spectrum seen in natural red spinels.

Luminescence: Pale pink (Mn) and yellow-green stones display strong green fluorescence in UV. Colorless stones fluoresce blue-white in UV. Pale blue stones fluoresce bright orange-red in SW, red in LW. Red stones fluoresce crimson in UV. Pale blue-green stones fluoresce intense yellow in UV.

Inclusions: Growth striae seen in corundum are not typical of Verneuil spinel. Bubbles are also not as diagnostic and may look like negative crystals. Also seen are tiny flat cavities. Flux material is also typically inclusion free. Crystals in natural stones remain a critical diagnostic feature.

Stone Sizes: Verneuil boules typically are about 3-5 inches long and 1-1½ inches in diameter.

Comments: The key diagnostic feature in distinguishing synthetic spinel is the higher R.I. and density produced by the alumina stabilizer in the Verneuil process. Octahedral crystals of red spinel have been grown from the flux.

However, stoichiometric red spinel grown by the Verneuil process may have no excess alumina and therefore display the same physical properties as natural spinel. The color of this material is attributable to traces of Cr and Ti. Faint curved striae and tadpole-shaped bubbles have been observed in the material. Chromium apparently produces a green color when introduced into Verneuil boules grown with excess alumina. If the chemistry is made stoichiometric, the boules crack, but some stones have been cut from this material. Some boules (uncharacteristically) show distinct growth striae and bubbles.

A lapis imitation has been made consisting of a sintered cobalt-rich blue spinel to which is added specks of gold to imitate the pyrite in natural lapis. The material has a strong cobalt absorption spectrum: S.G. = 3.52, hardness = 8, N = 1.725.

Asteriated synthetic spinel has also appeared on the market. The stars are, of course, 4-rayed. A weakly chatoyant moonstone simulant has also been reported. The properties given are: N = 1.728, S.G. about 3.64; strong greenish fluorescence in SW, no spectrum, weak, irregular star effect; inclusions include air bubbles, some hexagonal. Also strain knots and anomalous birefringence.

STRONTIUM TITANATE

Formula: $SrTiO_3$.

Crystallography: Isometric; crystals generally manufactured with Verneuil torch.

Colors: Colorless if pure; dopants produce colors as follows:

Dopant	Range of colors (% dopant)		
	0.001	0.02	3
Cr	Yellow-dark brown	dark red-red brown	black
Co	Yellow to yellow-orange	reddish	deep red to blackish red
Fe	Yellow to yellow-brown	brown	dark red-brown to black
Mn	Yellow/yellow-orange		deep red-orange to red to reddish black
Ni	Yellow to orange	reddish orange	deep red to reddish black
V	Yellow to dark red-brown	dark red-brown to black	black
Cb or Ta	Light blue to black or blue-purple		black

Luster: Subadamantine.

Hardness: 5-6.

Density: 5.13.

Cleavage: Indistinct; very brittle.

Optics: $N = 2.40$-2.41.

Birefringence: None.

Dispersion: 0.190 (approximately four times that of diamond).

Luminescence: None.

Comments: This material supplanted rutile in the marketplace. It is nearer to colorless than rutile but is just as soft and brittle and also unrealistically dispersive. Neither rutile nor strontium titanate were truly convincing diamond simulants. Crystals were mass produced by flame fusion, with the usual gas bubble inclusions.

SYNTHETIC TURQUOISE

Formula: Hydrous phosphate of Cu, Al; *totally free of Fe* (versus natural turquoise, which always contains Fe).

Colors: Various shades of blue, intense.

Hardness: 6.

Density: 2.68-2.75.

Cleavage: None; fracture conchoidal; tough.

Optics: $N = 1.59$-1.60; opaque.

Birefringence: None.

Pleochroism: None.

Spectral: No spectrum evident; the spectrum in natural turquoise is mainly due to Fe.

Luminescence: Inert in SW, gray-blue in LW.

Comments: This material was introduced by Pierre Gilson in 1972. It is not an imitation, but a true homocreate with the correct crystalline structure and no apparent binding agent. Most physical properties match those of natural turquoise. The best distinguishing test is the microscopic presence (50× or more) of a regular, fine-grained texture and a mottled appearance. Also, the material dissolves in HCl. It is sold by weight and it provided in sawn blocks by the manufacturer. It is very compact and tough, takes a high polish, and resembles the finest Persian turquoise in color.

MISCELLANEOUS SYNTHETIC MATERIALS

ALEXANDRIUM

Li Al Silicate (+ Nd). Amorphous (glass). Light blue to lavender. Hardness = 6.5. $N = 1.58$. Heat sensitive.

"BANANAS"

$Ba_2NaNb_5O_{15}$. Colorless (slightly yellowish). $N = 2.31$. Dispersive.

BARIUM TITANATE

$BaTiO_3$. Isotropic. Hardness = 6-6.5. S.G. = 5.90. $N = 2.40$.

BERYL

Be Al silicate, colored by Co, grown hydrothermally; (also blue beryl, dark color = Fe, light blue color = Co). Pleochroic: o = light brown; c = reddish-purple. Strong absorption lines at 5860, 5670, and 5430.

BISMUTH GERMANIUM OXIDE

$Bi_{12}GeO_{20}$ or $Bi_4Ge_3O_{12}$. Isotropic. Bright golden orange. Hardness = 4.5. $N = 2.07$. S.G. = 7.12.

BROMELLITE

BeO. Colorless. Hardness = 8-9. S.G. = 3.0-3.02. R.I. = 1.720-1.735. Birefringence = 0.015. Fluoresces faint orange in LW.

CALCIUM TITANATE (PEROVSKITE)

$CaTiO_3$. Orthorhombic. Hardness = 5-6. S.G. = 4.05. R.I. (mean) = 2.40.

CALCIUM FLUORIDE (FLUORITE)

CaF_2 (doped with rare earths). Isometric. Wide range of colors. Hardness = 4.
Colorless: R.I. = 1.44; S.G. = 3.20; no absorption spectrum; flouresces green in LW.
Green: R.I. = 1.43-1.45; S.G. = 3.19-3.21; spectrum shows band in deep red, fine bands at 6900, 5300, and 4900; may fluoresce blue.
Red (doped with U): R.I. = 1.44; S.G. = 3.18; RE spectrum, many lines in yellow-green, sharp line at 3650; inert in UV.

CADMIUM SULFIDE (GREENOCKITE)

CdS. Hexagonal. Hardness = 3-4. S.G. = 4.7-4.9. R.I. = 2.50-2.52. Inert in SW, faint orange in LW.

HEMETINE

Fe oxides + Pb oxide. Sintered product designed to imitate hematite. S.G. = 7. Streak black to reddish black. Magnetic; natural hematite is not.

LASERBLUE

Borosilicate + Cu. Amorphous (glass). Medium to dark blue, very intense. Hardness = 6.5. $N = 1.52$. Heat sensitive, difficult to cut.

LITHIUM TANTALATE

$LiTaO_3$. Trigonal. Colorless. Piezoelectric. Hardness = 5.5-6. R.I.: o = 2.175; e = 2.18-2.22. Birefringence =

0.006. S.G. = 7.3-7.5. Dispersion = 0.087 (about twice that of diamond).

LITHIUM NIOBATE (LINOBATE)

$LiNbO_3$. Trigonal. Colorless, violet, green, red, blue, yellow. Dichroic. Hardness = 5+. R.I.: o = 2.21; e = 2.30. Birefringence = 0.090. S.G. = 4.64-4.66. Dispersion = 0.130 (about three times that of diamond). Inert in UV.

LITHIUM FLUORIDE (+Cr)

LiF (+Cr). Hardness = 3-4. S.G. = 2.64. N = 1.392. Isotropic.

MAGNESIUM OXIDE (PERICLASE)

MgO. Isometric. Colorless. S.G. = 3.55-3.60. N = 1.734-1.738. Cleavage = cubic. Hardness = 5-6. May be colored (blue/dark blue/green) also by irradiation. Green: N = 1.738; S.G. = 3.75.

MAGNESIUM SILICATE (FORSTERITE)

Mg_2SiO_4. Colorless crystals grown by pulling, doped with Ni = green, with V = blue.

POWELLITE

$CaMoO_4$. Tetragonal. Colorless (pulled crystals). Ho-doped: S.G. = 4.34; R.I. = 1.924-1.984.

PHENAKITE

Be_2SiO_4. Hexagonal. Colorless; may be turned yellow by irradiation. Hardness = 7.5. Blue-green (V-doped): S.G. = 3.0; R.I. = 1.654-1.670.

TIN OXIDE (CASSITERITE)

SnO_2. Tetragonal. Colorless to slightly yellowish. R.I. = 1.997-2.093. Birefringence = 0.098. Dispersion = 0.071 (about 1½ times that of diamond). S.G. = 6.8-7.1. Hardness = 6-7.

VICTORIA STONE (= Iimori Stone)

A complex silicate glass, apparently with an amphibole structure; highly chatoyant, due to network of fibers. Made by melting various minerals. Made in wide color range.
Nephritelike: R.I. = 1.61; S.G. = 3.00; hardness = 6.
Jadeitelike: R.I. = 1.50; S.G. = 2.80; hardness = 6.

YTTRIUM ALUMINATE

$YAlO_3$. Isometric. Colorless, doped with rare earths to give many colors, including green, red, bluish, orangy pink, pink, blue-violet. N = 1.94-1.97. S.G. = 5.35. Hardness = 8.5. Dispersion = 0.033. (just below diamond). Shows rare earth spectrum; a good diamond simulant.

YTTRALOX

Y_2O_3 or $(Y,Th)_2O_3$. Isometric. Colorless (turns yellowish if impure). R.I. = 1.92. S.G. = 4.84. Hardness = 6.5-8. Dispersion = 0.050 (just above diamond). A reasonable diamond simulant; the Th-doped material is a sintered polycrystalline product, with about 10% Th oxide, and slightly lower dispersion (0.039).

ZINC ALUMINATE (GAHNITE)

$ZnAl_2O_4$. Isometric; a spinel mineral. N = 1.805. S.G. = 4.40. Hardness = 7.5-8.

ZINC SULFIDE (SPHALERITE, WURTZITE)

ZnS. Sphalerite: isometric; N = 2.30; S.G. = 4.06; hardness = 3.5-4.
Wurtzite: hexagonal; R.I.: o = 2.356; e = 2.378; birefringence = 0.022; S.G. = 4.03; hardness = 3.5-4.

ZINC OXIDE (ZINCITE)

ZnO. R.I. = 2.01-2.03. Hexagonal. Hardness = 4.5. S.G. = 5.43-5.70.

Homocreate Materials That Have Been Synthesized

ANDRADITE	GROSSULAR	RUTILE
APATITE	HALITE	SANMARTINITE
AZURITE	HEMATITE	SCAPOLITE
BADDELEYITE	IOLITE	SCHEELITE
BERLINITE	JADEITE	SODALITE
BERYL	KYANITE	SPHALERITE
BROMELLITE	LAZURITE	SPINEL
CALCITE	LEUCITE	SPODUMENE
CASSITERITE	MAGNETITE	TAAFFEITE
CERARGYRITE	MALACHITE	TOPAZ
CHRYSOBERYL	MIMETITE	TOURMALINE
CINNABAR	NANTOCKITE	UVAROVITE
CORUNDUM	OLIVINE	VANADINITE
CUPRITE	OPAL	VARISCITE
DIAMOND	PERICLASE	VILLIAUMITE
FLUORITE	PEROVSKITE	VIVIANITE
FORSTERITE	PHENAKITE	WULFENITE
GADOLINITE	POWELLITE	WURTZITE
GAHNITE	PROUSTITE	ZINCITE
GREENOCKITE	QUARTZ	ZIRCON

Trade Names of Synthetics

ALEXANDRITE
Alexandria-Created Alexandrite (Creative Crystals)
Crescent Vert Alexandrite (Kyocera)
Inamori Created Alexandrite (Kyocera)

COLORLESS SAPPHIRE
Brillite
Diamondette
Diamonflame
Emperor-lite
Gemette
Jourado Diamond
Ledo Frozen Fire
Mr. Diamond
Thrilliant
Vega Gem
Vesta Gem
Zircolite

CORUNDUM
Amaryl (pale green)
Crown Jewels (colorless)
Danburite (pink)
Diamondite (colorless)
Gemini Ruby
Gemini Sapphire
Syntholite (red-violet)
Ultralite (red-violet)
Violite (red-violet)
Walderite (colorless)
Zirctone (blue-green)

CUBIC ZIRCONIA
Cerene
C-Ox
Cubic-Z
Cubic Zirconia
Cubic Zirconia II
Cubic Zirconium
Cubic Zirconium Oxide
CZ
Diamonair II
Diamondite
Diamond-QU
Diamonesque
Diamonique III
Diamonite
Diamon-Z
Diconia
Djevalite
Fianite
Phianite
Phyanite
Shelby
Singh Kohinoor
Zirconia
Zirconium
Zirconium Yttrium Oxide

EMERALD
Chatham Created Emerald
Crescent Vert Emerald (Kyocera)
Gemerald
Gilson Created Emerald
Emerita (Lechleitner overgrowth)
Igmerald (I.G. Farben)
Inamori Created Emerald (Kyocera)
Linde Created Emerald
Lenix Emerald (Lenic Co.)
Regency Created Emerald (Vacuum Ventures)
Symerald (Lechleitner overgrowth)

GGG
Diamonique II
Galliant
Triple-G

RUTILE
Astryl
Brilliante
Capra; Capri
Diamothyst
Gava Gem
Jarra Gem
Java Gem
Johannes Gem
Kenya Gem
Kima Gem
Kimberlite Gem
Lusterlite
Meredith
Miridis
Rainbow Diamond
Rainbow Gem
Rainbow Magic Diamond
Rutania
Rutile
Sapphirized Titania
Sierra Gem
Tania-59
Tirium Gem
Titangem
Titania
Titania Brilliante
Titania Midnight Stone
Titanium
Titanium Rutile
Titan Stone
Ultimate
Zaba Gem

SPINEL
Alumag
Aquagem (pale blue)
Berylite (pink)
Brazilian Emerald (yellow-green)
Corundolite
Degussite (blue-lapis imitation)
Dirigem (yellow-green)
Emerada (yellow-green)
Erinide (yellow-green)
Jourado Diamond (colorless)
Lustergem

Magalux
Perigem (yellow-green)
Radient
Rozircon (pink)
Strongite
Wesselton Simulated Diamond (colorless)

YAG
Alexite
Amatite
Astrilite
Circolite
Dia-Bud
Diamite
Diamogem
Diamonair
Diamondite
Diamone
Diamonique
Diamonite
Diamonte
Di 'Yag
Geminair
Gemonair
Kimberly
Linde Simulated Diamond
Nier-Gem
Regalair
Replique
Somerset
Triamond
YAG
YAlG
Yttrium Aluminum Garnet
Yttrium Garnet
Yttrogarnet

STRONTIUM TITANATE
Bal de Feu
Brilliante
Continental Jewel
Counterfeit Diamond
Diagem
Diamontina
Dynagem
Fabulite
Jewelite
Kenneth Lane Jewel
Lustigem
Marvelite
Pauline Trigere

Rossini Jewel
Sorella
Starilian
Strontium Mesotitanate
Strontium Titanate
Symant
Wellington Jewel
Zeathite
Zenithite

MISCELLANEOUS

NAME	COMPOUND
EMERALDINE	Stained Chalcedony
LAVERNITE	Periclase
ROYALITE	Glass
SIERRA GEM	Rutile coated with sapphire
STAR TANIA	Star rutile
TRIPLITINE	Emerald-coated beryl triplet

Bibliography

General

Anderson, B. W., *Gem Testing* 9th ed. London: Butterworth, 1980.

Anderson, Frank J., *Riches of the Earth*. New York: Rutledge Press, 1981.

Arem, Joel E., *Gems and Jewelry*. New York: Bantam Books, 1975.

Bancroft, Peter, *Gem and Crystal Treasures*. Fallbrook, Calif.: Western Enterprises—Mineralogical Record, 1984.

Bank, Hermann, *From The World of Gemstones*. Innsbruck, Austria: Penguin, 1973.

Bauer, Max, *Precious Stones*. Charles Griffin & Co., 1904; reprinted in 2 volumes, New York: Dover Publications, 1968.

Cavenago-Bignami, Speranza, *Gemmologia,* 2nd ed. Milan, Italy: Editore Ulrico Hoepli, 1965.

Cipriani, C. and A. Borelli, *Simon and Schuster's Guide to Gems and Precious Stones*. New York: Simon and Schuster, 1986.

Desautels, Paul E., *The Gem Kingdom*. New York: Random House, 1970.

Eppler, W. F., *Praktische Gemmologie*. Stuttgart, Germany: Ruhle-Diebener-Verlag KG, 1973.

Greenbaum, Walter W., *The Gemstone Identifier*. New York: Arco Publishing, 1983.

Gubelin, Edward J., *Internal World of Gemstones*. Zurich: ABC Edition, 1974.

Hurlbut, C. S., and G. S. Switzer, *Gemology*. New York: Wiley, 1979.

Kraus, Edward H., and Chester B. Slawson, *Gems and Gem Materials*. New York: McGraw-Hill, 1939.

Kunz, George F., *Gems and Precious Stones of North America*. Scientific Publishing Co., 1892; reprinted New York: Dover Publications, 1968.

Liddicoat, Richard T., Jr., *Handbook of Gem Identification*. Los Angeles, Calif.: Gemological Institute of America, 1972.

O'Neil, Paul (ed.), *Gemstones*. Alexandria, Va.: Time-Life Books, 1983.

Parsons, Charles J., *Practical Gem Knowledge for the Amateur*. San Diego, Calif.: Lapidary Journal, 1969.

Read, Peter G., *Dictionary of Gemology*. London: Butterworth Scientific, 1982.

Read, Peter G., *Gemmological Instruments*. London: Newnes-Butterworth, 1978.

Sauer, Jules R., *Brazil: Paradise of Gemstones*. Published by author, 1982.

Schubnel, Henri-Jean, *Pierres Precieuses Dans Le Monde*. Paris: Horizons de France, 1972.

Shipley, Robert, *Dictionary of Gems and Gemology*. Los Angeles, Calif.: Gemological Institute of America, 1974.

Sinkankas, John, *Gemstones of North America*. Princeton, N.J.: D. Van Nostrand, 1959.

Sinkankas, John, *Gem Cutting*. New York: Van Nostrand Reinhold, 1962.

Sinkankas, John, *Van Nostrand's Standard Catalog of Gems*. Princeton, N.J.: D. Van Nostrand, 1969.

Sinkankas, John, *Gemstone and Mineral Data Book*. New York: Winchester Press, 1972.

Sinkankas, John, *Gemstones of North America,* Vol. 2. New York: Van Nostrand Reinhold, 1976.

Smith, G. F. Herbert, *Gemstones,* 13th ed. New York: Pitman, 1958.

Van Landingham, S. L. (ed.), *Geology of World Gem Deposits*. New York: Van Nostrand Reinhold, 1985.

Vargas, Glenn, and Martha Vargas, *Descriptions of Gem Materials*. Palm Desert, Calif.: Published by authors, 1972.

Webster, Robert, *Gems,* 3rd ed. Hamden, Conn.: Archon Books, 1975.

Jewelry

Bainbridge, Henry C., *Peter Carl Faberge*. London: B. T. Batsford, 1949, reprinted, London: Hamlyn Publishing Group, 1966.

Becker, Vivienne, *Antique and 20th Century Jewelry*. London: N.A.G. Press, 1980.

Black, J. Anderson, *The Story of Jewelry*. New York: William Morrow, 1974.

Bradford, Ernle, *Four Centuries of European Jewellery*. Country Life, 1953, reprinted, Feltham, Middlesex, England: Spring Books, 1967.

Evans, Joan, *A History of Jewellery, 1100-1870*. Boston: Boston Book & Art, 1970.

Flower, Margaret, *Victorian Jewellery*. New York: A. S. Barnes, 1967.

Fregnac, Claude, *Jewelery from the Renaissance to Art Nouveau*. London: Octopus Books, 1973.

Gere, Charlotte, *Victorian Jewelry Design*. Chicago: Henry Regnery, 1972.

Grigorietti, Guido, *Jewelry through the Ages*. New York: American Heritage Press, 1969.

Heiniger, Ernst A., and Jean Heiniger, *The Great Book of Jewels.* Boston: New York Graphics Society, 1974.

Kuntzsch, Ingrid, *A History of Jewels and Jewellery.* Leipzig, Germany: Edition Leipzig, 1979.

Meen, V. B., and A. D. Tushingham, *Crown Jewels of Iran.* Toronto: University of Toronto Press, 1968.

Menzhausen, Joachim, *The Green Vaults.* Leipzig, Germany: Edition Leipzig, 1970.

Sitwell, H. D. W., *The Crown Jewels and Other Regalia in the Tower Of London.* London: W. S. Crowell, 1953.

Snowman, A. Kenneth, *Carl Faberge: Goldsmith to the Imperial Court of Russia.* New York: Greenwich House, 1983 (reprint, first published 1979).

Diamonds

Argenzio, Victor, *Diamonds Eternal.* New York: David McKay, 1974.

Berman, R. (ed.), *Physical Properties of Diamond.* Oxford: Clarendon Press, 1965.

Blakey, George G., *The Diamond.* London: Paddington Press, 1977.

Bruton, Eric, *Diamonds,* 2nd ed. Philadelphia: Chilton, 1978.

Chapman, Leo, *Diamonds in Australia.* Sydney: Bay Books, 1980.

Copeland, Lawrence L., *Diamonds . . . Famous, Notable and Unique.* Los Angeles, Calif.: Gemological Institute of America, 1974.

DeBeers Consolidated Mines, Ltd., *Notable Diamonds of the World.* New York: N. W. Ayer Public Relations, 1971.

Dickinson, Joan Y., *The Book of Diamonds.* New York: Crown, 1965.

Field, J., *The Properties of Diamond.* London: Academic Press, 1979.

Freedman, Michael, *The Diamond Book.* Homewood, Ill.: Dow Jones-Irwin, 1980.

Gaal, Robert A. P., *The Diamond Dictionary,* 2nd ed. Santa Monica, Calif.: Gemological Institute of America, 1977.

Green, Timothy, *The World of Diamonds.* New York: William Morrow, 1981.

Grodzinski, Paul, *Diamond Technology,* 2nd ed. London: N.A.G. Press, 1942, 1953.

Koskoff, David E., *The Diamond World.* New York: Harper & Row, 1981.

Lenzen, Godehard, *The History of Diamond Production and the Diamond Trade.* New York: Praeger, 1966.

Maillard, Robert (ed.), *Diamonds: Myth, Magic and Reality.* New York: Crown, 1980.

Orlov, Yu L., *The Mineralogy of the Diamond.* New York: Wiley-Interscience, 1977.

Pagel-Theisen, Verena, *Diamond Grading ABC,* 7th ed. West Germany: published by author, 1980.

Sutton, Antony C., *The Diamond Connection.* Los Angeles: JD Press, 1979.

Tolansky, S., *The History and Use of Diamond.* London: Methuen, 1962.

Watermeyer, Basil, *Diamond Cutting.* Cape Town, South Africa: Purnell & Sons, 1980.

Wilson, A. N., *Diamonds from Birth to Eternity.* Santa Monica, Calif.: Gemological Institute of America, 1982.

Specific Gemstones

Beck, Russell J., *New Zealand Jade: The Story of Greenstone.* Wellington, Australia: A.H. and A.W. Reed, 1970.

Chu, Arthur, and Grace Chu, *The Collector's Book of Jade.* New York: Crown, 1978.

Dickinson, Joan Younger, *The Book of Pearls.* New York: Crown, 1968.

Dietrich, R. V., *The Tourmaline Group.* New York: Van Nostrand Reinhold, 1985.

Easby, Elizabeth K., *Pre-Columbian Jade from Costa Rica.* New York: Andre Emmerich, 1968.

Grabowska, Janina, *Polish Amber.* Warsaw: Interpress Publishers, 1983.

Gump, Richard, *Jade: Stone of Heaven.* New York: Doubleday, 1962.

Hansford, S. Howard, *Jade.* New York: American Elsevier, 1969.

Hartman, Joan M., *Chinese Jade of Five Centuries.* Rutland, Vt.: Charles E. Tuttle, 1969.

Kalokerinos, Archie, *In Search of Opal.* Sidney, Australia: Ure Smith, 1967.

Kunz, George F., and Charles H. Stevenson, *The Book of the Pearl.* New York: The Century Co., 1908.

Laufer, Berthold, *Jade—A Study in Chinese Archaeology and Religion,* Publ. 154, Anthroplogical Series, Vol. X, Field Museum of Natural History, Chicago, reprinted, New York: Dover Publications, 1974.

Leechman, Frank, *The Opal Book,* 5th ed. Sidney, Australia: Ure Smith, 1973.

Leiper, Hugh (ed.), *The Agates of North America.* San Diego, Calif.: The Lapidary Journal, 1966.

O'Leary, Barrie, *A Field Guide to Australian Opals.* Australia: Rigby, 1977

Palmer, J. P., *Jade.* London: Spring Books. 1967.

Pogue, Joseph E., *Turquoise,* Memoires of the National Academy of Sciences, Vol. XII, part 2, Mem. 2, 3, reprinted, Glorieta, New Mexico: Rio Grande Press, 1974.

Rice, Patty C., *Amber, the Golden Gem of the Ages.* New York: Van Nostrand Reinhold, 1980.

Sinkankas, John, *Emerald and Other Beryls.* Radnor, Pa: Chilton, 1981.

Mineralogy

Arem, Joel E., *Rocks and Minerals.* New York: Bantam Books, 1973.

Barth, Tom F. W., *Feldspars.* New York: Wiley, 1969.

Bloss, F. Donald, *An Introduction to the Methods of Optical Crystallography.* New York: Holt, Rinehart & Winston, 1961.

Dana, James D., *The System of Mineralogy,* 6th ed. New York: Wiley, 1898.

Deer, W. A., R. A. Howie, and J. Zussman, *Rock-Forming Minerals,* Vol. 1 (1962), Vol. 2 (1963), Vol. 3 (1962), Vol. 4 (1963), Vol. 5 (1962). New York: Wiley.

Evans, R. C., *An Introduction to Crystal Chemistry,* 2nd ed. Cambridge: Cambridge University Press, 1964.

Fleischer, Michael, *Glossary of Mineral Species.* Bowie, Md.: The Mineralogical Record, 1975.

Frondel, Clifford, *The System of Mineralogy,* Vol. 3, *The Silica Minerals.* New York: Wiley, 1962.

Frye, Keith, *The Encyclopedia of Mineralogy.* Stroudsburg, Pa.: Hutchinson Ross, 1981 (Encyclopedia of Earth Sciences, vol. IV B).

Gleason, Sterling, *Ultraviolet Guide to Minerals.* Princeton, N.J.: D. Van Nostrand, 1960.

Hey, Max, *An Index of Mineral Species and Varieties Arranged Chemically,* 2nd ed., with Appendix (1963). London: Trustees of the British Museum, 1962.

Hurlbut, Cornelius, *Dana's Manual of Mineralogy,* 18th ed. New York: Wiley, 1972.

Mitchell, Richard S., *Mineral Names: What Do They Mean?* New York: Van Nostrand Reinhold, 1979.

Palache, C., H. Berman, and C. Frondel, *The System of Mineralogy,* 2 vols. New York: Wiley, 1944, 1951.

Roberts, W. L., G. R. Rapp, and J. Weber, *Encyclopedia of Minerals.* New York: Van Nostrand Reinhold, 1974.

Synthetics

Arem, Joel E., *Man-Made Crystals.* Washington, D.C.: Smithsonian Institution Press, 1973.

Buckley, H. E., *Crystal Growth.* New York: Wiley, 1951.

Elwell, Dennis, *Man-Made Gemstones.* Chichester, England: Ellis Horwood; New York: Halsted Press, 1979.

Faraday Society, *Crystal Growth.* London: Butterworth Scientific Publications, 1959.

Gilman, J. J. (ed.), *The Art and Science of Growing Crystals.* New York: Wiley, 1963.

Holden, Alan, and Phyllis Singer, *Crystals and Crystal Growing.* Garden City, New York: Anchor Books (Doubleday), 1960.

Laudise, Robert A., *The Growth of Single Crystals.* Englewood Cliffs, N.J.: Prentice-Hall, 1970.

Lefever, Robert A., *Preparation and Properties of Solid Materials,* Vol. 1, *Aspects of Crystal Growth.* New York: Marcel Dekker, 1971.

MacInnes, Daniel, *Synthetic Gem and Allied Crystal Manufacture.* Park Ridge, N.J.: Noyes Data Corp., 1973.

Nassau, Kurt, *Gems Made by Man.* Radnor, Pa.: Chilton, 1980.

O'Donoghue, Michael, *A Guide to Man-Made Gemstones.* New York: Van Nostrand Reinhold, 1983.

O'Donoghue, Michael, *Synthetic Gem Materials.* London: Worshipful Company of Goldsmiths, 1979.

Peiser, H. Steffen (ed.), *Crystal Growth.* Oxford: Pergamon Press, 1967.

Westinghouse Research Laboratories, *Crystals Perfect and Imperfect.* New York: Walker and Co., 1965.

Yaverbaum, L. H. (ed.), *Synthetic Gem Production Techniques.* Park Ridge, N.J.: Noyes Data Corp., 1980.

Journals

Journal of Gemmology (London, Gemmological Association of Great Britain; quarterly).

Lapidary Journal (San Diego, California; monthly).

Gems & Gemology (Los Angeles, Gemological Institute of America; quarterly).

Zeitschrift der Deutsche Gemologische Gesellschaft (Idar-Oberstein, Germany; quarterly).

American Mineralogist (Mineralogical Society of America; monthly).

Gemstone Species and Ornamental Materials (Excluding Varieties)

Actinolite
Adamite
Albite
Algodonite
Allanite
Almandine
Amber
Amblygonite
Amphibole (G)*
Analcime
Anatase
Andalusite
Andesine
Andradite
Anglesite
Anhydrite
Ankerite
Anorthite
Anorthoclase
Antigorite
Apatite (G)
Apophyllite
Aragonite
Augelite
Axinite (G)
Azurite

Barite
Bayldonite
Benitoite
Beryl
Beryllonite
Bismutotantalite
Boleite
Boracite
Bornite

Brazilianite
Breithauptite
Bronzite
Brookite
Brucite
Buergerite
Bustamite
Bytownite

Calcite
Canasite
Cancrinite
Cassiterite
Catapleiite
Celestite
Ceruleite
Cerussite
Chabazite
Chambersite
Charoite
Childrenite
Chiolite
Chlorapatite
Chondrodite
Chromdravite
Chromite
Chrysoberyl
Chrysocolla
Chrysotile
Cinnabar
Clinochrysotile
Clinohumite
Clinozoisite
Cobaltite
Colemanite
Coral

Cordierite
Corundum
Covellite
Creedite
Crocoite
Cryolite
Cuprite

Danburite
Datolite
Diamond
Diaspore
Dickinsonite
Diopside
Dioptase
Dolomite
Dravite
Dumortierite

Ekanite
Elbaite
Enstatite
Eosphorite
Epidote
Ettringite
Euclase
Eudialyte
Euxenite

Feldspar (G)
Fergusonite
Ferridravite
Ferroaxinite
Ferrosalite
Fluorapatite
Fluorite

Forsterite
Friedelite

Gadolinite
Gahnite
Gahnospinel
Galaxite
Garnet (G)
Gaylussite
Grandidierite
Grossular
Gypsum

Hambergite
Hancockite
Haüyne
Hedenbergite
Hematite
Hemimorphite
Hercynite
Herderite
Hodgkinsonite
Holtite
Hornblende
Howlite
Huebnerite
Humite
Hureaulite
Hurlbutite
Hydrogrossular
Hydroxylapatite
Hypersthene

Idocrase
Inderite

*(G) indicates names referring to groups (not distinct species).

239

Jade (G)
Jadeite
Jeffersonite
Jeremejevite
Jet

Kämmererite
Kornerupine
Kurnakovite
Kyanite

Labradorite
Langbeinite
Lawsonite
Lazulite
Lazurite (lapis lazuli)
Legrandite
Lepidolite
Leucite
Liddicoatite
Linarite
Lizardite
Ludlamite

Magnesioaxinite
Magnesiochromite
Magnesite
Malachite
Manganaxinite
Manganotantalite
Marcasite
Marialite
Meionite
Meliphanite
  (= melinophane)
Mellite
Mesolite
Microcline
Microlite
Milarite
Millerite
Mimetite
Monazite
Montebrasite
Mordenite

Nambulite
Natrolite

Natromontebrasite
Nepheline
Nephrite
Neptunite
Niccolite
Norbergite

Obsidian
Oligoclase
Olivine (peridot) (G)
Opal
Orthoclase
Orthoferrosilite

Painite
Palygorskite
  (= attapulgite)
Papagoite
Pargasite
Parisite
Pearl
Pectolite
Pentlandite
Periclase
Petalite
Phenakite
Phosgenite
Phosphophyllite
Piedmontite
Pollucite
Powellite
Prehnite
Prosopite
Proustite
Pumpellyite
  (= chlorastrolite)
Purpurite
Pyrargyrite
Pyrite
Pyrope
Pyrophyllite
Pyroxmangite
Pyrrhotite

Quartz

Realgar
Rhodizite

Rhodochrosite
Rhodonite
Rutile

Salite
Samarskite
Sanidine
Sapphirine
Sarcolite
Scapolite (G)
Scheelite
Schefferite
Schorl
Schorlomite
Scolecite
Scorodite
Scorzalite
Sellaite
Senarmontite
Serandite
Serpentine (G)
Shattuckite
Shortite
Siderite
Sillimanite
  (= fibrolite)
Simpsonite
Sinhalite
Smaltite
  (= skutterudite)
Smithsonite
Sodalite
Sogdianite
Spessartine
Sphalerite
Sphene
  (= titanite)
Spinel
Spinel (G)
Spodumene
Staurolite
Stibiotantalite
Stichtite
Stolzite
Strontianite
Sturmanite
Sugilite
Sulfur

Taaffeite
Talc
  (= soapstone
   = steatite)
Tantalite
Tektite
Tephroite
Thaumasite
Thomsonite
Tinzenite
Topaz
Tourmaline (G)
Tremolite
Triphylite
Tsilaisite
Tugtupite
Turquoise

Ulexite
Uvarovite
Uvite

Vanadinite
Variscite
Väyrenenite
Vesuvianite
Villiaumite
Vivianite

Wardite
Wavellite
Weloganite
Whewhellite
Wilkeite
Willemite
Witherite
Wollastonite
Wulfenite

Xonotlite

Yugawaralite

Zektzerite
Zincite
Zircon
Zoisite
Zunyite

Mineral Groups of Gemological Interest

(NOTE: only species of gemological interest have been listed)

AMBLYGONITE GROUP
Amblygonite   Montebrasite   Natromontebrasite

AMPHIBOLE GROUP
Actinolite   Hornblende   Tremolite
Ferroactinolite   Pargasite

APATITE GROUP
Carbonate-hydroxylapatite   Carbonate-fluorapatite
Fluorapatite   Mimetite   Pyromorphite
Vanadinite

ARAGONITE GROUP
Aragonite   Cerussite   Strontianite   Witherite

BARITE GROUP
Barite   Anglesite   Celestite

CALCITE GROUP
Calcite   Magnesite   Rhodochrosite   Siderite
Smithsonite

EPIDOTE GROUP
Allanite   Clinozoisite   Epidote   Hancockite
Piedmontite   Zoisite

FELDSPAR GROUP
Albite   Oligoclase   Andesine   Labradorite
Bytownite   Anorthite   Anorthoclase   Celsian
Hyalophane   Microcline   Orthoclase

GARNET GROUP
Almandine   Andradite   Grossular
Hydrogrossular   Kimzeyite   Goldmanite
Pyrope   Schorlomite   Spessartine   Uvarovite
Knorringite   Yamatoite

HUMITE GROUP
Chondrodite   Clinohumite   Humite
Norbergite

OLIVINE GROUP
Fayalite   Forsterite   Tephroite

OSUMILITE GROUP
Milarite   Osumilite   Sogdianite   Sugilite

PYROXENE GROUP
Acmite   Augite   Clinoenstatite
Clinohypersthene   Diopside   Enstatite
Hypersthene   Jadeite   Spodumene

RUTILE GROUP
Cassiterite   Rutile

SODALITE GROUP
Hauyne   Lazurite   Nosean   Sodalite

SPINEL GROUP
Chromite   Franklinite   Gahnite   Galaxite
Hercynite   Magnesiochromite   Magnetite
Spinel

TOURMALINE GROUP
Buergerite   Dravite   Uvite   Elbaite
Schorl   Liddicoatite   Ferridravite
Chromdravite   Tsilaisite

ZEOLITE GROUP
Analcime   Chabazite   Gmelinite   Heulandite
Mesolite   Natrolite   Pollucite   Scolecite
Stilbite   Thomsonite   Yugawaralite

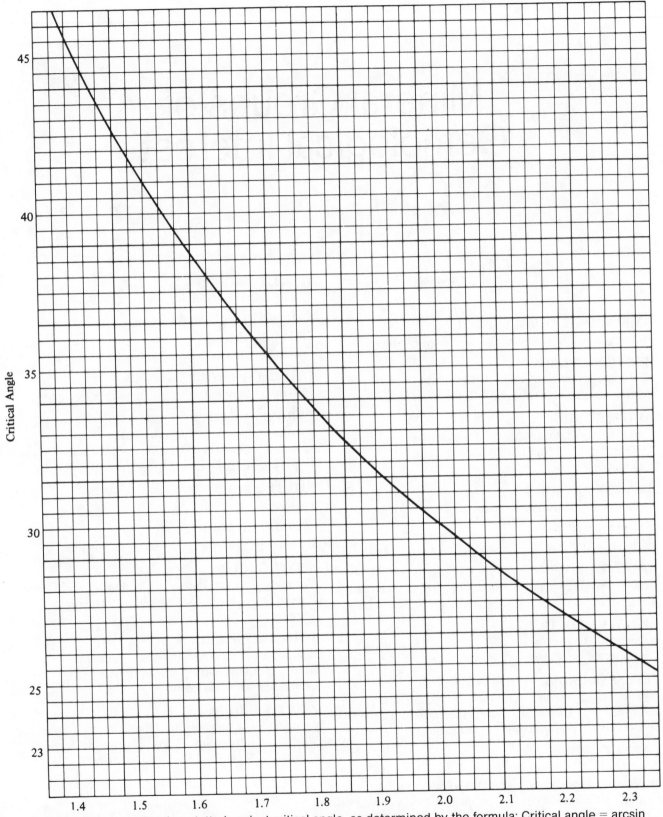

Graph of index of refraction plotted against critical angle, as determined by the formula: Critical angle = arcsin (1/*n*) where *n* is the refractive index. This graph is most useful to the gem cutter for determining main pavilion angles. Maximum brilliance is achieved when the pavilion main angle is slightly greater than the critical angle. This can be determined for any given gem material with a quick refractive index measurement on a polished surface prior to cutting the pavilion.

PERIODIC CLASSIFICATION OF THE ELEMENTS

IA	IIA	IIIB	IVB	VB	VIB	VIIB	VIIIB			IB	IIB	IIIA	IVA	VA	VIA	VIIA	0
1 **H** Hydrogen 1.0079																	2 **He** Helium 4.00260
3 **Li** Lithium 6.941	4 **Be** Beryllium 9.01218											5 **B** Boron 10.81	6 **C** Carbon 12.011	7 **N** Nitrogen 14.0067	8 **O** Oxygen 15.9994	9 **F** Fluorine 18.99840	10 **Ne** Neon 20.179
11 **Na** Sodium 22.98977	12 **Mg** Magnesium 24.305											13 **Al** Aluminum 26.98154	14 **Si** Silicon 28.086	15 **P** Phosphorus 30.97376	16 **S** Sulfur 32.06	17 **Cl** Chlorine 35.453	18 **Ar** Argon 39.948
19 **K** Potassium 39.098	20 **Ca** Calcium 40.08	21 **Sc** Scandium 44.9559	22 **Ti** Titanium 47.90	23 **V** Vanadium 50.9414	24 **Cr** Chromium 51.996	25 **Mn** Manganese 54.9380	26 **Fe** Iron 55.847	27 **Co** Cobalt 58.9332	28 **Ni** Nickel 58.71	29 **Cu** Copper 63.546	30 **Zn** Zinc 65.38	31 **Ga** Gallium 69.72	32 **Ge** Germanium 72.59	33 **As** Arsenic 74.9216	34 **Se** Selenium 78.96	35 **Br** Bromine 79.904	36 **Kr** Krypton 83.80
37 **Rb** Rubidium 85.4678	38 **Sr** Strontium 87.62	39 **Y** Yttrium 88.9059	40 **Zr** Zirconium 91.22	41 **Nb** Niobium 92.9064	42 **Mo** Molybdenum 95.94	43 **Tc** Technetium 98.9062b	44 **Ru** Ruthenium 101.07	45 **Rh** Rhodium 102.9055	46 **Pd** Palladium 106.4	47 **Ag** Silver 107.868	48 **Cd** Cadmium 112.40	49 **In** Indium 114.82	50 **Sn** Tin 118.69	51 **Sb** Antimony 121.75	52 **Te** Tellurium 127.60	53 **I** Iodine 126.9045	54 **Xe** Xenon 131.30
55 **Cs** Cesium 132.9054	56 **Ba** Barium 137.34	57* **La** Lanthanum 138.9055	72 **Hf** Hafnium 178.49	73 **Ta** Tantalum 180.9479	74 **W** Tungsten 183.85	75 **Re** Rhenium 186.2	76 **Os** Osmium 190.2	77 **Ir** Iridium 192.22	78 **Pt** Platinum 195.09	79 **Au** Gold 196.9665	80 **Hg** Mercury 200.59	81 **Tl** Thallium 204.37	82 **Pb** Lead 207.2	83 **Bi** Bismuth 208.9804	84 **Po** Polonium (210)a	85 **At** Astatine (210)a	86 **Rn** Radon (222)a
87 **Fr** Francium (223)a	88 **Ra** Radium 226.0254b	89** **Ac** Actinium (227)a	104 (260)a	105 (260)a	106 (263)*												

metals ← → nonmetals

Lanthanide series

58 **Ce** Cerium 140.12	59 **Pr** Praseo-dymium 140.9077	60 **Nd** Neodymium 144.24	61 **Pm** Promethium (145)a	62 **Sm** Samarium 150.4	63 **Eu** Europium 151.96	64 **Gd** Gadolinium 157.25	65 **Tb** Terbium 158.9254	66 **Dy** Dysprosium 162.50	67 **Ho** Holmium 164.9304	68 **Er** Erbium 167.26	69 **Tm** Thulium 168.9342	70 **Yb** Ytterbium 173.04	71 **Lu** Lutetium 174.97

Actinide series

90 **Th** Thorium 232.0381b	91 **Pa** Protactinium 231.0359b	92 **U** Uranium 238.029	93 **Np** Neptunium 237.0482b	94 **Pu** Plutonium (242)a	95 **Am** Americium (243)a	96 **Cm** Curium (247)a	97 **Bk** Berkelium (249)a	98 **Cf** Californium (251)a	99 **Es** Einsteinium (254)a	100 **Fm** Fermium (253)a	101 **Md** Mendelevium (256)a	102 **No** Nobelium (254)a	103 **Lr** Lawrencium (257)a

a Mass number of most stable or best known isotope.

b Mass of most commonly available, long-lived isotope.

Index

*1. ADAMITE: Ojuela Mine, Mapimi, Mexico (0.86)

2. ALGODONITE: Mohawk Mine, Keweenaw Peninsula, Michigan (each ~ 1 inch across)

3. AMBER: Baltic Sea area (various cut gems and utility objects)

4. AMBER: Dominican Republic (with insect inclusion)

All numbers refer to carat weights unless otherwise indicated. Sequential numbers refer to rows of gems, reading left to right, top row, middle rows, bottom row. Rows are separated by double slashes (//). The symbol ~ means *approximately*. The symbol * means that the gems illustrated have been color analyzed and the data appear on pages 28–35. The photos and data can most easily be matched using gemstone color, shape, and weight.

5. AMBLYGONITE: Brazil (5.2, 6.3)

*6. ANDALUSITE: Brazil
(7.55, 2.40, 2.92, 9.55)

*7. ANGLESITE: Morocco (6.99)

8. APATITE: *Catseye apatite,* India
(~ 2.4, 5.6)

*9. APATITE: Burma (colorless, 7.34), Mexico (antique, 8.70), Brazil (green, 1.09; blue, 0.86) // Madagascar (light blue, 1.07),
Brazil-? (green, 12.40; dark green, 2.87), Canada (green, 8.05) // Brazil (dark blue, 0.55), Madagascar (light blue, 1.07),
Maine (violet, 1.02).

10. APOPHYLLITE: India (1.3, 8.6, 2.4)

11. AUGELITE: California (~ 1.5, rough ½ inch across)

12. AXINITE: Baja California, Mexico
(~ 2.0, rough 1½ inches long)

13. ARAGONITE:
Czechoslovakia (5.35)

14. AZURITE with MALACHITE: Bisbee,
Arizona (~ 4 inches high)

15. BARITE: South Dakota (4.7), Colorado (9.4, 1.9)

*16. BERYL: Brazil (yellow, 40.98; green, 18.42; peach, 9.06 // peach, 6.92;
     colorless, 11.25; green, 4.54; blue, 18.08 // green, 19.09; pink, 17.33), Africa
     (blue, 21.80); Brazil (20.00)

*17. BENITOITE: San Benito County, California
      (1.19, 0.66, 1.07 // 1.08, 1.15, 1.30)

18. BERYL: *Aquamarine catseye,*
     Brazil (18.37)

19. BERYL: *Aquamarine,* Brazil (25.65)

20. BERYL: *Aquamarine,* Nigeria (3.10, 7.82, 2.81)

22. BORACITE: Hanover, Germany (0.6)

*21. BERYL: *Golden beryl,* Brazil (20.00, 19.85 // 18.98, 3.20)

23. BERYLLONITE: Maine (~ 2, rough 1 inch across)

25. BUSTAMITE: Broken Hill,
New South Wales,
Australia (2.6)

24. BORNITE: Butte, Montana (specimens 2 inches across)

26. BRAZILIANITE: Brazil (3.0, 2.7)

*27. CALCITE: Paramca, Spain
(cobaltian, 3.40), Mexico (12.55)

28. CALCITE: Canada (600.91)

29. CANASITE: Bur'atskaja, Urals,
Siberia, USSR
(∼ 2 inches across)

30. CANCRINITE: Bigwood Township,
Ontario, Canada (~ 3 inches across)

*31. CASSITERITE: Bolivia (14.25, 3.5)

32. CELESTITE: Madagascar (16.3)

33. CELESTITE: Canada (1.5)

34. CERULEITE: Arizona (specimens each ~ 1 inch across)

35. CHABAZITE: Nova Scotia (specimen ~ 3 inches across)

36. CHAMBERSITE:
Texas (0.5)

37. CERUSSITE: Tsumeb, Namibia (32.87)

*38. CHILDRENITE: Brazil (1.37)

39. CHIOLITE: Greenland (1.1)

40. CHONDRODITE: Tilly Foster Mine, Brewster,
New York (~ 2, rough 1 inch long)

*41. CHRYSOBERYL: Sri Lanka (7.80, 6.19, 7.51, 7.04) // Brazil (11.84), Sri Lanka (13.25, 9.30 // 21.30), Brazil (11.49), Sri Lanka (12.02)

42. CHRYSOBERYL: *Catseye,* Sri Lanka (~ 5)

43. CHRYSOBERYL: *Alexandrite,* USSR (~ 6); incandescent light (above) and daylight (below)

44. CHRYSOCOLLA: Arizona and New Mexico (large specimen ~ 4 inches high)

*45. CHRYSOCOLLA: Arizona (free form, 13.59)

*46. CLINOHUMITE: USSR
     (1.52)

*47. CINNABAR: Charcas,
     Mexico (1.37)

48. COLEMANITE: Boron,
California (26.50)

49. COPAL: New Zealand (yellow bead ~ 1 inch long)

50. CORAL: South China Sea (red carving ~ 4 inches tall)

*51. CORDIERITE: *Iolite,* India
(1.56, 8.51, 3.00)

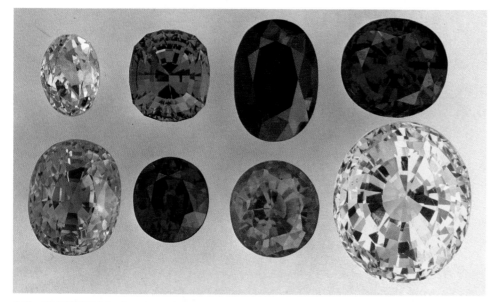

*52. CORUNDUM: *Sapphire,* Sri Lanka (2.12, 3.76, 4.25, 5.21 // 6.05, 3.60, 4.02, 16.12)

*53. CORUNDUM: *Sapphire,* Umba River, Tanzania (1.98, 1.40, 1.86, 3.41, 3.28 // 0.96, 3.77, 1.46, 2.56, 4.64)

*54. CORUNDUM: *Sapphire,* Montana (1.35, 1.77, 1.47, 1.66 // 1.19, 1.10, 1.40, 1.22, 1.30 // 1.03, 1.10, 0.96, 0.95, 2.30)

*55. CORUNDUM: *Sapphire,* Sri Lanka, heated geuda (6.13, 3.89 // 4.00, 2.21, 3.60)

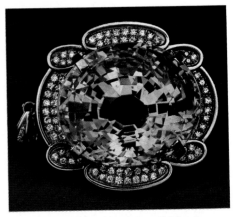

56. CORUNDUM: *Sapphire,* Sri Lanka (184, in gold pendant with diamonds)

*57. CORUNDUM: *Ruby,* Thailand (3.66), Burma (3.56), Thailand 2.23 // Burma (2.30), Thailand (2.11, 2.07, 3.56)

58. CORUNDUM: *Ruby,* Thailand (2.22, 3.68, 3.35)

59. CORUNDUM: *Ruby-Star ruby,* Sri Lanka (2.75),
Burma (2.6, 0.62), India (8.4)

60. CORUNDUM: *Sapphire-Star sapphire,*
Sri Lanka (31.87)

*62. CREEDITE: Chihuahua, Mexico (0.96)

63. CROCOITE: Dundas, Tasmania (3.4)

61. CORUNDUM: *Ruby,* Burma (gems 0.8-1.3, in
platinum pin with diamonds)

64. CUPRITE: Onganja,
South Africa (48.07)

66. DATOLITE: Paterson, New Jersey (4.0)

65. DANBURITE: Charcas, Mexico (8.5, crystal ~ 2½ inches long)

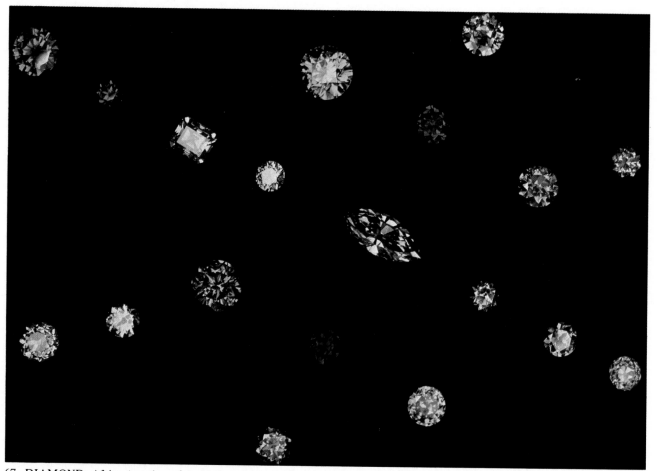

67. DIAMOND: Africa (portion of A. V. Gumuchian's "Spectrum Collection," New York City; ~ ½ to 5)

68. DIAMOND: South Africa; at sorting office of DeBeers Co., Kimberley (rough crystals, ~ 0.25 to 5)

69. DIAMOND: South Africa (~ 2)

*71. DIASPORE: Turkey (2.10)

*70. DIOPSIDE: New York (2.15), Kenya (0.75, chrome diopside), USSR (3.5, chrome diopside)

72. DOLOMITE: Spain (4.5)

73. DUMORTIERITE: Nevada (~ 2 inches across);
Ogilby, California (~ 1 inch across)

74. EKANITE: Sri Lanka (~ 0.5)

*75. ENSTATITE: Kenya (1.80),
Burma (0.55), Kenya (4.38)

76. ENSTATITE: *Star enstatite*, India (~ 3 to 15)

77. HYPERSTHENE: Africa (~ 6)

78. EPIDOTE: Baja California,
    Mexico (1.0), Kenya (1.2)

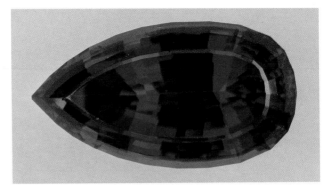

*79. ZOISITE: *Tanzanite,* Tanzania (26.54)

80. CLINOZOISITE:
    Mexico (1.18)

81. ZOISITE: *Tanzanite,* Tanzania, unheated, showing natural color range
    (~ 0.5 to 5)

82. PIEDMONTITE: Adams County, Pennsylvania
    (~ 4 inches across)

83. ZOISITE: *Thulite,* Norway (each specimen
    ~ 2 inches across)

84. EUCLASE: Brazil (5.49, 1.34)

85. FELDSPAR: *Orthoclase,* Madagascar (4.98), Zimbabwe (1.23), Sri Lanka (1.5), Madagascar (2.5)

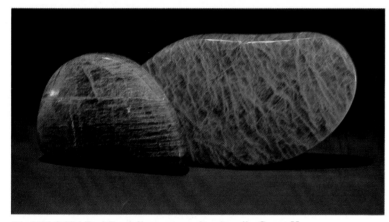

87. FELDSPAR: *Moonstone,* India and Sri Lanka (~ 5 each)

86. FELDSPAR: *Microcline-amazonite,* Amelia Court House, Virginia (1 inch); Ontario, Canada (~ 2 inches across)

88. FELDSPAR: *Albite,* Sri Lanka (4.6), New Mexico (3.9)

89. FELDSPAR: *Labradorite-"sunstone,"* Oregon, showing color range (~ 1 to 5)

90. FELDSPAR: *Labradorite-"sunstone,"* Oregon (~ 14)

91. FELDSPAR: *Labradorite,* Chihuahua, Mexico (36.45, 34.0, 24.26)

92. FELDSPAR: *Labradorite-"spectrolite,"* Finland (~ 2 inches across)

93. FELDSPAR: *Oligoclase,* Canada
    (3.96, 7.21)

94. FRIEDELITE: Franklin,
    New Jersey (1.74)

*95. FLUORITE: Colombia (3.05); Switzerland (0.92), Illinois (15.80) // Illinois
    (5.75), England (6.05), Illinois (8.80)

96. FLUORITE: Illinois (1031,
    world's largest of this color)

97. FLUORITE: Africa (62.55), New Hampshire (152.90), Illinois
    (17.55), New Hampshire (38.10)

*98. GARNET: *Grossular,* Asbestos, Quebec, Canada (9.81), Tanzania (4.15, 5.01 // 2.59, 4.48, 2.18, 3.88 // 2.47, 4.82, 4.14)

*99. GARNET: *Malaya,* Tanzania (12.80, 11.39, 6.38 // 8.23, 8.56, 14.46)

*100. GARNET: *Hessonite,* Orissa State, India (3.61, 3.81, 5.65)

*101. GARNET: *Grossular-tsavorite,* Tanzania (4.11, 2.47, 1.25, 4.01)

102. GARNET: *Andradite-demantoid,* USSR (stones ~ 0.25-0.50)

103. GARNET: *Andradite-demantoid,* USSR (1.93, 0.93, 4.37)

*104. GARNET: *Spessartine,* Brazil (4.05), Madagascar (15.40) //
Amelia, Virginia (4.65), locality unknown (6.41)

*105. GARNET: *Rhodolite,*
Tanzania (24.46)

107. GRANDIDIERITE:
Madagascar (1.1)

108. HEMIMORPHITE:
Mexico (0.75)

106. GARNET: *Almandine-
Star garnet,* Africa (~15)

109. HAMBERGITE:
Madagascar (1.5)

110. HEMIMORPHITE: Zacatecas, Mexico (~ 3 inches high)

111. HERDERITE: Brazil (9.6, 3.65, 9.25)

112. HODGKINSONITE:
Franklin, New Jersey
(0.35)

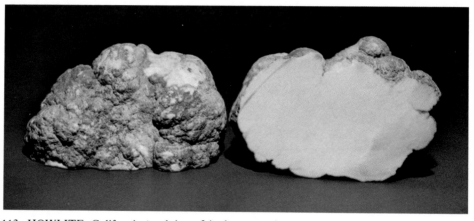

113. HOWLITE: California (nodule ∼ 3 inches across)

114. HUREAULITE: Pala County, California
(∼ 3 inches across)

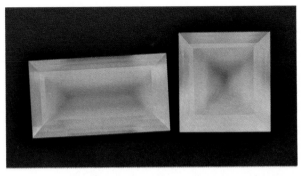

116. JADE: *Nephrite,* China (1.9); *Jadeite,* Burma (2.0)

*115. IDOCRASE: Africa (2.35), Italy (1.40) //
Africa (1.05), Switzerland (3.80)

117. JADE: *Jadeite,* Burma—"imperial jade" (4.77)

118. JADE: *Nephrite and Jadeite,* assorted carvings and beads, China and USSR (snuff bottles ∼ 2 inches high)

119. JADE: *Nephrite*, Siberia, USSR (owl ~ 2 inches tall)

120. JADE: *Jadeite*, Burma (statue ~ 8 inches high)

121. JADE: *Nephrite*, China, "chicken-bone jade."
Vase Ming Dynasty, 14th century
(~ 8 inches high)

122. JADE: *Chloromelanite*, Burma (~ 3 inches long)

123. JADE: *Jadeite*, Burma
(pin ~ 2 inches across)

*124. JEREMEJEVITE: Nerchinsk, Siberia, USSR (0.5, 0.4)

125. JET: Whitby, England (~ 3 each)

126. KORNERUPINE: Kenya (0.55), Madagascar (1.23), Kenya (1.47)

127. KYANITE: Brazil (4.55, 7.80)

128. LAZURITE: *Lapis Lazuli,* Afghanistan (solid blue), Chile (mottled), cabochons 5 to 25 carats.

*129. LAZULITE: Brazil (0.70, 0.44)

131. LUDLAMITE: Idaho (~ 0.5)

130. LEGRANDITE: Mexico (~ 2, rough 1½ inches long)

133. MALACHITE: Zaire (~ 4 inches high)

132. MAGNESITE: Brazil (134.5, world's largest cut magnesite)

134. MANGANOTANTALITE: Alta Ligonha, Mozambique (5.5)

135. COLUMBOTANTALITE: Brazil (2.9)

136. STIBIOTANTALITE: Mozambique (1.0)

137. MELLITE: Germany (0.42)

*138. MICROLITE: Brazil (0.14)

139. MILARITE: Tsumeb, Namibia (0.53)

140. MIMETITE: Tsumeb, Namibia (2.81)

141. OBSIDIAN: Mexico (banded and sheen varieties); Utah ("snowflake obsidian," cabochon 30 × 40 mm)

142. NATROLITE: Bound Brook, New Jersey (~5)

143. NICCOLITE: Cobalt, Ontario, Canada (polished cabochon ~ 1 inch long)

144. OPAL: *Black opal,* Australia (free-form cabochons ~ 30 carats each)

145. OPAL: *Semiblack opal,* Australia (~ 10 carats)

146. OPAL: *Black opal,* Australia (stone in bracelet ~ 20 carats)

147. OPAL: *Black opal,* Australia,
lighting position #1
(stone in ring ~ 10 cts)

148. OPAL: *Triplet,* Australian rough,
ceramic base/quartz top
(30 × 23 mm)

*149. OPAL: *Fire opal,* Idaho (11.74),
Mexico (5.15, hyalite)
// Mexico (0.76, 8.04)

150. OPAL: *Contraluz,* Mexico, illuminated
from front (~ 4)

151. OPAL: *Contraluz,* Mexico, illuminated
from rear (~ 4)

153. OPAL: *Moss opal,* Idaho (5.70)

152. OPAL: *Black opal,* Australia, lighting position #2 (stone in ring ~ 10 cts)

154. PEARL: Worldwide localities, selected to show color variation.

155. PERIDOT: Burma (83.01)

156. PECTOLITE: *"Larimar,"* Dominican Republic (cabochons ~ 6 to 30 carats)

*157. PERIDOT: Norway (4.51), Egypt (8.22) // Arizona (9.20, 8.25)

158. PETALITE: Brazil (15.65)

159. PHENAKITE: Colorado (stone ~ 2.5)

160. PHOSGENITE: Monte Poni, Sardinia (1.5)

161. PHOSPHOPHYLLITE: Potosi, Bolivia (8.1)

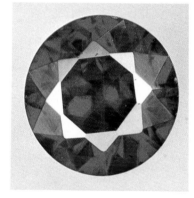

*163. PROUSTITE: Germany (7.53)

162. POLLUCITE: Maine (gem ~ 2 cts)

164. PREHNITE: Mexico (2.47), Australia (7.65)

165. PUMPELLYITE: Isle Royale, Lake Superior, Michigan (pebbles ~ ¼ inch)

166. PURPURITE: Usakos, Namibia (specimens ~ 2 inches across)

167. PYROXMANGITE:
    Japan (0.55)

*168. QUARTZ: Brazil (colorless, 11.0; green, 4.48; rose, 14.20)

*169. QUARTZ: *Citrine.* Brazil (7.55, 4.20, 8.81, 12.64 // 16.90, 19.72, 15.76)

171. QUARTZ: with inclusions, Brazil (dendrites, rutile, tourmaline, ~ 6, 12, 25, respectively)

*170. QUARTZ: *Smoky Quartz,* Brazil (23.78), 15.61 // 9.37, 13.57)

*172. QUARTZ: *Amethyst,* Brazil (6.22, 9.18), Zambia (8.52) // Brazil (4.40, 3.61, 6.41, 6.38)

173. QUARTZ: *Chrysoprase,* Australia (largest beads ~ 8 mm)

174. QUARTZ: *"Ametrine,"* Uruguay
     (∼ 15, 25)

175. QUARTZ: *Agate,* Mexico, "fortification agate"
     (slab ∼ 4 inches across)

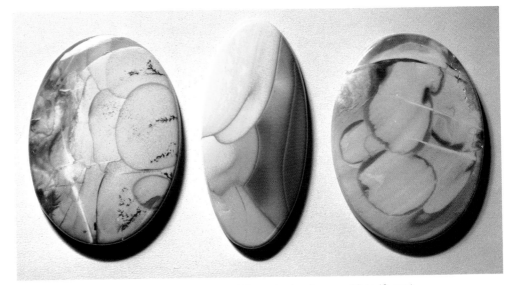

176. QUARTZ: *Jasper,* southwestern United States (cabochons ∼ 30 × 40 mm)

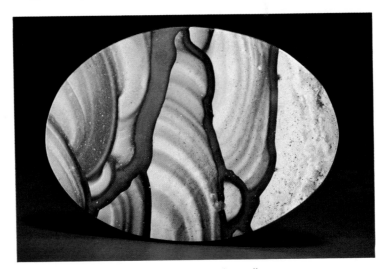

177. QUARTZ: *Jasper,* Oregon, "picture jasper"
     (cabochon ∼ 30 × 40 mm)

178. QUARTZ: *Petrified Wood,* Utah (slab ~ 4 inches across)

179. QUARTZ: *Tigereye,* South Africa (rough mass ~ 3 inches long; blue and red cabochons are dyed)

180. REALGAR: Washington (0.65)

181. RHODOCHROSITE: Argentina, cross-section of stalactite, with cabochons (15 × 20 mm)

182. RHODIZITE: Madagascar (0.49)

*183. RHODOCHROSITE: Peru (7.15), South Africa (9.42), Argentina (3.95)

184. RHODONITE: Australia
(beads, 15 mm)

185. RHODONITE: Broken Hill,
New South Wales, Australia (4.5)

186. SARCOLITE: Italy (0.33)

*187. SCAPOLITE: Tanzania (32.44, 32.00)

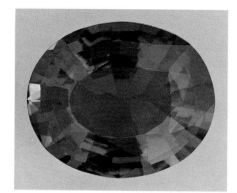

*188. SCAPOLITE: Tanzania (14.83)

189. SCAPOLITE: *Catseye scapolite,* Burma (7.0)

190. SCHEELITE: California (2.2), Mexico (2.4)

*191. SCORODITE: Tsumeb, Namibia (1.15, 1.50)

192. SERANDITE: Mt. Ste. Hilaire, Quebec, Canada (~ 1.5, rough ~ 2 inches long)

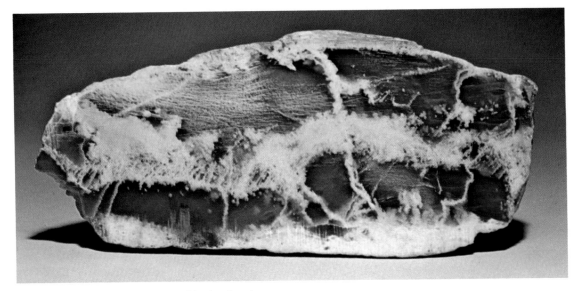

193. SERPENTINE: Pakistan (~ 4 inches long)

194. SERPENTINE, *Williamsite*, Maryland (2.3)

195. SHORTITE: Wyoming (0.5)

196. SIDERITE: Portugal (1.40)

197. SILLIMANITE: *Fibrolite*, Kenya (0.34), Burma (2.44)

198. SIMPSONITE: Brazil (0.27)

*199. SINHALITE: Sri Lanka (4.58, 7.07 // 4.18, 9.18)

200A. SMITHSONITE: Tsumeb, Namibia (cabochon ∼ 50,
       faceted gems ∼ 18, 12)

*200B. SMITHSONITE: Tsumeb, Namibia
        (8.00, 10.40)

201. SMITHSONITE: Kelly Mine, New Mexico (blue 5 inches), Mexico (other colors)

202. SODALITE: Namibia (~ 2 each)

203. HACKMANITE: Ontario, Canada (0.8, 4.7)

204. SPHALERITE: Spain (~ 6)

*205. SPHALERITE: Colorado (1.93), Spain (3.30), Mexico (4.65) // Spain (14.48, 5.57)

206. SPHENE: Baja California, Mexico (6.0, 6.4, 6.75)

207. SPINEL, *Gahnite,* Brazil
(1.56)

*208. SPHENE: Madagascar (6.22), Baja California, Mexico (1.55, 1.76), India (7.01) // Baja California, Mexico
(1.01, 1.44, 4.22), India (2.65)

209. SPINEL: Burma (~ 2 to 15)

*210. SPINEL: Sri Lanka (8.21, 7.65), Burma (5.23) // 9.02, 7.07, 5.89
// USSR (6.56, 8.87), Burma (11.40)

*211. SPINEL: Sri Lanka (8.35, 9.20, 9.30, 15.22 // 4.78, 11.23, 7.27, 5.46, 3.96 // 11.98, 8.53, 7.98, 14.96)

*212. SPINEL: Burma (5.30, 2.98
3.07 // 2.34, 10.98, 3.95
// 8.89, 2.68, 3.21

*213. SPODUMENE: Brazil (29.85), Afghanistan (16.06, 32.71) // California (17.76), Afghanistan (17.01), Brazil (47.33)

214. SPODUMENE: *Triphane,* Pakistan, (~ 170)

215. SPODUMENE: *Kunzite,* Brazil (720)

216. STICHTITE: Argent Hill,
Tasmania, Australia (specimen
~ 2 inches across)

217. STRONTIANITE: Austria
(2.1)

218. SUGILITE: Kuruman, South Africa (gem 3.66)

219. TEKTITE: *Moldavite*, Czechoslovakia
(6.4)

220. TAAFFEITE: Sri Lanka
(1.17, 1.52)

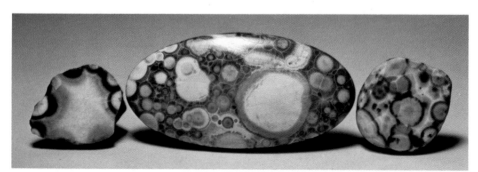

221. THOMSONITE: New Mexico (cabochon 23 ~ 47 mm), Isle Royale,
Lake Superior, Michigan (~ ½ inch each, rough stones)

*222. TOPAZ: USSR (6.72), Brazil (12.59), Mexico (5.29), Brazil (4.65) // Brazil (25.25, 8.76, 7.20, 8.45), USSR (17.84)

*223. TOPAZ: USSR, "imperial topaz" (17.84)

224. TOPAZ: Blue topaz, irradiated and heated (∼ 115)

225. TOPAZ: Blue topaz, "London Blue," irradiated and heated (∼ 8 each)

*226. TOURMALINE: Mozambique (color suite, 1.81-3.08)

*227. TOURMALINE: *Rubellite,* Madagascar (36.85), Brazil (13.16, 17.13 // 16.73, 10.26, 23.56)

*228. TOURMALINE: Brazil (9.84, 15.96), Africa (10.05, chrome), Brazil (9.68, 14.75)

*229. TOURMALINE: Mozambique (10.90), Tanzania (5.74, 5.84 // 10.39, 46.84)

*230. TOURMALINE, *Bicolor,* Brazil (4.92, 23.90, 14.32)

*231. TOURMALINE: Afghanistan (23.32), Brazil (10.95), Mozambique (11.13), Pala, California (21.32)

232. TOURMALINE: *Catseye tourmaline,* Brazil (20.85)

233. TOURMALINE, *Watermelon tourmaline,* Brazil (large slice ~ 1 inch across)

234. TREMOLITE: *Hexagonite,* Balmat, New York
    (~ 1, crystal ~ 1 inch long)

235. TUGTUPITE: Illimassauk, Greenland
    (specimen ~ 1 inch across)

236. TURQUOISE: Arizona and
    New Mexico (right-rear
    nugget ~ 2 inches long)

237. TURQUOISE: Iran, matched beads (~ 15 mm)

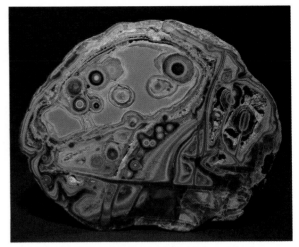

238. VARISCITE: Fairfield, Utah (slab ~ 6 inches across)

239. WILLEMITE: Franklin, New Jersey (0.5, 6.94, 0.6)

*240. WELOGANITE: Francon Quarry, Quebec, Canada (0.37)

241. WITHERITE: England (1.89)

242. WULFENITE: Tsumeb, Namibia (21+)

243. WULFENITE: Arizona (gem ~ 1.5, crystal 1 inch long, Red Cloud Mine)

244. ZINCITE: Franklin, New Jersey (gem ~1, rough 2 inches long)

245. ZIRCON: Cambodia (~ 25, 40 carats)

246. XONOTLITE: Laghi di Posina, Vicenza, Italy (gems ~ 2 carats each)

*247. ZIRCON: Sri Lanka (19.03, 17.43, 14.20, 9.26 // 4.36, 11.26, 15.70), Cambodia (5.56) // Sri Lanka (8.92, 16.63, 7.77, 5.34)

248. ZIRCON: Sri Lanka (blue = Cambodia) (~ 5-30 carats)

SYNTHETICS

[*Note:* The photographs of synthetic gemstones are purposely numbered beginning with 301 to distinguish them from the natural gemstones.]

301. VERNEUIL PROCESS: Boules grown by A. Verneuil and associates ~ 1900; upright boule ½ inch.

302. VERNEUIL RUBY: largest boule ~ 2 inches long

303. CORUNDUM GEMS: all 8 × 10 mm

304. CHATHAM RUBY: largest crystal ~ ½ inch

305. RAMAURA RUBY: gem ~ 5 carats, crystals ~ 2 inches across

306. CHATHAM SAPPHIRE: hexagonal crystal ~ 3 inches across

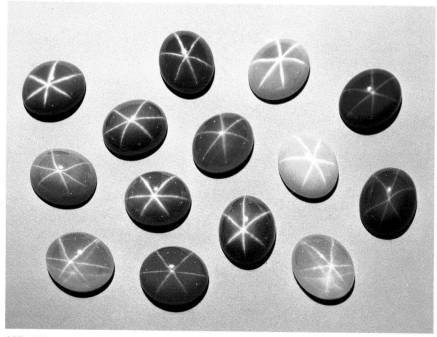

307. STAR CORUNDUM: cabochons 8 × 10 mm, "Heller Hope" stars.

308. CHATHAM SYNTHETICS: corundum, various colors, ~ 3-5 carat size (green heart is synthetic emerald)

309. CHATHAM EMERALD: largest crystal ~ 2 inches long

310. INAMORI SYNTHETICS: all ~ 2 carats, ruby, alexandrite // emerald, sapphire

311. GILSON OPAL: cabochons ~ 3-6 carats

312. GILSON EMERALD: very large crystal, 437 carats, ~ 60 × 40 × 10 mm

314. REGENCY EMERALD:
gem 2.88 carats,
crystal 20.25 carats

313. GILSON LAPIS, TURQUOISE: blocks, lapis 94.4 carats,
turquoise 96.5 carats

315. SLOCUM STONE: blocks ~ ½ inch square

316. GENERAL ELECTRIC SYNTHETIC
DIAMOND: crystals grown by G.E. process

317. CUBIC ZIRCONIA:
various colors,
~ 1-15 carats

318. YAG: various colors, 3.3 to 13.3 carats

319. STRONTIUM TITANATE: marquise ~ 25 carats

320. SYNTHETIC SPINEL: all 8 × 10 mm

321. RUTILE: emerald-cut, 7.84 carats

322. RUTILE: color suite, 1.45 to 7.25 carats

324. SYNTHETIC BLUE QUARTZ:
14.80 carats (USSR)

323. SYNTHETIC QUARTZ: amethyst (6.15, 10.45),
citrine (22.80)

326. SYNTHETIC GARNETS:
yttrium-aluminum-gallium-
garnet, doped with
chromium (dark green),
gem = 1.94 carats

325. SYNTHETIC GARNETS: yellow = dysprosium- aluminum; orange = samarium-
gallium; red = neodymium-gallium; all 1-5 carats.

328. SAMARIUM GALLIUM
GARNET: 6.19 carats

327. GGG: rounds, ~ 2-15 carats

329. LITHIUM NIOBATE: rounds, ~ 10, 15 carats

330. BARIUM TUNGSTATE:
     ~ 3 carats

331. LITHIUM TANTALATE: rounds, ~ 6, 15 carats

332. BISMUTH GERMANIUM
     OXIDE: 10.80 carats

333. CADMIUM SULFIDE
     (GREENOCKITE): ~ 5 carats

334. BARIUM SODIUM NIOBATE ("bananas"):
     ~ 4-5 carats

335. CADMIUM SELENIDE (50-50)/
     CADMIUM SULFIDE (25-75):
     ~ 5 carats

336. TELLURIUM OXIDE
     (TELLURITE): 8.10 carats

337. LEAD MOLYBDATE
     (WULFENITE): ~ 8 carats

338. LEAD MOLYBDATE (WULFENITE): 84.9 carats

339. MAGNESIUM OXIDE
     (PERICLASE): doped
     with nickel, ~ 5 carats

340. ZINC TUNGSTATE
(SANMARTINITE):
~ 3 carats

341. SILVER ARSENIC
SULFIDE (PROUSTITE):
6.98 carats

342. CALCIUM TUNGSTATE (SCHEELITE): gems ~ 3-15 carats

343. "LASERBLUE": 16.04, 11.30

344. "ALEXANDRIUM": 50.40 carats